Diversity and Indigenous Peoples in Canada

THIRD EDITION

Darion Boyington

Harpreet Aulakh

Shahé Kazarian

John Roberts

emond ▪ Toronto, Canada ▪ 2017

Emond Montgomery Publications Limited
60 Shaftesbury Avenue
Toronto ON M4T 1A3
http://www.emond.ca/highered

Printed in Canada.
Reprinted August 2018.

We acknowledge the financial support of the Government of Canada.   Canadä

Emond Montgomery Publications has no responsibility for the persistence or accuracy of URLs for external or third-party Internet websites referred to in this publication, and does not guarantee that any content on such websites is, or will remain, accurate or appropriate.

Publisher: Anthony Rezek
Managing editor, development: Kelly Dickson
Developmental editor: Heather Gough
Senior editor, production: Jim Lyons
Production supervisor: Laura Bast
Copy editor: Leslie Saffrey
Proofreaders: Jim Lyons, Lila Campbell, and David Handelsman
Permissions editor: Lisa Brant
Indexer: Belle Wong
Typesetter and cover designer: Tara Wells
Cover image: M. Cornelius/Shutterstock

Library and Archives Canada Cataloguing in Publication

Roberts, John A., 1944-
[Diversity and First Nations issues in Canada]
    Diversity and indigenous peoples in Canada / Darion Boyington, Harpreet Aulakh, Shahé Kazarian, John Roberts. — 3rd edition.

Revision of: Diversity and First Nations issues in Canada / John Roberts, Darion Boyington, Shahé S.
    Kazarian. — 2nd ed. — Toronto: Emond Montgomery Publications, © 2012.
Includes bibliographical references and index.
ISBN 978-1-55239-668-1 (paperback)

    1. Police-community relations—Canada.   2. Multiculturalism—Canada.   3. Native peoples—
Canada.   4. Native peoples—Canada—History.   5. Law enforcement—Canada.   6. Police—Canada.
7. Discrimination—Canada.   I. Kazarian, Shahe S., 1945-, author   II. Boyington, Darion, author
III. Aulakh, Harpreet, 1972-, author   IV. Title.   V. Title: Diversity and First Nations issues in Canada

HV8157.R62 2017   363.2'30971   C2016-905818-2

To my students, who both challenge my mind and keep me young. And to the next generation of justice professionals and police officers. As you move into positions of leadership in this country, lead with wisdom to create a fair and just society.

—Darion Boyington

To my father, Jagir Singh Sidhu, who inspires me.

—Harpreet Aulakh

Brief Contents

PART I   Diversity Issues in Canada

PART II   Indigenous Peoples in Canada

Detailed Contents

PART I

DIVERSITY ISSUES IN CANADA

1 A Portrait of Canadian Diversity

2 Human Rights and Freedoms

3 Cultural Diversity

4 Religious Diversity

5 Family Violence, Mental Health Issues, and Developmental Disabilities

6 Diversity Competency in the Criminal Justice System

PART II

INDIGENOUS PEOPLES IN CANADA

7 Colonization and Treaties

8 Current Issues over Land

9 Indian and Inuit Residential Schools

10 Current Socio-Economic Issues

11 Indigenous People and the Criminal Justice System

Preface

The third edition of *Diversity and Indigenous Peoples in Canada* has been extensively revised and updated in the light of comments and new developments. This edition extends its focus beyond Ontario and encompasses the whole country, including the Arctic. It also includes a look at international issues as they affect Canada in relation to terrorism, which has moved into the spotlight in recent years.

Diversity and Indigenous Peoples in Canada continues to support college and university courses that combine elements of diversity issues in law enforcement and Indigenous issues. Part I of the text explores the basic concepts of diversity, multiculturalism, and human rights in a Canadian context. A portrait emerges of the nature and scope of Canadian diversity, and its many benefits to our society. The text discusses the rights and freedoms enshrined in Canadian human rights legislation and highlights the role of police in upholding them. Readers will gain an understanding of cultural and religious diversity and achieve a greater awareness of topics including family violence, mental health issues, and developmental disabilities. Part I concludes with an in-depth examination of the efforts of Canadian police services both to diversify the face of policing itself and to increase the diversity competency of their officers. Throughout Part I, the focus remains on the relationship between law enforcement and the diverse communities they serve—specifically, perceptions of police in the community, the evolution of policing culture, and the benefits and challenges of diversity for policing, including the strategies and skills needed for policing with diversity competency. A greater awareness and understanding of diversity, and a focus on our many similarities rather than our differences, are critical to helping reduce conflict and misunderstanding.

Part II of the text offers a concise history of the relationship between Indigenous people in Canada and the new populations of settlers, and in doing so lays the foundation for understanding their past and present interactions and relations. The text explores the treaty process in which Indigenous people lost vast areas of their traditional lands, and with this necessary background discusses land claims, which are commonly misunderstood by many members of the Canadian public. The socio-economic issues facing Indigenous people today are a legacy of colonization and forced assimilation. The text examines the history of the residential school system and the Truth and Reconciliation Commission's report on that era. The text also examines the positive strides that Indigenous communities are making toward self-government and the stabilization of their economies in partnership with the government of Canada. New initiatives from the court system and Correctional Service Canada, as well as new approaches to policing, are evaluated with regard to their ultimate goal—to reduce the overrepresentation of Indigenous people in the criminal justice system.

Acknowledgments

I would like to thank the reviewers of the second edition for their helpful suggestions and comments: Simon Bradford (Georgian College), André Goh (Toronto Police Service, Diversity and Inclusion), and Fadel H. Zabian (Fanshawe College).

I would also like to thank the team at Emond Publishing for their guidance and help, especially Heather Gough, whose ideas, suggestions, and research improved this edition in countless ways.

Darion Boyington

I am indebted to the team at Emond Publishing for their work and assistance in completing this edition: Anthony Rezek, for his unstinting support; Heather Gough, for her attentive and meticulous editing, and for her patience and help in keeping the project moving; Laura Bast, for her effective supervision of design and production; and Holly Penick, for her efforts in the marketing of the book.

I am grateful to my colleagues for their encouragement and support. I thank my friends and family for listening and encouraging. I thank my parents for a lifetime of love and support. And finally, to Manmeet, Reet, and Harman, I owe my deepest appreciation and gratitude, for their love, encouragement, support, and understanding along the way.

Harpreet Aulakh

About the Authors

Darion Boyington served 14 years as a police officer, occupying various roles such as coaching new recruits and developing community services programs. She left policing to teach at Mohawk College in the Police Foundations program and to complete her degree at Wilfrid Laurier University. Her passion for the study of Indigenous Issues in Canada comes from her front-line experience with Indigenous people in the criminal justice system. Her research centres on understanding the past and present conditions of Indigenous people in Canada, and specifically their relationship with the criminal justice system. Her research goal is to create accurate, quality curricula to enable all students, especially justice students, to fully comprehend the multi-faceted challenges that currently face Indigenous populations in Canada, and to be prepared to partner with Indigenous communities in their efforts to improve their position in Canada, making a more equal society for everyone.

Harpreet Aulakh is an associate professor in the Department of Economics, Justice and Policy Studies at Mount Royal University, Calgary. She holds a PhD in sociology from the University of Saskatchewan, Saskatoon with a focus in criminology and sociology of law. Her primary academic areas of interest are diversity issues and the criminal justice system, Indigenous peoples and justice, youth gangs, youth crime, and youth justice. Since 2008, she has taught at Mount Royal University in the criminal justice program. She teaches courses in diversity and justice, young offenders in conflict with the law, and Indigenous people and the criminal justice system. She is currently the program coordinator of justice studies in the department.

PART I

Diversity Issues in Canada

1 A Portrait of Canadian Diversity

Young Syrian refugees gather around Minister of Immigration, Refugees and Citizenship John McCallum (second from left); Defence Minister Harjit Sajjan (centre); and Health Minister Jane Philpott (right) as they tour the Zaatari Refugee Camp, near the city of Mafraq, Jordan, in 2015.

LEARNING OUTCOMES

After completing this chapter, you should be able to:

- Understand the concepts of diversity and multiculturalism.
- Discuss the four state ideologies of host countries.
- Define Canada's concept of multiculturalism.
- Understand Canadian society, immigration, gender, sexuality, and Canadian diversity.

Introduction

Canadian citizens come from many different nations and cultural backgrounds. In demographic terms, Canada is heterogeneous with regard to race, ethnicity, culture, religion, gender, sexual orientation, age, and physical and mental abilities. Canada's multiculturalism policies, the *Canadian Charter of Rights and Freedoms*, provincial human rights legislation, and affirmative programs are institutional responses to this diversity. Canada is an advanced nation known around the world for its fairness and equality, but diverse minority groups face inequalities in life experiences and life chances, and there appear to be disparities in their interactions with the justice system. The tensions resulting from Canada's increasing diversity (Li, 1998) can be exacerbated by intersections of ethnicity, gender, and sexuality, and by the challenges to our security posed by threatened or actual terrorism. This book presents an up-to-date and critically stimulating introduction to issues surrounding diversity and social and criminal justice. The first part of the book looks at the facts of diversity in Canadian society, and the second part examines colonialism and the historical and current injustices experienced by Indigenous people in Canada, and their overrepresentation in the criminal justice system.

Diversity refers, in a general sense, to the variety of human qualities among different people and groups (University of Maryland, 2000). More specifically, it refers to the ethnic, social, or gender variety in a community of people. When we consider the diversity of a community, we look at its members in two aspects or dimensions: primary and secondary. *Primary* dimensions include a person's age, **ethnicity**, gender, physical abilities and qualities, race, and sexual orientation. *Secondary* dimensions include the person's educational background, geographic location, income, marital status, parental status, religious beliefs, and work experience. Secondary dimensions are less fixed than primary ones (Kazarian, Crichlow, & Bradford, 2007, p. 4).

The term **multiculturalism** has different meanings and associations. It can suggest an ideal of cultural variety, and it can describe the actual state of a society—its condition of having a diverse population. Multiculturalism exists in many countries, including Australia, the United Kingdom, and the United States. In some of these places, it is a cause for celebration as well as a plain fact. Only in Canada, however, is multiculturalism both a national ideology and a state policy. Canada is the first nation to make a policy of multiculturalism part of its national constitution (Kazarian et al., 2007, p. 39).

diversity
the variety of human qualities among different people and groups

ethnicity
the culture of origin with which an individual or group identifies within a multicultural context

multiculturalism
a policy relating to or designed for a combination of several distinct cultures

Four State Ideologies

Host cultures—cultures that receive immigrants and refugees—tend to have one of four ideologies, or belief systems, regarding how to incorporate new members of their society. These four ideologies are as follows: multiculturalism ideology, civic ideology, assimilation ideology, and ethnist ideology.

Multiculturalism Ideology

The **multiculturalism ideology** supports people of diversity in maintaining or promoting their distinctive culture, provided that this culture does not clash with the criminal and civil laws of the nation. Four main principles are associated with the ideology of multiculturalism. First, people of diversity are expected to adopt the public **values** of the host nation: its democratic ideals, constitutional and human rights provisions, and civil and criminal codes. A second principle is that the private values of individual citizens are protected. Private values are the attitudes and beliefs that people hold in private life, shown in their relations with family and friends as well as in their wider social circle. A third principle of multiculturalism ideology is that the state recognizes multicultural values and protects them from interference by other people and by the state itself. The fourth principle is that the state should fund the ethnocultural activities of both its long-standing citizens and its newcomers, since both groups contribute to the state through taxation.

Civic Ideology

The second approach a society may take to the diversity of its citizens is the **civic ideology**. This ideology is the same as the multiculturalism ideology except that it doesn't support state funding for the promotion of ethnocultural diversity. Great Britain is an example of a state that supports civic ideology.

Assimilation Ideology

The **assimilation ideology** is a homogenization or "melting pot" ideology. According to this ideology, newcomers to a country should give up their cultural and linguistic identities and adopt the culture of the host state. In return, the state protects the private values of individual citizens while reserving the right to limit the expression of these values under certain circumstances. The United States supports assimilation ideology.

Ethnist Ideology

The **ethnist ideology** is similar to the assimilation ideology except that the state exerts more control over which groups are permitted to assimilate (Kazarian et al., 2007, p. 39). For example, the state may require that an immigrant be part of a certain ethnicity, religion, or race to be accepted as a citizen. Japan and Israel subscribe to ethnist ideology.

Canada and the Concept of Multiculturalism

Canada has been defined by its dominant cultures. This occurred in three distinct historical stages:

1. Canada as a Colony of the British Empire
   a. An external authority in England exercised sovereignty.
   b. Canadians had limited democratic rights and were governed by a political elite.
   c. The dominant cultures were English and French, although the British sought to assimilate the French.
2. Canada as an Independent "White Dominion" in the British Empire/Commonwealth
   a. Sovereignty was increasingly exercised within the Dominion.
   b. Canadians had full democratic rights and were governed by Parliament.
   c. The dominant culture was British, although immigrants began arriving to colonize the West.
   d. Commitment to the British Empire and a policy of assimilation still produced cultural uniformity in Canada (except in Quebec). Canadians were British subjects until 1947.

multiculturalism ideology
ideology that recognizes and supports people of diversity in maintaining or promoting their diversity, provided that their practices do not clash with the laws of the nation

values
standards or principles; ideas about the worth or importance of certain qualities, especially those accepted by a particular group

civic ideology
ideology that subscribes to multiculturalism ideology principles but does not support state funding to maintain and promote ethnocultural diversity

assimilation ideology
ideology that expects people of diversity to relinquish their culture and linguistic identity and adopt the culture of the host state

ethnist ideology
ideology that expects people of diversity to assimilate, but the state defines which groups should assimilate and thus which ones are not rightful members of the state

3. Canada as a Fully Sovereign and Independent Nation-State
   a. Canada became completely independent of British sovereignty (1931–1949).
   b. The divide between French and English was temporarily settled through constitutional reform.
   c. European immigration slowed while people from other parts of the world began to immigrate to Canada.
   d. The subsequent immigration boom caused a substantial demographic shift in the latter half of the 20th century.
   e. The assimilation of French Canadians and Indigenous peoples was eventually replaced by the concept of multiculturalism.

Equal Rights and the Policy of Multiculturalism

Canada faces a difficulty when it comes to diversity issues. On the one hand, Canadians live in a rights-based culture; we assume that all citizens should be treated equally under civil law and that no one will receive any unearned benefits because of his or her identity. This is the rule of law upon which Canada was founded.

But there is tension between this assumption of equal rights and the principles of Canada's multiculturalism, which supports a cultural group's rights to retain its values and way of life within the wider sphere of Canadian society. The equal-rights culture focuses on the individual; multiculturalism focuses on the group.

Multiculturalism became a formal policy in Canada under Prime Minister Pierre Elliott Trudeau in 1971. The policy became law with the *Canadian Multiculturalism Act* of 1988. Further protections for minorities are enshrined in section 15 of the *Canadian Charter of Rights and Freedoms* (1982). These formal policies and laws are meant to address the needs of new Canadians and disadvantaged groups. However, the government's need to interpret multiculturalism from an equal-rights point of view—that is, from the standpoint that everyone is fundamentally equal—has weakened the formal policy of multiculturalism as a tool for addressing inequalities and **discrimination** related to culture. How does it weaken it? For one thing, an assumption of general equality can blur our understanding of just how deeply disadvantaged an immigrant population can be. Further, the equal-rights perspective is sometimes unaccepting of cultural practices that do not meet Canadian standards of equal treatment for all individuals. At what point, for example, does the government discourage the traditional custom of a minority group in Canada—perhaps a custom related to gender—on the grounds that it violates the liberal ideal of equal rights?

Informal multiculturalism refers to the popular idea of multiculturalism held by people in a society where diversity exists. In Canada, informal multiculturalism accepts social diversity as a given and takes it for granted that the relative lack of success of people from disadvantaged groups is owing to the persistence of discriminatory and stereotypical attitudes rather than to the failings of particular formalized policies. According to this viewpoint, the persistence of discriminatory attitudes needs to be examined, as do the ways in which the imbalances of power between minority and majority populations work themselves out in daily life (Baxter, 2003).

discrimination
a process by which a person is deprived of equal access to privileges and opportunities available to others because of prejudice

host community
comprises groups of people who have the power and influence to shape attitudes toward the remaining groups in society

settlement patterns
the variety of ways people physically establish themselves in a country, whether born there or as immigrants

Concept of the Host Community

A **host community** is sometimes called the host culture or nation, the dominant culture or society, or the majority culture. A host community consists of people long established in a country, though the history of their **settlement patterns** may differ. Whether descended from English settlers, from First Nations people, or from more recent immigrants, the members of a host community determine the basic character and attitudes of the society.

Host communities are made up of groups of people who have the power and influence to change attitudes toward the less established communities in the society. These people set the tone for how the rest of society views and deals with the less powerful *other*. In Canada, for example, the host culture might begin to change its views about the rights of gay and lesbian communities and cease to view marriage as an exclusively heterosexual institution, with the result that, after a time, legislation is introduced allowing for gay and lesbian marriages. Host communities also determine immigration policies—that is, who is a desirable addition to the host culture and who is undesirable. Finally, by assimilating newcomers and expecting them to accept its established patterns, the host community influences the settlement and adaptation patterns of those it accepts as newcomers. And the influence doesn't only go one way. Majority host communities are influenced in turn by the minority groups they come in contact with.

Acculturation Orientations of Host Communities

Acculturation refers to the process by which one cultural group acquires from another group new cultural attributes that may eventually be absorbed into its own system. With immigrant groups, host communities adopt one or more of the following acculturation orientations (in other words, approaches to cultural adaptation):

- An **integrationist** host community encourages immigrants both to adopt important features of the host culture and to maintain aspects of their heritage culture.
- An **exclusionary** host community is intolerant of the wishes of immigrants or other cultures to maintain their heritage cultures. At the same time, it does not allow them wholly to adopt the host culture. Host community members are ambivalent about newcomers.
- An **assimilationist** host community demands that immigrants give up their cultural identity and adapt totally to the host culture. In other words, new ethnic communities are expected to participate in ethnocultural institutions that are not their own (Kallen, 2003). Over time, the host culture accepts as full-fledged citizens those who have been culturally absorbed.
- A **segregationist** host community distances itself from immigrants and their cultures. It allows them to maintain their heritage culture, but would prefer that they return to their countries of origin. Members of the host community believe that immigrants "can never be incorporated culturally or socially as rightful members of the host society" (Bourhis, Moise, Perreault, & Senecal, 1997).

Acculturation Orientations of Settler Groups

Immigrants exhibit one of four modes of acculturation—marginalization, assimilation, separation, and integration—which together form the acronym MASI:

- **Marginalization** occurs when people reject the host culture as well as their heritage culture, disenchanted with both.
- **Assimilation** involves giving up one's traditional culture in favour of the host culture.
- **Separation** occurs when an individual rejects the host culture and maintains his or her culture of origin.
- **Integration** occurs when immigrants at once embrace the host culture and maintain their culture of origin.

Integration is generally seen as the most desirable mode of cultural adaptation (Berry, 2006). Immigrants who adapt in this way show good levels of psychological adjustment and personal satisfaction. These are important considerations from an economic perspective and also from

acculturation
process of change in the cultural patterns of an ethnic group as a result of contact with other ethnic groups

integrationist
supportive of immigrants' adopting features of the host culture while maintaining aspects of their heritage culture

exclusionary
intolerant of immigrants' heritage culture and of immigration in general

assimilationist
intolerant of immigrants' heritage culture, demanding that they relinquish the culture and adopt the host culture

segregationist
opposed to immigrants and other cultures, preferring that immigrants return to their countries of origin

marginalization
simultaneous rejection of the culture of origin and the host culture

assimilation
absorption of groups of different cultures into the main culture

separation
individual rejection of the host culture and maintenance of the culture of origin

integration
embrace of the host culture and maintenance of the culture of origin

a law-and-order perspective; members of ethnic groups who are integrated are less likely to engage in disorderly or criminal activity. Because integrationists do not practise separation—do not isolate themselves from the host culture—their allegiance to their heritage culture does not lessen their commitment to the welfare of the host nation (Berry & Sam, 1997).

History of Immigration and Diversity in Canada

Immigration is and always has been an important factor in Canadian society. The latest reports from Statistics Canada indicate that 1,306,764 people immigrated to Canada in the five-year period from 2010 to 2014, an average of about 261,353 people yearly. This process began several centuries ago, with the arrival of English and French explorers and settlers. At first contact between Indigenous peoples and European peoples in Canada, there were 56 Indigenous nations speaking more than 30 languages. The French and English colonized the eastern part of what is now Canada, and signed treaties with First Nations peoples acknowledging Indigenous nationhood.

In 1867, the English and French languages were given constitutional status at Confederation. Bilingualism became the core of Canada's approach to diversity. From the late 1800s to the mid-1900s, Canada's immigration policy was based on supplying a labour pool for settlement and agriculture; after this, immigration policy was based on establishing a Canadian industrial base. Canada recognized the right of minorities to maintain their culture and traditions, with some exceptions, such as the Japanese during the Second World War.

In 1950, as a result of the Massey-Levesque Commission, which linked cultural diversity and Canadian identity, ethnocultural diversity gradually came to be understood as an essential ingredient in a distinct Canadian society. At that time, 92 percent of Canada's population growth was the result of birth rate. By 2001, immigration had outpaced the natural birth rate, and now, birth rate accounts for less than one-third of Canada's population growth, whereas immigration contributes about two-thirds of population growth.

The 1960 *Canadian Bill of Rights* outlawed discrimination by federal agencies on the grounds of race, national origin, colour, religion, and gender. This policy was reflected in the *Immigration Act* of 1960, which stated that immigrants were not to be refused entry into Canada on the grounds of race, national origin, colour, or country of origin. This Act resulted in more immigration from Southern Europe, from Africa, and from the West Indies.

The *Official Languages Act* of 1969 required the government to give equal status, rights, and privileges to both official languages in federal institutions. It further required that these institutions must serve Canadians in the official language of their choice.

The 1970s and 1980s saw substantial numbers of refugees admitted to this country. In some cases, this was a result of Canada's official multiculturalism policy, established in 1971, which provided for programs and services to help individuals from diverse cultures overcome barriers to their full participation in Canadian society.

The 1982 *Canadian Charter of Rights and Freedoms* granted parents who are members of an English or French linguistic minority in the communities where they live to have their children educated in the official language of their choice. Section 27 of the Charter stated that the courts were to interpret the constitution in a manner that would preserve and enhance the multicultural nature of Canada:

> 27. This Charter shall be interpreted in a manner consistent with the preservation and enhancement of the multicultural heritage of Canadians.

Jean Chrétien, as minister of justice, commented on the importance of the Charter in protecting the rights of a multicultural and ethnically diverse population (1982, p. v):

In a free and democratic society, it is important that citizens know exactly what their rights and freedoms are, and where to turn for help and advice in the event that those freedoms are denied or those rights infringed. In a country like Canada—vast and diverse, with 11 governments, 2 official languages, and a variety of ethnic origins—the only way to provide equal protection for everyone is to enshrine those basic rights and freedoms in the Constitution.

The concept of diversity expanded from language, ethnicity, race, and religion to include gender, sexual orientation, ability (or disability), and age. The rights of diverse groups are enshrined in other Canadian legal responses to diversity, including the following federal legislation:

- the *Canadian Human Rights Act*,
- the *Employment Equity Act*, and
- the *Canadian Multiculturalism Act*.

Provinces have responded to diversity issues by passing similar legislation, including pay equity acts, and developing programs to promote diversity. On the international stage, Canada is signatory to, among others, the following agreements:

- the *Universal Declaration of Human Rights*, and
- the *International Covenant on Economic, Social and Cultural Rights*.

Refugee Policies

Article 1 of the 1951 United Nations *Protocol Relating to the Status of Refugees* (1983) defines a refugee as any person who

> owing to well-founded fear of being persecuted for reasons of race, religion, nationality, membership of a particular social group or political opinion, is outside the country of nationality and is unable or, owing to such fear, is unwilling to avail himself of the protection of that country; or who, not having a nationality and being outside the country of his former habitual residence as a result of such events, is unable or, owing to such fear, is unwilling to return to it.

Welcoming refugees should be seen not as an immigration issue, but as a human rights issue.

Canada has been home to refugees since before Confederation. The United Empire Loyalists, for example, flocked to Canada (along with many non-British subjects) during the American Revolution in 1776. Similarly, English Puritans found refuge in Canada in the 1600s after suffering religious persecution in their native country. Scots settled in Canada after the Highland Clearances of the 1600s, the Irish during the potato famine of the 1800s, Russians as a result of the Bolshevik Revolution, and Armenians after the genocide of 1923. The origins of Canada's refugees continue to change. Refugees just after the Second World War were primarily from Eastern Europe. Nowadays, the majority come from places such as South Asia, Somalia, Cambodia, Vietnam, Guatemala, and the Middle East.

Canada's humanitarian tradition with respect to refugees continues to be strong. From 1995 to 2004, Canada welcomed more than 2.1 million immigrants, among them 265,685 refugees (12 percent of all immigrants) who were granted permanent residence (Canadian Council for Refugees, 2005). In 2014, Canada gave permanent residence to 23,286 refugees (Statistics Canada, 2015a). Continuing Canada's commitment to respond to humanitarian crises, by the end of February 2016, the federal government had welcomed more than 25,000 refugees who were displaced as a result of armed conflict in Syria.

refugee policy
humanitarian policy, based on the United Nations definition of a refugee, that assesses eligibility for entry to a country based on refugee status

Immigration and refugee policies need periodic renovation, and such changes have occurred in Canada. The 1976 Canadian *Immigration Act* introduced a **refugee policy** that formalized the country's approach to identifying and selecting refugees. The Act identified three routes to granting qualified refugees permission to resettle in Canada: overseas selection, special programs, and inland refugee-status determination.

In 1996, a review of Canada's refugee and immigration policy was initiated with the aim of making fundamental policy reforms and introducing new legislation. This resulted in the reintroduction of the *Immigration and Refugee Protection Act* of 2001. This Act and its accompanying regulations had the following aims:

- to be simpler, more modern, and more coherent than previous legislation;
- to respond effectively to Canada's global challenges of the 21st century;
- to ensure that Canada can preserve immigration as a source of diversity, richness, and openness to the world;
- to enhance Canada's advantage in the global competition for skilled workers;
- to maintain and enhance the country's strong humanitarian tradition;
- to deter migrant trafficking and to punish those who engage in this form of slavery; and
- to maintain confidence in the integrity of the immigration and refugee protection program.

The main reason for these changes to the country's refugee policy was to clear the backlog of refugee cases. On June 29, 2010, Bill C-11, the *Balanced Refugee Reform Act*, received royal assent. This Act affects the Immigration and Refugee Board of Canada (IRB) and was intended to improve Canada's asylum system, resettle more refugees from abroad, and make it easier for refugees to start their lives in Canada (Citizenship and Immigration Canada, 2011). Another set of significant changes to the refugee determination system came into force on December 15, 2012 as a result of the *Balanced Refugee Reform Act* and the *Protecting Canada's Immigration System Act*. These changes have been widely criticized on the grounds that they create a two-tier system for refugee protection that discriminates against some refugee claimants based on the country of origin, requires mandatory detention of designated foreign nationals, provides limited recourse for negative decisions, and provides limited access to social safety nets such as health care services.

The Syrian Refugee Crisis

In 2011 in Syria, increasing hostilities and civil war between several factions forced many Syrians to flee to neighbouring countries. By 2013, over 2 million refugees had fled the country, in need of peaceful resettlement elsewhere. In January 2015, the Canadian government pledged to resettle 10,000 Syrian refugees over three years; after the fall 2015 federal election, the newly elected government revised this plan to accept 25,000 refugees by the end of 2015. The target date was later extended to February 2016 to allow more time to process refugee applications. A total of 29,713 Syrian refugees were resettled from November 4, 2015 to August 1, 2016 (Government of Canada, 2016).

Not all reactions to the newcomers have been positive. On January 8, 2016, a Muslim centre in Vancouver organized a welcome event for a group of Syrian refugees. After the event, around 30 attendees, including a number of children, were waiting for a bus when they were pepper-sprayed by a man bicycling past. The Vancouver police announced that they would treat the incident as a hate-motivated crime (see Chapter 2).

Source: Azpiri (2016).

EXERCISE 1

With the Vancouver pepper-spraying incident in mind, examine the following quotation. Do you feel that acceptance of and respect for diverse cultures have to be legislated? Do you believe that, with increasing immigration, Canadians might not so readily give this respect and acceptance? Give reasons for your answer.

> Compassion, acceptance, and trust; diversity and inclusion—these are the things that have made Canada strong and free. Not just in principle, but in practice. Those of us who benefit from the many blessings of Canada's diversity need to be strong and confident custodians of its character. (Trudeau, 2015)

Canada's Indigenous Peoples

As mentioned at the beginning of this chapter, there was a significant Indigenous presence in Canada when the first Europeans arrived. Indigenous cultures were greatly affected by contact with Europeans. From the first, Indigenous nations were at a disadvantage. They faced social changes, new technologies, and imported diseases, as well as the Europeans' quest for new lands.

The French and the British were the main European influences in North America from the 1500s to the early 1900s. They competed for dominance by establishing settlements. Both sides courted Indigenous peoples in their quest for trade and in their battles with each other over control of the continent. European settlement gradually pushed Indigenous peoples off the land, and they became dependent upon Europeans for their livelihood. Hunting skills disappeared, languages were lost, traditions were abolished. Indigenous peoples came to be seen as wards of the government, unable to take care of themselves. Missionaries moved in to "save" the lost Indigenous souls, one result of which was the infamous residential school system in which many Indigenous children were physically, culturally, and sexually abused.

In the second half of the 20th century, oppressed peoples around the world challenged the remnants of colonialism and demanded equality. Some of these peoples proclaimed their independence and forged new nations. Others, such as the First Nations, Inuit, and Métis of Canada, demanded the right to sovereignty and self-determination within the framework of Canada (Roberts, 2006).

Attempts to address the needs of Canada's Indigenous peoples began in 1973. This was when Indigenous land rights, based on a group's traditional use and occupancy of a certain area of land, were first recognized. In 1982, the *Charter of Rights and Freedoms* recognized and affirmed the treaty rights of Indigenous (Aboriginal) peoples to protect their cultures, traditions, and languages. In 1996, the Royal Commission on Aboriginal Peoples presented a comprehensive five-volume report to Parliament identifying the legal, political, social, economic, and cultural issues that need to be addressed to ensure the future survival of Canada's First Nations, Inuit, and Métis. Two years later, the government responded with a plan to work in partnership with Canada's Indigenous peoples to improve their health, housing, and public safety; to strengthen their economic development; and to help them implement self-government.

Indigenous peoples account for a significant portion of the Canadian population. The 2011 census revealed that 1,400,685 individuals in Canada reported Indigenous identity, representing 4.3 percent of the Canadian population (Statistics Canada, 2011a). Those claiming First Nations identity numbered about 851,560 people, making them the largest Indigenous ancestry group. Another 451,795 individuals reported Métis identity, and 59,445 individuals identified as Inuit.

Indigenous cultures will be lost if modern governments do not help protect them by enabling Indigenous peoples to continue their traditional ways of life on their ancestral lands. In both

North America and Australia, hundreds of Indigenous languages and cultural practices are either extinct or endangered. If the rights of Indigenous peoples to freely hunt, fish, or travel are not restored or maintained, their cultures will disappear (University of Maryland, 2000).

Immigration Trends

This section examines immigration into Canada around the beginning of the 21st century.

Ethnic Origins

Ethnic origin, as defined in the census, refers to the ethnic or cultural group to which an individual's ancestors belonged. The 1901 census recorded about 25 different ethnic groups in Canada. At that time, people of either Indigenous, British, or French origins made up the majority of the ethnic groups reported.

The list of ethnic origins in 2011 includes much greater variety (see Table 1.1); more than 260 different ethnic origins were reported in Canada's 2011 census (Statistics Canada, 2011c). Among these were the groups associated with Canada's Indigenous peoples and with the European groups—the English, French, Scottish, and Irish—that first settled in Canada. There were also groups associated with immigrants who came to Canada over the last century: Germans, Italians, Chinese, Ukrainians, Dutch, Polish, and East Indians, among others. Table 1.2 shows the most prevalent ethnic origins in Canada and how these origins have changed over three generations. The statistics concerning the third generation reflect responses to the 2011 National Household Survey.

By 2011, 13 Canadian groups with distinct ethnic origins had passed the 1 million mark. The largest group, just over 10 million people, reported their ethnic origin as Canadian, either alone or with other origins.

Visible Minorities

Visible minorities are legally recognized in Canada; they are one of four groups designated under the *Employment Equity Act*. (The other three such groups are women, Aboriginal people, and people with disabilities.) The 2011 National Household Survey enumerated 6,264,750 individuals who identified themselves as members of the **visible minority** population (Statistics Canada, 2011c). They made up 19 percent of the total population of Canada (see Figure 1.1).

The visible minority population in Canada has grown steadily over the past 35 years. In 1981, the estimated 1.1 million people in this group represented 4.7 percent of Canada's total population. In 1991, 2.5 million people were members of a visible minority group, 9.4 percent of the population. This number increased to 3.2 million in 1996, which was 11.2 percent of the total population. By 2001, their numbers had reached an estimated 3,983,800—13.4 percent of the total population. Between 2001 and 2006, the rate of growth of the visible minority population was 27.2 percent, five times greater than the whole population's 5.4 percent rate of growth. From 2006 to 2011, the visible population increased by 23.5 percent, almost four times faster than the increase for the Canadian population, which was only 5.9 percent.

If current trends continue, Canada's visible minority population will continue to grow more quickly than the rest of the population; by 2031, according to Statistics Canada projections, visible minority groups could represent roughly one-third (14.4 million people) of Canada's total population. In comparison, the rest of population is projected to increase by just 12 percent during this period.

visible minority
individuals, other than Indigenous peoples, who are non-Caucasian in race or non-white in colour

TABLE 1.1   Ethnic Origins, 2011 Counts, for Canada, Provinces, and Territories

	Total responses[1]	Single responses[2]	Multiple responses[3]
		number	
Total population	**32,852,320**	**19,036,295**	**13,816,025**
Ethnic origin			
Canadian	10,563,805	5,834,535	4,729,265
English.............................	6,509,500	1,312,570	5,196,930
French	5,065,690	1,165,465	3,900,225
Scottish	4,714,970	544,440	4,170,530
Irish	4,544,870	506,445	4,038,425
German	3,203,330	608,520	2,594,805
Italian	1,488,425	700,845	787,580
Chinese	1,487,580	1,210,945	276,635
First Nations (North American Indian)	1,369,115	517,550	851,565
Ukrainian...........................	1,251,170	276,055	975,110
Dutch (Netherlands)	1,067,245	297,885	769,355
Polish	1,010,705	255,135	755,565
East Indian	1,165,145	919,155	245,985
Russian	550,520	107,300	443,220
Welsh..............................	458,705	28,785	429,915
Filipino............................	662,600	506,545	156,060
Norwegian	452,705	44,075	408,630
Portuguese	429,850	250,320	179,530
Métis	447,655	68,205	379,445
Swedish...........................	341,845	26,080	315,770
Spanish	368,305	66,575	301,730
American (USA)	372,575	32,935	339,640
Hungarian (Magyar)	316,765	80,540	236,220
Jewish	309,650	115,640	194,010
Greek	252,960	141,755	111,205
Jamaican	256,915	142,870	114,040
Danish	203,080	31,370	171,705
Austrian...........................	197,990	22,945	175,040

NOTES:

1. The category "Total responses" indicates the number of respondents who reported a specified ethnic origin, either as their only ethnic origin or in addition to one or more other ethnic origins. The sum of all total responses for all ethnic origins is greater than the total population estimate due to the reporting of multiple origins.

2. A single ethnic origin response occurs when a respondent provides one ethnic origin only.

3. A multiple ethnic origin response occurs when a respondent provides two or more ethnic origins.

SOURCE: Statistics Canada (2011b).

TABLE 1.2   Top 10 Ethnic Origins by Generational Status, Canada, 2011

First generation[1]		Second generation[2]		Third generation or more[3]	
Ethnic origin	*number*[4]	*Ethnic origin*	*number*	*Ethnic origin*	*number*
Chinese	1,058,160	English	1,134,055	Canadian	9,447,975
East Indian	783,065	Canadian	958,725	English	4,833,750
English	541,695	Scottish	719,870	French	4,464,065
Filipino	496,015	German	612,200	Scottish	3,730,650
German	345,805	Irish	599,445	Irish	3,704,230
Italian	344,030	Italian	524,480	German	2,245,320
Scottish	264,450	French	386,755	First Nations (North American Indian)	1,268,980
Irish	241,195	Chinese	375,670	Ukrainian	924,485
French	214,870	East Indian	349,200	Italian	619,915
Polish	211,030	Dutch	303,725	Dutch (Netherlands)	614,075

NOTES:

1. First generation includes persons who were born outside Canada. For the most part, these are people who are now, or have ever been, immigrants to Canada.

2. Second generation includes persons who were born in Canada and had at least one parent born outside Canada. For the most part, these are the children of immigrants.

3. Third generation or more includes persons who were born in Canada with both parents born in Canada.

4. The table indicates the number of respondents who reported a specified ethnic origin, either as their only ethnic origin or in addition to one or more other ethnic origins. The sum of all total responses for all ethnic origins is greater than the total population estimate due to the reporting of multiple origins.

SOURCE: Statistics Canada (2011b).

FIGURE 1.1   Number and Share of Visible Minority Persons in Canada, 1981–2011

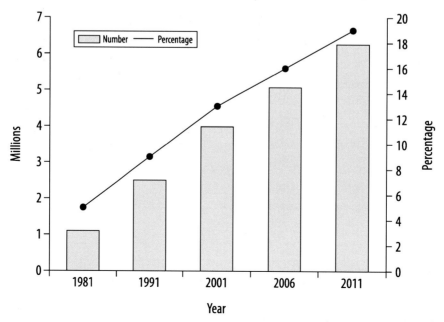

SOURCE: Statistics Canada (2006); Statistics Canada (2013).

The Distribution of Visible Minority Groups

South Asians—people from the southern part of Asia, including, among others, people from Bangladesh, East India, Pakistan, and Sri Lanka—made up Canada's largest visible minority group in 2011 (see Table 1.3).

The 2011 census listed 1,567,400 individuals who identified themselves as South Asian, an increase of 24 percent from 1,262,865 in 2006. They represented 25 percent of all visible minorities, or 4.8 percent of the total population of Canada. By comparison, between 2006 and 2011, the number of individuals in Canada who identified themselves as Chinese increased 8.9 percent, from 1,216,570 to 1,324,745. This group accounted for about 21 percent of the visible minority population and 4 percent of the total Canadian population. The number of people in Canada identifying themselves as Black rose 20.6 percent between 2006 and 2011, from 783,795 to 945,665, making them the third-largest visible minority group. They accounted for 15 percent of the visible minority population and 2.9 percent of the total Canadian population in 2011 (Statistics Canada, 2011c).

TABLE 1.3   Visible Minority Groups, 2011 Counts, for Canada, Provinces, and Territories

Geographic name	Total population by visible minority groups	Total visible minority population[1]	South Asian[2]	Chinese	Black	Filipino	Latin American	Arab	Southeast Asian[3]
Canada............	32,852,320	6,264,750	1,567,400	1,324,745	945,665	619,310	381,280	380,620	312,080
Newfoundland and Labrador	507,270	6,930	1,855	1,645	1,450	350	185	370	320
Prince Edward Island	137,375	4,255	490	1,830	385	90	235	200	205
Nova Scotia	906,170	47,270	4,960	6,050	20,785	1,890	1,360	6,285	1,160
New Brunswick	735,835	17,130	2,445	2,535	4,875	1,100	1,160	1,380	730
Quebec	7,732,525	850,240	83,320	82,850	243,625	31,490	116,380	166,260	65,855
Ontario	12,651,795	3,279,565	965,990	629,140	539,205	275,380	172,560	151,645	137,875
Manitoba..........	1,174,345	153,625	25,270	17,025	19,610	59,220	9,140	3,240	7,565
Saskatchewan	1,008,760	63,275	12,325	11,300	7,255	16,025	3,255	2,095	4,915
Alberta	3,567,975	656,330	156,660	133,390	74,435	106,030	41,305	34,920	41,025
British Columbia	4,324,455	1,180,870	313,440	438,145	33,260	126,035	35,465	14,090	51,970
Yukon.............	33,320	2,025	360	400	95	675	105	0	210
Northwest Territories	40,800	2,725	185	380	555	900	105	110	225
Nunavut..........	31,700	510	95	65	115	130	30	15	25

NOTES:

1. The *Employment Equity Act* defines visible minorities as "persons, other than aboriginal peoples, who are non-Caucasian in race or non-white in colour."

2. For example, "East Indian," "Pakistani," "Sri Lankan," etc.

3. For example, "Vietnamese," "Cambodian," "Malaysian," "Laotian," etc.

SOURCE: Statistics Canada (2011c).

Metropolitan Areas and Visible Minority Groups

According to the 2011 National Household Survey, most (about 85 percent) of visible minority groups resided in Canada's ten metropolitan areas, compared with almost half of the country's total population that lived in these areas. In 2011, more than 2.5 million visible minority persons lived in Toronto, making up 47 percent of the metropolitan's total population. In Vancouver, more than 1 million people were visible minorities, making up about 45 percent of Vancouver's total population (see Table 1.4). At least 100,000 visible minority persons lived in each of Montreal, Calgary, Ottawa-Gatineau, Edmonton, Winnipeg, and Hamilton (Statistics Canada, 2011f). The three largest visible minority groups in Toronto were South Asians, Chinese, and Blacks.

Other Trends Among Immigrant Groups

Some notable trends among newcomers to this country, according to Statistics Canada (2011c), include the following:

- In 2011, of the number of immigrants who reported a single mother tongue, about 24 percent reported English as their mother tongue. Of the top non-official languages, the Chinese languages were most common mother tongues, followed by Tagalog (a language of the Philippines), Spanish, and Punjabi (see Table 1.5).
- The incidence of people reporting multiple ethnic ancestries continued to rise in 2011. An estimated 45.4 percent reported more than one ethnic origin, compared with 41.4 percent in 2006, 38.2 percent in 2001, and 35.8 percent in 1996.
- Canada's visible minority population is ethnoculturally diverse (in other words, many of its members represent a blend of ethnic and cultural backgrounds), more so in some groups than in others.
- In 2011, the top ancestries among Blacks were Caribbean, including Jamaican, Haitian, and Trinidadian/Tobagonian, and African, including Somalian, Ghanaian, and Ethiopian. Members of Black visible minority groups also reported British Isles origins (10.9 percent), Canadian origin (10.8 percent), and French origin (4.3 percent).
- Most members of South Asian visible minority groups reported backgrounds from the Indian subcontinent: East Indian, sometimes in combination with other origins (66.0 percent), Pakistani (9.3 percent), Sri Lankan (8.5 percent), and Punjabi (4.7 percent).
- The most frequently reported origin among Latin, Central, and Southern American visible minorities was Mexican. Among the Arab visible minorities, the most frequent was Lebanese. Iranian was most frequent among West Asians, and Filipino among East and Southeast Asians.

TABLE 1.4   Visible Minority Population and Top Three Visible Minority Groups, Selected Census Metropolitan Areas, Canada, 2011

Census metropolitan areas	Total population Number	Visible minority population Number	Percentage	Top 3 visible minority groups
Canada	32,852,325	6,264,755	19.1	South Asian, Chinese, Black
Toronto	5,521,235	2,596,420	47.0	South Asian, Chinese, Black
Montreal	3,752,475	762,325	20.3	Black, Arab, Latin American
Vancouver	2,280,695	1,030,335	45.2	Chinese, South Asian, Filipino
Ottawa–Gatineau	1,215,735	234,015	19.2	Black, Arab, Chinese
Calgary	1,199,125	337,420	28.1	South Asian, Chinese, Filipino
Edmonton	1,139,585	254,990	22.4	South Asian, Chinese, Filipino
Winnipeg	714,635	140,770	19.7	Filipino, South Asian, Black
Hamilton	708,175	101,600	14.3	South Asian, Black, Chinese

SOURCE: Statistics Canada (2011f).

TABLE 1.5   Mother Tongue by Immigrant Status for Canada, 2011 National Household Survey

Mother tongue	Total population[1]	Non-immigrant population[2]	Immigrant population[3]
Total..	**32,852,325**	**25,720,170**	**6,775,765**
Single responses..............................	**32,369,380**	**25,462,830**	**6,562,050**
English	18,850,405	17,213,930	1,559,900
French.......................................	6,967,460	6,717,355	224,820
Non-official languages	6,551,515	1,531,545	4,777,330
Chinese languages[4].......................	1,066,950	171,355	852,710
Panjabi (Punjabi)	433,280	120,020	305,395
Spanish	399,815	65,410	306,685
Italian....................................	403,425	153,710	247,260
Arabic....................................	323,125	50,780	253,525
Aboriginal languages[5]	193,855	193,015	645
German	366,960	159,380	201,095
Tagalog (Pilipino, Filipino).................	371,500	16,230	320,075
Vietnamese	154,910	36,895	115,710
Portuguese	207,980	47,535	155,320
Urdu	165,380	33,585	128,695
Polish	187,455	44,000	141,770
Korean	137,215	11,135	106,565
Persian (Farsi)............................	169,545	19,290	144,475
Russian...................................	162,335	20,095	138,125
Tamil.....................................	146,710	28,910	114,655
Other languages[6]	2,635	415	2,155
Multiple responses	**482,945**	**257,340**	**213,715**
English and French...........................	57,820	54,255	3,355
English and non-official language	353,530	175,425	168,705
French and non-official language	65,320	23,865	39,260
English, French, and non-official language	6,280	3,800	2,390

NOTES:

1. The total population count includes the non-immigrant population, the immigrant population, and the non-permanent resident population. The non-permanent resident population is not shown separately.

2. Non-immigrants are persons who are Canadian citizens by birth. Although most Canadian citizens by birth were born in Canada, a small number were born outside Canada to Canadian parents.

3. Immigrants are persons who are, or have ever been, landed immigrants in Canada. A landed immigrant is a person who has been granted the right to live in Canada permanently by immigration authorities. Some immigrants have resided in Canada for a number of years, while others are more recent arrivals. Most immigrants were born outside Canada, but a small number were born in Canada. Includes immigrants who landed in Canada prior to Census Day, May 10, 2011.

4. All Chinese languages are grouped together. For a detailed breakdown of Chinese languages, see 2011 Census Dictionary.

5. All Aboriginal languages are grouped together. For a detailed breakdown of Aboriginal languages, see 2011 Census Dictionary.

6. This is a subtotal of all languages collected by the census that are not displayed separately. For a full list of languages collected in the census, see 2011 Census Dictionary.

SOURCE: Statistics Canada (2011d).

Immigration and Diversity

There has been a fundamental transformation in Canadian immigration since 1961. The "Old Canada" is still present—a country that resists multiculturalism; is predominantly rural, conservative, and white; and opposes social change. But this dated version of our country is no longer the main one, and it is under pressure from diverse ethnicities. This pressure will have a profound effect on, among other things, the ways people communicate and the ways public services are delivered. As we become aware of cultural barriers to communication and the need to communicate on a global scale, we will see the need to incorporate the languages of diverse cultures into the public sphere. This will lead, for example, to a requirement that public service and business workers be bilingual or even trilingual.

Before 1961, the Canadian government deliberately sought to retain the British nature of Canadian society. Canadian culture was bound by a fairly uniform code of moral attitudes and manners. Profound differences of opinion or culture were not readily tolerated. The general cultural emphasis was on work, the accumulation of wealth, the written word, codified laws and regulations, and punctuality.

Since 1961, immigration has produced a society where social customs and manners are more diverse, dynamic, and fluid. These changes pose a challenge to Canadian civil authorities. How will someone from a small African community be integrated into Canadian culture? How can we expect that person to understand something as complicated as Canada's *Criminal Code*? Most people whose families have been in Canada for more than three generations take for granted their understanding of what is socially acceptable, legal or illegal, or simply right and wrong; they have been raised within this cultural context. Such people also tend to assume that the predominant customs and laws in this country are somehow natural or superior to others. These assumptions are now being challenged, and the question of national identity—what is a Canadian?—remains open.

One of the challenges facing newcomers to this country is poverty. This condition is widespread among immigrant groups, and it is a problem not only for them but for our society as a whole. The children of immigrants and visible minorities are twice as likely as other Canadian children to live in poverty. Almost one in two recent-immigrant children lives in poverty (Brown, 2005). As Laurel Rothman (2005) has said,

> Here in one of the wealthiest countries in the world, with the lowest unemployment rate in 30 years, it seems an irony that so many [immigrant] children still live in poverty. All of these groups are growing … [O]ur national policy is to increase the number of immigrants … but at the most basic levels of food and housing and income, these groups are being marginalized.

One of the many reasons for this poverty is that male immigrants face barriers to good jobs. Earnings of full-time male workers who had recently immigrated to this country fell significantly in the period 1980–2006, while earnings of Canadian-born men rose slightly. Discrimination still influences hiring, despite the laws against it. Our society resists recognizing the professional credentials of immigrants, despite the shortage of qualified people in certain areas of our labour force, such as doctors in Ontario or skilled workers across the country. The low wages earned by immigrants put a strain on our social services. Some immigrants are returning to their homelands because they can't make a living here.

EXERCISE 2

Two problems facing immigrants—poverty and lack of acceptable credentials—are mentioned in the previous paragraph. List some of the other problems faced by immigrants, and give examples of each.

Developing a Canadian Identity

Demographic trends indicate that more and more people in this country are identifying themselves as Canadian. In the 2011 census, the most frequently reported ethnicities among third-generation immigrants were as follows (see also Table 1.2):

- Canadian (10.5 million),
- English (6.5 million),
- French (5 million),
- Scottish (4.7 million),
- Irish (4.5 million), and
- German (3.2 million).

These numbers tell us that in 2011 over 30 percent of the population identified themselves as Canadian. This fact might suggest the possibility of defining a Canadian identity. However, a study done by Rudolf Kalin and John W. Berry (2000) suggests that the majority of those who identify themselves as Canadian are members of the Charter groups—in other words, descendants of English and French settlers. Slightly fewer than one-half of people from other ethnic heritages chose to identify themselves as Canadian.

It is likely that as successive generations of immigrant families live in Canada, their members will lean more toward identifying themselves as Canadian. But this will be a gradual process. According to Statistics Canada (2006), immigrants were more likely than people born in Canada to report a strong sense of belonging to their ethnic or cultural group, and immigrants who had recently arrived indicated that their ethnic or cultural ancestry was important to them. This allegiance is reflected in the fact that there are more than 250 ethnic newspapers and magazines produced in the Toronto area alone. The mission of these media is to inform, to build community, and, as time goes on, to pass their cultural legacy on to the next generation.

Statistics show that the first generation of immigrants has the strongest sense of belonging to an **ethnic group**, with this sense of ethnicity declining considerably by the third generation (see Table 1.2). Identification with Canada increases with time in Canada, as does participation in non-ethnic organizations. Multiculturalism and cultural diversity seem to be working for Canada. It seems likely that, in time, a true Canadian identity will emerge—an identity that, instead of simply assimilating the country's new members into a uniform culture, will register their diverse values as contributions to Canadian society. And these new members, in turn, will come to see themselves as Canadian.

ethnic group
group of individuals with a shared sense of peoplehood based on presumed shared socio-cultural experiences and/or similar characteristics

The search for a Canadian identity is probably premature right now. But when this identity does emerge, it will be characterized by openness, tolerance, multiculturalism, and diversity. This identity won't define itself negatively—for example, against the melting-pot identity of the United States ("Our identity is that we're not like them"). It will be a positive identity of different textures and contours, expressing a society where people of all origins and ethnicities are free to maintain their cultures and traditional faiths and customs. There is still a way to go, but it's happening.

EXERCISE 3

How would you define the Canadian identity? What is a Canadian? How does a Canadian differ from a citizen of any other country in the world? How do Canadians differ from Americans? Be specific in your answers, and give concrete examples.

Gender

Immigration plays a significant role in determining the composition of Canada's population. However, diversity in Canada extends beyond ethnicity, immigration, visible minority, religion, and languages; it includes gender and sexual diversity.

There is a spectrum of terms that play a role in understanding gender diversity in Canada. The biological characteristics differentiating males and females are referred to as **sex**. The social or cultural characteristics associated with being male or female are referred to as **gender**. The World Health Organization defines gender as referring to the socially constructed roles, behaviours, activities, and attributes that a given society or culture considers appropriate for men and women. **Gender identity** is the extent to which one identifies as being either masculine or feminine (Diamond, 2002). The environments in which people grow up shape their understanding of gender, **gender roles**, and gender identity.

Female Population in Canada

The sex structure of Canada's population is changing and so are the socio-demographic and ethnocultural characteristics of females. Females account for just over half of Canada's population. In 2014, there were slightly more females than males; there were 17.9 million females (50.4 percent) compared with 17.6 million males (49.6 percent) (Statistics Canada, 2015b). Over the past century, female population has grown slightly faster compared with male population. In 1921, there were fewer females: 4.3 million (48.5 percent) compared with 4.5 million males (51.5 percent).

Like the general population, the female population in Canada is aging because of the combination of various factors such as low fertility rates, high life expectancy, and the aging of baby boomers (Statistics Canada, 2011e). The proportion of senior women aged 65 and over has increased over time, whereas that of girls under 14 years of age has decreased. The majority of both males and females reside in the four most populous provinces in Canada: Ontario, Quebec, British Columbia, and Alberta. In 2014, the female population of the three most populous provinces (Ontario, Quebec, and British Columbia) was younger than that of the Atlantic provinces and older than that of the Prairie provinces (Statistics Canada, 2015b). (These three provinces also have larger shares of immigrants compared with the rest of the country.) The female population in the Prairie provinces is the youngest; this is explained by the relatively large proportion of Indigenous population in Saskatchewan and Manitoba. The Indigenous population has high fertility rates and thus a higher proportion of younger people compared with the non-Indigenous population.

Canada's female population is becoming increasingly diverse in terms of ethnicity. Out of the total female population, 4.3 percent reported an Indigenous identity in the 2011 National Household Survey (Statistics Canada, 2015b). A similar proportion of males reported an Indigenous identity. Compared with Indigenous females, the median age for Indigenous males in 2011 was lower (26.1 years for Indigenous males and 29.1 years for Indigenous females). The Indigenous female population grew more than four times as fast as the non-Indigenous female population between 2006 and 2011: 20 percent for Indigenous females, compared with 4.8 percent for non-Indigenous females.

According to the 2011 National Household Survey, 3.5 million females or 21 percent of the total female population were immigrants, up from 20 percent in 2006, 19 percent in 2001, and 14 percent in 1951 (Figure 1.2). The most common country of birth of female immigrants who arrived in 2013 was China (14 percent), followed by 12 percent each from India and Philippines and more than 4 percent each from Pakistan and Iran. Correspondingly, for immigrant males who arrived in Canada in 2013, about 13 percent were born in each of India and China, followed by 10 percent in Philippines, 4.9 percent in Pakistan, and 4.3 percent in Iran (Statistics Canada, 2015b). A slightly higher number of females (67 percent compared with 63 percent of males) who reported visible minority status were immigrants in 2011.

sex
a person's biological status as assigned at birth, typically categorized as male, female, or intersex, and associated with physical attributes such as chromosomes, hormonal prevalence, and external and internal anatomy

gender
the culturally constructed roles, attitudes, feelings, and behaviours that are associated with a person's biological sex

gender identity
a person's self-perception of their gender, which may or may not be the same as their birth-assigned sex

gender roles
culturally informed norms of how males and females are expected to feel, think, and behave

FIGURE 1.2   Immigrant Females as a Percentage of the Total Population, Canada, 1921 to 2011

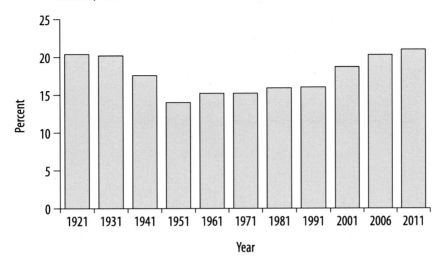

SOURCE: Statistics Canada (2015b).

Females are more likely (78 percent compared with 74 percent of males) to be affiliated with a religion. For both males and females, the most common religion was Christianity. More females (37 percent) than males (27 percent) reported that religious or spiritual beliefs play an important role in the way they live their life.

Gender Diversity and Inequality

Most people develop a gender identity that matches their biological sex. However, some have a gender identity different from their sex. Therefore, the terms *gender* and *sex* should not be used interchangeably. People who have a gender identity different from their biological sex and those who express their gender in ways different from social expectations are referred by the terms *trans*, **transgender**, and **transsexual**.

Gender (in)equality is a global issue because men and women around the world have unequal power relations. The disadvantages women and girls face in our society are a main source of inequality. Women do not benefit from the same rights and opportunities across all sectors of society compared with men. Even though the lives of many women have improved in Canada, gender inequality still remains (Grant, 2016).

Canadian women have made considerable progress in education over the past few decades. More women in Canada than ever before graduate from university and enter professions that were previously exclusively male. However, economic opportunities, pay equity, and job security have not seen as much progress, and sexual harassment in the workplace is still common. As reported by Status of Women Canada, Canada lags behind in the developed world in women's equality (Status of Women Canada, 2015):

- An income gap means that men are paid 20 percent more than their female colleagues.
- Immigrant women have lower rates of labour force participation and employment than other women.
- Indigenous women, women in rural areas, and elderly women are more likely to be living in poverty than non-Indigenous, urban, and younger women.
- Poverty rates for single-mother families and single elderly females increased between 2009 and 2011.
- Muslim women are far more likely to be victims of a hate crime than other women.

transgender
a person whose gender identity, gender expression, or behaviour differs from that typically associated with the biological sex that was assigned at birth

transsexual
a person whose gender identity differs from the biological sex that was assigned at birth

- Violence against males has declined but violence against females has increased.
- Women and girls are disproportionately victims of sexual violence.
- In 2013, most police-reported family violence victims were females.
- Canada has no comprehensive national strategy to address violence against women and lags behind countries such as the United Kingdom, Ireland, Australia, and New Zealand.

In a May 2014 report, the RCMP estimated that there were 1,181 cases of Indigenous women who had disappeared or were murdered since the 1980s. Indigenous women account for 16 percent of Canada's female homicide victims and 11.3 percent of missing women, while they form only 4.3 percent of the total female population of Canada.

Gender and Sexual Harassment in the Military

After media reports estimated that there were 1,780 sexual assaults per year in the Canadian Armed Forces (CAF), the military asked former Supreme Court of Canada justice Marie Deschamps to lead an External Review Authority (ERA) to investigate. Her inquiry targeted CAF policies, procedures, and programs that dealt with sexual misconduct and sexual harassment. In her final report, released March 2015, she found that there was an "underlying sexualized culture" in the CAF that was "hostile to women and LGBTQ members." She wrote:

> [T]he ERA's consultations revealed a sexualized environment in the CAF, particularly among recruits and non-commissioned members, characterized by the frequent use of swear words and highly degrading expressions that reference women's bodies, sexual jokes, innuendos, discriminatory comments with respect to the abilities of women, and unwelcome sexual touching.
>
> Although the most common complaints to the ERA related to this hostile, sexualized environment, the ERA also heard reports of quid pro quo sexual harassment. Some participants further reported instances of sexual assault, including instances of dubious relationships between lower rank women and higher rank men, and date rape. At the most serious extreme, these reports of sexual violence highlighted the use of sex to enforce power relationships and to punish and ostracize a member of a unit.
>
> The ERA found that members appear to become inured to this sexualized culture as they move up the ranks. For example, non-commissioned officers (NCOs), both men and women, appear to be generally desensitized to the sexualized culture. Officers tend to excuse incidents of inappropriate conduct on the basis that the CAF is merely a reflection of civilian society. There is also a strong perception that senior NCOs are responsible for imposing a culture where no one speaks up and which functions to deter victims from reporting sexual misconduct.
>
> As a result of these attitudes, there is a broadly held perception in the lower ranks that those in the chain of command either condone inappropriate sexual conduct, or are willing to turn a blind-eye to such incidents.

Madame Deschamps identified a number of other deficiencies in policy and procedure that discouraged the reporting of sexual harassment and assault and entrenched the culture of hostility. In her report, she made ten recommendations. The first two targeted the sexualized culture, including the recommendation that the CAF acknowledge the serious problem of inappropriate sexual conduct. Recommendation No. 2 stated:

> Establish a strategy to effect cultural change to eliminate the sexualized environment and to better integrate women, including by conducting a gender-based analysis of CAF policies.

Source: Deschamps (2015); Pugliese (2015).

Sexual Diversity

The term **sexual diversity** is often used with respect to sexuality or sexual orientation. Sexuality or **sexual orientation** refers to a person's emotional or sexual attraction. Canadians have become more tolerant and accepting of different sexual orientations. Not everyone is heterosexual; many are gay, lesbian, bisexual, transsexual, or queer (LGBTQ). A society that recognizes and accepts people of different sexual orientations demonstrates sexual diversity.

sexual diversity
variations in sexual behaviours, orientations, and identities

sexual orientation
a person's sexual preference, whether heterosexual, gay or lesbian, or bisexual

Sexual Diversity in Canada

Until the 21st century, sexual diversity in Canada was less visible than it is now. According to the 2011 census, about 2 percent of Canadians identify themselves as homosexual or bisexual (Statistics Canada, 2015c). There were 64,575 same-sex couples living together in 2011, which represents less than 1 percent of all couples. About one-third (21,015) of these couples were legally married; this number had nearly tripled between 2006 and 2011, following the legalization of same-sex marriage in 2005. Over 90 percent of all same-sex couples (married and common law) did not have a child living with them.

Sexual Inequality

Canada is recognized as a world leader in sexual minority rights. In 2005, Canada became the fourth country in the world to legally allow same-sex marriages. But, even with legal equality rights, social inequality still exists for the LGBTQ community in Canada. There are stigma and taboos related to sexual orientation among various ethnocultural groups, and construction of sexual identity differs across different cultures. Fear, hatred, and intolerance of people who are gay, lesbian, bisexual, or transsexual leads to intense feelings and prejudice, which often result in discrimination, harassment, and hate crimes. There has been an increase in the number of hate crimes motivated by intolerance of sexual diversity. In 2013, there were 186 police-reported hate-crime incidents connected to the victims' sexual orientation (Statistics Canada, 2015d). Following are some other facts on police-reported hate crimes motivated by sexual orientation:

- Hate crimes motivated by sexual orientation are more likely to be violent compared with hate crimes targeting other groups.
- Males under the age of 25 are more likely to be both the victims and the perpetrators of violent hate crimes motivated by sexual orientation.
- Most of these violent hate crimes are perpetrated by someone unknown to the victim.

CHAPTER SUMMARY

Canada is a diverse, multicultural country that encourages all groups to retain their cultures and cultural practices. The process of embracing diversity has been lengthy; beginning in colonial times, it has now reached the stage where Canada accepts more than 200,000 immigrants yearly. South Asians are now the most numerous immigrants. South Asians, Chinese, and Blacks are the largest visible minority populations. The trend of increasing immigration has many implications for the development of a Canadian identity.

Even though the sex structure of Canada's population encompasses a slim majority of females over males, gender inequality exists in power relations and pay equity in the workforce. Canada has legally recognized sexual equality; however, strong feelings of hatred toward sexual minority groups are evident in our society. Ethnic diversity intersects with gender and sexual diversity to form a collective Canadian experience.

REFERENCES

Azpiri, J. (2016, January 9). Police release updated suspect description after Syrian refugees pepper sprayed in Vancouver. *Global News*. http://www.globalnews.ca.

Balanced Refugee Reform Act. (2010). SC 2010, c. 8.

Baxter, P. (2003). *A portrait of Canadian diversity*. Unpublished manuscript. Barrie, ON: Georgian College.

Berry, J.W. (2006). Acculturation: A conceptual overview. In M.H. Bornstein & L.R. Cote (Eds.), *Acculturation and parent-child relationships: Measurement and development* (pp. 13–30). Mahwah, NJ: Lawrence Erlbaum Associates.

Berry, J.W., & Sam, D. (1997). Acculturation and adaptation. In J.W. Berry, M.H. Segal, & C. Kagitcibasi (Eds.), *Handbook of cross-cultural psychology: Social behavior and applications*. Vol. 3 (pp. 291–326). Needham Heights, MA: Allyn and Bacon.

Bourhis, R.Y., Moise, L.C., Perreault, S., & Senecal, S. (1997). Towards an interactive acculturation model: A social psychological perspective. *International Journal of Psychology, 32*, 369–386.

Brown, L. (2005, November 24). Native, minority kids twice as likely to be poor. *The Hamilton Spectator*, p. A11.

Canadian Charter of Rights and Freedoms. (1982). Part I of the *Constitution Act, 1982*, being Schedule B to the *Canada Act 1982* (UK), 1982, c. 11.

Canadian Council for Refugees. (2005, March). An overview of Canada's refugee policy. http://ccrweb.ca.

Canadian Multiculturalism Act. (1985). RSC 1985, c. 24 (4th Supp.).

Chrétien, J. (1982). *Canadian Charter of Rights and Freedoms: A guide for Canadians*. Ottawa: Supply and Services.

Citizenship and Immigration Canada. (2011). Balanced refugee reform. http://www.cic.gc.ca/english/refugees/reform.asp.

Deschamps, M. (2015). External review into sexual misconduct and sexual harassment in the Canadian Armed Forces. External Review Authority. http://www.forces.gc.ca/en/caf-community-support-services/external-review-sexual-mh-2015/summary.page.

Diamond, M. (2002). Sex and gender are different: Sexual identity and gender identity are different. *Clinical Child Psychology and Psychiatry, 7*(3): 320–334.

Government of Canada. (2016). Welcome refugees: Canada resettles Syrian refugees. http://www.cic.gc.ca/english/refugees/welcome/milestones.asp.

Grant, T. (2016, March 7). Women still earning less money than men despite gains in education: Study. *The Globe and Mail*. http://www.theglobeandmail.com.

Immigration and Refugee Protection Act. (2001). SC 2001, c. 27.

Kalin, R., & Berry, J.W. (2000). Ethnic and self-identity in Canada: Analyses of 1974 and 1991 national surveys. In M.A. Kalbach & W.E. Kalbach (Eds.), *Perspectives on ethnicity in Canada* (pp. 88–110). Toronto: Harcourt Brace.

Kallen, E. (2003). *Ethnicity and human rights in Canada: A human rights perspective on race, ethnicity, racism and systemic inequality*. New York: Oxford University Press.

Kazarian, S., Crichlow, W., & Bradford, S. (2007). *Diversity issues in law enforcement* (3rd ed.). Toronto: Emond Montgomery.

Li, Peter. (1998). *The Chinese in Canada* (2nd ed.). Toronto: Oxford University Press.

Protecting Canada's Immigration System Act. (2012). SC 2012, c. 17.

Pugliese, D. (2015, May 1). Q&A: Why Marie Deschamps was asked to examine sexual assault and harassment in Canada's military. *The National Post*. http://news.national post.com.

Roberts, J. (2006). *First Nations, Inuit, and Métis peoples: Exploring their past, present, and future*. Toronto: Emond Montgomery.

Rothman, L. (2005). Report card on child poverty in Canada by the coalition Campaign 2000. http://www.campaign2000.ca.

Statistics Canada. (2006). Canada's ethnocultural mosaic, 2006 census: Findings. http://www12.statcan.ca/census-recensement/2006/as-sa/97-562/index-eng.cfm.

Statistics Canada. (2011a). Aboriginal peoples in Canada: First Nations people, Métis and Inuit. https://www12.statcan.gc.ca/nhs-enm/2011/as-sa/99-011-x/99-011-x2011001-eng.cfm.

Statistics Canada. (2011b). 2011 National Household Survey: Data tables. Immigration and ethnocultural diversity. Catalogue no. 99-010-X2011028. http://www12.statcan.gc.ca/nhs-enm/2011/dp-pd/dt-td/Index-eng.cfm.

Statistics Canada. (2011c). 2011 National Household Survey: Data tables. Immigration and ethnocultural diversity. Catalogue no. 99-010-X2011029. http://www12.statcan.gc.ca/nhs-enm/2011/dp-pd/dt-td/Index-eng.cfm.

Statistics Canada. (2011d). 2011 National Household Survey: Data tables. Immigration and ethnocultural diversity. Catalogue no. 99-010-X2011033. http://www12.statcan.gc.ca/nhs-enm/2011/dp-pd/dt-td/Index-eng.cfm.

Statistics Canada. (2011e). Female population. http://www.statcan.gc.ca/pub/89-503-x/2010001/article/11475-eng.pdf.

Statistics Canada. (2011f). Visible minority population and top three visible minority groups, Canada, 2011. https://www12.statcan.gc.ca/nhs-enm/2011/as-sa/99-010-x/2011001/tbl/tbl2-eng.cfm.

Statistics Canada. (2013). Immigration and ethnocultural diversity in Canada: National household survey, 2011. http://www12.statcan.gc.ca/nhs-enm/2011/as-sa/99-010-x/99-010-x2011001-eng.pdf.

Statistics Canada. (2015a). Facts and figures 2014: Immigration overview. http://www.cic.gc.ca/english/resources/statistics/index.asp.

Statistics Canada. (2015b). Female population. http://www.statcan.gc.ca/pub/89-503-x/2015001/article/14152-eng.pdf.

Statistics Canada. (2015c). Same-sex couples and sexual orientation. http://www.statcan.gc.ca/eng/dai/smr08/2015/smr08_203_2015.

Statistics Canada. (2015d). Police reported hate crime in Canada, 2013. http://www.statcan.gc.ca/pub/85-002-x/2015001/article/14191-eng.htm#a20.

Status of Women Canada. (2015). Women and girls in Canada. https://www.documentcloud.org/documents/2363152-statusofwomen.html.

Trudeau, J. (2015, November 26). "Diversity is Canada's strength." http://pm.gc.ca/eng/news/2015/11/26/diversity-canadas-strength.

United Nations. (1983). *Convention and protocol relating to the status of refugees: Final act of the United Nations Conference of Plenipotentiaries on the Status of Refugees and Stateless Persons and the text of the 1951 Convention Relating to Refugees. Resolution 2198 adopted by the General Assembly and the text of the 1967 Protocol Relating to the Status of Refugees.* New York: United Nations.

University of Maryland. (2000). Diversity database. http://www.umd.edu/diversity.

REVIEW QUESTIONS

True or False?

____ 1. The term *multiculturalism* can suggest an ideal of cultural diversity.

____ 2. The term *ethnicity* refers to the ideologies of host cultures.

____ 3. Ethnist ideology is a "melting pot" ideology that accepts all immigrants indiscriminately.

____ 4. There is tension between Canada's assumption that all citizens should be treated equally under the law and its principles of multiculturalism.

____ 5. Multiculturalism became a formal policy in Canada under Prime Minister Pierre Trudeau in 1971.

____ 6. A host community is made up of groups of people who have the power and influence to change attitudes toward the less established communities in the society.

____ 7. "Assimilation" refers to an immigrant's rejection of his or her culture in favour of absorption into the main culture.

____ 8. Indigenous peoples were not recognized under the 1982 *Canadian Charter of Rights and Freedoms*.

____ 9. A person's gender identity refers to the culturally constructed roles, attitudes, and feelings that are associated with the biological sex that was assigned at birth.

____ 10. More visible minority people live in Toronto than in any other city in Canada.

Multiple Choice

1. *Diversity* refers to
   a. country of origin
   b. the variety of human qualities among different people and groups
   c. a national ideology of a country or state
   d. the prevailing attitude of the host country

2. Ethnist ideology is an ideology in which the state
   a. defines which groups are permitted to assimilate
   b. promotes a "melting pot" approach to assimilation
   c. promotes a "homogeneous" approach to assimilation
   d. creates funding for new Canadians

3. The *Canadian Multiculturalism Act* of 1988 was inaugurated to
   a. deny to new Canadians the rights that are held by other Canadians
   b. define the number of immigrants who could arrive in Canada
   c. address the needs of new Canadians and disadvantaged groups
   d. declare the dominant culture of Canada to be British

4. A host community consists of people who
   a. determine the basic character and attitudes of the society
   b. have a friendly attitude to all immigrants
   c. come from English and French cultures
   d. have a variety of marriage institutions

5. Marginalization occurs when
   a. the cultural patterns of an ethnic group change
   b. the host community rejects the immigrants' heritage culture
   c. an immigrant rejects the host culture as well as his or her heritage culture
   d. a visible minority immigrant group moves close to the host country's border

6. Canada has been home to refugees since
   a. 1967
   b. the Second World War
   c. the latest census
   d. before Confederation

7. From the 1500s to the early 1900s, the main European influences in North America were
   a. the Vikings and Norsemen
   b. priests and missionaries
   c. Spain and Portugal
   d. the English and French

8. Visible minorities are persons other than Indigenous people who are
   a. Caucasian in race or non-white in colour
   b. non-Caucasian in race or non-white in colour
   c. Caucasian in race or white in colour
   d. non-Caucasian in race or white in colour

9. Between 2001 and 2006, 75 percent of the immigrants who arrived in Canada were
   a. members of a visible minority group
   b. South Asian
   c. from Jamaica and/or Trinidad
   d. European and Asian

10. Most new Canadians come from
    a. South Asia
    b. the Philippines
    c. China
    d. Pakistan

Fill in the Blanks

1. Canada is the first nation to make a policy of _Multiculturalism_ part of its national constitution.

2. The assimilation ideology is a homogenization or _____ ideology.

3. When Canada was a colony of the British Empire, Canadians had limited _democratic rights_ and were governed by a political elite.

4. Discrimination is the process by which a person is _deprived_ of equal access to privileges and opportunities available to others.

5. Acculturation is the process of change in the _cultural_ patterns of an ethnic group as a result of contact with other ethnic groups.

6. The four designated groups under the *Employment Equity Act* are women, people with disabilities, _Aboriginal people_, and visible minorities.

7. The term *transgender* refers to a person whose _behaviour_ differs from that typically associated with the biological sex that was assigned at birth.

8. Immigrants to Canada are increasingly from _South Asia_.

9. Before 1961, the Canadian government deliberately sought to retain the _British_ nature of Canadian society.

10. The children of immigrants and visible minorities are twice as likely to live in _cities_ as other Canadian children.

2 Human Rights and Freedoms

Queen Elizabeth II signs the Proclamation of the *Constitution Act, 1982* on April 17, 1982, while Prime Minister Pierre Elliott Trudeau (left) looks on. The Proclamation marked the full transfer of legislative authority from the United Kingdom to Canada, granting Canada the power to amend its own constitution. The newly enacted *Constitution Act, 1982* included the *Canadian Charter of Rights and Freedoms*.

LEARNING OUTCOMES

After completing this chapter, you should be able to:

- Identify the major developments in the history of human rights in Canada.
- Understand the contents and key principles in Canada's federal human rights statutes and the Ontario *Human Rights Code*.
- Explain how human rights legislation influences people's individual and collective rights and freedoms.
- Discuss the impact of relevant policies and legislation on the rights of people of diversity.
- Discuss the prevalence of hate crimes and laws dealing with hate crimes.
- Discuss policing in the context of human rights and freedoms since 9/11.

Introduction

The evolution of civil rights has influenced human conditions around the world, inspiring nations and improving their peoples' quality of life. This chapter discusses human rights and freedoms, for four main reasons. First, they reflect the collective conscience of nations. Second, they provide the international community with basic standards of equality and fairness. Third, law enforcement agencies need to understand human rights and freedoms to fulfill their mandate. Fourth, the current tension between two very different ideals of law enforcement—democratic community policing as opposed to the dictatorship policing that has evolved in response to terrorist threats in Western countries—centres on questions about human rights and freedoms.

International Human Rights and Freedoms

The general idea of human rights—that is, the idea of basic claims or privileges to which all humans are entitled—originated with the ancient Greeks and Romans. Today's notion of human rights was strongly influenced by England's 1215 *Magna Carta*, or Great Charter, which was a response to the misuse of power by the monarchy and royal officials in medieval England. This document, which turned 800 years old in 2015, played a crucial role in the development of human rights, democracy, liberty, and justice. It established the principle of the rule of law and the due process of law. The *Magna Carta* informed many future attempts to establish human rights and freedoms, including the United States Declaration of Independence (1776) and the French Declaration of the Rights of Man and of the Citizen (1789). The ideals of liberty and equality are at the core of these documents, most of which affirm, for example, a person's right to pursue happiness, to own property, to enjoy free speech, and not to be imprisoned arbitrarily.

In 1946, the General Assembly of the United Nations established the Commission on Human Rights. Two years later, the Office of the United Nations High Commissioner for Human Rights (1948) set down the *Universal Declaration of Human Rights*. The 30 articles of this document recognize the equality and dignity of all people and grant people certain inalienable human rights, including the right to freedom, security, personal expression, an adequate standard of living, and education. The UN Human Rights Council replaced the UN Commission on Human Rights in 2006, with a mandate to uphold the highest standards in the promotion and protection of human rights. The council includes members from 47 states—13 each from African and Asian states, 6 from Eastern European states, 8 from Latin American and Caribbean states, and 7 from Western European and other states (including Canada and the United States)—and its purpose is to address human rights violations around the world and make recommendations on them. In June 2011, for example, the council established an independent expert to investigate the situation of human rights in Côte d'Ivoire, the African country formerly named Ivory Coast, and it initiated a study of discriminatory laws and practices around the world.

EXERCISE 1

Before beginning this section, read the five statements below. Indicate whether you agree or disagree with each statement, and give reasons for your view. Do you believe that Canadian human rights legislation would address each of these situations? As you go through this chapter, come back to these statements and indicate which act, code, right, or policy in Canada might address each situation.

1. If women want to breastfeed their infants, they should do so in the privacy of their homes, not in public.
2. Parents should be able to remove their children from school instruction that is contrary to their religious beliefs.
3. Human rights and freedoms provisions enable criminals to get away with murder.
4. Muslim women should have the right to wear a niqab (face veil) while testifying in court.
5. The law should protect police officers better, so that they can do their jobs without constant fear of reprisal.

Human Rights in Canada: Federal

Human rights legislation in Canada started 250 years ago. The *Royal Proclamation of 1763* gave provincial legislatures in Canada the right to pass laws in relation to property and civil rights and to local matters. The Proclamation was followed by the *British North America Act* (now called the *Constitution Act, 1867*), which gave the provinces power over property and civil rights and gave the federal government power over divorce and marriage. The *Canadian Bill of Rights* was introduced in 1960 to protect individual rights and freedoms. In 1977, the federal government passed the **Canadian Human Rights Act**.

Canadian Human Rights Act

The term **discrimination** means harassing someone or treating someone unfavourably based on prejudice. Examples of discrimination could include the following:

- refusing to hire someone because of his or her age;
- denying a promotion to a female employee because of her gender;
- having an office that is not accessible to people in wheelchairs;
- using racist language in the workplace;
- requiring job applicants to have work experience in Canada;
- refusing to hire a person who for religious reasons cannot work on certain days, even though this person's absences would not cause the employer undue hardship; and
- paying employees in female-dominated jobs less than those in male-dominated jobs of equal value.

The *Canadian Human Rights Act*, which the federal government passed in 1977, prohibits discrimination based on a person's race, national or ethnic origin, colour, religion, age, sex,

Canadian Human Rights Act
the federal statute that prohibits discrimination based on race, national or ethnic origin, colour, religion, age, sex, sexual orientation, marital status, family status, disability, or conviction for an offence for which a pardon has been granted

discrimination
a process by which a person is deprived of equal access to privileges and opportunities available to others because of prejudice

sexual orientation, marital status, family status, disability, or pardoned conviction (that is, a conviction for which a pardon has been granted). The Act was amended in 1996 to include sexual orientation (not included in the original 1977 Act) as a prohibited ground of discrimination, and in 2000 it underwent a comprehensive review by the Canadian Human Rights Act Review Panel.

The *Canadian Human Rights Act* is constantly in flux, subject to continual amendments. In 2008, section 67 of the Act was repealed, an important human rights development for First Nations peoples in Canada. Section 67 had the effect of exempting the *Indian Act* (an old piece of legislation, first enacted in 1876) from the provisions of the *Human Rights Act*. What this meant, practically speaking, was that any actions taken and decisions made by First Nations leaders or the federal government under the *Indian Act*—decisions and actions that affected First Nations people living or working on reserves—were not subject to the protections of the *Human Rights Act*. In other words, First Nations people on reserves were unable to file discrimination-related complaints with the Canadian Human Rights Commission if those complaints arose from actions taken under the *Indian Act*. With the amendment, First Nations peoples have full access to the human rights complaint-resolution mechanism available to other Canadians.

As of June 26, 2014, section 3 of the *Canadian Human Rights Act* that forbade communication of hate messages over the telephone or the Internet is no longer in force. The section was repealed on the grounds that it infringed on the fundamental freedom of expression guaranteed in the *Canadian Charter of Rights and Freedoms*. However, this does not make hate speech legal on the Internet or by phone. Section 319 of the *Criminal Code* continues to prohibit public incitement and wilful promotion of hatred, and indulgence in any of these acts is a criminal offence. (Hate crime laws are discussed in detail later in the chapter.)

The *Canadian Human Rights Act* is administered by the **Canadian Human Rights Commission** (CHRC), a government agency with the mandate to investigate human rights complaints against federally regulated employers and to develop policies and address issues related to discrimination. The commission—which is also empowered, under the *Employment Equity Act*, to ensure that employers within federal jurisdiction provide equal opportunity for women, Indigenous peoples, the disabled, and visible minorities—has developed policies on many matters, among them the following:

- harassment in the workplace;
- drug testing in the workplace;
- the employment rights of those with HIV/AIDS;
- pregnancy and human rights in the workplace;
- accommodating people with environmental sensitivities; and
- mental health issues in the workplace.

Section 40(1) of the *Canadian Human Rights Act* stipulates that "any individual or group of individuals having reasonable grounds for believing that a person is engaging or has engaged in a discriminatory practice may file with the [Canadian Human Rights] Commission a complaint in a form acceptable to the Commission." The commission investigates a suspected case and tries to reach agreement between the parties before referring the case to the **Canadian Human Rights Tribunal** (CHRT) for formal hearing. The CHRT is a separate agency that functions in an informal court-like setting and has its own rules and procedures. The tribunal hears arguments from all parties involved in the dispute, weighs all evidence, and decides whether a violation of the Act has occurred. If a violation has taken place, the tribunal will determine what remedy and/or sanctions are to be applied. If any party is dissatisfied and wants to appeal the decision of the CHRC or CHRT, they can do so by filing an application for judicial review of the decision to the Federal Court of Appeal.

Canadian Human Rights Commission the federal body responsible for investigating and adjudicating complaints concerning violations of the *Canadian Human Rights Act*

Canadian Human Rights Tribunal a quasi-judicial body that hears complaints of alleged discrimination referred by the Canadian Human Rights Commission

Violation of the *Canadian Human Rights Act* does not constitute a criminal offence and, therefore, does not result in a criminal record and/or imprisonment. If the tribunal decides that the Act has been violated, it can order the party to stop the discriminatory activity or practice, to take measures to rectify the practice, or to prevent it from occurring in the future. The tribunal can also order compensation to the victim for expenses and loss of wages or pain and suffering caused by the discriminatory practice.

Canadian Charter of Rights and Freedoms

The **Canadian Charter of Rights and Freedoms** was introduced in the *Constitution Act, 1982*; it forms the first part of the Act. The Charter sets out *minimum* rights for Canadian citizens, as well as certain rights for everyone in Canada. These ten basic rights and freedoms, which must be upheld by all levels of government (federal, provincial, and territorial), are summarized below.

Canadian Charter of Rights and Freedoms the part of the Canadian Constitution that protects the rights and freedoms that are deemed essential to maintaining a free and democratic society and a united country

Basic Rights and Freedoms Enshrined in the Canadian Charter of Rights and Freedoms

1. Guarantee of rights and freedoms
2. Fundamental freedoms
3. Democratic rights
4. Mobility rights
5. Legal rights
6. Equality rights
7. Official languages of Canada
8. Minority language educational rights
9. Enforcement
10. General

Guarantee of Rights and Freedoms, and Fundamental Freedoms

Guarantee of Rights and Freedoms

1. The *Canadian Charter of Rights and Freedoms* guarantees the rights and freedoms set out in it subject only to such reasonable limits prescribed by law as can be demonstrably justified in a free and democratic society.

Fundamental Freedoms

2. Everyone has the following fundamental freedoms:
    (a) freedom of conscience and religion;
    (b) freedom of thought, belief, opinion and expression, including freedom of the press and other media of communication;
    (c) freedom of peaceful assembly; and
    (d) freedom of association.

Source: *Canadian Charter of Rights and Freedoms* (1982).

fundamental freedoms
freedom of conscience and religion; freedom of thought, belief, opinion, and expression, including freedom of the press and other media of communication; freedom of peaceful assembly; and freedom of association

Section 1 of the Charter guarantees certain rights and freedoms to all persons in Canada subject to reasonable and legal limits, and section 2 lists the **fundamental freedoms**. For example, the Charter guarantees freedom of speech, thought, and belief, and freedom of the press and other media. The following measures, which were once considered legally acceptable, are contrary to the spirit of the Charter:

1. banning the propagation of certain political ideologies by closing down any premises used for that purpose;
2. prohibiting the distribution of any book, pamphlet, or tract without permission of a chief of police; and
3. restricting a religious group's right to free expression and religious practice.

The Charter also ensures the right to gather in peaceful groups and—a similar protection— ensures freedom of association, which is each individual's right to come together with other people and collectively express, promote, pursue, and defend common interests. These freedoms are not absolute. For example, freedom of speech is subject to laws governing libel and slander, in recognition of the fact that speech is capable of harming people. We can see the need for such a restriction when we consider such things as hate literature.

Democratic Rights

democratic rights
rights to vote and to run in an election and the assurance that no government has the right to continue to hold power indefinitely without seeking a new mandate from the electorate

In addition to enshrining certain fundamental freedoms, the Charter gives all Canadian citizens **democratic rights** to vote or run in an election (s. 3), as well as the assurance that no government has the right to continue to hold power indefinitely without seeking a new mandate from the electorate (s. 4). It should be noted that section 46 of the Ontario *Police Services Act* restricts police officers' right to run for office: "No municipal police officer shall engage in political activity, except as the regulations permit." The regulations under the Act state that a serving police officer may run for federal, provincial, or municipal office only if granted a leave of absence (O. Reg. 268/10, s. 16(1)).

Mobility Rights

mobility rights
the freedom to enter, remain in, or leave the country, and to live and seek employment anywhere in Canada

Section 6 of the Charter grants **mobility rights** to Canadian citizens and permanent residents. This guarantees their freedom to enter, remain in, or leave the country, as well as to live and seek employment anywhere in Canada. Provinces reserve the right to set residence requirements for certain social and welfare benefits, and to establish employment standards applicable to both newcomers and long-time residents.

Legal Rights

Legal Rights

7. Everyone has the right to life, liberty and security of the person and the right not to be deprived thereof except in accordance with the principles of fundamental justice.
8. Everyone has the right to be secure against unreasonable search or seizure.
9. Everyone has the right not to be arbitrarily detained or imprisoned.
10. Everyone has the right on arrest or detention
    (a) to be informed promptly of the reasons therefor;
    (b) to retain and instruct counsel without delay and to be informed of that right; and
    (c) to have the validity of the detention determined by way of *habeas corpus* and to be released if the detention is not lawful.

11. Any person charged with an offence has the right
    (a) to be informed without unreasonable delay of the specific offence;
    (b) to be tried within a reasonable time; ...
    (d) to be presumed innocent until proven guilty ... ; ...
12. Everyone has the right not to be subjected to any cruel and unusual treatment or punishment.
13. A witness who testifies in any proceedings has the right not to have any incriminating evidence so given used to incriminate that witness in any other proceedings, except in a prosecution for perjury or for the giving of contradictory evidence.
14. A party or witness in any proceedings who does not understand or speak the language in which the proceedings are conducted or who is deaf has the right to the assistance of an interpreter.

Source: *Canadian Charter of Rights and Freedoms* (1982).

The **legal rights** section of the Charter (ss. 7–14) provides basic legal protection for persons in their dealings with the state and its justice system. More specifically, the right to life, liberty, and security entails a prohibition against unreasonable search or seizure by the police as well as against police officers' execution of these functions in an unreasonable manner—for example, with unnecessary force. These legal rights also prohibit a person's being detained or held arbitrarily. This means that a police officer has to show reasonable cause for detaining an individual.

The legal rights concerning arrest and detention protect people from arbitrary or unlawful actions by law enforcement agencies. When being held or arrested by any authority, people have the following rights:

1. to be informed of the reasons for their being taken into custody;
2. to be instructed of their right to contact and consult a lawyer without delay; and
3. to have a court determine quickly whether the detention is lawful.

Finally, the legal rights set out in the Charter prohibit subjecting any individual to cruel and unusual treatment or punishment.

> **legal rights**
> the basic legal protections granted to all Canadian citizens in their dealings with the state and justice system

Equality Rights

Equality Rights

15(1) Every individual is equal before and under the law and has the right to the equal protection and equal benefit of the law without discrimination and, in particular, without discrimination based on race, national or ethnic origin, colour, religion, sex, age or mental or physical disability.

(2) Subsection (1) does not preclude any law, program or activity that has as its object the amelioration of conditions of disadvantaged individuals or groups including those that are disadvantaged because of race, national or ethnic origin, colour, religion, sex, age or mental or physical disability.

Source: *Canadian Charter of Rights and Freedoms* (1982).

Section 15 of the Charter, dealing with **equality rights**, establishes that all Canadians, regardless of their race, national or ethnic origin, colour, religion, sex, age, or mental or physical disability, are equal before the law and are to enjoy equal protection and benefit of the law. Sexual orientation is not specifically mentioned in this section, but a Supreme Court ruling in

> **equality rights**
> the rights of all Canadians, regardless of race, national or ethnic origin, colour, religion, sex, sexual orientation, age, or mental or physical disability, to be equal before the law and to enjoy equal protection and benefit of the law

CLOSE-UP   The G20 Toronto Protests

A striking example of how the imperative of law and order can come into conflict with civil liberties was the G20 summit, held in downtown Toronto over two days in June 2010. This event occasioned a multi-million-dollar security operation, mass demonstrations, and rioting. Clashes between members of the public and the police were highly publicized and resulted in a slew of investigations and public inquiries. In all, more than 1,100 people were arrested—the largest mass arrest in Canadian history—though the majority were never charged. Ombudsman André Marin called the events "the most massive compromise of civil liberties in Canadian history" (CBC News, 2010).

In the aftermath of the summit, various groups cited the alarming number of illegal arrests, detentions, and incidents of police brutality, including the use of excessive force by some police in making arrests. The highly publicized example of Adam Nobody, tackled and punched repeatedly by officers, is perhaps the best-known case in point; one officer who was involved in the incident was later convicted of assault with a weapon, while another officer was acquitted. Many individuals were detained for hours and then released without any charges being laid; others were packed into paddy wagons and dropped off outside city limits or taken to the G20 temporary jail.

Following the summit, the Canadian Civil Liberties Association (CCLA) called for a joint federal–provincial public inquiry to determine responsibility for the violations of fundamental rights and freedoms, including the following:

- the violent dispersal of protesters gathered in the designated "free speech zone" at Queen's Park, in the course of which tear gas and rubber bullets were used;
- mass detentions and arrests, and delays in providing or failure to provide medical care to those arrested;
- an incident in which a group of protesters who had arrived from Quebec were awoken at a University of Toronto residence building and arrested en masse; and
- a prolonged mass detention in which police used, for the first time in the city's history, a controversial tactic known as "kettling"—the corralling of people by large cordons of police officers—to indiscriminately confine about 300 protesters and innocent bystanders for hours in torrential rain.

Throughout the summit, Toronto Police Chief Bill Blair emphasized the police responsibility to maintain security. He stressed that the police were working hard "to maintain order and restore the rule of law" and advised members of the public to leave areas when asked to do so if they did not wish to be involved with police. However, according to the chair of the police services board, the summit "stained the credibility of the Toronto Police" (Kennedy, 2011, p. A1). In light of the G20 controversy, the CCLA has called for changes to police practices and training in situations where public order is concerned. This organization has emphasized the role that policing is supposed to play in facilitating the right to peaceful protests (CBC News, 2011). The CCLA cited incidents of police officers' removing their badges and telling protesters that martial law had been declared and that they no longer had any rights and could be held as long as necessary. After five years, in August 2015, the Toronto police force's disciplinary tribunal found a senior officer guilty of misconduct under the *Police Services Act*. Superintendent Mark Fenton, who was responsible for two incidents of kettling of innocent protesters, was found guilty of two charges of unlawful arrest and one of discreditable conduct.

One year after the summit, the *Toronto Star* interviewed 43 of the people who had been kettled—a technique that, at the time of writing, the Toronto police have decided never to use again—to find out how the experience changed them (Yang & Kennedy, 2011). For many, the experience sparked political activism, and nearly all reported that they now distrust police and have become reluctant to report minor incidents, to cooperate with investigations, or even to ask officers for directions.

An important element in any analysis of the G20 summit is Ontario Regulation 233/10, passed by the Ontario government without debate. This regulation brought some areas within the G20 security fence under the authority of the *Public Works Protection Act* (PWPA), a statute passed in 1939 to protect infrastructure works from Nazis during the Second World War. Initially, the public was told that the regulation gave officers authority to demand identification from anyone within five metres of the fence and to detain them as necessary. In fact, there was no five-metre rule. But even after this misconception was corrected, searches and arrests continued to occur "well beyond the security zone" (CBC News, 2010).

The Toronto Police Services Board, Ontario's Office of the Independent Police Review Director, and the Ontario ombudsman have reviewed the events of the summit and the controversy surrounding Regulation 233/10. The government has been criticized for passing the regulation without debate and for not clarifying precisely how it would affect civilians. The ombudsman's report recommended that the government provide the public with better information whenever police powers are temporarily expanded. The PWPA was repealed on June 24, 2015 and replaced with the *Security for Courts, Electricity Generating Facilities and Nuclear Facilities Act, 2014*.

1995 found sexual orientation to be a prohibited ground of discrimination. This section applies to government departments, government officials, and agencies closely related to government. It does not protect against discrimination by private citizens, businesses, or organizations.

EXERCISE 2

When carrying out their duties, law enforcement officials must take human rights and freedoms, such as equality, into consideration. Provide examples of how that consideration might affect the discharge of the following duties:

1. preventing crimes and other offences, and providing assistance and encouragement to other persons in the prevention of crimes and other offences
2. apprehending criminals, other offenders, and others who may lawfully be taken into custody
3. laying charges, prosecuting, and participating in prosecution
4. executing warrants and performing related duties

Official Languages of Canada

Official Languages of Canada

16(1)   English and French are the official languages of Canada and have equality of status and equal rights and privileges as to their use in all institutions of the Parliament and government of Canada.

(2)   English and French are the official languages of New Brunswick and have equality of status and equal rights and privileges as to their use in all institutions of the legislature and government of New Brunswick. ...

17(1)   Everyone has the right to use English or French in any debates and other proceedings of Parliament.

(2)   Everyone has the right to use English or French in any debates and other proceedings of the legislature of New Brunswick.

18(1)   The statutes, records and journals of Parliament shall be printed and published in English and French and both language versions are equally authoritative.

(2)   The statutes, records and journals of the legislature of New Brunswick shall be printed and published in English and French and both language versions are equally authoritative.

19(1)   Either English or French may be used by any person in, or in any pleading in or process issuing from, any court established by Parliament.

(2)   Either English or French may be used by any person in, or in any pleading in or process issuing from, any court of New Brunswick.

20(1)   Any member of the public in Canada has the right to communicate with, and to receive available services from, any head or central office of an institution of the Parliament or government of Canada in English or French, and has the same right with respect to any other office of any such institution where

(a)   there is a significant demand for communication with and services from that office in such language; or

(b)   due to the nature of the office, it is reasonable that communications with and services from that office be available in both English and French.

(2)   Any member of the public in New Brunswick has the right to communicate with, and to receive available services from, any office of an institution of the legislature or government of New Brunswick in English or French.

> 21. Nothing in sections 16 to 20 abrogates or derogates from any right, privilege or obligation with respect to the English and French languages, or either of them, that exists or is continued by virtue of any other provision of the Constitution of Canada.
>
> 22. Nothing in sections 16 to 20 abrogates or derogates from any legal or customary right or privilege acquired or enjoyed either before or after the coming into force of this Charter with respect to any language that is not English or French.
>
> Source: *Canadian Charter of Rights and Freedoms* (1982).

official languages
English and French, as confirmed by the Charter, which guarantees that the federal government will serve members of the public in the official language of their choice

Sections 16 to 22 of the Charter confirm that English and French are Canada's two **official languages** but do not require any member of the public to become bilingual. Rather, these sections give people the right to communicate with the federal government in either language, to receive federal government services in the official language of their choice, and to use either language in Parliament or in all courts of law that are under federal jurisdiction.

Minority Language Educational Rights

Minority Language Educational Rights

> 23(1) Citizens of Canada
> (a) whose first language learned and still understood is that of the English or French linguistic minority population of the province in which they reside, or
> (b) who have received their primary school instruction in Canada in English or French and reside in a province where the language in which they received that instruction is the language of the English or French linguistic minority population of the province,
> have the right to have their children receive primary and secondary school instruction in that language in that province.
>
> (2) Citizens of Canada of whom any child has received or is receiving primary or secondary school instruction in English or French in Canada, have the right to have all their children receive primary and secondary school instruction in the same language.
>
> Source: *Canadian Charter of Rights and Freedoms* (1982).

Section 23 of the Charter uses three criteria to determine which Canadian citizens of the English- and French-speaking minorities in each province are entitled to have their children educated in their own language. The first criterion is *mother tongue*. The Charter stipulates that individuals whose first-learned and still-understood language is French and who live in a mainly English-speaking province have the constitutional right to have their children educated in French; those whose mother tongue is English and who live in a mainly French-speaking province have the right to have their children educated in English. The second criterion is the *language in which the parents were educated in Canada*. The Charter stipulates that individuals who were educated in one of the official languages—whether English or French—and live in a province where that language is in the linguistic minority have the right to send their children to a school that uses that minority language.

The third criterion relates to the *language in which other children in the family are receiving or have received their education*. The Charter protects the right of children whose siblings have received primary or secondary school instruction in either official language to be educated in the same language. In a separate section (s. 29), the Charter guarantees the establishment and operation of religious schools and provides them with immunity from other provisions. Thus, the Charter ensures that neither the provision concerning freedom of conscience and religion nor the equality rights provision can override existing constitutional rights with respect to the establishment and state financing of religious schools.

Enforcement

Enforcement

24(1) Anyone whose rights or freedoms, as guaranteed by this Charter, have been infringed or denied may apply to a court of competent jurisdiction to obtain such remedy as the court considers appropriate and just in the circumstances.

(2) Where, in proceedings under subsection (1), a court concludes that evidence was obtained in a manner that infringed or denied any rights or freedoms guaranteed by this Charter, the evidence shall be excluded if it is established that, having regard to all the circumstances, the admission of it in the proceedings would bring the administration of justice into disrepute.

Source: *Canadian Charter of Rights and Freedoms* (1982).

Section 24 allows a person or group whose rights have been denied or infringed upon by law or by action taken by the state to apply to a court for a remedy. An example of a potential infringement would be a case where police have broken into and searched a person's premises and discovered incriminating evidence. In the subsequent trial, the court could exclude the evidence if it is established that a right under the Charter was infringed and that the admission of the evidence would bring the administration of justice into disrepute.

General Rights of Indigenous Peoples, Multiculturalism, and the Rights of Women

General

25. The guarantee in this Charter of certain rights and freedoms shall not be construed so as to abrogate or derogate from any aboriginal, treaty or other rights or freedoms that pertain to the aboriginal peoples of Canada including
    (a) any rights or freedoms that have been recognized by the Royal Proclamation of October 7, 1763; and
    (b) any rights or freedoms that now exist by way of land claims agreements or may be so acquired. ...
27. This Charter shall be interpreted in a manner consistent with the preservation and enhancement of the multicultural heritage of Canadians.
28. Notwithstanding anything in this Charter, the rights and freedoms referred to in it are guaranteed equally to male and female persons.

Source: *Canadian Charter of Rights and Freedoms* (1982).

The rights of Canada's Indigenous peoples (First Nations, Inuit, and Métis), the protection of Canada's multicultural character, and the rights of women are addressed in sections 25, 27, and 28 of the Charter, respectively (the Charter uses the term *aboriginal*).

Section 25 provides that Charter rights must not interfere with **Indigenous rights** to preserve their culture, identity, customs, traditions, and languages; their treaty rights; and any special rights that they have currently or rights that they may acquire in the future. (Section 35 of the Constitution recognizes and affirms existing Indigenous and treaty rights.) Section 25 also ensures that any new benefits that Indigenous peoples may gain from a settlement of land claims would not conflict with the general equality rights as set out in the Charter.

Indigenous rights the rights of Canada's Indigenous peoples to preserve their culture, identity, customs, traditions, and languages, and to maintain any special rights that they have currently or may acquire in the future

**multicultural
heritage**
the unique and
constitutionally en-
shrined character of
Canadian society

Section 27 is a unique provision within the Charter in that it enshrines the multicultural character of Canadian society—that is, the maintenance and enhancement of Canada's **multicultural heritage**.

Finally, section 28 ensures that all rights in the Charter are guaranteed equally to both sexes.

Disputes over Multiculturalism

Federal human rights legislation has had its critics and its controversies in Canada. Reconciling the cultural practices of immigrant communities with the mainstream values of Canadian liberal democracy is not always simple or straightforward. In the past few decades, the debate between multicultural religious accommodation and the secular "one law for all" approach has played out repeatedly around such issues as the right of Sikh police officers to wear turbans, the right of Sikh students to wear the ceremonial dagger known as the kirpan in schools, and the right of Jews to build temporary *succahs*, or huts, on balconies.

In 2003, a debate ignited in Ontario surrounding religiously based arbitration. The 1991 *Arbitration Act* made it possible for private parties to designate a religious arbitrator to resolve civil disputes; the arbitrator's decision would be legally binding, and the parties would have the right to appeal any decision that was not in accordance with Canadian law to a Canadian court. Since then, various groups have set up arbitration boards that render decisions based on religious principles.

In 2003, the Islamic Institute of Civil Justice announced that it would start offering family arbitration founded on sharia law. A major public firestorm erupted that pitted the values of religious freedom and multicultural accommodation against perceived threats to gender equality and the primacy of secular law.

In the debate, some charged that multiculturalism was eroding women's rights and argued that allowing religious courts to function would impede the integration of cultures into Canadian society; others worried that banning religious arbitration would simply drive the practice underground and deny community members the protection of the law. The debate ended in 2005, when Ontario Premier Dalton McGuinty announced that the *Arbitration Act* would be amended to end faith-based arbitration in family law matters and to mandate that Canadian law be followed in the resolution of such disputes.

An ongoing topic of debate in this country, as well as in Britain and France, is the niqab, or face veil, worn by some Muslim women. In 2009, a judge ordered a Toronto woman to testify without her niqab at a sexual assault trial (Muslim Matters, 2009). This raised the general question of whether Muslim women should be allowed to appear as witnesses wearing a veil that covers everything but their eyes. The conflict here is between the right of a defendant to face an accuser in open court and the right of religious freedom. In October 2010, the Ontario Court of Appeal ruled that a Muslim woman is allowed to wear her niqab while testifying in court so long as her doing so does not compromise the fairness of the trial. Further complicating this issue is that, according to many Muslim scholars like Gora (2015), a Muslim woman is not required to cover her face; it is a personal choice. In March 2011, the woman in the 2009 case appealed to the Supreme Court of Canada to have an unimpeded right to wear her niqab while testifying (MacKinnon, 2012). In a split decision, the top court upheld the lower court's ruling that she may have to remove the niqab if wearing it poses a serious risk to the fairness of the trial (*R v. N.S.*, 2012).

Visible Minority Canadians in the Labour Market

Canada's increasingly diverse society has a number of problems to address. One problem concerns inequities in the Canadian labour market. These were featured in a report, *Canada's Colour Coded Labour Market* (Block & Galabuzi, 2011). This report compared work and income

CLOSE-UP   Zunera Ishaq

Zunera Ishaq, a Toronto woman, challenged the federal government's policy banning the wearing of the niqab and other face
coverings during citizenship ceremonies. The policy was intended
to ensure that the new citizens were actually saying the oath and
that the oath was "taken freely and openly—not with faces hidden" (Kenney, 2011). This policy meant that a woman who refused
to remove her face covering to take the oath would be denied
citizenship.

> My religious beliefs would compel me to refuse to take
> off my veil in the context of a citizenship oath ceremony,
> and I firmly believe that based on existing policies, I
> would therefore be denied Canadian citizenship. I feel
> that the governmental policy regarding veils at citizen-
> ship oath ceremonies is a personal attack on me, my
> identity as a Muslim woman and my religious beliefs.
> (*Ishaq v. Canada*, 2015)

The Federal Court of Appeal ruled in 2015 that such a policy
violates the Canadian *Citizenship Act*, which states that citizenship
judges must allow the greatest possible religious freedom when
administering the oath (*Ishaq v. Canada*, 2015). On October 9,
2015, Zunera Ishaq took her oath of citizenship while wearing her
niqab.

Quebec's controversial *Charter of Values*, introduced as a proposed bill by the governing Parti Québécois (PQ) in Quebec's
legislature in 2013, would have prohibited public sector employees from wearing or displaying conspicuous religious symbols.
However, the bill died following the 2014 provincial election in
which the PQ was defeated. A new religious neutrality bill, Bill 62,
was introduced in summer 2015 and was undergoing review in fall
2015 in the Quebec National Assembly. This bill, if passed, would
ban provincial employees from wearing religious face coverings
at work and would also prevent people from covering their faces
while receiving provincial government services (CTV News, 2015).

---

trends among visible minority members of the Canadian population and the rest of the population (Myrie, 2011). Among the report's findings were the following:

- Immigrants from visible minority groups earn only 81 percent of what white immigrants earn.
- Earnings by male immigrants from visible minorities were 68.7 percent of white males'
  earnings.
- Canadian-born visible minority individuals earn less than other Canadian-born individuals with the same level of education.
- Visible minority women make 56.5 cents for every dollar white males earn, while visible
  minority males earn 75.6 cents.
- Canadian-born visible minority men earn 18 percent less than Canadian-born white
  men.

Despite our society's apparent adherence to the *Canadian Human Rights Act* and the *Canadian Charter of Rights and Freedoms*, the economic situation of many immigrants suggests
that racism and discrimination are still factors in our society.

Human Rights in Provinces and Territories

At the time that the *Canadian Bill of Rights* was enacted, the provincial and territorial governments started to develop their own human rights codes. These codes are administered and
enforced by independent human rights commissions and tribunals. Like the *Canadian Human
Rights Act*, provincial and territorial human rights legislation has "quasi-constitutional status."

This means that it prevails over other laws—you must comply with human rights law before other laws, unless there is a specific exception. Human rights codes differ from one Canadian jurisdiction to another. Generally, provincial human rights laws prohibit discrimination in all aspects of employment; the leasing and sale of property; public accommodation, services, and facilities; membership in labour unions and professional associations; and the dissemination of hate propaganda. There are slight variations in the grounds of discrimination from one jusrisdiction to another, so it is important to examine current human rights legislation. The box below provides links to provincial and territorial human rights laws.

Provincial and Territorial Human Rights Legislation

Provinces and territories	Human rights law	Human rights agencies
Alberta	*Alberta Human Rights Act*, RSA 2000, c. A-25.5	Alberta Human Rights Commission, http://www.albertahumanrights.ab.ca
British Columbia	*Human Rights Code*, RSBC 1996, c. 210	BC Human Rights Tribunal, http://www.bchrt.bc.ca
Manitoba	*The Human Rights Code*, CCSM c. H175	Manitoba Human Rights Commission, http://www.manitobahumanrights.ca
New Brunswick	*Human Rights Act*, RSNB 2011, c. 171	New Brunswick Human Rights Commission, http://www.gnb.ca/hrc-cdp/index-e.asp
Newfoundland and Labrador	*Human Rights Act, 2010*, SNL 2010, c. H-13.1	Newfoundland and Labrador Human Rights Commission, http://www.justice.gov.nl.ca/hrc/
Northwest Territories	*Human Rights Act*, SNWT 2002, c. 18	Northwest Territories Human Rights Commission, http://nwthumanrights.ca
Nova Scotia	*Human Rights Act*, RSNS 1989, c. 214	Nova Scotia Human Rights Commission, http://humanrights.gov.ns.ca
Nunavut	*Human Rights Act*, SNu 2003, c. 12	Nunavut Human Rights Tribunal, http://www.nhrt.ca/english/general_information
Ontario	*Human Rights Code*, RSO 1990, c. H.19	Human Rights Tribunal of Ontario, http://www.sjto.gov.on.ca/hrto/
Prince Edward Island	*Human Rights Act*, RSPEI 1988, c. H-12	Prince Edward Island Human Rights Commission, http://www.gov.pe.ca/humanrights/
Quebec	*Charter of Human Rights and Freedoms*, CQLR c. C-12	Commission des droits de la personne et des droits de la jeunesse (Human Rights and Youth Rights Commission), http://www.cdpdj.qc.ca/en/commission/
Saskatchewan	*The Saskatchewan Human Rights Code*, SS 1979, c. S-24.1	Saskatchewan Human Rights Commission, http://saskatchewanhumanrights.ca
Yukon	*Human Rights Act*, RSY 2002, c. 116	Yukon Human Rights Commission, http://www.yhrc.yk.ca

Source: Canadian Human Rights Commission (2013).

Ontario Human Rights Code

Owing to space limitations, this section focuses on a single one of these provincial codes: the **Ontario** *Human Rights Code*, which was enacted in 1962.

In its preamble, the Ontario *Human Rights Code* recognizes that "the inherent dignity and the equal and inalienable rights of all members of the human family is the foundation of freedom, justice and peace in the world and is in accord with the *Universal Declaration of Human Rights* as proclaimed by the United Nations." Part I of the Code, which deals with **freedom from discrimination**, is provided below.

Ontario *Human Rights Code*
the Ontario statute that protects the dignity and worth of every person and provides for equal rights and opportunities without discrimination that is contrary to law

freedom from discrimination
the standard set out in part I of the Ontario *Human Rights Code*, granting freedom from discrimination with respect to services, goods, facilities, accommodation, contracts, employment, and vocational associations, and freedom from sexual solicitation in the workplace and by those in a position of power

Ontario Human Rights Code

Part I: Freedom from Discrimination

Services

1. Every person has a right to equal treatment with respect to services, goods and facilities, without discrimination because of race, ancestry, place of origin, colour, ethnic origin, citizenship, creed, sex, sexual orientation, gender identity, gender expression, age, marital status, family status or disability.

Accommodation

2(1) Every person has a right to equal treatment with respect to the occupancy of accommodation, without discrimination because of race, ancestry, place of origin, colour, ethnic origin, citizenship, creed, sex, sexual orientation, gender identity, gender expression, age, marital status, family status, disability or the receipt of public assistance.

Harassment in accommodation

(2) Every person who occupies accommodation has a right to freedom from harassment by the landlord or agent of the landlord or by an occupant of the same building because of race, ancestry, place of origin, colour, ethnic origin, citizenship, creed, sexual orientation, gender identity, gender expression, age, marital status, family status, disability or the receipt of public assistance.

Contracts

3. Every person having legal capacity has a right to contract on equal terms without discrimination because of race, ancestry, place of origin, colour, ethnic origin, citizenship, creed, sex, sexual orientation, gender identity, gender expression, age, marital status, family status or disability.

Accommodation of person under eighteen

4(1) Every sixteen or seventeen year old person who has withdrawn from parental control has a right to equal treatment with respect to occupancy of and contracting for accommodation without discrimination because the person is less than eighteen years old.

Idem

(2) A contract for accommodation entered into by a sixteen or seventeen year old person who has withdrawn from parental control is enforceable against that person as if the person were eighteen years old.

Employment

5(1) Every person has a right to equal treatment with respect to employment without discrimination because of race, ancestry, place of origin, colour, ethnic origin, citizenship, creed, sex, sexual orientation, gender identity, gender expression, age, record of offences, marital status, family status or disability.

Harassment in employment

(2) Every person who is an employee has a right to freedom from harassment in the workplace by the employer or agent of the employer or by another employee because of race, ancestry, place of origin, colour, ethnic origin, citizenship, creed, sexual orientation, gender identity, gender expression, age, record of offence, marital status, family status or disability.

Vocational associations

6. Every person has a right to equal treatment with respect to membership in any trade union, trade or occupational association or self-governing profession without discrimination because of race, ancestry, place of origin, colour, ethnic origin, citizenship, creed, sex, sexual orientation, gender identity, gender expression, age, marital status, family status or disability.

Sexual harassment

Harassment because of sex in accommodation

7(1) Every person who occupies accommodation has a right to freedom from harassment because of sex, sexual orientation, gender identity or gender expression by the landlord or agent of the landlord or by an occupant of the same building.

Harassment because of sex in workplaces

(2) Every person who is an employee has a right to freedom from harassment in the workplace because of sex, sexual orientation, gender identity or gender expression by his or her employer or agent of the employer or by another employee.

Sexual solicitation by a person in position to confer benefit, etc.

(3) Every person has a right to be free from,

(a) a sexual solicitation or advance made by a person in a position to confer, grant or deny a benefit or advancement to the person where the person making the solicitation or advance knows or ought reasonably to know that it is unwelcome; or

(b) a reprisal or a threat of reprisal for the rejection of a sexual solicitation or advance where the reprisal is made or threatened by a person in a position to confer, grant or deny a benefit or advancement to the person.

Reprisals

8. Every person has a right to claim and enforce his or her rights under this Act, to institute and participate in proceedings under this Act and to refuse to infringe a right of another person under this Act, without reprisal or threat of reprisal for so doing.

Infringement prohibited

9. No person shall infringe or do, directly or indirectly, anything that infringes a right under this Part.

Source: Ontario *Human Rights Code* (1990).

Ontario Human Rights Commission the provincial body that promotes, protects, and advances human rights by engaging in research, education, legal actions, and policy development to prevent discrimination

Part III of the Code concerns the **Ontario Human Rights Commission** (OHRC) and describes its mandate: to promote, protect, and advance human rights in Ontario. The OHRC once had the task of hearing complaints, but—since 2008, when the *Human Rights Code Amendment Act* (Bill 107) was passed—it now focuses on human rights issues of broad public interest and cases of systemic discrimination. The OHRC is also responsible for developing new partnerships with communities, individuals, and the government to ensure that human rights are protected in Ontario.

Part IV of the Code outlines the complaint process. As of 2008, individuals who believe their rights have been infringed under the Code can file a complaint with the Human Rights Tribunal of Ontario (HRTO). A person has the right to file a complaint up to one year after the date the discrimination occurred. The tribunal has procedures in place to ensure that claims of discrimination are

- addressed in a timely manner,
- resolved fairly, and
- based on the facts and the law.

Bill 107 also created the Human Rights Legal Support Centre. The centre offers legal services to individuals in Ontario who believe they have experienced discrimination.

Ontario Human Rights Commission Policies and Initiatives

The OHRC has issued a number of policies to clarify or complement the Code, some of which are described below. In advancing its various policies, the OHRC makes reference to harassment, to a poisoned environment, and to constructive discrimination. As defined in the Code (part II, s. 10(1)), **harassment** is a "course of vexatious comment or conduct that is known or ought reasonably to be known to be unwelcome." A poisoned environment is defined by the OHRC as one in which a person or a group of people are treated differently for reasons related to prohibitory grounds, such as gender, race, and sexual orientation.

According to the Code (part II, s. 11(1)), **constructive discrimination** refers to "a requirement, qualification or factor … that is not discrimination on a prohibited ground but that results in the exclusion, restriction or preference of a group of persons who are identified by a prohibited ground of discrimination." In other words, constructive discrimination refers to policies or practices that may not be obviously discriminatory but that have a discriminatory effect on a group protected under the Code. For example, an employer that requires all employees to work on Saturdays would be practising constructive discrimination against an employee who, for religious reasons, is unable to work on that day. But the notion of constructive discrimination comes with a significant restriction: the Code provides that constructive discrimination does not apply in a case where accommodating the employee's special needs would cause the employer undue hardship—for example, if the employee's religion prevented him from working on Saturdays, but the employer's business was only open on weekends.

A requirement, qualification, or factor is not discriminatory if it can be established that it is reasonable and bona fide (in good faith) in the circumstances. In the context of hiring, for example, two conditions are required to establish that a factor is bona fide: first, it must be demonstrated that there is an objective relationship between the selection criteria and the job in question; second, it must be shown that the standards required for the job are imposed in good faith.

The Ontario Human Rights Commission periodically publishes human rights policies, including the following recent ones:

- Policy on preventing discrimination based on creed (September 17, 2015)
- Policy on preventing discrimination because of pregnancy and breastfeeding (October 29, 2014)
- Policy on preventing discrimination based on mental health disabilities and addictions (June 18, 2014)
- Policy on preventing discrimination because of gender identity and gender expression (April 14, 2014)
- Policy on removing the "Canadian experience" barrier (February 1, 2013)

harassment
unwelcome comments or conduct toward another person

constructive discrimination
a kind of discrimination that may not be obviously discriminatory and may seem to be based on reasonable criteria, but that effectively excludes, restricts, or favours some people contrary to human rights laws

- Policy on preventing sexual and gender-based harassment (May 2013)
- Policy on competing human rights (January 26, 2012)
- Policy on human rights and rental housing (July 21, 2009)
- Policy on discrimination because of family status (April 3, 2007)

The following sections describe some other Ontario Human Rights Commission policies.

Policy on Discrimination and Harassment Because of Sexual Orientation

The Ontario *Human Rights Code* prohibits discrimination on the grounds of sexual orientation and same-sex partnership status. The Code defines **sexual orientation** as "more than simply a 'status' that an individual possesses; it is an immutable personal characteristic that forms part of an individual's core identity. Sexual orientation encompasses the range of human sexuality from gay and lesbian to bisexual and heterosexual orientations" (OHRC, 2000).

The Code's current view of *spouse* and *partnership* can be traced to May 20, 1999, when the Supreme Court of Canada found the opposite-sex definition of *spouse* in part III of Ontario's *Family Law Act* to be unconstitutional. In response to this decision, Ontario introduced Bill 5 (1999), which amended the *Family Law Act* so that its provisions concerning support obligations applied to same-sex partners. Bill 5 also amended the Ontario *Human Rights Code* by defining marital status to include same-sex partnership status and defining spouse to include same-sex partner. Same-sex partner is further defined to mean the individual with whom a person of the same sex is living in a conjugal relationship outside marriage. Similarly, *same-sex partnership status* is defined to mean the status of living with an individual of the same sex in a conjugal relationship outside marriage. Further amendments to the Code, in 2005, sought to improve understanding of discrimination experienced by lesbian, gay, and bisexual individuals, and to assist organizational development of harassment-free environments.

Policy on Preventing Discrimination Because of Gender Identity and Gender Expression

The OHRC's policy on discrimination and harassment because of **gender identity**, first published in 2000, was completely revised and updated in 2014. The purpose of the new policy is to create and promote understanding and awareness about trans people and their rights under the Ontario *Human Rights Code*. It also provides guidelines to organizations and employers to meet their legal responsibilities to prevent discrimination based on gender identity and gender expression. Although the Ontario *Human Rights Code* does not explicitly define *gender identity* and *gender expression*, the policy defines these terms based on tribunal and court decisions. *Gender identity* is defined as a person's internal and individual experience of gender, which may be the same as or different from their birth-assigned sex (OHRC, 2014). It refers to an individual's experience of being a woman, a man, both, or neither. Gender expression is the way in which a person publicly chooses to express or present their gender in the form of hair, dress, makeup, body language, and voice. Gender identity is fundamentally different from sexual orientation (OHRC, 2014). *Trans* or *transgender* are umbrella terms that refer to people with diverse identities and expressions that differ from stereotypical gender norms. The policy reminds employers that trans people are vulnerable to harassment because of their gender identity and gender expression and that they have a duty to provide and maintain an environment free from discrimination.

Policy on Preventing Sexual and Gender-Based Harassment

The OHRC revised its policy on sexual harassment in 2013. The new policy focuses on sexual harassment and discrimination in employment, housing, and education. Sexual harassment is discrimination based on sex, and the policy highlights the fact that sexual harassment is against

sexual orientation
a person's sexual preference, whether heterosexual, gay or lesbian, or bisexual

gender identity
a person's self-perception of their gender, which may or may not be the same as their birth-assigned sex; involves self-image, physical appearance, behaviour, and gender-related conduct

the law. The Ontario *Human Rights Code* prohibits all forms of discrimination based on sex and protects both men and women from sexual harassment (OHRC, 2013). The policy supports a person's fundamental right to freedom from sexual harassment and from other forms of unequal treatment expressed through demeaning comments and actions based on gender. The policy clearly distinguishes between, on the one hand, accepted social interaction or consensual relations and, on the other hand, behaviour that is known or ought reasonably to be known to be unwelcome. Also, the policy provides a framework for educational initiatives (for example, the development of training materials and anti-harassment policies) by employers and others.

There are two views of *sexual harassment*. Narrowly speaking, sexual harassment is an objectionable comment or conduct of a sexual nature. Broadly speaking, sexual harassment is not necessarily overtly sexual in nature; it may simply be conduct that is related to the recipient's gender and that demeans that person or causes him or her personal humiliation or embarrassment. Most cases of sexual harassment involve men harassing women. But women sometimes harass men, and sexual harassment between members of the same sex has been known to occur.

A person can be guilty of sexual harassment or discrimination without making explicit reference to gender or sex. Sexual discrimination may involve harassing comments or conduct whose gender basis is unspoken. Specific examples of sexual harassment and inappropriate gender-related comments and conduct include the following (OHRC, 2013, s. 2.1):

1. gender-related comments about an individual's physical characteristics or mannerisms;
2. the invasion of personal space;
3. unnecessary physical contact, including unwanted touching;
4. demanding hugs;
5. suggestive or offensive remarks or innuendoes about members of a specific gender;
6. propositions of physical intimacy;
7. gender-related verbal abuse, threats, or taunting;
8. leering or inappropriate staring;
9. bragging about sexual prowess;
10. demands for dates or sexual favours;
11. offensive jokes or comments of a sexual nature about an employee, client, or tenant;
12. display of sexually offensive pictures, graffiti, or other materials;
13. questions or discussions about sexual activities;
14. paternalism based on gender that a person feels undermines his or her self-respect or position of responsibility; and
15. rough and vulgar humour or language related to gender.

The revised policy also states that gender-based harassment is a form of sexual harassment and defines it as any behaviour that reinforces traditional heterosexual gender norms. Gender-based harassment is different from other forms of sexual harassment because it is generally not motivated by sexual interest or intent. The Ontario *Human Rights Code* policy regarding sexual harassment is consistent with the laws in several countries on workplace discrimination and harassment. A harassment-free work environment is one without a hostile or abusive atmosphere—one in which an employee is not subjected to offensive remarks or behaviour or to intimidating, hostile, or humiliating working conditions.

Policy and Guidelines on Racism and Racial Discrimination

This policy (OHRC, 2005) describes racism, racial discrimination, and racial harassment. It replaces the previous policy on racial slurs, harassment, and jokes. The policy now addresses a number of considerations related to racism, including racial profiling and employment-related discrimination. The policy also stresses the importance of developing an organizational culture that respects human rights and prevents racial discrimination.

This policy has had an impact on law enforcement. Numerous law enforcement agencies have been developing projects and offering education aimed at preventing racism and discrimination in policing, including employment practices in policing. In 2011, the Windsor Police Service, the Windsor Police Services Board, the Ontario Police College, and the Ontario Human Rights Commission launched the Human Rights Project to address policing and human rights issues. The main purpose was to develop and implement initiatives to identify, eliminate, and prevent any possible discrimination in the Windsor Police Service's employment practices and service delivery. The three-year project highlighted that Windsor Police is not representative of the community it serves, and the recruitment services do not reach out to the underrepresented groups of community members. The project's final report brought forward a number of strategies and policy directives. These include development of a human resources policy in accordance with the Ontario *Human Rights Code*; development of outreach recruitment programs that target diverse community members; improvement of public relations and communication with diverse community members; improvement in translation services; accommodation of the diverse needs of Windsor Police Service members; and development of training programs and materials that addressed the issues of equity, diversity and non-discrimination requirements of the Ontario *Human Rights Code* (Windsor Police Service, 2014).

CLOSE-UP   Mike McKinnon

Mike McKinnon, an Indigenous corrections officer working at the Toronto East Detention Centre, filed a human rights complaint against the Ontario Ministry of Community Safety and Correctional Services because of racial discrimination and harassment at his workplace. In his complaint, McKinnon alleged that, beginning in 1977, he and his wife were subjected to racist slurs and racist behaviour by his co-workers and even by his supervisors:

> "I was called 'chief,' conversations were referred to as 'powwows'; my wife, who was then my girlfriend was referred to as a 'squaw,'" recalled McKinnon who never hid his Indigenous ancestry, as some of his colleagues did.

In 1998, 20 years after the incidents that spurred the complaint, the Ontario Human Rights Tribunal ruled that the failure of

management to take action against the discrimination was an infringement of McKinnon's right to a workplace free of harassment and discrimination. Mr. McKinnon's complaint became a leading case in Canada on human rights remedies in race discrimination. This case is noteworthy also because of the length of time taken to finally resolve the matter. The complaint was filed in 1988 and settled in 2011 after 23 years. The terms of the settlement have not been published; however, a spokesman for the Ministry of Community Safety and Correctional Services said that the ministry will "undertake and continue a number of actions focused on enhancing accountability, recruitment and training with respect to Aboriginal employees."

Source: Infantry (2011).

Hate Crimes

In the context of Canada's increasingly diverse population, hate crimes and discrimination remain a source of concern. Hate crimes can be defined as crimes motivated by hatred or prejudice toward one's perceived membership in a particular social group, which may be according to race, gender, sexual orientation, religion, disability, class, age, nationality, or political affiliation (Perry, 2011, p. 367). Despite the increased use of this term, there is no one national-level definition of hate crime. There are some clear differences between jurisdictions, as some police services tend to be more inclusive in defining hate crime (Roberts, 1995). For example, in the definition used by the Edmonton Police Service, the phrase "in whole or in part" can include crimes in which hate plays a role but may not be the sole motivation for the crime (Pruegger, 2009, p. 9):

> A hate crime is an offence committed against a person or property, which is motivated, in whole or in part, by the suspect's hate, bias or prejudice towards an identifiable group based on, real or perceived, race, national or ethnic origin, language, colour, religion, sex, age, mental or physical disability, sexual orientation or any other similar factor. (Edmonton Police Service, n.d.)

On the other hand, from 1993 to 1997 the Toronto Police Service used a more restrictive definition of hate crime, in which the act must have been "based solely upon a victim's race, religion, nationality, ethnic origin, sexual orientation, gender or disability" (Roberts, 1995). This definition was very restrictive and hid the extent of hate crimes in Toronto during this period. After much criticism, the Toronto police dropped "solely" from its definition. Many other police agencies (such as the Montreal police force) do not explicitly recognize that hate can partly influence the commission of crime:

> A crime is considered to be a hate crime when it is motivated by prejudice or hate based on factors such as the victim's race, national or ethnic origin, language, colour, religion, gender, mental or physical disability or sexual orientation. (SPVM, n.d.)

Another concept worth noting is that the Edmonton Police Service uses the phrase "real or perceived" to refer to the victim's characteristics that motivate a hate crime (Pruegger, 2009, p. 9). This language covers many hate crimes that are perpetrated against people presumed to be a member of the target group. For example, a person who attacks a Sikh believing him or her to be Muslim or Arab can be charged with a hate crime; such an incident is not treated as a case of mistaken identity. These variations in defining hate crime make it difficult to collect information and statistics about the nature and extent of the problem of hate crimes in Canada.

Prevalence of Hate Crimes in Canada

Differences in definitions generate inconsistency in measuring the nature and extent of prevalence of hate crime in Canada (Roberts, 1995). According to Statistics Canada, hate crimes represent only a small percentage of all police-reported crime in Canada. In 2013, police forces across Canada reported 1,167 hate-motivated criminal incidents; the number is 17 percent lower (247 fewer incidents) than in 2012 (Allen, 2015). The majority of all reported hate crimes (585 incidents or 51 percent) were racially or ethnically motivated, whereas 326 incidents (28 percent) were related to religion; 186 incidents (16 percent) were motivated by hatred of sexual orientation; and the remaining 70 incidents (5 percent) were motivated by hatred of language, mental or physical disability, sex, age, occupation, or political beliefs.

Black people in Canada are the most highly targeted group for hate crimes motivated by race or ethnicity. Of 585 incidents of racially or ethnically motivated hate crimes in 2013, 255 reported incidents were targeted against the Black population (44 percent). Significantly fewer members of other populations were reported as victims, including East and Southeast Asian (10 percent), South Asian (about 9 percent), Arab and West Asian (8 percent), and Indigenous (5.5 percent). Of the 326 reported religion-related hate crimes, more than half (55.5 percent) were against Jewish people, followed by 20 percent against Muslims.

Statistics Canada notes that violent incidents made up 40 percent of police-reported hate crimes in 2013 (Allen, 2015). The most violent hate crime offence reported is assault (all levels). Even though fewer hate crime incidents were related to sexual orientation than to ethnicity or race and religion, they were the most likely to be violent. Two-thirds of incidents motivated by hatred of a sexual orientation were violent (66 percent), whereas only 44 percent of those motivated by hatred of a race or ethnicity and 18 percent of those motivated by hatred of a religion were violent.

Canada's three largest cities (Toronto, Montreal, and Vancouver) together accounted for 43 percent of all the police-reported hate crime incidents. However, none of these cities had the highest hate crime rates; Thunder Bay, Ontario and Hamilton, Ontario reported the highest rates of hate crimes in Canada.

Hate Crime Laws in Canada

Hate Propaganda Laws

The *Criminal Code* of Canada was amended in 1970 to include anti-hate propaganda provisions. The box below gives specific sections from the *Criminal Code* that outline hate promotion offences and related provisions. Sections 318 and 319 make it a criminal offence to (1) advocate genocide; (2) publicly incite hatred; and (3) wilfully promote hatred in public places against an "identifiable group" based on colour of skin, race, religion, national or ethnic origin, age, sex, sexual orientation, or mental or physical disability (*Criminal Code*, s. 318(4)). These sections do not address hate on the Internet in particular; however, they have been used to prohibit online postings of hate propaganda. Sections 320 and 320.1 of the Code give judges the authority to order the removal of hate propaganda stored on a computer system that is available to the public, including the Internet. Such authority extends to all computer systems located within Canada.

Hate Crime Laws

Hate Propaganda

Advocating genocide

318(1) Every one who advocates or promotes genocide is guilty of an indictable offence and liable to imprisonment for a term not exceeding five years.

(2) In this section, *genocide* means any of the following acts committed with intent to destroy in whole or in part any identifiable group, namely,

(a) killing members of the group; or

(b) deliberately inflicting on the group conditions of life calculated to bring about its physical destruction.

Consent

(3) No proceeding for an offence under this section shall be instituted without the consent of the Attorney General.

(4) In this section, *identifiable group* means any section of the public distinguished by colour, race, religion, national or ethnic origin, age, sex, sexual orientation, or mental or physical disability.

Public incitement of hatred

319(1) Every one who, by communicating statements in any public place, incites hatred against any identifiable group where such incitement is likely to lead to a breach of the peace is guilty of

(a) an indictable offence and is liable to imprisonment for a term not exceeding two years; or

(b) an offence punishable on summary conviction.

Wilful promotion of hatred

(2) Every one who, by communicating statements, other than in private conversation, wilfully promotes hatred against any identifiable group is guilty of

(a) an indictable offence and is liable to imprisonment for a term not exceeding two years; or

(b) an offence punishable on summary conviction.

Defences

(3) No person shall be convicted of an offence under subsection (2)

(a) if he establishes that the statements communicated were true;

(b) if, in good faith, the person expressed or attempted to establish by an argument an opinion on a religious subject or an opinion based on a belief in a religious text;

(c) if the statements were relevant to any subject of public interest, the discussion of which was for the public benefit, and if on reasonable grounds he believed them to be true; or

(d) if, in good faith, he intended to point out, for the purpose of removal, matters producing or tending to produce feelings of hatred toward an identifiable group in Canada.

Forfeiture

(4) Where a person is convicted of an offence under section 318 or subsection (1) or (2) of this section, anything by means of or in relation to which the offence was committed, on such conviction, may, in addition to any other punishment imposed, be ordered by the presiding provincial court judge or judge to be forfeited to Her Majesty in right of the province in which that person is convicted, for disposal as the Attorney General may direct.

Exemption from seizure of communication facilities

(5) Subsections 199(6) and (7) apply with such modifications as the circumstances require to section 318 or subsection (1) or (2) of this section.

Consent

(6) No proceeding for an offence under subsection (2) shall be instituted without the consent of the Attorney General.

Definitions

(7) In this section,

communicating includes communicating by telephone, broadcasting or other audible or visible means;

identifiable group has the same meaning as in section 318;

public place includes any place to which the public have access as of right or by invitation, express or implied;

statements includes words spoken or written or recorded electronically or electromagnetically or otherwise, and gestures, signs or other visible representations.

Warrant of seizure

320(1) A judge who is satisfied by information on oath that there are reasonable grounds for believing that any publication, copies of which are kept for sale or distribution in premises within the jurisdiction of the court, is hate propaganda shall issue a warrant under his hand authorizing seizure of the copies.

• • •

Consent

(7) No proceeding under this section shall be instituted without the consent of the Attorney General.

• • •

Warrant of seizure

320.1(1) If a judge is satisfied by information on oath that there are reasonable grounds to believe that there is material that is hate propaganda within the meaning of subsection 320(8) or computer data within the meaning of subsection 342.1(2) that makes hate propaganda available, that is stored on and made available to the public through a computer system within the meaning of subsection 342.1(2) that is within the jurisdiction of the court, the judge may order the custodian of the computer system to

(a) give an electronic copy of the material to the court;

(b) ensure that the material is no longer stored on and made available through the computer system; and

(c) provide the information necessary to identify and locate the person who posted the material.

. . .

Mischief relating to religious property

430(4.1) Every one who commits mischief in relation to property that is a building, structure or part thereof that is primarily used for religious worship, including a church, mosque, synagogue or temple, or an object associated with religious worship located in or on the grounds of such a building or structure, or a cemetery, if the commission of the mischief is motivated by bias, prejudice or hate based on religion, race, colour or national or ethnic origin,

(a) is guilty of an indictable offence and liable to imprisonment for a term not exceeding ten years; or

(b) is guilty of an offence punishable on summary conviction and liable to imprisonment for a term not exceeding eighteen months.

. . .

Other sentencing principles

718.2 A court that imposes a sentence shall also take into consideration the following principles:

(a) a sentence should be increased or reduced to account for any relevant aggravating or mitigating circumstances relating to the offence or the offender, and, without limiting the generality of the foregoing,

(i) evidence that the offence was motivated by bias, prejudice or hate based on race, national or ethnic origin, language, colour, religion, sex, age, mental or physical disability, sexual orientation, or any other similar factor.

Source: *Criminal Code* (1985).

Section 2 of the *Canadian Charter of Rights and Freedoms* guarantees freedom of thought, belief, opinion, and expression to Canadians. Charges laid under *Criminal Code* section 318 or 319 infringe freedom of speech and can raise Charter challenges. Therefore, the prosecution has a heavy burden of proof and requires consent of the provincial attorney general before initiating proceedings under sections 318 and 319(2). Charges under section 319(1) do not require such consent. The Supreme Court of Canada upheld the constitutional legality of hate propaganda laws in *R v. Keegstra* (1990). Jim Keegstra, a high school teacher in Alberta, taught his students that Jews are "power hungry," "treacherous," "subversive," "money-loving," and "child killers," along with other anti-Semitic beliefs. He also taught that the Holocaust was a myth promoted as part of a Jewish conspiracy. His students were expected to accept these notions as facts and were tested on them. He was charged and found guilty under section 319(2). However, the conviction was later overturned by the Alberta Court of Appeal based on a constitutional challenge of the validity of the law. The Supreme Court of Canada upheld Keegstra's conviction and the law by stating that even though section 319(2) does limit freedom of speech, it is a reasonable limit justified within a democratic society, and, therefore, this section does not violate the Charter.

Another section of the *Criminal Code*, section 181, prohibited wilfully spreading false news that was injurious to the public interest. This law was invoked in the case of Ernst Zündel (*R v. Zündel*, 1992), but did not withstand a Charter challenge. Zündel denied the Holocaust had occurred by publishing a brochure, "Did Six Million Really Die?" in which he claimed that the Holocaust was a myth emanating from a Jewish world conspiracy. He was charged and convicted for spreading false news in 1985. The Supreme Court of Canada found that Zündel did violate section 181 of the Code but overturned his conviction on the grounds that this section infringes section 2(b) of the *Charter of Rights and Freedoms*, which guarantees the right to freedom of expression. Section 181 of the *Criminal Code* was, therefore, struck down as unconstitutional because it cannot be justified under the reasonable limits clause of section 1 of the Charter.

Sentencing in Hate-Motivated Crimes

There are other offences that are not specifically designated as hate crimes but in which hate plays a role. A charge under one of the general offences of the *Criminal Code* could be deemed as a hate crime if bias is proven to be its motivation. Proof of motivation makes hate crimes different from other crimes. Section 718.2(a)(i) of the *Criminal Code* allows for enhanced penalties for hate-motivated crimes because such crimes are believed to traumatize not only the victim but also the group or community to which the victim belongs. For example, an assault committed out of hatred toward a person's religious affiliation can be punished more severely than an assault arising from personal disagreement between the two people. However, determining and proving hate motivation is difficult.

Convictions in such cases rely on proving that the offender acted on his or her bias when he or she committed the crime. Law enforcement officers must bring concrete evidence of hate and prosecutors must prove beyond a reasonable doubt that the suspect's crime was solely motivated by bias against a group of people to which the victim belongs. The burden of proof is very high, which discourages prosecutors from charging suspects with hate crimes.

Human Rights and Freedoms: Police Abilities, Knowledge, and Skills

The importance of human rights and freedoms to the quality of people's lives is increasingly recognized. Many countries actively uphold these rights for their citizens, and law enforcement plays a significant role in such initiatives. In recent years, however—in particular, following the 9/11 terrorist attacks on the United States—many Western governments, including Canada's, have become increasingly focused on national and international security concerns. This has created tensions between two police responsibilities: the duty to ensure civil order and the duty to ensure that civil liberties are upheld.

Police services operate in contexts of international, national, and provincial human rights provisions that enshrine basic individual and collective rights and freedoms at social and institutional levels. These provisions act as a society's "collective conscience," so that it can protect the ideals of democratic citizenship and social justice. The human rights and freedoms acts, codes, and policies are more than just abstract principles and goals; their purpose is to transform a society plagued by human rights violations into one that treasures and preserves equal treatment and protection under the law.

At the international level, the United Nations Centre for Human Rights has developed international human rights standards specific to law enforcement. The standards address policing ethics and legal conduct, policing in democracies, non-discrimination in law enforcement, police investigations, arrest, detention, the use of force and firearms, civil disorder, states of emergency, armed conflict, protection of juveniles, community policing, and police violations of human rights, as well as the rights of women, refugees, non-nationals, victims, police command, and management.

Police legislation in Canada is consistent with international standards and with federal and provincial laws regarding human rights and freedoms. In its declaration of principles, the **Ontario *Police Services Act*** stipulates that police services shall be provided at the provincial level in accordance with the safeguards that guarantee the fundamental rights enshrined in the *Canadian Charter of Rights and Freedoms* and the Ontario *Human Rights Code* (principle 2). A police culture in which all police officers uphold the letter and the spirit of human rights laws and foster a climate of justice, respect, acceptance, and harmonious coexistence is key to maintaining both the integrity of the profession and a positive relationship with the general public.

However, the focus of law enforcement on counterterrorism and national security represents a challenge to policing that seeks to balance civil liberty and civil order; law enforcement must negotiate two conflicting approaches to policing. On the one hand, democratic community policing honours equally the imperatives of law and order and of due process; on the other hand, democratic dictatorship policing emphasizes law and order more than it does civil liberties. In practical terms, law enforcement agents must at once honour human rights standards, respect the civil rights of citizens, and establish a trusting relationship with the communities they serve and protect. At the same time, they must do whatever is necessary to prevent threats to individual and collective rights and freedoms, and to national security.

While police officers are charged with protecting the rights and freedoms of citizens, in some cases police abuse their authority. Three types of police abuse of authority have been identified (Freeman, 1996):

- *Physical abuse/excessive force.* This involves the use of more force than is necessary to carry out an arrest or search, or the "wanton use of any degree of physical force against another by the police officer under the colour of the officer's authority."
- *Verbal/psychological abuse.* "Relying on authority inherently vested in them based on their office, police verbally assail, ridicule, harass, and/or place persons who are under the actual or constructive dominion of the officer in a situation where the individual's esteem and/or self-image is threatened and/or diminished; threat of physical harm under the supposition that a threat is psychologically coercive and instills fear in the average person."
- *Violation of civil rights.* This includes "any violation of a person's constitutional rights, federally protected rights, and provincially protected rights even though the person may not suffer any apparent physical or psychological damage in the purest sense."

Ontario *Police Services Act*
a statute requiring that the police services provided throughout Ontario reflect the safeguards enshrined in the *Canadian Charter of Rights and Freedoms* and the Ontario *Human Rights Code*

CLOSE-UP The Maher Arar Case

Maher Arar is a Canadian software engineer. CBC News (2006) reported that on September 26, 2002, during a stopover in New York en route from Tunis to Montreal, Arar was detained by American authorities, who may have been acting upon false and misleading information supplied by the Royal Canadian Mounted Police (RCMP). Despite carrying a Canadian passport, Arar was deported to Syria, held in solitary confinement in a Syrian prison where he was regularly tortured for over a year, and eventually released and returned to Canada in October 2003.

Arar's case reached new heights of controversy when an Ottawa journalist wrote an article, published on November 8, 2003, containing information leaked to her from an unknown security source, possibly within the RCMP. This information suggested that Arar was a trained member of an al Qaeda terrorist cell. The RCMP raided the journalist's house while investigating the leak. The raid was widely denounced and led to a public inquiry.

The episode strained Canada–US relations and led to a public inquiry in Canada, which cleared Arar and was sharply critical of the RCMP, other Canadian government departments, and the United States over its treatment of Arar. The United States did not participate in the inquiry, but maintained that Arar's removal to Syria was legal. Human rights groups dispute this. The Canadian government paid Arar $10.5 million in compensation for its part in his ordeal.

There are questions concerning the role of various government officials in the Arar case. RCMP Commissioner Giuliano Zaccardelli resigned in December 2006 over contradictions in his testimony to the House of Commons Committee on Public Safety and National Security with respect to what he knew at the time and what he told government ministers. Arar himself appealed to the United States Supreme Court, where he attempted to hold American officials accountable for labelling him an al Qaeda suspect and deporting him to Syria. In 2010, the Supreme Court declined to hear the appeal due to national security considerations.

Source: CBC News (2006).

EXERCISE 3

A police service allows a Sikh officer to wear his turban on duty, a Muslim officer to wear her hijab, and an Indigenous officer to continue the practice of wearing long braids (traditional for many Indigenous peoples). Do you consider that allowing these traditional cultural practices within a police service represents the weakening of an official institution? Why or why not?

CHAPTER SUMMARY

Human rights laws and policies enshrine basic rights and freedoms. With the institutions that administer them, they protect both citizens and social justice. They support equality and respect for all citizens, regardless of their culture, race, religion, gender, age, sexual orientation, gender identity, socio-economic status, or physical or mental ability. The problem of hate-motivated crimes is inevitable in a diverse country like Canada. The response of governments to the 9/11 terrorist attacks has increased the tension between the imperatives of national security and law and order, on the one hand, and of civil liberties on the other.

REFERENCES

Allen, M. (2015). Police-reported hate crime in Canada, 2013. http://www.statcan.gc.ca/pub/85-002-x/2015001/article/14191-eng.htm#tb3.

Block, S., & Galabuzi, G.-E. (2011). *Canada's colour coded labour market: The gap for racialized workers*. Ottawa: Canadian Centre for Policy Alternatives. http://www.policyalternatives.ca/sites/default/files/uploads/publications/National%20Office/2011/03/Colour%20Coded%20Labour%20Market.pdf.

Canadian Bill of Rights. (1960). SC 1960, c. 44.

Canadian Charter of Rights and Freedoms. (1982). Part I of the *Constitution Act, 1982*, being Schedule B to the *Canada Act 1982* (UK), 1982, c. 11.

Canadian Human Rights Act. (1977). RSC 1985, c. H-6, as amended.

Canadian Human Rights Act Review Panel. (2000). Promoting equality: A new vision. http://dsp-psd.pwgsc.gc.ca/Collection/J2-168-2000E.pdf.

Canadian Human Rights Commission. (2013). Provincial and territorial human rights agencies. http://www.chrc-ccdp.ca/eng/content/provincial-and-territorial-human-rights-agencies.

CBC News. (2006, September 18). The Maher Arar inquiry: frequently asked questions. *CBC News*. http://www.cbc.ca.

CBC News. (2010, December 7). G20 police rule slammed by ombudsman. *CBC News*. http://www.cbc.ca.

CBC News. (2011, February 28). G20 "rights violations" require public inquiry: Report. *CBC News*. http://www.cbc.ca.

Citizenship Act. (1985). RSC 1985, c. C-29.

Constitution Act, 1982. (1982). Being Schedule B to the *Canada Act 1982* (UK), 1982, c 11.

Criminal Code. (1985). RSC 1985, c. C-46.

CTV News. (2015, June 11). Secular values, the Liberal way: Quebec tables new legislation. *CTV News*. http://montreal.ctvnews.ca.

Edmonton Police Service. (n.d.). What is a hate crime? http://www.edmontonpolice.ca/CommunityPolicing/OrganizedCrime/HateBiasCrime.aspx.

Family Law Act. (1990). RSO 1990, c. F.3, as amended.

Freeman, A.P. (1996). Unscheduled departures: The circumvention of just sentencing for police brutality. *Hastings Law Journal, 47*, 677.

Gora, T. (2015, February 19). Wearing a niqab or a veil is not a requirement of Islam. *Huffington Post*. http://www.huffingtonpost.ca/tahir-gora/niqab-canada_b_6712172.html.

Human Rights Code. (1990). RSO 1990, c. H.19, as amended.

Infantry, Ashante. (2011, August 22). 23 years later, jail guard compensated for racial taunts. *The Toronto Star*. https://www.thestar.com.

Ishaq v. Canada (Citizenship and Immigration). (2015). 2015 FC 156.

Keegstra, R v. (1990). [1990] 3 SCR 697.

Kennedy, B. (2011, June 25). New poll finds "monumental shift" in public perception of Toronto police because of G20 actions. *The Toronto Star*, p. A1.

Kenney, J. (2011). Speaking notes for The Honourable Jason Kenney, P.C., M.P. Minister of Citizenship, Immigration and Multiculturalism. http://www.cic.gc.ca/english/department/media/speeches/2011/2011-12-12.asp.

MacKinnon, L. (2012, December 20). Top court rules judges may order witness to remove niqab. *CBC News*. http://www.cbc.ca.

Muslim Matters. (2009, February 3). Canadian judge orders witness to remove niqaab. http://muslimmatters.org/2009/02/03/canadian-judge-orders-witness-to-remove-niqaab/.

Myrie, E. (2011, March 24). Oh, Canada: Diverse but not inclusive. *The Hamilton Spectator*, p. A13.

N.S., R v. (2012). 2012 SCC 72, [2012] 3 SCR 726.

Office of the United Nations High Commissioner for Human Rights. (1948). *Universal declaration of human rights*. http://www.un.org/en/universal-declaration-human-rights/index.html.

Ontario *Human Rights Code*. (1990). RSO 1990, c. H.19, as amended.

Ontario Human Rights Commission (OHRC). (2000, January 11). Policy on discrimination and harassment because of sexual orientation. http://www.ohrc.on.ca/en/resources/publications.

Ontario Human Rights Commission (OHRC). (2005). Policy and guidelines on racism and racial discrimination. http://www.ohrc.on.ca/en/policy-and-guidelines-racism-and-racial-discrimination.

Ontario Human Rights Commission (OHRC). (2013). Policy on preventing sexual and gender-based harassment. http://www.ohrc.on.ca/en/policy-preventing-sexual-and-gender-based-harassment-0.

Ontario Human Rights Commission (OHRC). (2014). Policy on preventing discrimination because of gender identity and gender expression. http://www.ohrc.on.ca/en/policy-preventing-discrimination-because-gender-identity-and-gender-expression.

Perry, B. (2011). *Diversity, crime, and justice in Canada*. Don Mills, ON: Oxford University Press.

Police Services Act. (1990). RSO 1990, c. P.15, as amended.

Pruegger, V. (2009). *Alberta hate/bias crime report*. http://www.threesource.ca/documents/December2010/hate_crime_report_card.pdf.

Public Works Protection Act. (1990). RSO 1990, c. P.55.

Roberts, J.V. (1995). Disproportionate harm: Hate crime in Canada. http://www.justice.gc.ca/eng/rp-pr/csj-sjc/crime/wd95_11-dt95_11/toc-tdm.html.

Security for Courts, Electricity Generating Facilities and Nuclear Facilities Act, 2014. (2014). SO 2014, c. 15.

SPVM (Montreal Police). (n.d.). Hate crimes. http://www.spvm.qc.ca/en/Fiches/Details/Hate-Crimes.

Windsor Police Service. (2014). *Human rights project: Final report*. http://www.police.windsor.on.ca/about/human-rights/Documents/WPS%20Human%20Rights%20Project%20Final%20Report%20Oct%202014.pdf.

Yang, J., & Kennedy, B. (2011, June 25). Inside the G20 kettle. *The Toronto Star*, pp. IN1, IN3.

Zündel, R v. (1992). [1992] 2 SCR 731.

REVIEW QUESTIONS

True or False?

1. Human rights reflect the collective conscience of nations.
2. The *Canadian Human Rights Act* of 1977 prohibited discrimination based on sexual orientation.
3. The *Canadian Charter of Rights and Freedoms* applies only to the federal government.
4. The purpose of human rights legislation is not to punish the individual or employer that has discriminated.
5. A serving police officer may run for political office only if granted a leave of absence.
6. Legal rights on arrest and detention do not protect Canadian citizens from arbitrary or unlawful actions by law enforcement agencies.
7. The *Canadian Charter of Rights and Freedoms* states that every Canadian citizen must be able to speak either English or French.
8. Harassment involves unwelcome comments or conduct toward another person.
9. Police legislation in Canada is consistent with international standards and federal and provincial laws covering human rights and freedoms.
10. Democratic community policing honours equally the imperatives of law and order and of due process.

Multiple Choice

1. Understanding human rights and freedoms enables police to
   a. create tensions within the community
   b. measure the way that police treat non-diverse communities
   c. fulfill their mandate
   d. deal with the international community

2. The principle of the rule of the law and the due process of law was first established by
   a. the *Canadian Charter of Rights and Freedoms*
   b. the *Universal Declaration of Human Rights*
   c. the *Magna Carta*
   d. the French *Declaration of the Rights of Man and of the Citizen*

3. An employer has a rule that male employees must be clean-shaven. Using this rule, the employer refuses to hire a Sikh man who, according to his religion, is not allowed to shave. This is
   a. direct discrimination
   b. constructive discrimination
   c. harassment
   d. marginalization

4. If a person has a reason to believe that he or she has been discriminated against by a restaurant employer because of his or her sexual orientation, he or she may file a complaint with
   a. the local police department
   b. the Canadian Human Rights Commission
   c. the provincial human rights commission
   d. the Court of Queen's Bench

5. Which of the following is not explicitly stated as a prohibited ground of discrimination in the equality rights section of the *Canadian Charter of Rights and Freedoms*?

    a. age

    b. race

    c. mental disability

    d. sexual orientation

6. Police breaking into a person's residence and discovering incriminating evidence

    a. does not violate a person's legal rights

    b. always violates a person's legal rights

    c. may be deemed to violate a person's legal rights, in which case the evidence may be inadmissible in court

    d. is not covered under the *Canadian Charter of Rights and Freedoms*

7. A person can be guilty of sexual harassment or discrimination

    a. only if the event occurs in the workplace

    b. only if physical contact is made between two people

    c. only if a specific reference to gender or sex is made

    d. without making specific reference to gender or sex

8. Programs put in place to improve employment opportunities for minorities or persons with disabilities are permitted in the *Charter of Rights and Freedoms* under

    a. equality rights

    b. legal rights

    c. minority language rights

    d. democratic rights

9. Counterterrorism efforts since 9/11 have caused all of the following except

    a. broadening of police powers

    b. restrictions on civil liberties

    c. tension between civil liberties and police powers

    d. enhanced protection of legal rights

10. Democratic community policing

    a. favours individual rights over law and order

    b. denies due process to people

    c. honours equally the imperatives of law and order and of due process

    d. makes allowances for people from other countries

Fill in the Blanks

1. The *Royal Proclamation of 1763* gave provincial legislatures in Canada the right to pass laws in relation to property and ___Civil Rights___. /local matters

2. Any person in Canada who believes he or she has been discriminated against can file a complaint with the ___CHRC___.

3. The *Charter of Rights and Freedoms* guarantees rights and freedoms to all Canadians subject to reasonable and _____ limits.

4. A Supreme Court ruling in 1995 made ___Sexual Orientation___ a prohibited ground of discrimination.

5. The right to vote in an election is an example of a ___Democratic___ right.

6. Individuals who believe their rights have been infringed under the Ontario *Human Rights Code* can file a complaint with the ___CHRT___.

7. ___Constructive Discrimination___ refers to policies or practices that may not be obviously discriminatory but that have a discriminatory effect on a group protected under the Ontario *Human Rights Code*.

8. Verbal/psychological abuse is deemed to occur where a person under the dominion of a police officer receives a threat of physical harm that would instill fear in the ___Average___ person.

9. Overtightening handcuffs is an example of ___Physical Abuse/ Excessive force___ abuse.

10. Having national security as a priority is a challenge to policing that tries to balance civil liberty and civil ___order___.

3 Cultural Diversity

Zoya Khan, originally from Pakistan, joins her parents and others in pledging the oath of citizenship.

Introduction

Canada's more than 35 million inhabitants compose a cultural, ethnic, and linguistic mosaic not found anywhere else on earth. According to the 2011 National Household Survey, 6,775,800 individuals in this country were born outside Canada, which accounted for about 20 percent of the Canadian population (Statistics Canada, 2013b). Most of these immigrants were attracted here by Canada's quality of life and its reputation for being peaceful, open, and welcoming toward people of different cultures.

The diversity of Canada—geographic, political, and ethnocultural—is a challenge for Canadian police. Canada is a federation of ten provinces and three northern territories, with 81 percent of the country's population living in urban areas (Statistics Canada, 2011b). The different geographic regions of Canada pose varied problems with respect to distance, population, climate, and political jurisdiction. On the political side, some communities are served by federal services, some by regional services, and others by city services, with different laws and bylaws applying accordingly. In the cities, boundaries between regions and, in some cases, dense populations offer their own unique challenges. Nowadays, police have to contribute to international strategies against terrorism while continuing to combat crime and protect civil order domestically. In the course of these varied tasks, police encounter many different types of people from all walks of life.

Accounts of Canada's diverse population usually neglect the complex background of each cultural group and fail to consider the similarities and differences between the various groups. This is regrettable, because a better understanding of one another's cultures would improve social relations between Canadians, which might strengthen our national identity. And this, in turn, could enhance security and lawful conduct. This chapter focuses on the primary ethnocultural communities in Canada, and touches on some of the challenges associated with policing in the post-9/11 world.

Concepts of Culture, Ethnicity, Race, and Minority

There is a great deal of confusion over the terms *culture*, *ethnicity*, *race*, and *visible minority* (Kazarian & Evans, 1998). For example, the English and the French are sometimes called Canada's "two founding races" despite the fact that both cultural groups belong to the Caucasian race.

Culture

The term *culture*, in a narrow sense, means "folk tradition." The anthropological term for culture in this sense is *ethnoculture* (Kallen, 2003). This notion of culture refers to the distinctive ways of viewing and doing things shared by members of a particular ethnic community—practices they transmit to one another and to the next generation through a process of "enculturation." In a slightly broader sense, **culture** refers to the patterns of behaviour and behavioural consequences that are shared and transmitted among the members of a particular society (Linton, 1945). Triandis (1995, p. 36) refers to culture as "the man-made part of the environment" and describes it as having two aspects: the objective (for example, roads and bridges) and the subjective (beliefs, attitudes, norms, roles, and values). A person's culture shapes his or her unique world view, influencing how that person thinks, feels, acts, communicates, and interprets his or her environment. Culture is inherited—an accident of birth—but it is also a learned phenomenon; it is acquired, for the most part, through the ordinary process of growing up and participating in the daily life of a particular ethnic community (Kallen, 2003).

culture
the patterns of behaviour and behavioural consequences that are shared and transmitted among members of a particular society

Ethnicity

The term **ethnicity** (also known as *ethnic identity*) refers to the cultural origin (for example, British or Armenian) with which a person or group identifies *within a multicultural context*, such as Canada. Self-identification is the essence of ethnicity; a Canadian man of Armenian descent is legally a citizen of this country, but might (or might not) define himself, ethnically, as an Armenian Canadian. Ethnicity can be mostly symbolic, involving an attachment to and pride in one's cultural origin; or it can be behavioural, comprehensively expressed through participation in cultural behaviours and activities and the active wish to pass them on to one's children.

ethnicity
the culture of origin with which an individual or group identifies within a multicultural context

Census Canada defines ethnic origin as "the ethnic or cultural group(s) to which an individual's ancestors belonged" (Statistics Canada, 2006). But there is a difference between "ethnic group" and "cultural group." Again, *ethnicity* implies self-identification. A person who is part of an "ethnic group" is one who sees himself or herself as part of that group, who identifies with its culture. A person who belongs to a "cultural group" has a particular cultural heritage but may not identify with it. A person does not choose the cultural group to which he or she belongs; it is inherited. A person's ethnicity, on the other hand, depends on his or her identifying with a particular cultural group. For example, a woman may be a member of the Estonian cultural group but choose to identify herself as Canadian. An interesting feature of today's society—an effect of globalization and intermarriage among ethnic groups—is that many individuals have multiple ethnic ancestries and identities.

Race

The word *race* first appeared in the English language about CE 1500. It comes from the French word *race*, which has equivalents in Italian (*razza*) and in Spanish (*raza*). Beyond this, the origin of the word is obscure (Kallen, 2003). It was not until the 18th century that the term *race* was used to indicate major divisions of humankind, classified according to certain common physical characteristics such as skin colour (Kallen, 2003). Categorizing people by race is essentially a way of identifying them according to the ancestry or origin indicated by their physical characteristics. In the end, race is not an absolute marker of identity but a social concept, nowadays often rejected as a means of classifying people.

Originally, **race** referred both to biological characteristics (as in "white race," "black race," "yellow race," or "red race") and to cultural traits and values (as in "peasant race") (Berry & Laponce, 1994). The term is increasingly used in reference to such group markers as language, national origin, ethnicity, culture, and religion. In fact, the meaning of *race* has become so broad and loose that it has lost its value as a defining term. Social scientists and others use the term strictly in reference to physical or biological features.

race
a classification based on ancestry or origin as indicated by physical characteristics

Minority

For the purposes of this text, a minority (or subordinate) group within a society is one that has less social status than the majority group; its members wield less political and economic and/or social power than the majority (Kallen, 2003). For example, Blacks in South Africa are the numerical majority insofar as they constitute most of the country's population, but we would classify them as a minority in that country because they hold relatively little power politically, economically, and socially. The term *minority* is not and should not be used merely as a racial classification, to refer to those who are not white. In other words, any racial group in any society can hold the majority power and be considered the "majority group."

In short, the term *minority* applies to groups within a society that have less social, political, and economic power than the majority or host group. The minority group may also differ from the majority on the basis of race, religion, political affiliation, nationality, culture, or some other characteristics. But lack of power is their main defining feature. In Canada, a **visible minority** is a group of people, other than Indigenous peoples, who are non-Caucasian in race or non-white in colour (*Employment Equity Act*, 1995, s. 3), and the term is mainly used in the context of employment; visible minorities are one of the four groups—along with women, Indigenous peoples, and people with disabilities—designated under the *Employment Equity Act* as beneficiaries of employment equity.

As discussed in Chapter 1, visible minorities are a growing presence in Canada. By 2011, our visible minority population had reached 6.2 million people, 19.1 percent of the total Canadian population. This means that one in every five people in Canada belongs to a visible minority group (Statistics Canada, 2013b). Visible minorities include both Canadian-born and foreign-born (immigrant) individuals. The increase in the visible minority population is attributed to the number of immigrants that came to Canada from non-European countries (Statistics Canada, 2013b). In 2011, more than 80 percent of newcomers came from Asia, the Middle East, the Caribbean and Central and South America, Africa, and Oceania. The rest of the immigrants were born in Europe (nearly 14 percent) and the United States (4 percent) (Statistics Canada, 2013b).

The vast majority of visible minorities live in Ontario, British Columbia, Quebec, and Alberta. More than one-quarter of Ontario's population belongs to visible minority groups, and they constitute more than half of the total visible minority population in Canada. Visible minorities in British Columbia accounted for more than one-quarter (27.3 percent) of the province's population in 2011. According to the 2011 census, visible minorities constituted about 18 percent of the population of Alberta, followed by Quebec with 11 percent of the province's population. Close to half of Toronto's population belongs to a visible minority (47 percent), with the largest visible minority group being South Asian. Visible minorities constitute 45 percent of Vancouver's population, followed by Calgary (28 percent), and Montreal (20 percent). According to the 2011 National Household Survey, about 91 percent of immigrants, especially recent arrivals, lived in urban areas (called census metropolitan areas or CMAs by Statistics Canada); the corresponding figure for those born in Canada was 63.3 percent (Statistics Canada, 2013b).

visible minority
individuals, other than Indigenous peoples, who are non-Caucasian in race or non-white in colour

---

EXERCISE 1

Newcomers to Canada, who are often especially vulnerable to crime, may fear police for a number of reasons. Immigrants and refugees may have experienced police corruption and brutality in their countries of origin; newcomer women may be reluctant to disclose gendered violence to male officers; or undocumented immigrants may be reluctant to draw the attention of law enforcement for fear of deportation. What are some things that police services could do to encourage these newcomers to cooperate with police when serious crimes occur in their neighbourhoods?

Stereotypes and Prejudices

Historically and, in some cases, to this day, stereotypes and prejudice have attached themselves to certain races, ethnicities, and minorities. A **stereotype** is a standardized, usually oversimplified conception of something, whether a person, group, event, or issue. Stereotypes falsify reality through overgeneralization and strip their subjects of individuality. To say, for example, that all English people love tea and soccer is to affirm a stereotype, albeit a relatively harmless one. An example of a more harmful stereotype is that of the "drunken Indian," which continues to be a powerful one in mainstream society. Many believe that Indigenous people "can't handle their liquor" or that "once they start drinking, they can't stop," or that, for biological reasons, Indigenous people are, as a race, more susceptible than others to alcoholism and alcohol abuse. However, none of these stereotypes has any scientific basis. Many have suggested that alcohol abuse among Indigenous people should be viewed as a consequence of social, psychological, and economic disadvantages, not as a cause of these factors (Moynes, 1999).

A **prejudice** is an adverse judgment or opinion formed with little or no knowledge or experience or examination of the facts; a predetermined preference, idea, or bias. To be prejudiced is to hold unreasonable preconceived judgments or convictions about something. Prejudice can involve the irrational suspicion or hatred of a particular group, race, or religion. Prejudices cause people to judge prematurely and irrationally. When strongly held, they can be contagious, encouraging other people to succumb to them and become biased against someone or something. Prejudices affect their targets detrimentally, often forming the foundations of, among other things, racist and sexist attitudes.

Police in Canada need to ensure that stereotypes and secret prejudices do not influence their interactions with people in our diverse communities. In preparation for encountering different cultures and ethnicities, police officers should do the following: avoid being judgmental; increase their understanding of different cultures; understand that people of diversity are neither all saints nor all villains; recognize that they can learn a lot from people of diversity; and focus on similarities among people as much as on differences (Kazarian, Crichlow, & Bradford, 2007, p. 148).

stereotype
conventional, formulaic, and usually oversimplified conceptions that falsify reality through overgeneralization and strip their subjects of individuality

prejudice
an adverse judgment or opinion formed with little or no knowledge or experience or examination of the facts; a predetermined preference, idea, or bias

---

EXERCISE 2

Consider a few of the stereotypes that you have encountered with respect to people of diversity. What effects do you think stereotypes have on the people who are subjected to them and on society generally?

Cultural Beliefs and Practices: Core Dimensions

There are 10,000 cultures and 7,102 distinct languages in the world (Lewis, Simons, & Fennig, 2015; Moynihan, 1993; Triandis, 1995). It would be impossible to study all cultures in detail, but we can familiarize ourselves with the key characteristics of some of them—what we might consider their "personalities," and what psychologists call their *dimensions*. Several such dimensions or "personalities" of cultures have been identified, and we describe them below. Note that these dimensions are continuums, not categories; in other words, cultures are seen not as being entirely one thing or the other but as having more of some characteristics than others. A "dimensional" approach to cultures and cultural beliefs and practices allows us to see them in relation to one another, and works against the tendency to stereotype people, cultures, or cultural beliefs and practices.

- **Achievement Versus Relationship Culture**
  In achievement cultures, people primarily live to work, whereas in relationship cultures, they work to live. Individuals from achievement cultures tend to focus on work and on getting the job done. Individuals from relationship cultures emphasize leisure and fun, the separation of work life from private life, close family ties, and nurturing social relations.

CLOSE-UP   The Komagata Maru Incident

During the first half of the 20th century, Canadian immigration policies were ethnically selective and created a division between preferred and non-preferred immigrants. Preference was given to British and American immigrants, along with immigrants from northern and central European countries. Immigrants from Asia fell under the category of non-preferred immigrants.

In 1908, the federal government amended the *Immigration Act* of 1906 and enacted the *Continuous Passage Act*, which included the text below:

> … THEREFORE the Governor general in Council is pleased to Order and it is hereby Ordered that, … immigrants may be prohibited from landing or coming into Canada unless they come from the country of their birth, or citizenship, by a continuous journey and on through tickets purchased before leaving the country of their birth, or citizenship. Wednesday, 8th Day of January, 1908. (Citizenship and Immigration Canada, 2008)

The *Continuous Passage Act* did not refer to race or nationality; however, its requirement that immigrants travel directly to Canada from their country of origin without stopping restricted immigrants from South Asian countries from entering Canada. No routes from these countries at that time offered a direct passage to Canada. Even though Indians were British subjects, this Act did not allow them to enter Canada as immigrants. This regulation was in response to the recommendation of the deputy minister of labour, William Lyon Mackenzie King, that Ottawa should limit the entry of Oriental people. The Act remained in effect until 1947.

The *Komagata Maru* was a Japanese steamship that arrived in Canadian waters on May 23, 1914. Upon its arrival, 356 passengers from British India were not allowed to disembark. This incident is an example of Canadian immigration laws that excluded immigrants of those ethnicities that were deemed unfit to enter Canada.

A Sikh merchant, Gurdit Singh, had chartered the *Komagata Maru*, which began its journey in Hong Kong en route to Vancouver. When the ship docked at English Bay, out of the 376 passengers, only 20 were permitted to go ashore. These 20 passengers included returning residents of British Columbia and the ship's doctor and his family. The 356 people who were forbidden entry to Canada were British subjects, because India was a British colony

at the time. The Canadian government maintained that these passengers could not be allowed entry to Canada because the ship did not make a continuous journey from India to Canada (it had stopped in China and Japan) and was, therefore, in violation of the *Continuous Passage Act*. The ship remained docked at Vancouver for two months while Canadian courts tested the legality of the *Continuous Passage Act*. During this time, immigration officers did not permit food and water to be taken on board. After the British Columbia Court of Appeal upheld the legislation and ruled in favour of the immigration board's decision to deny entry, the *Komagata Maru* was escorted out of the harbour on July 23, 1914.

Passengers on the *Komagata Maru* in English Bay, Vancouver.

With local citizens cheering at the docks, the naval cruiser HMCS *Rainbow* and troops from the BC regiment were deployed to enforce the departure of *Komagata Maru*. Upon its arrival in India, a clash with British soldiers killed 19 passengers, and the others were arrested. The Canadian government was criticized for the way it handled the whole incident. Although Canada was accepting vast numbers of immigrants from Europe—more than 400,000 alone in 1913—the denial of entry of over 300 immigrants from India demonstrated racial discrimination in Canada's immigration system. In 2008, Prime Minister Stephen Harper issued an informal apology to the Indo-Canadian community over the incident, and in May 2016, Prime Minister Justin Trudeau issued an apology for the incident on the floor of the House of Commons.

- **Tight Versus Loose Culture**

  Tight cultures impose clear-cut societal norms. Such cultures have only minimal tolerance for people who deviate from established norms and expectations. Predictability, certainty, and security are dominant values in tight cultures. Unlike individuals from loose cultures, which are less concerned about rules and conformity, individuals from tight cultures tend to be more anxious, insecure, and fearful of the consequences of violating the norms.

- **Low-Context Versus High-Context Culture**

  Cultures can also be described in terms of communication style. In low-context cultures, words are extremely important because they convey most of the message being sent. Low-context cultures include the host cultures of Canada, Britain, France, Germany, the United States, and most Scandinavian countries. In these countries, police officers use direct and logical language, usually without emotion, and they expect their words alone to convey their message. Low-context cultures are also time-oriented—that is, schedules are an important part of completing tasks.

  In high-context cultures, by contrast, words without emotion and context have very little meaning; words convey only part of the message being sent. Here, the spoken message needs to be understood in the context of the larger communication or social interaction. People from high-context cultures prefer to get to know strangers before developing a work relationship with them. Having long personal conversations prior to reaching agreements or carrying out instructions is common in these cultures, to the annoyance of individuals from low-context cultures. Individuals from high-context cultures are also task-oriented—completing a task is more important to them than the schedule. Lateness or missing appointments may be less problematic in high-context cultures than it is in low-context ones. High-context cultures include Indigenous cultures and African, Caribbean, Asian, and Latin American cultures.

- **Collectivism Versus Individualism**

  Cultures can also be viewed in terms of being *collectivist* ("we"-oriented) as opposed to *individualist* ("me"-oriented). Collectivist cultures are characterized by hierarchical structures and by identification with, loyalty to, and dependence on in-groups. The self-concepts of individuals from these cultures tend to depend on the in-groups rather than on distinct identities. The interdependence of the individual and the group is a critical feature of collectivist cultures, in which people value immediate and extended family (sometimes including ancestors), family honour, security, hierarchical relationships, obedience, conformity, group decisions, group "face," and group harmony. People from these cultures are likely to downplay their own goals and remain loyal to group goals. They believe that parents have an obligation to care for their children, and that children have an obligation to care for their aging parents. In collectivist cultures, elderly parents are expected to live with their children and command their respect.

  People from individualist cultures are likely to pursue personal goals and, when faced with a conflict between the group's goals and their own, are likely to follow the latter. They tend to value independence, self-reliance, and competition over cooperation. They may also mistrust authority. Table 3.1 summarizes the differences between individualist and collectivist cultures.

  Relative to European peoples, Indigenous, African, Asian, and Latin American peoples are collectivist, given their relative de-emphasis on the welfare of the individual in favour of the welfare of the community. Canada has been a collectivist country in the sense that it has "recognized collectivities as fundamental units and emphasized group rights over those of individual citizens" (Lock, 1991, p. 87). Universal health

TABLE 3.1   Differences Between Individualist and Collectivist Cultures

Individualism	Collectivism
Pursuit of one's own goals	Loyalty to one's group
Nuclear family structure	Extended family structure
Self-reliant	Group-reliant
Time and energy invested for personal gain	Time and energy invested for group gain
Receptive to career changes	Relatively unreceptive to career changes
Relatively little sharing of material/ non-material resources	Sharing of material/non-material resources
Emphasis on competition	Emphasis on cooperation
Relatively non-conformist	Conformist
Mistrust of authority	Respectful of status and authority

care, employment insurance, and social welfare assistance are examples of areas where the majority of Canadians believe that government should help those who need it. This is essentially an idea of collective responsibility. As Lock (1991) describes, "Whereas in America 'life, liberty, and the pursuit of happiness' were enshrined as fundamental ideals, in Canada 'peace, order, and good government' were laid down as overarching goals" (p. 87).

It is important to note that collectivist individuals may be found in individualist cultures, and individualist individuals may be found in collectivist cultures. Individuals may also embrace individualism and collectivism at the same time.

EXERCISE 3

How could focusing on cultural differences rather than similarities affect the practice of law enforcement?

Cultural Beliefs and Practices: Specific Cultural Groups

Canada is a multicultural and multi-ethnic society comprising more than 200 ethnic groups (Statistics Canada, 2013b). The nation's minority cultural groups can be divided into three major categories, as follows: Indigenous peoples, non-visible ethnic minority peoples, and visible minority ethnic peoples. The following sections will discuss the three major cultural groups and the major subgroups in each. Space limitations prevent us from discussing the many smaller groups. (A single chapter simply cannot begin to cover the international world within Canada.)

The 2011 National Household Survey revealed that 13 different ethnic origins in Canada have populations of more than 1 million. The ethnic origin most often reported by people who have lived in Canada for three or more generations is Canadian, followed by English, French, Scottish, Irish, and German. In the case of first-generation immigrants, Chinese and East Indian are now the most common ethnic origins, with English now ranking third (see Table 1.2 in Chapter 1).

Indigenous Peoples

Indigenous peoples make up almost 4.3 percent of the population in Canada. This minority community, more than half of whom live in Canada's cities, is growing fast compared with the rest of the country's population. The Indigenous population increased by 20 percent between 2006 and 2011, which is almost four times as much as the 5.2 percent increase in the non-Indigenous population within the same time period. As shown in Table 3.2, in 2011, the number of Canadians who reported being Aboriginal (the term used by Statistics Canada, which includes First Nations, Métis, and Inuit) reached 1.4 million (Statistics Canada, 2013a).

TABLE 3.2   Population Counts, by Aboriginal Identity, Canada, 2011

	Population counts
Total Aboriginal identity population	1,400,685
First Nations	851,560
Métis	451,795
Inuit	59,445
Multiple Aboriginal identities	11,415
Aboriginal identities not included elsewhere	26,475

NOTES:
Excludes data for one or more incompletely enumerated Indian reserves or Indian settlements.
The three Aboriginal groups are based on the population reporting a single identity of "First Nations," "Métis," or "Inuit."
SOURCE: Statistics Canada (2015).

At the time of first European contact, more than 56 Indigenous nations existed in Canada, speaking more than 50 languages (Dickason, 1997, p. 5). These numbers have radically diminished. Infringements on the human rights of Indigenous peoples began with the first European contact and have continued through our country's history. The effects of this historical mistreatment are evident in the higher rates of poverty, poorer health, higher death and suicide rates, and far greater unemployment compared with other Canadians, as discussed in Chapter 10.

Attempts to address the needs of Canada's Indigenous peoples began in 1973. This was when the Supreme Court of Canada first recognized Indigenous land rights, which were based on an Indigenous group's traditional use and occupancy of a certain area of land. In 1982, the *Canadian Charter of Rights and Freedoms* recognized and affirmed the treaty rights of Indigenous peoples (it uses the term *aboriginal*) to protect their cultures, customs, traditions, and languages. In 1996, the Royal Commission on Aboriginal Peoples presented a comprehensive five-volume report to the Parliament of Canada identifying the legal, political, social, economic, and cultural issues that need to be addressed to ensure the future survival of Canada's First Nations, Inuit, and Métis peoples. One year later, the federal government responded with *Gathering Strength: Canada's Aboriginal Action Plan*, a proposal to work in partnership with Canada's Indigenous peoples to improve health, housing, and public safety, strengthen economic development, and assist with the implementation of self-government (Aboriginal Affairs and Northern Development Canada, 1997).

In 2008, the federal government issued a Statement of Apology to survivors of the residential schools and established the Truth and Reconciliation Commission (TRC) to deal with the devastation that the schools wrought. The TRC had a five-year mandate to gather the written and oral history of residential schools and to work toward reconciliation between former students and the rest of Canada. The TRC held seven national events between 2010 and 2013, with the closing event held in Ottawa in June 2015. During this time, the commission collected more than 6,200 statements from former students.

The history of Indigenous peoples in Canada, including the federal–Indigenous relationship and residential schools, is discussed in detail in the second part of this book.

The Culture of Indigenous Peoples

Underlying Indigenous ethics, values, and rules of behaviour is a traditional need to promote social harmony within the community and thereby ensure the community's survival in harsh natural environments. Indigenous cultures have a collectivist orientation; they value group harmony over individual success. Indigenous peoples have always cultivated a cooperative social climate, encouraging the members of an extended family, clan, band, or tribe to adopt patterns of behaviour that involve the suppression of conflict (Brant, 1990). Indigenous ethics or principles of behaviour, which still apply today, are listed in Table 3.3.

TABLE 3.3   Indigenous Ethics of Behaviour

Non-interference	Physical, verbal, and psychological coercion are avoided, as is exertion of pressure by means of advising, instructing, coercing, or persuading.
Non-competitiveness	Rivalry is averted and social embarrassment of individuals is prevented.
Emotional restraint	Both positive (joy and enthusiasm) and negative (anger and hostility) emotions are suppressed.
Sharing	Generosity is encouraged while hoarding material goods is discouraged.
Concept of time	There is a belief in "doing things when the time is right."
Attitude toward gratitude and approval	Gratitude and approval are rarely shown, verbalized, or expected.
Principle of teaching by modelling	To learn, one is *shown* how rather than *told* how. Actions convey useful and practical information.

SOURCE: Brant (1990, p. 536).

Indigenous peoples believe that *non-interference* helps promote positive relations between people. Teaching in Indigenous culture is done by modelling—that is, by example—rather than by commanding or dictating. In adult–child relationships, this policy of non-interference takes the form of permissiveness. Brant (1990, p. 535) describes how this approach might be expressed in an Indigenous family:

> A Native child may be allowed at the age of six, for example, to make the decision on whether or not he goes to school even though he is required to do so by law. The child may be allowed to decide whether or not he will do his homework, have his assignment done on time, and even visit the dentist. Native parents will be reluctant to force the child into doing anything he does not choose to do.

Non-competitiveness is another principle of Indigenous peoples' behaviour that enables them to avoid conflict between groups and between individuals. It is a policy in keeping with their collectivist orientation—their emphasis on group harmony over individual success.

Indigenous cultures value *emotional restraint* because it promotes self-control and discourages the expression of strong, violent feelings, which often lead to conflict. But this social principle comes at a paradoxical price. Suppressing emotions may create a need for alcohol as an outlet, and alcohol abuse often leads its users back to violence. Alcohol-related domestic violence and violence within the community are serious issues for Indigenous peoples living on reserves.

Sharing is an important part of Indigenous collectivist cultures. In addition to its historical value as a survival tactic, sharing helps to suppress conflict by minimizing the likelihood of greed, envy, arrogance, and pride within the community. It also contributes to equality and democracy. Striving for individual gain—for prosperity and success and other assets, such as a superior education—is inconsistent with the ethic of sharing. Indigenous society tends to be disapproving of individual ambition. This disapproval has been a factor in the "skimming" of Indigenous society, a process by which young, talented Indigenous people or those with a post-secondary education leave the reserve to live in non-Indigenous society and marry non-Indigenous people (Brant, 1990).

The *concept of time* in contemporary Indigenous life is also connected to Indigenous peoples' emphasis on harmonious relationships (Brant, 1990). They tend to be less perturbed by delay or impressed by punctuality than are people from more individualistic cultures, in which personal success depends on meeting deadlines and excelling at time management. Indigenous people are unlikely to be inconvenienced or annoyed by delays in starting scheduled meetings or social functions.

In Indigenous cultures, excellence is expected at all times. A negative consequence of this core value is performance anxiety. Indigenous people may avoid taking risks for fear of making mistakes or subjecting themselves to public scrutiny. At the same time, Indigenous people do not expect or welcome praise or rewards when they achieve excellence. Being good is expected of everyone. Praise of the individual is likely to be seen as deceitful or, in group contexts, as embarrassing, because it does not credit the whole group. Praise that is not shared with peers is seen as damaging to peer relationships. By a similar principle, gratitude and approval are rarely expressed in Indigenous culture. Both are considered superfluous because doing something for someone else is thought to carry its own intrinsic reward.

The ethical principles described above can bring Indigenous people into conflict with mainstream cultural values. For example, the Indigenous emphasis on the collective rather than the individual can create an impression of uncompetitiveness that does not sit well with the contemporary business world. Mainstream North American culture expects people to be competitive, and labels them "lazy" or "indifferent" if they behave otherwise.

EXERCISE 4

For each of the following principles of Indigenous ethics, think of situations where the principle might be in conflict with "mainstream" North American ethics:

- non-interference
- non-competitiveness
- emotional restraint
- sharing
- concept of time
- attitude toward gratitude and approval
- principle of teaching by modelling

Non-Visible Ethnic Minority Peoples

Non-visible ethnic minority groups in Canada include two of the founding peoples of Canada—that is, the English and the French—and a host of other cultural groups originally from Europe, including Germans, Italians, the Dutch, Australians, and New Zealanders. As we saw in

Chapter 1 (see Table 1.2), English, French, Scottish, and Irish are the most frequently reported non-visible ethnic minority groups in Canada for third-generation or more Canadians.

While there are differences among the English, Scottish, Irish, and Welsh cultures, they have certain values in common. Traditionally, they have been individualistic, emphasizing work ethic, self-reliance, emotional reserve, the nuclear family structure, privacy, and democracy. Self-reliance and work ethic are connected; a reluctance to express affection is common, as is respect for personal privacy and an unwillingness to disclose personal concerns or difficulties to others. This unwillingness stems from the belief that personal problems reflect personal failures, which are best met with greater individual effort.

People of French heritage are likely to value their language and its preservation, their French culture and its distinctiveness, their families, and, in some cases, their religion.

Visible Minority Populations

As stated above, the term *visible minority* refers to whether a person belongs to a visible minority group as defined by the *Employment Equity Act*. This includes "persons, other than aboriginal peoples, who are non-Caucasian in race or non-white in colour." There is significant variation among Canada's visible minority populations in terms of origin, linguistic characteristics, and religious affiliation. In Canada, the visible minority population consists primarily of South Asian, Chinese, Black, Arab, West Asian, Filipino, Southeast Asian, Latin American, Japanese, and Korean peoples.

Visible minority groups in Canada are, first of all, statistically significant, constituting 19.1 percent of the entire population (Statistics Canada, 2013b). Over 6.2 million individuals who identify themselves as belonging to visible minorities have made Canada their home. Their population in Canada increased from 16.2 percent in 2006. In 1981, 1 in 20 Canadians belonged to a visible minority; in 2001, it was 1 in 7; in 2006, it was nearly 1 in 6; and in 2011, it was 1 in 5 (Statistics Canada, 2013b).

Today, the three largest visible minority groups in Canada are South Asians, Chinese, and Blacks, in that order; collectively, these three groups constitute more than two-thirds of the visible minority population in Canada (Statistics Canada, 2013b). The following sections discuss these three groups, as well as Arabs. Space considerations preclude a detailed discussion of other visible minorities.

South Asians

The largest group of visible minority identified themselves as South Asian, with over 1.5 million people in Canada in 2011. This amounts to one-quarter of the total visible minority population (Statistics Canada, 2013b). South Asians include anyone whose ancestry can be traced, directly or indirectly, to the Indian subcontinent, a complex miscellany of states and ethnic groups (Tran, Kaddatz, & Allard, 2005). Hence the term *South Asian* encompasses a great variety of ethnic backgrounds, including, among various others, Bangladeshi, Bengali, East Indian, Goan, Pakistani, Sikh, Sri Lankan, and Tamil. It also includes people who, though born in Canada or elsewhere—for example, the Caribbean or Great Britain—identify themselves as belonging to one of the ethnic groups that make up the population of South Asia. In short, *South Asian* is an umbrella term equivalent to *North American*, more a convenience for Canadian statisticians than an ethnicity that someone from the region would actually claim.

The first South Asian immigrants to Canada were Sikhs, whom, although they were relatively few in number (5,000 in 1908), white society viewed with the same animosity as it did Blacks, Chinese, and Japanese. The presence of Sikhs in British Columbia at the turn of the century prompted talk of a "Hindu invasion" in the popular press (despite the fact that the Sikh religion, known as Sikhism, is in fact opposed to Hinduism). As the First World War approached, white

Canadians became even more obsessed with racial purity. The following screed, quoted in Henry and Tator (2005, p. 71), is typical of the period:

> To prepare ourselves for the irrepressible conflict, Canada must remain a White Man's country. On this western frontier of the Empire will be the forefront of the coming struggle ... . Therefore we ought to maintain this Country for the Anglo-Saxon and those races which are able to assimilate themselves to them. If this is done, we believe that history will repeat itself and the supremacy of our race will continue.

The prevalence of such white supremacism in the province led British Columbia to pass laws barring South Asians from participating in elections, even though they were British citizens. Most people of Asian descent of any kind, whether British citizens or not, were denied voting rights in Canada. This disenfranchisement had a negative economic impact on Asian Canadians. Excluded from voters' lists, they could neither bid on government contracts nor enter professions such as law, education, or medicine. South Asians did not get the franchise until the late 1940s (Baxter, 2003).

Despite the wide variety of their national and ethnic origins, South Asians have certain cultural values in common. Compared with other visible minority groups in Canada, they are remarkable for having strong ties not only to family and community but also to their linguistic, religious, and ethnic origins, as well as to Canada and its ideals (Tran, Kaddatz, & Allard, 2005).

It is not surprising, given South Asians' varied origins, that linguistic diversity is a conspicuous feature of their culture in Canada. The linguistic collective of the Indian subcontinent includes more than 75 languages, of which Punjabi, English, and Tamil are the three most common (Tran et al., 2005). Their traditional languages are important to South Asians. Compared with other visible minority cultures (the Chinese, for example), they are considerably more concerned about maintaining their mother tongues and passing them on to their children.

South Asians are also diverse in their religious beliefs. Sikhism, Hinduism, Islam, and Christianity are the religions most often practised in the South Asian community, with each ethnic subgroup adhering strongly to its particular faith. Of all visible minority groups in Canada, South Asians are the most likely to say that their religion is important to them, and the most likely to have participated in a religious activity within the past year (Tran et al., 2005). This commitment to religion is not only evident in newcomers; it is maintained by second-generation South Asians, too.

South Asians maintain close ties both with their countries of origin and with their ethnocultural communities in Canada. This community closeness has a historical basis; it is partly a consequence of the harsh conditions and prejudice that South Asians faced on arriving in Canada a century ago, when community ties and support were crucial to their survival. More than other visible minority groups, South Asians tend both to work and to socialize with members of their own ethnic group. Many South Asians in Canada have co-workers with the same ancestral origins, and South Asians are the least likely of all visible minority groups to marry outside their own communities (Tran et al., 2005).

A strong sense of family obligation and belonging is common among South Asians, who, like the Chinese and other visible minority groups, are more likely to live in multi-generational households made up of parents, children, spouses, and other relatives. In 2001, only 8 percent of seniors of South Asian origin lived alone, compared with 29 percent of all seniors. More South Asian seniors (25 percent) lived with relatives such as the family of a son or daughter, whereas only 5 percent of all Canadian seniors lived with relatives (Lindsay, 2001).

In keeping with their generally retentive attitude to origins, South Asians set much store by their cultural customs and traditions—for example, celebrations, food, and clothing—and they believe in the importance of maintaining them. Time does little to alter this attitude; second-generation South Asians feel as strongly about retaining their original culture as more recent arrivals do (Tran et al., 2005).

CLOSE-UP   Harjit Sajjan

Harjit Sajjan, Canada's defence minister in Prime Minister Trudeau's Liberal government, garnered attention not only because he took on the role of defence minister with grassroots knowledge of military service, but also because of his identity as a visible minority immigrant sporting a turban and a beard.

Harjit Sajjan was born in the Punjab state of India and came to Canada at the age of five, along with his mother and sister, to join his father. His father had immigrated a few years before and worked in a sawmill in Vancouver. Growing up in Vancouver, Sajjan and his sister would accompany their mother during the summer months to pick berries on the farms of BC's Lower Mainland area. "'I hated it,' Sajjan says. 'Imagine every single day getting picked up at 5 a.m. and you're not going to get back until 7 or 8 p.m.'" (Geddes, 2016).

His teenage years were a crucial period, when Sajjan decided to attend a different high school to avoid trouble, and he also decided to wear a turban and follow the principles of Sikhism. "'I needed a commitment to stay out of trouble, including alcohol and other things,' he says" (Geddes, 2016). Growing up wearing the turban in Vancouver's multicultural community, he did not face much racism until he joined the army reserves after high school. The first unit he applied to reportedly rejected him. Sajjan talks about facing overt racism during his training:

> Instructors told him he didn't belong in the army, and, as Sajjan terms it, "beasted" him more than other recruits. He talked to his father about quitting. "He said, 'Yeah, sure, come on home. But do realize that every other person who wears a turban, or every other person in a minority, will be labelled a failure if you leave now.' So I sucked it up." (Geddes, 2016)

Harjit Sajjan's first overseas deployment was to Bosnia on a peacemaking mission. He was deployed three times to Afghanistan and was awarded one of the military's highest recognitions, the Order of Military Merit, for his role in reducing the Taliban's influence in Kandahar.

The Honourable Harjit Sajjan addresses the ship's company of HMCS *Winnipeg* on the ship's flight deck on December 23, 2015.

Source: National Defence and the Canadian Armed Forces.

After he returned from Bosnia, Sajjan joined the Vancouver Police Department in 1999 and served on the police force for 11 years. He worked his way up to become a detective-constable with the Gang Crime Unit, specializing in combatting organized crime including gang violence and drug crimes.

After returning from his third mission in Afghanistan, Sajjan became the first Sikh Canadian to command a Canadian military regiment and became a commander of the British Columbia Regiment (Duke of Connaught's Own) in 2011. In 2014, on the 100th anniversary of the *Komagata Maru* incident, many media reports highlighted the fact that Harjit Sajjan, a Sikh, commands the same regiment "that was involved in forcing the *Komagata Maru* out of Vancouver harbour 100 years ago" (Roberts, 2014). Sajjan commented that "Canada has grown in the past century … and progress has been made. I look at our diversity in Canada as an example for the rest of the world. If we don't succeed with it, it will not succeed anywhere else" (Roberts, 2014).

Sources: Geddes (2016); Roberts (2014).

An interesting characteristic of South Asians in Canada is that, despite strong and persistent allegiance to their original cultures, they are also very patriotic to Canada. Of all visible minority groups in Canada, South Asians feel the strongest about being Canadian and about belonging to Canada, and are the most likely to vote. They are also more likely than other Canadians to feel an allegiance to their province and to the cities and towns where they live. For South Asians, pride in and awareness of ethnic origin does not lead to insularity; they are very active in the civic life of this country.

Chinese

The second-largest visible minority group in 2011 was Chinese, with over 1.3 million people. They made up 21.1 percent of the visible minority population (Statistics Canada, 2013b). The Chinese in Canada, though varied in their languages, countries of birth, and religious affiliations, are strongly linked by a single ethnicity, a majority identifying themselves as Chinese. A small proportion (8.6 percent) of Chinese visible minorities reported multiple ethnic origins.

Chinese immigration to Canada has occurred in three distinct waves over the past 150 years. The first immigrants settled in British Columbia in 1860, drawn north from California, where they had gone in search of gold, by news of gold in the Fraser River area. When the Fraser River gold rush ended, many of the Chinese prospectors stayed on in Western Canada and moved into other kinds of labour—domestic service, farming, and, eventually, railway building (Chui, Tran, & Flanders, 2005).

The next wave of immigration came two decades later, when Chinese workers, known derogatorily as "coolies," were brought in as part of the manual labour force to build the Canada Pacific Railway (1881–1885). This was a vast, dangerous undertaking that brought the Chinese work-gangs much hardship and scandalously low pay; they were exploited, then released without prospects once the railway was finished. (In 2006, the government of Canada issued Chinese Canadians a formal apology for their treatment during and after the building of the CPR.)

A long spell of official discrimination against Chinese people followed, beginning with the 1885 *Act to Restrict and Regulate Chinese Immigration*. This Act introduced a "head tax" of $50 (later increased to $500), required of any person of Chinese origin seeking to enter Canada. The *Chinese Immigration Act* (1923) followed, denying Chinese residents of Canada the right to vote, obtain citizenship, or work in certain occupations. This legislation effectively put an end to Chinese immigration until the 1940s, when the Act was repealed (Chui et al., 2005).

The next wave of Chinese immigration had its beginnings in the late 1960s, when Canada's immigration policy changed; national origin was removed as a selection criterion and replaced by a concern for skills and education. By the mid-1980s, Chinese immigration had gained momentum, and this continued for the next two decades, with an average of 35,400 immigrants arriving in Canada annually between 1981 and 2001 (Chui et al., 2005). By the beginning of the 21st century, the Chinese formed the largest visible minority group in Canada. Approximately two-thirds of recent Chinese immigrants have come from the People's Republic of China. Most of the remainder come from Hong Kong, and a smaller proportion from Taiwan. The socio-economic profile of these latter-day Chinese immigrants, most of them wealthy, educated urbanites, differs significantly from that of earlier Chinese immigrants, who were manual labourers with few resources. Most Chinese immigrants of the new wave have chosen to live in big urban centres, such as Vancouver and Toronto (Chui et al., 2005).

The Chinese language, which after English and French is the third-most common mother tongue in Canada, is composed of different dialects. These vary according to the speaker's region of origin, though all are based on the same written language of Chinese characters. The two most common dialects are Cantonese and Mandarin (Chui et al., 2005).

Religion is not an important factor in the lives of many Chinese, more than half of whom have no religious affiliations. This number is higher for those with roots in the People's Republic of China, but still significant among those from Hong Kong and Taiwan. The religions most common among Chinese who do claim religious affiliations are Buddhism and Christianity (Roman Catholicism and Protestantism) (Chui et al., 2005).

The Chinese in Canada today perceive themselves as hard-working, industrious people, and the employment statistics bear this out. During the past 20 years, Chinese immigration has accounted for a significant percentage of the growth in the Canadian labour market. Gravitating toward white-collar occupations, many Chinese have found employment in the business and administrative spheres and in the natural and applied sciences. They are a family-centred community—the main reason given by Chinese immigrants for choosing to live in the urban centres of Toronto and Vancouver was that they had family living there already. Like the South Asians, Chinese individuals are more likely than those in the general population to live in a family household, often with several generations living under one roof. Respect for the elderly and responsibility for aging parents are traditional in Chinese culture, and their elderly, as with seniors in the South Asian community, are much less likely than those in the general population to live alone (Chui et al., 2005).

Blacks

According to the 2011 National Household Survey, close to 945,700 people in Canada identified themselves as Black (Statistics Canada, 2013b). They made up close to 15 percent of the visible minority population. More Blacks reported multiple ethnic origins (29.8 percent) compared with South Asians and the Chinese. Blacks have a long and tragic history of colonization and slavery in North America. In the United States, a small number of captured Africans were brought to Jamestown, Virginia to work as farm labourers early in the 17th century. By the 19th century, many more Africans had been taken by force to North America, and grew to a slave population in the millions.

One of the great myths of Canadian society is that it has never had slavery; in fact, slavery was practised in Canada from the beginning of the 17th century. It was legalized in 1709 and continued until the abolition of slavery throughout the British Empire in 1834. The passage of the *Fugitive Slave Act* in the United States in 1850 greatly increased the number of Blacks coming to Canada; it required that all runaway slaves—even those who had escaped to non-slaveholding areas of the United States—be returned to their masters. But these Black refugees were unwelcome in Canada; they were subjected to racial prejudice and ridicule both personally and in the press, and were seen as responsible for a disproportionate amount of crime.

Historically, the Canadian government has consistently resisted the immigration of Blacks. In the early 1900s, when the government was attempting to lure experienced farmers from the United States, the Immigration Branch informed its American agents that Blacks should not be among those encouraged to come to Canada. The government often rejected Blacks on medical or other non-racial grounds, so as not to be accused of overt racism (Baxter, 2003).

The history of racism in Canada toward people of African descent should not be understated. In 1903, J.S. Woodsworth, the founder of the CCF political party, expressed an antipathy toward Blacks that is startling, though perhaps typical of the time; he asserted that the "very qualities of intelligence and manliness which are the essentials for citizens in a democracy were systematically expunged from the Negro race" (Henry & Tator, 2005, p. 66). Following are some other examples of racism from Canada's past:

- 1785: Sheriffs in Saint John, New Brunswick were instructed to deny Blacks the right to vote.
- 1795: Blacks in Saint John were denied fishing rights.
- 1830s: Some churches in Canada consigned Black worshippers to back galleries.
- 1850s: Blacks were denied admission to hotels in Ontario cities such as Chatham, Hamilton, and Windsor.
- 1850: The *Separate School Act* enabled whites to relegate Blacks to all-Black schools with exclusively Black teachers. This practice continued up to the 1960s.
- 1920s: The Ku Klux Klan grew to the point of having 119 chapters throughout Canada.
- 1924: The City Commissioner of Edmonton banned all Blacks from public parks and swimming pools.
- 1918–1939: McGill University had racial segregation regulations that were maintained until well after the Second World War.
- 1954: A teacher was dismissed from a teaching position in Victoria, British Columbia merely for being married to a Jamaican woman.

As can be seen from the timeline above, discrimination against Blacks continued long after the abolition of slavery in 1834. All provinces with significant Black populations had segregation laws on the books for most of the 20th century. In Ontario, school segregation continued to be legal until 1964, while residential segregation was imposed through restrictions on deeds and leases. When a Black person applied for an apartment, for example, he or she might be told untruthfully that it was already taken.

Although African Canadians have been resilient in the face of slavery, segregation, and racist theories and practice, their battle against discrimination is ongoing. In Canada, Blacks continue to face particularly harsh obstacles to success. Census data continue to show that they suffer more unemployment than those in the general adult population, and that they have lower incomes (Milan & Tran, 2004). They are also more likely to feel discriminated against on the basis of their ethnicity, culture, race, skin colour, language, accent, or religion. After Indigenous peoples, they are the most stigmatized of all visible minorities in Canada, and this has cost them heavily in terms of economic success and in their relationships with the justice system (Baxter, 2003).

Arab Peoples

The fastest-growing visible minority group in Canada, after South Asians, are people of Arab heritage. According to the 2011 census, the population of the Arab community in Canada increased from 563,315 in 2006 to 750,925 in 2011. This is an increase of 33.25 percent in five years. In comparison with the 2001 census, the Arab population has almost doubled in ten years (368,530 in 2001) (Dajani, 2014a). An overwhelming majority of people (five in six) of Arab ethnic origin tend to settle in either Ontario or Quebec. The first Arabs arrived in Canada over 100 years ago, in the late 19th century, most of them emigrating from a small region of Syria. The majority went to Montreal, where they worked as unskilled labourers and, very often, as peddlers, an occupation that eventually led to their dispersion throughout Canada and to their establishing themselves as settled merchants and wholesalers (Hayani, 2015). The second wave of Arab immigration began a century later, after 1961, when Canada's immigration policy changed, and the country became more receptive toward non-European ethnic groups. Arab immigration to Canada has accelerated since then, and between 2006 and 2031 the Arab population is expected to more than triple, which is the fastest population growth among all ethnic groups in Canada (Statistics Canada, 2011a).

Originally denoted "Syrians and Turks," Arab immigrants are now identified for immigration purposes according to their countries of birth, which are very diverse. The majority of Arabs living in Canada are Lebanese, Syrian, Egyptian, Chaldean/Iraqi, and Palestinian/Jordanian, and more than half of all Arab Canadians were born outside the country. Arabs, like Chinese people, tend to be very conscious of sharing a common ethnocultural origin that transcends variations in original citizenship, dialect, and political affiliation (Hayani, 2015).

There are various dialects of spoken Arabic, with significant regional differences in vocabulary and accent. The written Arabic language, however, is the same everywhere, used and recognized throughout the Arab world. It is a significant factor in Arab ethnicity—in their strong sense of belonging to a single ethnocultural group.

Religion is more important to Arab Canadians than it is to people in the general population; in 2001, Arabs were much more likely than those in the general population to report a religious affiliation. Early Arab immigrants to Canada were Christian, but since 1961 the majority have been Muslim. In 2001, Arabs in Canada were divided almost equally between Christianity and Islam (44 percent each). However, according to 2011 census, more Arabs reported belonging to the Muslim faith (55 percent) than to the Christian faith (34 percent) (Dajani, 2014c). The immigration trends of the last ten years suggest that Islam is now the leading religion of Arab Canadians. But it is worth reminding ourselves that the Muslim community in Canada is not entirely composed of Arabs. According to the 2011 National Household Survey, there were approximately 1,053,945 Muslims in Canada and about 600,000 residents of Canada of Arab origin (Statistics Canada, 2013b).

Arabs in Canada put great emphasis on education and are very well educated compared not only with other visible minority groups but also with the general population. Young Arab Canadians are more likely to be in school than most young Canadians are, and are much more likely to have university degrees or post-graduate degrees. In 2011, 60 percent of Arabs in Canada held university certificates, diploma, or degrees at the bachelor's level or higher, compared with 40 percent of the general Canadian population (Dajani, 2014b). Concerned about academic accomplishment, Arabs are also very conscious of their cultural heritage and proud of their many intellectual contributions to Western civilization in language, mathematics, and science (Dajani, 2014b).

The family is a central institution for Arab Canadians, who are less likely than other Canadians to live alone and more likely to be married (Statistics Canada, 2007). They hold marriage, child-bearing, and child-rearing in high regard, and prefer to marry within their own local community (Dajani, 2014c.). Kinship ties are strong, with family obligation extending beyond the immediate nuclear family of husband, wife, and children. In the Arab community, as in the South Asian and Chinese communities, seniors are less likely to live alone than are seniors in the general population (Statistics Canada, 2007). Unmarried daughters are more likely to continue to live with their parents, regardless of age.

In Arab culture, the concepts of honour and shame are very important, and family members are interdependent in matters of reputation. For example, a woman's losing her virginity before marriage brings shame and dishonour to her family, as do certain medical conditions, such as mental illness. In Arab culture, such events and conditions may be concealed because of the shame they bring to the family and because of the damage they may do to the marriage opportunities of other family members.

Discrimination has been a concern in the Arab Canadian community for decades, with the media at times presenting a simplistic and stereotypical image of Arab culture. Statistics confirm that the incomes of Arab people do not reflect their levels of academic accomplishment (Statistics Canada, 2007). Since 9/11, this discrimination has intensified and manifested itself in new contexts as a result of factors that include heightened security concerns, simplistic media coverage, and Islamophobia. Many Arabs feel demonized and unfairly associated with terrorism. Despite this sense of being discriminated against, many Canadians of Arab origin, like South Asians, feel a strong sense of belonging to Canada and are active in Canadian society. A large proportion of Arabs, compared with other visible minority groups, vote in elections and participate in community associations (Statistics Canada, 2007).

Cultural Diversity: Police Abilities, Knowledge, and Skills

Culture, race, and ethnicity influence individual values, practices, and codes of conduct. Diverse values and customs enrich a country's quality of life, but they may also be a source of conflict, misunderstanding, and violence.

Ethnocultural groups and their community leaders have certain responsibilities:

- to respect others' rights and freedoms;
- to live peacefully with diversity;
- to recognize that there is one secular law for all;
- to obey the law of the land; and
- to protect the civil order of the nation.

Conflict and misunderstanding are more likely where certain ethnocultural groups consider themselves superior and others inferior, or where different laws apply to different groups. All of these groups, as well as the police, need to respect diversity and to uphold a core value called

diversity equity, according to which no ethnocultural group is superior or inferior to any other.

Police must resist simplistic perceptions of ethnocultural groups. In Western countries, the post-9/11 demonization of Arab communities showed how these distortions can occur. Some people equated "Arab" and "Muslim Arab" with "terrorist," on the grounds that some Arab communities and their leaders failed to condemn terrorism absolutely after 9/11 or were slow to do so, or, as in a few cases, reacted jubilantly to news of the tragedy. Police need to remember that very few Arabs are fundamentalists, extremists, radicals, fascists, or terrorists, and that terrorists are likely to defy demographic, racial, or ethnic profiles. They may emerge from any demographic category—male or female, young or old, immigrant or citizen—and from any ethnocultural group or nationality, whether African, Asian, European, Hispanic, or Middle Eastern.

Colour-blind and democratic law enforcement is needed to protect civil order and curb terrorist threats. All those who pose a real terrorist threat, whatever their race, ethnicity, or religion, must be subject to democratic policing measures, including screening, scrutiny, surveillance, and criminal prosecution. Of course, targeting the terrorist danger itself can only do so much; it combats the outward expression of the problem while ignoring its underlying causes. Sound, mutually respectful relations between police and community, marked by trust and open communication, are key counterterrorism measures.

Police should be neither complacent nor overzealous. Protection of civil order is critical. Ethnocultural groups and their leaders must understand the responsibilities police have in Canada and the practices they are obliged to follow. And police must offer these groups the reassurance of a democratic approach to policing. By declining to identify terrorism with a particular ethnic group and by maintaining diversity equity in the law enforcement psyche, police recognize all people's humanity and thereby promote the humanity of policing. This creates a climate of mutual trust and, ultimately, a safer, more secure Canada.

diversity equity
a value according to which there are no superior or inferior cultural groups

CHAPTER SUMMARY

It is important to remember that most ethnocultural categories—South Asians, for example—include a variety of cultures and ethnic origins, and that within the various sub-categories are individuals with highly personal beliefs and attitudes. Stereotyping people is a simplistic and lazy substitute for getting to know and understand them. By studying people carefully and focusing on the common ground between them and ourselves, we can reduce conflict and misunderstanding. Establishing a mutually respectful and trusting relationship between law enforcement and the communities they serve helps protect civil order.

REFERENCES

Aboriginal Affairs and Northern Development Canada. (1997). *Gathering strength: Canada's Aboriginal action plan.* http://www.ahf.ca/downloads/gathering-strength.pdf.

Baxter, P. (2003). A portrait of Canadian diversity: The 2001 census and its implications for multiculturalism. In *Issues in diversity and First Nations policing.* Unpublished manuscript, Georgian College, Barrie, ON.

Berry, J.W., & Laponce, J.A. (1994). Evaluating research on Canada's multiethnic and multicultural society. In J.W. Berry & J.A. Laponce (Eds.), *Ethnicity and culture in Canada* (pp. 3–16). Toronto: University of Toronto Press.

Brant, C.C. (1990). Native ethics and rules of behaviour. *Canadian Journal of Psychiatry, 35,* 534–539.

Canadian Charter of Rights and Freedoms. (1982). Part I of the *Constitution Act, 1982,* being Schedule B to the *Canada Act 1982* (UK), 1982, c. 11.

Chui, T., Tran, K., & Flanders, J. (2005, Spring). Chinese Canadians: Enriching the cultural mosaic. *Canadian Social Trends.* Statistics Canada. Catalogue no. 11-008. http://www.statcan.gc.ca/pub/11-008-x/2004004/article/7778-eng.pdf.

Citizenship and Immigration Canada. (2008). The 100th anniversary of the Continuous Passage Act. http://www.cic.gc.ca/english/multiculturalism/asian/100years.asp.

Dajani, G. (2014a). 750,925 Canadians hail from Arab lands. http://www.canadianarabinstitute.org/publications/reports/750925-canadians-hail-arab-lands/.

Dajani, G. (2014b). A highly educated, yet under-employed Canadian Arab community. http://www.canadianarabinstitute.org/publications/reports/highly-educated-yet-under-employed-canadian-arab-community/.

Dajani, G. (2014c). Religion and marital status in the Canadian Arab community. http://www.canadianarabinstitute.org/publications/reports/religion-and-marital-status-canadian-arab-community/.

Dickason, O.P. (1997). *Canada's First Nations: A history of founding peoples from earliest times* (2nd ed.). Toronto: Oxford University Press.

Employment Equity Act. (1995). SC 1995, c. 44.

Geddes, J. (2016, January 8). Harjit Sajjan: Canada's "bad-ass" defence minister. *Macleans.* http://www.macleans.ca.

Hayani, I. (2015). Arabs in Canada. http://www.globalresearch.ca/arabs-in-canada/5415869.

Henry, F., & Tator, C. (2005). *The colour of democracy: Racism in Canadian society* (3rd ed.) Toronto: Nelson Thomson.

Kallen, E. (2003). *Ethnicity and human rights in Canada: A human rights perspective on race, ethnicity, racism and systemic inequality.* New York: Oxford University Press.

Kazarian, S., Crichlow, W., & Bradford, S. (2007). *Diversity issues in law enforcement* (2nd ed.). Toronto: Emond Montgomery.

Kazarian, S.S., & Evans, D.R. (1998). Cultural clinical psychology. In S.S. Kazarian & D.R. Evans (Eds.), *Cultural clinical psychology: Theory, research and practice.* New York: Oxford University Press.

Lewis, M.P., Simons, G.F., & Fennig, C.D. (Eds.). (2015). *Ethnologue: Languages of the world* (18th ed). Dallas, TX: SIL International. Online: http://www.ethnologue.com.

Lindsay, C. (2001). The South Asian community in Canada. Statistics Canada. http://www.statcan.gc.ca/pub/89-621-x/89-621-x2007006-eng.pdf.

Linton, R. (1945). *The cultural background of psychology.* New York: Appleton-Century.

Lock, M. (1991). Nerves and nostalgia: Greek-Canadian immigrants and medical care in Quebec. In B. Pfleiderer & G. Bibeau (Eds.), *Anthropologies of medicine: A colloquium on West European and North American perspectives* (pp. 87–103). Braunschweig, Germany: Vieweg+Teubner Verlag.

Milan, A., & Tran, K. (2004, Spring). Blacks in Canada: A long history. *Canadian Social Trends.* Statistics Canada. Catalogue No. 11-008. http://www.statcan.gc.ca/pub/11-008-x/2003004/article/6802-eng.pdf.

Moynes, J. (1999). *Social competence and deviant behaviour: Native community care, counselling and development.* Hamilton, ON: Mohawk College.

Moynihan, D.P. (1993). *Pandaemonium: Ethnicity in international politics.* Oxford: Oxford University Press.

Roberts, N. (2014, May 24). B.C. regiment that once forced out the Komagata Maru is now commanded by a Sikh. *The Globe and Mail*. http://www.theglobeandmail.com.

Statistics Canada. (2006). Ethnic origin reference guide, 2006 census. http://www12.statcan.ca/census-recensement/2006/ref/rp-guides/ethnic-ethnique-eng.cfm.

Statistics Canada. (2007). The Arab community in Canada. http://www.statcan.gc.ca/pub/89-621-x/89-621-x2007009-eng.htm.

Statistics Canada. (2011a). Canada year book, 2011: Ethnic diversity and immigration. http://www.statcan.gc.ca/pub/11-402-x/2011000/chap/imm/imm-eng.htm.

Statistics Canada, (2011b). Population, rural and urban by province and territory (Canada). http://www.statcan.gc.ca/tables-tableaux/sum-som/l01/cst01/demo62a-eng.htm.

Statistics Canada. (2013a). *Aboriginal peoples in Canada: First Nations people, Métis and Inuit*. http://www12.statcan.gc.ca/nhs-enm/2011/as-sa/99-011-x/99-011-x2011001-eng.pdf.

Statistics Canada. (2013b). Immigration and ethnocultural diversity in Canada. National Household Survey, 2011. http://www12.statcan.gc.ca/nhs-enm/2011/as-sa/99-010-x/99-010-x2011001-eng.cfm.

Statistics Canada. (2015). *Aboriginal statistics at a glance* (2nd ed.). Catalogue no. 89-645-X. http://www.statcan.gc.ca/pub/89-645-x/2015001/pop-concept-eng.htm.

Tran, K., Kaddatz, J., & Allard, P. (2005, Autumn). South Asians in Canada: Unity through diversity. *Canadian Social Trends*. Catalogue no. 11-008. http://www.statcan.gc.ca/kits-trousses/pdf/social/edu04_0128a-eng.pdf.

Triandis, H.C. (1995). A theoretical framework for the study of diversity. In M.M. Chemers, S. Oskamp, & M.A. Costanza (Eds.), *Diversity in organizations: New perspectives for a changing workplace* (pp. 11–36). Thousand Oaks, CA: Sage.

REVIEW QUESTIONS

True or False?

1. The terms *culture*, *ethnicity*, *race*, and *minority* are often used interchangeably.

2. In its anthropological sense, culture is synonymous with ethnoculture.

3. Ethnicity can be symbolic or behavioural.

4. Indigenous people are considered one of Canada's visible minorities.

5. The Indigenous population in Canada is growing almost twice as fast as the rest of the population.

6. The English and French in Canada are considered non-visible ethnic minority peoples.

7. The term *South Asian* identifies a single ethnic group from the Indian subcontinent.

8. A stereotype is an adverse judgment or opinion formed without knowledge or an examination of facts.

9. Slavery had been practised in Canada since the early years of the 17th century.

10. Studying other people carefully and focusing on the common ground between them and ourselves can help reduce conflict and misunderstanding.

Multiple Choice

1. Both English and French people belong to the same

   a. paralanguage group

   b. ethnocentral group

   c. cultural majority

   d. Caucasian race

2. *Culture* can be narrowly defined as

   a. historical tradition

   b. a socialization group

   c. a generalization

   d. folk tradition

3. *Ethnicity* refers to

   a. the cultural origin with which a person or group identifies within a multicultural context

   b. a factor of globalization

   c. a person's colour

   d. a pattern of behaviour

4. *Race* is a means of categorizing people according to

   a. religion

   b. gender

   c. common beliefs and practices

   d. common ancestry or origin

5. A nuclear family structure is

   a. a characteristic of Asian racial minority cultures

   b. a social pattern of behaviour

   c. an attempt to ensure the survival of a culture

   d. a characteristic of an individualist culture

6. Australians in Canada are an example of

   a. a non-visible ethnic minority

   b. a visible ethnic minority

   c. a non-visible ethnic majority

   d. a visible ethnic majority

7. Slavery was legal in Canada until
   a. 1709
   b. 1834
   c. 1850
   d. 1903

8. The first Chinese immigrants came to Canada in 1860
   a. to build the railway
   b. to farm
   c. to prospect for gold
   d. to work as pedlars

9. The first South Asians who came to Canada were
   a. Vietnamese
   b. Sikhs
   c. Chinese
   d. Laotians

10. *Diversity equity* refers to a core value according to which
    a. all cultural groups should earn the same amount of money
    b. there are no superior or inferior cultural groups
    c. different laws for different cultural groups should prevail
    d. some cultural groups should be considered as potential terrorists

Fill in the Blanks

1. The _English_ and the _French_ have been called the "two founding races" of the Canadian Confederation.

2. Individuals belonging to a particular ethnic community have unique world views that are shaped by their _Environment_.

3. Race is not an absolute marker of identity but a _social_ concept that can be rejected as a means of categorizing people.

4. A _Minority_ group within a society may constitute most of population, but they hold relatively little political, economic, and social power.

5. The majority of Indigenous people live in _Cities_ across Canada.

6. Teaching in Indigenous cultures is done by _Modelling_ rather than by commanding or dictating.

7. The fastest-growing visible minority group in Canada are people of _Arab_ heritage.

8. _Stereotypes_ falsify reality through overgeneralization and strip their subjects of individuality.

9. _South Asian_ are now the largest visible minority group in Canada.

10. All of the provinces with significant Black populations had _segregation_ laws on the books for most of the last century.

4 Religious Diversity

The Aga Khan Museum in Toronto, which opened in September 2014 alongside the Ismaili Centre, incorporates elements of traditional Islamic and contemporary Canadian architecture. The museum houses a permanent collection of over 1,000 artifacts from Muslim civilizations in Europe, the Middle East, Africa, and Asia. Its stated mission is to foster an understanding and appreciation of the contributions made by Muslim civilizations.

LEARNING OUTCOMES

After completing this chapter, you should be able to:

- Explain the concept of religion.
- Recognize that there is a wide variety of religious beliefs and practices in our pluralistic society.
- Understand how knowledge of the various religions in our society can help in community policing.
- Discuss how misconceptions about different religions and Islamophobia contribute to hate crimes.
- Understand the role religion plays in radicalization and terrorism.
- Understand how religious profiling has become normalized in the "war on terrorism."
- Understand the significance of religion in the rehabilitation of inmates.

Introduction

This chapter discusses the concept of religion and describes the current trends in the beliefs and religious practices of a number of communities in our society. It also examines the post-9/11 experiences of Muslims and discusses the significance of these experiences for policing in Canada, and how the criminal justice system can respond effectively in the post-9/11 environment. Adherence to religious beliefs plays a significant role in changing one's lifestyle. This notion is the basis of various religious programs for rehabilitating prison inmates.

What Is Religion?

religion
a spiritual belief system that addresses matters of ultimate reality, such as life and death, and instructs people in how to live

All human beings have basic spiritual needs that **religion** offers ways of satisfying. Those needs and the solutions offered vary according to religion; each religious tradition evolves in a unique historical context. For example, Christianity identifies sin as a fundamental human problem and offers salvation from sin through Jesus Christ as a solution. Buddhism, on the other hand, regards ignorance, not sin, as the fundamental problem and prescribes enlightenment as the solution and the goal. In their rites, religions use sacred speech and narrative (myth, prayer, song) and sacred acts and rituals, and they designate sacred places for religious expression (Forman, 1993).

Let us define *religion*, then, as a set of teachings and/or rituals that address issues of ultimate reality—the meaning of life, for example—and that try to tell us how to find fulfillment, spiritual health, and salvation within our mortal existence and beyond it (Religion Facts, 2010).

Religious Beliefs and Practices

religious beliefs
tenets of particular faiths

religious practices
concrete expressions of religious beliefs

Religion plays a significant role in the lives of many people. Each religion has its own world view and its own concept of a higher power. For example, both the Ten Commandments of Christianity and the Five Pillars of Islam provide the spiritual foundation of the religion and serve as the central tenets to be followed by adherents. (See Tables 4.1 and 4.2.) Within a religious family, the members' common faith gives them a link to their past and to their future (White, 1997). However, **religious beliefs** and **religious practices** in pluralistic societies have the potential to create divisiveness, animosity, and intolerance. People tend to misunderstand one another's religious beliefs and to view their own as the only valid one. For example, many

TABLE 4.1   The Ten Commandments

1. I the Lord am your God. . . . You shall have no other gods beside Me.
2. You shall not make for yourself a sculptured image. . . . You shall not bow down to them or serve them.
3. You shall not take in vain the name of the Lord your God.
4. Remember the Sabbath day and keep it holy.
5. Honour your father and your mother.
6. You shall not murder.
7. You shall not commit adultery.
8. You shall not steal.
9. You shall not bear false witness against your neighbour.
10. You shall not covet.

TABLE 4.2   The Five Pillars: Basic Religious Practices of Islam

Iman (faith)	*Iman* signifies the belief that the sole purpose of life is to serve and obey God through the teachings and practices of Muhammad. Muslims are required to declare their faith by bearing witness that there is no God but Allah and that Muhammad is his final messenger.
Salat (prayer)	Muslims are required to pray five times a day: at dawn, noon, afternoon, evening, and night.
Zakat (alms giving)	A certain percentage of earnings is expected to go to the poor or needy. This obligation is based on the belief that everything belongs to Allah.
Siyam (fasting)	Fasting is beneficial for health, self-purification, and self-restraint; it reminds Muslims of their purpose in life and promotes empathy for poor and hungry people. All adult Muslims are expected to fast (abstain from food, drink, and sexual relations) from sunrise to sunset during the holy month of Ramadan.
Hajj (pilgrimage)	Adult Muslims with the physical and financial means are required to make at least one pilgrimage to Mecca (in Saudi Arabia), the birthplace of Islam, during the 12th month of the Islamic calendar.

Americans interviewed by CNN after the 9/11 terrorist attacks believed that what America needed to do was go into Iraq and turn all Iraqi Muslims into Christians so as to "save" and "humanize" them.

Powerful nations have always sought to impose religious conversion on the peoples they oppress and colonize. Consider, for example, the colonists' attempts to Christianize Canada's Indigenous peoples. Throughout history, conquered peoples have been forcibly converted to new religions, and these coercive conversions have left scars. Understanding an ethnocultural group's history of religious struggle can give us clues about its attitudes—its levels of trust and resistance—toward being integrated into mainstream society. Generally, if we know something about the major religions and about the beliefs and practices associated with them, we will better understand the cultures within our society that these religions inform and influence.

Needless to say, not everyone has a religion or professes religious beliefs. For example, **atheists** profess no particular religion and do not believe in a higher power. Similarly, **agnostics** neither believe nor disbelieve in a higher power, and some believe that it is impossible to know with

atheist
a person who does not believe in a higher power

agnostic
a person who believes it impossible to know God or to determine how the universe began

certainty whether one exists. Nonetheless, atheists and agnostics have their own values and individual codes of ethical conduct. They deserve as much recognition, respect, and protection as those with strong religious beliefs and practices. It has been estimated that in 2010 worldwide there were nearly 1.1 billion atheists, agnostics, and people who do not affiliate with any religion, and this number is projected to increase to more than 1.2 billion by 2050 (Pew Research Center, 2015).

Religion in Canada

Canada is a multicultural, multi-ethnic, multilingual, and multi-faith country, one of the most religiously diverse countries in the world. New immigrants to Canada have brought not only new cultures and languages, but also new faiths. Nearly 7.2 percent of the Canadian population reported affiliation with the Muslim, Hindu, Sikh, or Buddhist religions. This figure increased from just under 5 percent in 2001, which is consistent with changing immigration patterns. Immigration is continuously changing Canada's religious makeup; the demographic trends suggest that the number of Canadian residents reporting Protestant and Catholic affiliations is bound to decrease as the numbers reporting affiliations with Islam, Hinduism, Sikhism, and Buddhism increase. (See Table 4.3.)

Christianity is the most popular religion in the world. About 33 percent of the world's population is Christian, and there are over 34,000 separate Christian groups in the world (Ontario Consultants on Religious Tolerance, 2009). During the 20th century, prior to 1990, Christianity's popularity was stable in North America. About 87 percent of adults identified themselves as Christian. After 1990, however, substantial numbers of people began to disaffiliate themselves from Christianity and other organized religions. By 2010, the proportion of Christians in North America had fallen to about 77 percent, and it is projected to drop to 66 percent by 2050 (Pew Research Center, 2015). Canada is not immune to this trend. The percentage of Christians in Canada is dropping, with a decrease of almost 10 percent in the first decade of the 21st century. Just over two-thirds of the Canadian population (67.3 percent) reported an affiliation with a Christian religion in 2011 (Statistics Canada, 2013), a decrease from 77 percent in 2001. Owing to fewer attendees (especially younger ones) and aging congregations, many churches in Canada are "facing an uphill battle to stay open" (Brown, 2015).

TABLE 4.3 Religious Affiliation in Canada, 2011

Religion	Number of Canadian residents
Buddhist	366,830
Christian	22,102,745
Hindu	497,960
Jewish	329,500
Muslim	1,053,945
Sikh	454,965
Indigenous spirituality	64,940
Baha'i	18,945
Other religions	111,890
No religious affiliation	7,850,605
Total	32,852,320

SOURCE: Statistics Canada (2011).

Roman Catholics are the largest religious group in Canada. The Roman Catholic Church is the most popular and widespread of the Christian churches. In 2011, 39 percent of Canadians identified themselves as Roman Catholic. Most of these reside in Quebec (45.3 percent), followed by Ontario (31 percent). In 2011, members of Protestant denominations made up 27 percent of the Canadian population (Statistics Canada, 2013).

Other faith groups are increasing in number. In 2011, 498,000 Canadian residents identified themselves as Hindu, which represents 1.5 percent of the Canadian population. In 2001, their number was 297,200, an increase of over 1.5 times in a decade. Close to three-quarters (74 percent) of the Hindu population in Canada lives in Ontario, with the vast majority (89 percent) in the census metropolitan area (CMA) of Toronto. Hindus account for 3 percent of Ontario's population (Statistics Canada, 2013). Sikhism in Canada displayed a similar increase. In 2011, about 455,000 Canadian residents, 1.4 percent of the population, identified themselves as Sikhs (Statistics Canada, 2013). Most Sikhs in Canada live in British Columbia (44.2 percent) and Ontario (40 percent). They accounted for close to 5 percent of British Columbia's population in 2011, with more than three-quarters living in the Vancouver CMA. Buddhists also displayed an increase of 1.2 times between 2001 and 2011. Over 366,000 Canadian residents identified themselves as Buddhists in 2011; nearly half of them live in Ontario, and they form 1.3 percent of that province's population (Statistics Canada, 2013).

Islam may become the dominant religion of the world during the 21st century. In 2010, one out of five people in the world was a Muslim, and this is expected to increase to about three in ten people by 2050. Islam is one of the fastest-growing faiths in Canada, where the Muslim population more than doubled in the decade between 2001 and 2011. More than 1 million people identified themselves as Muslims in 2011. This represents 3.2 percent of Canada's population (Statistics Canada, 2013). About half of the Muslim population lives in Ontario and two-thirds in the three major CMAs of Toronto, Montreal, and Quebec City combined (Statistics Canada, 2013). The main demographic reason for Islam's growth is that Muslims tend to have more children than adherents of the other major world religions (Lipka & Hackett, 2015). In addition to the high fertility rates of Muslim women, Muslims tend to be younger than members of other major religions. These factors combined will accelerate the growth of the Muslim population in Canada; it is projected that there will be 2.7 million Muslims in Canada by 2030, or approximately 6.6 percent of the population (Pew Research Center, 2011).

The First Mosque in Canada

In the early 1930s, the total Muslim population in Canada was 645, with highest concentrations in Saskatchewan, Alberta, and British Columbia. Edmonton was home to the largest Muslim community whose members became increasingly concerned about preserving and passing on their faith and traditions to their children.

In May of 1938, a small lot was purchased for $5,000 as the future site of the first Muslim place of worship, or mosque, built in Canada. Although incomplete in November of the same year, Al Rashid Mosque housed its first religious event—a funeral for Ali Tarrabain, a Muslim pioneer who immigrated to Canada at the turn of the century.

Finally, on December 12, 1938, the official opening of Al Rashid was held, with attendance by the Mayor of Edmonton and the Mayor of Hanna, Alberta. The dedication was performed by Abdullah Yusuf Ali, a prominent Muslim scholar and translator of the Qur'an, the Muslim holy book.

In the following years, Al Rashid was used as a community centre and gathering place for Muslims and non-Muslims. It was a significant religious centre that attracted Muslims from other parts of Canada. In November 1982, a new mosque, also named Al Rashid, was built to accommodate an expanding Muslim community, leaving the old mosque vacant for years.

Threatened to be demolished to make room for an expanding school and later, hospital, the old Al Rashid was moved and now stands as a historic building in Fort Edmonton Park.

Today, the Al Rashid Mosque is one of six mosques in Edmonton, all serving a community of about 20,000 Muslims. The new centre offers funeral services, housing, educational programs, and runs a full-time, independent school.

Source: Milo Productions Inc. (2015).

The 2011 census indicates that 329,500 Canadian residents identify themselves as religiously Jewish, accounting for 1 percent of the total Canadian population. This number decreased slightly from 329,995 in 2001. Statistics Canada differentiates between those who identify as ethnically Jewish and those who identify as religiously Jewish. More than half of Canada's religious Jews live in Ontario (58 percent), followed by Quebec (24 percent).

The census data from 2011 indicate that the median age of those affiliated with minority religious groups in Canada was lower than the median age of those affiliated with Christianity. Muslims, Sikhs, and Hindus each had relatively young populations. The median age of Muslims was 29 years; Sikhs, 30; and Hindus, 32—all well below the median age of Christians, which was over 43 years. As described above, most of these minority religions are overwhelmingly concentrated in metropolitan cities such as Montreal, Toronto, and Vancouver and, to a lesser extent, in mid-sized cities such as Ottawa, Quebec City, Calgary, Edmonton, Winnipeg, and Halifax.

The number of Canadian residents who have no religious affiliation has been increasing rapidly in past decades, rising from 4 percent in 1971, to 16.5 percent in 2001, to nearly 24 percent in 2011. There are regional variations in religious disaffiliation across Canada, with the highest number (44 percent) in British Columbia. This is almost three times higher than in Atlantic Canada (16 percent) and almost four times higher than in Quebec (12 percent).

The number of Canadians who reported attendance at religious services has declined significantly in recent decades. Younger generations of Canadians report attending religious services less frequently than do older generations. Attendance at religious services is higher among immigrants than native-born Canadians.

Interestingly, the number of Canadian residents identifying themselves as Jedi—based on the *Star Wars* movie series—has dropped significantly in the past decade, from 20,000 people in 2001 to about 9,000 people in 2011.

EXERCISE 1

1. Do you currently have any impressions of the following people? Consider your reactions.
   a. a Muslim woman wearing a niqab
   b. a Chinese Buddhist
   c. a Christian Scientist
   d. a Jehovah's Witness
   e. a traditional Indigenous man
   f. a Sikh man wearing a turban
   g. a Hindu woman wearing a sari
   h. a Muslim man with a beard

        i.   a white Protestant woman
        j.   a Roman Catholic priest
   2. Identify factors that may have contributed to your impressions. Identify which factors are irrational and which are rational.

Religion and Hate Crimes

In Canada, hate crime is committed to intimidate, harm, or terrify not only a person but also an entire group of people to which the victim belongs. More than one-quarter (28 percent) of all hate crime incidents reported to police in 2013 in Canada were motivated by hatred toward a religious group. There were 326 incidents of hate crimes targeting Jewish, Muslim, Catholic, and other religious groups (Allen, 2015). Jewish people are the most frequently targeted victims of religious hate crimes; more than half (181 incidents or 56 percent) were reported to be committed against Jewish populations. Jews have been persecuted for centuries (Office of Democratic Institutions and Human Rights, n.d.), and anti-Semitism continues to cause hate crimes against Jewish people. Most religious hate crimes are not violent but are mischief motivated by hate, including mischief to religious property. Around the world, anti-Semitic hate incidents are reported to spike close to Holocaust remembrance days and Nazi-related anniversaries (Office of Democratic Institutions and Human Rights, n.d.).

Muslims are the second most frequently targeted victims of religious hate crimes in Canada, after Jews. In 2014, 99 incidents of hate crimes targeting Muslims were reported to the police (Paperny, 2016), more than doubling from 45 incidents reported in 2012. Table 4.4 shows that while hate crimes targeting other religious groups decreased from 2012 to 2013, those against Muslims increased.

Anti-Muslim sentiments have a profound impact on the victimization of Muslims in Western countries. Although more than half of the hate crimes (67 percent) targeting Muslim populations from 2010 to 2013 were non-violent, hate crimes targeting Muslims were more likely to be violent compared with those targeting other religions. The most common offence against Muslims during this period was mischief and mischief to religious property. During the same period, the religious group with the highest percentage of female victims of hate crimes was Muslims (47 percent). The National Council of Canadian Muslims suggests that Muslim women wearing hijabs are more likely to be victims of attacks against individuals because their religious affiliation is more visible than Muslim men's (as cited in Allen, 2015).

TABLE 4.4   Police-Reported Hate Crime Incidents, by Religious Motivation, Canada, 2012 and 2013

Religious motivation	2012	2013
Jewish	242	181
Muslim	45	65
Catholic	37	29
Other	54	41
Religion not specified	41	10
Total	419	326

Other—Includes motivations based upon religions not otherwise stated (e.g., Sikh, Hindu, Buddhist).

SOURCE: Allen (2015).

Islamophobia and Hate Crimes

Islamophobia
irrational fear of
or hostility toward
Muslims that results
in fear or dislike of all
or most Muslims or
those who are per-
ceived to be Muslims

The term **Islamophobia** is defined as an "unfounded hostility towards Muslims and therefore, fear or dislike of all or most Muslims" (Canadians for Justice and Peace in the Middle East, 2015). Islamophobia is common in Western societies, including Canada. In a 2013 Angus Reid poll, 54 percent of Canadians held an unfavourable view of Islam (this figure had risen sharply from 46 percent in 2009), with numbers as high as 69 percent among residents of Quebec (Angus Reid, 2013). In recent years, violent terrorist acts perpetrated by self-identified Islamic groups have appeared more frequently in the media. The rise of the so-called Islamic State (often referred to as ISIS) and the media coverage of it likely contribute to the negative stereotypes and misunderstandings associated with Islam. As a result, the Muslim population in Western countries has come under prejudicial scrutiny. Since 2001, there has been a significant increase in remarks painting Muslims as threats to national security. When public and political figures use xenophobic and racist language, the impact is far-reaching. Such rhetoric perpetuates misconceptions and stereotypes about the targeted communities. It also generates support for policies and practices that harm people of colour, immigrants, and religious minority groups.

Islamophobia affects targeted individuals in a number of ways, and it is particularly troubling when it threatens rights to citizenship, access to employment, and community integration. Some of the policies of Immigration, Refugees and Citizenship Canada (formerly Citizenship and Immigration Canada) discussed in Chapter 2 discriminated against individuals who observe particular religious practices. One example was the initial denial of citizenship to a Muslim woman who failed to remove her niqab during the citizenship oath ceremony. Islamophobia also presents barriers to community integration of Muslim populations, particularly when it is expressed by government officials. In Shawinigan, Quebec, the city council refused to rezone an industrial park to allow the building of a mosque in response to what the mayor called "irrational fears" (Rukavina, 2015a). In a similar incident in New York in 2010, numerous elected officials and politicians opposed the construction of the Park 51 Muslim community centre in Lower Manhattan because of its perceived proximity to the site of the World Trade Center and the 9/11 attacks (Ratnesar, 2010). In February 2015, a Quebec judge refused to hear the case of a Muslim woman because she would not remove her hijab (Rukavina, 2015b). Incidents like these, which restrict access to the judicial process, present barriers to the *social* integration of any religious minority group.

Misconceptions About Religions

Islamophobia can also greatly affect those outside the Muslim community. Religious ignorance can have serious costs, and one minority religious group that has suffered some dangerous consequences of Islamophobia is Sikhism. Recent analysis and scholarship has expanded the definition of Islamophobia to include discrimination against individuals who may be perceived as Muslims. This perception can be based on dress, race, name, language, accent, or other cultural markers (Canadians for Justice and Peace in the Middle East, 2015). Muslims are thus seen as the visible "other"—the hijab, the beard, the foreigner, and the one looking different from "us." Sikh men, who wear beards and turbans, are often confused with Muslims. They are abused for their appearance and become victims of misdirected Islamophobia and hate-motivated crimes in Western countries. A nationwide survey conducted on the behalf of the National Sikh Campaign in the United States showed that 60 percent of the Americans who participated in the survey admitted they knew nothing about Sikhs or Sikhism. Only 11 percent said that they had a close friend or acquaintance who was a Sikh. When Americans were shown a picture of a man or boy in a turban, they were far more likely to assume that he was Middle Eastern or Muslim than Sikh (Hart Research Associates, 2015).

Ignorance about Sikhs and Sikhism presents a significant danger to the community. There has been a dramatic increase in hate-based violent crimes against Sikhs since September 2001.

Four days after the 9/11 attacks, Balbir Singh Sodhi, a turbaned Sikh gas station owner in Arizona, was killed after being mistaken for a Muslim by a gunman looking to "shoot a Muslim." One of the worst acts of violence against a faith community in the United States happened in Wisconsin at a Sikh *gurudwara* (place of worship) in 2012, which left six people dead. In September 2013, Prabhjot Singh, an associate professor of International and Public Affairs at Columbia University in New York, became the victim of a hate crime when a mob of 12 people attacked him shouting "Osama" and "terrorist." Many of these acts of violence may be classified as misdirected aggression intended for Muslims. The fact that Sikhs are mistaken for Muslims demonstrates a profound lack of knowledge about the fifth-largest religion in the world with approximately 30 million adherents.

Ignorance prevails not only at the local level; until recently, the US Federal Bureau of Investigation (FBI) categorized hate crimes against Sikhs as anti-Islamic, with no separate monitoring of anti-Sikh hate crimes. It was only in March 2015 that the Department of Justice and the FBI updated their databases to track hate crimes against Sikhs, recording the number of hate crimes and data on the perpetrators, dates, and methods. These data should shed light on the causes of the crimes and how such crimes can be prevented.

Misconceptions about different religious symbols and minority faiths shape the dominant society's attitudes and responses at the individual and the societal level. The Sikh kirpan (religious sword or dagger) is one such symbol that has been the subject of media and public attention and has raised questions of religious freedom and public safety. The kirpan can be misunderstood to be a knife that could be used as an offensive weapon (Sikhiwiki, 2012). An important legal question is whether Sikhs should be allowed to carry the kirpan in a particular venue. Courts have allowed kirpans in public places where safety is not an overriding issue, given that the blade of the kirpan is carefully sealed in clothing.

In 2006, the Supreme Court of Canada decision in *Multani v. Commission scolaire Marguerite-Bourgeoys* allowed kirpans in schools. In 2002, a Montreal-area school board banned a 12-year-old Sikh boy from wearing his kirpan in school. The Supreme Court of Canada's unanimous ruling overturned the ban and clearly stated that the ban infringed the Sikh boy's guarantee of religious freedom under the *Canadian Charter of Rights and Freedoms*. The court did, however, establish certain conditions under which the kirpan may be carried, including that it must be worn under the clothes and should be covered by a sheath. Wearing the kirpan to school was again raised in another case in Quebec in 2009. A 13-year-old Sikh boy had an altercation with a group of boys outside school, in which he was accused of using his kirpan as a weapon. The boy maintained that he had not used the kirpan to assault the victims, and the judge acquitted him based on his "'clear and coherent' testimony … against the 'vagueness and contradictions' in the victims' version of events" (MacPherson, 2009). On this ruling, MacPherson reported, "This left intact the clean criminal record of the kirpan in schools: In the more than 100 years that Sikhs have been in Canada, a kirpan has never been used as a weapon in a school (or in this case, near one)" (2009). Along with the kirpan, there are five articles of faith that baptized Sikhs must wear (see Table 4.5). They are often called the "five Ks" because they all begin with that letter.

Highlighting the significance of safety as a real concern, the Canadian Human Rights Tribunal allowed an airline to disallow kirpans, along with any other sharp objects, on any of its flights. The tribunal upheld that it is legitimate to prohibit kirpans in aircraft to protect passengers and staff because air travel is a unique environment where strangers are brought together in a confined space for a prolonged period of time (*Nijjar v. Canada 3000 Airlines Ltd.*, 1999). Within the context of safety and security in public places, various levels of government have implemented kirpan accommodation policies in their buildings, including courthouses. For example, Sikh members of Parliament can wear a kirpan in the House of Commons, and even visitors are allowed to wear it in the public gallery. Alberta and British Columbia allow Sikhs to wear a kirpan in provincial courthouses, and Toronto has a similar policy.

TABLE 4.5   The Five K's (Articles of Faith) in Sikhism and Their Significance

Kesh	Uncut hair, a symbol of spirituality and dedication. Sikh men must wear a turban, a symbol of royalty and dignity; it is optional for Sikh women. The turban cannot be covered by anything else and cannot be replaced with a hat.
Kanga	Comb, a symbol of cleanliness and discipline.
Kara	Steel bracelet, to remind its wearer to show restraint.
Kachha	Undergarments, a symbol of self-control and chastity.
Kirpan	Ceremonial dagger or sword, a symbol of dignity and the Sikh struggle against injustice. The kirpan is a religious symbol only and is never used as a weapon.

SOURCE: Brar (1998).

Other religious symbols have been subjected to scrutiny because of the various misconceptions surrounding them. A jewellery store in New York gained public and media attention in 2012 when it was reported that it was selling earrings shaped like swastikas. Complaints from local politicians led the New York Police Department to intervene and ask the owner to stop selling the earrings. The owner complied but maintained that the earrings were based on the Tibetan Buddhist symbol of eternity (Miller, 2012). Many people, to whom the swastika is a Nazi symbol associated with hate, are unaware that it is a symbol of peace and holiness in Buddhism and Hinduism and is used during religious ceremonies or when doing good deeds. Such misconceptions can cause tensions and pose challenges to the social inclusion of minority religious groups.

Radicalization and Terrorism

Radicalization and terrorism are of increasing concern for a diverse society and the criminal justice system. In 2015 and 2016, the attacks in Paris and Nice, France, Belgium, and Germany and shootings in Copenhagen and San Bernardino, among other incidents, mark the continuation of radical terrorism in the West after 9/11. Assessments of these attacks seem to focus on the radicalization of the perpetrators. It is essential to point out that people can become radicalized for a variety of reasons, and they are not necessarily driven by religion. However, a disturbing trend is such attackers' frequent claims to be associated with Islamic radicalism.

Scholars and governments around the world have made quite an effort to define **radicalization**, to understand and tackle it. This has resulted in a number of definitions that lack conformity and consistency. In Canada, the Royal Canadian Mounted Police (RCMP) describes radicalization as when an individual is "introduced to an overtly ideological message and belief system that encourages movement from moderate, mainstream beliefs towards extreme views" (Royal Canadian Mounted Police, 2009). Radicalization is described as a process by which individuals and groups adopt a particular socio-political and/or religious world view that is considered radical or extreme (Royal Canadian Mounted Police, 2009). Some scholars argue that the process of radicalization is gradual and requires a slow, difficult progression through different stages (Horgan, 2005; Silber & Bhatt, 2007). Therefore, a person does not become radicalized overnight, although the process may be accelerated by a particular incident that acts as a catalyst (such as experiencing discrimination or perceiving war in Iraq or air strikes on ISIS in Syria as attacks on Islam). The process of radicalization differs from person to person, and there is no standard profile of the "typical" radicalized individual. However, all studies agree that there is

radicalization
process by which individuals or groups become socialized to radical or extreme views or beliefs

a stage of individual change (for example, an increase in religiosity or a search for one's identity) that is enhanced through these external incidents. The move to violent radicalization usually takes place when the individual socializes with like-minded people. Prison, the Internet, social media, and personal ties to friends and family members who are already radicalized are the most common settings for being exposed to extremist ideologies.

Becoming radicalized is not the same as becoming a terrorist. Not all individuals who adopt radical or extremist views engage in violence. Also, radicalization is not unique to one religion, ethnicity, nationality, or gender identity. For example, two white former US Army soldiers who were unhappy with the federal government perpetrated the 1995 bombing in Oklahoma City. While radicalization may occur among various groups, the radicalization among Muslim populations in Europe, Australia, and North America is currently the greatest threat. Many governments today are concerned about the threat of terrorism and radical Islamic terrorist groups.

Terrorism is often seen as a byproduct of radicalization; however, many scholars argue that the root cause of terrorism is not radicalization, because not all radicals become terrorists (Rahimullah, Larmar, & Abdalla, 2013). In recent decades, many scholars and governments have come up with definitions of terrorism. The FBI defines terrorism as "the unlawful use of force and violence against persons or property to intimidate or coerce a government, the civilian population, or any segment thereof, in furtherance of political or social objectives" (National Institute of Justice, 2011). The Canadian *Criminal Code* defines terrorist activity as an act "committed in whole or in part for a political, religious or ideological purpose, objective or cause" (1985, s. 83.01); unlike in the FBI definition of terrorism, the act does not need to be violent, but it does need to have the intention of intimidating the public (Canada, Department of Justice, 2015). The common element in these definitions is that terrorism includes acts that are meant to advance a cause. It is a substantive issue for governments because it can endanger the society they are trying to protect.

terrorism
an act committed in whole or in part for a political, religious, or ideological purpose, objective, or cause

The Role of Religion in Radicalization

In the wake of various terrorist attacks in the Western world in the post-9/11 era, it is true that Islamic radicalization is a real phenomenon, one that raises questions about the role of religion in radicalization. Since 2001, numerous studies have attempted to establish the relationship between religion and violent radicalization. According to Awan (2007), one striking commonality among those who had committed bombings in the United Kingdom is that their political radicalization was linked to their increasing religiosity. Among incarcerated terrorists in Europe, a strong religious commitment was stated as the primary motivation for involvement in Islamic terrorism (Wadgy, 2007). Even though these studies establish the causal link between Islamic faith and radicalism, there is much dispute on this point in the literature.

Religious Profiling

In Western countries, the general public has largely approved of racial profiling of minority groups since 9/11. In 2002, Canadian's attitudes toward profiling based on ethnicity and religion were surveyed (EKOS Research Associates, 2002). Findings indicated that about 48 percent of Canadians approved of racial/ethnic profiling. Respondents also agreed that it is acceptable for airline, police, and customs officials to single out individuals of Arabic origin for increased scrutiny. Overall, Canadians were more negative about and less tolerant of Arabs/Muslims.

Since 2001, Western governments, under the guise of national security, engaged in many practices that led to discriminatory treatment of Arab or Muslim people or those originating from South Asian or Middle Eastern countries. Immediately following 9/11, the Canadian government enacted two laws that indirectly discriminated against people based on their race, ethnicity, or religion. Kruger, Mulder, and Korenic (2004) observed that the *Immigration and Refugee Protection Act* (IRPA), which came into effect in 2002, increased police powers to arrest, detain, and deport immigrants who aroused suspicion of involvement in terrorist activities. The IRPA denied immigrants many rights they had previously enjoyed and characterized immigrants and refugees as potential security concerns (Jantzi, 2014). Another law introduced in October 2001, the *Anti-terrorism Act*, included measures to prosecute, convict, and punish terrorists as well as definitions of terrorism, terrorists, and terrorist groups. Bhabha (2003) asserts that the introduction of these laws in a climate of "war against terrorism" unsurprisingly became parallel to a "war against Islam." The broad powers given to administrators to define and blacklist terrorist groups have disproportionately impacted Muslims.

Violation of human rights in the name of national security has become an acceptable norm. The controversial Bill C-51, the *Anti-terrorism Act, 2015*, became law in June 2015. This law further expands police powers to arrest people on suspicion of terrorism without a warrant; police can arrest someone whom they believe *may* carry out terrorist acts (Canadian Civil Liberties Association, 2015). Canada's spy agency, the Canadian Security Intelligence Service (CSIS), can now disrupt *perceived* terrorist acts. Amendments to the *Secure Air Travel Act* empower officials to place Canadian residents on a no-fly list based merely on the suspicion that the individual *may* cause a threat to air transportation or *may* engage in terrorism. This lowering of standards of proof to mere suspicion raises concerns about religious and racial profiling of Canadian Muslims.

There are numerous cases where Muslims or those who are thought to be Muslims were subjected to discriminatory treatment at border crossings or airports. A couple of months after 9/11, a refugee claimant from Palestine, Ribhi Sheikha, was arrested at Toronto's Pearson International Airport and detained for 57 days. Immigration authorities claimed that he was from a country that CSIS had listed as "terrorist-harbouring" (Adelman, 2002). The infamous case of Maher Arar, a Canadian citizen who was wrongfully accused of having terrorist ties, deported by the United States to Syria, imprisoned, and tortured, was discussed in detail in Chapter 2. Project Thread, in which 23 South Asian Muslims in the Greater Toronto Area were arrested as "possible Al-Qaeda sleeper cell" members (the allegations of terrorism were later found to be unsubstantiated) is an example of **religious profiling** and moral panic (Odartey-Wellington, 2009). Such cases reflect religious profiling of Muslims as potential terrorists; some use the term "Muslim terrorism," a discourse that inevitably associates all Muslims, as well as Arabs and some ethnic minorities, with terrorism (Odartey-Wellington, 2009). In 2011, just a few days before the anniversary of 9/11, Prime Minister Stephen Harper in a CBC interview stated that "the major threat is still Islamicism" (CBC News, 2011). Over time, Western countries have normalized this discourse in which religious profiling is rarely questioned.

religious profiling the targeting of an individual, for safety or security reasons, on the basis of stereotypes about the person's religion, including ethnic and racial stereotypes, rather than on the basis of reasonable suspicion

Religious Diversity: Police Abilities, Knowledge, and Skills

Police officers need to be aware of the important role that religious beliefs and practices often have in the lives of those they serve and protect. Police officers may sometimes have to intervene in conflicts that have religious overtones, and they can be subject to accusations of racism if these situations are not handled with awareness and sensitivity. Knowledge of religion can assist police in resolving these kinds of conflicts successfully and can help them, more generally, in the practice of community policing and in their interactions with community members.

Many police services in multicultural countries have incorporated cross-cultural awareness in their diversity training of police officers and new recruits. For example, in order to improve the capacity of police officers to meet the needs of diverse communities, police forces in Australia and New Zealand have jointly produced a reference guide for officers that includes numerous questions about religious diversity and police protocols. *A Practical Reference to Religious and Spiritual Diversity for Operational Police* (Australia New Zealand Policing Advisory Agency, 2010) outlines information regarding nine religions (see Table 4.6) that is relevant to police's day-to-day interaction with religiously diverse people. For example, if an officer deals with a member of the Sikh religion, the guide explains that baptized Sikhs may be offended if an officer asks them to undo their turban, because it is a sacred object in their faith. Similarly, a Muslim woman wearing a full-faced hijab or niqab may find it objectionable to reveal her face to male officers or in public places. This is because the dress code of Islam requires women to cover certain parts of the body in order to dress modestly. In such situations, a police officer may have to make additional arrangements to conduct a search or follow the protocol in a manner that protects human dignity. This would mean taking a Sikh man to a private room where he can undo his turban or having a female officer confirm the identity of a Muslim woman (Queensland Police Service, 2016).

Following airport security protocol without knowledge and awareness of religious significance of faith objects sparked just such an incident in February 2016. An Aeromexico officer at a security checkpoint at Mexico City International Airport ordered a Sikh man to remove his turban in front of other people. Waris Ahluwalia, a Sikh actor and designer, refused and was barred from boarding his flight. He had offered to comply if he were taken to a private screening room, but the officer refused. Such incidents display lack of awareness and respect for cultural and religious values of minority groups and are "humiliating and dehumanizing." Aeromexico in its apology to Ahluwalia stated that a directive had been issued to the "staff regarding the religious significance of the Sikh turban and plans to make a formal request to the TSA [Transportation Security Administration] and the Mexican government to implement religious and diversity sensitivity training regarding screening of passengers with religious headgear into its airport security training curriculum" (Johnson & Shoichet, 2016). No doubt, officers who know about diverse religions are better equipped to work, solve crimes, and maintain law and order in diverse communities.

There are practical strategies available to law enforcement. Grossman, Bruck, Stephenson, Dwyer, and Roose (2013) in their review of the cross-cultural training practices of the Victoria Police in Australia highlighted the importance of such practices in understanding and appreciating key differences between diverse religious communities. Front-line officers become sensitive to specific customs and religious practices that will affect their interactions with these communities, such as whether to remove their shoes when entering a mosque or how to deal with a deceased body in a Hindu family. However, they suggested that cross-cultural education and training material should be regularly checked for accuracy by members of the relevant community, because such material may inadvertently reinforce stereotypes. Grossman et al. (2013) also emphasized that identifying best practices nationally and internationally in policing approaches to cross-cultural/religious training (such as those described in Table 4.6) is problematic in many ways. For example, cross-cultural materials may not acknowledge diversity within religious groups.

At the theoretical level, the best practices model tends to suggest that culture and religion can be "reduced to a technical skill for which [service providers] can be trained to develop expertise" (Kleinman & Benson, 2006, para. 3). Practically, best practices guides tend to condense diverse religious differences and become a series of "do's and don'ts" that offer shorthand explanations for complex variables and, therefore, may end up perpetuating stereotypes when an entire religious group can be described "by simple slogans" (Kleinman & Benson, 2006, para. 3). Grossman et al. (2013) also stress that "awareness of different habits, customs, preferences or behaviours on its own (technical competence) outside the context of what these mean for the people who value them is not enough" (p. 37). This narrow approach, without broader understanding of religious values, risks stereotyping and profiling of religious differences.

TABLE 4.6   A Practical Reference to Religious and Spiritual Diversity for Operational Police

Key Topics	Aboriginal and Torres Strait Islander	Bahá'í	Buddhism	Christianity
13 Protocols for dealing with strangers	• **Greeting:** Initially, same sex communication • **Silence:** Important part of communication • **Handshaking:** Not generally given • **Touching:** Usually viewed as inappropriate • **Eye contact:** Common to lower eyes to show respect • **Pointing:** Using the finger is seen as disrespectful	None	• **Handshaking:** Not appropriate with monks or nuns • **Touching:** Not appropriate with monks or nuns • **The head:** Not appropriate to touch the head	None
18 Special considerations when approaching or entering a place of worship or person's house; or acknowledging or searching sacred objects	• Approval from Traditional Owners, local elders and/or government authority • Follow local protocols (eg: men attending sacred men's sites) • Modest attire	• Contact guides	• Contact head monk or nun • Remove weapons where safe • Care when seated facing religious objects • Lift religious objects by base	• Remove weapons where safe • Modest attire • Care when touching the altar
6 Special clothing, jewellery or ornaments	• Ceremonial items during secret or sacred ceremonies • String sometimes worn by family members during bereavement • Care when touching • Standard protocols for searching and detention apply	No	• Monks and nuns may have short/shaved hair, wear robes • Threaded beads (mala) sometimes carried • Care when touching • Standard protocols for searching and detention apply	• Religious leaders often wear robes/other religious clothing • Threaded beads (rosary beads) sometimes carried • Standard protocols for searching and detention apply

Hindu	Islam	Judaism	Māori	Sikhism
• **Handshaking:** Not appropriate with observant Hindus • **Eye contact:** Not appropriate in some traditions between males and females • **Hands:** Left hand not used for general interaction • **Pointing at people:** Usually viewed as disrespectful	• **Handshaking:** Not appropriate between males and females with observant Muslims • **Hands:** Left hand not used for general interaction • **Eye contact:** Sustained contact often not appropriate • **Comforting:** Avoid physical contact	• **Handshaking:** Not appropriate with many Orthodox Jews • **Physical contact:** Not appropriate with many Orthodox Jews	• **Touching:** Not appropriate to touch the head • **Eye contact:** Minimal eye contact common	• **Handshaking:** Sometimes viewed as inappropriate between males and females • **Touching:** Sometimes viewed as inappropriate between males and females • **The head:** Not appropriate to touch the head or turban
• Remove hats and shoes • Seek assistance when handling objects • Food offered	• Contact Imam of mosque • Modest attire • Remove shoes • Avoid walking in front of Muslims while praying	• Contact security at Synagogue	• Remove shoes	• Contact community leaders • Remove shoes • Care when touching the Sikh Holy Script
• Married Hindu women may wear a necklace (**mangalsutra**) or wedding bangles; and a marking over third eye (**bindi** or **pottu**) • Thread sometimes worn around body • Care when touching • Standard protocols for searching and detention apply	• Muslim women may wear the following: headscarf (**Hijab**); face veil (**Niqab**); covering for the whole body (**Burqa**); and covering for the whole body thrown over the head (**Chador**) • Standard protocols for searching and detention apply	• Orthodox men may dress in black, wear hats, and grow beards and earlocks • Orthodox women may wear wigs and long dresses • Jewish men often wear a skullcap (**kippah**) • Standard protocols for searching and detention apply	• Green stone (**pounamu**) and/or bone necklaces sometimes worn • Standard protocols for searching and detention apply	• Some Sikhs wear a turban • Some Sikhs wear 5 articles of faith (**Five Ks**): a small sacred sword (**Kirpan**); an iron bangle (**Kara**); a special undergarment (**Kachera**); a small wooden comb (**Kanga**); and uncut hair (**Keshas**) • Care when touching these; removal from the body is viewed as a severe punishment • Standard protocols for searching and detention apply

(The table is concluded on the next pages.)

TABLE 4.6 Concluded

Key Topics	Aboriginal and Torres Strait Islander	Bahá'í	Buddhism	Christianity
20-22 Death, bereavement and mourning	• Traditional Aboriginal belief that death is caused by another person (no natural death) • Bereavement (sorry business) may take precedence over all else • **Marigeth** (in-laws) often announce a death amongst Torres Strait Islanders • Requesting to keep the deceased for a time to prepare is common in Aboriginal communities • Spending considerable time with the deceased is common in Torres Strait Island communities • Preference is not to have post mortems conducted unless required by law • Performing a smoking ceremony is common in Aboriginal communities	• Family members may wish to place a burial ring on the deceased • Preference is that the deceased is not to be transported more than one hour's travelling distance • Cremation is forbidden • Burial is preferred to take place as soon as reasonably possible • Burial is preferred to take place within one hour's travelling distance	• Contact Buddhist monk or nun, and maintain a peaceful environment • Some may request that the body be left undisturbed for up to eight hours • Chinese, Tibetan and Vietnamese Buddhists would generally prefer to stay with the deceased	• Some may want a priest or other clergy member to give "last rites" (prayers)

SOURCE: Australia New Zealand Policing Advisory Agency (2010, pp. 8–9).

Hindu	Islam	Judaism	Māori	Sikhism
• Contact the Hindu community • Place the deceased in a north-south direction with the head pointing towards the south • Some may prefer identification by a senior male relative • Preference is not to have post mortems conducted unless required by law • Hindus are usually cremated, except for children under three, who are buried • Cremation is preferred within 24 hours of death • Some may want the deceased to go home before cremation	• Burial is preferred within 24 hours of death • A mourning period of 40 days is generally observed by the family of the deceased • Preference is not to have post mortems conducted unless required by law	• Contact immediate family or a Rabbi, and the Jewish Burial Society (**Chevra Kadisha**) • Strict observance of religious practices in relation to death and burial • Preference that touching of the deceased is kept to a minimum, and the deceased is covered or screened • Preference that all body parts, including tissue and blood, be retrieved for burial with the body • Preference is not to have post mortems conducted unless required by law • Cremation is forbidden • Burial is preferred within 24 hours of death	• Contact members of the Māori community to allow for blessing of the area before the body is moved, particularly in the event of suicides • Preference that all body parts be kept together • Common for the community to gather around the **tūpāpaku** (deceased) so it is not left on its own at any stage • Pictures of the living should not be placed with the deceased	• Contact family of the deceased • Care when touching the deceased where the 5 Ks and/or turban are worn; preference is that the 5 Ks are not removed from the deceased at the scene or during post mortem • Where the 5 Ks are removed, care should be taken to replace them • Sikhs are cremated, and cremation is preferred as soon as possible after death • Some may want the deceased to go home before cremation

In the post-9/11 environment, the religion most in need of understanding by police is the Muslim faith practised by Arab and other communities. Law enforcement agencies need to do what they can to cultivate good relations between Muslims and their host cultures. Police also need to separate, in their own minds, the Muslim people and their Islamic religion from the concepts of terrorism and suicide bombers. One constructive measure in this regard would be to eliminate the practice of racial profiling, by which Arabs and Muslims are automatically seen as threats to national security. In fostering good relations between themselves and the Arab/Muslim communities, police need to be aware that very few Muslims and Arabs are terrorists. There is currently a struggle within Islam between moderates and radicals, and the vast majority of Muslims identify with and support the moderates. Law enforcement agencies need to recognize that cultivating good relations with Muslims is good business for law enforcement, both in general and as a counterterrorism measure. It is also a good way to nourish a culture of peace. Reaching out to Muslims in the post-9/11 climate—trying to understand their culture and to create dialogue with their communities—should be seen as a duty for law enforcement. This may help to reduce the influence of implicit bias and strengthen relationships between police and Muslims. Implicit bias arises from the associations between groups of people and stereotypes about those groups. These are automatic associations that under certain conditions can "influence behavior, making people respond in biased ways even when they are not explicitly prejudiced" (National Initiative for Building Community Trust and Justice, 2015, para. 1).

Religious beliefs strongly influence an ethnocultural group's values, moral code, and social conduct. How their religious beliefs are viewed by others, especially by those in the host culture, also strongly affects such groups. Police may find the beliefs and practices of various religions puzzling or objectionable. But for a police officer to allow such personal disapproval—to label these unfamilar practices primitive or savage—would be irresponsible. Religious intolerance in any form is wrong.

National and international strategies for intelligence gathering are important, as are cutting-edge technologies in border security and counterterrorism. Equally important, however, is some understanding of the "clash of civilizations" within our multicultural society. Such understanding can contribute to a trusting relationship between law enforcement and our society's diverse cultural and religious communities.

EXERCISE 2

Some religious groups in our society have survived official persecution in their countries of origin, persecution in which police were involved. Consider some of these groups, and consider what core values and beliefs contributed to their persecution. How might this past mistreatment affect their attitudes and behaviour in their new country, and what might be the consequences for policing in Canada?

Religious Diversity: Prisons and Rehabilitation

Religious diversity within the Canadian population in general has been expanding in the past few decades. This diversification is also reflected in the federal prison population. The comparative numbers for the years 2006–7 and 2011–12 in Table 4.7 show the growing diversity of the religious affiliation of offenders over five years (Public Safety Canada, 2012).

Religion plays a vital role in the day-to-day lives of many prisoners. For incarcerated persons, a connection to religious and spiritual beliefs can provide comfort during periods of isolation

TABLE 4.7   The Religious Identification of the Offender Population

	Offender population			
	2006–7		2011–12	
	#	%	#	%
Catholic	9,237	41.1	8,412	36.3
Protestant	4,580	20.4	4,070	17.6
Muslim	857	3.8	1,091	4.7
Indigenous spirituality	844	3.8	998	4.3
Buddhist	381	1.7	493	2.1
Jewish	172	0.8	188	0.8
Orthodox	115	0.5	104	0.4
Sikh	123	0.5	175	0.8
Other	1,437	6.4	1,976	8.5
None	3,551	15.8	3,770	16.3
Unknown	1,185	5.3	1,879	8.1
Total	**22,482**	**100.0**	**23,156**	**100.0**

SOURCE: Public Safety Canada (2012).

from their family and community. Some prisons, especially maximum-security prisons, are known for their harsh environments; for many inmates, religion is one of the methods used to cope with the prison environment (Clear et al., 1992). Religion offers a set of practices for inmates, such as the proclamation of faith, prayer, charity, and fasting. These practices help develop discipline and structure in individuals whose lives are characterized by chaos and instability. Religious programming is easily the most common form of correctional rehabilitation available to prisoners.

From a policy perspective, it has been established that spiritual development and religious practice promote rehabilitation and reduce recidivism among inmates (Clear et al., 1992). An evaluation of a Texas faith-based pre- and post-release prison program, InnerChange, highlighted that graduates of this program had lower recidivism rates than offenders who did not participate in the program. It is a Christian-oriented program that provides education, work, life skills, values, and mentoring in a religious environment. The program starts with biblical and life skills education while the inmates are in prison and follows them for 6 to 12 months of aftercare while the offenders are on parole (Griffiths, Dandurand, & Murdoch, 2007). In Canada, this program is offered through Prison Fellowship Canada. A similar international program that runs in about 50 correctional institutions in Canada is Alpha for Prisons. It is a 10-week course offered to inmates in prison to explore the Christian faith and help them transform their lives and prepare them for life upon release. Once released, ex-offenders are connected to a local church community. Alpha Canada claims that the reoffending rates decrease significantly among offenders who participate in this course (Alpha Ministries Canada, n.d.). Many such programs primarily focus on rehabilitation of the offenders. Prison Fellowship Canada not only offers various programs on Christian teachings and adjustment to life after prison; its programs also strive for positive development of relationships between inmates and their children and families. The box below provides a brief description of all programs offered by Prison Fellowship Canada.

Prison Fellowship Programming

Prison Fellowship Canada is a community-based volunteer organization with chapters across Canada that works with inmates, ex-offenders, and their families and victims to promote reconciliation and rehabilitation. It offers a range of programs to inmates both during and after incarceration. These programs, based on Christian teachings, use a rehabilitative and restorative approach to help offenders understand the consequences of their behaviour, develop empathy, and take responsibility for their actions.

During incarceration, inmates can participate in the InnerChange program, which includes Bible study, one-on-one and group mentoring, pen-pal friendships, and chapel services. Prison Fellowship Canada also helps support family ties, with particular emphasis on inmates' relationships with their children. Together with local churches, Prison Fellowship Canada helps offenders' children participate in community events, attend summer camp, and ensure that they receive a Christmas gift from their incarcerated parent.

Prison Fellowship Canada recognizes that reintegrating into the community can be a great challenge for ex-offenders. Reconnecting with family, finding a place to live, and looking for work are all difficult and stressful. To help reduce the likelihood of reoffending, Prison Fellowship Canada works with ex-offenders to strengthen their support networks through churches and other local organizations.

Prison Fellowship Canada also offers a restorative justice program that supports the victims of crime through mediation with offenders. By bringing victims and offenders together, the program seeks to help them understand the consequences of crime and begin the process of recovery and transformation.

Source: Prison Fellowship Canada (n.d.).

Chapter 11 discusses similar programs that emphasize and support Indigenous spirituality during incarceration.

Freedom of religion is one of the basic rights offenders retain during incarceration. Correctional Service Canada (CSC) makes provisions for the exercise of offenders' religious rights as guaranteed by the *Canadian Charter of Rights and Freedoms*. The principle of religious and spiritual accommodation is mandated in the *Corrections and Conditional Release Act* (CCRA). Religious and spiritual accommodation means "providing access to an adequate level of resources (leadership, opportunities for worship, educational resources, religious articles, dietary requirements) to allow offenders to practice their religion or spirituality as fully as they desire (up to a level that is generally available to people in the community) within the correctional setting" (Correctional Service Canada, 2006, p. 4).

Chaplaincy services are important because they provide a positive environment for prisoners to express themselves and can help them in rehabilitation. Interfaith chaplaincy services are also mandated in federal prisons in Canada. CSC regulations indicate the responsibility of chaplains to exercise their profession in a multi-faith setting. Chaplains are directed to

- seek to provide pastoral care to persons of a different faith with the same commitment as they do to members of their own faith;
- ensure that inmates have access to literature (and religious articles, as applicable) pertaining to their faith;
- consult authorities of a given religion about questions that arise in the course of life in the institution; and
- make arrangements for other religious representatives to visit, and accompany them during their visits; the only exception is Indigenous spirituality, which is the purview of the institutional elder (see Chapter 11 for more information on programs for Indigenous inmates).

These services are intended to strengthen the participation of offenders in the faith life of their own communities (CSC, 2006). CSC chaplaincy and food services have made a significant effort to address the religious rights of offenders whose faith entails dietary obligations and/or prohibitions. In a practical sense, religion is a central aspect of the modern prison system. However, making accommodations for the changing religious demographics of the prison population has been challenging. In 2012, the Conservative government cancelled contracts of part-time non-Christian chaplains, stating that "full-time Christian chaplains were capable of providing spiritual advice to those outside their faith, much like they've done in the Canadian Forces" (Cohen, 2013). CSC has been criticized (more so recently) for not providing consistent religious services to inmates of minority faiths. The Canadian Human Rights Tribunal and British Columbia's Human Rights Tribunal received complaints of religious discrimination experienced by Muslim inmates where correctional facilities allegedly failed to provide a halal diet or adequate time and religious materials for prayers and ceremonies in the prison chapel (Brosnahan, 2015; *Globe and Mail*, 2015).

Prisons and Radicalization

In *From Rehabilitation to Recruitment*, Wilner (2010) points out that prison authorities should be careful in finding ways to uphold inmates' right to practise their religion and also in ensuring that prisons do not unintentionally facilitate radicalization. As mentioned earlier, prisons are by nature hostile environments, characterized by isolation and predisposition to violence. It therefore comes as no surprise that inmates can be susceptible to radicalization and terrorism. There is growing concern that extreme religious radicalization ideologies can flourish in prisons. The January 2015 terrorist attacks in Paris spurred the debate on how to deal with radicalization in prisons. Amedy Coulibaly shot a police officer and four hostages at a kosher grocery store in Paris before police killed him. Coulibaly is believed to have been radicalized in prison, where he met one of the Kouachi brothers responsible for the *Charlie Hebdo* killings a week before. Chérif Kouachi, one of the brothers who massacred 12 people in the attack at the *Charlie Hebdo* weekly newspaper, came under the influence of Djamel Beghal, a known figure of French radical Islamism, while incarcerated at the prison. A few other examples are often mentioned. Kevin Lamar James recruited more than a dozen fellow prisoners into a terrorist group called Jam'iyyat Ul-Islam Is-Saheeh (JIS). Jamal "el Chino" Ahmidan, who embraced jihadist principles while serving time, was the mastermind behind the 2004 Madrid train bombings. Richard Reid, known as the "shoe bomber," who attempted to blow up an American Airlines flight between Paris and Miami in 2001, also converted to Islam while serving time for a string of muggings (Ballas, 2010).

Compared with other Western countries, Canada has fewer terrorists in its prisons. However, as Canada has just started to incarcerate terrorists, it may see the problem of prison radicalization in the near future. Wilner (2010) suggests some key recommendations specifically for prison authorities to deal with the potentially growing issue. Muslim inmates have the right to access religious leaders of their faith. CSC should carefully screen prison imams before granting them access to inmates and monitor what they say to prisoners. Inmates have the right to access religious literature. However, they should not be reading radical manifestos advocating terrorism. Prison libraries should be regularly screened for radical literature. Terrorists can be placed in separate units away from the general prison population and denied access to other prisoners. CSC can develop a policy to move them frequently within the system to disrupt their social networks. CSC should deal with prisoners' grievances sensitively, especially those regarding inmates' religious rights being violated. Radicals are more likely to use these incidents to promote their message of hate, anger, and resentment of authority. Staff should receive more training to identify warning signs of radicalization.

CHAPTER SUMMARY

Pluralistic societies include many religions. Lack of awareness and misconceptions about different religions cause intolerance and hate crimes. The "war on terrorism" in Western countries has normalized the use of religious profiling and justified the violation of human rights. Religiously diverse countries are facing the challenges of separating increasing religiosity, radicalization, and terrorism. Law enforcement's responses to the potential or real threat of radicalization have affected the lives of religious minority groups. Cross-cultural education and diversity training equip police officers to better understand and respect various religions in order to effectively respond to the diverse religious beliefs and practices they encounter in their day-to-day interactions with members of different religious groups. Growing religious diversity is seen within prisons. Freedom to practise religion is a fundamental right that correctional facilities need to accommodate. However, the growing concern that extreme religious radicalization ideologies can flourish in prisons poses another challenge for correctional facilities.

REFERENCES

Adelman, H. (2002). Canadian borders and immigration post 9/11. *The International Migration Review, 36*(1), 15–28.

Allen, M. (2015). Police reported hate crime in Canada, 2013. Statistics Canada. http://www.statcan.gc.ca/pub/85-002-x/2015001/article/14191-eng.htm#r6.

Alpha Ministries Canada. (n.d.). Alpha for prisons. http://www.alphacanada.org/alpha-in-prisons/.

Angus Reid. (2013). Canadians view non-Christian religions with uncertainty, dislike. Angus Reid Global. http://angusreidglobal.com/wp-content/uploads/2013/10/Canadians-view-non-Christian-religions-with-uncertainty-dislike.pdf.

Anti-terrorism Act. (2001). SC 2001, c. 41.

Anti-terrorism Act, 2015. (2015). SC 2015, c. 20.

Australia New Zealand Policing Advisory Agency (ANZPAA). (2010). *A practical reference to religious and spiritual diversity for operational police* (3rd ed.). http://www.anzpaa.org.au/our-work/publications/religious-spiritual-diversity-for-police.

Awan, A. (2007). Virtual jihadist media: Function, legitimacy and radicalizing efficacy. *European Journal of Cultural Studies, 10*(3), 389–408.

Ballas, D. (2010, October). Prisoner radicalization. *FBI Law Enforcement Bulletin, 79*, 1–5. https://leb.fbi.gov/2010/october/leb-october-2010.

Bhabha, F. (2003). Tracking "terrorists" or solidifying stereotypes? Canada's Anti-terrorism Act in light of the Charter's equality guarantee. *Windsor Review of Legal and Social Issues, 16*, 95–136.

Brar, S. (1998). Introduction to Sikhism. http://www.sikhs.org/summary.htm.

Brosnahan, M. (2015, November 3). 2 Muslim inmates file rights complaints against Alberta prison. *CBC News*. http://www.cbc.ca.

Brown, C. (2015, May 17). Keeping faith: The changing face of religion in Canada. *CBC News*. http://www.cbc.ca.

Canada, Department of Justice. (2015). Memorializing the victims of terrorism. http://www.justice.gc.ca/eng/rp-pr/cj-jp/victim/rr09_6/p3.html.

Canadian Charter of Rights and Freedoms. (1982). Part I of the *Constitution Act, 1982*, being Schedule B to the *Canada Act 1982* (UK), 1982, c. 11.

Canadian Civil Liberties Association. (2015). Understanding Bill C-51: The Anti-terrorism Act, 2015. https://ccla.org/understanding-bill-c-51-the-anti-terrorism-act-2015/.

Canadians for Justice and Peace in the Middle East. (2015). Islamophobia in Canada. Factsheet series no. 192. https://d3n8a8pro7vhmx.cloudfront.net/cjpme/pages/1086/attachments/original/1431614167/192-En-Islamophobia-in-Canada-v4.pdf?1431614167.

CBC News. (2011, September 6). Harper says "Islamicism" biggest threat to Canada. *CBC News*. http://www.cbc.ca.

Clear, T., Bruce, R., Stout, B., Dammer, H., Kelly, L., Hardyman, P., & Shapiro, C. (1992, November). Does involvement in religion help prisoners adjust to prison? *NCCD Focus*. http://www.nccdglobal.org/sites/default/files/publication_pdf/religion-and-prisoners.pdf.

Cohen, T. (2013, November 10). Prison chaplaincy program gets facelift following review. *Postmedia News*. http://o.canada.com.

Correctional Service Canada (CSC). (2006). Religious and spiritual accommodation in CSC institutions. http://www.csc-scc.gc.ca/chaplaincy/092/doc_e.pdf.

Corrections and Conditional Release Act. (1992). SC 1992, c. 20.

Criminal Code. (1985). RSC 1985, c. C-46.

EKOS Research Associates. (2002). *September 11 in hindsight: Recovery and resolve*. http://www.ekospolitics.com/articles/9sept2002.pdf.

Forman, R. (Ed.). (1993). *Religions of the world* (3rd ed.). New York: St. Martin's Press.

Globe and Mail. (2015, April 21). Muslim files complaint after B.C. jail tells him to use towel as prayer mat. *The Globe and Mail*. http://www.theglobeandmail.com.

Griffiths, C., Dandurand, Y., & Murdoch, D. (2007). *The social reintegration of offenders and crime prevention*. Ottawa: National Crime Prevention Centre. https://www.public safety.gc.ca/cnt/rsrcs/pblctns/scl-rntgrtn/scl-rntgrtn -eng.pdf.

Grossman, M., Bruck, D., Stephenson, P., Dwyer, R., & Roose, J. (2013). *Learning to engage: A review of Victoria Police cross-cultural training*. Centre for Cultural Diversity and Wellbeing, Victoria University. https://www.vu.edu.au/ sites/default/files/ccdw/pdfs/learning-to-engage-cross -cultural-training-practice-review-victoria-police -2013.pdf.

Hart Research Associates. (2015). *Sikhism in the United States: What Americans know and need to know*. http://www .sikhcampaign.org/report.

Horgan, J. (2005). *The psychology of terrorism*. London: Routledge.

Immigration and Refugee Protection Act. (2001). SC 2001, c. 27.

Jantzi, M. (2014). "Stranger danger": A critical discourse analysis of the Immigration and Refugee Protection Act. Master's research paper, Wilfrid Laurier University. http://scholars.wlu.ca/cgi/viewcontent.cgi?article=1005 &context=soci_mrp.

Johnson, D., & Shoichet, C. (2016, February 10). Sikh actor Waris Ahluwalia: Education must follow apology over turban incident. *New York Daily News*. http://www.cnn.com.

Kleinman, A., & Benson, P. (2006). Anthropology in the clinic: The problem of cultural competency and how to fix it. *PLOS Medicine, 3*(10), e294. http://journals.plos.org/ plosmedicine/article?id=10.1371/journal.pmed.0030294.

Kruger, E., Mulder, M., & Korenic, B. (2004). Canada after 9/11: New security measures and "preferred" immigrants. The Prairie Centre of Excellence for Research on Immigration and Integration Working Paper Series. http://www .ualberta.ca/~pcerii/WorkingPapers/WP09-04.pdf.

Lipka, M., & Hackett, C. (2015). Why Muslims are the world's fastest growing religious group. http://www.pewresearch .org/fact-tank/2015/04/23/why-muslims-are-the-worlds -fastest-growing-religious-group/.

MacPherson, D. (2009, April 18). Student's kirpan survives latest court challenge. *Montreal Gazette*. http://vigile.quebec/ Student-s-kirpan-survives-latest.

Miller, J. (2012, January 12). Swastika earrings reportedly no longer for sale at Brooklyn jewelry store. *Fox News*. http://www.foxnews.com.

Milo Productions Inc. (2015). Al Rashid Mosque: The first mosque in Canada. *A New Life in a New Land*. http://www .anewlife.ca/alrashid.

Multani v. Commission scolaire Marguerite-Bourgeoys. (2006). 2006 SCC 6, [2006] SCR 256.

National Initiative for Building Community Trust and Justice. (2015). *Implicit bias*. Community-oriented trust and justice briefs. Washington, DC: Office of Community Oriented Policing Services. https://uploads.trustandjustice.org/ misc/ImplicitBiasBrief.pdf.

National Institute of Justice. (2011). Terrorism. http://www.nij .gov/topics/crime/terrorism/pages/welcome.aspx.

Nijjar v. Canada 3000 Airlines Ltd. (1999). 1999 CanLII 19861 (CHRT).

Odartey-Wellington, F. (2009). Racial profiling and moral panic: Operation Thread and the Al-Qaeda sleeper cell that never was. *Global Media Journal, 2*(2), 25–40.

Office of Democratic Institutions and Human Rights. (n.d.). What is hate crime: Anti-Semitism. http://hatecrime.osce .org/what-hate-crime/anti-semitism.

Ontario Consultants on Religious Tolerance. (2009). Numbers of adherents of major religions, their geographical distribution, date founded, and sacred texts. http://www .religioustolerance.org/worldrel.htm.

Paperny, A. (2016, April 13). Hate crimes against Muslim-Canadians more than doubled in 3 years. *Global News*. http://globalnews.ca.

Pew Research Center. (2011). *The future of the global Muslim population*. http://www.pewforum.org/files/2011/01/ FutureGlobalMuslimPopulation-WebPDF-Feb10.pdf.

Pew Research Center. (2015). The future of world religions: Population growth projections, 2010–2050: North America. http://www.pewforum.org/2015/04/02/north-america/.

Prison Fellowship Canada. (n.d.). Prison Fellowship Canada: Our programs. http://prisonfellowship.ca.

Public Safety Canada. (2012). Annual report: Corrections and conditional release statistical overview 2012. http://www .publicsafety.gc.ca/cnt/rsrcs/pblctns/ccrso-2012/index -en.aspx.

Queensland Police Service. (2016, March). Chapter 6: Special needs. *Operational Procedures Manual*, Issue 51. https://www.police.qld.gov.au/corporatedocs/ OperationalPolicies/opm.htm.

Rahimullah, R., Larmar, S., & Abdalla, M. (2013). Understanding violent radicalization amongst Muslims: A review of the literature. *Journal of Psychology and Behavioral Science, 1*(1), 19–35.

Ratnesar, R. (2010, August 18). Ground zero: Exaggerating the jihadist threat. *Time*. http://www.time.com.

Religion Facts. (2010). The big religion chart: Comparison chart. http://www.religionfacts.com/big_religion_chart.htm.

Royal Canadian Mounted Police. (2009). *Radicalization: A guide for the perplexed*. https://cryptome.org/2015/06/rcmp-radicalization.pdf.

Rukavina, S. (2015a, February 13). Shawinigan mayor explains decision to reject mosque. *CBC News*. http://www.cbc.ca.

Rukavina, S. (2015b, February 26). Quebec judge wouldn't hear case of woman wearing hijab. *CBC News*. http://www.cbc.ca.

Secure Air Travel Act. (2015). SC 2015, c. 20, s. 11.

Sikhiwiki. (2012). Misconceptions of the kirpan. http://www.sikhiwiki.org/index.php/Misconceptions_of_the_Kirpan.

Silber, M.D., & Bhatt, A. (2007). *Radicalization in the West: The homegrown threat*. New York City Police Department. http://www.saneworks.us/uploads/application/16.pdf.

Statistics Canada. (2011). 2011 National Household Survey, Data tables. Catalogue no. 99-010-X2011032.

Statistics Canada. (2013). *Immigration and ethnocultural diversity in Canada: National household survey, 2011*. http://www12.statcan.gc.ca/nhs-enm/2011/as-sa/99-010-x/99-010-x2011001-eng.pdf.

Wadgy, L. (2007). The psychology of extremism and terrorism: A Middle-Eastern perspective. *Aggression and Violent Behaviour, 12*(2), 141–155.

White, G.C. (1997). *Beliefs and believers*. New York: Berkley Books.

Wilner, A. (2010). *From rehabilitation to recruitment*. Ottawa: Macdonald-Laurier Institute. http://www.macdonaldlaurier.ca/files/pdf/FromRehabilitationToRecruitment.pdf.

REVIEW QUESTIONS

True or False?

_____ 1. Diverse religious beliefs and religious practices in a pluralistic society can create divisiveness, animosity, and intolerance.

_____ 2. Some agnostics believe that it is impossible to know with certainty whether a higher power exists.

_____ 3. It has been estimated that in coming years, the number of atheists, agnostics, and people who do not affiliate with any religion will decrease.

_____ 4. The latest census data indicate that the number of Canadian residents reporting Protestant and Catholic religious affiliations is bound to increase, whereas the numbers reporting Islam, Sikhism, and Buddhism will decrease.

_____ 5. The percentage of Christians in Canada has dropped at a rate of almost 10 percent over the past decade.

_____ 6. Most of Canada's Roman Catholics reside in Ontario.

_____ 7. The median age of Roman Catholics is higher than that of Muslims in Canada.

_____ 8. Attendance at religious services is higher among immigrants than native-born Canadians.

_____ 9. For the most part, Canadian courts have allowed kirpans in public places where safety is not an overriding issue.

_____ 10. Around the world, anti-Semitic hate incidents are reported to spike close to Holocaust remembrance days and Nazi-related anniversaries.

Multiple Choice

1. The largest religious group in Canada is
   a. Roman Catholics
   b. Protestants
   c. Muslims
   d. Buddhists

2. _____ profess no particular religion and do not believe in a higher power.
   a. Agnostics
   b. Atheists
   c. Jedis
   d. Monotheists

3. The majority of Hindus in Canada live in the province of
   a. Quebec
   b. Ontario
   c. British Columbia
   d. Alberta

4. One demographic reason for the increase in the Muslim population in Canada is
   a. high fertility rates
   b. the high median age of Muslims
   c. high conversion rates to Islam
   d. all of the above

5. The number of people who identified themselves as religiously unaffiliated is highest in
   a. British Columbia
   b. Atlantic Canada
   c. Quebec
   d. Ontario

6. The majority of hate crimes motivated by religious hatred in Canada are
   a. violent
   b. theft
   c. mischief
   d. assault

7. After Jews, _____ are the second most frequently targeted victims of religious hate crimes in Canada.

    a. Christians

    b. Muslims

    c. Sikhs

    d. Hindus

8. _____ is an irrational fear or unfounded hostility toward Muslims that results in fear or dislike of all or most Muslims and those who are perceived as Muslims.

    a. Moral panic

    b. Islamophobia

    c. Hate crime

    d. Radicalization

9. A pre- and post-release faith-based program, InnerChange, is offered in Canadian prisons through

    a. Alpha for Prisons

    b. Correctional Service Canada

    c. Prison Fellowship Canada

    d. InterFaith Chaplaincy

10. _____ is the automatic association that people make between groups of people and stereotypes about those groups.

    a. Implicit bias

    b. Discrimination

    c. Religious profiling

    d. Moral panic

Fill in the Blanks

1. Religion is a set of _teachings_ and/or rituals that address issues of ultimate reality.

2. Agnostics believe in the _impossibility_ of knowing God.

3. _Radicalization_ is the process by which individuals or groups become socialized to radical or extreme views or beliefs.

4. The reasons for closure of churches in Canadian cities are _fewer attendees_ and _aging congregations_

5. _Roman Catholics_ make up the largest Christian religious group in Canada.

6. The majority of Sikhs in Canada live in the province of _British Columbia_.

7. _Jews_ are the most frequently targeted victims of religious hate crimes.

8. Hate crimes targeting Muslims were more likely to be _violent_ offences compared with hate crimes targeting other religions.

9. One minority religious group other than Muslims who have suffered dangerous consequences of Islamophobia are the _Sikhism_.

10. Compared with other Western countries, Canada has _fewer_ terrorists in its prisons.

5 Family Violence, Mental Health Issues, and Developmental Disabilities

This mural, located outside the Centre for Addiction and Mental Health (CAMH) in Toronto, has multiple meanings. One meaning comments on the recent changes to CAMH. Once a closed institution called the Provincial Lunatic Asylum, it has changed over the years to reflect society's changing attitudes toward mental illness. Most recently, CAMH rebuilt its campus to integrate treatment buildings with the community, to break down barriers and reduce the stigma of mental health care, and to provide a whole-community approach to mental health treatment.

LEARNING OUTCOMES

After completing this chapter, you should be able to:

- Understand how various groups in Canada are affected by family and intimate partner violence.
- Understand various mental illnesses and their characteristics.
- Understand intellectual and developmental disabilities, and how they are defined.
- Identify the justice system's strategies for addressing family violence and for responding to individuals with mental health issues and intellectual disabilities.

Introduction

Everyone has the right to a safe home environment, one that is free from neglect and from economic, physical, psychological, and spiritual abuse. But there are people who lack such an environment and are exposed to neglect, intimidation, domination, and physical or sexual assault. These people have the right to protection and assistance. Society once regarded intimate partner violence as a "private matter." However, since the 1980s, the criminal justice system and social service networks have shifted their strategies for responding to family violence and intimate partner violence, including the development of specialized domestic violence courts. Despite this, for complex reasons, many victims of domestic violence remain reluctant to involve the criminal justice system.

Becoming involved with people who suffer from mental illness, a developmental disability, or a substance-abuse problem can pose a particular challenge for police and for the criminal justice system. Traditional police training has not equipped officers with the tools that they need to understand how to tailor their responses to people with these special needs (*CBC News*, 2014). Several high-profile encounters with police that have ended in death, such as the 2013 shooting of 18-year-old Sammy Yatim in Toronto, have led to increased calls for effective training in de-escalation and crisis intervention.

diversity policing
the use of effective policing practices in response to the issues of diverse populations

This chapter discusses family violence and mental illness from the perspective of **diversity policing**. The chapter's aim is to help you better understand the realities of family violence and mental health issues, and the ways in which police can respond most appropriately to them.

Family Violence and the Law

family violence
the different forms of abuse, mistreatment, or neglect that adults or children may experience in their intimate, kinship, extended, or dependent relationships

The term **family violence** covers the many different forms of abuse, mistreatment, or neglect that adults or children may experience in their intimate, kinship, extended, dependent, or trust relationships (Statistics Canada, 2015a). While family violence typically involves either the abuse of one partner in a relationship by the other or the abuse of a child by a parent, it can also entail the abuse of children by a caregiver or the abuse of a parent by a child.

Abuse in families may take a variety of forms, including physical abuse, sexual abuse, emotional and psychological abuse, financial and economic abuse, neglect, and spiritual or religious abuse. There are numerous behaviours that can be classified as forms of abuse. An abuser may use one or more of these tactics with the intention of establishing and maintaining control over a person or a household (Government of Newfoundland and Labrador Violence Prevention Initiative, 2015). Not all forms of abuse are crimes in Canada; many are more subtle, and it can be difficult for law enforcement to take action against them. Nevertheless, police officers must be alert in looking for signs of abuse, since abuse tactics that are not offences may be warning signs for other, more actionable forms of abuse.

Although the *Criminal Code* does not set out specific family violence offences, there are many general offences defined under the Code that could be involved in family violence—for example, assault, sexual assault, criminal harassment (such as stalking and threatening harm), and murder. The relationship between the accused and the victim in incidents of violent crime are examined to identify the presence of family violence.

Physical Abuse

Physical abuse is a broad category. It varies in the degree of force or violence used against another person. It can be smaller actions, such as scratching, pushing, shoving, biting, hair-pulling, or throwing objects, or very severe actions that can threaten someone's life. It can also include preventing a person from leaving, locking a person out of their home, or withholding medication. Threats of any of these actions may also constitute physical abuse. Physical abuse is assault when someone purposely uses or tries to use force directly or indirectly against another person without that person's consent, such as throwing an object at a person. Other forms of physical abuse may also constitute crimes; for example, preventing a person from leaving a room during an argument by blocking a door may constitute kidnapping and forcible confinement (*Criminal Code* ss. 279(1) and (2)).

Physical Abuse

Physical abuse is the intentional use of force against a person without that person's consent. Physical abuse includes

- pushing or shoving
- hitting, slapping, or kicking
- pinching or punching
- strangling or choking
- stabbing or cutting
- shooting
- throwing objects at someone
- burning
- holding someone down for someone else to assault
- locking someone in a room or tying them down
- killing someone

Sources: Department of Justice (2015a); Benedictis, Jaffe, & Segal (2014).

Sexual Abuse

Sexual abuse within the family may victimize children or adults. Any sexual activity with an adult, even a spouse, common law partner, or dating partner, without consent is a crime. Sexual abuse of a child involves any sexual activity with a child where consent is not or cannot be obtained. The World Health Organization defines child sexual abuse as the "involvement of a child in sexual activity that he or she does not fully comprehend, is unable to give informed consent to, or for which the child is not developmentally prepared and cannot give consent, or that violates the laws or social taboos of society" (2003, p. 75). Forms of child sexual abuse include but are not limited to rape, sexual assault, fondling, exposure, voyeurism, prostitution, and child pornography. Children and youth are more likely to be sexually assaulted by someone known to them, including parents, siblings, extended family members, caregivers or guardians, or other people in their lives.

In Canada, until 1983, rape was considered an offence only outside of marriage, meaning that a husband could rape his wife without committing a crime. While this is no longer the case in Canada, it remains the case in many other countries around the world.

Sexual Abuse

Any sexual contact with anyone without consent is a crime. Sexual abuse of an adult can include

- sexual touching or sexual activity without consent
- continued sexual contact when asked to stop
- forcing someone to commit unsafe or humiliating sexual acts

Sexual abuse of children can include a number of acts, including but are not limited to

- sexual touching of any part of the body
- encouraging a child to engage in sexual activity, including masturbation
- intentionally engaging in sexual activity in front of a child
- showing children pornography or using children to create pornography
- encouraging a child to engage in prostitution

Sources: Department of Justice (2015a); Benedictis, Jaffe, & Segal (2014).

Emotional Abuse

Emotional abuse (also referred to as psychological abuse) involves a series of incidents or patterns of behaviour that occur over a period of time. Like physical abuse, it is a broad category involving many types of behaviour, some of which are subtle and can appear benign without the context of the pattern of abuse. Emotional abuse may range from emotional violence (verbal abuse, put-downs, humiliation, constant criticism, threats, harassment, and intimidation through the damage or destruction of property) to less obvious types of behaviours: excessive possessiveness, forced isolation from friends and family, or emotional withdrawal or neglect (Munro, 2001). Most forms of emotional abuse are not crimes, although threats and harassment can be.

This type of abuse is difficult to identify because it does not leave physical marks. Victims often are unable to recognize its occurrence for a number of reasons. Abusers may deny that abuse has taken place or tell the abused person that nobody would believe them if they spoke about the abuse, and over time, victims of abuse may become habituated to see this behaviour as normal and expected.

Emotional Abuse

Emotional or psychological abuse happens when a person uses words or actions to control, frighten, or isolate someone or take away their self-respect. It can include

- threats, put-downs, name calling, or insults
- constant yelling or criticism
- controlling or preventing contact with friends or family
- destroying belongings, hurting pets, or threatening to do so
- bullying: intimidation or humiliation (including on the Internet)

Sources: Department of Justice (2015a); Benedictis, Jaffe, & Segal (2014).

Financial Abuse

Financial or economic abuse involves exerting control over a person's money or belongings. It is often used to make it difficult for the victim to leave the abuser, and it is sometimes considered to be a form of emotional abuse. It can involve control over finances and can range from denying money to buy necessities, to controlling bank accounts, pressuring someone for money or property, or denying access to finances and imposing a financially dependent relationship. Preventing a person from obtaining a job, controlling a person's access to financial information, or demanding that a person account for every purchase that they make can constitute financial or economic abuse. Some more serious forms of financial abuse can be crimes, including fraud and theft.

Financial Abuse

Financial abuse happens when someone uses money or property to control or exploit someone else. It can involve

- taking someone's money or property without permission
- withholding or limiting money to control someone
- pressuring someone to sign documents
- forcing someone to sell things or change a will
- withholding money intended to buy food or medical treatment
- controlling bank accounts and paycheques
- controlling or limiting someone's spending on groceries
- checking the gas gauge in the car to ensure that no extra trips are taken
- denying access to finances
- preventing a person from working

Sources: Department of Justice (2015a); Benedictis, Jaffe, & Segal (2014).

Neglect

Neglect is the failure to provide necessary care, assistance, guidance, or attention that causes or is likely to cause the person physical, mental, or emotional harm. Some people have a legal or social responsibility to care for and support a child or an adult who is unable to meet those needs himself or herself. Spouses and common law partners may have a duty to care for each other. Adults have a duty to care for their dependent children, and in some jurisdictions, may have a duty to care for their dependent parents.

In some cases, neglect may rise to the level of a crime. Section 215 of the *Criminal Code* reads:

215(1) Every one is under a legal duty
   (a) as a parent, foster parent, guardian or head of a family, to provide necessaries of life for a child under the age of sixteen years;
   (b) to provide necessaries of life to their spouse or common-law partner; and
   (c) to provide necessaries of life to a person under his charge if that person
      (i) is unable, by reason of detention, age, illness, mental disorder or other cause, to withdraw himself from that charge, and
      (ii) is unable to provide himself with necessaries of life.

Failure to provide the necessaries of life constitutes an offence when "the failure to perform the duty endangers the life of the person to whom the duty is owed, or causes or is likely to cause the health of that person to be endangered permanently" (*Criminal Code* s. 215(2)(a)(ii)). The "necessaries of life" are not defined in the *Criminal Code* but can include medical attention.

Neglect

Neglect happens when someone who has a duty to care for a relative fails to provide them with their basic needs. It can involve

- not providing proper food or warm clothing
- failing to provide adequate health care, medication, and personal hygiene
- failing to prevent physical harm
- failing to ensure proper supervision (if needed)

Spouses and common law partners have a duty to care for each other. Adults have a duty to care for their dependent children as well as their dependent parents.

Source: Department of Justice (2015a); Benedictis, Jaffe, & Segal (2014).

Spiritual or Religious Abuse

Spiritual or religious abuse involves a situation where a person is not allowed to express their own opinion about religion, cultural beliefs, and values. It can also involve a situation where a person's spiritual beliefs are manipulated to keep him or her feeling powerless. Some common examples are ridiculing a person's beliefs and culture, withholding access to religion, or using religion as a cover for other types of abuse.

Spiritual or Religious Abuse

Spiritual or religious abuse includes

- using the spouse's or intimate partner's religious or spiritual beliefs to manipulate them
- preventing the partner from practising their religious or spiritual beliefs
- ridiculing the other person's religious or spiritual beliefs
- forcing the children to be reared in a faith that the partner has not agreed to

Source: Department of Justice (2015a); Benedictis, Jaffe, & Segal (2014).

Child-Specific Offences

child abuse
physical and psychological abuse of children

Child abuse is the physical or psychological mistreatment or violence or neglect of a child by someone whom the child trusts or depends on, such as a parent, sibling, other relative, caregiver, guardian, or anyone known to the child (Department of Justice, 2002, p. 1). There are different types of abuse a child may be subjected to: physical abuse, sexual abuse, emotional abuse, and neglect. Neglect occurs when the caregiver fails to provide (deliberately or otherwise) for the child's basic needs such as adequate clothing, food, shelter, supervision, or medical or dental care. Most often there is a combination of individual, family, and social factors that increase the child's risk for abuse. Some believe that social inequalities and power imbalances are linked to child abuse. Colonialism, racism, sexism, poverty, and social isolation increase a child's vulnerability to abuse (Department of Justice, 2002).

Many types of child abuse are crimes under the *Criminal Code*, such as assault, sexual assault, child abandonment, child abduction, and failure to provide the necessaries of life. Provincial and territorial laws also ensure the safety of children by enabling child welfare agencies to look into suspected cases of abuse and neglect. These laws protect children from abuses that are not defined as crimes under the *Criminal Code* (Department of Justice, 2012c). These laws also set an age of protection for children, which varies from one jurisdiction to another. For example, the age of protection in Nunavut, Nova Scotia, New Brunswick, Ontario, and Saskatchewan is 16; in Quebec, Manitoba, and Alberta, 18; and in British Columbia and Yukon, 19. The *Criminal Code* generally defines a child as someone under 18 years of age.

Child sexual abuse refers to a situation when a person in a position of authority or trust takes advantage of a child for sexual purposes (Department of Justice, 2012c). Child sexual abuse occurs when an adult or adolescent has any kind of sexual activity with the child. The two main categories of child sexual abuse offences are non-contact sexual offences (such as exposing a child to sexually explicit acts) and contact sexual offences (such as touching the genital area). Child sexual abuse offences can occur with or without the use of violence. Over the past few decades, these offences have increasingly involved the use of technology and social media—for example, to create images of sexual abuse for child pornography and to lure children into prostitution.

child sexual abuse
the sexual exploitation of a child under the age of 18

According to the Department of Justice Canada (2012c, p. 18), sexual abuse of a child includes

- any sexual contact between an adult and a child under 16,
- any sexual contact with a child between the age of 16 and 18 without consent, or
- any sexual contact that exploits a child under 18.

Acts of violence against children may fit within one of the previous categories or may be one of the number of child-specific offences in the *Criminal Code*. These range from failure to provide the necessaries of life to a number of child-specific sexual offences. The *Criminal Code* and the *Canada Evidence Act* include provisions concerning family violence and are amended periodically to address growing concerns in the area of family violence, such as child pornography, sexual exploitation of youth, the luring of children on the Internet, child sex tourism, and the admissibility of testimony by child victims and witnesses (Department of Justice Canada, 2006). Canada's provinces and territories all have child protection legislation to allow intervention where a child is in need of protection and to permit child welfare agencies to assess the safety of children who may be at risk of being abused or neglected by their parents or guardians.

Although the topic is controversial, Canadian law establishes that not all corporal punishment of children rises to the level of prohibited physical abuse. Section 43 of the *Criminal Code* permits parents, guardians, and schoolteachers to use reasonable corporal punishment toward children for corrective purposes. In 2004, the Supreme Court of Canada narrowed the scope of this section to disallow corporal punishment directed toward children under the age of two or toward teenagers; the court also interpreted the reasonableness requirements to disallow punishment using objects (such as belts) and punishment that is more than merely transitory and trifling, that harms or degrades the child, or that goes beyond what is appropriate based on the gravity of the wrongdoing (Barnett, 2008). Because of this, while some maintain that all corporal punishment constitutes physical abuse, spanking and other forms of physical force toward children may not be actionable offences.

Children are especially likely to be subjected to emotional abuse (Doherty & Berglund, 2008). In addition to the behaviours associated with emotional abuse (described above), children are considered to be at a risk of emotional abuse if they live in situations of family violence, since this can affect their cognitive, emotional, and psychological well-being and development. Emotional abuse, including exposure to domestic violence, is the most prevalent form of child abuse. Despite that fact, however, this type of child abuse is the least likely to lead to criminal charges (Doherty & Berglund, 2008).

Recourse for Family Violence

The *Criminal Code* provides special provisions to protect the victims of family violence. These provisions include release on "no contact" orders, peace bonds or recognizances, protection orders, and other procedures (Department of Justice Canada, 2015b). The accompanying box describes some of the criminal and civil protection orders often used in domestic violence cases.

Criminal and Civil Protection Orders in Domestic Violence Cases

Peace Bond

Section 810 of the *Criminal Code* authorizes a criminal court to issue a peace bond. This is a protection order that is used when a defendant appears likely to commit a criminal offence but there are not reasonable grounds to believe that an offence has actually been committed. The court may impose specific conditions to prevent the defendant from committing harm to the person named in the bond, their spouse or common law partner, or their child, or from committing damage to their property (Department of Justice, 2015c). Peace bonds are preventive measures and require the defendant to "keep peace and be of good behaviour," along with any other conditions that the court imposes, such as prohibitions against being within a certain distance of the person, possessing weapons, or using alcohol or non-prescription drugs.

The peace bond does not create a criminal record, but the defendant must obey its conditions. Failure to comply with the conditions is a criminal offence that can result in up to four years' imprisonment. Peace bonds are valid for up to one year, with the possibility of renewal by the court.

Restraining Order

A restraining order is a non-criminal court order issued by a civil court, available through provincial or territorial family or child protection legislation. For a restraining order, there must be past violence, threats of violence, or other actions that make the victim afraid for his or her physical safety. A judge may order a person to stay away from another person and prohibit the abuser from hurting or threatening to hurt the victim. A restraining order lists conditions that the defendant must obey. These conditions can be very general, such as requiring the defendant to stay away from the victim, or specific, such as requiring the defendant to stay 200 metres from the victim's home, place of work, children's school, or place of worship. The duration of a restraining order is determined by the judge and can be extended.

The consequences of breaching the conditions of a civil restraining order are set out in the relevant provincial or territorial legislation. Legislation that is silent on enforcing restraining orders, as it is in British Columbia, Manitoba, and Ontario, allows for the "default enforcement mechanism" of section 127 of the *Criminal Code*. Breach of a restraining order under section 127 is a criminal offence. Alberta's *Protection Against Family Violence Act* sets out provisions for enforcing restraining orders, including ordering police to immediately arrest and bring the person before the court. If the breach is proved in court, the offender can be fined or jailed. In this case, breach of a restraining order is not a criminal offence.

Source: Department of Justice (2015c); Student Legal Services of Alberta (2011).

In addition to these federal legislative provisions, provincial and territorial laws are designed to provide civil measures to protect the victims of family violence. These measures may include issuing emergency intervention orders that may, for example, grant the right for only the victim to remain in the home and use the family vehicle, or issuing a restraining order for the abuser to have no communication with the victim or his or her family members (Department of Justice Canada, 2015b). As of 2015, six provinces (Alberta, Manitoba, Nova Scotia, Prince Edward Island, Newfoundland and Labrador, and Saskatchewan) and all three territories have specific legislation on family violence. British Columbia's legislation provides for family violence protection orders to shield victims of family violence.

However, criminal and civil protection orders do not proactively protect victims of intimate partner violence. Among women who had obtained a restraining or protective order against a violent partner, one-third reported a breach of that order (Brennan, 2011).

How Big a Problem Is Family Violence?

Family violence is a pervasive social and policing problem in Canada, but its real extent is unknown. Victims often do not report the problem to police, and most victims who do report it have suffered multiple incidents before coming forward. The federal government is working to increase public awareness of family violence through research, studies, and surveys (Department of Justice Canada, 2011).

Abuse and Violence Between Adults

Intimate partner violence is violence or mistreatment suffered at the hands of a current or former marital, common law, or same-sex partner. It may involve spiritual, emotional, psychological, sexual, or economic abuse, or varying degrees of physical violence. It is more likely to occur between ex-spouses or partners than between current spouses or partners (Statistics Canada, 2011, p. 9). The term *intimate partner violence* is often used interchangeably with related terms such as *domestic abuse, domestic violence,* **dating violence**, and **spousal violence**. In 2014, more than 88,000 people aged 15 to 89 were victims of police-reported intimate partner violence (Statistics Canada, 2016). This represents more than one-quarter (27 percent) of all victims of police-reported violent crime. Of all the victims of police-reported intimate partner violence, 52 percent were victims of dating violence and 46 percent were victims of spousal violence. Nearly two-thirds of victims of intimate partner violence were being victimized by a current intimate partner—either a current dating partner (33 percent) or a current spouse (33 percent). Emotional abuse is more than twice as common between partners as physical abuse; in 2004, about one in six people reported experiencing emotional or financial abuse during a relationship.

Spousal violence is suffered by both sexes, but in 2014 the great majority of victims (80 percent) of police-reported intimate partner violence were women (Statistics Canada, 2016). Common assault (the least violent kind of assault; it includes pushing, grabbing, slapping, and face-to-face threats) is the most frequent type of spousal violence, accounting for nearly two-thirds of offences, followed by major assault, uttering threats, and criminal harassment (Statistics Canada, 2016). Young adults have the highest rate of intimate partner victimization. The risk of intimate partner victimization decreases as age increases. Within intimate partner violence, victims of dating violence tend to be younger than the victims of spousal violence. The proportion of those victimized by a dating partner declined as the victim's age increased, whereas the proportion of those victimized by their spouses rose as the victim's age increased (Statistics Canada, 2016). Socio-demographic factors—education and income levels, for example—have no influence on spousal violence rates; it is as common among the affluent as among the financially disadvantaged (Statistics Canada, 2011, p. 11).

Violence in an intimate relationship remains a risk after the end of the relationship. Of women who reported being assaulted by their partners after the dissolution of the relationship, one-third stated that the violence began or became more severe after separation (Statistics Canada, 2006). Women are particularly at risk of being killed immediately after leaving an abusive partner: 26 percent of female homicide victims were killed by their spouses during marital separation, and half of those women were killed within two months of the end of the relationship.

intimate partner violence
violence committed within an intimate relationship

dating violence
violence committed by a current or former dating partner or by a person with whom the victim had a sexual relationship or a sexual attraction

spousal violence
violence or mistreatment suffered at the hands of a marital or common law partner

Children and Youth

Police-reported data for 2014 indicate that about 16,300 children and youth under the age of 18 were victims of family-related violence. Physical assault was the most common type of police-reported family violence against children and youth, followed by sexual assault. When children and youth were victims of family violence, a parent was identified as the abuser in nearly six of ten incidents (Statistics Canada, 2016). (See Table 5.1.) The psychological and behavioural consequences of child sexual abuse include post-traumatic stress disorder and disturbed interpersonal relations.

TABLE 5.1   Accused Perpetrators of Family Violence Against Children and Youth by Relationship to the Victim, Sex of the Accused, and Type of Assault, 2007

Accused by relationship to victim and sex	Total assault		Sexual assault[1]		Physical assault[2]	
	number	percent	number	percent	number	percent
Total family	**11,621**	**100**	**3,217**	**100**	**8,404**	**100**
Female	2,604	22	130	4	2,474	29
Male	9,017	78	3,087	96	5,930	71
Parent[3]	6,454	56	1,094	34	5,360	64
Female	1,748	15	50	2	1,698	20
Male	4,706	40	1,044	32	3,662	44
Sibling[4]	2,380	20	887	28	1,493	18
Female	420	4	32	1	388	5
Male	1,960	17	855	27	1,105	13
Extended family[5]	2,440	21	1,218	38	1,222	15
Female	416	4	46	1	370	4
Male	2,024	17	1,172	36	852	10
Spouse/ex-spouse[6]	347	3	18	1	329	4
Female	20	0	2	0	18	0
Male	327	3	16	0	311	4

NOTES:

1. Includes sexual assault (level 1), sexual assault with a weapon or causing bodily harm (level 2), aggravated sexual assault (level 3), and the "other sexual crimes" category, which includes sexual interference, sexual touching, sexual exploitation, incest, etc.
2. Physical assault includes common assault (level 1), assault with a weapon or causing bodily harm (level 2), aggravated assault (level 3), unlawfully causing bodily harm, discharge firearm with intent, criminal negligence causing bodily harm, and other assaults.
3. Includes a small number of cases where age or the relationship between the accused and the victim may have been miscoded.
4. Includes natural, step, half, foster, or adopted siblings.
5. Includes others related by blood, marriage, adoption, or foster care.
6. Includes legally married and common law partners and ex-spouses. Rates are calculated per 100,000 population for the geographic areas policed by the Incident-based Uniform Crime Reporting Survey respondents. Population counts by marital status are not available for this geographic level.

      Children and youth include all those under the age of 18. Excludes incidents where the sex and/or age of the victim was unknown. Data are not nationally representative. The Incident-Based Uniform Crime Reporting Survey collected data from 153 police services representing approximately 94 percent of the population of Canada in 2007. The Hamilton Police Service is excluded from the analysis due to data quality of the relationship variable. Rate per 100,000 population for the geographic areas policed by the Incident-Based Uniform Crime Reporting Survey respondents, based on populations provided by Demography Division, Statistics Canada.

SOURCE: Statistics Canada (2009).

Girls under the age of 18 reported higher rates of both physical and sexual assault by a family member than boys did; in 2014, the rate of family-perpetrated sexual assault was four times higher for girls than for boys (Statistics Canada, 2016). (See Figure 5.1.)

FIGURE 5.1   Rate of Police-Reported Family Violence, by Sex and Age Group of Victim, Canada, 2014

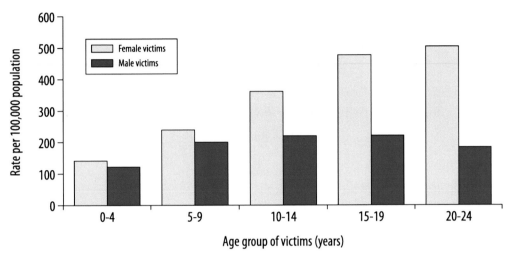

NOTE: Excludes incidents where the sex or age of victim was unknown. Excludes spousal victims under the age of 15 years. Excludes a small number of victims in Quebec whose age was unknown but was miscoded as 0. Rates are calculated on the basis of 100,000 population. Populations based on July 1st estimates from Statistics Canada, Demography Division.

SOURCE: Statistics Canada (2016).

Older Adults

Elder abuse is the physical, sexual, emotional, or psychological abuse or neglect, or the financial exploitation (fraud and theft), of an older person by

- a caregiver (spouse or partner, adult child, or relative);
- a staff member in an institution, such as a nursing home;
- a person in a relationship of trust; or
- a criminal.

For the victims of elder abuse, the psychological effects may include—apart from the trauma of the abuse itself—feelings of shame, embarrassment, self-blame, and inadequacy.

In 2013, police reported over 2,900 incidents of family violence against seniors (Statistics Canada, 2015a). Seniors represent a relatively small proportion of all family violence victims (about 3 percent) and they had lower rates of family violence compared with any other age group. Adult children and current or ex-spouses were the family members most likely to commit violence against senior women, while adult children were most often accused of violence against senior men (see Figure 5.2). Police-reported incidents of family violence against senior women were higher than those against senior men. Family violence accounted for one-third of all violent acts committed against seniors. Just over half of police-reported family violence incidents against seniors were common assaults (Statistics Canada, 2015a).

elder abuse
the physical, sexual, emotional, or psychological abuse or neglect, or the financial exploitation, of an older person by a caregiver, a staff member in an institution, or a criminal

FIGURE 5.2 Relationship of Accused to Senior Victim, 2007

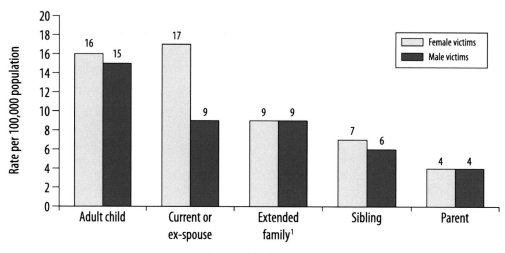

NOTE:

1. Extended family includes aunts, uncles, cousins, sisters or brothers-in-law, etc.

Data are not nationally representative. The Incident-Based Uniform Crime Reporting Survey collected data from 153 police services representing approximately 94 percent of the population of Canada in 2007. The Hamilton Police Service is excluded from the analysis due to data quality of the relationship variable. Excludes incidents where the victim's sex, age, and/or relationship of the accused to the victim was unknown.

SOURCE: Statistics Canada (2009).

Diversity and Family Violence

People of diversity, whatever the basis of their minority status—age, gender, ethnocultural identity, educational deficit, socio-economic status, occupation, race, religion, sexual orientation, physical or developmental disabilities—may be especially vulnerable to family violence (Canadian Women's Foundation, 2015; Green, 1996; Biesenthal et al., 2000; Law Commission of Canada, 2001). Members of the gay and lesbian communities are more than twice as likely as heterosexuals to report having experienced spousal violence, as are Indigenous people (Statistics Canada, 2011, p. 11). In many cultures, family violence tends to be kept secret; people are embarrassed by it and do not want to discuss it. As a result, no one really knows exactly how many people are victims or survivors of this kind of violence. Table 5.2 lists some myths associated with family violence.

TABLE 5.2 Myths About Family Violence

- Family violence is rare.
- Family violence is confined to lower socio-economic classes.
- Family violence happens only in heterosexual relationships.
- People with disabilities are unlikely to be victims of family violence.
- Substance abuse is the real cause of family violence.
- Victims of family violence have masochistic personalities.
- Victims of family violence exaggerate the abuse.
- Abusive behaviour can be justified.
- Abusers cannot control their abusive behaviours.
- Victims of family violence provoke the abuse.
- Victims of family violence consider abuse a sexual turn-on.
- Diversity (for example, culture, disability) is the root cause of family violence.

EXERCISE 1

Consider the myths about family violence listed in Table 5.2. How might a belief in some of these myths affect the way in which police respond to perpetrators and victims of family violence?

Gender and Family Violence

While women and men experience similar levels of violence and emotional abuse in their relationships, the violence experienced by women tends to be more severe and more often repeated than the violence directed at men. Women are one and a half times more likely than men to report multiple experiences of abuse (Public Health Agency of Canada, 2015a). Women are three times more likely than men to report being sexually assaulted, beaten, choked, or threatened with a gun or a knife. They are also nearly two and a half times more likely than men to report higher rates of injury caused by abuse. Women are more likely to be victims of criminal harassment, uttering threats, abduction, kidnapping, hostage taking, and criminal negligence causing bodily harm (Statistics Canada, 2015a).

Immigrants and Refugees and Family Violence

Mainstream Canadian conceptions of acceptable behaviour, including what constitutes violence and abuse, differ from accepted norms in other cultures. For example, early marriage is a common practice in many parts of the world, especially Africa and South Asia, but in the West the practice is considered a form of sexual violence; forcing young girls into marriage and sexual relations poses risks to their health, including exposure to HIV/AIDS, and decreases their chance of attending school.

When considering what constitutes "abuse," we must apply this country's currently accepted legal definitions, and require that *all* Canadians act in accordance with them. At the same time, we must recognize that there are cultural practices—the piercing of infant girls' ears, for example, or the circumcision of infant boys—that, while considered objectionable by some, do not qualify as "abuse."

Immigrants and refugees from diverse cultures bring with them a variety of attitudes, beliefs, and practices that must be understood when examining family violence in a Canadian context. Not all cultures, for example, espouse the equality of men and women or have a conception of women's rights; some permit or regard as minor crimes practices such as honour killing, forced suicide, marital rape, and female genital mutilation, which are considered reprehensible in Canada and constitute serious crimes.

Immigrant women's vulnerability to family violence is greater as a result of a number of factors, including economic dependence, social isolation, language and cultural barriers, lack of understanding of legal rights, and lack of knowledge about available community services (Canadian Women's Foundation, 2015). Law enforcement agencies are often aware that immigrant and refugee women are reluctant to report their violent victimization; refugee women especially, who may have been traumatized by war or oppressive governments, may not report for fear of further victimization or deportation.

Significant domestic tensions can arise when traditionalist families, accustomed to controlling their children according to strict familial and religious codes, suddenly find themselves in a liberal, secular environment where women have considerable freedom. Under these circumstances, conflict can arise between women and their families, and the conflict may result in violence. Police services and governments across Canada are attempting to increase awareness of human rights in the West, particularly women's rights, and urging community groups to help fight such crimes.

Honour Crimes

Honour crimes are the assault or murder of a female family member by male family members for having, in the family's eyes, tarnished the family's honour. Acts that have given rise to honour crimes include a girl or woman having been raped, engaging in consensual sex out of wedlock, going out alone, refusing an arranged marriage, eloping, committing adultery, wearing revealing clothing, flirting, and attempting to escape an abusive relationship. The belief is that killing the girl or woman will restore the family's name in the community. In such cases, girls and women are often killed solely on the basis of a family member's suspicions, without being given an opportunity to defend themselves. The simple fact of the allegation is considered enough to defile the family's honour, and therefore sufficient justification for the killing. Typically, those who commit such murders in their countries of origin go unpunished or receive reduced sentences.

While less well known than the honour crimes targeting women and girls described above, honour crimes targeting homosexual men and women have been reported in the media in recent years. The practice of "corrective rape"—sexual assault targeting men and women who are or are perceived to be LGBTQ—has received increasing attention, as have a number of killings targeting LGBTQ people (Carter, 2013). In some cases, these crimes are committed by or sanctioned by the families of the victims.

Although honour crimes are most often associated with conservative Islam, it is important to note that many Muslims strongly condemn the practice, holding that it is contrary to Islam and in no way justified by Islamic law. It is also important to note that honour crimes are found not only in Islamic communities; they tend to occur in communities with strong patriarchal values in which women are subordinate to men (Department of Justice Canada, 2010). For example, in 2000, a Roman Catholic woman from Israel was granted refugee protection in Canada on the basis that she feared becoming the victim of an honour killing (*I.F.X. (Re)*, 2000).

Related to the practice of "honour" killing is the practice of forced suicide. They are related insofar as the suicide takes the place of a murder (thus ensuring that no male relative will risk punishment for murder).

CLOSE-UP   Honour Crimes and the Shafia Murders

The case of the Shafia family illustrates both the nature of honour killings and the difficulties that police may face when policing diverse communities. In 2012, three members of the Shafia family—Mohammad Shafia, his second wife, Tooba Yahya, and their son, Hamed Shafia—were convicted of first-degree murder in the deaths of four of their family members in what was described as an honour killing. The prosecution described the three convicted family members conspiring to kill Mohammad's first wife, Rona Amir Mohammad, and Mohammad and Tooba's three daughters: Zainab, 19; Sahar, 17; and Geeti, 13. While it is unclear precisely how the four women died, the prosecution asserted that they were hit over the head, drowned, and placed in a car, which was subsequently rammed into the water of the Kingston Mills locks, near Kingston, Ontario, to simulate a car accident.

What emerged during the investigation was a series of failures on the parts of agencies and the police to protect Zainab, Sahar, and Geeti. Mohammad Shafia's abuse had spanned years, arising from anger that his three daughters were acting contrary to his perception of their cultural and religious obligations. In 2008, child services had been called to Sahar's school after her suicide attempt. Despite a troubling interview, the agency concluded that she was not at risk at that time and closed the case. In early 2009,

Zainab left the home after an outburst of physical abuse from her father, and the police became involved. They interviewed each child, who disclosed abuse but later recanted when their father became involved. Child services were again called, and Geeti requested to be removed from the home, but no action was taken and the file was again closed. Two months later, Sahar's school phoned child services yet again on her behalf but received only a referral to a shelter.

During the murder investigation, wiretaps in the Shafia's van caught Mohammad Shafia ranting about the behaviour of his daughters. As *Maclean's* reported:

> "I am happy and my conscience is clear," Shafia proclaimed the night before his arrest, unaware that a police wiretap was recording his every word. "They haven't done good and God punished them." …"They committed treason from beginning to end," Shafia declared, during another one of his intercepted rants. "They betrayed kindness, they betrayed Islam, they betrayed our religion and creed, they betrayed our tradition, they betrayed everything."

Source: Friscolanti (2016).

Explanations for and Causes of Family Violence

In a society composed of diverse cultures, family violence is a complex social issue and can be a product of various factors. In the past, explanations for family violence pointed to stress, alcohol and drug use, a history of abuse as a child, or even characteristics of the abused person. Some current explanations focus on the abuser's desire for power and control and the relative lack of consequences for abusive behaviour. Essentially, violence and intimidation are effective ways of gaining and keeping control, and their successful use both reinforces the abuser's choice to use violence and weakens the victim's ability to leave the situation (Canadian Resource Centre for Victims of Crime, n.d.).

The social explanation for family violence points to several factors: men's socially ingrained expectation of control and power, women's fear of disclosure (which can prolong the abuse), economic hardship, and society's lax attitude toward abusers (Champagne, Lapp, & Lee, 1994). The social view identifies patriarchy as the main culprit, arguing that patriarchal societies institutionalize the social control of women and perpetuate their lack of power in relation to men.

Religion, too, can be a factor in domestic violence. Some religions may practise **gendered apartheid**, based on the belief that women are morally inferior to men and constitute a subordinate class of human being (Okin, 1999). Gendered apartheid is opposed by feminism, which views women and men as moral and human equals and promotes a culture in which women have the same advantages and opportunities as men (Okin, 1999).

gendered apartheid
a policy of segregation, followed in certain religions, based on a belief that women are inferior to men and constitute a subordinate class of human being

Although the following are not causes of family violence, they are correlated with it (National Institute of Justice, 2007):

- early parenthood,
- problem drinking,
- severe poverty, and
- unemployment.

The Cycle of Abuse and Barriers to Leaving Violent Relationships

Many victims of abuse are silent about and tolerant of abuse for complex reasons that may include

- a sense of privacy or shame,
- a fear of social stigma falling on the family and a desire to keep up appearances,
- a desperate need to be in a relationship,
- fear of reprisal and harm to their children,
- financial or emotional dependence,
- lack of social support, and
- inadequate support from the criminal justice system.

Abuse and domestic violence often occur in predictable ways that make it more difficult to leave the relationship. For example, emotional abuse is intended to wear down a victim's self-esteem, and as a result, victims may come to feel that they deserve ill-treatment and violence; abusers who isolate their victim from family or friends often do so to reduce the victim's escape routes. The **cycle of abuse** theory describes a predictable pattern of abuse that reinforces itself and keeps the victim close to the abuser (see Figure 5.3).

cycle of abuse
a social cycle theory that describes four stages of behaviour in an abusive relationship

During the tension-building stage, the abuser begins to act out toward the victim, who feels the need to placate the abuser (often described as "walking on eggshells"). This leads to an episode

FIGURE 5.3   The Cycle of Abuse

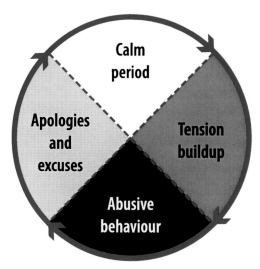

SOURCE: Department of Justice Canada (2009).

of major abuse, which may include acute physical violence. After the abusive episode, the abuser may express remorse, minimize the abuse, or justify it by blaming the victim for provoking it. The abuser may then exhibit loving behaviour, generosity, kindness, or other behaviours intended to convince the victim that the abusive episode will not happen again. This stage eventually leads again to the tension-building stage. Over time, the violent episodes may become more frequent, more severe, or both (Department of Justice Canada, 2009).

The Canadian government has funded projects through the Family Violence Initiative aimed at helping people leave abusive relationships. These projects have developed, among other things, resources for victims regarding how to get safely out of a violent relationship and for people encountering victims of family violence (Department of Justice Canada, n.d.). Among these resources is one developed by the Department of Justice Canada, *Abuse Is Wrong in Any Language* (2012a), which focuses on behaviours occurring in immigrant and ethnic families that are not always recognized as family violence or crimes. This booklet, available in ten languages as well as English, teaches immigrant women about their rights when it comes to abuse in the family.

Social Responses to Family Violence

Canada supports a policy of zero tolerance for all types of violence. This policy states that

- all perpetrators of violence should face appropriate consequences from the criminal justice system;
- victims should receive necessary protection from the criminal justice system; and
- victims and survivors of violence should be provided with diversity-sensitive supports and services in their communities.

Supports and Services

Organizations providing community support and services are essential for an effective response to family violence. Shelters for abused women, in particular, fulfill an important role; they provide refuge and services to women and children fleeing family violence. In 2014, the 627 shelters serving abused women across Canada recorded admissions of more than 60,000 women (Beattie

& Hutchins, 2015). In 2013–14, half of women's admissions to shelter facilities were to transition homes, which provide abused women with short- to medium-term housing. Another 41 percent of admissions were to emergency shelters and centres that provide short-term accommodations. These shelters provide a range of services, including transportation, counselling, advocacy, housing referral, and life skills training, as well as services and programs for residents' children. They also provide continued support for former residents (see Figure 5.4).

Organizations providing community support and services to victims of family violence need to recognize diversity as a factor in that violence. For example, gay and lesbian victims of family violence can feel ill at ease in mainstream shelters, where they may fear encountering homophobia. There are a number of diversity-oriented initiatives, including the Family Violence Initiative's culturally sensitive resource guide, *Guidelines for Service Providers: Outreach Strategies for Family Violence Intervention with Immigrant and Minority Communities*. It identifies outreach strategies that mainstream service agencies can use to encourage minority communities and their leadership to address family violence issues (Changing Ways, 2010; Department of Justice Canada, n.d.).

It has been noted (Justice Institute of British Columbia, 2007; Kazarian & Kazarian, 1998) that abused immigrant and refugee women have unique vulnerabilities, including

- worries about their immigration status (for example, their lack of permanent status or the threat of their abuser's sponsorship being withdrawn if they complain), about their work permits, and about deportation;
- lack of knowledge about host country laws (for example, women from some cultures may not realize that spousal assault is a criminal act) and about the personal rights and freedoms they are entitled to in this country;
- lack of familiarity with the system and its available community supports and services; and
- language barriers.

FIGURE 5.4   Annual Number of Admissions of Women to Shelters, by Type of Shelter, 2013–2014

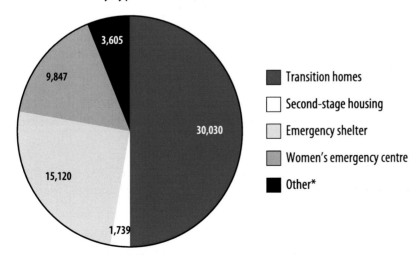

* Includes all other facilities not otherwise specified. For example, in 2013–14, there were 746 admissions to family resource centres (Ontario only) and 95 admissions to interim housing (Manitoba only).

SOURCE: Adapted from Beattie & Hutchins (2015, table 2).

The various needs of abused immigrant and refugee women are listed in Table 5.3. Canadians should view it as a social responsibility to inform immigrant women in abusive relationships that Immigration, Refugees and Citizenship Canada does not expect them to remain silent about their partners' violent behaviour or to live in danger.

TABLE 5.3 Major Needs of Abused Immigrant and Refugee Women

1. Accessible information about Canadian laws and rights, social infrastructure, and available services
2. Help from interpreters or service providers who speak the languages of the immigrant women and who can help them leave abusive relationships, maintain their health and safety, and realize their rights
3. Help in addressing sponsorship and immigration barriers, with specific information about these matters and about the rights of women as immigrants or refugees
4. Material assistance in meeting a wide range of interrelated practical and material needs, including pre-employment or bridging programs, employment, income assistance, child care, transportation, affordable housing, and medical care
5. Assistance from the community to overcome their (the women's) isolation and self-blame for the abuse

SOURCE: Justice Institute of British Columbia (2007).

In the past, community supports and services for victims of family violence took little notice of the issue of diversity. This *adiversity* ("a-" as in *asocial*) tradition is changing; programs are gradually becoming more diversity-oriented. Specialized community-based programs are following a support-and-service philosophy that aims to

- respect diversity, individual autonomy, and safety;
- support a community-wide response to reduce violence against women; and
- promote systemic change at the legal and medical levels and in our society's overall response to victims.

Family Violence and the Criminal Justice System
Police Response to Family Violence

mediative policy
a non-arrest police approach to family violence calls

Police have had three major response policies regarding family violence: the mediative policy, the pro-arrest policy, and the mandatory arrest policy. The **mediative policy**, which is now obsolete, favoured a non-arrest, hands-off approach by police. In other words, police officers responding to family violence calls mainly tried to get everyone in the household to calm down. Then they left it to the family to resolve their difficulties or they referred the offender or victim to social agencies.

The mediative approach to family violence was based partly on the fact that, in the past, police did not consider violence in intimate relationships a real crime. Two mindsets prevailed in this regard, the practical and the patriarchal. The following assumptions informed the practical mindset:

- the victim probably does not want the offender arrested;
- the victim depends financially on the offender and cannot afford to have him or her arrested;
- the offence may be culturally acceptable;
- the offender may cause harm to the victim once he or she is released;

- an arrest may have the unfortunate effect of breaking up the relationship; or
- the court is likely to dismiss charges when the victim chooses not to prosecute.

The patriarchal mindset resulted from a police officer's having been socialized in a patriarchal and hierarchical societal structure in which sexist attitudes prevailed, including the assumption that men should have power and control over women. Police officers with this mindset had little interest in enforcing laws against men who abused women, because they viewed such abuse as natural.

Since the mid-1970s, there have been major changes in the way police respond to family violence. Two policies now prevail. The **pro-arrest policy** encourages arrest in family violence cases, but it leaves the decision about arrest to the discretion of the officers. The **mandatory arrest policy**, on the other hand, dictates that arrest must take place whenever probable cause exists, even in the case of less serious offences. Police services in many countries, including Canada, have adopted a policy of laying criminal charges in family violence cases. Nonetheless, many police officers are still reluctant to take this approach.

To understand the complex nature of family violence, police departments across Canada have put increased emphasis on police training. Police officers receive ongoing training and education, with some jurisdictions having mandatory domestic violence training for police officers in order to effectively respond to the needs of victims of family violence. Police departments have also created specialized domestic violence units staffed by officers who have received extensive training to investigate spousal abuse cases and provide services to victims.

pro-arrest policy
a policy that favours arrest in family violence cases but leaves the decision to the discretion of the officers

mandatory arrest policy
a policy dictating that arrest must take place in family violence cases

Justice System Response to Family Violence

Over the decades, the criminal justice system, in consultation with advocacy groups and community service providers, has developed many innovative policies in response to the issue of family violence. In the early 1980s, Canadian jurisdictions developed a prosecutorial policy called the "no-drop" policy, which limits a Crown prosecutor's discretion to drop charges on the grounds that the victim is unwilling to cooperate and does not want to continue with the complaint. The no-drop policy was put in place to deal with the issue of many victims of family violence dropping charges before trial (Brown, 2000).

To improve the court system for family violence cases, many provincial and territorial jurisdictions have implemented specialized domestic violence courts or court processes to facilitate the prosecution of these cases and treat them seriously. Nine jurisdictions have established provincial/territorial domestic violence courts because most family violence offences are prosecuted in provincial court (Department of Justice Canada, 2013). Domestic violence courts not only facilitate prosecution of cases by expediting court processing time but also provide early intervention for low-risk offenders, tough sentences for serious and repeat offenders, specialized counselling services, and pre-sentencing programs for the accused; thus, they increase offender accountability and provide improved support and services for the victims.

Domestic violence cases usually have multiple charges from different incidents, and dealing with them in separate courts with different judges makes the criminal and non-criminal proceedings cumbersome for the accused, the victim, and the family as a whole. For example, a violent incident of abuse may lead to criminal charges, child protection proceedings, and divorce proceedings. Dealing with each of these in a separate court may lead to conflicting orders, such as an order for access to a child that conflicts with a bail condition to refrain from contacting that child (Department of Justice Canada, 2012b). Domestic violence courts allow for the consolidation of all such matters; having one judge assigned to each set of cases provides consistency and increases the efficiency of the system for the victims and the offenders. Since the implementation of the first domestic violence court in Winnipeg in 1990, several research studies found evidence of increases in both victim reporting rates and conviction rates in this specialized court (Department of Justice Canada, 2013). In Saskatchewan, offenders who completed treatment programs prior to sentencing had lower recidivism rates compared with those who completed programs after sentencing (Department of Justice Canada, 2013).

Mental Illness

mental illness
a group of disorders marked by disturbances in thinking, feeling, and relating

Mental illness is more common than many people think, and traditionally has not been discussed openly. It is estimated that 20 percent of Canadians are likely to experience mental illness during their lifetime, and that the remaining 80 percent are likely to be affected by a family member, friend, or colleague who is mentally ill (Canadian Mental Health Association [CMHA], 2011).

Mental illness occurs in people of all ages, education and income levels, and ethnocultural backgrounds (CMHA, 2011). While mental illness can be treated effectively, social stigma and discrimination represent a major barrier to treatment, and as a result, nearly half of people who have experienced depression or anxiety have never sought medical attention.

The Cost of Mental Illness

- The cost to the Canadian economy of mental illness, which includes health care costs, lost productivity, and reduced quality of life, is estimated at $51 billion per year.
- At the beginning of the 21st century, $6.3 billion was spent on uninsured mental health services and on time off work for mental health needs that were not treated by the health care system.
- Mental illness was the reason for 3.8 percent of all admissions to general hospitals (1.5 million hospital days).

Source: CMHA (2011).

homelessness
the condition of having no fixed, regular, and adequate address

Homelessness is significantly correlated with diagnoses of mental illness and substance abuse, although it is not clear whether mental illness and substance abuse are factors that contribute to homelessness or whether the opposite is true—that homelessness contributes to mental illness and substance abuse. Two acknowledged facts are that a history of mental illness or substance abuse increases the *risk* of homelessness, and that the increased stress and anxiety associated with homelessness can lead to mental health issues and can cause individuals to use substances as a coping strategy (Mental Illness Awareness Week, 2010). The Canadian Mental Health Association found that between 23 percent and 67 percent of homeless persons in Canada report having a mental illness (CMHA, 2011).

Although research indicates that people with mental illness are less likely than the general population to commit crimes, the number of interactions between police and people with mental illnesses has increased significantly in recent years (Coleman & Cotton, 2014). Some of these interactions result in negative outcomes, which poses a challenge for law enforcement agencies. According to the 2012 Canadian Community Health Survey—Mental Health, approximately one in five contacts with police involved someone with a mental health or substance-use disorder (Statistics Canada, 2015b). New psychiatric and psychological treatment approaches to mental illness contribute to the deinstitutionalization of the mentally ill and their reintegration into the community. However, shortcomings in community mental health services, including insufficient funding for health and social services, have led to increased police involvement in calls from the community concerning mental health episodes.

This part of the chapter focuses on policing mental illness; its aim is to increase your understanding of mental illness and to consider how police can respond more effectively in situations involving mental illness. The emphasis here is on the mental illnesses that most commonly bring individuals into contact with the criminal justice system: substance-related disorders, mood disorders, schizophrenia and psychosis, and intellectual and developmental disabilities (Latimer & Lawrence, 2006).

Defining Mental Illness

Mental illness is a generic term for a variety of disorders. The Police Executive Research Forum (1997) has defined mental illness as a group of distinct disabilities marked by disturbances in thinking, feeling, and relating. The Public Health Agency of Canada (2011) has stated that mental illnesses are characterized by alterations in thinking, mood, or behaviour (or some combination thereof) that are associated with significant distress and impaired functioning over an extended period of time. The causes of mental illness are complex, involving an interplay of genetic, biological, personality, and environmental factors (CMHA, 2011).

Although mental illness causes disturbances in behaving, feeling, relating, and thinking, such disturbances can also be caused by other factors, including head injury, medical conditions such as diabetes and epilepsy, and substance abuse. For example, people who use stimulants (including cocaine and methamphetamines) may experience **formication**, a hallucinatory experience in which the users feel that insects or snakes are crawling over or under their skin. Similarly, people in the aftermath of a cocaine high may become irritable and depressed.

Mental illness ranges from mild to severe. Severe mental illnesses can include schizophrenia, mood disorders, organic brain syndrome (a general term referring to physical disorders that negatively affect brain function), and paranoia and other psychoses. According to the Public Health Agency of Canada (2015b), mental illness can occur in the form of

> **formication**
> a hallucinatory experience, sometimes undergone by stimulant users, that involves feeling that insects or snakes are crawling over or under one's skin

- mood disorders,
- psychoses (for example, schizophrenia),
- anxiety disorders,
- personality disorders,
- psychosexual disorders,
- substance-abuse disorders,
- intellectual disability,
- dementia, and
- other non-psychotic mental disorders, such as eating disorders.

Mental disturbances can be categorized as *non-psychotic* or **psychotic**; the latter involves losing touch with reality. Hallucinations and delusions are the two most common symptoms of a psychotic mental disturbance. Anxiety and depression are the two most common types of non-psychotic mental disturbance.

> **psychosis**
> a form of mental disturbance that involves a person's losing touch with reality

Substance-Related Disorders

In 2012, more than 20 percent of Canadians (about 6 million people) met the criteria for a substance-use disorder at some point in their lifetime (Pearson, Janz, & Ali, 2013). Men, in general, had higher rates of substance-use disorders compared with women. Overall, men were 2.6 times more likely than women to meet the criteria for substance dependence (CMHA, 2011). People with **substance-related disorders** may show both psychotic and non-psychotic mental disturbances. For example, consuming alcohol can have serious effects such as blackouts and aggression. Phencyclidine (PCP or "angel dust") is known to produce severe anxiety, depression, disorientation, unpredictable aggression, and paranoid thoughts (Levinthal, 1996). Alcohol and drug abuse are also associated with crime and social violence such as robbery, burglary, shoplifting, human trafficking, prostitution, and the trafficking and distribution of illicit drugs for income.

> **substance-related disorders**
> mental disorders caused by substance dependence and abuse, and by substance withdrawal

In responding to a person with a substance-related disorder, police need to

- ensure their own safety and the safety of others,
- recognize the symptoms the person is displaying,
- expect irrational behaviour,
- decide whether the situation is a medical emergency, and
- ensure that an interim use of physical restraint is safe and unlikely to cause the person added harm.

Mood Disorders and Suicidal Behaviour

mood disorders
mental disorders, including depression and bipolar disorder, that affect a person's mood

depression
a mood disorder characterized by extended periods of despair and hopelessness and a lack of interest in life

Mood disorders include depression and bipolar disorder. No one is immune to depression, which affects children as well as adults. Women are diagnosed with depression more often than men are. Approximately 12 percent of Canadians in 2012 met the criteria for a mood disorder at some point during their lifetime (Pearson, Janz, & Ali, 2013), while about 1 percent of Canadians will experience bipolar disorder (CMHA, 2011). Mood disorders among both males and females were highest among youth and young adults (15 to 24 years of age); however, in all age groups females were more likely than males to suffer from mood disorders. **Depression** is characterized by extended periods of despair and hopelessness and a lack of interest in life. Contrary to popular belief, it is not simply sadness or feeling down. People who suffer from depression may have trouble facing each day. Symptoms of depression may include

- sleep disturbance (sleeping too much or too little),
- a change in eating habits (overeating or loss of appetite),
- irritability or agitation,
- anhedonia (loss of pleasure or interest in activities that used to be enjoyable),
- poor concentration,
- suicidal ideation (thoughts of and plans for suicide),
- headaches or stomach aches, and
- feeling alienated or separated from the rest of society.

Like mood disorders in general, depression is more common among women than men in all age groups—except among seniors, when men and women have equal chances of suffering from depression.

bipolar disorder
a mood disorder, previously known as manic depression, that involves emotional swings between depression and mania

Bipolar disorder, previously called manic depression, is a condition in which a person has emotional swings between depression and mania. **Mania** is a mood state of high emotion, agitation, and impulsivity. In 2012, about 2.6 percent of the population displayed a profile consistent with bipolar disorder (Pearson, Janz, & Ali, 2013). Men and women are equally prone to bipolar disorder. Table 5.4 lists the symptoms of depression and mania.

mania
a mood disorder characterized by an emotional high, agitation, and impulsivity

People with mood disorders may exhibit psychotic or non-psychotic symptoms. Psychotic symptoms tend to be consistent with their mood state. For example, a man in a manic state may have the psychotic belief that his blood can cure all the sicknesses in the world, and he may insist, in his elated mood, that as much blood as possible be drawn from his arm and taken around the world to cure people of their diseases.

suicide
a consequence of mood disorder, with suicidal mood disorder taking the possible forms of ideation, threat, gesture, attempt, and completed suicide

Suicide may be a consequence of a mood disorder; the symptoms of a suicidal mood disorder include *ideation* (thinking about suicide), *threat* (expressing the intention to commit a self-destructive act), *gesture* (a self-destructive act with little or no death intent), *attempt* (a self-destructive act with clear death intent), or *completed suicide*.

People with mood disorders are at a particularly high risk of suicide. Studies indicate that more than 90 percent of suicide victims have a diagnosable psychiatric illness, and suicide is the most common cause of death for people with schizophrenia. Major depression and bipolar disorder account for 15 to 25 percent of all deaths by suicide in patients with severe mood disorders (CMHA, Toronto, n.d.).

TABLE 5.4   Symptoms of Depression and Mania

Depression	Mania
• Feelings of sadness or emptiness	• Inflated self-esteem or grandiosity
• Loss of interest or pleasure	• Talkativeness
• Sleep disturbance (too much or too little sleep)	• Extreme irritability
• Change in eating habits (increase or decrease in appetite)	• Distractibility
	• Decreased need for sleep
• Change in weight (loss or gain)	• Increased sexual, social, school, and work activities
• Psychomotor disturbance (agitation or slowness in movement)	• Increased pleasurable activities (overspending, sexual indiscretion)
• Fatigue or loss of energy	
• Loss of self-esteem	
• Feelings of guilt or self-blame	
• Cognitive disturbance (poor concentration, indecisiveness)	
• Suicidal or homicidal thoughts	

In 2012, 3,926 people in Canada committed suicide (Statistics Canada, 2015c). Suicide accounts for 25 percent of all deaths among 15- to 24-year-olds and 20 percent among 25- to 34-year-olds. Men succeed in killing themselves four times more often than women do (CMHA, Toronto, n.d.), even though women attempt suicide more often than men do. Methods of suicide commonly used by both men and women are

- hanging (46 percent for men, 37 percent for women);
- use of firearms (20 percent for men, 3 percent for women);
- poisoning (20 percent for men, 42 percent for women); and
- other (14 percent for men, 18 percent for women) (Statistics Canada, 2010).

Table 5.5 lists risk factors for suicidal behaviour. It is interesting to note that the media rarely report on public suicides—cases where people jump in front of trains or off bridges. Even cases with sensational circumstances may not make it into the media. The Canadian Psychiatric Association discourages the publication of information about completed suicides, since publicizing suicide and making notorious those who commit it may encourage others to imitate them (Canadian Psychiatric Association, n.d.).

In responding to a depressed and suicidal person, police need to

- avoid telling the person to cheer up or snap out of it;
- assess the risk of suicide by asking direct questions and making explicit use of the words *kill* or *die* (for example, "Are you thinking of killing yourself?" "Have you made plans to kill yourself?" "Why do you want to die?");
- take suicide threats seriously;
- be empathetic (for example, "I would like to help because I know you are in pain");
- avoid promising secrecy;
- not leave the person alone;
- draw on the person's social support system (family, friends, counsellor); and
- present the person with two options to choose from (for example, "Would you like to go to the hospital with me, or would you rather I called an ambulance?").

TABLE 5.5   Risk Factors for Suicidal Behaviour

- Suicide plan
- History of past suicide attempts
- Absence of community support
- Recent loss (actual, threatened, or imagined)
- Physical illness, including AIDS or other terminal illness
- Change in lifestyle, behaviour, or personality
- Giving away possessions or valuables
- Putting personal affairs in order (for example, making a will)
- Depression, including feelings of hopelessness and helplessness
- Postpartum depression
- Substance use
- Recent discharge from psychiatric hospital care
- Psychosis
- Anniversaries (birthday, wedding, death of a loved one)

In responding to a manic person, police need to

- reduce all extraneous stimulation (for example, noise from a TV);
- avoid arguments;
- allow the person to discharge energy in appropriate ways, such as by pacing;
- be firm, empathetic, and direct;
- draw on the person's social support system; and
- present the person with options to choose from.

Psychosis and Schizophrenia

Psychosis may be a symptom of a number of mental illnesses, although it is most commonly known as a symptom of schizophrenia. The Centre for Addiction and Mental Health describes the symptoms of psychosis as positive or negative, also known as excess and deficit symptoms. Table 5.6 lists the major symptoms of psychosis.

Some of these symptoms will be more fully discussed below.

While many people most often associate psychosis with schizophrenia, it can occur in a number of other mental illnesses and physical illnesses, including

- bipolar disorder,
- depression with psychotic features,
- drug- or alcohol-induced psychosis,
- postpartum psychosis,
- brain tumours,
- brain infections, and
- stroke (CAMH, n.d.; MedlinePlus, n.d.).

schizophrenia
a serious mental illness marked by a breakdown in the connection between thoughts, feelings, and actions, and often accompanied by strong psychotic disturbances and delusions

Schizophrenia, which afflicts 1 percent of the Canadian population (CMHA, 2011), is one cause of psychotic mental disturbances. Men tend to be afflicted by it at a younger age than

TABLE 5.6   Excess and Deficit Symptoms of Psychosis

Excess symptoms	Deficit symptoms
• Hallucinations	• Mood disturbances
• Thought disorders	• Impaired interpersonal functioning and motivation
• Delusions	• Restricted emotional expression
• Disorganized speech, thought, or behaviour	• Restricted speech and verbal fluency

SOURCE: CAMH (n.d.).

women are. Its symptoms differ from those of mood disorders in that the psychotic symptoms of schizophrenia tend to be inconsistent with the person's mood. For example, a person suffering from schizophrenia may break into laughter and show signs of elation while discussing some delusional event—the imaginary death of a parent, for example—that would normally bring feelings of sadness or distress.

Thought disorders are ideas and speech that make sense to the psychotic person but not to others. **Hallucinations** are delusional sensory experiences that are often disturbing to the person having them. Things that appear in hallucinations can be felt, heard, seen, smelled, or tasted. Hearing voices and seeing things are the most common forms of hallucination. People who are hallucinating may talk to themselves, display concentration problems, or make head movements toward the source of the voices they hear. A person who is having visual hallucinations may jerk the eyes or the head. **Delusions** are ideas that have no basis in reality, and they are another common symptom of psychosis. A person with paranoid schizophrenia may believe, for example, that he is Jesus and the subject of persecution, or that valuable thoughts are being sucked out of his mind and stolen. A variety of psychotropic drugs are used in the treatment of psychosis and schizophrenia (for example, clozapine). When persons with psychosis, including schizophrenic persons, discontinue taking their medication, they may do things that lead to a need for police intervention.

In responding to a person showing psychotic symptoms, police need to

- be firm, empathetic, reassuring, and helpful;
- avoid using deception or humour;
- validate and acknowledge the person's hallucinatory experience (do not argue against it), but also communicate that the experience is in fact a hallucination and does not correspond to reality (for example, "I don't see the man, but I understand that you do");
- avoid invading the personal space of a paranoid person and avoid implying special knowledge of the person's paranoid beliefs;
- employ the standard Use of Force Continuum if a schizophrenic person presents a threat;
- draw on the person's social support system, if necessary; and
- offer the person options to choose from.

Intellectual and Developmental Disabilities

Intellectual disability is not the same as mental illness. Three criteria are used to establish intellectual disability: significantly subaverage intelligence (an IQ below 70), significant limitation in adaptive functioning, and onset before the age of 18 years. *Intellectual disability* is the current term for the condition. Terms that were previously used, the main one being "mental retardation," are being eliminated from diagnostic manuals and legislation (Harris, 2013).

The terminology surrounding these kinds of disabilities can be confusing. Although *intellectual disability* and *developmental disability* are sometimes used as synonyms, the latter is, in the

thought disorders
a pattern of vague or disorganized thinking that may appear illogical to others

hallucinations
delusional sensory experiences that may be disturbing to the person having them; a common symptom of schizophrenia

delusions
ideas that have no basis in reality; a common symptom of schizophrenia

intellectual disability
a condition characterized by significantly subaverage intelligence, significant limitation in adaptive functioning, and onset before the age of 18 years

current usage, a much broader term; it is used in reference to a variety of disabling conditions, including intellectual disability, autism spectrum disorders (autism and Asperger syndrome), cerebral palsy, fetal alcohol spectrum disorders, and Down syndrome, as well as a variety of physical disabilities, such as congenital blindness. In other words, intellectual disability is a subcategory of developmental disability. A person may have more than one developmental disability, and they may be related; a person with the developmental disability of Down syndrome, for example, is very likely to have an IQ below 70, which meets the criteria for intellectual disability. On the other hand, a person with cerebral palsy or Asperger syndrome, which qualify as developmental disabilities, may have very strong cognitive functioning (American Association on Intellectual and Developmental Disabilities, 2011).

The communication and behavioural development of people with intellectual disability may be limited in a variety of ways. They may have a short attention span, impaired speech, or difficulty understanding or answering questions. They may act inappropriately with peers or with the opposite sex, become easily frustrated, be excessively eager to please, or be easily influenced by others. Finally, they may have difficulty carrying out the activities of daily living, such as using the telephone and telling time.

In responding to a person with an intellectual disability, police need to

- treat the person with respect and dignity,
- use simple language and short sentences,
- be patient but firm, and
- avoid asking confusing or leading questions.

Mental Illness and the Criminal Justice System

People with mental illness are overrepresented in the criminal justice system (CMHA, British Columbia Division, 2005). This is in part due to the criminalization of mental illness and the difficulty of obtaining proper treatment. As CMHA, British Columbia Division explains (2005), mental illness is often correlated with poverty, inadequate housing, substance abuse, trauma, and homelessness. When a person with mental illness cannot access treatment, they may act in ways that attract police attention—this may involve committing a crime, or police may become involved in obtaining treatment for the person.

When the United Nations' *Principles for the Protection of Persons with Mental Illness and the Improvement of Mental Health Care* were adopted by resolution of the UN General Assembly on December 17, 1991, the international community officially recognized the fundamental right of mentally ill people to be protected from discrimination (Office of the United Nations High Commissioner for Human Rights, 1991). Despite this development, mental health legislation in many countries still allows the removal of the civil liberties of people with mental illness (Persad & Kazarian, 1998). The essential criteria for determining whether someone should be forcibly confined in a psychiatric hospital are whether the person is a danger to self, a danger to others, or incompetent to care for himself or herself.

In Canada, mental health laws in each province and territory specifically set out the parameters of police involvement with mentally ill people and their powers in detaining an involuntary patient at a mental health facility. Individuals with mental illness are admitted to a psychiatric or mental health facility when they pose a threat to the safety of themselves or others. Police officers have discretionary powers when intervening in a situation involving a mentally ill person. They can admit the person to a psychiatric hospital, arrest the person, or resolve the situation informally (Commission for Public Complaints Against the RCMP, 2010).

The Ontario *Mental Health Act* (1990) regulates the administration of mental health care, including the involuntary admission of people into a psychiatric hospital. The Act was amended by Bill 68, also known as Brian's Law, on June 23, 2000. Brian Smith was a popular sportscaster and former National Hockey League player who was shot and killed by a man with a history of serious mental illness. Brian's Law enables seriously mentally ill people to be treated in a community setting that is less restrictive and less intrusive than a psychiatric hospital. Other provinces (for example, Saskatchewan) have similar laws.

The power of a police officer to admit someone against his or her will to a psychiatric hospital or unit is dealt with under section 17 of the *Mental Health Act*. Brian's Law stipulates that a police officer may take a person into custody provided that the officer has reasonable and probable grounds to believe that disorderly conduct has occurred and has reasonable cause to believe that the person fulfills the prescribed conditions of threat and lack of competence to care for one's self. Section 33 of the Act states that a police officer must stay with a person who has been involuntarily admitted until the facility decides whether or not to admit the person.

Brian's Law also stipulates that a justice of the peace may issue an order authorizing a police officer to take a person in custody to an appropriate place for examination by a physician, provided that—based on information that the officer must give under oath—there is evidence of *threat* and *mental disorder* (s. 16). As evidence of *threat*, the statute requires information to the effect that

1. the person has threatened or attempted or is threatening or attempting to cause bodily harm to himself or herself;
2. the person has behaved or is behaving violently toward another person or has caused or is causing another person to fear bodily harm from him or her; and
3. the person has shown or is showing a lack of competence to care for himself or herself.

As for taking a person into custody on the grounds of mental disorder, the statute requires information, based on the officer's reasonable cause or belief, that the person's mental disorder is of a nature or quality that will result in (1) serious bodily harm to the person, (2) serious bodily harm to another person, or (3) serious physical impairment of the person.

Mental Disturbances and Police Response

The majority of people with mental health disorders are not involved in criminal behaviour; however, someone with a mental illness is more likely to have an interaction with police (Statistics Canada, 2015b). In 2012, one in three Canadians with a mental health disorder reported having contact with the police. It is worth mentioning that not all of these interactions are criminal in nature. Brink et al. (2011, p. 29) indicated that

- 2 in 5 people with mental illness have been arrested in their lifetime;
- 3 in 10 people with mental illness have had the police involved in their care;
- 1 in 7 referrals to emergency psychiatric inpatient services involve the police; and
- 1 in 20 police dispatches or encounters involve persons with mental health problems.

In their day-to-day duties, police are very likely to encounter people with one (or a combination) of the following conditions: a substance-related disorder, a mood disorder, schizophrenia, or an intellectual disability. Police are also very likely to deal with mental disturbances in connection with

- suicidal behaviour;
- threatening, destructive, assaultive, or violent behaviour;
- psychotic thinking and ideation (losing touch with reality);
- confusion in thought or action; and
- strange or unusual behaviours that exceed public tolerance.

When police interact with someone who has a mental illness, it is important to realize that officers may not immediately be aware that mental illness is involved. They may approach the situation as usual but not get the expected compliance, which may escalate the situation and result in a negative outcome.

Some recent high-profile cases of police use of force with mentally ill people have caused some serious concerns, such as the deaths of Sammy Yatim and Andrew Loku (see the Close-Up: Andrew Loku box in Chapter 6). These incidents have led to calls for better training and education of police officers to effectively deal with mentally ill persons. You will learn more about policing and mental health in Chapter 6.

Trial, Sentencing, and Treatment

Intent is an important aspect of most criminal offences. Accused persons may have a psychiatric or developmental condition that renders them unable to appreciate the nature and consequences of their actions or unable to know that their actions are wrong at the time of the offence. These persons may raise the mental disorder defence; they may be found **not criminally responsible** (NCR) for the crime of which they are accused. While this is an important step in safeguarding the rights of mentally ill persons, the defence is quite narrow, and the test is difficult to meet (Roach et al., 2015). A majority of accused persons diagnosed with mental illness are held criminally responsible for committing a criminal offence.

When the accused person's mental illness persists to trial, the *Criminal Code* provides that they may be found **unfit to stand trial**. Accused persons must be able to participate in their full answer and defence; when a person cannot do so, holding a trial is not considered to be in accordance with the principles of fundamental justice. Unlike an NCR finding, a finding of unfitness to stand trial is a temporary measure designed to allow the accused person access to treatment until he or she is fit to stand trial (Latimer & Lawrence, 2006).

It is important to understand that an NCR finding or a finding of unfitness to stand trial does not mean that the criminal justice system is "going easy" on an offender. These measures are meant to prevent people who are not morally blameworthy from receiving an unjust punishment. These findings are difficult to raise, and their successful use is quite rare: only 1.8 persons in 1,000 are diverted to review boards through either of these findings (Latimer & Lawrence, 2006).

Persons who are found to be NCR are not punished traditionally but are given forensic treatment through the mental health system. The goal is to balance public safety with the treatment and rehabilitation needs of mentally ill offenders. Individuals must participate in treatment in a psychiatric hospital or in the community through partnerships with mental health care agencies. They are ordered to periodically meet with review boards to assess their progress and review any risk they pose to public safety.

Through the review board system, an offender who has been found NCR may ultimately spend more time in custody than a similarly situated offender who has been found guilty, especially for non-violent offences that would otherwise be associated with relatively short sentences. This is because the provincial review boards are mandated to consider above all the safety of the public. Section 672.54 of the *Criminal Code* reads:

> 672.54 When a court or Review Board makes a disposition under subsection 672.45(2), section 672.47, subsection 672.64(3) or section 672.83 or 672.84, it shall, *taking into account the safety of the public, which is the paramount consideration*, the mental condition of the accused, the reintegration of the accused into society and the other needs of the accused, make one of the following dispositions that is necessary and appropriate in the circumstances:
>
> (a) where a verdict of not criminally responsible on account of mental disorder has been rendered in respect of the accused and, in the opinion of the court or Review

not criminally responsible
a criminal defence that may apply when a person, at the time of committing a crime, was unable by reason of a mental disorder to appreciate the nature or quality of the crime or to know that it was wrong

unfit to stand trial
a determination that a person is unable on account of a mental disorder to understand the nature, object, and possible consequences of a criminal proceeding, and that the person is unable to communicate with counsel

Board, the accused is not a significant threat to the safety of the public, by order, direct that the accused be discharged absolutely;

(b) by order, direct that the accused be discharged subject to such conditions as the court or Review Board considers appropriate; or

(c) by order, direct that the accused be detained in custody in a hospital, subject to such conditions as the court or Review Board considers appropriate. [Emphasis added.]

Because of these provisions, persons found NCR may be detained in a hospital for treatment until the review board is satisfied that the safety of the public would not be compromised by their release.

In many Canadian jurisdictions, specialized mental health courts have been established to deal with the unique challenges and needs of mentally ill people who are accused of committing a crime. The main objective of these courts is to provide special care to mentally ill people and divert them from the regular justice system. Depending on the crime, a mental health court may divert the accused to medical or therapeutic treatment before sentencing.

As an example, let us look at Nova Scotia's mental health court program. An entirely voluntary program, it began in November 2009 and accepts persons with mental disorders that affect their judgment, which may include psychotic disorders, developmental delays, organic brain injuries, and concurrent mental health and substance-abuse issues. The court team includes traditional court actors, including a judge, Crown attorney, and defence counsel, but also includes or consults a probation officer, a social worker, a psychiatric nurse, a forensic psychologist, and an addictions social worker (Provincial Court Nova Scotia, 2014). The program requires that the offence with which the accused person is charged be linked in some way to their mental disorder, and that the accused person acknowledge responsibility for the act or omission that forms the basis of the criminal charge. The accused person receives a treatment plan and is placed in contact with the appropriate community agencies; he or she also checks in regularly (in some cases, weekly) with the court. Successful completion of the program may lead to charges being withdrawn by the Crown.

Mental Illness and Corrections

Individuals with mental illness are overrepresented in corrections as well as the criminal justice system generally. Ontario's Ministry of Community Safety and Correctional Services reported that in 2008, 15 percent of inmates in provincial prisons required an intervention for mental illness (Public Services Foundation of Canada, 2015). In British Columbia, the Ministry of Justice estimated that more than half of the inmates admitted to provincial correctional facilities had a substance-abuse or mental health problem, or both (Public Services Foundation of Canada, 2015). The Office of the Correctional Investigator's report (Sapers & Zinger, 2012) indicates that the number of federal inmates with mental health needs at the time of intake almost doubled between 1997 and 2008. Relatively more females (29 percent) than males (13 percent) were identified as having mental health problems at the time of admission to a federal correctional facility.

Prisons are difficult and challenging places for everyone and especially for people with mental illness because of the stressful environment, social isolation, and overcrowding. Mentally ill inmates may react to the situation by acting out and displaying disruptive behaviour, self-harm, and violence. Correctional officers who misunderstand the symptoms of mental illness often treat these behaviours as security issues. In order to maintain discipline, common interventions to manage self-injury in correctional facilities include physical handling, restraints, pepper spray, and segregation (Sapers & Zinger, 2012). Research indicates that prolonged segregation can aggravate the symptoms of mental illness and cause long-term psychological harm (Metcalfe, 2014). The suicide rate is also very high in prisons—for federal inmates, more than seven times the Canadian average (Sapers & Zinger, 2012).

Correctional Service Canada is required to provide inmates with essential health care, including mental health care, in order to successfully rehabilitate and reintegrate them into the community. Inmates with mental illness are entitled to the same treatment as people in the general population. Male federal inmates suffering from acute or chronic mental illness or cognitive disorders are sent to one of the five regional treatment centres. Female federal inmates are provided mental health services at the Regional Psychiatric Centre in Saskatoon.

You will learn more about mental health initiatives in corrections in Chapter 6.

Police Abilities, Knowledge, and Skills

Family Violence

Police, Crown attorneys, judges, probation officers, victim-witness assistance personnel, and correctional personnel provide supports and services in the area of family violence, and they develop public information resources. Policing in Canada is becoming more responsive to family violence issues (Department of Justice Canada, n.d.); police executives attend national forums on family violence with the following goals in mind:

- to educate themselves about facts, initiatives, and approaches related to family violence;
- to learn about effective police and community responses to family violence; and
- to develop—with other police chiefs, professionals, and government agencies—networks for dealing with family violence.

Police are also becoming more effective in responding to family violence calls. Most have shifted from a victim-blaming approach to an approach that holds the abuser accountable. Traditional victim-blaming attitudes not only failed to intercede against the abuser; they also revictimized the victim by giving tacit approval to the abuse.

Police recognize that they cannot fight family violence alone and that they need community support systems. Among the positive changes police have made in this regard are

- organizing family-response teams,
- identifying at-risk households on the beat, and
- providing the community with family violence training programs.

In addition to developing these outward initiatives to address family violence in the community, police services are acknowledging the need for internal initiatives. They are recognizing that police are not immune to the problems of family violence in their own lives.

Mental Illness

Policing mental illness is challenging for several reasons. Many of the incidents to which police are called involve mental illness, and such incidents are on the rise. If the police response is not successful, the outcomes of these incidents can be tragic. Also, such incidents call for a specialized response from police. When police respond to a person in a mental health crisis in the same way they respond to a typical emergency criminal situation (that is, with a show of force and authority), they may in fact escalate the situation to the point of putting people at risk of injury or death (CMHA, British Columbia Division, 2005).

Cases where police have injured or killed mentally ill people indicate the need for specialized police training in mental health (Lucas, 2015). The Ontario Ministry of the Solicitor General *Policing Standards Manual* (2000) has advised chiefs of police to ensure that their police services' training programs teach officers about conflict resolution in connection with the mentally ill or the emotionally disturbed.

Several Canadian police services have implemented special training policy guidelines and / or specialized intervention teams for managing incidents involving the mentally ill. In Ontario, these police services include those in Ottawa-Carleton, Toronto, Niagara, Guelph, Hamilton-Wentworth, and Chatham-Kent, as well as the Ontario Provincial Police. The specialized approach entails teaching police officers about mental health legislation and mental disturbances, and about specific interventions such as

- tactical communication;
- crisis resolution;
- containment of potentially volatile situations (for example, a mentally ill person threatening other people with a gun); and
- partnership with available community supports and services.

The supports and services available in the community may include advocacy representatives, consumer and family education, family support, medical and dental services, medication, peer support, police support, and rehabilitation centres (Fernando & Kazarian, 1995; Kazarian & Joseph, 1994). Many of these support systems, including crisis response services (crisis lines, mental health teams, and hospital emergency wards), are insufficiently funded; the deinstitutionalization movement has caused a sharp increase in the demand for such resources and has led to shortages in certain areas, such as hospital beds. To function effectively and efficiently, community support systems also require skilled coordinators.

Finally, police are not immune to mental health issues of their own. It may be difficult for police to accept this fact, since it shatters the image of their invulnerability and indomitable emotional strength (Violanti, 1996). But police are no less susceptible to problems of this sort than other people are. Furthermore, police work involves confronting trauma and adversity on a regular basis, and these experiences can affect even the most resilient minds. Initiatives for promoting the mental well-being of police are absolutely necessary.

EXERCISE 2

Based on your reading in this chapter, analyze each of the following scenarios. For each one, consider the following questions:

- What is the problem, what are the issues, what are the solutions?
- Is your response appropriate?
- If not, what would an appropriate response be?

1. A 24-year-old man is threatening to punch his mother. As the police officer on the scene, you assess the situation and decide that the man is unlikely to act out his anger, and that there is no real possibility that anyone will get hurt. You say, "If you don't stop threatening your mother, you'll have a real battle on your hands. Now what's it going to be?"

2. A 28-year-old homeless woman has been drinking and is now threatening passersby with a knife. As the police officer on the scene, you decide that the woman is unlikely to attack anyone or hurt anyone accidentally. You say, "All you homeless people are drunk. What are we going to do with you?"

3. You are called to an incident involving a teenager who tells you that the dentist put a microchip in his mouth when he went for a filling, so now everyone can hear his private thoughts all the time. You say, "You believe people are spying on you. That must be very scary."

4. A 65-year-old mentally ill woman tells you that her husband and children are trying to get rid of her by poisoning her food. You tell the family that the woman is "psycho" and that you have to take her to the "nuthouse."

CHAPTER SUMMARY

Family violence is a serious problem for society and for the justice system. It affects both men and women. Over the decades, various legal responses to family violence have been adopted within the justice system, including mandatory arrest policies, no-drop policies, and specialized courts to change the work culture and effectively respond to the needs of victims and offenders. Effective policing requires seeing this kind of violence for the criminal action that it is, understanding family violence in the context of Canada's ethnocultural diversity, and forming partnerships with community supports and services.

In preparing to police mental illness, police must understand as best they can the various types of illnesses, common symptoms, and most appropriate responses, and recognize the established connections between mental illness, substance abuse, and homelessness. Police must also understand how mental illness differs from intellectual and developmental disabilities, and how best to respond in situations involving the latter. To serve and protect *all* people effectively, police need to work in partnership with families, professionals, and community services.

REFERENCES

American Association on Intellectual and Developmental Disabilities. (2011). Developmental disabilities. http://www.aamr.org.

Barnett, L. (2008). The "spanking" law: Section 43 of the Criminal Code. Parliament of Canada, Law and Government Division. PRB 05-10E. http://www.lop.parl.gc.ca/content/lop/researchpublications/prb0510-e.htm.

Beattie, S., & Hutchins, H. (2015). Shelters for abused women in Canada, 2014. *Juristat*. http://www.statcan.gc.ca/pub/85-002-x/2015001/article/14207/tbl/tbl02-eng.htm.

Benedictis, T., Jaffe, J., & Segal, J. (2014). Domestic violence and abuse: Types, signs, symptoms, causes, and effects. American Academy of Experts in Traumatic Stress. http://www.aaets.org/article144.htm.

Biesenthal, L., Sproule, L.D., Nelder, M., Golton, S., Mann, D., Podovinnikoff, D., Roosendaal, I., Warman, S., & Lunn, D. (2000). *The Ontario rural woman abuse study: Final report.* Ottawa: Department of Justice Canada.

Brennan, S. (2011). Section 1: Self-reported spousal violence, 2009. *Family Violence in Canada: A statistical profile.* Statistics Canada. http://www.statcan.gc.ca/pub/85-224-x/2010000/part-partie1-eng.htm.

Brink, J., Livingston, J., Desmarais, S., Greaves, C., Maxwell, V., Michalak, E., Parent, R., Verdun-Jones, S., & Weaver, C. (2011). *A study of how people with mental illness perceive and interact with the police.* Calgary: Mental Health Commission of Canada. http://www.mentalhealthcommission.ca.

Brown, T. (2000). Charging and prosecution policies in cases of spousal assault: A synthesis of research, academic, and judicial responses. Department of Justice Canada. http://www.justice.gc.ca/eng/rp-pr/csj-sjc/jsp-sjp/rr01_5/rr01_5.pdf.

Canada Evidence Act. (1985). RSC 1985, c. C-5.

Canadian Mental Health Association. (2011). Fast facts about mental illness. http://www.cmha.ca/media/fast-facts-about-mental-illness/.

Canadian Mental Health Association, British Columbia Division. (2005). Police and mental illness: Increased interactions. http://cmha.bc.ca/wp-content/uploads/2016/07/policesheets_all.pdf.

Canadian Mental Health Association, Toronto. (n.d.). Suicide statistics. https://toronto.cmha.ca/mental_health/suicide-statistics/.

Canadian Psychiatric Association. (n.d.). Media guidelines for reporting suicide. http://www.cpa-apc.org/browse/documents/273.

Canadian Resource Centre for Victims of Crime. (n.d.). Spousal abuse. http://crcvc.ca/docs/spousalabuse.pdf.

Canadian Women's Foundation. (2015). Fact sheet: Moving women out of violence. http://www.canadianwomen.org/sites/canadianwomen.org/files/FactSheet-StopViolence-ACTIVE%20-%20May2015.pdf.

Carter, C. (2013, July 27). The brutality of "corrective rape." *New York Times.* http://www.nytimes.com.

CBC News. (2014, August 27). Mental health commission calls for more experts in police training. http://www.cbc.ca.

Centre for Addiction and Mental Health. (n.d.). Psychosis. https://www.camh.ca/en/hospital/health_information/a_z_mental_health_and_addiction_information/psychosis/Pages/Psychosis.aspx.

Champagne, C., Lapp, R., & Lee, J. (1994). *Assisting abused lesbians: A guide for health professionals and service providers.* London, ON: London Battered Women's Advocacy Centre.

Changing Ways. (2010). *Guidelines for service providers: Outreach strategies for family violence intervention with immigrant and minority communities*. London, ON: Author.

Coleman, T., & Cotton, D. (2014). Tempo: Police interactions—A report towards improving interactions between police and people living with mental health problems. http://www.mentalhealthcommission.ca/English/document/36596/tempo-police-interactions-report-towards-improving-interactions-between-police-and-pe.

Commission for Public Complaints Against the RCMP. (2010). Policing persons with mental illness: Issues and trajectories. https://www.crcc-ccetp.gc.ca/en/archived-policing-persons-mental-illness-issues-and-trajectories.

Criminal Code. (1985). RSC 1985, c. C-46, as amended.

Department of Justice Canada. (n.d.). Projects funded by the Department of Justice Canada under the Family Violence Initiative (April 2008–March 2009). http://www.justice.gc.ca/eng/rp-pr/cj-jp/fv-vf/appro/a2008_09.html.

Department of Justice Canada. (2002). Child abuse: A fact sheet from the Department of Justice Canada. http://publications.gc.ca/collections/Collection/J2-295-2002E.pdf.

Department of Justice Canada. (2006). About family violence. http://www.justice.gc.ca/eng/cj-jp/fv-vf/about-apropos.html.

Department of Justice Canada. (2009). Abuse is wrong. http://justice.gc.ca/eng/rp-pr/cj-jp/fv-vf/aiw-mei/index.html.

Department of Justice Canada. (2010). Preliminary examination of so-called "honour killings" in Canada, section 9: Socio-cultural influences and honour killings. http://www.justice.gc.ca/eng/rp-pr/cj-jp/fv-vf/hk-ch/p5.html.

Department of Justice Canada. (2011). Family Violence Initiative. http://www.justice.gc.ca/eng/fund-fina/cj-jp/fv-vf.html.

Department of Justice Canada. (2012a). Abuse is wrong in any language. http://www.justice.gc.ca/eng/rp-pr/cj-jp/fv-vf/fe-fa/index.html.

Department of Justice Canada. (2012b). Best practices where there is family violence (criminal law perspective). http://www.justice.gc.ca/eng/rp-pr/cj-jp/fv-vf/bpfv-pevf/p6.html.

Department of Justice Canada. (2012c). Child abuse is wrong: What can I do? http://www.justice.gc.ca/eng/rp-pr/cj-jp/fv-vf/caw-mei/pdf/caw_2012.pdf.

Department of Justice Canada. (2013). Making the links in family violence cases: Collaboration among the family, child protection and criminal justice systems. http://www.justice.gc.ca/eng/rp-pr/cj-jp/fv-vf/mlfvc-elcvf/mlfvc-elcvf.pdf.

Department of Justice Canada. (2015a). About family violence. http://www.justice.gc.ca/eng/cj-jp/fv-vf/about-apropos.html.

Department of Justice Canada. (2015b). Family violence laws. http://www.justice.gc.ca/eng/cj-jp/fv-vf/laws-lois.html.

Department of Justice Canada. (2015c). Peace bonds fact sheet. http://www.justice.gc.ca/eng/cj-jp/victims-victimes/factsheets-fiches/peace-paix.html.

Doherty, D., & Berglund, D. (2008). *Psychological abuse: A discussion paper*. Public Health Agency of Canada. Catalogue no. HP20-12/2008E. http://www.phac-aspc.gc.ca/sfv-avf/sources/fv/fv-psych-abus/index-eng.php.

Fernando, M.L.D., & Kazarian, S.S. (1995, April). Patient education in the drug treatment of psychiatric disorders: Effect on compliance and outcome. *CNS Drugs, 3*, 291–304.

Friscolanti, M. (2016, March 3). Inside the Shafia killings that shocked a nation. *Maclean's*. http://www.macleans.ca.

Government of Newfoundland and Labrador Violence Prevention Initiative. (2015). Defining violence and abuse. http://www.gov.nl.ca/VPI/types/index.html.

Green, K. (1996). *Family violence in Aboriginal communities: An Aboriginal perspective—Information from the national clearinghouse on family violence*. Ottawa: Health Canada.

Harris, J. (2013). New terminology for mental retardation in DSM-5 and ICD-11. *Current Opinion in Psychiatry, 26*(3), 260–262.

I.F.X. (Re). (2002). [2000] CDD No. 166.

Justice Institute of British Columbia. (2007). *Empowerment of immigrant and refugee women who are victims of violence in their intimate relationships: Final report*. New Westminster, BC: Author.

Kazarian, S.S., & Joseph, L.W. (1994). A brief scale to help identify outpatients' level of need for community support services. *Hospital and Community Psychiatry, 45*, 935–937.

Kazarian, S.S., & Kazarian, L.Z. (1998). Cultural aspects of family violence. In S.S. Kazarian & D.R. Evans (Eds.), *Cultural clinical psychology: Theory, research and practice* (pp. 316–347). New York: Oxford University Press.

Latimer, J., & Lawrence, A. (2006). The review board systems in Canada: An overview of results from the mentally disordered accused data collection study. Department of Justice Canada. http://www.justice.gc.ca/eng/rp-pr/csj-sjc/jsp-sjp/rr06_1/rr06_1.pdf.

Law Commission of Canada. (2001). *Restoring dignity: Responding to child abuse in Canadian institutions*. Ottawa: Minister of Public Works and Government Services.

Levinthal, C.F. (1996). *Drugs, behavior, and modern society*. Needham Heights, MA: Allyn and Bacon.

Lucas, L. (2015, July 6). Changing the way police respond to mental illness. *CNN*. http://www.cnn.com/2015/07/06/health/police-mental-health-training/.

MedlinePlus. (n.d.). Psychotic disorders. US National Library of Medicine. https://www.medlineplus.gov/psychotic disorders.html.

Mental Health Act. (1990). RSO 1990, c. M.7. Amended by Bill 68 (Brian's Law) on June 23, 2000. Amended 2010 and 2015.

Mental Illness Awareness Week. (2010). Homelessness and mental illness. http://miaw.ca/en/mental-illness/what -is-mental-illness/homelessness.aspx.

Metcalfe, J. (2014). PLS on BC Corrections: Use of solitary confinement. West Coast Prison Justice Society. https://prisonjustice.org/2014/01/20/pls-on-bc -corrections-use-of-solitary-confinement.

Munro, K. (2001). Emotional abuse: The most common form of abuse. http://kalimunro.com/wp/articles-info/sexual -emotional-abuse/emotional-abuse-the-most-common -form-of-abuse.

National Institute of Justice. (2007). Causes and consequences of intimate partner violence. http://www.nij.gov/topics/ crime/intimate-partner-violence/pages/causes.aspx.

Office of the United Nations High Commissioner for Human Rights. (1991, December 17). Principles for the protection of persons with mental illness and the improvement of mental health care. http://www.ohchr.org/EN/Professional Interest/Pages/PersonsWithMentalIllness.aspx.

Okin, S.M. (Ed.). (1999). *Is multiculturalism bad for women?* Princeton, NJ: Princeton University Press.

Ontario Ministry of the Solicitor General. (2000, February). Police response to persons who are emotionally disturbed or have a mental illness or a development disability, section 29. *Policing Standards Manual.* Toronto: Queen's Printer for Ontario.

Pearson, C., Janz, T., & Ali, J. (2013). Mental and substance use disorders in Canada. http://www.statcan.gc.ca/pub/82 -624-x/2013001/article/11855-eng.htm.

Persad, E., & Kazarian, S.S. (1998, November). Physician satisfaction with review boards: The provincial psychiatric hospital perspective. *Canadian Journal of Psychiatry, 43*(9), 905–909.

Police Executive Research Forum. (1997). *The police response to people with mental illnesses.* Washington, DC: Author.

Protection Against Family Violence Act. (2000). RSA 2000, c. P-27.

Provincial Court Nova Scotia. (2014). *Nova Scotia Mental Health Court report: Celebrating 5 years.* http://www.courts .ns.ca/News_of_Courts/news_docs/NS_MHC_Report _2014.pdf.

Public Health Agency of Canada. (2011). *A report on mental illness in Canada.* http://www.phac-aspc.gc.ca/publicat/ miic-mmac/index-eng.php.

Public Health Agency of Canada. (2015a). Family violence: How big is the problem in Canada? http://www.phac -aspc.gc.ca/sfv-avf/info/fv-problem-eng.php.

Public Health Agency of Canada. (2015b). *Report from the Canadian Chronic Disease Surveillance System: Mental illness in Canada, 2015.* http://healthycanadians.gc.ca/ publications/diseases-conditions-maladies-affections/ mental-illness-2015-maladies-mentales/index-eng.php.

Public Services Foundation of Canada. (2015). *Crisis in correctional services: Overcrowding and inmates with mental health problems in provincial correctional facilities.* http://www.bcgeu.ca/sites/default/files/page/attachments/ Crisis in Correctional Services April 2015[2].pdf.

Roach, K., Berger, B.L., Cunliffe, E., & Stribopoulos, J. (2015). *Criminal law and procedure: Cases and materials* (11th ed.). Toronto: Emond Montgomery.

Sapers, H., & Zinger, I. (2012). Annual report of the Office of the Correctional Investigator 2011–2012. Ottawa: Correctional Investigator of Canada. http://www.oci-bec .gc.ca/cnt/rpt/annrpt/annrpt20112012-eng.aspx.

Statistics Canada. (2006). Measuring violence against women: Statistical trends 2006. Catalogue no. 85-570-XIE. http:// www.unece.org/fileadmin/DAM/stats/gender/vaw/ surveys/Canada/2006_Publication_VAW.pdf.

Statistics Canada. (2009). *Family violence in Canada: A statistical profile 2009.* Canadian Centre for Justice Statistics, Incident-Based Uniform Crime Reporting Survey. http://www.statcan .gc.ca/pub/85-224-x/2009000/t020-eng.htm.

Statistics Canada. (2010). Suicides and suicide rate, by sex and by age group. http://www.statcan.gc.ca/tables-tableaux/ sum-som/l01/cst01/hlth66a-eng.htm.

Statistics Canada. (2011). *Family violence in Canada: A statistical profile.* Catalogue no. 85-224-X. http://www.statcan.gc.ca/ pub/85-224-x/85-224-x2010000-eng.pdf.

Statistics Canada. (2015a). *Family violence in Canada: A statistical profile, 2013.* http://www.statcan.gc.ca/ pub/85-002-x/2014001/article/14114-eng.pdf.

Statistics Canada. (2015b). Mental health and contact with police in Canada, 2012. http://www.statcan.gc.ca/pub/ 85-002-x/2015001/article/14176-eng.htm.

Statistics Canada. (2015c). Suicides and suicide rate, by sex and by age group (both sexes no.). http://www.statcan.gc.ca/ tables-tableaux/sum-som/l01/cst01/hlth66a-eng.htm.

Statistics Canada. (2016, January 21). Family violence in Canada: A statistical profile, 2014. *Juristat.* http://www.statcan.gc.ca/ pub/85-002-x/2016001/article/14303-eng.htm.

Student Legal Services of Alberta. (2011). Domestic abuse. http://www.slsedmonton.com/userfiles/file/Domestic %20Abuse%202011-%20with%20icons.pdf.

Violanti, J.M. (1996). *Police suicide: Epidemic in blue.* Springfield, IL: Charles C. Thomas.

World Health Organization. (2003). Child sexual abuse. In *Guidelines for medico-legal care for victims of sexual violence.* http://www.who.int/violence_injury_prevention/ resources/publications/en/guidelines_chap7.pdf.

REVIEW QUESTIONS

True or False?

F **1.** Abuse of a parent by a child is not included in the definition of family violence.

T **2.** Psychological abuse may involve forced isolation from friends or family.

F **3.** In Canada, all forms of family violence are against the law.

T **4.** Substance abuse is often correlated with mental health issues.

F **5.** Psychosis occurs only in schizophrenia.

T **6.** Family violence tends to be kept secret in many cultures.

T **7.** It is a myth that substance abuse is the real cause of family violence.

F **8.** In responding to a person showing psychotic symptoms, police should use humour.

T **9.** Gay and lesbian victims of family violence sometimes feel ill at ease in mainstream shelters.

F **10.** People with mental illness are underrepresented in the correctional system.

Multiple Choice

1. Psychological abuse may involve
- **a.** humiliation
- **b.** sexual abuse of children
- **c.** withholding money to buy food
- **d.** discrediting a person's religious beliefs

2. Legal provisions to deter family violence are found in the
- **a.** Constitution
- **b.** *Highway Traffic Act*
- **c.** *Criminal Code*
- **d.** *Canadian Bill of Rights*

3. The symptoms of depression may include all of the following, except
- **a.** anhedonia
- **b.** headaches
- **c.** agitation and impulsivity
- **d.** psychotic symptoms

4. According to the social explanation, family violence is caused in part by
- **a.** substance abuse
- **b.** stress
- **c.** provocation by women
- **d.** lack of consequences for abusive behaviour

5. In the past, community supports for victims of family violence gave little thought to
- **a.** consequences under the *Canadian Bill of Rights*
- **b.** the financial implications of family violence
- **c.** the needs of diverse communities
- **d.** effective responses to family violence

6. The mediative approach to family violence involved which of the following assumptions?
- **a.** the victim wants the offender arrested
- **b.** a restraining order will be an effective intervention once the offender is released
- **c.** the offence may be culturally acceptable
- **d.** men and women should be equal

7. One police response to family violence is the pro-arrest policy, which involves
- **a.** leaving an arrest to the discretion of officers
- **b.** mandatory arrest
- **c.** encouraging mediation between the offender and victim
- **d.** a hands-off approach

8. *Mental illness* is a generic term for
- **a.** a variety of disorders
- **b.** a specific disorder
- **c.** issues relating to family violence
- **d.** the disorders of homeless people

9. *Formication* is a hallucination involving
- **a.** snakes and insects
- **b.** dead relatives
- **c.** hearing voices
- **d.** suicide

10. In responding to a depressed and suicidal person, police need to
- **a.** encourage the person to cheer up
- **b.** be empathic
- **c.** leave the person alone
- **d.** use physical restraint

Fill in the Blanks

1. Extreme emotional highs are a symptom of _Mania_.

2. Mistreatment at the hands of a common law partner in a relationship is considered to be _Physical_ abuse.

3. A _Gesture_ is the term for a self-destructive act with little or no death intent.

4. Men and women experience _similar_ levels of both violence and emotional abuse in their relationships.

5. Psychotic symptoms may be either _Hallucinations_ or _delusions_.

6. An accused person who is unable to communicate with counsel may be found _unfit to stand trial_

7. _Delusions_ are ideas that have no basis in reality and are a common symptom of psychosis.

8. In corrections, prolonged _Segregation_ can aggravate the symptoms of mental illness and cause psychological harm.

9. _Brian's Law (Ontario Mental Health Act)_ authorizes Ontario police officers to take a person into custody for mental health treatment under certain circumstances.

10. In responding to a manic person, police need to present the person with _options_ to choose from.

6 Diversity Competency in the Criminal Justice System

Officers from the Durham Regional Police Service ride in a specially decorated cruiser in the 2013 Toronto Pride Parade. The Pride cruiser is a yearly tradition for the DRPS, and it makes appearances at community events celebrating the LGBTQ community.

LEARNING OUTCOMES After completing this chapter, you should be able to: ■ Describe self-perceptions of police and community perceptions of police. ■ See how diversity can be both a challenge and a strategic advantage for police. ■ Describe some of the initiatives police services have taken to diversify the face of policing and to reach out to diverse communities. ■ Understand how police are increasing their diversity competency with all communities, including LGBTQ communities. ■ Identify the initiatives taken by police to ensure safe interventions for people with mental illness. ■ Understand the initiatives taken by corrections to accommodate the needs of diverse inmate populations.

Introduction

Police and the communities they serve have common goals. Both want safe, crime-free neighbourhoods and a good quality of life. A police officer whom the community views as an ally is more likely to be effective in policing communities; when people respect the police, they are more likely to assist them. In Canada's pluralistic, multicultural society, the communities served by law enforcement are very diverse. In the 2011 census, over 200 different ethnic origins were reported in Canada, from English (6,509,500 persons) to Gambian (595 persons) (Statistics Canada, 2006). Amid this diversity, police and police services have been rethinking how they can

- better represent the diverse ethnic backgrounds and diverse groups they serve;
- perform their jobs in a way that respects diversity;
- cultivate and maintain the resources—the confidence, openness, education, support, and cultural awareness—to serve their diverse communities effectively; and
- address issues of diversity in policing proactively (Durham Regional Police Service, 2010).

This chapter focuses on several related topics: perceptions of police in the community, the evolution of policing culture, the benefits and challenges of diversity for policing today, and the strategies, structures, and skills needed for policing with **diversity competency**—in other words, policing with an inclusive, responsive attitude to diversity. The chapter also discusses the initiatives taken by corrections to deal with diversity and mental illness in inmate populations.

diversity competency possessing the cultural knowledge and understanding to serve diverse communities effectively

Perceptions of Police

How well a free society administers justice is one measure of its health. Within the criminal justice system, the police are the only element that has a direct relationship with the community. What is the role of police in relation to the community? We can consider this question from two perspectives: the police's perception of themselves and the community's perception of the police.

Self-Perception of Police

The roots of policing stretch far back in time and began with a community-based focus. Sir Robert Peel set the precedent for public police services with his adage "the police are the public and the public are the police." Consider the first two of Peel's nine principles of policing, written in England in 1829:

1. The basic mission for which police exist is to prevent crime and disorder as an alternative to the repression of crime and disorder by military force and severity of legal punishment.
2. The ability of the police to perform their duties is dependent upon *public approval* of police existence, actions, behavior and the ability of the police to secure and maintain *public respect*. (Ottawa Police Service, n.d.)

Within the first hundred years of public policing, the role and identity of police forces strayed from Peel's principles and moved toward military-like enforcement of the law in order to meet the needs of the government. The Royal Canadian Mounted Police was started by Sir John A. Macdonald on the advice of the army, which recommended that a mounted force of riflemen be assigned to keep law and order in the North-West Territories in 1873. Originally named the North-West Mounted Police (later given its current name when it merged with the Dominion Police, who mainly patrolled further southeast), the RCMP quickly established a reputation for effective enforcement of the law. The famous saying "the Mounties always get their man" reflects their reputation.

The RCMP, besides having a proud heritage of law enforcement, was also very much used as an arm of the government to enforce its will. Less proud elements of the RCMP's history were the targeting of the Chinese community for deportations on suspicion of involvement in opium dens, the apprehension of Indigenous children for forced attendance at residential schools, strike-breaking in the period of labour unrest between the First and Second World Wars, and infiltrating political and ethnic groups considered to be a danger to the Canadian government, including the Communist Party of Canada in 1921. Similarly, as recently as 1981, the Toronto police were used to enforce laws against gay men in Toronto when they raided bath houses, an event for which the current chief Mark Saunders publicly apologized in 2016 (CBC News, 2016).

Police services in Canada have a tradition of paramilitary operations. The RCMP, for example, provided contingents in the Boer War and the First and Second World Wars. This reinforced police forces' image of themselves as military-like enforcers. All police services in Canada maintain a paramilitary structure with regard to rank, discipline, uniform, and many other elements of police culture. This is part of police identity and is not to be viewed as negative. Because we authorize police officers to use force, including deadly force, police services must have a discipline structure for accountability and a rank structure for decision-making. Because police are essential services, being part of a police service means voluntarily coming under the authority of provincial police services legislation. Officers cannot in each situation simply behave as they choose or take action as they see fit.

The paramilitary image of police agencies and their officers defined policing for a century. The identity and culture of policing often led to an "us versus them" mentality that at times labelled not just criminals but the community as "them." Many police agencies and their officers isolated themselves from the community and only interacted to enforce law and order. Policing is a vocation in which its members tend to overidentify with their role as police officers and underidentify with their roles outside of their work; they see policing not as what they do, but who they are. This would lead many police officers to interact less with their communities and more among themselves, which in turn would lead to increased isolation from the community. This was commonly referred to as the **police force approach**, which was often measured by

police force approach the approach to policing that emphasizes the crime-control, enforcement aspect of the job, on the assumption that police need to be hard on crime

- the number of patrols they carried out to deter criminal activity,
- their response rate to police calls, and
- their tally of arrests and convictions.

In the mid-1990s, the direction of policing turned back toward Peel's principles and truly embraced the concept that the police are the public and the public are the police. There was a recognition that police could only be effective with the support of the community. The change in identity was reflected in a change of name: many a "police force" began calling itself a "**police service**." (See Table 6.1.) The focus was now on building positive community relationships rather than alienating the community through exclusively confrontational enforcement. With this change, officer self-perceptions had to change as well.

police services
the name given to policing that emphasizes the helpful, supportive aspect of the role, with a focus on problem-solving, crime prevention, and partnership between police and communities

TABLE 6.1 Police Force Approach Versus Police Services Approach

Police Force	Police Services
Crime fighting	Crime preventing
Incident-driven	Problem-driven
Reactive	Proactive
Us versus them	Partner with community
Centralized	Decentralized
Hierarchical	Egalitarian
Diversity-blind	Diversity-sensitive
Inwardly focused	Outwardly focused

Many different community-based policing models were developed, such as problem-oriented policing (POP) and community-oriented policing services (COPS). Even hiring practices changed, with a strong emphasis placed on hiring young people who were already deeply involved in their communities, playing leadership roles in volunteer organizations.

Today, police services are also moving toward more autonomy in choosing how to serve their communities rather than following government directives. All police services are involved in community consultation processes to gauge the needs of the communities they serve and to work collaboratively with community members to address problems and create novel solutions that result in win–win solutions for all stakeholders. Today, police services are part of the community more than ever, and **community policing** is the norm with police services. (See Table 6.2.)

Consider a recent model, community mobilization, adopted by most police services across the country around 2010. It is defined as "a capacity-building process through which community individuals, groups, or organizations plan, carry out, and evaluate activities on a participatory and sustained basis to improve health and other needs, either on their own initiative or stimulated by others" (Howard-Grabman & Snetro, 2003, p. 3). In Figure 6.1, notice that only one-quarter of the wheel represents enforcement or roles strictly assigned to police agencies, but three-quarters is completely community-driven, including determining what level of police assistance is needed. For this model to work effectively, excellent relationships must be fostered between the police and the entire community, including all age groups, religious organizations, mental health providers, LGBTQ communities, and people of all income levels and service needs.

community policing
policing that is associated with the police services approach and with the mandate of policing for and with communities

TABLE 6.2 Principles of Community Policing

- Empowering police officers and supervisors to solve community issues without having to seek a stamp of approval from the police hierarchy.
- Actively listening, at all police levels, to community issues, concerns, and solutions.
- Providing needs-based police services determined by public input.
- Adopting a style of internal police management that is responsive to the recruitment of police with attributes and skills conducive to effective community-oriented policing.
- Applying a people-oriented philosophy to the organization of police services, to law interpretation, and to law enforcement.
- Communicating with citizens in languages they understand, including mandatory police acquisition of second languages for the purposes of communication and the minimization of conflict, doubt, and distrust.
- Selecting and training police officers to ensure that the best people are entrusted with the job of policing.
- Using police officers as effectively as possible with respect to the jobs and neighbourhoods to which they are assigned.
- Ensuring that the employees of a police service reflect the cultural diversity of the community served.
- Assigning officers to work with residents, schools, and community groups for the purpose of resolving community issues.
- Treating employees of police services fairly by fostering an environment within the ranks that is free of sexual harassment, discrimination, and bias.

SOURCE: Williams & Henderson (1997, pp. 219–220).

Community Perception of Police

Just as the police's self-image has changed over the years, so has the public's image of the police. Rather than avoiding contact with police or calling them only in an emergency, citizens and agencies are engaging with police; for example, community members may attend a "citizens' police academy" and agencies may involve police in their safety planning and intervention programs. A positive public image benefits police in several ways:

- it enhances self-respect and job satisfaction,
- it makes policing a safer profession,
- it increases the willingness of the public to voluntarily comply with laws as well as assist police in their investigations, and
- it makes police more effective in solving problems and combatting crime.

Most people in our society are satisfied with police most of the time. In the late 1990s, a survey in 11 Western industrial nations showed that satisfaction with police performance was highest in Canada. In fact, the study found that "Canadians love their cops far more than the English love their famed British Bobby" (Durkan, 1998, p. A9). In 2012, the Ontario Provincial Police Community Satisfaction Survey found that 95.8 percent of respondents felt safe or very safe in their community, and 92.4 percent were satisfied or very satisfied with the level of service offered by the OPP (Ontario Provincial Police, 2012).

FIGURE 6.1 Ontario's Mobilization & Engagement Model of Community Policing

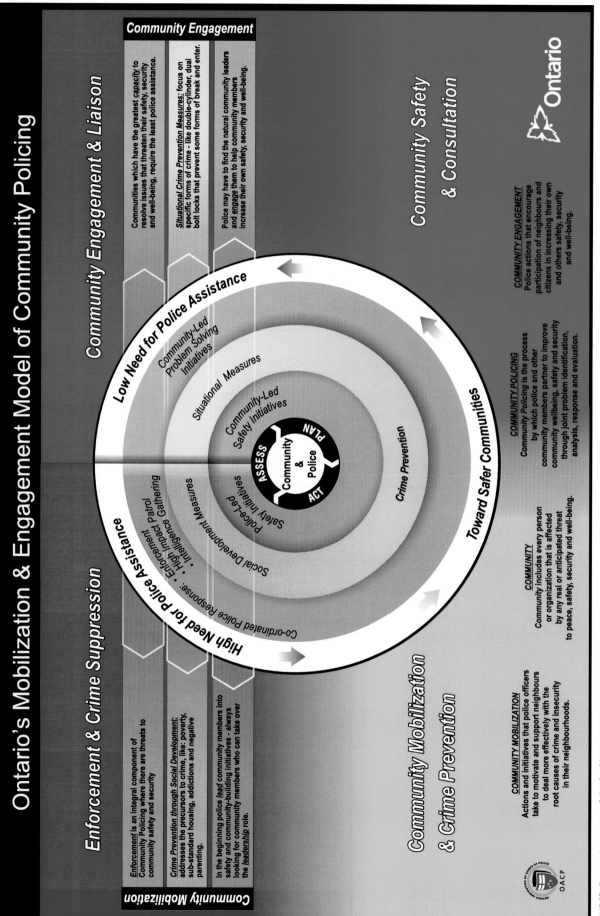

SOURCE: Ontario Association of Chiefs of Police (2015).

The General Social Survey of 2013 by Statistics Canada reports that policing in Canada has the highest level of public confidence, with 76 percent of Canadians reporting either some or a great level of confidence in the institution. Established and new immigrants showed more confidence in police than did non-immigrants. The school, banking, and judicial court systems ranked below police at 61 percent, 59 percent, and 57 percent respectively (Cotter, 2015). (See Figure 6.2.) The General Social Survey on Victimization in 2014 indicated that 73 percent of Canadians believed police were doing a good job at being approachable and easy to talk to, 70 percent believed that they promptly responded to calls, and 68 percent believed they treated people fairly. Perceptions of police performance were higher in Quebec and lowest in the Western provinces. Winnipeg and Vancouver rated lower among municipal services and Ottawa rated higher than average (Cotter, 2015).

A community's personal interactions with police officers will determine its perception of them. It is a circular process that can work for or against police. The police set the tone: if they show positive, helpful attitudes toward the people they serve, the community will view them favourably—and this public approval will, in turn, reinforce the positive attitude taken by police. (See Figure 6.3.) On the other hand, antagonistic encounters between police and community will generate negative perceptions on both sides. This reciprocal relationship is at the core of police–community relations (Coffey, 1990).

FIGURE 6.2   Confidence in Institutions, by Immigrant Status, 2013

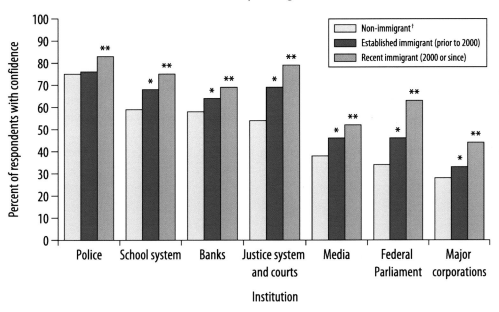

*   significantly different from reference category (p < 0.05)

**   significantly different from reference category (p < 0.05) and established immigrants (p < 0.05)

†   reference category

NOTE: Includes those who stated they had a great deal of confidence or some confidence. Responses of don't know/not stated are excluded from the calculation of percentages. Immigrants whose length of time in Canada is unknown are excluded.

SOURCE: Cotter (2015).

FIGURE 6.3   The Circular Process of Police–Community Interactions

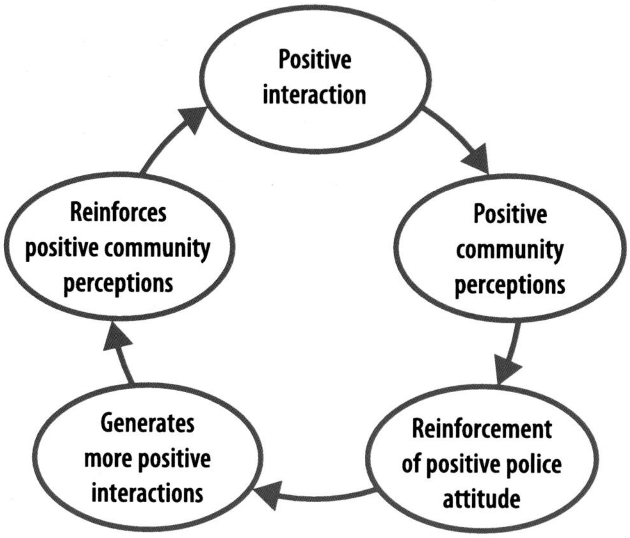

Negative Perceptions of Police

Certain kinds of police conduct are extremely damaging to the image of police in the community. People particularly object to rudeness and authoritarianism. Rudeness is one of the most common complaints. In fact, the Office of the Independent Police Review Director (OIPRD) (2014) states in its 2013–14 annual report that incivility is the most common complaint it receives about officers, and that this usually occurs in the context of a traffic stop. People object to **authoritarianism** from police—that is, "badge-heavy" conduct that insists on obedience. Such conduct is appropriate and necessary in certain situations, such as when police are confronted by violence or when they are interrogating a suspect, handling a crime scene, conducting an investigation, or resolving a domestic dispute. But if it appears too often or in situations where it is not called for, authoritarian conduct will prevent a strong police–community alliance. Most situations that police find themselves in are better served by cooperation and compromise. Visibility, accessibility, problem-solving ability, fairness, and openness to partnership—these are what communities want from police.

authoritarianism
policy of demanding
obedience to authority

EXERCISE 1

Visit the website of the Office of the Independent Police Review Director (OIPRD) at www.oiprd .on.ca. Under "Education & Resources," review the most recent annual report and consider the most common types of complaints. Then read some of the summaries of incident complaints; critically analyze the officers' behaviour as described in the summaries and look for commonalities in the incidents.

The general belief in Canada, therefore, is that *most* of the public is content with the service provided by police. But not *all* Canadians are content, since we see public advocacy groups such as Black Lives Matter openly criticize the treatment that minority groups receive from police and from the criminal justice system at large. The perception of unequal treatment must be examined, because perception is everything. It flavours interactions and defines relationships. In police interactions with all people, including those of diverse backgrounds, "justice

CLOSE-UP   Black Lives Matter

Black Lives Matter is an activist movement originating in the United States that campaigns against police's negative attitude toward Black people, which leads to racial profiling, unequal treatment, and police brutality. In the summer of 2014 the movement grew and became very active in the protests in Ferguson, Missouri after the shooting of Michael Brown by Ferguson police. The Toronto chapter of Black Lives Matter camped outside Toronto police headquarters on March 20, 2016 after the Ontario Special Investigations Unit (SIU) decided not to lay charges against the officer who fatally shot Andrew Loku, a Black man with mental health issues, at a disturbance at his apartment building the previous year (see the Close-Up: Andrew Loku box below). The protesters remained for over two weeks, demanding to meet with Ontario premier Kathleen Wynne and demanding changes to the police accountability processes. In response to the protest, some details of the SIU investigation were released, and the province has promised to review the SIU police accountability system. In a rare move, Premier Wynne met with protesters on the steps of the Ontario legislature on April 4, 2016 and promised to schedule future meetings to address their concerns.

must not only be done but it must be seen to be done." Are certain groups subjected to incivility and authoritarian treatment more than others? There is very little empirical research done in Canada on this issue, but statistics suggest that this is true.

In 2006, one of the more comprehensive studies that examined perceptions of police attitudes in Canada was conducted by University of Toronto researchers on behalf of the African Canadian Legal Clinic in Toronto (Wortley, 2006). The study was an exhaustive data review of Special Investigations Unit (SIU) reports. The Ontario SIU has a mandate to investigate all incidents in which police are involved that result in non-trivial injuries to civilians. The researchers also interviewed a panel of Black leaders in Toronto. In the portion of this study on perception it was found that 55 percent of Black Torontonians believe that police are more likely to use force against Black people than white people, and only 33 percent felt there was no difference. In contrast, only 26 percent of white Toronto residents believed that the police were more likely to use force against Black people than white people, and 61 percent of white people believe that there was no difference.

The review of the SIU reports found that both Black and Indigenous Canadians are over four times more likely than others to be an injured party in an SIU investigation. The difference is larger when the Greater Toronto Area (GTA) population alone is considered: statistics show that the Black population of the GTA is 6.7 percent, but Black involvement is 25.9 percent in SIU investigations and 50 percent in police shootings. The authors of the study had to investigate themselves to discover the race of the involved parties, because the SIU did not keep race-based statistics during the time frame of the study's data (2000 to 2006). Since the OIPRD also does not track race in its records of complaints statistics, it is difficult to quantify how many complaints are based on incivility of police toward members of different races or ethnic minorities.

The professional standards branch of the Toronto Police Service (TPS) does not keep or disclose complaint numbers based on the race of complainants when it creates data surrounding the internal police complaints system either, but it does record the number of complaints against the police service made to the Human Rights Tribunal of Ontario. The human rights complaint system records the reason for complaint, which may shed light on the identity of complainants and on the treatment of people of colour in Toronto. For example, the 2013 annual report of the TPS records that there were 25 human rights applications filed against the various branches of the TPS. Of those, 15 were based on race and 13 on colour (applications can list more than one basis for the alleged discrimination); the next highest, at 10, were complaints of discrimination against ethnic origin, followed by disability, ancestry, and place of origin at 7 each (Toronto Police Service, 2014).

Keeping race-based statistics on crime was a hotly contested debate in the late 1990s. It was in fact forbidden by the province of Ontario. At that time Julian Fantino, then head of Toronto's 31 division, released race-based crime statistics to the public. He reported on the Jane and

Finch area of Toronto, which was plagued by crime, noting that although the area's population at that time was only 6 percent Black, 82 percent of robberies, 55 percent of purse snatchings, and 51 percent of drug offences were committed by Blacks. The release of that information caused great controversy for the TPS, which denied that it collected race-based statistics, as well as for Fantino and the Black communities of Toronto. Fantino's reporting did not provide context for understanding the statistics and created a public backlash of racist sentiment. Subsequent investigations revealed that the Black community was subject to overpolicing and was targeted for investigations and arrests, and that Black people would often plead guilty due to poor representation in court (DiManno, 2015). Today, researching race-based complaints against police comes up against the same difficulty of accessing accurate information; race-based statistics are unavailable or not disclosed to the public.

Racial Profiling

One of the practices most damaging to relationships between police services or enforcement agencies and racialized groups is racial profiling. In racial profiling, certain racialized or ethnic groups are targeted for extra scrutiny in police stop and search practices, customs searches at airports and border crossings, police patrols, and undercover activities or sting operations. There is no better example of this than the "carding" or "street check" process, which has been under review by the Ontario Human Rights Commission (OHRC) since the early 2000s. Carding is "non-detention, non-arrest interactions between the Service and community members that involve the eliciting and/or recording of personal information" (Ontario Human Rights Commission, 2015a). Its purpose is intelligence gathering for investigative purposes, and both pedestrians and people in vehicles may be stopped. Racialized minorities in Toronto, Ottawa, and Montreal have long complained about the practice, asserting that their overrepresentation in this practice is a violation of their Charter rights against racial or ethnic discrimination. Although they represented only 8 percent of the population of Toronto between 2003 and 2008, 25 percent of the contact cards filled out by TPS officers over that time were for Black persons. Almost 80 percent of contact cards listed the reason for the stop as "general investigative purposes," which is permissible by law. The statistics are similar in major cities across the

CLOSE-UP   Andrew Loku

In July 2015, an unidentified officer of the Toronto Police Service fatally shot Andrew Loku after a brief confrontation. His death and the SIU's subsequent report, in which the watchdog declined to lay charges against the officer involved, catalyzed a controversy about the unequal treatment of Black people, especially those with mental health problems, and led to protests (see the Close-Up: Black Lives Matter box above).

Andrew Loku was a 45-year-old Black man originally from South Sudan. He arrived in Canada in 2004 as a refugee fleeing the civil war in his home country. In 2009, given his history of mental health issues, the Canadian Mental Health Association helped him find an apartment in a building that primarily housed people with mental illness.

According to the SIU report, just before midnight on July 5, 2015, two officers responded to a 911 call about a man wielding a hammer and threatening to kill someone. Mere moments after making contact with Loku, one officer shot him twice, killing him. The SIU report suggested that Loku had advanced upon the

officers with the hammer raised, and that the shooting was in response to the officer's fear for his own life. However, a civilian witness disputes that finding, saying that she was walking back to Loku's apartment with him when the officers arrived:

> We turned around, started to walk toward the female officer, and the male cop showed up and he was saying, "freeze." I just had a bad feeling come over me. I said, "Wait, wait a minute" and then—bang, bang. That was it. Andrew was finished.

After the SIU report was released, the organization Black Lives Matter held a protest in front of TPS headquarters in downtown Toronto, targeting especially the secrecy of the SIU process. In response, the province of Ontario announced that Justice Michael Tulloch, the first Black judge on the Ontario Court of Appeal, would head a review of the SIU system.

Sources: Warnica (2015); Ross (2016); Gallant (2016).

country, indicating that Black people are stopped by the police three to five times more frequently than whites (Ontario Human Rights Commission, 2013). The perception of racial profiling seems to be borne out by the statistics, and this unequal treatment damages relationships.

In 2015, the OHRC completed its recommendations and submission to the Ontario Ministry of Community Safety and Correctional Services regarding the draft regulations on carding and street checks (Ontario Human Rights Commission, 2015b). This report is based on the OHRC's years of community and law enforcement consultation and mediation. The OHRC considers that the proposed legislation does not restrict officer discretion sufficiently to eliminate racial discrimination on the carding process but will, however, reduce it. The draft regulation strictly prohibits the random and arbitrary collection of identifying information by police and establishes rules for interactions where identifying information is collected. These rules include the following:

- The officer must be able to articulate detailed reasons for the stop that ensure the stop is for gathering information about individuals known or reasonably suspected to be engaged in illegal activities and for inquiring into suspicious activity.
- Police officers must inform the individual that he or she is not required to remain in the presence of the officer and must explain why the information is being collected.
- Officers must provide a document that gives the officer's name and badge number; the date, time, and location of the stop; and the reason for the stop. The document must also tell the individual how to contact the OIPRD to file a complaint and how to access the information collected.

Police services will be required to provide training to officers on the new regulations and how to record details of these interactions as well as training in areas such as bias awareness, discrimination, and racism. This draft legislation is expected to be in place by September 2016. The new rules will be reviewed for their effectiveness with a view to improving the fairness of this practice and assessing its impact on the relationships between police and racialized minorities.

EXERCISE 2

Visit the Ontario Human Rights Commission website at www.ohrc.on.ca. Under "Our Work > Legal," choose a case related to police action (for example, *Phipps v. Toronto Police Services Board*). Critically analyze the case by considering the actions of the officers involved. How were their actions or behaviours discriminatory? What effect did their actions have on the offended party and the community? What could the officers have done to avoid discrimination of this sort?

Recruiting Diversity: Changing the Face of Policing

Returning to Peel's adage that "the police are the public and the public are the police," police services have attempted to recruit people of diversity so that their staffs better reflect the communities they serve. Canada has made progress in moving away from a male-dominated police culture, but a gender imbalance persists. In 2014, out of nearly 70,000 police officers 14,175 were women, which is about one in five (Statistics Canada, 2015). Police services in Canada continue to recruit women in order to overcome this gender imbalance by holding women-only recruitment sessions and by promoting the career in a way that appeals to both genders. Police services also have to overcome the perception that there is gender bias inside policing in order to attract women.

Some of the very public struggles that supported the perception of gender bias were the human rights complaints by female RCMP officers as well as the lawsuits that followed complaints of sexual harassment. In 2007, RCMP officer Janet Merlo filed a claim against the RCMP stating that the constant sexual harassment she faced at work caused her emotional distress, leaving her unable to continue in her career. After Merlo came forward, almost 400 female RCMP employees joined the case with similar complaints, making it a class action suit. The action asserts that sexual harassment and discrimination by many perpetrators has been rampant inside the RCMP for decades and that complaints to RCMP management are not taken seriously. In 2011, Corporal Catherine Galliford, an accomplished officer who had moved up the ranks of the RCMP, launched a lawsuit alleging she had been the victim of sexual harassment as far back as 1991, when she graduated from the RCMP academy. In 2016, former Inspector Linda Davidson came forward with similar allegations and has filed a lawsuit against the RCMP.

These complaints should not surprise the RCMP, since in the early to mid-1990s they conducted a regular member survey in which 60 percent of female members reported being victims of sexual harassment in the workplace. The RCMP put complaints processes in place and made immediate efforts to stop the behaviour, but in retrospect it seems these measures were insufficient.

In response to the flood of sexual harassment complaints, the RCMP conducted a public interest investigation. A commission was struck to investigate all internal complaints between February 2005, when the RCMP harassment policy was updated, and November 2011, when the public interest investigation began. The aim was to analyze all allegations of harassment, including those that were not of a sexual nature, and to place in context the sensational media coverage of some cases. The difficulty, of course, is that the commission could investigate only the complaints filed. It can be assumed that some incidents were not reported because the victims may have feared that filing a complaint would hinder their career, particularly if the perpetrator was a senior officer. The investigation determined that 44 percent of those initiating any type of harassment complaint were female and 49 percent were male. The overwhelming majority of complaints were of bullying, belittling, and demeaning behaviour; abuse of authority; and psychological abuse. Only 4 percent of complaints were sexual in nature, and 6 percent were based on disability or ethnicity. The report does not give a gender breakdown of the sexual harassment complaints. The commission sought statistics on complaints from other police services across the country to compare with the RCMP's record of complaints. Although direct comparisons were difficult due to differences in complaints procedures, it was clear that the RCMP was not alone in its struggle to combat harassment in the workplace.

The RCMP has since implemented new complaints processes and training programs and given new powers to its leadership to discipline or dismiss those who perpetrate sexual harassment in the workplace. Although these changes may be too late for some already embroiled in lawsuits, there is hope that they will make the RCMP a more gender-equitable place to work.

Other people of diversity—for example, Indigenous peoples (see Chapter 11) and members of minority immigrant groups—are also underrepresented in law enforcement. Law enforcement services themselves are not entirely to blame for this situation; it is at least partly due to the perception in some cultures that law enforcement is not an appropriate career choice. In some cases, immigrant families have had negative experiences with law enforcement in their countries of origin. And members of visible minority immigrant families may have the mistaken impression that *all* law enforcement agencies are pervaded by the "**white machismo culture**." Another factor is that immigrant communities sometimes know little about career opportunities in policing, or else they assign higher status to traditional professions—the legal or medical professions, for example—than they do to policing.

Some departments have been more successful in recruiting diversity to reflect the diversity of the communities they serve and some less so. A 2015 *Toronto Star* report compared the diversity

white machismo culture

a culture that values white skin colour, masculinity, and hierarchy while devaluing non-whites, women, and non-traditional sexual orientation statistics of the Toronto Police Service (TPS) and the Peel Regional Police Service. Although 60 percent of the population of the region of Peel were visible minorities or racialized persons, only 13 percent of the service's nearly 2,000 members were visible minorities. The TPS has been more successful in recruiting visible minorities: 24 percent minority representation of its members in a population in which 49 percent are visible minorities (Grewal, 2015). The TPS has actively recruited in diverse communities. A brief look at its website for June and July 2016 shows recruitment events at an Asian cultural centre as well as at the Pride Toronto Street Fair and the Caribbean Carnival Kickoff (Grewal, 2015). Other examples of directed recruitment target the Indigenous population, such as the Vancouver Police Service's Aboriginal Cadet Program, the Regina Police Service's Aboriginal/Diversity Summer Student Program, the RCMP's Indigenous pre-cadet program, and the OPP's PEACE program (Police Ethnic and Cultural Exchange) targeting Indigenous students who may have an interest in policing.

Simply recruiting will most likely enhance a law enforcement organization's ability to serve a diverse public, but such a result is neither guaranteed nor the final stage. The 2006 University of Toronto study mentioned above included comments from the panel of Black community representatives that warned of making this assumption. As one panellist said:

> Sometimes, when Blacks go into policing—of course, some of them can be coopted. They will act just like the White officers. Because if there's any evidence in the research that says there are Black officers, whether because of self protection, or career advancement, or just to get along with their White colleagues, whether they are just coopted, they often act similarly. I mean, the Black youth I interviewed, they had negative experiences with Black police officers as well as—as a matter of fact, they talk about the fact that sometimes the worst experience they ever had was with Black police because they are trying to prove they are a cop first. They want to look good to the White officers. (Wortley, 2006, p. 22)

Following the panel discussion, the following point was made: a marginal increase in the minority composition of a police service will most likely lead to those officers being absorbed into the existing culture of the police service rather than changing the culture. It is only when the minority composition is significantly increased that the culture changes, since the minority members can support one another and press for change (Wortley, 2006).

Minority groups in law enforcement often form associations to unite and support one another in their careers. One of the first such organizations was the International Association of Women Police (IAWP), founded in 1915 to support women in the criminal justice field and now with a presence in 60 countries. Ontario Women in Law Enforcement (OWLE) began in the early 1990s to encourage, promote, and advance women in all branches of law enforcement, including corrections, private security, and the Canadian Border Services.

In 1992, the Association of Black Law Enforcers (ABLE) was formed in Ontario as an offshoot of the American organization of the same name. It is open to members of all branches of law enforcement for membership and includes other racial minorities. Its goals and objectives are

- to build bridges between law enforcement agencies and the community at large
- to support the pursuit of post-secondary education for and to provide scholarship opportunities to racial minority youth
- to improve the image of law enforcement in the community
- to promote racial harmony and cultural pride within the law enforcement community
- to educate the community about and promote understanding of the law
- to encourage membership from among Black and Racial Minority Law Enforcers as well as persons and organizations who are interested in furthering A.B.L.E.'s objectives
- to provide information, support, counseling and professional advice to all members
- to promote professionalism among A.B.L.E.'s members (Association of Black Law Enforcers, n.d.b)

ABLE acknowledges the existence of racial profiling, and in its submissions to the Ontario Human Rights Commission and Ontario's Ministry of Community Safety and Correctional Services, it questions the validity and reliability of street checks. It strongly claims that racial profiling is the intended byproduct of street checks (Association of Black Law Enforcers, n.d.a). Its input on developing policies for equitable delivery of police services is very valuable.

Serving with Pride (SWP) is an Ontario-based organization formed in 2006, providing support and advocacy for the LGBTQ community in all branches of law enforcement as well as outreach to the LGBTQ community, and advising leaders in law enforcement on LGBTQ issues. Although all law enforcement branches, including correctional and border services, have long been perceived as homophobic, this is changing. Testimony from many gay and lesbian officers on the SWP website prove that they have positive relationships with their peers and supervisors and that their disclosure of their sexual preference has not had negative consequences. Many police services, including the TPS, as mentioned above, are actively recruiting from the LGBTQ community.

Table 6.3 provides an overview of diversity initiatives in policing.

TABLE 6.3   Diversity Initiatives in Policing

- Relaxing weight and height requirements for recruits
- Increasing recruitment of people of diversity (for example, women and those from diverse cultures and sexual orientations) and those with higher education
- Introduction of race relations training programs
- Introduction of cultural awareness training programs
- Introduction of diversity awareness training programs
- Implementation of anti-racism and anti–sexual harassment programs
- Improvement in communication between police and people of diversity
- Increased citizen participation in crime prevention initiatives
- Increased community involvement in review of police activity (for example, civilian review boards)
- Introduction of police, ethnic, and cultural exchange (PEACE) programs
- Creation of Indigenous policing programs to improve Indigenous–police relations and quality of policing services to Indigenous peoples
- Inclusion of courses on diversity issues in policing as part of police foundations programs

EXERCISE 3

Visit the websites of the organizations mentioned in this section:

- International Association of Women Police: www.iawp.org
- Ontario Women in Law Enforcement: www.owle.org
- Association of Black Law Enforcers: www.ableorg.ca
- Serving with Pride: www.servingwithpride.ca

Describe the work that each does and its achievements over the last several years.

Serving Diverse Communities

Police in Canada serve and protect a diverse public. In their day-to-day working lives, police officers will encounter individuals who vary widely from one another—and from the officers themselves—in terms of cultural background, language, gender, age, socio-economic class, religion, sexual orientation, physical and mental ability, and psychological well-being. In response to the increased diversity of Canada's population and to other national initiatives, police services across the country are increasingly adopting a diversity-oriented policing structure and function.

So far, we have discussed communities' perceptions, both positive and negative, of police and some other law enforcement agencies. We have discussed police services' recruiting diversity in order to reflect the communities they serve. Looking back to the community mobilization model (Figure 6.1), we see that perhaps the most important part of providing the best possible service to diverse communities is developing relationships based on cooperation and respect.

CLOSE-UP   Somali Liaison Unit

The community engagement and liaison section of the community mobilization model is very important, and there is an excellent example in the Somali Liaison Unit (SLU) of the Toronto Police Service. The unit formed in 2013 in response to poor community relationships, gun violence, and youth crime. The six officers of the unit are trained to a high degree of cultural competence with that community; they even take Somali language classes. Their role is to build relationships and to collaborate with the community in the resolution of community-identified problems; they have been very effective in achieving these goals. According to Superintendent Scott Baptist,

> The Somali community outreach project strives to achieve meaningful dialogue and build trusting relationships with Toronto's Somali-Canadian community through the provision of highly visible, proven and community-supportive policing services. And really, in a nutshell, that says it all.

As part of the outreach, SLU officers offer a variety of youth programming at local parks, schools, mosques, and community centres. They are also working on a youth police academy, intended to encourage Somali youth to consider the Toronto Police Service as a career option; about this, Baptist said:

> We have worked very diligently to enhance the TPS as a career opportunity within the Somali community. It's absolutely critical in policing that Toronto police represent the community it serves, and it is so vital that we get Somali representation, and that all of the skills and cultural knowledge from the Somali community be part of our organization.

Source: Reason (2014).

For any initiative, such as the Somali Liaison Unit, it is important to know the community, starting with the push and pull factors that brought them to Canada. Approximately 25,000 Somalis settled in Canada in the 1980s and 1990s, "pushed" out of their home country by violence and persecution. Somalia is a Third World country, so those who fled had few economic resources. After waiting two years or more for refugee status, they arrived in Canada and settled predominantly in Ottawa and Toronto. They then waited another two years before attaining permanent resident status. The refugees were mainly Muslim, between 20 and 40 years old, and practised their culture's traditional gender roles. Few of them spoke English fluently. These circumstances determine a very different set of needs for resettlement than those of, for example, a Chinese economic immigrant drawn to Canada by the "pull" factor of starting a business. The challenges and risks for each of these groups are very different and require different types of assistance from their police services.

The importance of understanding a group's culture and their needs cannot be overestimated. The experience gained from the Somali migration can be put to good use in assisting Canadian law enforcement agencies in developing knowledge, skills, and abilities to serve future immigrant and refugee groups, such as the wave of refugees from Syria who began arriving in 2015.

Most police services have resources or a specialized unit devoted to serving diversity in their jurisdictions, such as

- York Region's Diversity, Equity and Inclusion Bureau
- Vancouver's Diversity and Aboriginal Policing Section
- RCMP Cultural Diversity Advisory Committee
- Halifax Equity and Diversity Officer
- Peel Regional Police Diversity Relations Unit

Programs similar to the Somali Liaison Unit will be run out of these dedicated resource units and will take different shapes and serve different communities, depending on the makeup of their jurisdictions.

Specialized Units, Hate Crimes, and Radicalization

Often larger police services have a unit assigned to hate crimes. Recall the definition of hate crime presented in Chapter 2:

> A hate crime is an offence committed against a person or property, which is motivated, in whole or in part, by the suspect's hate, bias or prejudice towards an identifiable group based on, real or perceived, race, national or ethnic origin, language, colour, religion, sex, age, mental or physical disability, sexual orientation or any other similar factor. (Edmonton Police Service, n.d.)

Most police services have a similar definition. However, variations in the definition can affect how hate crimes are counted in different jurisdictions. Fifty-one percent of all hate crimes in Canada are directed at racial minorities, 28 percent at religious minorities, and 16 percent at LGBTQ people (Allen, 2015). We must remember that we can quantify only reports made to the police. In Toronto, the LGBTQ hotline run by The 519 community centre receives an exponentially higher volume of calls than there are assaults against LGBTQ people reported to police, which indicates that these crimes may be vastly underreported and therefore difficult to quantify (Quan, 2016). Hate crime is particularly damaging because it does not victimize just one person; it victimizes and instills fear in an entire community. Consider the June 2016 mass shooting at a gay nightclub in Orlando, Florida: the deadliest rampage by a single gunman in US history, leaving 49 dead and 53 injured. Imagine the fear experienced by the LGBTQ community in countries around the world as a result of that attack.

Investigating hate crimes that have already occurred is only one part of police's involvement. They also gather intelligence on groups that may be planning incidents of hate crime or other extremist activities. The Ontario Provincial Police has a dedicated Hate Crime/Extremism Unit (HCEU) that consists of a detective sergeant, a crime analyst, and four detective constables who divide their efforts between gathering intelligence, assisting front-line service members, and giving lectures and presentations to policing agencies. They collect, evaluate, analyze, and disseminate intelligence and maintain a database on activities that fall within their mandate. They also facilitate the exchange of information with other agencies including the RCMP, municipal and regional police services, the Canadian Security Intelligence Service (CSIS), and government agencies. There are also numerous joint forces across the country, made up of officers seconded from various law enforcement services, with similar mandates.

Although any offence may be considered a hate crime if it is caused in whole or in part by hatred or bias against a specific group, there are sections of the *Criminal Code* that pertain particularly to hate crimes:

- section 318: advocating or promoting genocide
- section 319: public incitement and wilful promotion of hatred
- section 430(4.1): mischief to religious property

There are provisions in the *Criminal Code* to increase the sentences of offenders convicted of hate crimes in Canada. If the offence is motivated by hate and prosecuted as such, following a conviction the judge must treat hate as an aggravating factor and increase the sentence accordingly.

Another area where police are involved in intelligence gathering and prevention initiatives is in efforts to stop the recruitment of Canadian youth to radicalized terrorist organizations such as ISIS. In 2012, Canadian-born Andre Poulin of Timmins, Ontario left Canada to fight with ISIS in Syria. He had converted to Islam and went by the name Abu Muslim. Poulin was involved in making a recruitment video for ISIS aimed at Canadian youth before he was killed in battle in the summer of 2013. His death was filmed and used by ISIS in the recruitment video. Poulin was involved in recruiting five young Muslim men from the Toronto area to go to Syria, but four of these were stopped by family members before they reached Syria (Baksh & Arsenault, 2015). This is not the first incident of such recruitment. Three high school friends from London, Ontario—Ali Medlej, Xristos Katsiroubas, and Aaron Yoon—became Islamist terrorists. Two died in Algeria in a terrorist attack on a gas plant in 2013 that left 37 hostages dead. Like Andre Poulin, two of these teenagers were not from Muslim families (Humphreys, Bell, Keidan, & Blackwell, 2013). This serves as a reminder of the danger of making assumptions that connect race or ethnicity to the risk of terrorism.

ISIS has been successful in recruiting young women to travel to Syria as well. In 2014, a 23-year-old woman from Edmonton, born to a moderate Muslim family, left for Syria to join ISIS. CSIS had approached the family with concerns over her online social networking activity, but the family was not aware of the extent of the threat to their daughter (Clancy, 2015). In 2015, three Canadian girls aged 15, 18, and 19 were tracked by the RCMP to Cairo, where they were intercepted before they could board a plane to Syria (Bell, 2015).

The Standing Senate Committee on National Security and Defence produced a 2015 report entitled *Countering the Terrorist Threat in Canada: An Interim Report*. The committee reported that 93 Canadians had been identified by CSIS as seeking to join Islamist extremist groups such as ISIS, Al Qaeda, and Boko Haram. Eighty radicalized Canadians had been identified as participating in terrorist activity overseas and later returning to Canada; it is estimated that 145 Canadians are abroad providing support to terrorist organizations (Standing Senate Committee on National Security and Defence, 2015, p. iii). Although more recent threats come from organizations based in Iraq and Syria, the majority of CSIS files deal with extreme right-wing organizations such as neo-Nazis and white supremacists. The Canadian Network for Research on Terrorism, Security and Society defines right-wing extremism as encompassing "a large, loose, heterogeneous collection of groups and individuals espousing a wide range of grievances and positions, including: anti-government/individual sovereignty, racism, fascism, white supremacy/white nationalism, anti-Semitism, nativism/anti-immigration, anti-globalization/anti-free trade, anti-abortion, homophobia, anti-taxation, and pro-militia/pro-gun rights stances" (Parent & Ellis, 2014).

A comprehensive three-year study led by researchers at Simon Fraser University in BC suggests that more than 100 white supremacist organizations are operating in Canada. The membership of these groups ranges from three to a dozen or more. They feed off Internet-proliferated ideologies of racial supremacy and hate and spread anti-authority messages. Police agencies monitor these groups closely and CSIS also keeps files on their operations. They appear to be disorganized; they pose threats of public disorder and violence but not threats to national security (Perry & Scrivens, 2016). Canadian Paul Fromm is probably the most infamous representative of this movement. He has ties to the Ku Klux Klan in the United States and has run for political office in Mississauga, Ontario. He was a teacher with the Peel Region school board until he was dismissed after his speeches at white supremacist rallies came to light (Southern Poverty Law Center, n.d.).

The Standing Senate Committee on National Security and Defence made a total of 25 recommendations. Some of those recommendations are as follows:

- The government should work to establish a program that provides information about clear and specific indicators of radicalization to front-line workers including teachers, police officers, prison workers, nurses, and doctors.
- The government should establish a program to support families who report radicalization and are seeking help.
- The government should work with Muslim communities to create an effective counter-narrative to denounce the ideology of fundamentalism (Standing Senate Committee on National Security and Defence, 2015, pp. vi–viii).

The committee heard from police that the stigmatization of families as terrorist threats was counterproductive to their investigative efforts. Police report that they need the trust of community members to do outreach in the "pre-criminal space" in which individuals connect through social media to view extremist propaganda and seek out extremist teachings but have yet to act on the ideologies. The TPS reported to the committee that 600 of its officers had received training on recognizing indicators of radicalization so that front-line officers can report these signs that they may encounter in communities (Standing Senate Committee on National Security and Defence, 2015, p. 5).

The RCMP launched its Countering Violent Extremism program in the winter of 2015. The first phase is concentrated on training the service's front-line providers to recognize people at risk of radicalization; the second is building community capacity so that when they find someone at risk or in the process of radicalization, a "community hub" can be assembled, made up of mentors, psychologists, religious leaders, and others who can help the individual to de-radicalize and to assist the family (Robertson, 2014).

Representatives of Correctional Service Canada (CSC) also spoke to the committee regarding their experience of radicalization in custody. CSC had been advised by its European Union counterparts that custody facilities had been sites of recruitment and radicalization. CSC confirmed that Islam is the fastest-growing religion of choice for inmates (Standing Senate Committee on National Security and Defence, 2015, p. 8). The CBC reported in 2015 that Mohammed Shafia, whom you learned about in Chapter 5, appeared to have become radicalized, was leading prayers while in custody, and had a significant number of faithful followers (CBC News, 2015). The Shafia murder case itself is an example of how training in detecting signs of radicalism and risks to safety is lacking in front-line services, as the Shafia family had come to the attention of both the school board and child protection services in the months leading up to the murders.

As a proactive initiative, CSC hosted an international roundtable and symposium in December 2015 that brought together correctional services from countries such as France, the United Kingdom, New Zealand, Spain, and the Netherlands to discuss the risks of radicalization in prison populations. CSC is working on a more comprehensive plan to prevent radicalization in prison populations.

Cross-Cultural Criminal Investigations

Efforts to bring diversity training to community policing are also based on the importance of diversity factors in cross-cultural criminal investigations. For such investigations to be successful, police must have

- an understanding of diversity as a factor in crime;
- personnel from diverse communities who can interact with and gain the confidence of these communities and their leaders and thereby secure critical information for the investigation; and

- policies that require investigators or cultural experts to work with leaders of communities that are likely to be affected by an investigation (Perry, 2004).

An underlying assumption of cross-cultural criminal investigations is that if police engage in open and honest dialogue with community leaders, identify problems specific to the leaders' particular culture, and involve these leaders in the investigative process, they will not only have a successful investigation but also establish strong, long-lasting relationships with the community.

Policing People with Mental Illness

Dealing with people with mental illness is a common experience for police officers in contemporary policing in Canada. As you learned in Chapter 5, people with mental illnesses are more likely than others to have interactions with the police. Police officers encounter people with mental illnesses under numerous circumstances including

- Attending persons experiencing mental health crises, including apprehensions under the *Mental Health Act*;
- Calls in which the public is concerned about the behaviour of a person who may not have actually done anything wrong or illegal but is making people uncomfortable;
- Situations in which the [person with mental illness] has been victimized by crime or social disorder;
- Incidents in which a call is received by police for any reason—a crime in progress perhaps—and it turns out that the person involved is displaying signs of mental illness;
- Incidents in which the [person with mental illness] might be taken into custody for his/her own protection;
- Social contacts (those situations in which mentally ill people with little in the way of social or community support come to rely on the police or the 911 line as "friends"). (Cotton & Coleman, 2008, p. 2)

To interact adaptively with people with mental illnesses, police officers require the necessary skills and knowledge, which they acquire through education and training at the police academy, training centre, or college they attended. This is referred to as basic level training, also commonly known as recruit or cadet training. A systematic review of the training material of different police colleges and academies in Canada by Cotton and Coleman (2008, p. 15) indicated that all police academies provided education about mental illness at the basic training level; however, the curriculum varied significantly in terms of the content and delivery of the information. Despite variations, programs addressed

- verbal strategies,
- assessing suicidal intent,
- signs and symptoms of mental illnesses,
- mental health law, and
- use-of-force options.

In addition to the basic training, police organizations support the skills and knowledge of police personnel through ongoing in-service training. The Canadian Association of Chiefs of Police has formulated the *Contemporary Policing Guidelines for Working with the Mental Health System* (Coleman & Cotton, 2010). These guidelines provide policies and processes that can inform and support the work of individual police officers who encounter people with mental illness. As with basic level training, police agencies vary in the education and in-service training they provide to their officers. Despite these variations, the consensus is that appropriate education and training will result in more positive outcomes in interactions between police and people with mental illness. Therefore, according to Coleman and Cotton (2010, p. 8), the focus of in-service training should include

- more client-focused intervention,
- decreased use of force,
- more effective and efficient linkages with the mental health system when appropriate or desired, and
- a reduction of stigma.

The Ontario Police College now offers mental health training to new recruits. Many police jurisdictions have adopted some type of mental health crisis response service based on the crisis intervention team model, which is regarded as a best practice in responding to mentally ill people (Watson & Fulambarker, 2012). Police officers are trained to recognize the signs and behaviours of mental illnesses that can help mitigate negative interactions and de-escalate intense situations.

The new mobile crisis response or mental health intervention teams in many police services should accomplish most of the goals described above. When such a team attends a call, many people in crisis with a mental health issue will respond better to the mental health worker than to the officer on the team. These teams not only respond to calls but also make "house calls" as follow-up for people who have been in crisis or to people who they have reason to believe are headed for crisis (Bennett, 2015).

The British Columbia Division of the Canadian Mental Health Association (2005) has identified several programs, developed through a collaboration between police and mental health service providers, for helping people with mental health crises. These programs include

- mobile teams of police and mental health professionals;
- police "reception centres," where police can take a person who shows signs of mental illness for further assessment and referral;
- "crisis intervention teams" within each police catchment area to respond to mental health crises;
- joint protocols between police and the local mental health centre;
- ongoing mental health awareness training for all officers and specialized crisis-intervention skills training for specialized officers; and
- an information system that tracks crisis interventions and outcomes and trains dispatchers to recognize and address mental health issues.

Policing and LGBTQ Communities

Police services in Canada have taken various steps to improve relationships with LGBTQ communities, which historically have been marked by prejudice, discrimination, and harassment. These steps include but are not limited to (1) developing inclusive hiring practices for LGBTQ police personnel; (2) creating LGBTQ liaison committees; (3) sensitivity training for police personnel; and (4) developing policies and procedures to address the lived realities of members of the community (Ontario Association of Chiefs of Police, 2013, p. 6).

The Ontario Association of Chiefs of Police developed a best practices manual and recommended that police services consider the Self-Audit Checklist (see Table 6.4) in their initiatives to improve relationships with LGBTQ communities and workplace culture for LGBTQ police personnel. Some of the key elements of this checklist include developing language that reflects equity, targeted hiring, support for LGBTQ police officers, and continuous engagement of the local LGBTQ community through development of liaison committees and seeking their consultation in developing sensitivity training for police officers.

TABLE 6.4   The Self-Audit Checklist

(1) What Terminology Should Be Used?

- Consider developing a guidebook for fair and equitable language after consulting broadly with local LGBTQ community organizations and the Ontario Human Rights Commission.

(2) Community Engagement

- Consider creating an LGBTQ liaison committee in consultation with local LGBTQ community organizations.
- If your police service already has an LGBTQ liaison committee, consider consulting with local LGBTQ community organizations for feedback about how to improve the relationship with members of the community.
- Consider reviewing and revising the structure of your liaison committee to ensure that it has the power to bring about concrete policy and procedural changes within the organization.

(3) Recruitment and Retention of LGBTQ Police Personnel

- Consider developing a strategy to recruit LGBTQ police personnel. If your police service already has a strategy to recruit LGBTQ police personnel, consider evaluating its effectiveness.
- If your police service has not already done so, consider developing a strategy to retain LGBTQ police personnel. If your police service already has a strategy to retain LGBTQ police personnel, consider evaluating its effectiveness.

(4) Internal Support for LGBTQ Police Personnel

- Consider proactively developing a strategy to combat homophobia and transphobia in the workplace.
- Consider supporting the creation of an Internal Support Network (ISN) for LGBTQ-identified police personnel. Particularly, if your police service is a small one, consider inviting LGBTQ "allies" (those who do not identify as LGBTQ themselves, but support workplace inclusion) to join the ISN.
- If your police service already has an ISN, consider evaluating its effectiveness.
- Consider proactively developing policies and training programs that foster inclusion in the workplace for transgender and transsexual police personnel.
- Consider developing a policy to facilitate transitioning in the workplace for transgender and transsexual police personnel.

(5) Training

- Consider developing and implementing LGBTQ inclusivity training after consulting with local LGBTQ community organizations.
- Consider inviting LGBTQ community organizations to deliver LGBTQ inclusivity-training sessions on specific topics, such as hate crimes or transgender and transsexual policing issues.
- If your police service already has LGBTQ inclusivity training in place, consider consulting with local LGBTQ community organizations for feedback about how to improve it.
- If your police service already has LGBTQ inclusivity training in place, consider regularly reviewing legislation and case law to ensure that the material is accurate and up-to-date.

(6) Selected Topics

Hate Crimes

- Consider developing an anti-LGBTQ hate crime campaign that encourages members of LGBTQ communities to report hate-motivated violence to the police.
- Consider partnering with local LGBTQ community organizations to ensure that local issues related to LGBTQ hate crimes are appropriately addressed.
- Consider partnering with LGBTQ community organizations to deliver training about how to effectively respond to LGBTQ-motivated violence.

Youth Bullying

- Consider proactively addressing issues related to LGBTQ youth bullying in places such as schools and community centres.
- Consider developing anti-bullying campaigns using social media sites such as Twitter, Facebook, and YouTube to help promote the campaign.
- Consult with LGBTQ community organizations to empower youth to develop training related to policing and bullying.
- Consider working with school liaison officers to ensure that they have the skills necessary to support LGBTQ-identified youth in schools.

HIV Non-Disclosure

- Consider engaging in a dialogue with community organizations in order to develop practices including:
  - (1) training for police about HIV transmission and the realities of living with HIV today
  - (2) guidelines for police handling matters of alleged HIV (and possibly other sexually transmitted infections) non-disclosure.

Sexual Assault

- Consider working with LGBTQ community organizations (including shelters and counseling providers) to ensure that police personnel have the skills necessary to support LGBTQ-identified individuals who have experienced sexual assault.
- Consider creating a sexual assault awareness and survivors guide detailing the process of a sexual assault investigation, as well as police policies and procedures for investigating sexual assaults experienced by members of LGBTQ communities.

Age of Consent

- Consider developing training about section 159 of the *Criminal Code*, which has been struck down in five provinces, including Ontario.

Intimate Partner Violence (Domestic Violence)

- Consider working with LGBTQ community organizations (including shelters and counseling providers) to ensure that police personnel have the skills necessary to support LGBTQ-identified individuals who have experienced intimate partner violence.
- Consider creating an awareness campaign or publication that highlights the issues of intimate partner violence, including how police personnel investigate it.

Women's Only Spaces

- Consider developing a "Police Attendance at Locations Occupied Solely by Women in a State of Partial or Complete Undress" policy in consultation with local community organizations.
- Consider developing a training program to ensure that all police officers within the service are aware of the policy.

Sex Work

- Consider developing a policy and/or guidelines on policing and sex work in consultation with local community organizations, those that understand the lived experiences of sex workers.
- Consider developing a training program to ensure that all police officers within the service are aware of the policy and/or guidelines.

Strip Searches
- Consider developing a policy on transgender and transsexual strip searches.
- Consider developing a training program to ensure that all police officers within the service are aware of the policy.

Safe Lodging
- Consider developing a policy used to determine where to safely lodge transgender and transsexual detainees and to ensure that they have access to gender-affirming healthcare, such as prescribed hormones.
- Consider developing a training program to ensure that all police officers within the service are aware of the policy.

Recordkeeping and Statistics
- Consider developing a recordkeeping policy on LGBTQ-related issues, including hate-motivated incidents, transgender and transsexual detention and searches, and attendance in "women's only" spaces.
- Consider developing a training program to ensure that all police officers within the service are aware of the policy.

(7) Measurement and Accountability
- Consider clearly articulating SMART (Specific, Measurable, Actionable, Realistic and Timelined) human rights organizational change goals and desired outcomes at the start of the project (in other words, defining what success looks like).
- Consider developing and agreeing upon appropriate performance measures (including outcome measures).
- Consider regularly evaluating and assessing the impact of human rights organizational change efforts, and revising and updating strategies and action plans in light of incoming information.
- Consider partnering with academics or other better-resourced police organizations to conduct evaluations.
- If human rights organizational change begins as a time-limited project, consider making sure there is post project evaluation and follow-up to establish and guide more enduring human rights processes and systems.
- Consider tying data collection, analysis, and reporting to a specific human rights goal.

SOURCE: Ontario Association of Chiefs of Police (2013).

In relation to the detention of transgender persons, the best practices manual recommends that cell-area supervisors consider three questions:

- What facility would provide the safest environment for the transgender detainee—male or female cell-block areas?
- What is the detainee's general appearance; as what gender does the detainee live and identify?
- What is the physiology of the detainee? (Ontario Association of Chiefs of Police, 2013, p. 65)

The manual also suggests that the transgender person be respectfully asked where they would be most comfortably lodged, which seems to be common sense. Their request can be accommodated as long as there are no safety concerns. This is more easily accomplished for police because they will have custody of an arrested person for less than 24 hours.

The same reasoning is also recommended for searches. If a pre-detention search or a strip search is necessary and if officers of both genders are immediately available, the transgender person can be respectfully asked if they would prefer a female or male officer to conduct the search.

Diversity Initiatives in Corrections

Ethnic Minorities

As with the Canadian population as a whole, the Canadian prison population is also becoming increasingly diverse. Visible minorities made up 18 percent of the total federal inmate population in 2011–12, which is consistent with their proportion in the general population (about 19 percent in 2011) (Office of the Correctional Investigator, 2013). The proportion of Black inmates is increasing at a much faster rate than that of other visible minority groups. They increased by 75 percent from 2002–3 (767 inmates) to 2011–12 (1,340 inmates). Black inmates accounted for 6.1 percent of the total federal prison population in 2002–3 and 9.3 percent in 2011–12 (see Figure 6.4).

To better address the needs of ethnoculturally diverse inmates, the CSC has created an Ethnocultural Services section at its national headquarters supported by regional managers and ethnocultural coordinators within institutions. It also established national and regional Ethnocultural Advisory Committees to better identify and manage the needs and cultural interests of a diverse inmate population. Other CSC initiatives include cultural programs and awareness activities; sensitivity and diversity training for staff; and initiatives to increase the representation of visible minority groups on its staff, such as targeted hiring campaigns, a Diversity and Employment Equity Committee, and mentorship and leadership programs (Office of the Correctional Investigator, 2013). Despite these efforts, the CSC continues to face challenges in accommodating the diverse needs of visible minority groups.

Mentally Ill Inmates

Since 2008, the number of inmates with mental health and addiction-related issues has grown significantly in both provincial and federal prisons (Public Services Foundation of Canada, 2015). Recall from Chapter 5 that people with mental illness are generally overrepresented in the correctional system.

FIGURE 6.4 Ten-Year Federal Inmate Population Trends

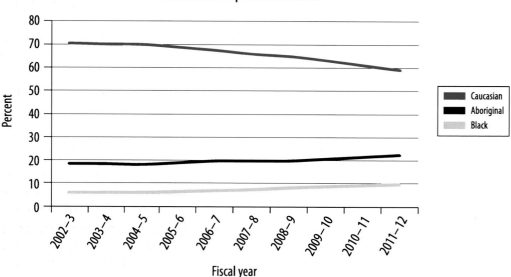

SOURCE: Office of the Correctional Investigator (2013).

CLOSE-UP   Ashley Smith

Nineteen-year-old Ashley Smith died in October 2007 in a segregation unit at the Grand Valley Institution for Women in Kitchener, Ontario by self-induced strangulation while on suicide watch. Smith was suffering from various forms of mental illness, which exhibited in behaviour that was difficult to manage, including self-harm. An inquest followed her death and a jury released its findings in 2013 containing much criticism of CSC's treatment of Smith in particular, and also concerns over the treatment of mentally ill inmates generally. CSC is now trying to incorporate into its system the jury's 105 recommendations. This case brought the issues of mental health in custody to the attention of the Canadian public and is a catalyst for change in the corrections system.

In 2010 the CSC identified addressing mental health needs in the population under its care as one of its top five priorities. It uses the term *mental health care* to mean "the care of a disorder of thought, mood, perception, orientation or memory that significantly impairs judgement, behaviour, the capacity to recognize reality or the ability to meet the ordinary demands of life" (Office of the Correctional Investigator, 2015, p. 13). The CSC faces the challenge not only of mental illness but also that two-thirds of its population in 2014 had addiction issues (Correctional Service Canada, 2014b). Its mental health and addictions services are for not only the approximately 15,000 offenders in custody but also the 7,700 offenders under supervision in the community (Correctional Service Canada, 2014b).

The Office of the Correctional Investigator 2014–2015 report indicates the prevalence of types of mental illness among the male population (Office of the Correctional Investigator, 2015, p. 12):

- mood disorders: 16.9 percent
- primary psychotic disorders: 3.3 percent
- alcohol or substance-use disorders: 49.6 percent
- anxiety disorders: 29.5 percent
- pathological gambling: 5.9 percent
- borderline personality disorder: 15.9 percent
- anti-social personality disorder: 44.1 percent

All of these rates are much higher than in Canada's general population, of whom one in five will suffer from a mental illness at some point during their lifetime. In fact, this report asserts that federal prisons in Canada house some of the largest concentrations of people with mental illnesses in the country. In response, the CSC planned in March 2015 to increase the total number of "mental health beds" to 778, including 150 psychiatric beds for acute levels of care and 628 beds for intermediate-level care (Office of the Correctional Investigator, 2015, p. 14). The increased costs were offset by eliminating 500 acute psychiatric treatment beds because the need for intermediate-level care was more pressing. The new distribution reflects more accurately the needs of the population based on the prevalence data commissioned by CSC in 2013 (Office of the Correctional Investigator, 2015, p. 14).

As part of its Mental Health Initiative, CSC aims to have offenders assessed for mental health at least four times within the first 14 days of incarceration, with the first assessment within 24 hours of admission. As in all illnesses, different levels of care are required. Those inmates assessed with less severe mental health needs can receive treatment within the primary penitentiary where they are assigned. This treatment includes counselling and support through nurses and psychologists. Inmates with higher needs may require intermediate care if they are unable to cope within the institution (Office of the Correctional Investigator, 2015). This intermediate care is not available in all institutions, but after recent pilot projects, the goal is to have this level of care widely available soon. The structured living environments in the five minimum- and medium-security women's institutes are an example of this care. For those with acute needs such as psychosis, there are regional treatment centres that act as both penitentiaries and psychiatric institutions. These cases are rare, since most offenders have medium or low levels of mental health needs (Correctional Service Canada, 2013).

When an offender is released into the community on a conditional release or warrant expiry, the CSC assesses his or her mental health and offers mental health supports through the Community Mental Health Initiative. The CSC has found that offenders receiving this kind of support have a 34 percent lower risk of suspension of conditional release and a 59 percent lower risk of revocation of parole than a control group receiving no such support (Dupuis, MacKay, & Nicol, 2013).

CSC also offers a variety of treatment programs for substance abuse. Again, there are streams for different levels of needs. High-intensity programs consist of 89 two-hour sessions intermixed with some individual sessions with addictions counsellors. The offenders learn new skills to cope with stress without using drugs or alcohol. Research shows that men who complete these programs are less likely to reoffend. Moderate intensity programs consist of 26 group sessions and one individual session. There is a pre-release program to prepare the offender closer to the time of release, as well as a substance-abuse maintenance program (Correctional Service Canada, 2014a).

CSC's mental health strategy (see Figure 6.5) is supplemented by providing mental health awareness training to case management staff, health care nurses, and correctional officers. Correctional officers have regular contact with inmates and they can build relationships and identify signs and symptoms of problematic behaviour. It is imperative that correctional officers are provided with various tools to understand the complex behaviour of mentally ill inmates such as aggression, violence, self-harm (for example, head-banging, self-mutilation, use of ligatures), and suicide. The training equips correctional workers in identifying and managing these behaviours. Dvoskin and Spiers (2004) advocate and foster the role of correctional staff as therapeutic agents. They outline four ways in which correctional officers can participate in the treatment of mental health of inmates:

- counselling and psychotherapy—talking with inmates;
- consultation—talking about inmates;
- special housing, activities, and behavioural programs; and
- medication.

FIGURE 6.5   CSC's Mental Health Strategy

Intake	Throughout incarceration	Pre-release	Community supervision	WED
Mental health screening and assessment for timely identification of mental health needs	Primary and intermediate mental health services in regular institutions. Treatment centre admissions for offenders with severe acute mental health needs	Clinical discharge planning to prepare offenders with mental health needs for their return to the community	Enhanced mental health support and linkages to partner agencies to prepare for transfer of care at WED	Transfer of care to provincial/territorial health services

NOTE: WED stands for warrant expiry date, meaning the date a criminal sentence officially ends.

SOURCE: Correctional Service Canada (2012).

CHAPTER SUMMARY

While diversity was once considered purely a challenge for police, it is now seen as offering benefits and strategic advantages for policing culture, for police–community relations, for criminal investigations, and, ultimately, for public safety. In short, the diversification of policing makes police more effective.

Policing has come a long way in recognizing the value of diversity. Police services have changed their traditional "tough" culture, benefiting both police and society through the cultural competence they have acquired. There is always room for improvement, but Canadian police organizations have made great strides in diversifying the face of policing. This includes providing support to personnel belonging to diverse groups.

Correctional facilities are becoming increasingly diverse, which poses challenges in meeting the needs of visible minority groups and mentally ill inmates. Organizational changes, targeted hiring, and cultural programs are some of the steps taken by correctional facilities to accommodate diverse inmates. The biggest challenge is providing continuous care, treatment, and support to an increasing number of mentally ill inmates.

REFERENCES

Allen, M. (2015). Police-reported hate crime in Canada, 2013. http://www.statcan.gc.ca/pub/85-002-x/2015001/article/14191-eng.htm.

Association of Black Law Enforcers. (n.d.a). Racial profiling and street check submissions. http://www.ableorg.ca/index.php?option=com_k2&view=item&id=184:racial-profiling-and-street-check-submissions&Itemid=435.

Association of Black Law Enforcers. (n.d.b). Who we are. http://www.ableorg.ca/index.php?option=com_content&view=article&id=126&Itemid=776.

Baksh, N., & Arsenault, A. (2015, March 2.) Timmins, Ont.-born jihadist recruited 5 others for ISIS. *CBC News*. http://www.cbc.ca.

Bell, S. (2015, April 15). How RCMP officers tracked three Canadian girls in Egypt before they could join ISIL in Syria. *The National Post*. http://news.nationalpost.com.

Bennett, K. (2015, April 8.) Hamilton police send mental health pros to the front lines with cops. *CBC News*. http://www.cbc.ca.

Canadian Mental Health Association, British Columbia Division. (2005). Police and mental illness: Increased interactions. http://www.cmha.bc.ca/wp-content/uploads/2016/07/policesheets_all.pdf.

CBC News. (2015, May 5). Mohammad Shafia intimidated prisoners into attending prayers. *CBC News*. http://www.cbc.ca.

CBC News. (2016, June 22). Toronto police chief Mark Saunders apologizes for 1981 gay bathhouse raids. *CBC News*. http://www.cbc.ca.

Clancy, N. (2015, February 25). ISIS recruited Canadian woman to join fight in Syria. *The Huffington Post*. http://www.huffingtonpost.ca.

Coffey, A. (1990). *Law enforcement: A human relations approach*. Englewood Cliffs, NJ: Prentice Hall.

Coleman, T., & Cotton, D. (2010). Police interactions with persons with a mental illness: Police learning in the environment of contemporary policing. http://www.mentalhealthcommission.ca/sites/default/files/Law_Police_Interactions_Mental_Illness_Report_ENG_0_1.pdf.

Correctional Service Canada. (2012). Towards a continuum of care. http://www.csc-scc.gc.ca/002/006/002006-2000-eng.shtml.

Correctional Service Canada. (2013). Intensive intervention strategy in women's institutions. http://www.csc-scc.gc.ca/acts-and-regulations/578-cd-eng.shtml.

Correctional Service Canada. (2014a). National substance abuse programs: National pre-release substance abuse program. http://www.csc-scc.gc.ca/correctional-process/002001-2009-eng.shtml#s4.

Correctional Service Canada. (2014b). The federal offender population profile 2014. http://www.csc-scc.gc.ca/publications/005007-3033-eng.shtml.

Cotter, A. (2015, December 7). Spotlight on Canadians: Results from the General Social Survey—Public confidence in Canadian institutions. Statistics Canada. http://www.statcan.gc.ca/pub/89-652-x/89-652-x2015007-eng.htm.

Cotton, D., & Coleman, T. (2008). A study of police academy training and education for new police officers related to working with people with mental illness. http://www.pmhl.ca/webpages/reports/AApoliceacademy.pdf.

DiManno, R. (2015, August 17). A thorny history of race-based statistics. *The Toronto Star*. https://www.thestar.com.

Dupuis, T., MacKay, R., & Nicol, J. (2013). *Current issues in mental health in Canada: Mental health and the criminal justice system*. Library of Parliament background paper. Publication no. 2013-88-E. http://www.parl.gc.ca/content/lop/researchpublications/2013-88-e.pdf.

Durham Regional Police Service (DRPS). (2010, May 20). *2005–2010 diversity strategic plan*. http://www.drps.ca/upload_files/Diversity_Strategic_Plan_DRPS1.pdf.

Durkan, S. (1998, March 24). Canadian cops top the list in most-popular survey. *The London Free Press*, p. A9.

Dvoskin, J., & Spiers, E. (2004). On the role of correctional officers on prison mental health. *Psychiatric Quarterly*, *75*(1), 41–59.

Edmonton Police Service. (n.d.). What is a hate crime? http://www.edmontonpolice.ca/CommunityPolicing/OrganizedCrime/HateBiasCrime.aspx.

Gallant, J. (2016, March 18). No charges for police officer who shot Andrew Loku. *The Toronto Star*. https://www.thestar.com.

Grewal, S. (2015, October 8). Peel police don't mirror community's racial makeup, data shows. *The Toronto Star*. https://www.thestar.com.

Howard-Grabman, L., & Snetro, G. (2003). How to mobilize communities for health and social change. https://www.msh.org/sites/msh.org/files/2015_08_msh_how_to_mobilize_communities_for_health_social_change.pdf.

Humphreys, A., Bell, S., Keidan, M., & Blackwell, T. (2013, April 6). How three Canadians graduated from a rebellious high-school friendship to the world of Islamist terrorism. *The National Post*. http://news.nationalpost.com.

Office of the Correctional Investigator. (2013). *A case study of diversity in corrections: The Black inmate experience in federal penitentiaries*. http://www.oci-bec.gc.ca/cnt/rpt/pdf/oth-aut/oth-aut20131126-eng.pdf.

Office of the Correctional Investigator. (2015). *Annual report of the Office of the Correctional Investigator 2014–2015*. http://www.oci-bec.gc.ca/cnt/rpt/pdf/annrpt/annrpt20142015-eng.pdf.

Office of the Independent Police Review Director. (2014). *Annual report 2013–14*. http://www.oiprd.on.ca/EN/PDFs/Annual-Report-2013-2014_A_E.pdf.

Ontario Association of Chiefs of Police. (2013). *Best practices in policing and LGBTQ communities in Ontario*. http://www.oacp.on.ca/Userfiles/Files/NewAndEvents/OACP LGBTQ final Nov2013.pdf.

Ontario Association of Chiefs of Police. (2015). Ontario's mobilization and engagement model of community policing. http://www.oacp.on.ca/Userfiles/Files/NewAndEvents/CrimePreventionCampaign/COMMUNITY POLICING WHEEL-2.pdf.

Ontario Human Rights Commission. (2013). TPS racial profiling and carding: OHRC deputation at November 18, 2013 public meeting inviting public comment on PACER report and Mukherjee report. http://www.ohrc.on.ca/en/news_centre/tps-racial-profiling-and-carding-ohrc-deputation-november-18-2013-public-meeting-inviting-public.

Ontario Human Rights Commission. (2015a, August 11). OHRC submission to the Ministry of Community Safety and Correctional Services on street checks. http://www.ohrc.on.ca/en/ohrc-submission-ministry-community-safety-and-correctional-services-street-checks.

Ontario Human Rights Commission. (2015b, December 11). OHRC submission to the Ministry of Community Safety and Correctional Services on street checks. http://www.ohrc.on.ca/en/ohrc-submission-ministry-community-safety-and-correctional-services-street-checks-0.

Ontario Provicial Police. (2012). *2012 annual report*. http://www.publicsafety.gc.ca/lbrr/archives/cnmcs-plcng/cn31065-2012-eng.pdf.

Ottawa Police Service. (n.d.). Sir Robert Peel's principles of law enforcement 1829. http://www.ottawapolice.ca/en/about-us/Peel-s-Principles-.asp.

Parent, R.A., & Ellis III, J.O. (2014, May). *Right-wing extremism in Canada*. Canadian Network for Research on Terrorism, Security and Society working paper series no. 14-03. Public Safety Canada. http://www.publicsafety.gc.ca/lbrr/archives/cnmcs-plcng/cn31894-eng.pdf.

Perry, B., & Scrivens, R. (2016). Uneasy alliances: A look at the right-wing extremist movement in Canada. *Studies in Conflict and Terrorism*, *39*(9), 819–841.

Perry, D. (2004, Fall). Complexities of cross-cultural investigations. *Canadian Police Chief Magazine*, 22–24.

Public Services Foundation of Canada. (2015). *Crisis in correctional services: Overcrowding and inmates with mental health problems in provincial correctional facilities*. http://www.bcgeu.ca/sites/default/files/page/attachments/Crisis in Correctional Services April 2015[2].pdf.

Quan, D. (2016, June 12). "We still are targets": LGBT activists say Orlando shooting a stark reminder of violence they face. *The National Post*. http://news.nationalpost.com.

Reason, C. (2014, February 19). Crime down, relationships improve between police and Somali community: 23 Division police. *Etobicoke Guardian*. http://www.insidetoronto.com.

Robertson, D. (2014, December 17). RCMP poised to roll out program to prevent radicalization. *Ottawa Citizen*. http://ottawacitizen.com.

Ross, S. (2016, April 29). For Black Lives Matter, small win on Andrew Loku may go a long way. *The Globe and Mail*. http://www.theglobeandmail.com.

Southern Poverty Law Center. (n.d.). Extremist files: Paul Fromm. https://www.splcenter.org/fighting-hate/extremist-files/individual/paul-fromm.

Standing Senate Committee on National Security and Defence. (2015). *Countering the terrorist threat in Canada: An interim report*. http://www.parl.gc.ca/Content/SEN/Committee/412/secd/rep/rep18jul15-e.pdf.

Statistics Canada. (2006). Ethnic origins, 2006 counts, for Canada, provinces and territories—20% sample data. http://www12.statcan.ca/census-recensement/2006/dp-pd/hlt/97-562/pages/page.cfm?Lang=E&Geo=PR&Code=01&Table=2&Data=Count&StartRec=1&Sort=3&Display=All.

Statistics Canada. (2015). Police resources in Canada. Table 7: Police officers by sex, Canada, 1986 to 2014. http://www.statcan.gc.ca/pub/85-002-x/2015001/article/14146-eng.htm#a12.

Toronto Police Service. (2014). *Professional standards annual report, 2013*. https://www.torontopolice.on.ca/publications/files/reports/prs2013annualreport.pdf.

Warnica, R. (2015, July 17). The life and bloody death of Andrew Loku: Toronto police officer's face "went white as a ghost" after shooting. *The National Post*. http://news.nationalpost.com.

Watson, A., & Fulambarker, A. (2012). The crisis intervention team model of police response to mental health crises: A primer for mental health practitioners. *Best Practices in Mental Health*, 8(2), 71–78.

Williams, W.L., & Henderson, B.B. (1997). *Taking back our streets: Fighting crime in America*. New York: Lisa Drew/Scribner.

Wortley, S. (2006). Police use of force in Ontario: An examination of data from the Special Investigations Unit. https://www.attorneygeneral.jus.gov.on.ca/inquiries/ipperwash/policy_part/projects/pdf/AfricanCanadianClinicIpperwashProject_SIUStudybyScotWortley.pdf.

REVIEW QUESTIONS

True or False?

___ 1. Immigrants have greater confidence in the institution of policing than non-immigrants.

___ 2. It is misleading to describe a police officer's job as law enforcement.

___ 3. Authoritarian conduct is what the community wants and expects from police.

___ 4. Women and minorities are underrepresented in law enforcement.

___ 5. Ontario's Mobilization and Engagement Model of Community Policing focuses on enforcement and crime suppression.

___ 6. Federal prisons in Canada house some of the largest concentrations of people with mental health conditions in the country.

___ 7. Ontario's draft regulations on carding and street checks would permit officers to stop individuals without requiring reasonable suspicion of illegal activities.

___ 8. Police are unlikely ever to encounter a situation where a person's accent is a barrier to communication.

___ 9. Black and Indigenous Canadians are over four times as likely as others to be involved as an injured party in an SIU investigation.

___ 10. The Toronto Police Service makes race-based statistics available to researchers.

Multiple Choice

1. When determining where to house a transgender detainee, correctional officers should consider all of the following except
   a. the detainee's safety
   b. the detainee's gender identity
   c. the length of the detainee's detention
   d. the detainee's wishes

2. Most people are satisfied with police
   a. most of the time
   b. some of the time
   c. all of the time
   d. very little of the time

3. It can be argued that the functions police perform are by necessity
   a. coercive
   b. antagonistic
   c. secretive
   d. passive

4. The majority of harassment complaints in the RCMP were based on
   a. sexual harassment
   b. harassment as a result of ethnicity
   c. bullying or belittling behaviour
   d. harassment as a result of disability

5. Police services in Canada are organized
   a. according to Peel's principles
   b. as a military structure
   c. according to the police force approach
   d. as a paramilitary structure

6. Community mobilization is defined as
   a. community resistance to policing
   b. the process of police enforcement in the community
   c. a capacity-building, community-led process with police assistance
   d. the process of improving police image within the community

7. Complaints of incivility by police officers most often arise during
   a. street checks (or "carding")
   b. detention
   c. the arrest process
   d. traffic stops

8. Most reported hate crimes in Canada are directed at
   a. religious minorities, including Muslims
   b. gays and lesbians
   c. transgender people
   d. racial minorities

9. The majority of CSIS's files relate to
   a. overseas terrorism
   b. Islamist extremism, including ISIS
   c. right-wing extremism
   d. none of the above

10. The most common mental illness in the male federal correctional population is
    a. schizophrenia
    b. alcohol or substance-use disorders
    c. mood disorders
    d. anti-social personality disorder

Fill in the Blanks

1. The _police_ are the only element in the criminal justice system that has a direct relationship with the community.

2. The police practice of stopping people for non-arrest, non-detention investigations and eliciting their personal information is also known as _carding_.

3. Assaults and hate crimes against LGBTQ people are vastly _under reported_.

4. Two approaches have come to dominate policing worldwide: the authoritarian police force approach and the _police service_ approach.

5. According to the General Social Survey, immigrants show a _higher_ level of confidence in police than non-immigrants do.

6. In pluralistic Western countries, _____ have historically been overrepresented in police services.

7. Police services in Canada in the 21st century sees diversity as a strategic _____.

8. If an offence is motivated by _hate_ and prosecuted as such, the judge must treat this as an aggravating factor on sentencing.

9. The current best practice model for responding to a mental health crisis is the _crisis intervention team_ model.

10. Correctional Services Canada has identified offenders' _mental health needs_ as a top priority.

PART II

Indigenous Peoples in Canada

7 Colonization and Treaties

Six Nations Iroquois (Haudenosaunee) chiefs reading wampum belts on September 14, 1871.

LEARNING OUTCOMES

After completing this chapter, you should be able to:

- Identify the differences between the Western European world view and the world view of Indigenous peoples.
- Consider how differences in world view will affect the continuing relationship between mainstream culture and Indigenous cultures.
- Identify the core issues in the long-standing debate over Indigenous claims to land and authority in the Americas.
- Discuss the relationship between the new European arrivals and the Indigenous people in Canada up to the time of the *Royal Proclamation of 1763*.
- Explore the treaty-making process and consider the benefits and disadvantages to all parties involved.
- Identify the assimilation policies and legislation set out by the Dominion of Canada and discuss the moral and ethical implications of those policies.

Introduction

This chapter contrasts pre-contact Europe and pre-contact North America with the goal of understanding what the two cultures were like before they collided. Once this is established, we go on to examine the colonization of Canada and its effects on the original inhabitants of the land.

We gain insight into a culture's world view by examining its creation story. This chapter looks at Indigenous creation stories and at Western European creation stories. We will reflect briefly on Western creation stories. Not all Canadians today are familiar with the Christian religion. But at the time of colonization and well into the 20th century, the majority of Canadians were people of Western European origin—that is to say, overwhelmingly Christian. Their European culture was the dominant culture in Canada during colonization and arguably remains so today. Despite the fact that Canada is widely considered to be a cultural mosaic, the fundamental principles of Indigenous cultures have always been quite different from the European principles that underlie the mainstream world view in Canada.

After examining the creation stories and differences in world view between Indigenous culture and mainstream culture, we will examine the relationship between Indigenous people and Europeans as it developed from the time of first contact through to the period in which Indigenous people went from being partners in trade and allies in war to being displaced and subjugated peoples.

World View

A world view is the set of assumptions and beliefs on which a people's comprehension of the world is based. The stories, symbols, analogies, and metaphors that compose a people's mythology express a world view in coded form. Such expression occurs in informal, formal, unconscious, and conscious ways through family and community, through arts and media, and through economic, spiritual, governmental, and education institutions. (Cajete, 2000, p. 62)

What distinguishes the world view of the dominant culture in Canada? Amid the many cultures that compose Canada, there is a dominant, mainstream culture. Members of a mainstream culture are sometimes hardly aware of its existence, but people from outside that culture tend to be acutely aware of it. According to Cajete, our culture gives us a particular world view that affects the way we live and our social and political actions. What are the stories, metaphors, symbols, and myths that express the mainstream Canadian world view?

Foundations of the Mainstream Canadian World View

The foundations of the mainstream Canadian world view before and during the centuries of colonization include stories of creation, 17th-century philosophy, structures of governance, and capitalist assumptions about land and property.

Religious Creation Story

Our society is still influenced by the Christian religion. The Christian belief is that humans are created in the image of God and that they, alone among the world's creatures, are endowed with a spirit. God has given humans "dominion over the fish of the sea, and over the fowl of the air, and over the cattle, and over all the Earth" (Genesis 1:25). This belief has profoundly shaped mainstream Western culture's view of humanity's relationship with the natural world. Christian principles, including the concept of the Protestant work ethic, were in part responsible for the emphasis on industry in Western European society and the development of capitalism, which continues to be the dominant economic ideology in North America. The Bible's assertion that humans were made to cultivate the earth is in part responsible for the emphasis on agriculture in Western European society, while the biblical view that the human purpose is to populate the earth was, historically, one of the factors in the high populations of Western European societies.

Our conceptions of justice are rooted in religion. Until very recently, our principles of sentencing for criminal offences were based on notions of retribution and punishment that are biblical in origin. Although the purpose of sentencing, as expressed in section 718 of the *Criminal Code*, is now more in line with modern thinking, various signs and symbols within mainstream culture (for example, in film, books, and stories) still promote a biblical, "eye for an eye" view of justice.

Finally, the Christian faith is a proselytizing religion, based on the belief that there is only one God and one true religion and that others must convert to it or be damned. At the same time, it contains many factions. This state of affairs produced much religious intolerance and dissension and conflict in Europe, one of the many reasons Europeans came to settle in new lands. Christianity's proselytizing tendency has affinities with ethnocentrism—the idea that others must live as we do because ours is the best way to live and all other ways are inferior. Not just Indigenous people but all people from cultural traditions outside the mainstream one will have come across this ethnocentric propensity in members of the cultural majority.

Scientific Creation Story

Mainstream culture has a second creation story, the scientific one based on Charles Darwin's theory of evolution. This story locates the creation of humanity in the "Cradle of Humankind" in South Africa. (According to some Christian scientists seeking to validate the biblical story, this is the true site of the Garden of Eden.) It is a story that has humans evolving from apelike ancestors to their current form, then gradually migrating outward to occupy the earth.

Darwin's theory of evolution has had a huge impact on mainstream culture's world view. That impact is reflected in colloquialisms such as "dog eat dog" and "only the strong survive." The creation story based on Darwin's theory has profoundly affected the way we see both ourselves and life on this planet. It supports our view that life is about competition for resources and survival. For mainstream Western culture, the scientific view of creation has displaced to some extent the religious view of creation.

Philosophy and Governance

Philosopher Thomas Hobbes wrote *Leviathan* in 1651, after the discovery of the Americas but prior to their full-scale colonization. Hobbes theorized that life in a state of nature, where there is no strong centralized government with absolute power, is "nasty, brutish, and short." His view of human nature was not a positive one. He presumed that men would kill one another in order to survive. He advocated investing absolute power in a sovereign in order to maintain both structure and peace in society. Hobbes's historical circumstances influenced his opinion. Europe in that period experienced political instability, war, and plagues that wiped out large portions of the population. There were huge class divisions between the wealthy and the poor, with wealth concentrated in the Church and monarchy. Europe was a long way from democracy. The Church and the sovereign were seen as a single concentrated source of power, while ordinary people had very little political control. It was a top-down structure of governance. This is the conception of government that many Europeans subscribed to when they embarked on the process of colonization.

Our political structure today is very different. While the Canadian political structure is in many ways based on the British political structure, some academics maintain that our current form of democratic government was to some extent modelled on the forms of government practised by Indigenous peoples at the time of their first contact with European explorers.

Locke's Theory of Landownership

When we discuss land rights, we tend to think in terms of rights to private ownership of property; that is our cultural understanding of people's relationship to land. This understanding is rooted in biblical texts and in political structures that date back to medieval times. Early in European history, the division of the "haves" and "have-nots" was determined by private landownership. By the time the Americas were "discovered," most of the land in Europe was already in the hands of private landowners. Those who worked the land for landowners would almost certainly never own land; they would be labourers their entire lives. When the Americas were discovered, philosopher John Locke wrote a theory of landownership that reinforced the established Western European notion of man's relationship to land. Locke's theory would rationalize the European seizure of land in the Americas. In brief, his theory went like this:

1. All land is owned by all of mankind.
2. Land can be transferred from general to private ownership by mixing one's labour with it.
3. Once converted to private ownership, land requires delineated boundaries (physically represented by fencing).
4. In order to have delineated boundaries, a society must have an established government and laws for enforcing private ownership.
5. Proviso: A man could take as much land as he required, provided that he left "enough, and as good" for others. (Bishop, 2003)

Locke's theory is an important one: it will come up again later in this book in connection with the clearing of Indigenous people from the land and our society's justifications for doing so. It is also relevant to our discussion later in this chapter; it provides a contrast to Indigenous concepts of land and methods of government.

The concepts we have discussed thus far should be very familiar to all members of mainstream Canadian culture. They are the building blocks of our society's world view. Many other concepts could be discussed, particularly the rise of capitalism, but space limitations preclude a fuller treatment. Now we must look at another world view, one that is very different from the mainstream one.

Indigenous World View

Before Europeans arrived on the shores of what would become Canada, there were self-governing nations of people living in organized groups throughout the land. Archaeologists estimate that the land sustained 500,000 to 2,000,000 people in all (Dickason, 1997, p. 43). These nations have rich histories that are tens of thousands of years old; conservative archaeological estimates put Indigenous occupancy at around 15,000 years. (According to Indigenous people, they have been here since time began.) In other words, European history on the continent represents less than one-tenth of the histories of these nations, who occupied every territory of the continent, using natural resources for sustenance.

Pre-contact population density estimates demonstrate Indigenous peoples' symbiotic relationship with the land. The highest population densities were in areas of plentiful resources that could support many people. Population densities in deserts and in temperate zones, where there is a short growing season, were smaller. Although the population of what would become Canada was low because of the climate, the population in Central and South America has been estimated as high as 37 million. The Aztec population alone was estimated at 11 million; their main city was said to be larger than Madrid, Spain. On the Caribbean island of the Dominican Republic, the site of the first European landing, the population density was very high.

FIGURE 7.1   Cultural and Language Groups Prior to Contact

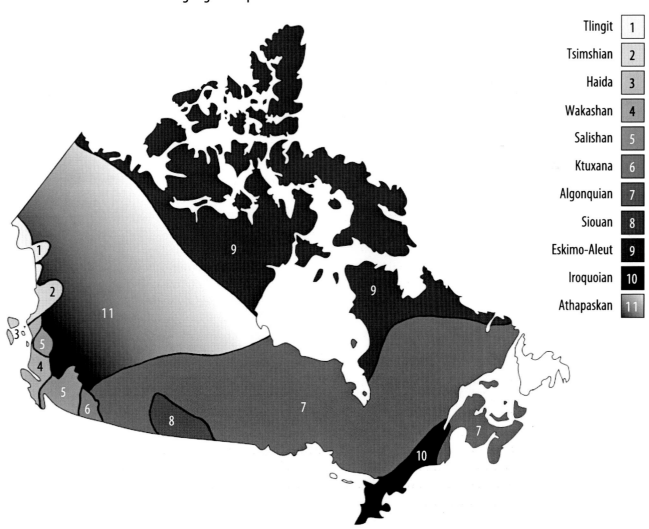

Tlingit	1
Tsimshian	2
Haida	3
Wakashan	4
Salishan	5
Ktuxana	6
Algonquian	7
Siouan	8
Eskimo-Aleut	9
Iroquoian	10
Athapaskan	11

In the 16th century, an estimated 2,200 languages were spoken across the continents of Central and South America (Dickason, 1997, p. 5). In what would become Canada, 50 languages were spoken, which have been classified into 11 language families (see Figure 7.1). Not all people who speak the same language can understand one another. Many languages have a number of different dialects—variations of a common language. Since language is the conduit of culture, we know that the cultures are as diverse as their languages. Often we approach Indigenous people across Canada as if they are all part of one homogeneous group. This misconception often damages relationships between Indigenous people and mainstream Canadians.

Oral Tradition

Language conveys culture from one generation to the next. Indigenous culture accomplishes this through an oral tradition in which storytelling is the means of conveying values, social expectations, history, and knowledge. Storytellers hold a special place in Indigenous communities; storytelling is a tremendous responsibility that is taken very seriously. Stories are not passed down in a spontaneous manner; they are told and retold by the storyteller in teaching circles and formal ceremonies. Traditionally, few Indigenous cultures found a need to write; their storytellers have always been like living books. The stories they tell have certain features in common:

- They include various aspects of the storyteller's physical environment—the people, the local animals, and plants. Mythical creatures in the stories combine human characteristics with characteristics of local animals.
- They provide spiritual guidance and ethical instruction, exemplifying cultural values and expectations.
- They often include places that would be familiar and of spiritual significance to the listeners.
- They are rich in symbolism that sheds light on the origin of the people as well as on their world view.

European historians have tended to question the reliability of oral histories, believing that they are susceptible to being embellished, misinterpreted, or misunderstood. But they have found that the earliest recordings of Indigenous stories, which were compiled by Jesuit priests in the early 1600s, are identical to the stories being told by Indigenous elders and other storytellers today. This attests to the accuracy and completeness of oral transmission from one generation to the next and to the fact that these stories are timeless. Heirs to the text-centred European tradition would do well to remember that many of their culture's central narratives—the Bible, for example, and the seminal works of Homer—were in fact derived from oral renderings that subsisted for hundreds or thousands of years before anyone wrote them down. The oral and the written modes are not as distinct as is sometimes assumed. Stories about the Garden of Eden and Noah's ark, and other European creation stories, are, like Indigenous stories, filled with allegory and symbolism.

Creation Stories

One of the most important subjects in First Nations and Inuit stories is their origins. In all stories, the people either were created from the land in which they have traditionally lived or came to the land from some other spiritual place. Creation stories are important to a culture because they situate it in the world and shape its world view. Animals figure prominently in Indigenous stories of creation, working collaboratively with humans. Not only humans but animals and other natural elements are endowed with spirit by the Creator. The Creator gives humans stewardship of the natural world and compels them to live in harmony with it. This is remarkably different from Western ideas about the role of humans, which were based on the Christian concept of humankind having dominion over the natural world.

Concepts of Land and Spirituality

From these creation stories come foundations for a distinct world view. Intrinsic to this view is the connection to land. In these stories, land is more than merely a geographic territory or a potential source of wealth. It is *Land*—a sacred living entity, with its own rhythms and cycles. The life and spirituality of Indigenous peoples have always been connected to the land in a close, symbiotic relationship. They believe that because the people were born with the land as part of the common creation, they cannot be separated or differentiated from it.

All Indigenous peoples' spirituality is connected to the land. Their spiritual practices developed to reflect this connection, and these practices are as diverse as the nations themselves.

Mi'kmaq Creation Story—Two Creators and Their Conflicts

Before the earth was new, the sun was all that existed in the great universe. The sun divided the earth into several parts separated by many great lakes. In each part he caused one man and one woman to be born. They bore children and lived for many years. Wickedness pervaded this family, and slowly they killed one another. The sun wept and wept with grief. The tears became rain that fell from the skies until water covered the entire earth. The family had to set sail in bark canoes to save themselves from the flood. A violent wind overturned their boats. All perished in the sea but the old man and the old woman, who were best of all people, and it was they who populated the earth.

Source: Whitehead (1991).

Community Organization

Indigenous people organized themselves in different ways depending on their unique environments and spiritual beliefs. Generally, they organized themselves into communal groups that were egalitarian, self-sufficient, and connected to the land and its resources. Often they were connected to other specific nations in cooperative relationships for trade and the sharing of resources. These relationships were often set out in treaties that outlined each nation's responsibility to the others and, at times, delineated territorial boundaries for the purpose of resource management and harvest. Several nations would often be unified in a confederacy.

The Haudenosaunee, for example, were a collection of five nations: Mohawk, Seneca, Oneida, Onondaga, and Cayuga. Each nation had its own distinctive clan system. The Mohawk were bear, turtle, or wolf clan. The other nations had their respective clans. The Five Nations were united in a "League of Peace," otherwise known as the Iroquois Confederacy. The Confederacy was governed by a council of 50 chiefs representing the participant nations. Decisions were made by **consensus** among the chiefs and by the chief's consultation with the people whose interests he represented. Women had tremendous influence in the governmental system since they selected the chiefs and had the right also to remove a chief who proved to be unsatisfactory. Clarkson, Morrissette, and Régallet (1992, p. 16) have described the Indigenous decision-making process as follows:

> [W]hen decisions had to be made that affected the whole community, each clan would sit around a central fire with all other clans. Decisions the clan made together may include when to move, conservation of the resources of the territories, the striking of alliances and relationships with other nations and how to implement these decisions. Usually after

consensus government
a form of government that requires all parties to agree with a decision

much discussion and further consultation with their clan members, decisions would be made that would respect the interests of all clans and their members. Decisions were not arrived at in the same manner as western society today through majority vote. When decisions had to be made it would be through a consensus process. All people had to agree with the action or no action would be taken.

These forms of government indicate that cooperation and consensus are among the foundations of the Indigenous world view. Their spiritual teachings, by advising that decisions be made in the best interests not only of all living people but also of all people of the next seven generations, encourage a far-sighted concern for the community. Indigenous forms of governments are based on equality and on balancing individual interests against group interests, with group interests always taking precedence.

Because everything is connected in the Indigenous world view, spirituality influences land use, and both influence governance structures. There is no separation between these elements as there is in mainstream tradition. The conception of individual rights is not alien to the Indigenous system of social organization; it just is less important than group or collective rights. Negotiated rights to harvest territories are not individual rights; they are collective rights of the group. The harvest does not belong to the individual harvester but to the collective group and is distributed according to subsistence needs. The focus of Indigenous teachings is the individual's responsibilities to the group rather than the individual's rights within the group.

International Organization

Individual Indigenous nations did not exist in a vacuum. They were very aware of one another and entered into relationships to exchange knowledge and to trade material goods. In this way, they influenced one another's cultures. Sometimes nations traded for natural resources not available within their own territory. Agricultural societies such as the Iroquois traded their excess agricultural products. Trade took place over vast areas of the Americas.

Contact

First contact with Indigenous peoples in what would become Canada was made not by the British or the French, but by Vikings travelling from Greenland, drawn by the great supply of fish. They arrived in Newfoundland sometime between the 11th and 13th centuries and settled at L'Anse aux Meadows, which is today a UNESCO World Heritage Site. Little is known about the presence of the Vikings in North America; however, they did record their encounter with the Indigenous people of Newfoundland, whom they referred to as the "Skraelings." Although this group is known by several names, the most common is Beothuk. They were a small community of hunter-gatherers who depended upon the coastline for the fish and seals that they stored for consumption throughout the winter.

Explorer John Cabot arrived on the coast of Newfoundland in 1497, then carried news of the rich fishing waters back to Europe. Many Europeans were drawn by the opportunity to make their fortune exporting fish to Europe. In 1501, Portuguese explorer Gaspar Corte-Real captured 50 Beothuk and took them back to Europe as slaves. Probably as a result of this incident, the Beothuk subsequently avoided contact with whites.

By 1578, over 400 European fishing ships came to the region every summer. They began to occupy the coastline to dry fish, limiting the Beothuk's access to the ocean. Growing hostilities by the Europeans forced the Beothuk further inland, and, without access to the resources of the sea, they faced great hardship.

In 1713, the French were expelled, and the British increased their coastal settlements, further cutting off the Beothuk from the ocean and the resources that had sustained them for thousands of years. After taking control of the land and the resources, the British decided to attempt to protect the remaining Beothuk, whose population they recorded in 1768 as a mere 400. The British captured the last few Beothuk in 1810. The last known Beothuk, Shanawdithit, died of tuberculosis in 1829 (Dickason, 1997, pp. 73–74).

The first true voyage of discovery into what would become Canada was Jacques Cartier's exploration of the Gulf of St. Lawrence in 1534. Cartier met with the St. Lawrence Iroquois and engaged in trade with them. They described to him the route to the interior of the continent, where he hoped to find gold. With the help of his Iroquois guides, Cartier made it all the way to Hochelaga, present-day Montreal. He counted 14 villages on the north shore, of which Hochelaga was the largest, numbering 50 longhouses, with an estimated population of 1,500.

Europeans continued to arrive on Canada's eastern shores, drawn by a variety of hopes—of growing wealthy through the region's natural resources, of acquiring land, or of escaping poverty or religious persecution in the Old World. These Europeans continued to make contact with various Indigenous nations, each with its own form of governance and economic system.

Initially, contact involved a spirit of cooperation between the Indigenous groups and the colonists, and respect for one another's sovereignty. The reasons were threefold, and quite practical:

1. The Indigenous nations vastly outnumbered the colonists, who were poorly equipped for the harsh conditions of the land.
2. The economic interests of the newcomers depended on maintaining a good relationship with the Indigenous communities, who in turn benefited in terms of trade.
3. Indigenous people were desperately needed as military allies by the French and the English in their wars against each other, and, later, against the newly independent United States.

In the relationship between the Europeans and the Indigenous nations, the latter clearly had the upper hand at this point. This was made most clear in the Two-Row Wampum, or the *Guswentha*, the first agreement entered into between the Five Nations of the Iroquois and the British. To the Iroquois, the *Guswentha* was international law, recorded in wampum beads as was their custom. The two coloured rows of wampum represented an English trading ship and an Iroquois canoe. They travel parallel paths along the river of life. These paths never meet; the two nations are bound together in peace and friendship, with an agreement for reciprocal aid and defence. At the same time, neither nation is to interfere with the other or attempt to impose laws on it.

This agreement is well documented by the British, referred to as the **covenant chain**. The covenant chain was a clear recognition by both sides that their political systems would remain separate even as their systems of trade and alliance bound them. The British historical record, until it reaches the early 1800s, contains many references to this agreement.

covenant chain
first agreement entered into between the Five Nations of the Iroquois and the British; a clear recognition by both sides that their political systems would remain separate even as their systems of trade and alliance bound them

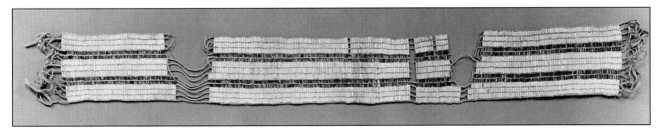

The Two-Row Wampum Belt (*Guswentha*).

This military alliance with the Iroquois served the British well and led to their defeat of the French in 1760. The French and British continually accused one another of bribing their allies with gifts and also of using Indigenous people, who during battles sustained great losses on the front lines, as "cannon fodder."

First Nations on both sides considered the battle to be between the French and the English and allied themselves with their traditional trade partners, viewing the outcome as a matter of trade dominance alone; they had no concept that their lands were at stake. They viewed the land as their sacred territory, which they had allowed Europeans to settle on under certain terms and conditions, such as trade alliances and gift distributions.

Upon the defeat of the French, many Indigenous leaders remarked to the English that it was not the Indigenous people that were conquered but the French. Ojibwe Chief Minweweh, whose warriors had fought on the side of the French, reminded the English: "Although you have conquered the French you have not conquered us. We are not your slaves. These lakes, woods and mountains were left us by our ancestors. They are our inheritance, and we will part with them to none" (Dickason, 1997, p. 155).

To address the Indigenous people's fears concerning the loss of their ancestral lands, the British included article 40 in the Capitulation of Montreal between the French and English. This section guaranteed First Nations protection of their lands from the encroachment of new settlers. It immediately proved difficult to enforce, however, as settlers began to pour in once peace had been established. Colonial governments displayed little will to enforce the legislation (Dickason, 1997, p. 153).

After the defeat of the French, First Nations found their position worsening. They had been holding the balance of power between two rivals, but now found themselves becoming irrelevant to both the British and the French. Gift distributions ended quickly, as did the supply of guns and ammunition. The Europeans no longer respected boundaries that First Nations set out as hunting grounds or sacred territories. Discontent among various nations led to a formidable uprising led by a remarkable man named Pontiac, an Odawa war chief, who was able to unite a number of nations in his quest to defeat the Europeans and drive them from the land. Within the span of two months in 1763, nine British forts fell to Pontiac with almost no casualties sustained by his men. The British feared being overrun and resorted to the first ever recorded case of biological warfare. They distributed smallpox-infected blankets to Indigenous settlements, wiping out entire communities, including women, children, and elders.

In this intense political climate, the British tried to justify their acquisition of land in the Americas. It was apparent to them that the land was in fact occupied by organized nations of people, albeit non-Christians. The British sought to reconcile their principles of justice with acquiring land for resource extraction and settlement. Securing the land for these purposes would be impossible without the help of the Indigenous nations. Britain was facing a growing rebellion in the 13 colonies and would require the allegiance of Indigenous nations again in war to avoid the loss of the New World altogether. Britain would never be able to secure the necessary allegiance if Europeans continued to trespass on the Indigenous peoples' territories, which was causing great animosity toward the British.

Royal Proclamation of 1763 the cornerstone of Indigenous land claims today; has been called the "*Magna Carta* of Indian Rights" and has been deemed by the courts to have the "force of a statute which has never been repealed"

The Royal Proclamation

In 1763, the British drew up an important piece of legislation to address the dilemma. The *Royal Proclamation of 1763* would become the cornerstone of Indigenous land claims today. This document has been called the "*Magna Carta* of Indian Rights" and has been deemed by the courts to have the "force of a statute which has never been repealed."

The first purpose of the Proclamation was to reserve a large piece of land for Indigenous occupation and use; under the Proclamation, the lands west of the Appalachian mountains were recognized as Indian lands. The second purpose was to appease Indigenous leaders in order to secure military allegiance and to stop the mounting Indigenous resistance movement. The third purpose was to create a treaty process by which the Crown alone could purchase Indigenous land for settlement.

Consider the wording of the Proclamation itself:

> And We do hereby strictly forbid, on Pain of our Displeasure, all our loving Subjects from making any Purchases or Settlements whatever, or taking Possession of any of the Lands above reserved [for Indians], without our especial leave and Licence for that Purpose first obtained.
>
> And We do further strictly enjoin and require all Persons whatever who have either wilfully or inadvertently seated themselves upon any Lands within the Countries above described, or upon any other Lands which, not having been ceded to or Purchased by Us, are still reserved to the said Indians as aforesaid, forthwith to remove themselves from such Settlements.
>
> And whereas great Frauds and Abuses have been committed in purchasing Lands of the Indians, to the great Prejudice of our Interests, and to the great Dissatisfaction of the said Indians: In order, therefore, to prevent such Irregularities for the future, and to the end that the Indians may be convinced of our Justice and determined Resolution to remove all reasonable Cause of Discontent, We do, with the Advice of our Privy Council strictly enjoin and require, that no private Person do presume to make any purchase from the said Indians of any Lands reserved to the said Indians, within those parts of our Colonies where We have thought proper to allow Settlement: but that, if at any Time any of the Said Indians should be inclined to dispose of the said Lands, the same shall be Purchased only for Us, in our Name, at some public Meeting or Assembly of the said Indians.

This powerful piece of legislation has never been repealed and therefore is still in effect and legally binding. The 13 colonies were very displeased with the limitations the Proclamation imposed on them; it became one of the many reasons for their rebellion against the British. The *Royal Proclamation* is legislation, drawn up by an imperial power, designed to protect the rights of Indigenous peoples to their land. As you continue to read, consider whether the British kept the terms of the Proclamation. Are we honouring these terms today?

The *Royal Proclamation* did accomplish what it set out to do: it drew a line between British territory and Indigenous land, and it convinced Indigenous people of Britain's "Justice and determined Resolution to remove all reasonable Cause of Discontent" where the Indigenous people were concerned. Its reassurances secured Indigenous support for the British in the upcoming American War of Independence and in Britain's later battles to repel the American invasion of what would become Canada.

The British government's third objective in establishing a treaty process to acquire land was to give the Crown a monopoly over land sales in Canada; it established itself as the only legal purchaser of Indigenous land. This was a source of enormous wealth for the British. In some of the first treaties in Ontario, the Crown purchased land for a mere 3 pence an acre from Indigenous people, who could not drive up the prices of their land by selling to any other party. The British then sold the land to private investors for settlement for 6 to 15 pence per acre, making a healthy profit.

The *Royal Proclamation* does not refer to Indigenous nations as sovereign nations, but neither does it refer to them as subjects of the Crown. It was not until after Confederation in 1867 that Canada began to aggressively and harshly subjugate Indigenous people.

The Fur Trade

During the early period of European–Indigenous contact, when settlement was still sparse, the fur trade was well under way. The French aligned with the Huron and other East Coast nations, and the English aligned with the Iroquois and their Indigenous allies. Both in trade and in war, the British and the French managed to exploit the divisions that had existed among Indigenous nations prior to contact.

The British set up the Hudson's Bay Company and the French, the Compagnie du Nord. The companies were in direct competition for the harvest and export of furs. Both attempted to extend their trade northward so as to gain control over trade routes. As early as 1632, the French were exporting up to 15,000 kilograms of furs a year. The French had 500 to 700 men on the canoe routes travelling to Huronia. Furs were the next best thing to gold (Dickason, 1997, p. 103).

The balance of power at this time was still very much in favour of the Indigenous nations. Consider, for example, that in 1633 the French colonies had 3,000 people, while the Huron nation alone numbered over 30,000. However, the Huron would shortly experience a rapid population decline as a result of European diseases brought by the missionaries and traders.

seigneurial farms a system in which a man, usually a soldier, was granted land in the name of France

The French established a system of **seigneurial farms**, in which one man, usually a soldier, was granted land in the name of France. The soldier would bring over his family from France to labour on the farm to produce food for the fledgling colonies. The French did not enact any treaties to acquire this land for farming; they simply considered themselves as sole proprietors of the land by their mere presence. They declared the land to be *terra nullius*—empty land. The French did not recognize Indigenous nations as rightful possessors of land, on the grounds that the Indigenous people were not Christian. The French were, however, very careful to maintain good relationships with Indigenous nations and never made any open assertions to them about the ownership of the land on which they settled. The lack of treaties or legal arrangements to clear the land of Indigenous title became problematic later; upon the defeat of the French, the British also did not enact any legislation to clear the land of Indigenous title, assuming that the French had already done so.

As the fur trade expanded, forts were erected to house staff and government officials. The fur trade extended into northern Ontario in search of fresh supplies and to advance British interests. The fur trade was not conducted at a sustainable rate; beavers were all but extinct south of today's Canada–US border and soon neared extinction in southern Ontario in 1830 once the traders moved in.

The trading posts created new, non-Indigenous communities in Indigenous territory in the North, and had an impact on Indigenous people who came to sell furs. Posts were often established in strategic proximity to Indigenous campsites, and Indigenous groups who had traditionally been hunter-gatherers, travelling continuously with the seasons, began to create permanent dwellings around the trading posts.

Indigenous people began to barter for objects such as sewing needles, copper pots, knives, and hatchets. This improved their immediate quality of life; they traded for items they could not easily produce themselves. This trading system, however, could not create long-term economic prosperity in Indigenous communities. The real profits were being exported back to Europe in the form of furs, and the resources that had sustained Indigenous people for thousands of years were quickly being depleted beyond recovery.

Changes to Indigenous Communities

Contact with Europeans brought fundamental changes to Indigenous communities. For example, they began to develop notions of cumulative wealth. Before contact, Indigenous people had never viewed furs in terms of wealth. Animals were killed for food, shelter, clothing, and

CALL TO ACTION

The Truth and Reconciliation Commission (TRC) was established in 2008 with the goal of hearing the stories of First Nations people who had been affected by the residential school system, a part of Canada's systemic attempt to subjugate and assimilate Indigenous peoples. You will read more about this in Chapter 9. As part of its final report, issued in 2015, the TRC made 94 Calls to Action—steps to be taken to help redress the legacy of Canada's residential school system in particular and repair Canada's relationship with Indigenous peoples in general.

You will see some of these Calls to Action placed throughout the text near the historical incidents that they address. When you read them, consider how the repercussions of these historical incidents continue to affect the lives of Indigenous people today.

> 45. We call upon the Government of Canada, on behalf of all Canadians, to jointly develop with Aboriginal peoples a Royal Proclamation of Reconciliation to be issued by the Crown. The proclamation would build on the Royal Proclamation of 1763 and the Treaty of Niagara of 1764, and reaffirm the nation-to-nation relationship between Aboriginal peoples and the Crown. The proclamation would include, but not be limited to, the following commitments: Repudiate concepts used to justify European sovereignty over Indigenous lands and peoples such as the Doctrine of Discovery and *terra nullius*.

tools. Anything that the hunter did not need would be given to another family. The proceeds generated by the hunt were shared among community members. Hunting for more than the community needed simply did not make any sense; collecting and storing hides was ill-adapted to the Indigenous peoples' traditional lifestyle. Arrangements for trade of excesses could be made with neighbouring nations, but the scale of this trade was never such that it would outstrip the environment.

Economic imperatives, previously non-existent, began to influence the process by which Indigenous leaders were selected. The clan system, which had previously maintained the groups' cohesiveness by maintaining strict rules, values, and social mores, slowly lost its influence.

Indigenous groups became increasingly dependent on European traders and less reliant on their own natural environment and on the traditional web of trade established between Indigenous nations prior to contact. The introduction of alcohol through trade created new societal problems that have persisted to this day in some Indigenous communities. For many Indigenous nations, this dependence on European trade became entrenched; for others it remained insignificant. Europeans were eager to foster this dependence because it provided an advantage in trade. For Indigenous people, the fur trade did not provide economic stability; the prices of furs were dependent on the whims of fashion, and the fur harvest fluctuated according to environmental conditions and animal populations. The rate of harvest was unsustainable, and the fur trade was destined to collapse.

Many animals that were hunted for their fur neared extinction by the early 1800s. As a result, many trading posts closed, bringing extreme hardship to those Indigenous people who had come to rely on their commerce. Many faced starvation and diseases unknown before contact. The government provided food and other necessities but could never restore the economy of Indigenous people. Animal resources had been depleted beyond recovery in the first phase of harvest. Indigenous lands later underwent a second harvesting of natural resources in the form of logging and mining, which proved no less devastating to their society.

Along with trade goods, Europeans brought Christian religion—English Protestant and French Catholic—and missionaries to spread the faith. Indigenous people were not eager to accept missionaries or their faith. Traders brought practical benefits such as guns and copper pots, but new spiritual beliefs were something Indigenous people simply did not value. Eventually, however, most Indigenous groups began to accept missionaries into their communities, sometimes for self-serving reasons. In some instances, traders and missionaries assisted one another's causes; Indigenous trappers who had converted to Christianity were often given better prices for their furs and were permitted to purchase guns and ammunition while their non-Christian peers were not. The missionaries often became frustrated with these incentives, believing that Indigenous people were converting for convenience rather than from genuine desire for the Christian religion.

The Indigenous conversions may often have been half-hearted or purely mercenary, but the impact of European religion on Indigenous communities was unquestionably profound. Missionaries restricted or forbade Indigenous ceremonies, traditions, and cultural practices, pronouncing them "from the devil." With these elements of their culture gone—elements that had been the foundations of their values, unity, and governance for thousands of years—Indigenous communities began to unravel. Differences arose between those who accepted European religion and those who did not, and this disrupted communities and families. In extreme cases, such as in Oka, Quebec, the churches or religious orders were given authority to govern reserve land and resources. Resources were extracted and the churches reaped the financial profits while the Indigenous people were driven into poverty.

Following the American Revolution, a massive influx of settlers into Upper Canada began. Land was needed for settlement, and in keeping with the *Royal Proclamation of 1763* the British began the tedious process of acquiring Indigenous land through treaty. Although Indigenous people did not fully understand the treaty-making process, they had no choice but to engage in it; with Canada competing with its US neighbours for occupancy and therefore title over lands and access to resources, the British felt pressure to expand westward.

CLOSE-UP   Oka

In 1717, King Louis XV of France granted land 30 kilometres northwest of Montreal to the Seminary of Saint-Sulpice on the condition that it be used as a mission for the Mohawk people who had settled there. The grant was made to the seminary since it was deemed that the Mohawk could not manage the land themselves. The condition of the grant was such that if the Mohawk later abandoned the land, its ownership would revert to the Crown. The documents did not state whether the Sulpicians were the sole proprietors of the land or the trustees of the land for the Mohawk. As far as the Mohawk were concerned, the land had always been and continued to be their territory. The particular location was chosen so that the Mohawk territory, Kanesatake, was far enough from Montreal to limit negative influences from the French settler population, but close enough that the Mohawk could quickly be called into military action in defence of the French.

After the French lost their North American colonies, the Mohawk of Kanesatake unsuccessfully tried in 1781 to prove in court their proprietorship of the land. In 1841, the British issued a special ordinance confirming the seminary's title amid continuing disputes over the land and its resources. As the Mohawk began to turn from the Catholic faith to Methodism, the seminary encouraged them to leave Kanesatake so that French Canadians could settle there, establishing the town of Oka. To relieve tensions, in 1853 the Indian Department set aside land in Ontario and elsewhere in Quebec for the Mohawk of Kanesatake; however, most refused to leave. The Mohawk continued to assert

their rights to the land, cutting wood and building cabins. Some were jailed for cutting trees, since the seminary claimed rights to the timber. Violence ensued in many skirmishes, including one in which a church was burned down. In 1869, and again in 1878 and 1912, the government affirmed the seminary's ownership of the land.

In 1936, facing a financial crisis, the Church sold parts of this land for development, causing such strife that the Indian Department purchased the unsold portions of the land and managed it as a reserve, even though it was not granted reserve status. In 1961 the Mohawk requested that the land be granted reserve status so that it had protection from sale under the *Indian Act*; this was not granted. In 1975, as a new land claims process was outlined, the Mohawk put forward a comprehensive land claim, which was rejected. They filed a specific land claim two years later, which was rejected in 1986.

The claim, still unresolved, reached a boiling point in 1990 when the town of Oka announced that a nine-hole golf course on the contested land would be expanded and luxury condominiums built there also. In the resulting violent confrontation between Quebec police and the Indigenous residents of Kanesatake, an officer of the Sûrete du Québec was shot and killed. A 78-day standoff between the Canadian army and the Mohawk of Kanesatake cost millions and failed to resolve the land question.

Source: Dickason (1997, pp. 319–322).

Once occupancy was established, the "Indian question" remained. What would the colonies do with regard to the Indigenous peoples with whom they had entered into treaties? The newly formed government of Canada chose to embark upon a journey of forced assimilation by carefully enacting legislation designed to eliminate the Indigenous peoples as a special group within Canadian society.

Treaties Background

Most **treaties** in Canada were signed between 1800 and the early 1900s. They are documents drawn up by the Canadian government as purchase agreements for land recognized as having Indigenous title. In 1982 the treaties were protected in section 35 of the *Canadian Charter of Rights and Freedoms*, which reads as follows: "The existing aboriginal and treaty rights of the aboriginal peoples of Canada are hereby recognized and affirmed." This is a recent affirmation of the legitimacy of these treaty documents. Indigenous people continue to petition the government of Canada to fulfill its treaty promises and to have the original spirit of the treaties interpreted by the courts to uphold Indigenous rights to resources and land.

treaty
an agreement between two states that has been formally concluded and ratified

Treaties were not unknown to Indigenous people prior to the arrival of Europeans. Since time immemorial, Indigenous nations had made treaties among themselves to settle wars, establish ties of peace and friendship, create military alliances, delineate harvest territories, and facilitate trade. The records of these treaties were passed down orally and were honoured by the groups who entered into them.

When Europeans arrived, Indigenous people entered into treaties with them as well, such as the Two-Row Wampum treaty between the Iroquois and the British described above and the British–Mi'kmaq Treaty of 1725, which covered Nova Scotia as well as other territories. The British secured military neutrality and assistance from the Mi'kmaq in their war against the French in exchange for facilitating trade and guaranteeing protection of the Mi'kmaq people's traditional economy of hunting and fishing.

Indigenous people expected that the principles that had governed their earlier agreements—treaties of peace and friendship, military and trade alliances—would carry over into their negotiations with the Europeans over land. To them, mutual respect and understanding were essential components of negotiations. And they assumed, in keeping with the principles of their oral culture, that terms negotiated by way of discussion would be included in the final agreement.

This was not the case for Europeans; they had a different conception of written documents as opposed to spoken assurances, and different goals for the negotiations. Indigenous people believed that no one could own the land in the European sense of ownership. The land was a gift from the Creator, and they were stewards of the land, not owners of it. Indigenous people viewed the treaties as laying out the terms of a mutual sharing of resources, including their own compensation for consenting to share with Europeans.

Europeans understood the treaties, according to their own cultural context, as requiring First Nations to yield the land to the Europeans, thus giving the Europeans absolute ownership of the land. The intention was to erase First Nations title to the land so that it could be parcelled out for sale for new ownership. Although both parties had interpreters present, it was difficult to translate the European understanding of ownership into terms the First Nations negotiators would grasp. In retrospect, too, one must wonder how diligently the Crown tried to convey its intended meaning; a full understanding on the part of the First Nations people would most certainly have brought negotiations to an unsuccessful conclusion. Many times it was not until the Europeans began the process of removing First Nations people from their land that the latter fully understood what they had signed.

There are three categories of treaties in Canada: (1) pre-Confederation treaties, which were entered into before 1867; (2) numbered treaties, signed between 1871 and 1921, and intended to unite the interior of Canada and formally recognize these territories as part of Canada, as well as to clear title to build a railway to facilitate the extraction of resources; and (3) land claims agreements, which were made after 1973, when the government established a formal land claims policy.

All treaties before 1973 were initiated by Europeans. Indigenous people never began any negotiations to sell their land. Following the defeat of the British in the American Revolution of 1776–1783, the British sought land to compensate both their Indigenous allies—primarily, the Six Nations (Mohawk, Onondaga, Cayuga, Seneca, Oneida, and Tuscarora), who had performed military services and sustained considerable losses for the British—and their other military allies. In 1784, Frederick Haldimand purchased 3 million acres (1.2 million hectares) from the Mississauga for £1,180 worth of goods to facilitate the settlement of the Loyalists. The Iroquois loyalists were granted a tract 6 miles (10 kilometres) wide on either side of the Grand River, a total of almost 1.2 million hectares in what is today southwestern Ontario. This is known as the Haldimand Grant, which provided a land base for the Six Nations reserve. In Chapter 8 we will look at this grant and discuss its implications for today.

Until 1798, the government had no problem obtaining Indian land, through treaty, for about 3 pence per acre in either cash or goods, then selling that land for a healthy profit to private investors and settlers for 6 to 15 pence per acre. By 1912, there were 483 treaties listed for Canada, comprising a considerable body of law (Dickason, 1997, p. 163).

Indigenous allies became the deciding factor in yet another war—the War of 1812—as the newly independent United States attempted to make its way north into British-held territory. The British were victorious and in the end established a border between the United States and Canada. In the following years of peace, the European population in Canada once again exploded. Between 1821 and 1851, the European population rose from 750,000 to 2.3 million (Dickason, 1997, p. 198). Once again the Crown was desperate for land to accommodate the population growth. With peace in sight, the British had less need of their Indigenous allies, who thus lost one of their key means of maintaining a balance of power. The government began to offer First Nations people annuities for their land rather than the considerably larger one-sum payments. This was a more economical way for the Crown to obtain land through treaty, since the annuities could be paid from the profitable sale of the land to settlers.

The treaty-making process was quite irregular. The Crown representative was included as a negotiator, but otherwise there seems to have been no standard policy, especially concerning the price of land. In 1790, for example, 2 million acres (809,000 hectares) were purchased by the Crown for £1,200 from the Ojibwe and Odawa in southern Ontario. Two years later, 3 million acres (1.2 million hectares) were purchased from the same group for the same amount (Dickason, 1997, p. 164). Many of these land transactions were not properly recorded or were imprecise in their terms regarding boundaries, giving rise to later disputes. For example, one treaty, aptly named the "gunshot treaty," describes a boundary as being "from the lakeshore to as far back as you can hear a gunshot." Many of the original treaties were lost. By the mid-1830s, a sequence of over 30 treaties had been concluded, effectively covering southern Ontario.

There were many problems with the treaty process. First, as discussed previously, there was the problem of making the First Nations people understand such concepts as exclusive possession of property. Second, there was the government's unscrupulous tendency to weight the written terms of the agreement more heavily than the oral ones that the First Nations negotiators considered binding. Today, efforts have been made to research the recorded minutes of council meetings before and after the signing of a treaty. This research has brought to light promises that were clearly made by the government but never written into treaty documents, which were then signed by individuals who could not read. Third, there was the problem of obtaining signatures from the leaders of First Nations affected by the treaty. Many First Nations were left out of the treaty-signing process simply because government officials did not know they were there. With a stroke of a pen, the government seized the land of these people without their permission or signatures. Adhesions (subsequent signings) had to be made later to the treaties to include some groups who had been overlooked.

Numbered Treaties

Following Confederation in 1867, treaty negotiations began with a large number of First Nations across Canada. These treaties are referred to as the "numbered treaties"; they were made in the interest of nation building and to acquire land for a national railway. These treaties cover very large land areas (see Figure 7.2). The terms of the 1850 Robinson–Huron treaty became a precedent for the other numbered treaties. These terms included the following:

- Sale of reserved lands and mineral rights was to be conducted by the government for the sole use and benefit of the First Nations.
- Negotiations were to be open and accessible to the public.

FIGURE 7.2   Treaties and Comprehensive Land Claims in Canada

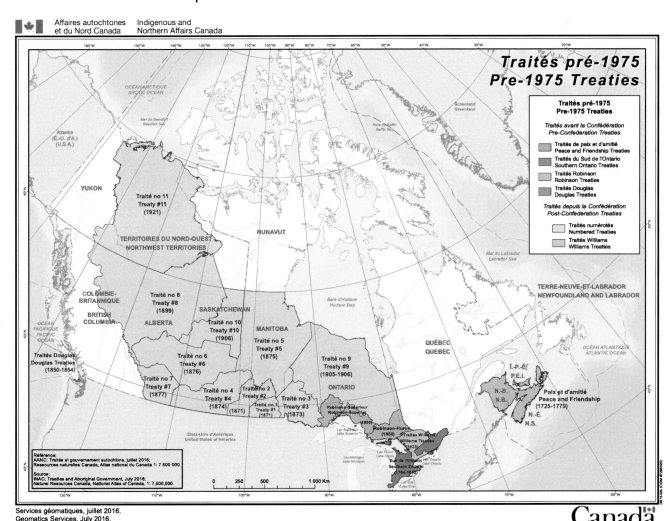

This map shows the boundaries of the land surrender treaties made between Indigenous peoples and the Crown between 1725 and 1975.

- Land was to be surrendered only to the Crown.
- Annexed to each treaty, a schedule of reserves was to be held in common by each group affected by the treaty.
- Annuities were to be paid in cash to signing members.
- First Nations retained "the full and free privilege to hunt over the Territory now ceded by them, and to fish in the waters thereof … saving and excepting such portions of the said Territory as may from time to time be sold or leased to individuals or companies of individuals" (Aboriginal Affairs and Northern Development Canada, 1939).

The numbered treaties based the quantity of land reserved for First Nations people on their population in the treaty area at the time. These populations were smaller than pre-contact populations, since Indigenous peoples had sustained at least an 80 percent death toll due to European diseases. Among other items, agreements regarding schooling, annuities, and agricultural equipment for First Nations were included in most numbered treaties.

This brings us to a common misconception among Canadians. Some believe that federally funded education, housing, or taxation exemption are special and generous provisions from the federal government for First Nations. This is not the case; the federal government has frequently tried to escape these obligations but has been instructed by the courts that the treaties hold the force of law and must be honoured. These benefits were granted to First Nations people in negotiated treaties by which the Crown acquired the land that is now Canada. In the words of the treaties, these terms are to be upheld "as long as the grass is green, as long as the sun shines and the rivers flow."

Western Expansion

The pressure to populate the West with white settlers intensified following the conclusion of the American Revolution in 1783. It was apparent that the western lands and all the wealth and resources therein would belong to whoever could get there first and was prepared to defend it. The newly independent United States had severed its ties with Britain and therefore was no longer bound by the *Royal Proclamation*, and it embarked on a series of wars against the Indigenous inhabitants of the Americas in order to clear them from the land.

The British colonies created incentives for immigrants and other white settlers to move west, enticing agricultural settlers with 64 hectares of free "Crown land." Rapid work was required to obtain that land from the current occupants by way of treaty. The protection of this western land would be provided in part by the Indigenous peoples themselves. Recall that the United States concluded terms of independence in 1783. After this, the British were concerned about the Americans moving west and northward, as well as about the possibility of an American attack on the remaining British colonies, which would ultimately happen in 1812. The British had learned a valuable lesson in their wars against the French: the side with the most Indigenous allies would win. Between 1784 and 1788, the British spent £20,000 on gift distributions to Indigenous people, hoping to secure military allegiance as they moved westward. This was more than the British had paid to secure land through most of the treaties to that date. They were successful in securing the allegiance of Tecumseh, who was a powerful Shawnee leader. He sided with the British and united more than 30 nations to lead in the defence of British-held territories. Together they helped the British repel the Americans in the War of 1812. Tecumseh sided with the British not only for the gift distributions but also because he believed them to be the lesser of two evils, since the British continued to make assurances of protecting Indian lands, an assurance that the United States would not make.

VOICES

Tecumseh

My heart is a stone. Heavy with sadness for my people; cold with the knowledge that no treaty will keep the whites out of our land; hard with determination to resist as long as I live and breathe. Now we are weak and many of our people are afraid. But hear me; a single twig breaks but the bundle of twigs is strong. Someday I will embrace our brother tribes and draw them into a bundle and together we will win our country back from the whites.

Following the War of 1812, western expansion accelerated again. Northwestern Indigenous peoples such as the Sioux, Blackfoot, and Plains Cree, as well as the Métis, had built an economy based on the buffalo. Upon the arrival of traders, a market was quickly created for buffalo products. The hides became fashionable to wear, and the bones were exported to create bone china, popular in Europe. Bison bones were used in a wide variety of other applications as well, including as fertilizer; as part of the refining of sugar, liquor, and vinegar; and during the manufacture of dyes. At the peak of the bison slaughter, a ton of dried bones could sell for as much as $10. In less than a century, by 1889, the number of buffalo had been reduced from 70 million to 635. Needless to say, this caused extreme hardship among the Indigenous peoples of the plains at a time when treaty negotiations were fully under way.

Ultimately, Europeans made it all the way to the west coast of Canada. In 1785 the first trading ships arrived, drawn by the lucrative trade in sea otter pelts. Contact and trade were done by ship because an overland route was not found until 1804. Within the first 100 years of contact, West Coast peoples suffered an 80 percent population decrease due to European diseases, one of the most dramatic declines in an Indigenous population since first contact (Dickason, 1997, p. 180).

Sea otter pelt trading was in full swing by 1792, and by 1825 the sea otter population was devastated. One trader, John Kendrick, reported that he traded £100 worth of chisels and iron tools for 200 sea otter pelts. He then received £8,000 for the pelts in Europe (Dickason, 1997, p. 181).

In 1852, Vancouver Island had only 500 settlers; however, the discovery of gold brought 25,000 miners to Queen Charlotte Island in 1858. Salish First Nations and miners clashed regularly, sometimes violently. The destruction of Indigenous territories was rapid, and their land base eroded with the building of roads and mines.

Salmon resources were being exploited for export to European markets. Salmon was a main source of subsistence for many First Nations such as the Nisga'a, and the depletion of this resource caused them significant hardship. James Douglas, governor of Vancouver and the British Columbia mainland at this critical time, attempted to acquire land by way of treaty. He had signed 14 treaties with Salish bands on Vancouver Island by 1854, but this amounted to only 3 percent of the island's territory. The First Nations were not eager to enter into treaties, and James Douglas quickly ran out of money. Although the colony offered no further finances, Douglas was undeterred and continued to establish reservations for the First Nations people based on their favourite locations and on their numbers. He allotted 200 acres (81 hectares) per head of family, then simply assumed the rest of Vancouver Island and British Columbia to be territory of the Crown. He retired in 1864 and was succeeded by Frederick Seymore, who appointed a commissioner of Crown lands, Joseph Trutch. Trutch refused to recognize the legitimacy of the reserves established by Douglas, and was hostile to First Nations land claims. He wrote:

> The Amerindians have no rights to the land as they were of no actual value to them, and I cannot see why they should either retain these lands to the prejudice of the general

interests of the colony. Or be allowed to make a market of them to either the government or individuals. (Dickason, 1997, p. 234)

Trutch proceeded to reduce the size of the reserves surveyed by Douglas from 200 to 10 acres (81 to 4 hectares) per head of family, again without compensation.

British Columbia entered Confederation with Canada in 1871 and was allowed to retain control over "Crown land." But the federal government assumed responsibility for "Indians and lands reserved for Indians" as per the *British North America Act* of 1867. Arguments between provincial and federal governments began over how much land was to be granted for reserved First Nations land. British Columbia tried to reduce the lands even further, to 4 acres (1.6 hectares) per head of family, but the federal government insisted on 80 acres (32 hectares). British Columbia persisted in assigning reserves for First Nations without compensation, and by 1900 there were over 90 reserves established at an average of 185 acres (75 hectares) each (Dickason, 1997, pp. 234–235).

Note the emerging pattern here with regard to the seizure of land and resources. Most of the resources were exported to Europe; however, much of the wealth produced from the resources went toward building what is now our very affluent country. In fact, Canada still relies for its wealth on natural resources such as timber, oil, and gas; owners of land often grow wealthy from its natural resources. Unfortunately, Indigenous peoples generally do not share in this wealth. As we will see in Chapter 10, Indigenous people still suffer from higher than average levels of poverty and today live on only one-half of 1 percent of Canada's land mass.

EXERCISE 1

Consider the concept of "progress" from different cultural world views. How did the Western concept of progress affect Canada's Indigenous peoples?

Vanishing Race

The size of almost all reserves established through the treaty process was based on the population of the First Nation at the time of the treaty. But First Nations populations were low during this period, and the treaties made no provision for an increase in numbers. This seems evidence of a strong belief that Indigenous people were vanishing. And in fact they were dying at a rapid rate from disease, and many were lost in the numerous wars among the colonists. It was generally believed that within three generations of treaty-making there would be no Indigenous people left; they would either die of disease or be assimilated into mainstream Canada.

The Canadian government's intent regarding First Nations was never made so clear as it was by Deputy Superintendent of Indian Affairs Duncan Campbell Scott in 1920:

I want to get rid of the Indian problem. I do not think as a matter of fact that this country ought to continually protect a class of people who are able to stand alone. That is my whole point. … That has been the whole purpose of Indian Education and advancement since earliest times. One of the very earliest enactments was to provide for the enfranchisement of the Indian. So it is written in our law that the Indian was eventually to become enfranchised. … Our object is to continue until there is not a single Indian in Canada that has not been absorbed into the body politic and there is no Indian question, and no Indian department, that is the whole object of this Bill. (Leslie & Maguire, 1978)

Scott's view was reflected in the actions of certain Canadians during this period. Indigenous graves, often fresh, were dug up so that the remains could be put on display at Wild West

VOICES

Repatriating the G'psgolox Totem Pole

The G'psgolox totem pole was carved and raised in British Columbia in 1872 by the Raven Clan of the Haisla Nation after its chief, G'psgolox, had had a spiritual experience. An avalanche drove the nation to abandon its home, where the pole stood. Shortly thereafter, collectors from Sweden, who had been looking for a totem pole for their museum, found and removed it. The Haisla did not know where the pole had gone, and its whereabouts remained a mystery until it was located in the Museum of Ethnography in Stockholm, Sweden in 1991. The chief of the Haisla and a descendant of the pole's creator went to Sweden to request the pole's return. After long negotiations, the support of the BC government, and many delays, the return of the pole was celebrated in 2006 in Kitamaat, BC. The G'psgolox totem pole was the first to be repatriated to its people and began the return of many artifacts that have been housed for a century or more in European museums.

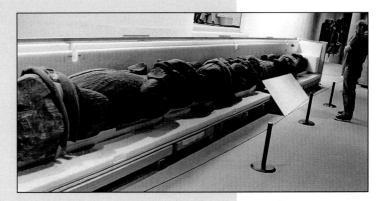

Source: Gersten (2007).

shows. Spiritual and cultural artifacts still in use by Indigenous people were taken and sold to collectors, who anticipated their value increasing as the Indigenous people themselves vanished. Today, Indigenous nations have undertaken serious efforts to repatriate these items and bring them back to their communities from museums around the world.

The idea of the Indigenous peoples' vanishing was appealing to the British for one very important reason: the treaties they had entered into with First Nations were binding in perpetuity. The British could see that the cost of maintaining these promises forever could be high, particularly because the depletion of resources was impoverishing First Nations people and creating a need among them for the relief assistance guaranteed by the treaties. Assimilation of those who survived disease and poverty became a paramount concern for the British in the years to come. The complete assimilation of First Nations meant no obligation to honour treaties and free access to reserve lands.

Assimilation Legislation

In the 1830s, as settlers and resource speculators increasingly encroached on reserve land, it became necessary to define who was an Indian and who therefore could reside on reserves. The following were considered Indians under the definition fashioned by the Crown:

- All individuals of Indian blood belonging to a tribe, band, or body of Indians and their descendants.
- Any person residing among such Indians whose parents were or are descended on either side from Indians, and the descendants of this person.
- All women lawfully married to an Indian and their children. First Nations women who married non–First Nations men would not be entitled to be Indian; nor would their children.

In 1830, the British began attempts to assimilate Indigenous people into mainstream culture, pushing them to become agriculturalists, to set up communities similar to white settlements, and to adopt the Christian religion and ways of life. Some Indigenous nations accepted this transition and requested assistance with it; they recognized that the industrialization of their lands would make the hunting way of life impossible. Furthermore, they believed that conversion to the "ideal" might help protect their lands. Model villages were set up and overseen by missionaries; many were quite successful. However, regardless of their success, as white communities expanded, the model villages lost land, and many were relocated. From the perspective of the British government, the genius of this plan was that the finances required to set up these communities and begin the "civilizing" process would come from the funds generated through the sale of reserve land or through the extraction of resources such as lumber from reserve lands. In effect, Indigenous people would pay their own way to "civilization" (Dickason, 1997, p. 199).

CALL TO ACTION

60. We call upon leaders of the church parties to the Settlement Agreement and all other faiths, in collaboration with Indigenous spiritual leaders, Survivors, schools of theology, seminaries, and other religious training centres, to develop and teach curriculum for all student clergy, and all clergy and staff who work in Aboriginal communities, on the need to respect Indigenous spirituality in its own right, the history and legacy of residential schools and the roles of the church parties in that system, the history and legacy of religious conflict in Aboriginal families and communities, and the responsibility that churches have to mitigate such conflicts and prevent spiritual violence.

The Crown passed legislation in 1857 called the *Gradual Civilization Act* to create a process of enfranchisement for First Nations people, so that they could cease being considered Indigenous. Enfranchisement began as a voluntary process. The legislation set out that if a First Nations male was self-supporting, debt-free, and deemed by the superintendent to be a suitable candidate for enfranchisement, he could forfeit his Indian status and receive 50 acres (20 hectares) of land cut from his people's reserve. Furthermore, he would thereafter have all the rights of a regular citizen, including the right to vote in provincial and federal elections. If it had been successful, this legislation would have eroded the reserve land base as well as First Nations sovereignty. Very few First Nations people accepted this offer (Dickason, 1997, p. 225).

In 1869, the *Enfranchisement Act* was introduced to limit blood quantum to at least one-quarter Indian in order to qualify to remain a status Indian. All others would be removed automatically from treaty entitlements. The purpose of this legislation, in the words of a bureaucrat in 1871, was "to lead the Indian people by degrees to mingle with the white race in the ordinary avocations of life" (Miller, 2004). The result would be fewer treaty Indians. Amazingly, this focus continued to be central to all legislation designed to administer Indian people until 1985.

During Confederation in 1867, at a time when efforts were focused on nation building, the British Parliament passed the **British North America Act**, also known now as the *Constitution Act, 1867*. Indigenous people were not consulted in the creation of the Act, and the Act did not recognize the right of Indigenous self-government. Section 91(24) of this Act gave Canada authority over "Indians, and Lands reserved for Indians." Many historians believe this was a turning point in history that marked the beginning of an era of serious oppression of Indigenous people in Canada. Through the BNA Act, the power of Indigenous governments was reduced to less than that of a municipality. Power would be held by the federal government with no regard to the diversity of First Nations peoples, their cultures, or their historical relationships with the Crown. They would all be treated as one homogeneous group and governed by a one-size-fits-all policy. They would no longer have the right to negotiate with the British

British North America Act
a statute enacted on March 29, 1867, by the British Parliament providing for the Confederation of Canada

Crown in regard to legislation affecting them or their lands; rather, they would have to negotiate with the federal government, which had a keen interest in acquiring the lands occupied by Indigenous people.

CALL TO ACTION

45. We call upon the Government of Canada ... to ... [r]econcile Aboriginal and Crown constitutional and legal orders to ensure that Aboriginal peoples are full partners in Confederation, including the recognition and integration of Indigenous laws and legal traditions in negotiation and implementation processes involving Treaties, land claims, and other constructive agreements.

The Indian Act

Within nine years of Confederation, the legislation regarding First Nations was consolidated into one act called the **Indian Act**. The *Indian Act* retained the earlier definition of an Indian but, continuing to broaden its scope of authority, now defined a band as well (Dickason, 1997, p. 259). The original *Indian Act* defined a band as follows:

> The term "band" means any tribe, band or body of Indians who own or are interested in a reserve or in Indian lands in common, of which the legal title is vested in the Crown, or who share alike in the distribution of any annuities or interest moneys for which the Government of Canada is responsible; the term "the band" means the band to which the context relates; and the term "band," when action is being taken by the band as such, means the band in council.

Indian Act
a statute created in 1876 to consolidate all policies aimed at the administration of Indian populations in Canada and giving the federal government exclusive jurisdiction over Indians and reserves

According to the current *Indian Act*, a band is

a body of Indians
    (a) for whose use and benefit in common, lands, the legal title to which is vested in Her Majesty, have been set apart before, on or after September 4, 1951,
    (b) for whose use and benefit in common, moneys are held by Her Majesty, or
    (c) declared by the Governor in Council to be a band for the purposes of this Act.

The lands mentioned in paragraph (a) refer to a reserve. Many First Nation groups are still awaiting designation as bands in accordance with this legislation; without such designation, the government does not afford them any benefits or protection. There are currently 617 recognized bands in Canada and 126 in Ontario.

The *Indian Act* did not include the Inuit because there was little contact between Canada and the Inuit at the time. The government was intent on reducing rather than increasing the number of status Indians. So when the Inuit question arose in the 1930s, Ottawa's position was that since the Inuit are not culturally Indians, they were not included in the *British North America Act*, section 91(24), which designated the federal government's responsibility for Indians. In the 1930s, the Inuit of northern Quebec were hard hit by a scarcity in the game that were their traditional source of sustenance, and they needed relief assistance. Neither level of government wanted any responsibility to provide this assistance, even though fur traders, miners, and whalers had spent decades extracting resources from Inuit land without compensating the land's inhabitants. The Quebec government took the federal government to court, arguing that the Inuit were Indians for all intents and purposes and should fall under the authority of the federal government. In 1939, the Supreme Court of Canada ruled that the Inuit, although culturally distinct, would be considered Indians, but would not be included in the *Indian Act*.

Despite the Inuit's being legally classified as Indians, the government neglected them until after the Second World War, when the need arose for military expansion into the North. Between

1941 and 1970, the federal government used a disk system to identify those Inuit for which it accepted responsibility. Each disk, which could be worn on a string around the neck, bore the Canadian coat of arms and the identity number of the wearer. This simplified record keeping, since the naming system used by the Inuit was unfamiliar to the government. The disk evolved into proof of status: those who had disks were eligible for government services; those without were not.

Other groups were also left out of the legislation aimed at Indians, including the Innu of Newfoundland and Labrador. When these territories entered Confederation in 1949, the rights of Indians to be defined and dealt with in accordance with Canadian legislation such as the *Indian Act* were originally included in the documents but were deleted prior to ratification, leaving the Innu with no protection for their territories and no guarantees of any assistance in times of need.

The Métis

As a result of the fur trade, many French and English traders married Inuit and First Nations women, creating a new and culturally distinct group of people in Canada. This group—the Métis—were also not included as Indians within the Act. The children of these unions grew up predominantly in their mothers' cultures—commonly Cree, Ojibwe, Saulteaux, or Inuit—but they were also introduced to French Catholicism and English Protestantism. As these communities grew in number, they became even more distinct as second and third generations intermarried. They occupied settled communities in Rupert's Land, owned under Crown patent by the Hudson's Bay Company; spoke French or English; and were predominantly employed by the Hudson's Bay Company or the North West Company as trappers, traders, buffalo hunters, exporters of pemmican, and interpreters. The Métis settlements in the Red River Colony (today's Winnipeg area) and Saskatchewan each developed a unique culture. When the government of Canada took over Rupert's Land in 1869, the ownership of the Red River Colony land was called into question.

The Métis as a distinct group did not enter into treaties but were occasionally included in treaty documents, listed as "half-breeds." They had settled all over Rupert's Land, and its sale to Canada left them with claims to settlements that had never been treated. The Métis united to set up a provisional government under Louis Riel, who negotiated the passage of the *Manitoba Act* in 1870, which brought the Red River Colony into Confederation as the province of Manitoba shortly thereafter. The Act provided Métis with 1.4 million acres (570,000 hectares) of reserve land. This was intended to give the Métis, who already lived there, a head start on land acquisition and to secure their settlements before a massive influx of European settlers arrived. After Manitoba joined Confederation, the transfer of land did not proceed as promised. However, the Supreme Court of Canada's recent decision in *Daniels v. Canada (Indian Affairs and Northern Development)* (2016) confirmed that Métis peoples are recognized as Indians under section 91(24) of the *Constitution Act, 1867*. This may open the door to the future settlement of historic Métis land claims.

When Ottawa sent out surveyors to assess and survey Rupert's Land to prepare for additional settlement, the Métis became very concerned over their position in their territories and the preservation of their unique culture. The Métis blocked the surveyors' access to the territory and rebelled against the settler government. Louis Riel, as leader of the rebellion, ordered the execution of one of its representatives and, as a result, was himself later hanged for treason.

The Métis did not fall under the strict definition of the *Indian Act* since they had no formally recognized bands, although they were defined as a distinct people. The *Indian Act* therefore did not provide the Métis land protection rights nor rights to education or relief. They are today recognized as one of Canada's founding Indigenous peoples, and their Indigenous rights are protected under section 35 of the *Constitution Act, 1982*. To be recognized as Métis today, an individual must fulfill the following three conditions: self-identification as a Métis, ancestral connection to a historic Métis community, and acceptance by a Métis community (*R v. Powley*, 2003).

Imposed System of Government

The *Indian Act* quickly provided for the removal of First Nations traditional systems of governance and replaced them with a system called the band council. It is similar in nature to municipal governments in that it comprises one chief and several councillors elected through a process that is strictly regulated by the Act. This system was implemented for all First Nations in a one-size-fits-all fashion with no consideration given to the diverse forms of government and culture across First Nations. Furthermore, a person called the Indian agent (a white government official set in place to oversee the functions of the reserve) had authority under the Act to remove the chief or council members for any number of reasons.

Some nations resisted this intrusion on their established systems of government, the Six Nations being one of them. This band tried to resist the transition to an elected band council by agitating for change to the system and petitioning the Queen, insisting that they were allies, not subjects, of the British Crown, and had never given up their sovereignty. In 1924, Deputy Superintendent General of Indian Affairs Duncan Campbell Scott ordered the overthrow of the Six Nations' traditional council by force. Lt. Col. Morgan was charged with the responsibility of overseeing troops provided by the RCMP to overthrow the traditional council and oversee the institution of the first elected band council for the Six Nations.

Tax Exemption

The *Indian Act* included laws surrounding taxation. First Nations people living on reserves were not to be taxed either on any purchases they made while living on a reserve or on income generated from on-reserve activities. This provision was included in recognition of the special status accorded to "reserved territories" and was rooted in principles concerning nationhood and self-government. This tax exemption still exists today and is misunderstood by some non-Indigenous people, who perceive it as an unfair advantage. Many Indigenous people assert that this tax exemption signifies that Indigenous land is sovereign land and not a part of Canada, based on the fact that Indigenous people have never surrendered their sovereignty and right to self-government. Many non-Indigenous people overestimate the benefits of tax exemption. It is only for people living on the reserve and does not exempt income earned off-reserve. Since on-reserve employment is hard to find and on average generates income levels that are less

CLOSE-UP   The Métis National Council

Today, the Métis National Council is made up of five provincial organizations: Métis Nation British Columbia, Métis Nation of Alberta, Métis Nation—Saskatchewan, Manitoba Métis Federation, and the Métis Nation of Ontario. The provincial organizations have regional councils to represent Métis throughout each province. This council represents the voice of the Métis to the federal government and argues for the rights of the Métis under section 35 of the *Constitution Act, 1982*. The Métis have their own flag, which depicts the joining of two nations and the eternal existence of a people, represented by the infinity symbol on a blue background.

The councillors of the Métis Provisional Government in 1870. Louis Riel is seated in the centre.

than half the average Canadian income, most Indigenous people work off-reserve and are subject to income tax and all other taxes that other Canadians pay.

Sixty percent of First Nations people live off-reserve and therefore work off-reserve. Since tax-exemption status is attached to the territory of a reserve, not to the person, fully 60 percent of First Nations people pay all of the taxes that other Canadians pay, apart from provincial sales tax on purchases. Status Indians living off-reserve do not access provincial dollars to obtain services as non-First Nations members of the community do. They are the sole responsibility of the federal government and therefore must access federal funds allocated through Indian Affairs for services. For example, the province funds non-Indigenous education, while the federal government funds status Indians attending provincial schools in an agreed sum per student. It makes sense, then, that First Nations people are not forced to contribute to a provincial tax base that they are unable to access for services.

Changes Through Time

The first change to the *Indian Act* in 1880 was to withdraw "half-breeds" (Métis) from treaty agreements. This measure was calculated to quickly reduce the number of Indians that held status and therefore had treaty rights. At the same time, treaties were being made in the western plains area. The government could see that the buffalo population was in sharp decline and that the Métis, a distinguishable group who had already asserted their right to land, would require assistance in rebuilding their economy. In order to avoid any obligation of assistance, the government encouraged the Métis to accept **scrip**—a one-time payment and small land allocation—in lieu of the assistance they would have been entitled to as treaty Indians.

scrip
a one-time payment issued to Métis to discharge treaty rights

In the same year, the Indian Branch became its own department, with inside staff based in Ottawa, including a superintendent general, a chief clerk, an accountant, and clerical staff, as well as outside staff comprising 460 field workers responsible for the implementation of policies directed at Indians. These outside workers were called **Indian agents**, and were invested with tremendous authority over the reservation and the people with whom they worked.

Indian agent
a federal employee of Indian Affairs in charge of administration on reserves

A 1958 job study lists the authorities of the Indian agent as follows: dealing with the recording of property; registering births, deaths, and marriages; administering band funds; and holding elections. The Indian agent interviewed people who needed farming equipment, those who complained about land encroachments, and those applying for loans. He encouraged people to marry legally and to enlist in the armed forces. He adjusted property when members left or joined the band. He dealt with the estates of the deceased and supervised the building of infrastructure, including schools. He negotiated the surrender of band lands for highways or other purposes, and applied for relief funds to house those in need. He informed the court of matters concerning Indians who were on trial for criminal matters. He was the justice of the peace and the health inspector for the community and, later, for the schools. He presided over band council meetings and could vote to break a tie. Finally, he enforced the *Indian Act* and policies directed at Indians.

In some cases, Indian agents were capable people with integrity; in others, they were not. In all cases, they were non-Indigenous. This continued for decades. Slowly, bands have wrested authority for these matters back from the federal government.

In 1880, the "unmaking" of Indians continued, with mandatory enfranchisement of Indigenous people who held a university degree, joined the clergy or the armed forces, or voted in a federal election. The 1880 changes to the *Indian Act* dispensed with recognition of hereditary chiefs and recognized only elected band council chiefs. Indigenous peoples in the West were prohibited from selling their agricultural products because the government did not want them to purchase liquor or other "worthless" things.

In 1884, First Nations people complained that the government was not fulfilling the treaty agreements that would enable them to use the land; agricultural equipment promised in the treaties was not delivered. The government conceded that this was a legitimate complaint but excused the breach, explaining that the bands were not sufficiently advanced to benefit from the promised tools, livestock, and schools.

The potlatch and other Indigenous ceremonies were banned in 1884, with a two- to six-month jail term for those who contravened this prohibition. This prohibition was included in the Act but was not enforced until the 1920s under the leadership of Deputy Superintendent General of Indian Affairs Duncan Campbell Scott. Cultural practices and ceremonies went underground to avoid the watchful eye of the Indian agent. These practices had always played a critical part in the Indigenous oral culture, conveying to the next generation the people's history, their principles of governance, and their spirituality. Repressing these practices resulted in the beginning of loss of culture.

In 1889, the *Indian Act* was amended to allow the federal government to override a band that did not wish to lease land. By 1894, any Indian lands that were not worked (agriculturally) due to illness or injury could be leased to non-Indigenous Canadians under the authority of the superintendent. Idle or surplus Indian land was also seen as fair game.

In 1911, section 46 of the *Indian Act* allowed portions of land to be taken by municipalities or companies for roads or railways without consent of the band but with permission of the superintendent. Section 46(a) permitted the removal of Indians, against their wishes, from any reserve next to or partly within a town of 8,000 inhabitants. For example, a Mi'kmaq reserve in Sydney, Nova Scotia and the Songhees reserve in Victoria, British Columbia were moved outside these cities to free up urban land for development. In the West, between July 1, 1896 and March 31, 1909, First Nations received $74,343 for surrendered land. The Department of Indian Affairs subsequently received $2,156,020 for that land.

The promise of reserved lands through treaty was in some cases not fulfilled; in other cases, the power given to the Indian agent through the *Indian Act* resulted in large sections of reserved lands, coveted by settlers and resource speculators, being carved out of the First Nation's territory, sometimes without compensation. Railways expropriated reserved lands freely, often splitting communities down the centre. The railway towns that were springing up often grew to displace Indigenous people, and more land was seized, often without compensation, as the towns expanded.

In 1918, the enfranchisement of Indigenous people was made easier for those who wished to apply; however, the plan still did not meet with success. Subsequently, in 1921, legislation changed to provide the Indian agent with the authority to enfranchise any Indian who was deemed suitable regardless of his or her wishes. In other words, without giving consent, an Indian could lose his or her status with the stroke of a bureaucrat's pen.

You may be wondering why Indigenous people did not rebel against this oppressive legislation and continued seizure of their lands. In fact they did respond and organize resistance, but it seemed futile. In 1880, in response to political movement in the West to oppose land seizure, a pass system was implemented, requiring any Indian leaving the reserve to have a pass issued by the Indian agent. The goal of the system was to inhibit Indigenous people's mobility and discourage Indigenous alliances that might threaten Canadian authority. Many reserves were impoverished due to the depletion of resources, and any sign of political activism was quickly met with governmental threats of withdrawal of its relief funds.

In 1927, in a heavy-handed response to Six Nations' resistance to the authority of the Act and the West Coast Nisga'a's continued appeals to England, the *Indian Act* was again amended to proclaim that no person could raise money to fund any form of claims to land against the federal government without the express permission of the Indian agent.

VOICES

Deskaheh

Deskaheh was Cayuga, born in 1873 in western New York. He moved to the Six Nations reserve in Ontario, married, and had a family. In 1917, he became hereditary Chief of the Cayuga Nation. In 1921, Deskaheh travelled to London, England on a passport issued by the Iroquois Confederacy because the Canadian government would not allow him to travel. He went to Europe with an attorney hired by the band to speak on behalf of the Six Nations against the subjugation of his people by the Canadian government. He petitioned to join the League of Nations but was ultimately unsuccessful; he did, however, garner support from many European nations when he presented his "Petition and case of the Six Nations of the Grand River." With his lawyer, he returned to the United States to petition in Washington, DC. He was denied re-entry into Canada and spent his last days in Tuscarora, New York. Although he gained the support of nations such as Ireland, Switzerland, and the Netherlands, he was unable to achieve his goal of obtaining recognized international nation status for the Six Nations. In 1924, the hereditary council was forcibly removed from Six Nations and a band council imposed while Deskaheh was in exile in the United States. One of his most famous statements commented on Canadian policies of assimilation:

> Over in Ottawa, they call that policy "Indian Advancement." Over in Washington they call it "Assimilation." We who would be the helpless victims call it tyranny. If it must go on to the bitter end we would rather that you come with your guns and poison gases and get rid of us that way. Do it openly and above board.

It is believed that Deskaheh's actions resulted in Ottawa's oppression of Six Nations in the following years.

EXERCISE 2

The legislated disempowerment of Indigenous people through legislation such as the *Indian Act* led to the federal government assuming fiduciary responsibility for First Nations in Canada. **Fiduciary responsibility** is the legal or ethical responsibility to manage something, usually money or property, in trust for another person (or people) and act in their best interests. Do you think that the federal government has fulfilled this duty? Why or why not?

fiduciary responsibility
the legal or ethical responsibility to manage something, usually money or property, in trust for another person (or people) and act in their best interests

1951: Changes to the Act

The *Indian Act* was overhauled in 1951 in an attempt to create a more equitable piece of legislation. The ban on potlatches and other traditional dances and ceremonies was lifted. Over the previous 30 years, however, the passing of Indigenous culture and oral history to new generations, which was a central function of these practices, had been seriously disrupted. Added to this was the residential school system, to be addressed in Chapter 9, which all but eliminated Indigenous languages and culture through the education department's primary goal of assimilation.

The Act established the Indian Register as a centralized record of all individuals entitled to be registered as status Indians. The registrar was given authority to add or delete names from the general band lists. In response to complaints from Indians who were unilaterally removed from the band list or who could not be included on the band list because their births had never been registered, new rules required the posting of the band list. An appeal process was instituted for those who were removed from the list, with a limit of six months for appeal.

Despite the overhaul of the Act, there was still no agreement to set up a land claims commission as requested by Indigenous people. Furthermore, the 1951 revisions to section 88 of the Act allowed "all laws of general application in force in any Province to apply as well to Indians on and off reserves." This was undoubtedly a precursor to the federal government's intention to slowly devolve the responsibilities for Indians onto the provinces. The problem with this amendment was that certain provincial laws, such as hunting and fishing regulations, if applied to Indians, violated treaty rights. Today, Canadian courts are attempting to navigate their way through layers of treaty and provincial law to provide an equitable interpretation of that law and to define Indigenous rights in Canada.

It was not until the early 1960s that First Nations people were given the right to vote in federal elections. Soon after, they would use this right to become politically active in opposing the White Paper of 1969, proposed by Liberal Indian Affairs Minister Jean Chrétien. This paper called for the elimination of the *Indian Act*, reserved land for Indians, and the special legal category of status Indian. It further proposed to transfer all responsibilities for First Nations to the provinces and promised to look into land claims. Although it was claimed that the White Paper laid out a path to equality for First Nations people in Canada, they viewed it as the final stroke of assimilation. The National Indian Brotherhood stated: "We view this as a policy designed to divest us of our aboriginal, residual, and statutory rights. If we accept this policy, and in the process lose our rights and our lands, we become willing partners in culture genocide. This we cannot do" (Dickason, 1997, p. 364).

Once again, a policy had been created with little consultation with Indigenous people. In the words of Dave Courchene, president of the Manitoba Indian Brotherhood from 1967 to 1974: "Once again the future of the Indian people has been dealt with in a high-handed and arbitrary manner. We have not been consulted; we have been advised of decisions already taken. I feel like a man who has been told he must die and am now to be consulted on the methods of implementing that decision" (Dickason, 1997, p. 364). Cree leader Harold Cardinal wrote:

> We do not want the Indian Act retained because it is a good piece of legislation. It is not. It's discriminatory from start to finish. But it is a lever in our hands and an embarrassment to the government, as it should be. No just society with even pretensions to being just can long tolerate such a piece of legislation, but we would rather continue to live in bondage under the inequitable Indian Act than surrender our sacred rights. Any time the government wants to honor its obligation to us we are more than ready to help devise new legislation. (Cardinal, 1969, p. 140)

Many treaties had originally been made with the British, and legislation passed the responsibility to honour those treaties to the federal government upon the transfer of power during Confederation. The federal government could not simply exonerate itself of those obligations by passing them on to provincial governments. In 1971, the federal government abandoned the White Paper, but the idea of devolving responsibilities for First Nations onto the provinces had not disappeared. It resurfaced in 1986, when the Nielson report recommended that the cost of delivering services to First Nations be shared by the provinces. This was motivated by the rising costs of program delivery, since First Nations populations increased dramatically around this time, and their communities were suffering from the effects of the residential school system, which increased the need for social services. This recommendation was abandoned after much protest from First Nations people.

The fight against the White Paper resulted in a positive change to policy and practice under the *Indian Act*; for the first time, the federal government agreed to fund research into land claims and to set up processes by which those claims could be negotiated. We will discuss land claims in Chapter 8.

CHAPTER SUMMARY

Although the mainstream political structure in Canada today borrows from Indigenous government structure, the two systems are based on very different world views, particularly in regard to land and relationships between peoples and nations. Though Indigenous people held significant political power in their relationship with Europeans until the signing of the *Royal Proclamation*, they were quickly divested of that power following the collapse of their traditional economies during rapid expansion and multiple waves of harvest of natural resources by new arrivals.

The dispossession and disempowerment of Indigenous people in Canada has been a long process that has spanned generations. This dispossession was purposefully conducted by many levels of government to facilitate expansion and economic growth for Canada; however, Indigenous people in Canada rarely benefited from the economic growth. Aggressive policies of assimilation were created to ensure that status Indians with treaty entitlements would slowly disappear. But Indigenous people, against all odds, managed to cling to their heritage and status; today we grapple with the important task of defining Indigenous rights in Canada in accordance with the treaties. Indigenous people in Canada struggle to reclaim authority over their own affairs, to reclaim lost culture, to rebuild healthy communities, and to create economic growth and prosperity for themselves within Canada.

REFERENCES

Aboriginal Affairs and Northern Development Canada. (1939). Copy of the Robinson Treaty made in the year 1850 with the Ojibewa Indians of Lake Huron conveying certain lands to the Crown. https://www.aadnc-aandc.gc.ca/eng/1100100028984/1100100028994.

Bishop, J.D. (2003). The Lockean basis of Iroquoian land ownership. In R.B. Anderson & R.M. Bone (Eds.), *Natural resources and Aboriginal people in Canada: Readings, cases, and commentary*. Toronto: Captus Press.

British North America Act. (1867). 30 & 31 Vict., c. 3, reprinted in RSC 1985, app. II, no. 5.

Cajete, G. (2000). Philosophy of native science. In G. Cajete, *Native science: Natural laws of interdependence*. Santa Fe, NM: Clear Light.

Canadian Charter of Rights and Freedoms. (1982). Part I of the *Constitution Act, 1982*, being Schedule B to the *Canada Act 1982* (UK), 1982, c. 11.

Cardinal, H. (1969). *The unjust society: The tragedy of Canada's Indians*. Edmonton: Hurtig.

Clarkson, L., Morrissette, V., & Régallet, G. (1992). *Our responsibility to the seventh generation: Indigenous peoples and sustainable development*. Winnipeg: International Institute for Sustainable Development. http://www.iisd.org/pdf/seventh_gen.pdf.

Criminal Code. (1985). RSC 1985, c. C-46.

Daniels v. Canada (Indian Affairs and Northern Development). (2016). 2016 SCC 12.

Dickason, O.P. (1997). *Canada's First Nations: A history of founding peoples from earliest times* (2nd ed.). Toronto: Oxford University Press.

Gersten, P. (2007). Cultural heritage legal summary. *Journal of Field Archaeology*, *32*(1), 86.

Indian Act. (1985). RSC 1985, c. I-5.

Leslie, J., & Maguire, R. (Eds.). (1978). *The historical development of the Indian Act* (2nd ed.). Ottawa: Indian and Northern Affairs Canada.

Miller, J.R. (2004). *Lethal legacy: Current Native controversies in Canada*. Toronto: Macfarlane Walter & Ross.

Powley, R v. (2003). 2003 SCC 43, [2003] 2 SCR 207.

Royal Proclamation of 1763. (1763). RSC 1970, app. II, no. 1.

Whitehead, R.H. (Ed.). (1991). *The old man told us: Excerpts from Micmac history, 1500–1950*. Halifax: Nimbus Publishing.

REVIEW QUESTIONS

True or False?

F **1.** Prior to European arrival in what today is Canada, there were 20,000 people living on this land mass.

T **2.** In the oral tradition, spoken language is used to convey culture from one generation to the next.

F **3.** The idea of collective rights was more prominent in European culture than in Indigenous culture.

T **4.** According to Iroquois history, the Two-Row Wampum is an agreement between the British and the Iroquois to respect each other's sovereignty and to form a military alliance.

T **5.** The *Royal Proclamation of 1763* is deemed to carry the force of law and has never been repealed.

F **6.** Through the *Indian Act*, the government recognizes traditional forms of Indigenous government.

T **7.** The *Constitution Act, 1982* recognizes existing treaty rights.

F **8.** Treaties are a strictly European creation; Indigenous peoples never entered into treaties prior to European arrival.

_F_   **9.** It was not until the 1940s that First Nations people were given the right to vote in federal elections.

_T_ **10.** The White Paper of 1969 proposed the elimination of reserved lands for Indians.

Multiple Choice

1. Indigenous peoples' creation stories most often assert that

  a. they travelled across the Bering Sea

  b. they travelled across the Atlantic Ocean

  c. the people were born from the land or came to the land from a spiritual place

  d. they travelled from the South Pacific on ocean currents

2. Many academics assert that our current form of democracy was influenced by

  a. Locke's theory of landownership

  b. Indigenous forms of government at the time of European contact

  c. Thomas Hobbes's philosophy

  d. Charles Darwin

3. In Europe, the Christian religion was a "proselytizing religion." This means that

  a. Christians believed in one God manifested in many forms

  b. Christians believed that others must convert to Christianity or be eternally damned

  c. Christians were very tolerant of others' spiritual beliefs

  d. the Christian religion was not central to European culture at that time

4. Which of the following is not true of the outcomes of the fur trade as it affected Indigenous people?

  a. Indigenous people became increasingly dependent on European traders for goods.

  b. Many animal species neared extinction due to overhunting.

  c. Indigenous people incorporated the accumulation of wealth into their culture, which upset traditional balances.

  d. The fur trade created long-term and permanent economic stability for Indigenous nations.

5. The term _terra nullius_ means

  a. empty land

  b. unfertile land

  c. land whose ownership is contested

  d. lawfully purchased land

6. A treaty is

  a. a promise that is not legally binding

  b. an agreement between states in written form and governed by international law

  c. an agreement that is informal in nature

  d. an agreement between two states that has been formally concluded and ratified

7. The Robinson–Huron treaty of 1850 set a precedent for all future treaties made to acquire lands for settlement. Which of the following is not true of those precedent-setting inclusions to treaties?

  a. Sales of reserve lands and mineral rights were to be conducted by the government for the sole use and benefit of the Indians.

  b. Land was to be surrendered only to the Crown.

  c. Annuities were to be paid.

  d. Indigenous people were to forfeit hunting and fishing rights over the land that was ceded in the treaty.

8. The government accepted fiduciary responsibility for First Nations people when it passed the _Indian Act_. Fiduciary responsibility means

  a. the responsibility to cultivate the natural resources on land granted by the government

  b. the responsibility to educate

  c. the legal or ethical responsibility to manage something, usually money or property, in trust for another person (or people) and act in their best interests

  d. the responsibility to civilize

9. Indigenous people opposed Chrétien's White Paper, which proposed legislation that would in effect eliminate the _Indian Act_. Why?

  a. Because they believed that the _Indian Act_ was fair and equitable.

  b. Because they were resistant to change of any kind.

  c. Because the White Paper did not address the issue of land claims.

  d. Because the White Paper proposed to eliminate reserve land and treaty status for Indians.

10. Special rights accorded to Indigenous people in Canada today in the areas of education and taxation are

  a. an attempt at reconciling the inequalities of the past

  b. acts of generosity by the Canadian government

  c. attempts to resolve social problems prevalent on reserves

  d. obligations of the federal Crown that are rooted in treaty law

11. After the _Indian Act_ was established, who had control over the sale of Indian reserve lands?

  a. Indians

  b. the federal government through the Indian agent

  c. band-elected First Nations representatives

  d. traditional councils established by the band

8 Current Issues over Land

Tensions flare and police advance during an anti-fracking (hydraulic fracturing to extract shale gas) protest at Elsipogtog First Nation, New Brunswick, in October 2013.

LEARNING OUTCOMES

After completing this chapter, you should be able to:

- Connect contemporary land claims to historical treaties and case law.
- Examine the importance of access to land and resources for Indigenous self-determination and independence.
- Understand the present-day process of defining Indigenous rights to land and resources.
- Analyze how police services can benefit from understanding the background and context of Indigenous land claims.
- Describe the particular issues in some specific land claims cases.

Introduction

In January 2013 the *Globe and Mail* reported on a recent Ipsos Reid survey of Canadian attitudes toward Indigenous peoples and issues (Mahoney, 2013). This coincided with the Canada-wide "Idle No More" campaign in which Indigenous people protested their unequal living conditions in Canada. The protests included the blockade of some railway lines and highways, as well as many generally peaceful gatherings. There were harsh feelings expressed by non-Indigenous Canadians in response to the poll questions. Two-thirds of those polled felt that Indigenous Canadians get too much support from tax dollars and 81 percent believed reserves should not get any further funds until external auditors reviewed their financial records. Only 31 percent felt that shutting down roads and rail lines was a legitimate form of protest. However, 63 percent felt that immediate action was required from government to raise the standard of living for Indigenous Canadians, and the same number supported resolving land claims to provide Indigenous people with the land and resources necessary to become self-sufficient. Almost two-thirds of Canadians supporting land claims resolution is a remarkable move forward from 2003, when 50 percent of Canadians surveyed believed there was no validity to any Indigenous land claims in Canada (Curry, 2003).

Members of police services are drawn from all segments of the Canadian population, so we can infer that they are similar to the "average Canadians" polled by Ipsos Reid. And yet it is their responsibility to keep the peace when land claims issues arise in the form of roadblocks or peaceful (and sometimes not so peaceful) demonstrations and reclamations. Provincial and federal governments have sometimes used police as enforcement in resolving land and resource disputes with Indigenous people—for example, in the case of the Ipperwash incident (see Appendix 8.1 at the end of this chapter). The results of this have been disastrous for both officers and Indigenous people, ending in severely strained relationships between the two.

Police services today see the need to ensure that their officers have a broader understanding of the legal landscape surrounding land claims. If an officer believes that Indigenous protesters have no legal grounds for their actions or grievances, or does not understand the legal landscape that surrounds civil action, he or she will have trouble maintaining an objective and unbiased approach to peacekeeping. This chapter will outline the legal background of Indigenous land and resource claims in Canada. This will involve reviewing the constitutional rights granted to Indigenous people and the case law that has evolved to define those rights. It also requires understanding the current process for claims resolution in Canada and the challenges that it faces.

Background

The *British North America Act* of 1867 (also known now as the *Constitution Act, 1867*) established the legislative powers of Canadian government, dividing them between the federal government and the provinces. Under section 91(24) of the Act, jurisdiction and governance over territories reserved for Indigenous people were given to the federal government of Canada. Indigenous nations were not party to the creation of this Act, nor were they consulted about it. Nine years after the implementation of the BNA Act, policies regarding Indigenous people were consolidated in the *Indian Act*, an oppressive statute designed to strip away the governing rights of First Nations. The government also used the *Indian Act* to force relocations and land seizures upon Indigenous people. As the land base of Indigenous people dwindled, their level of poverty increased and their dependence on the government deepened. In a country whose economy was, and still is, based on the harvest and export of natural resources, Indigenous people, now divested of land, would become the poorest group in the country.

Many of the over 600 Indigenous territories in Canada today are economically dependent on the federal government for support, much to their dismay. Economic independence for these communities often hinges on gaining access to the harvest of natural resources on lands that are part of their traditional territory but outside their small reserves—that is, areas to which they have been granted access under the Constitution. Until recently, the government of Canada has used legislation to deny Indigenous people access to lucrative harvests, in favour of large corporations, and to trap Indigenous people in a cycle of economic dependency.

Historical Case Law

One of the first cases concerning the land claims of Indigenous people in Canada was *St. Catherine's Milling & Lumber Company v. The Queen* (1888). It set a precedent for the land claims of all Indigenous nations in Canada. Indigenous people were not represented and were not even involved in this litigation process.

The Ojibwe people in northern Ontario entered into Treaty No. 3 with the federal government of Canada in 1873. Shortly thereafter, Sir John A. Macdonald, acting in his capacity as prime minister of Canada and superintendent of Indian Affairs, issued a timbering licence to St. Catherine's Milling and Lumber Company (an interest with which he is alleged to have been closely connected) (Monture-Angus, 1999, p. 68). The company had cut 2 million feet of lumber when Ontario filed for an injunction to prevent both further cutting of the lumber and its removal. Ontario asserted that the province, not the federal government, was entitled to licensing fees and royalties for timber, since Treaty No. 3 areas fell within the boundaries of Ontario. The province cited section 109 of the BNA Act as its authority. Section 109 of the Act reads as follows:

> All Lands, Mines, Minerals, and Royalties belonging to the several Provinces of Canada, Nova Scotia, and New Brunswick at the Union, and all Sums then due or payable for such Lands, Mines, Minerals, or Royalties, shall belong to the several Provinces of Ontario, Quebec, Nova Scotia, and New Brunswick in which the same are situate or arise, subject to any Trusts existing in respect thereof, and to any Interest other than that of the Province in the same.

The federal government was the defendant in this case. Its argument was that the Indians had owned the land and had passed that ownership on to the federal government through Treaty No. 3; therefore, the federal government owned the land and the resources within it despite the fact that it lay within Ontario's provincial boundaries. The federal government cited section 91(24) of the BNA Act, which states that the responsibility for "Indians, and Lands reserved for the Indians" falls to the federal government. Ontario argued, successfully, that

Indian title to land did not constitute full ownership since Indians had no concept of property rights as recognized in British law. Ontario argued that the Crown had title to all lands of North America and that any rights to land asserted by Indians were granted by the generosity of the Crown. This, of course, is inconsistent with both the *Royal Proclamation of 1763* and the treaties themselves. Nevertheless, the result of the decision was that Indian title in the land was defined as less than full title. It was held that Indian interest in the land was mere "personal and usufructuary right"; in other words, Indigenous people's right to use the land was held at the pleasure of the Crown, which had the power to remove that right at any time.

Since this decision was made by the Judicial Committee of the Privy Council in England, the highest court in the land, it became binding on all future land issues involving Indian title to land. It is one of those precedents in the Canadian court structure that was a huge obstacle to anyone attempting to move forward in Indigenous rights cases (Monture-Angus, 1999, p. 67), and it was followed for almost a century, until the *Calder* case in 1973. During the hundred years separating these two cases, the movement toward Indigenous land and resource rights was also hindered by amendments to the *Indian Act* in 1927, which prohibited First Nations from hiring lawyers or pursuing claims to land. These provisions were not repealed until 1951.

The *Calder* case began in 1971, when four Nisga'a communities in British Columbia's Nass Valley brought their case to the Supreme Court of Canada, asserting their claim to traditional territory that was outside the reserve created for them by the federal government. The communities based their claim on the fact that they had never entered into any treaties and had never relinquished their lands to either the federal government or the province of British Columbia. They and their ancestors had in fact occupied the land since time immemorial, and they had never agreed to relinquish any land or resources. The Supreme Court was split three to three on whether the claim to the land was valid (the seventh judge dismissed the case on a technicality). In his decision, Justice Judson stated:

> [T]he fact is that when the settlers came, the Indians were there, organized in societies and occupying the land as their forefathers had done for centuries. This is what Indian title means and it does not help one in the solution of this problem to call it a "personal or usufructuary right." What they are asserting in this action is that they had a right to continue to live on their lands as their forefathers had lived and that this right has never been lawfully extinguished. (*Calder et al. v. Attorney General of British Columbia*, 1973, p. 328)

Justice Hall discussed the process of extinguishment further. He stated that should the Crown claim to have extinguished Indigenous title to land, it must do so in a clear and plain manner; it cannot rely on implied extinguishment. The most significant part of this judgment is that all six judges agreed that

- Indigenous title to land existed, as defined by British law, prior to and at the time of colonization; and
- the Crown must act in a clear and plain way to extinguish that title.

Although the *Calder* case did not provide a clear test of extinguishment—this did not come until the case of *Sparrow*, in 1990—it did force the federal government to work toward settling Indigenous claims in regions of the country where treaties had not extinguished Indigenous title. This was something Indigenous activists had long wanted; since the 1951 revision of the *Indian Act*, which had repealed the prohibition against First Nations' pursuit of land claims, they had been pressing the government, to no avail, to create a process for settling land claims.

Another case that significantly affected Indigenous land and resource claims in Canada was *Guerin v. The Queen* (1984). Prior to the verdict in *Guerin*, the Department of Indian Affairs had a *moral duty* to act in the best interest of First Nations in the administration of reserve lands and resources. But this duty, known as a *fiduciary duty*—in other words, the duty to act in the best interest of another—was not recognized in law. Accordingly, the department had limited accountability to the Indigenous people it administered; it was accountable only to the federal government, whose interests were opposed to those of the Indigenous people, particularly in financial matters.

In *Guerin*, the Musqueam Indian Reserve had agreed to lease 66 hectares of reserve land in the city of Vancouver to the Shaughnessy Golf Club in 1955. In keeping with the *Royal Proclamation of 1763*, which provides that Indian land is "alienable"—in other words, can be surrendered or leased—only to the Crown, the band was required to surrender the 66 hectares to the Crown before the lease could take place. In a meeting, the band and the Indian agent agreed upon the terms of the lease to be put in place with the golf club. However, these terms were misrepresented to the band. The land was surrendered and the Crown entered into a lease agreement with the golf club on terms that were unfavourable to the band and inconsistent with what it had agreed to. The band attempted to grieve this action, but to no avail. The band was unable even to procure a copy of the lease agreement, which it had never received at the time the land was transferred, until 1970. When the band obtained a copy of the lease, it attempted to sue the Crown for damages. The case made its way to the Supreme Court of Canada, which issued its decision in 1984. At the heart of the argument was the Crown's responsibility to act in the best interest of the band. The Crown argued that the responsibility amounted to a "political trust" enforceable by Parliament but not to a "true trust" enforceable by the courts. The Crown was unsuccessful in its argument, and the SCC ruled as follows (*Guerin v. The Queen*, 1984, p. 376) in its final verdict:

> An Indian Band is prohibited from directly transferring its interest to a third party. Any sale or lease of land can only be carried out after a surrender has taken place, with the Crown then acting on the Band's behalf. The Crown first took this responsibility upon itself in the Royal Proclamation of 1763. It is still recognized in the surrender provisions of the *Indian Act*. The surrender requirement, and the responsibility it entails, are the source of a distinct fiduciary obligation owed by the Crown to the Indians.

Justice Dickson also stated the following:

> After the Crown's agents had induced the Band to surrender its land on the understanding that the land would be leased on certain terms, it would be unconscionable to permit the Crown simply to ignore those terms. ... Equity will not countenance unconscionable behaviour in a fiduciary, whose duty is that of utmost loyalty to his principal. (*Guerin v. The Queen*, 1984, pp. 388–389)

There have been many cases like *Guerin*—that is, cases that bring into doubt the Crown's responsible administration of band resources and band land. *Guerin* set a precedent; the government would be held responsible for mismanagement. In the *Guerin* case, the band was awarded $10 million in restitution. The sum of the settlement was based on what the lease value of the land would have been to that point had the band never surrendered the land to the government to facilitate the unfavourable lease (Henderson, 1996). The settlement of the case came at the end of a long, slow process. There were a number of appeals; the final decision was rendered a full 14 years after the band first obtained a copy of the lease and the Crown's misdealings were seen in their full extent. This was 29 years after the original proposed lease.

Constitution

During the litigation of the *Guerin* case, the Canadian Constitution was **patriated**. Prior to the patriation of the Constitution, Indigenous activists had appealed to international powers and to governments in Canada and Europe for the inclusion of Indigenous rights within the Constitution. Their work culminated in the inclusion of section 35 of the *Constitution Act, 1982*, which states the following:

patriation
the process by which Canada gained control over the Constitution; previously, amendments to the Canadian Constitution required an act of British Parliament

35(1) The existing aboriginal and treaty rights of the aboriginal peoples of Canada are hereby recognized and affirmed.

(2) In this Act, "aboriginal peoples of Canada" includes the Indian, Inuit and Métis peoples of Canada.

(3) For greater certainty, in subsection (1) "treaty rights" includes rights that now exist by way of land claims agreements or may be so acquired.

(4) Notwithstanding any other provision of this Act, the aboriginal and treaty rights referred to in subsection (1) are guaranteed equally to male and female persons.

Since the introduction of this provision in 1982, Canadian courts have been trying to clarify the extent of Indigenous rights in this country. It is important to note the wording of the section; the *existing* rights of Indigenous people are *recognized and affirmed*. This section does not provide any new rights for Indigenous people in Canada. Of course, Indigenous rights existed in common law in Canada prior to the enactment of the Constitution. The source of those common law rights was the Indigenous people's original occupation of land and their social and political organization, which existed prior to Canada's assertion of sovereignty. Some of those rights were expressly terminated by the Crown through treaty, but many were not. Some Indigenous rights were established through the treaty process. Section 35 of the Constitution, rather than creating new rights, elevates the rights that existed already, through common law and treaty, to constitutional status. This restricts the right of the Crown to modify or extinguish Indigenous rights (Bell & Paterson, 2003, p. 108).

Section 35 provided protection for Indigenous rights but did not simplify the process of defining what is and is not an Indigenous right. So—what is protected under section 35 of the Constitution? Indigenous people have been taking their cases to court continually over the years to have the courts define these rights.

EXERCISE 1

Indigenous activist, author, and lawyer Ardith Walkem (2003, p. 198) has written the following about the purpose of Indigenous people's battle for rights in the Canadian courts:

> When Indigenous Peoples speak of Aboriginal Title and Rights, it is a much broader conception than that which has evolved under Canadian Law. Indigenous Peoples are not seeking to have distinct practices protected, nor title recognized to small parcels of land. The reason that Indigenous Peoples engage in the court process stems from a simple desire and imperative: Our continued existence as peoples and maintenance of our ability to continue to exist and thrive on the territories on which the Creator placed us and according to the laws which bind us to the lands and waters and govern the relationships between all living things and the spiritual beings that also live within and through the lands and waters. These elements, at a minimum, embrace the fundamental aspects of Indigenous Peoples' aspirations:
>
> 1. Territory (both land and water) and recognition of our responsibility to manage, protect and benefit from that territory.
> 2. Recognition of the laws, traditions, languages and cultures of Indigenous peoples which flow, and are intricately tied to, our territories, and
> 3. Recognition of a right to self determination which ensures that we are able to survive into the future governed by, and accountable to, our own laws.

With reference to Walkem's description above, consider the importance and role of land within an Indigenous and a non-Indigenous framework, including its connection to identity and survival. How do you think this has shaped modern conflicts over land rights?

The right to self-determination is one of the fundamental aspirations of Indigenous people, and achieving it requires a certain degree of independence from the control of the Canadian government. This independence will require a degree of economic self-sufficiency, which means, in turn, that Indigenous people must rebuild their economies to thrive in today's world. Such rebuilding will require both land and control over resources of the land.

Many cases that have been brought before the Supreme Court involve rights to the harvest of natural resources—hunting and fishing rights, for example, as in *R v. Sparrow* (1990). Ronald Sparrow is a Salish and lives on the Musqueam Indian Reserve, which is located within Vancouver's city limits. He fishes commercially and for food. In May 1984, he was charged with using a drift net that was longer than British Columbia fishing regulations allowed. Sparrow did not dispute the facts at issue in the case but argued that he had an Indigenous right to fish in the area, as his forefathers had for generations, and that this right was protected under section 35 of the Constitution. An *Indigenous right* to fish in the area—so Sparrow's argument went—meant that he was not bound by the British Columbia fishing regulations applicable to non-Indigenous fishers. Sparrow did not decide lightly to embark upon this case; he was aware that the outcome would affect Indigenous fishing rights across Canada. He was supported in his decision by the band. Its members were being charged more and more frequently under the fishing regulations, and relations between the band and the Department of Fisheries were growing hostile. Sparrow's decision to embark on the case was in the interest of his community, not simply himself (Monture-Angus, 1999, pp. 88–89).

Sparrow's case was heard by the Supreme Court of Canada in 1990. In reviewing the case, the court recognized that the main issue was whether Parliament had the right to regulate Indigenous fishing in light of section 35 of the Constitution. The first matter to be decided was whether the rights of the Salish to fish were "recognized and affirmed" in the Constitution at the time of its patriation in 1982. The Crown's position was that the right claimed by Sparrow was extinguished prior to 1982 amid the myriad provincial fishing regulations enacted over time in British Columbia. The Crown was unsuccessful in its argument due to the precedent set by the *Calder* case in 1973, wherein the court stated that the Crown must articulate in a plain and clear manner its intent to extinguish an Indigenous right and cannot rely on implied extinguishment. Justices Dickson and La Forest stated the following in the *Sparrow* case: "The test of extinguishment to be adopted, in our opinion, is that the Sovereign's intention must be clear and plain if it is to extinguish an aboriginal right" (*R v. Sparrow*, 1990, p. 1099).

The Supreme Court found that the enactment of provincial regulations prior to 1982—the rationale for extinguishment cited by the Crown in the *Sparrow* case—is implied extinguishment only and did not meet the test for extinguishment. On this basis, the Supreme Court concluded that Sparrow's right to fish was constitutionally entrenched in 1982.

Since the Constitution is the supreme law of the land, statutes cannot be enacted to alter rights guaranteed in it. However, the Supreme Court in *Sparrow* recognized that the rights of Indigenous people to the fisheries are not absolute. In *Sparrow*, the Supreme Court set out a two-part test for determining whether infringement on an Indigenous people's constitutional right to fish is justified. The first part of the test asks whether the Crown has "compelling and substantial objectives" for infringement—for example, the protection of the resources in order to ensure the continuation of the right. The second part of the test requires that any legislation aiming to limit Indigenous people's constitutional rights to fisheries must be consistent with the Crown's fiduciary obligation to Indigenous people. Other compelling objectives may involve balancing the constitutional rights of Indigenous people to the fisheries with those of non-Indigenous people. In the latter circumstance, the test of fiduciary duty would come first.

The judgment rendered in *Sparrow* was seen as a victory for Indigenous people, whose aim in establishing a right to the resource was not to exclude non-Indigenous access but to increase their own economic self-sufficiency. Ultimately, of course, this victory was significantly limited by the power the decision gave the Crown to restrict Indigenous access through the two-part test. Still, the onus was now on the Crown to justify infringement, including minimal infringement. If the rights were to be infringed for justifiable reasons, this must be established through a process of negotiation. Bell and Paterson (2003, p. 107) offer a concise summary of the litigation process used to determine what Indigenous rights are constitutionally protected:

1. identification of the nature and content of the right;
2. determining whether the right is an "existing right" recognized and affirmed by section 35 (or whether it has been lawfully extinguished prior to the enactment of section 35);
3. determination of whether federal or provincial legislation constitutes a prima facie infringement with the exercising of an existing Aboriginal right; and
4. analysis of the legitimacy of justification for government interference.

The *Sparrow* decision shows how a common law Indigenous right to fish becomes protected under the Constitution. Later, in *R v. Badger* (1996), the Supreme Court clarified that rights set out in treaties must be protected in the same manner. This will have far-reaching consequences; many of the more than 500 treaties give Indigenous people the right to hunt and fish without interference by the Crown, and many treaties give them hunting and fishing rights over territories ceded in the treaties that are now Crown land or over territories in which interest has been vested in third parties due to grants by the Crown. The same two-part test set out in *Sparrow* must be applied to infringement of an Indigenous right that is set out in a treaty.

A number of cases since *Sparrow* have elaborated on the two-part test. The *R v. Van der Peet* case, decided by the Supreme Court of Canada in 1996, offered a new twist on the *Sparrow* two-part test. Dorothy Van der Peet was charged with violating BC fishing regulations, which prohibited the sale and barter of fish. Van der Peet was a member of the Sto:lo First Nation. She sold 10 salmon for $50 to a non-Indigenous person. In this case, the Supreme Court set new criteria for characterizing and interpreting Indigenous rights. It narrowed the definition of what could be considered an Indigenous right to a right that existed pre-contact. It held that a right is not an Indigenous right if it exists because of European influence. In this case, the Supreme Court held that the pre-contact activity of exchanging fish among nations or people did not correspond to an unlimited commercial right to fish for contemporary Indigenous people; it corresponded to a right to fish for livelihood. According to the principle in *Van der Peet*, contemporary Indigenous rights must in some cases be grounded in pre-contact activities. This decision would set a precedent for the battle between mainstream Canada and Indigenous people over the latter's right to access the forestry industry, one of Canada's greatest exports and sources of wealth. The Supreme Court would later rely on the *Van der Peet* decision to disallow Indigenous people increased commercial access to the forestry industry, on the basis that logging is not an activity in which they engaged pre-contact.

Indigenous Title to Land

The *Delgamuukw v. British Columbia* case (1997) began its journey through the Canadian court system in the early 1980s. It developed in the following way. The Gitksan and Wet'suwet'en people sought to force the province of British Columbia to recognize Indigenous title over the two bands' traditional territory, which they had never ceded to the province or federal government through treaty or by any other means. The area encompasses approximately 58,000 square kilometres in north-central British Columbia. The province asserted that Indigenous title to land in British Columbia had been extinguished in 1871, upon the incorporation of the province into the Dominion of Canada. The case was decided by the Supreme Court in 1997.

The case set precedents for Indigenous rights, including Indigenous title to land, and for Crown sovereignty, which the courts assert can coexist with Indigenous rights.

The BC Crown argued the following:

1. Indigenous peoples were so low on the scale of social organization that their lands can be treated as vacant and unoccupied for the purpose of issuing Crown grants pursuant to laws enacted by settler governments without regard to the prior occupation of Indigenous peoples (Mandell, 2003, p. 166).
2. Colonial land legislation before Confederation extinguished Indigenous peoples' relations to the land; once the colony (soon to become a province) enacted legislation regulating Indigenous peoples' rights to the land and resources, their rights were extinguished by implied extinguishment and by the powers vested in the colony/province (Youngblood Henderson, 1999).
3. The creation of land grants by British Columbia to settlers extinguished Indigenous tenure because Indigenous people were precluded from sustaining their relationship with the land; once settlers were granted land and began occupying it, Indigenous peoples' relationship to the land was broken. The existence of third-party interests displaces Indigenous use, right, and title (Youngblood Henderson, 1999; Mandell, 2003).
4. The establishment of federal First Nations reserves in British Columbia extinguished Indigenous tenure because Indigenous people "abandoned" their territory (Youngblood Henderson, 1999). An underlying assertion of this argument is that the benefits of colonization, such as "civilization" and "Christianity," were compensation enough for voluntarily vacating traditional lands (Mandell, 2003).
5. Section 88 of the *Indian Act* allowed provincial laws of general application to apply as well to Indians, extinguishing Indigenous title and rights (Youngblood Henderson, 1999).
6. Indigenous title and rights vanish with the passage of time (Mandell, 2003, p. 169).

These arguments, made by the Crown to assert the absence of Indigenous title over the land, are the same ones put forward initially by many students who are studying land claims for the first time. It is important to understand that the Supreme Court heard—and rejected—all of these arguments in the *Delgamuukw* decision. Arguments 2 to 5 rest on the assumption that the colony or province of British Columbia has the power to extinguish Indigenous title to land. The court ruled that the province never had the constitutional authority to extinguish Indigenous title, and since that title had never been extinguished, it is protected under section 35 of the Constitution.

The court did not recognize the passage of time as extinguishing title or rights, nor did it recognize the argument that Indigenous people, because "uncivilized," were not a people capable of holding territory.

In its decision, the court identified three components of Indigenous title:

1. It encompasses the right to exclusive use and occupancy of the land.
2. It gives Indigenous people the right to choose what uses the land can be put to, with the limitation that the land cannot be altered so as to destroy its capacity to sustain future generations of Indigenous people.
3. The lands held pursuant to Indigenous title have an economic component.

The first component of the Supreme Court's ruling in *Delgamuukw* displaced the *St. Catherine's* ruling of 1888, which had stated that Indigenous interest in the land was merely "personal and usufructuary"—that is, held at the pleasure of the Crown. It elevates the Indigenous interest in the land to exclusive use and occupancy. The second component of the ruling states that Indigenous people must be consulted over decisions pertaining to the uses of the land held under

Indigenous title. In other words, holding title to land gives Indigenous people mineral rights and rights to make decisions over resource harvesting and development. The third part of the court's ruling in *Delgamuukw*, by which the economic component of the land's value is recognized, suggests that the fiduciary responsibility of the Crown must be scrutinized in the dealings with Indigenous land, and that Indigenous people must benefit from the lands and resources. The Supreme Court also established a test for infringement on the rights inherent in Indigenous title. It specified that the Crown must provide justifications for infringement and that compensation must be paid for the infringement based on the nature of the infringement, in recognition of the economic component of Indigenous land title.

As in all cases involving Indigenous rights, a move forward would not be complete without a limitation being placed on it. The *Delgamuukw* decision set out a two-part test for determining whether infringement on Indigenous title is justified. The first requirement is that the infringement be for a valid legislative directive. The Supreme Court definition of "valid legislative directives" was very broad; it included the following:

1. the development of agricultural, forestry, mining, and hydroelectric power;
2. the general economic development of the province;
3. the protection of the environment or endangered species;
4. the building of infrastructure; and
5. the settlement of foreign populations to support those aims (McDonald, 2003, p. 231).

The second part of the test for justifiable infringement asks whether the infringement is consistent with the fiduciary responsibility of the Crown to Indigenous people. It makes it mandatory for the government to consult with Indigenous people before reaching a decision about infringement and compensation. This consultation process has not always gone smoothly, and breakdowns can lead to serious and sometimes dangerous confrontations. For an example of such a breakdown, we will look briefly at the East Coast lobster fisheries dispute between the Crown and the Mi'kmaq.

Case Study: Mi'kmaq Fishing Rights

Originally, the Mi'kmaq were partners in the Wabanaki Confederacy, which comprised five nations: Mi'kmaq, Passamaquoddy, Penobscot, Maliseet, and Abenaki. The traditional territory of this group included Atlantic Canada, Maine, and parts of Quebec. Post-contact, the Mi'kmaq were aligned with the French but made treaties with the British after France was forced to cede its territories in Acadia to the British. Settlers and the original inhabitants of the territory signed a series of treaties, beginning in 1725, to establish peace. These treaties reserved the Mi'kmaq the right to fish and hunt in the territory as they had always done. The treaties did not contain any provisions about transferring the land's ownership. Renewed in 1749, 1752, 1760, 1761, and 1794, this series of treaties was characterized as a covenant chain, with each treaty connected and linked to the others. The highlights of those treaties were as follows:

> British laws would be a great hedge about the Mi'kmaq property and rights. Mi'kmaq could traffic and barter or exchange commodities in any manner with managers of truck-houses (trading posts). Mi'kmaq would receive gifts in the form of goods on the First day of each October and the nation to nation relationship between the British and the Mi'kmaq would be respected and the Mi'kmaq way of life would be preserved. (Knockwood, 2003, p. 47)

This is the same chain of treaties that currently affects New Brunswick in terms of protection of land use for traditional purposes and conflict with the development of a shale gas extraction industry.

Following this chain of treaties, the BNA Act was instated, followed by the *Indian Act*, which essentially denied the treaty rights of the Mi'kmaq. Following this, myriad federal and provincial laws were enacted to regulate and limit the Mi'kmaq rights to fish and hunt. Nevertheless, the Mi'kmaq continued to press for the recognition of the treaties and continued to hunt and fish outside the regulations that had been unilaterally imposed. In 1928, Mi'kmaq Gabriel Sylliboy was charged with hunting out of season. He was found guilty when the trial judge asserted that the treaty protection did not extend to Mi'kmaq outside the small band of the Shubenacadie, and since Sylliboy was not a member of that band, he had no protection under the treaty. Furthermore, the judge ruled that even if Sylliboy were a member of that small band, he would still be found guilty on the following grounds: when the treaty was signed in 1752, the Mi'kmaq were not an independent power legally capable of entering into a treaty. One must question the logic of this statement. Why would the British negotiate a treaty with a group whom they did not recognize as having the legal capacity to enter into a treaty?

The precedent was set; in a subsequent case, *Francis v. The Queen* in 1969, Justice Richard of the New Brunswick Magistrate's Court convicted Martin Francis of fishing without a licence (Knockwood, 2003, p. 52). Francis asserted that the treaties set out his right to fish. Although the judge was sympathetic to the issues, he found it his "painful duty" to convict because, he said, previous case law meant that the law did not recognize the treaty.

A number of cases ensued involving the Mi'kmaq, who, seemingly undaunted, continued to battle in the courts to assert their rights. The first case that followed the constitutional provisions enshrined in section 35 was *Simon v. The Queen*, in 1985. The *Sylliboy* decision, stating that the Mi'kmaq were not capable of entering into treaties, was overturned. James Simon, charged with hunting infractions, was not convicted. The basis given by the Supreme Court for his acquittal was that the treaty of 1752 was a valid treaty that the Mi'kmaq had legitimately entered into and that ought to protect them against infringements on their hunting rights. The Supreme Court also found that the right was not an "absolute right" and was subject to federal regulation. Nevertheless, this was a victory, since it was the first time the Mi'kmaq treaties had been recognized, affording them protection under section 35.

The last relevant decision of the Supreme Court came in 1999, in the case of *R v. Marshall*. Donald Marshall Jr., a Mi'kmaq fisherman, was charged with violating federal fishing regulations by selling eels without a licence, fishing without a licence, and fishing during the closed season with illegal nets. Marshall had caught 463 pounds of eels that he sold for $787.10 (*R v. Marshall*, 1999, para. 4; Donham, 2003, p. 366). Entered into evidence for the defence were minutes from the treaty negotiations from 1760–61. Those minutes included requests from the Mi'kmaq for truckhouses in which to sell their peltries (animal skins), and agreements by which the Mi'kmaq could barter and trade their catches and hunting spoils with the managers of the truckhouses for "necessaries." In 1999, the Supreme Court interpreted this as the Mi'kmaq having retained not only their right to harvest resources but also the right to sell and trade to their best advantage. The court interpreted "necessaries" to mean "a modest livelihood." The court, as in other cases previously discussed, did not give the Indigenous group the right to an unlimited commercial harvest; it provided that federal regulations might restrict the Indigenous right if the resource needed to be protected. In keeping with the *Delgamuukw* decision, it was agreed that decisions about restricting or impinging on Indigenous rights must involve negotiation with the Mi'kmaq, as well as close attention to the Crown's performance of its fiduciary duty.

Approximately 40 Mi'kmaq boats took to the water to celebrate the recognition of their rights and began to fish lobster. The same waters were home to some 2,893 lobster boats owned by non-Indigenous people. The backlash from non-Indigenous fishers, particularly commercial fishers, was fierce. They lobbied the government to re-open the *Marshall* case and insisted that the conservation of lobster fisheries was at stake. Violence broke out in some communities between Indigenous and non-Indigenous fishers. The Department of Fisheries quickly pressured

Mi'kmaq and other bands to sign agreements limiting their newly recognized rights to fish. Twenty-seven bands signed agreements with the department within a year. Bands at Indian Brook and Burnt Church refused to sign, and continued to fish and develop their own conservation plan. They were portrayed in the media as renegades, adamant and unreasonable in their determination to fish illegally. The media failed to point out that the quantity of Indigenous traps was in fact less than 0.2 percent of the non-Indigenous traps (Donham, 2003, p. 371). (Similarly, today we see media portrayals of violent acts to oppose shale gas development but no explanation of the peace and friendship treaties, their history, and the duties mandated by the Supreme Court that exist as a result, as well as no media investigation of the level of consultation that is or is not happening surrounding those obligations.)

As Indigenous traps were destroyed by angry non-Indigenous fishers, and violence broke out, the RCMP was called upon to keep the peace, and the Department of Fisheries was sent in to save the lobsters from Indigenous fishers who, according to the media, were about to drive the lobsters to extinction. The Department of Fisheries arrested Mi'kmaq fishers and participated in sinking several of their vessels (Obomsawin, 2002). The RCMP did what it could to keep the peace. By 2002, the Mi'kmaq had acquiesced and signed agreements to severely limit their take of the resource. Ten Mi'kmaq fishers had been arrested for fishing violations and for further criminal offences related to resisting Department of Fisheries officers' arrests. The conflict is not over; the Mi'kmaq continue to attempt to inch their way into the commercial fishing business, but the conflict has taken on the form of constructive negotiations. The Mi'kmaq Rights Initiative has assembled a unified team of Mi'kmaq negotiators who together with the Province of Nova Scotia and the federal government meet to examine and agree upon the manner in which the Mi'kmaq will exercise their constitutional rights to land, fisheries, and natural resource harvesting. The Mi'kmaq had 300 consultation processes under way at the time of writing, and many of Nova Scotia's prominent corporations involved in resource industries participate in the consultation process (Mi'kmaq Rights Initiative, n.d.).

What all of this means is that in 2004 one of the poorest Indigenous groups on the East Coast, a group with the greatest right—according to the Supreme Court of Canada—to harvest resources, was assigned a negligible amount of the harvest. The Supreme Court decision in *Marshall* was intended to increase Mi'kmaq access to the fishery and to provide economic hope for the community. As constructive negotiations continue, the consultation process will lead to a more equitable distribution of resources and the inclusion of co-management plans, as discussed in the next section.

Shale Gas Extraction (Fracking) and Indigenous Rights

The chapter opening photo (see p. 205), taken in October 2013 in Rexton, New Brunswick, shows the RCMP enforcing a court-ordered injunction to remove Indigenous protesters from a blockade of seismic exploration trucks on Highway 134. The trucks were being used by SWN Resources, a Houston-based resource extraction company, for shale gas exploration in the area. Forty protesters were arrested following a clash with police in which six police vehicles were set ablaze. The conflict once again brings Indigenous land issues to the forefront, highlighting the Supreme Court–mandated "duty to consult" Indigenous people who have an underlying interest in the lands under development. Two weeks following the incident, the Assembly of First Nations' Chiefs in New Brunswick issued a statement that condemned acts of aggression by protesters but at the same time said, "First Nations are not anti-development but will never support development at the expense of the environment" (Assembly of First Nations' Chiefs in New Brunswick, 2013).

First Nations in the exploration area have concerns over the impact of shale gas extraction on local land and water and are not satisfied with the level of consultation on the matter.

The New Brunswick government subsequently placed a moratorium on shale gas drilling, and in March 2016 SWN Resources closed its New Brunswick office. Despite this, many businesses continue to pressure New Brunswick to permit shale gas extraction to create jobs and increase income for the province.

Working Together

Thus far we have examined the litigious and adversarial nature of defining Indigenous rights to land and resources. Because our system is based on Western European legal structures, it is adversarial in nature. However, there are other ways of defining rights and reaching mutually acceptable agreements about resource sharing and management. Because pursuing land claims through litigation is so slow and costly, it often happens that development continues on the contested lands until, by the time settlements are reached, the land's resources are already harvested or the land is permanently altered by, for example, mining or oil or gas exploration.

One of the new approaches to land claims is co-management. Co-management is a more inclusive and consensus-based approach to resource harvesting and development; it involves government and private industry sharing decision-making power with non-traditional actors—environmental groups, Indigenous groups, and local users of the resources—in the process of resource management. Co-management emphasizes resolving conflict through negotiation rather than litigation (Campbell, 1996). It has been implemented in areas where Indigenous rights to lands have not been extinguished and seems to have been most successful in more remote areas, where settlement and the harvesting of resources are just beginning.

As discussed earlier in this chapter, particularly in the *St. Catherine's Milling* case, the protection of Indigenous treaty rights, such as hunting and fishing, is seen as the responsibility of the federal government. However, the management of natural resources is seen as a provincial responsibility. Confusion can result when Indigenous people choose to exercise their treaty rights to natural resources on provincial Crown land. Whether they are permitted to do so depends on how developed that provincial land is.

Concepts of co-management fit well with the Supreme Court ruling in *Delgamuukw*, particularly the second component of the ruling, which set out the right of Indigenous people to determine the uses to which the land can be put. The process of co-management is a good answer to that component of the ruling, which makes sincere negotiations over land usage mandatory.

Current co-management schemes vary in the degree of control they allow Indigenous people in the management of resources. Provincial governments sometimes call their proposals "co-management" when what they are actually doing is informing Indigenous people about decisions already made with regard to the contested territories; they are not consulting with them on how to minimize the harmful effects to their communities. This kind of process is inconsistent with the true spirit of co-management. Even with real co-management, the degree of control allowed Indigenous people tends to vary; it can range from cooperation, to communication with advisory committees, to participation on management boards, all the way to partnership and community control. Ideally, the co-management process means a partnership of equals and completely joint decision-making. This requires commitment and a delicate balance of interests.

Co-Management: Torngat Mountains National Park

Torngat Mountains National Park is the 42nd and newest national park in Canada, created when the Nunavik Inuit Land Claims Agreement came into legal effect on July 10, 2008. This agreement was the first comprehensive land claims agreement in Atlantic Canada. The Park Impacts and Benefits Agreement formalized the ongoing relationship between Parks Canada and the Labrador Inuit and includes provisions that allow the Inuit to continue traditional activities such as land and resource uses in the park.

A seven-member cooperative management board comprises two members from Parks Canada; two from Makivik Corporation, which represents Quebec Inuit; and two from the Nunatsiavut government, as well as an independent chair appointed by all three parties.

Land Claims

comprehensive land claims
claims to territory that are not covered by treaty or land cession agreements

Land claims are divided into two categories: comprehensive land claims and specific land claims. **Comprehensive land claims** affect land that has not been covered by treaty, meaning approximately 50 percent of Canada's land mass. Since no treaty involving that land was made, Indigenous people have an interest in any land that, as per *Delgamuukw*, has a distinct economic nature. Treaties are not a thing of the past; the processes through which these contemporary claims are settled constitute modern-day treaties. Their settlement can involve terms and conditions touching on a variety of matters, including money, land, forms of local government, rights to wildlife, the protection of Indigenous language and culture, and the joint management of lands and resources. These modern treaties set out conditions concerning resource allocations, structures for self-government, and many other matters related to economic interests in the land. Government negotiators often offer an increase in the existing Indigenous land base in return for the extinguishment of Indigenous title over an even larger portion of land. Such exchanges are highly controversial for Indigenous people, since the extinguishment of rights over territory is precisely what they are fighting against. As previously discussed, Indigenous people have a special sense of their connection to the land.

Some negotiations have led to portions of urban land being added to reserve holdings. The Manitoba Treaty Land Entitlement Framework Agreement, signed in 1997 by Canada, Manitoba, and Indigenous representatives, sets out that land should be added to Indigenous peoples' reserved land base to compensate for land improperly expropriated from them. The land is to come from Crown holdings. But the agreement allows for the purchase of private land, on a willing buyer–seller basis, by Indigenous groups who do not have sufficient Crown land to choose from in their immediate vicinity, with the federal government supplying $76 million for this purpose (Treaty Land Entitlement Committee of Manitoba Inc., n.d.). The Manitoba Treaty Land Entitlement includes 21 First Nations. Purchases of this sort have gone forward in a number of agreements in Western Canada. In some cases, Indigenous bands have used settlement money to purchase properties in urban centres to provide housing for urban Indigenous people, and they have started economic ventures in traditionally non-Indigenous areas where proximity to urban centres increases their chances of business success.

FIGURE 8.1   Manitoba Treaty Land Entitlement

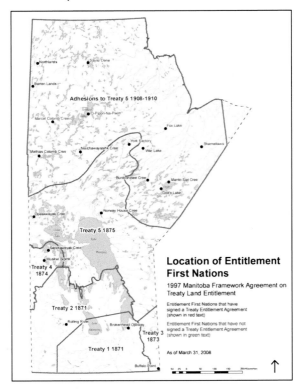

The First Nations involved in the Manitoba Treaty Land Entitlement, showing which nations have finalized their negotiations with the province and federal government in order to add to their reserve land base.

SOURCE: Implementation Monitoring Committee (2008).

Specific land claims are based on lawful obligation and involve claims related to the management of Indigenous lands and assets. With specific claims, the main issue is the loss of established band lands and their natural resources as a result of unilateral action by the Crown. The *Guerin* case discussed earlier in this chapter is an example of a specific land claim.

specific land claims claims that relate to specific misdealings of the Crown with relation to land or resources

---

EXERCISE 2

Research a specific land claim that interests you (for example, the Mississaugas of the New Credit claim regarding the Toronto Purchase) and reflect on the length of the process. Consider in what ways the land has changed while the claim was under way.

Each claim is distinct, reflecting the particular needs and history of each area. Take, for example, the claim put forward in 1988 by the Golden Lake Algonquin (Steckley & Cummins, 2001a). This claim is still under negotiation 30 years after the process began, and remains a long way from settlement. The Golden Lake Algonquin live 140 kilometres west of Algonquin Park, Ontario. They have never surrendered their rights to the land and have never signed a treaty. The government originally signed a treaty with an Ottawa band who spent a few years in the Algonquin area around 1680 but did not claim the area, at the time, as their traditional territory. The Algonquin, who claimed the area as traditional territory, were overlooked in the treaty process. This is not unusual and has happened to different Indigenous groups in Canada—the Lubicon Cree in Alberta, for example, and the Temagami Anishinaabe in northern Ontario.

The Golden Lake Algonquin have been asserting their claim to the land since 1772, when they petitioned the government to recognize their title. Sir William Johnson, superintendent of Indian Affairs for the northern district, assured the Algonquin that their title was protected under the *Royal Proclamation*—despite the fact that, at the time, they were being overwhelmed by white settlement. The government, after promising several times to keep settlers off the land, abruptly announced in 1836 that the Algonquin had already surrendered the land to the Crown under treaty and had been compensated accordingly. The 1845 Bagot commission, which investigated the uncompensated alienation of Indigenous people from their lands, looked at the Algonquin situation and recommended that the Algonquin be compensated for their land and that a tract of land be set aside for them. This recommendation was not followed.

In 1857, hemmed in by settlers on all sides, five Algonquin families petitioned the government for reserve land. Six years later, they were granted 631 hectares of land on which to live. Soon, other families joined the group and the population grew to the point that the established acreage could not sustain them. Algonquin Provincial Park was created in 1893 from Crown land that was for sale for settlement. Other groups of Algonquin were living in the area that would become the provincial park, and they petitioned the government to set aside lands for them, given that they had been displaced by the creation of the park. The government advised them to join the Golden Lake group on the area already set aside. (The government wished to avoid creating more reserves because it believed that the price of real estate would drop if there were too many Indigenous people in the area.) The Algonquin continued to petition the government, insisting that they had neither surrendered their land nor been compensated for its loss; furthermore, they had been told—and had believed—that their title to the land was protected under the *Royal Proclamation*. Their petitions were ignored.

In the mid-1980s, a Provincial Court judge agreed with the Algonquin that they had not ceded their traditional land and that therefore their title to the land was protected under the *Royal Proclamation*. The Supreme Court of Ontario overturned that decision; regardless, the Algonquin entered a claim that involved 8.8 million hectares, which included most of the park and much of the surrounding area, including small municipalities.

The Algonquin wished to reclaim unoccupied Crown land only, not private, commercial, or municipal lands. Four subjects were brought forward in this claim: land, natural resources, self-government, and compensation for the loss. The province began the negotiation process in response to the claim, but the public was outraged. The loss of the park and of Crown land meant that there was no room for non-Indigenous communities to expand.

By 1991, the two sides reached an interim agreement outlining hunting and fishing rights in the area. This agreement gave the Algonquin rights within the park, much to the dismay of non-Indigenous hunters. In 2013–14, members of the Ontario negotiations team scheduled over 150 meetings with landowners, cottage associations, and those who hold direct interests in Crown lands, including municipalities within the claim area. In June 2015, a proposed agreement-in-principle was finally reached and voting by the Algonquin was complete in March 2016, with the majority voting to accept the agreement-in-principle. An agreement-in-principle is something sought after in all negotiations. It is an interim point in the process; it is not legally binding, but it determines the scope of the negotiation and its goals. An agreement-in-principle requires ratification by all negotiating parties. The agreement-in-principle between the province, the federal government, and the Algonquins includes the following:

- the transfer of 117,500 acres of Crown lands to Algonquin ownership;
- defined Algonquin rights to resources, including hunting and fishing rights;
- $300 million as settlement capital from the federal and provincial governments;
- no creation of new reserves;

FIGURE 8.2 Algonquins of Ontario Settlement Area Boundary

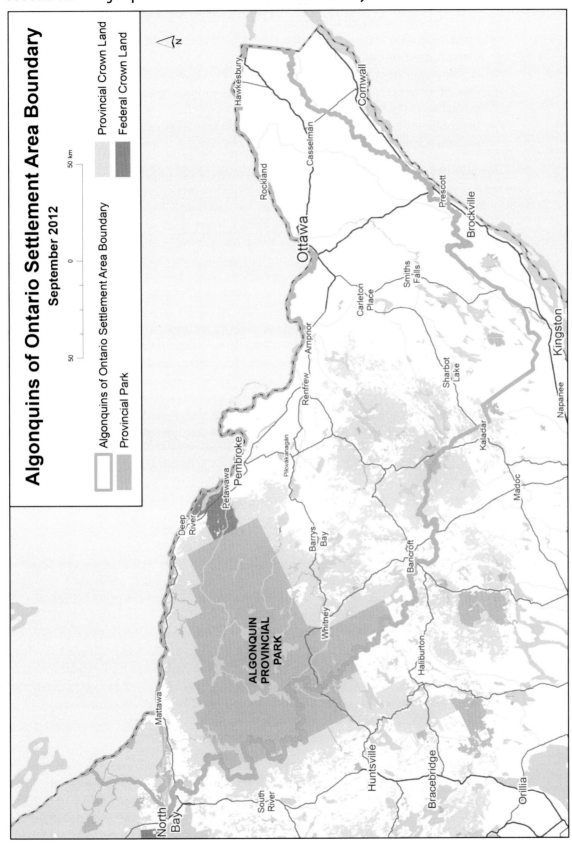

The original claim area of 36,000 square kilometres, or approximately 8.9 million acres; the claim settlement area is merely 117,500 acres, only a small fraction of the original claim area.

SOURCE: Aboriginal Affairs and Northern Development Canada (2012).

- the preservation of Algonquin Provincial Park for the enjoyment of all;
- no expropriation of land from private owners;
- the restoration of historically significant sites to the Algonquins;
- the development of moose harvesting plans by the Algonquin in consultation with the Ontario government;
- the development of fisheries management for the Algonquin settlement area by the Ontario government in consultation with the Algonquin, with the first priority being protection of the fisheries; and
- the continued provincial management of Algonquin Provincial Park in consultation with the Algonquin.

The next step is to begin drafting the detailed legal wording of a final agreement. In the case of the Algonquin land claim, the final agreement will be a modern treaty, which means it will be ratified by special legislation protected under the Canadian Constitution.

The considerable time it takes to negotiate a claim is obviously a major problem. Proposals have been put forward to speed the process along, but it remains painfully slow. Many claims have taken or will take much longer than the Algonquin's. Most claims are negotiated without protests or violence; however, when the negotiations break down, Indigenous people sometimes take action in the form of protests and/or setting up blockades. This most often happens when resource harvesting or development is occurring rapidly on contested land. Indigenous groups cannot afford to wait 20, 30, or 50 years while their claim makes its way through stages of research and negotiation. If they wait too long, there will be nothing left to negotiate for. These protests and/or blockades have the potential for violence: investors and construction or forestry crews become angry with the work stoppages, and Indigenous people become frustrated that their petitions are being ignored.

For specific claims, which are far easier to resolve than comprehensive claims, the resolution process has taken 13 years on average. In October 2008, the government passed the *Specific Claims Tribunal Act* (SCTA), which set a limit on how long a claim could remain outstanding. It was intended to reduce the backlog of 800 claims waiting for negotiation. The Act was given the slogan "Justice at Last" and was approved by the Assembly of First Nations. It was meant to increase impartiality and fairness, provide greater transparency, result in faster processing of claims, and provide better access to mediation.

The specific claims process has four steps:

1. Submission: A First Nation submits a well-researched claim to the minister responsible for Indigenous affairs.
2. Early review: The minister reviews the claim within six months to see if it meets the minimum standard articulated in the policy.
3. Research and assessment: The minister has three years to assess the validity of the claim and either accept it for negotiation or reject it on grounds that Canada has no obligation to negotiate. If a claim is rejected, the First Nation can file its claim with the Specific Claims Tribunal for a decision on the validity of the claim and compensation.
4. Negotiation and settlement: If a claim is accepted and negotiations cannot be concluded within three years, the First Nation can withdraw from negotiations and go to the tribunal for a binding decision on compensation.

As we approach the sunset of this program, scheduled for 2016–17, we reflect on the fact that the Act has not produced the results hoped for by Indigenous leaders. Aboriginal Affairs and Northern Development Canada (AANDC) reported in 2011 that the SCTA had resulted in the resolution of 445 specific claims since 2007. However, when the three-year deadline for negotiation (October 16, 2011) passed, the claims that had not been successfully negotiated started making their way to the new Specific Claims Tribunal. The tribunal opened in June

2011, after a delay in appointing judges and developing rules and procedural guidelines. A report published by the Union of British Columbia Indian Chiefs (2011) asserted that since the opening of the tribunal, Indigenous groups were being forced into take-it-or-leave-it offers from the government, on claims that have spent years under negotiation. They perceived that Canada had stopped negotiating in good faith and was intent on transferring the many outstanding specific claims to the newly created tribunal, which quickly became overwhelmed.

As Canada moves toward severely reducing the funding for the Justice at Last action plan in 2016–17, AANDC has published its success with the program, listing its achievements as

1. having fewer claims entering the system;
2. eliminating the backlog of claims;
3. negotiating specific claims that have been accepted by the minister;
4. establishing access to mediation for First Nations; and
5. fulfilling its requirements and meeting First Nations' expectations through the Specific Claims Tribunal providing final, just, and timely resolution of claims. (Aboriginal Affairs and Northern Development Canada, 2015)

However, in 2015 the Assembly of First Nations reviewed the process and refuted the AANDC statements of its achievements in a research document entitled *In Bad Faith: Justice at Last and Canada's Failure to Resolve Specific Land Claims*. While AANDC said that fewer claims are entering the system, the report's authors assert that AANDC omitted from its calculations the 230 claims that were in the research and development stage by the Claims Research Unit in 2014, which had yet to be submitted. AANDC also did not include 40 new claims that were rejected by the Claims Research Unit due to lack of funding; these claims also are yet to be submitted. Because the research and development process is so cumbersome and has had its funding drastically cut, there are an estimated 200 to 300 claims that will likely be submitted in the next five years, once the necessary funding is secured.

AANDC states that the backlog of 800 claims has been eliminated, but the way it has been eliminated requires closer inspection. First Nations claim that the "backlog" has been transferred to the Specific Claims Tribunal by the failure to negotiate in good faith to meet the three-year deadline, or by the rejection of claims through the early review, requiring additional research for resubmission.

Concerning AANDC's assertion that specific claims are being negotiated, First Nations point out that the early review includes a valuation of the claim. Claims are assessed as small value

FIGURE 8.3   Breakdown of Closed Claims per Fiscal Year

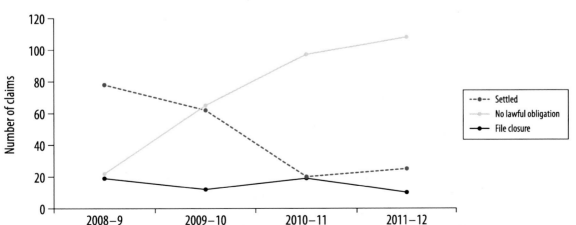

SOURCE: Aboriginal Affairs and Northern Development Canada (2013).

(less than $3 million), normal value ($3 million to $150 million), large value (over $150 million), or "unsure" value. This valuation allows proportional resources to be assigned to process the claim, including funding for negotiations and legal costs. Small-value claims are assigned limited funds and are often negotiated not in good faith but with a take-it-or-leave-it offer; however, these claims are listed as "negotiated" by the minister. The small-value claimants receive notification that their claim has been accepted for negotiation along with a one-time sum to cover legal costs and a 60- to 90-day window to accept the offer or have the file closed.

AANDC established a mediation unit as promised in the Justice at Last policy; however, this unit is housed within AANDC and the mediators are selected by AANDC, which brings into question their neutrality and independence in the mediation process.

The Specific Claims Tribunal, which is now handling the rejected claims and the claims that did not settle in the three-year time frame, has become overwhelmed. On November 14, 2014 the tribunal chair in his annual report warned that "crippling understaffing and considerable funding shortages will impair the ability of the Tribunal to function" (Assembly of First Nations, 2015, p. 27). He warns that the current and future caseload cannot be handled by the tribunal.

The Justice at Last negotiation and claims settlement process is to be completed by 2016–17. Time will tell what the final outcome will be as the measures of its achievements are presented in the future.

Ontario

Generally, there are three kinds of land claims in Ontario.

(1) **Claims relating to the fulfillment of terms of treaties.** These claims are usually the result of disagreements between the Crown and First Nations about the size and location of the reserves that were set aside in accordance with the treaties. These claims may also involve the wording of treaties and the understanding of the parties at the time of treaty signing. Claims can also arise as a result of events that occurred after the treaty signing, such as the flooding of reserve land for hydroelectric power and the expropriation of reserve land for public purposes such as highways, infrastructure, or military building without compensation. The Ipperwash land dispute falls into this category. (See Appendix 8.1 for details.)

(2) **Claims arising from the surrender for sale of reserve land.** These occur when an Indigenous community seeks compensation for, or the return of, land that had been surrendered to the Crown for sale for the benefit of the band. These surrenders did take place, and the funds generated from the sale of land were to be set aside for the sole benefit of the band. In many cases, however, the band did not receive these funds, or the land remained unsold and the band was not compensated.

(3) **Claims arising from Indigenous title.** There are few of these claims in Ontario, since most of the province is covered by treaty; however, other large areas of Canada are not covered by treaty. These claims are based on the allegation that lands traditionally used and occupied by Indigenous people were never surrendered to the Crown by Indigenous people. The Golden Lake Algonquin claim is an example of this type of claim in Ontario.

When it comes to negotiating land claims, the Ontario government has adopted the following policy:

> Ontario will not expropriate private property to reach a land claim settlement. However, when it would help to reach a settlement, Ontario may agree to buy land from an owner who wants to sell, in order to include it in a claim settlement.
>
> During negotiations, Ontario considers how Crown lands are being used. Potential impacts on current uses are reduced as much as possible. For example, the province will not cancel Crown land leases, easements, mining claims, timber allocations, and other licences and permits during their term. (Ontario Ministry of Aboriginal Affairs, 2011)

claims relating to the fulfillment of terms of treaties claims that are usually a result of disagreement between the Crown and First Nations about the size and location of reserves set aside by treaties

claims arising from the surrender for sale of reserve land claims occurring when First Nations seek compensation for, or the return of, land that had been surrendered to the Crown for sale for the benefit of the band

claims arising from Indigenous title claims based on the allegation that lands traditionally used and occupied by Indigenous people were never surrendered to the Crown by Indigenous people

In other words, Ontario residents need not fear a loss of land or loss of economic revenue as a result of a land claims negotiation or settlement. If a settlement indicates that acreage should be added to reserve holdings, the Crown would seek to negotiate the transfer of Crown land or would seek to purchase land from a willing seller.

Caledonia Land Claim

One well-known Ontario land claim involves the Six Nations of the Grand River, near Brantford, in what is now Caledonia. The history of this claim dates back to the Haldimand Grant of 1784, when Britain allowed the Six Nations to "take possession of and settle" approximately 385,000 hectares of land along the Grand River as a reward for their loyalty during the American Revolution. In 1792, the grant was reduced to 111,000 hectares by Lieutenant Governor John Graves Simcoe, and over the next two hundred years, much of the land was the subject of various transactions, with portions sold, leased to the Crown and then sold to third parties, surrendered (although this has been disputed), and set aside for a reserve.

In 1992, another element was added to the land's complex history when Henco Industries bought a company that owned about 40 hectares of land in the area. In 1995, Six Nations sued the Canadian and Ontario governments, asserting a land claim that included the land allegedly owned by Henco Industries. Ten years later, in July 2005, Henco registered plans for the Douglas Creek Estates subdivision with the province of Ontario and was granted title. In February 2006, when Henco began building homes on the land, a small group of Six Nations protesters moved onto the construction site and set up tents, a teepee, and a wooden building, and refused to leave. On March 10, Henco was granted a court order that required the protesters to leave the site by March 22, but they continued their occupation. During a pre-dawn raid by the OPP on April 20, which police stated was in response to "an escalation of activity," 16 people were arrested, and officers used pepper spray and Tasers against protesters. Protesters returned by 9 a.m. and blocked off the road using a dump truck and burning tires (CBC News, 2006a). OPP commissioner Julian Fantino underscored the role of law enforcement—it is to "preserve the peace, deal with offences and bring those who transgress the laws of the land to justice" (CBC News, 2006b).

The initial protests were followed by counterprotests from some residents of Caledonia, who were frustrated by the chaos and disruption of the protests; by the building and removal of barricades; and by general looting, vandalism, and violence. On May 19, the Ontario government announced an indefinite construction ban, and in mid-June the government bought out the disputed land for $12.3 million; the settlement was also to include compensation for the loss of future profits, to be determined later (CBC News, 2006a). Despite further judicial efforts to have the protesters removed, on August 27 the Ontario Court of Appeal ruled against ordering the protesters off the land.

In 2011, the government agreed to pay $20 million to compensate residents and business owners for the disruption caused by the protests. To resolve the claim, however, one must determine which part of the original land grant was surrendered by Six Nations legitimately, which part was kept, and which part was taken without Six Nations' consent (Darling, n.d.). Negotiations to settle the land claim are ongoing at the time of writing.

EXERCISE 3

Caledonia offers examples of the competing interests and obligations involved in any dispute over land—in this case, those of Henco Industries, the Six Nations protesters, the residents of Caledonia, the government, the court, and the police. In a dispute like this, what do you think the first priority should be? How would you balance the other interests against the priority you identified? Comment on the way this balance was struck in the case of Caledonia.

Political Activism

The cases discussed in this chapter, as well as the history of Indigenous people in Canada discussed in Chapter 7, have not progressed without organized political activity by Indigenous people. The earliest forms of activism were met with severe consequences from the federal government, which was able to control unrest through the *Indian Act*. However, since 1960 Indigenous people have been successful in bringing cases to court and pressuring the federal government to honour the treaties. Attempts have been made throughout Canada's history to organize political associations beyond the band level so that the common interests of Indigenous people in Canada could be advanced.

One of the first organizations to press land claims issues was the Allied Tribes of British Columbia, which formed in 1916 in an attempt to lobby the British Privy Council to adjudicate land claims. This organization folded in 1927 but was succeeded in 1931 by the Native Brotherhood of British Columbia, which emerged from Indigenous labour-related activities in the fishing industry.

In 1919 the League of Indians of Canada was formed in Ontario to address concerns over loss of reserve lands and the restriction of hunting and trapping rights, culturally destructive educational policies, poor economies on reserve, and poor health conditions. The league was ultimately unable to expand to include bands across Canada due to linguistic and cultural differences.

In the 1930s and 1940s the Indian Association of Alberta and the Union (later Federation) of Saskatchewan Indians were formed. In 1945 the North American Indian Brotherhood was another short-lived attempt to establish a national organization.

The National Indian Brotherhood emerged in 1967—finally, a national organization for Indigenous people in Canada. This was followed by a wave of activism sparked by the federal government's 1969 White Paper, which proposed to eliminate the *Indian Act* as well as transfer responsibilities for Indians to the provinces. The National Indian Brotherhood and affiliated activist groups successfully defeated the White Paper. The organization became the Assembly of First Nations in 1982, which today represents 634 member chiefs across Canada. The Native Council of Canada formed in 1970 to pursue changes in government policy with respect to Métis and non-status Indians. In 1993 this organization became the Congress of Aboriginal Peoples.

Indigenous protesters march through Ottawa to Parliament Hill in January 2013.

Between 1978 and 1982, all Indigenous political organizations worked together toward the inclusion of Indigenous rights in the Canadian Constitution. Today, much Indigenous political organization and activism centres on negotiating land claims and redefining treaties in the 21st-century political context, as well as pressing forward the issues of education, poverty, and equality previously discussed in this text. Indigenous activism and advocacy have helped achieve Canada's adoption of the United Nations' *Declaration on the Rights of Indigenous Peoples*, which the federal government at first opposed adopting. The advocacy of Indigenous political organizations was instrumental in obtaining the Indian Residential Schools Settlement Agreement as well as the Canadian government's apology for its part in the residential school system.

In December 2012, a younger Indigenous grassroots movement called "Idle No More" emerged. This movement effectively used social media to spread across Canada and into the United States, New Zealand, and Australia. It began as a "teach-in" in Saskatchewan about fears that federal omnibus Bill C-45 would weaken environmental protections and threaten Indigenous sovereignty. The timing of the event coincided with the announcement that Chief Theresa Spence of Attawapiskat First Nation was embarking on a hunger strike to bring attention to the poor living conditions on her reserve. The movement grew nationwide and included flash mobs of traditional dancing and drum circles as well as highway and railway blockades. It is important to understand that forward movement for Indigenous rights in Canada does not happen without political action, which sometimes takes the form of peaceful protest, blockades, and demonstrations. These actions inevitably require police involvement in one form or another. Today, police services plan ahead for the best interventions for all parties involved.

The Nishiyuu Walkers

In January 2013 seven Cree youth, wearing snowshoes and towing their supplies, began a 1,600-kilometre trek through the bush, in snow and freezing temperatures, from Whapmagoostui First Nation in Quebec to Ottawa. They became known as the Nishiyuu ("the people" in Cree) Walkers. They walked to Ottawa to bring attention to the poor living conditions in their community, to demonstrate unity among First Nations, and to show that the Cree are dedicated to keeping their language, culture, traditions, and laws of their ancestors. Along the way, around 270 others joined the trek. They reached Ottawa in March 2013, where they met with Aboriginal Affairs Minister Bernard Valcourt and invited him to visit their community.

Sources: CTV News (2013); Journey of Nishiyuu (n.d.).

CHAPTER SUMMARY

The Mi'kmaq fishing crisis and the dispute in Caledonia are two of the many conflicts between Indigenous protesters and police in Canada that have escalated into violence. Whenever these situations occur, police are called in to keep the peace. For police officers, the importance of remaining neutral cannot be overstated; understanding the issues helps. Of course, police are not required to actually *resolve* the larger issues. When Caledonia residents called police to forcibly end the crisis by removing the demonstrators from the disputed land, OPP commissioner Julian Fantino underscored the role of law enforcement—to "preserve the peace, deal with offences and bring those who transgress the laws of the land to justice."

Of course, we all have biases that may emerge under stress. When it comes to Indigenous land and resources disputes, these biases are increasingly fed by the media. It is important to look behind the press coverage, behind the immediate events, and outside the traditional tactical box of policing. It is crucial to look at the issue in its historical context to understand how emotionally charged these situations can be for all parties involved. Again, police are responsible for ensuring the safety of all persons and remaining neutral.

This chapter has shown that Indigenous land and resource claims have their foundations in law. The Supreme Court has clearly laid out the obligations of all parties in negotiating these claims. Problems arise, however, when governments allow the prospect of gaining income through development and commercial industry to take precedence over legal obligations.

REFERENCES

Aboriginal Affairs and Northern Development Canada. (2011). Fact sheet—Three-year time frames for negotiating specific claim settlements. http://www.aadnc-aandc.gc.ca.

Aboriginal Affairs and Northern Development Canada. (2012). Fact sheet: Algonquins of Ontario land claim negotiations. https://www.aadnc-aandc.gc.ca/eng/1355436558998/1355436749970.

Aboriginal Affairs and Northern Development Canada. (2013). *Summative evaluation of the Specific Claims Action Plan.* https://www.aadnc-aandc.gc.ca/DAM/DAM-INTER-HQ-AEV/STAGING/texte-text/ev_spcap_1385136300660_eng.pdf.

Aboriginal Affairs and Northern Development Canada. (2015). Specific claims. https://www.aadnc-aandc.gc.ca/eng/1100100030291/1100100030292.

Amnesty International. (2005, December 19). It is time to comply: Canada's record of unimplemented UN human rights recommendations. Ottawa.

Assembly of First Nations. (2015). *In bad faith: Justice at last and Canada's failure to resolve specific land claims.* http://www.ubcic.bc.ca/files/PDF/InBadFaith_JusticeatLast_CanadaFailureResolveSpecificClaims.pdf.

Assembly of First Nations' Chiefs in New Brunswick. (2013). First Nations, consultation, and fracking. http://www.chiefsnb.ca/index.php/news/item/first_nations_consultation_and_fracking.

Badger, R v. (1996). [1996] 1 SCR 771.

Bell, C., & Paterson, R. (2003). Aboriginal rights to repatriation of cultural property in Canada. In A. Walkem & H. Bruce (Eds.), *Box of treasures or empty box? Twenty years of section 35* (pp. 104–154). Penticton, BC: Theytus Books.

British North America Act. (1867). 30 & 31 Vict., c. 3, reprinted in RSC 1985, app. II, no. 5.

Calder et al. v. Attorney General of British Columbia. (1973). [1973] SCR 313.

Campbell, Tracy. (1996, March). Co-management of Aboriginal resources. *Information North, 22*(1). Arctic Institute of North America. http://arcticcircle.uconn.edu/NatResources/comanagement.html.

CBC News. (2006a). In-depth: Caledonia land claim, historical timeline. *CBC News.* http://www.cbc.ca.

CBC News. (2006b). OPP's job to "preserve the peace" in Caledonia: Top cop. *CBC News.* http://www.cbc.ca.

Churchill, W. (1992). *Last stand at Lubicon Lake: Struggle for the land.* Toronto: Between the Lines.

CTV News. (2013, March 25). "Nishiyuu Walkers" complete 1,600 km trek to Ottawa. *CTV News.* http://www.ctvnews.ca.

Curry, B. (2003, November 27). Half of Canadians disbelieve land claims. *The National Post.*

Darling, G. (n.d.). Land claims and the Six Nations in Caledonia Ontario. University of Alberta, Centre for Constitutional Studies. http://ualawccsprod.srv.ualberta.ca/index.php/constitutional-issues/aboriginal-rights/61-land-claims-and-the-six-nations-in-caledonia-ontario.

Delgamuukw v. British Columbia. (1997). [1997] 3 SCR 1010.

Donham, P.B. (2003). Fishery: Lobster wars. In R. Anderson & R. Bone (Eds.), *Natural resources and Aboriginal people in Canada: Readings, cases and commentary.* Concord, ON: Captus Press.

Francis v. The Queen. (1969). [1969] 1 NBR (2d) 886 (Prov. Ct.).

Friends of the Lubicon. (2006). United Nations holds Canada in continuing violation of Lubicon human rights. http://www.lubicon.ca/pa/humanr.htm.

Gibson, G., Higgs, E., & Hrudey, S. (1998). Sour gas, bitter relations. *Alternatives Journal: Environmental Thought, Policy and Action*, 24(2).

Goldi, J., & Goldi, J. (Producers). (2004). *Ipperwash: A Canadian tragedy*. [Motion picture].

Guerin v. The Queen. (1984). [1984] 2 SCR 335.

Henderson, B. (1996). Guerin v. The Queen [A brief introduction to Aboriginal law in Canada]. Welcome to my Virtual Law Office. http://www.bloorstreet.com/200block/rguerin.htm.

Implementation Monitoring Committee. (2008). Location of entitlement First Nations. http://www.tleimc.ca/index.php/entitlement-first-nations/map-of-entitlement-first-nations.

Indian Act. (1985). RSC 1985, c. I-5.

Journey of Nishiyuu. (n.d.). The quest of Wisjinichu-Nishiyuu, quest for unity. http://nishiyuujourney.ca/#!/?page_id=10.

Knockwood, C. (2003). The Mi'kmaq-Canadian treaty relationship: A 277-year journey of rediscovery. In A. Walkem & H. Bruce (Eds.), *Box of treasures or empty box? Twenty years of section 35* (pp. 43–60). Penticton, BC: Theytus Books.

Mahoney, J. (2013, January 16). Canadians' attitudes hardening on Aboriginal issues: New poll. *The Globe and Mail*. http://www.theglobeandmail.com.

Mandell, L. (2003). Offerings to an emerging future. In A. Walkem & H. Bruce (Eds.), *Box of treasures or empty box? Twenty years of section 35*. Penticton, BC: Theytus Books.

Marshall, R v. (1999). [1999] 3 SCR 533.

McDonald, M. (2003). Aboriginal forestry in Canada. In R. Anderson & R. Bone (Eds.), *Natural resources and Aboriginal people in Canada. Readings, cases and commentary*. Concord, ON: Captus Press.

Mi'kmaq Rights Initiative. (n.d.). Consultation. http://mikmaqrights.com/consultation/.

Monture-Angus, P. (1999). *Journeying forward: Dreaming First Nations independence*. Halifax: Fernwood Publishing.

Obomsawin, A. (2002). *Is the Crown at war with us?* [Motion picture.] National Film Board of Canada.

Ontario Ministry of Aboriginal Affairs. (2011). Ontario's approach to land claim negotiations.

Royal Proclamation of 1763. (1970). RSC 1970, app. II, no. 1.

Simon v. The Queen. (1985). [1985] 2 SCR 387.

Sparrow, R v. (1990). [1990] 1 SCR 1075.

Specific Claims Tribunal Act. (2008). SC 2008, c. 22.

St. Catherine's Milling & Lumber Company v. The Queen. (1888). 14 App. Cas. 46 (PC).

Steckley, J., & Cummins, B. (2001a). The Golden Lake Algonquin and Algonquin Park: Missed by treaty. In *Full circle: Canada's First Nations* (chap. 14). Toronto: Prentice Hall.

Steckley, J., & Cummins, B. (2001b). Social issues: The Dudley George story. In *Full circle: Canada's First Nations* (chap. 20). Toronto: Prentice Hall.

Sylliboy, R v. (1929). [1929] 1 DLR 307.

Treaty Land Entitlement Committee of Manitoba Inc. (n.d.). http://www.tlec.ca.

Union of British Columbia Indian Chiefs. (2011). Canada's undermining of the specific claims process—A summary and analysis. http://www.ubcic.bc.ca/News_Releases/UBCICNews07261101.html#axzz4JhOudtg6.

Van der Peet, R v. (1996). [1996] 2 SCR 507.

Walkem, A. (2003). Constructing the constitutional box: The Supreme Court's section 35(1) reasoning. In A. Walkem & H. Bruce (Eds.), *Box of treasures or empty box? Twenty years of section 35* (pp. 196–222). Penticton, BC: Theytus Books.

Youngblood Henderson, J. (1999). Impact of Delgamuukw guidelines in Atlantic Canada. Cape Breton University. http://www.cbu.ca/indigenous-affairs/unamaki-college/mikmaq-resource-centre/essays/impact-of-delgamuukw-guidelines-in-atlantic-canada/.

REVIEW QUESTIONS

True or False?

_____ 1. *St. Catherine's Milling & Lumber Company v. The Queen* concerned a dispute between the Ojibwe people and Ontario over logging leases.

_____ 2. Section 91(24) of the *British North America Act* gave jurisdiction over Indians and lands reserved for Indians to the provincial governments.

_____ 3. In the case of *Guerin v. The Queen*, the Supreme Court ruled that the Crown's responsibility was only a "political trust" rather than a true trust and that therefore the Crown was not accountable for the $10 million that had gone missing through the leasing of land to the golf club.

_____ 4. Section 35 of the *Constitution Act, 1982* created entirely new rights for Indigenous people, which had never existed in law before.

_____ 5. In *Delgamuukw*, the Supreme Court ruled that the Crown can never infringe on an Indigenous right in any circumstances.

_____ 6. Of the six arguments put forward by the Crown in the *Delgamuukw* case, the Crown was successful with the argument that a third-party interest in unceded Indigenous land displaces Indigenous title.

_____ 7. In the *Marshall* case of 1999, the court gave an unlimited right to the Mi'kmaq to fish, which led to the lobster-fishing dispute in the Maritimes.

_____ 8. The *Calder* case, in which four Nisga'a communities asserted rights over traditional territory outside the reserve created by the federal government, is an example of a specific land claim.

_____ **9.** With reference to the *Sparrow* case, it has been found that the enactment of provincial fishing regulations is evidence of clear and plain extinguishment of an Indigenous right.

_____ **10.** The management of natural resources is a provincial responsibility.

Multiple Choice

1. In the case of *R v. Sparrow*, a two-part test for limiting an Indigenous right was created. The first part of that test says that the Crown must have a compelling and substantial objective if it is to limit an Indigenous right. An example of this is
  a. protection of a resource
  b. protection of the economy
  c. obtaining votes
  d. there is no such thing as a compelling or substantial objective

2. The 1888 *St. Catherine's Milling* case set the precedent for the definition of Indigenous title to land for ____ years.
  a. 10
  b. 30
  c. 50
  d. 100

3. In the *St. Catherine's Milling* case, the court came to the conclusion that Indigenous groups had a "personal and usufructuary right" to land, which means
  a. the right to use the land at the pleasure of the Crown, so that the Crown has the authority to remove the right at any time
  b. the right to use the land but never own it
  c. the right to sole possession of the land
  d. no rights to the land whatsoever

4. In the *Calder* case, the decision over whether or not Indian title to land can be extinguished without treaty resulted in the setting of a standard by which such extinguishment can occur. Which of the following defines that standard?
  a. by implication through other laws
  b. by a failure to occupy the land
  c. in a clear and plain way
  d. by assumption

5. In the *Sparrow* case, the Crown set out a two-part test for limiting an Indigenous right. The first part was that the Crown must have a compelling and substantial objective, and the second part was that
  a. the limit must be fair
  b. the limit must be consistent with the Crown's fiduciary responsibility to Indigenous peoples
  c. the limit must protect the Canadian economy
  d. the limit must be temporary

6. The framework of the litigation process to determine an Indigenous right has four steps. Which of the following is not one of those steps?
  a. identification of the nature and content of the right
  b. determining whether the right is an "existing right" recognized and affirmed in section 35 of the *Constitution Act, 1982* (or whether it was extinguished prior to the Constitution)
  c. determination of whether the provincial or federal legislation or regulation interferes with the right
  d. paying out for loss of the right

7. A comprehensive land claim is
  a. a claim to an entire province
  b. a claim to territory that is not covered by treaty or land cession agreements
  c. a claim to resources but not to land
  d. a claim to privately and individually owned land

8. Co-management of land and resources has been implemented in some areas where Indigenous rights have not been extinguished. Co-management effectively is
  a. the inclusion of non-traditional groups such as environmentalist groups, Indigenous groups, and industry in decision-making over resources
  b. the division of management over resources strictly between federal and provincial governments
  c. the division of responsibility for the area among a vast number of government agencies
  d. the granting of exclusive authority to Indigenous groups to manage the area

9. A specific land claim is
  a. a claim that relates to a specific surveyed parcel of land
  b. a claim that relates to specific misdealings of the Crown with relation to land or resources
  c. a claim that results because Indigenous title was never extinguished by treaty
  d. a claim that cannot be legitimized

10. Which of the following is not one of the three types of land claims active in Ontario?
  a. claims relating to the fulfillment of terms of treaties
  b. claims arising from the surrender for sale of reserved lands
  c. claims arising from Indigenous title
  d. claims of abuse

APPENDIX 8.1

The Dudley George Story

During the American Revolution and the War of 1812, the Anishinaabe, originally from northern Ontario, were allies with the British. They settled in southern Ontario following the wars and became known as the Chippewa. The government of the Chippewa signed a treaty in 1825 that created four reserves: Sarnia, Walpole Island, Kettle Point, and Stoney Point. In 1928, the provincial government pressured the Stoney Point people to sell 152 hectares of prime waterfront land to private interests. Although they were against the idea of selling their land, the band had little control. Indian Affairs, through the oppressive *Indian Act*, sold the land without the band's permission. A large part of that land was reserved to create the Ipperwash Provincial Park in 1936. The Stoney Point people were unhappy about the sale and unhappier still when their burial site was disturbed in the creation of the park.

In 1942, the federal government asked the Stoney Point people to relinquish what remained of their land so that a military base could be built to support the war efforts. (Many of the Stoney Point men were, in fact, overseas serving as soldiers.) The federal government offered $23 per acre for 2,211 acres of land (895 hectares). The Stoney Point people voted on the offer and declined. Invoking the *War Measures Act*, the federal government expropriated the land regardless. The Stoney Point people were paid the said amount and were promised that the land would be returned to them at the end of the war, provided the military had no further need for it. The Stoney Point people were forced to leave and live with their neighbours at Kettle Point.

At the end of the war, the Stoney Point people requested to enter into negotiations for the return of their land. The armed forces continued, however, to make peacetime use of the land as a cadet training camp and therefore did not return the land. In 1981, 36 years after the end of the war, the federal government agreed to pay the Stoney Point band $2.4 million in compensation for the 40-year use of the land and agreed to return the land pending an environmental assessment. The cost of cleaning the area environmentally was expected to be high because of the way it was used by the military. The Department of National Defence then decided that it did not want to relinquish the land. The department promised to review the requirements for the training camp every three years; if the training camp was deemed unnecessary, the department would turn it over to the Stoney Point people.

A recommendation was put forward in 1992 by the Standing Committee on Aboriginal People that the federal government return the land. The committee insisted that the government's reasons for failing to relinquish the land were "without substance." The recommendation was not followed. In May 1993, the Stoney Point people, bringing tents and trailers, moved onto the military property. They maintained a tenuous relationship with the military they were living alongside. In September of that same year, they walked for three weeks to Ottawa to insist that action be taken to return the land. No action was forthcoming.

On September 4, 1995, Indigenous protesters moved into the adjacent provincial park after it had closed for the season. One of the contentious issues about the park was the burial ground, which the Stoney Point people had requested be protected and fenced off. This had never been done despite clear archaeological records of the existence and location of the burial ground. The Ontario government would deny that a burial ground was even located in the park; the government was subsequently proven wrong.

Newly elected Premier Mike Harris held an emergency meeting the day following the occupation. OPP Inspector Ron Fox was at that meeting. It was alleged that Premier Mike Harris insisted that the protesters be removed from the park. This allegation appears to have been substantiated: years later, at the 2006 inquiry into the incident, on a tape-recorded conversation from 1995 between Fox and OPP Inspector John Carson, made directly following the emergency meeting, Fox can be heard saying the following: "No question they don't give a shit about Indians";

and "They just want us to kick ass." During the course of the inquiry Mike Harris would deny saying, "Get the fucking Indians out of the park." Various people present at the meeting would testify that they heard Mike Harris say this; others would testify that he did not. Regardless, after four days of testimony at the inquiry, Harris stated that he would not make any changes in the way he had handled the Ipperwash incident.

Following the September 5, 1995 meeting, the OPP prepared themselves for the altercation they expected. They ordered night-vision goggles, gas masks, and helicopters, and brought in 250 officers from across the province. The OPP had received intelligence information that the protesters were unarmed.

On September 6, the order was given to the OPP to get the protesters out of the park. After dark, the OPP advanced on the 30 unarmed protesters in the park. Sergeant Kenneth Deane, a sniper for the Tactics and Rescue unit, then shot Indigenous protester Dudley George, who later died from his injuries. Deane would testify that he witnessed a muzzle flash and saw George with a rifle. The investigation would reveal that there was no rifle and that George was unarmed at the time of the shooting. The police did not call an ambulance for George; the protesters attempted to call for one but were arrested. George was driven to the hospital by family members; a car breakdown en route delayed medical treatment even further. George's family members were arrested at the hospital; it was too late to save George, who died from his wound.

Kenneth Deane was charged and found guilty of criminal negligence causing death. He was sentenced to two years less a day to be served in the community plus 180 community service hours. He appealed his conviction unsuccessfully. Deane did not testify at the 2006 inquiry because he died in a car accident before it took place.

The Indigenous protesters were arrested and faced 62 charges, most of which were dropped. Charges that stemmed from their entry into the park were dismissed because it was decided that they had colour of right to the park—that is, interest in the property—because the burial ground, previously alleged to be non-existent, was now acknowledged to be there.

Indigenous rights groups immediately demanded an inquiry into the incident. Ontario's Conservative government refused, and it was not until the election of a new government in 2003 that an announcement was made that an inquiry would begin.

Following the announcement of the inquiry, the CBC received OPP surveillance tapes that were aired on the news. The tapes show OPP officers at the scene just prior to the shooting making racist comments about the protesters. These tapes brought the OPP's actions and motives into question.

The inquiry's report, released May 31, 2007, ruled that the OPP, the government of former Ontario premier Mike Harris, and the federal government all bore responsibility for the events that led to Dudley George's death. Both federal and provincial governments had more than 50 years to resolve these issues and chose not to. This choice led to a violent confrontation between police and Indigenous protesters, which culminated in the death of Dudley George. This tragedy could certainly have been avoided. Police services in Canada would be wise to study and learn from these events to ensure that they are not repeated in the future, because confrontations involving Indigenous land and resources are likely to occur for decades to come.

In December 2007, the Ontario government announced that it would return the 56-hectare Ipperwash Provincial Park to the Chippewas of the Kettle and Stoney Creek First Nation, after a period of co-control between the Chippewas and the government. On May 28, 2009, the province officially signed over control of Ipperwash Park to the Chippewas. In April 2016, the military base Camp Ipperwash was also turned over to the Chippewas, along with the $95 million negotiated settlement.

Sources: Goldi & Goldi (2004); Steckley & Cummins (2001b).

APPENDIX 8.2
The Lubicon Cree

The Lubicon Cree were traditionally hunters and gatherers. From time immemorial, they had lived in a 10,000 square kilometre area surrounding Lubicon Lake in northern Alberta. In 1899, a delegation from the Canadian government travelled through northern Alberta to secure for Treaty No. 8 the signatures of bands occupying the area. However, treaty commissioners failed to contact a number of small bands scattered throughout the vast territory covered by the treaty. The Lubicon were one of those bands; members did not hear of the treaty until 1912. The band never signed a treaty, nor did they ever cede or relinquish rights to their traditional territory.

Under the provisions of Treaty No. 8, each band was to receive a "reserved" land, the acreage depending on the population of the band, and each member was to receive an annuity in payment for the alienation of the land. Bands that were not notified of the treaty could go to designated locations and be added to the pay list for annuities. When the Lubicon band members were notified of the treaty by other bands, they made their way to Whitefish Lake and received an annuity there. Government officials then added the Lubicon names to the band list at Whitefish Lake, although the Lubicon group had no connection to that band and were a separate and individual band, as they had always been.

In 1935, the Indian Department sent notice to the Lubicon band that they were living off their designated reserve, and must relocate to live at Whitefish Lake. The Lubicon protested that they had never lived there and were a separate and distinct band that resided at Lubicon Lake; they requested that they be declared a band by the Indian Department. The department investigated, concluded that the Lubicon were indeed a separate and distinct band, and approved the creation of a new reserve at Lubicon Lake. In 1940, that reserve was surveyed by the department according to the population of the band at the time, which was set by the Indian agent at 127 members. At 52 hectares per person, the reserve was surveyed for 6,500 hectares.

Prior to the completion of the deal in 1942, Indian Affairs official Malcolm McCrimmon was sent to northern Alberta to see that the pay lists for annuities for Indians were in order. Because Second World War expenses were mounting, the federal government was looking to reduce expenditures elsewhere, and the Indian Department seemed a logical place to cut costs. McCrimmon rewrote the rules for addition to treaty annuity lists and eliminated all members who joined after 1912. He insisted that birth records be provided to prove that only pure-blood Indians were on the lists—but this was in a remote area where children were born at home and it was common to have no birth record. McCrimmon eliminated 700 names from the annuity pay list, including 90 members of the Lubicon Cree band. He then argued against the establishment of a reserve for the Lubicon, saying that there were insufficient members of the band to warrant one. As a result, the Indian Department postponed the creation of a reserve indefinitely.

The Lubicon continued to live at Lubicon Lake, but a renewed interest in the area occurred in 1950 when Alberta Lands and Forest Division received inquiries from a large mining corporation regarding the Lubicon area. The company wanted the provincial government to open it for exploration. The province of Alberta requested that the Indian Department relocate the proposed reserve for the Lubicon to a "less isolated area." However, the federal government failed to respond to the province, which was anxious to lease the land. The province eventually sent a letter with an ultimatum, that the federal government respond within 30 days or the province would deem the proposed reserve not to exist. The federal government failed to respond. Alberta then requested that Indian Affairs strike the band from the record as an official band. The federal government could not comply with this request because it had declared the Lubicon a distinct band in 1939 even though it had failed to finalize a reserve for the band. Alberta insisted that the Lubicon band be reduced through enfranchisement where possible, and the remainder of the band be relocated to live with the Whitefish band. The two levels of government could not come to an agreement on how to resolve this issue.

In 1971, Alberta secured oil company financing to build an all-weather road into Lubicon territory for the purposes of exploration. The Lubicon lobbied the government to stop the encroachment of corporations, insisting on their right to their traditional territory. The Alberta government insisted that the Lubicon were squatters on provincial Crown lands with no land rights to negotiate. In 1975, as developers began exploration, the Lubicon filed a caveat under provincial law to place would-be developers on notice that title to the land was contested. The provincial government asked for a postponement of the caveat and rewrote legislation under Bill 29 to end grounds for Lubicon legal action.

In 1979 the all-weather road was completed and people poured into the area, severely disrupting the Lubicon way of life. In 1980, the Lubicon appealed to the federal government to provide them with financial assistance to seek an injunction to stop development until a resolution could be reached over the land title issues. The federal government denied the request. In 1981 Alberta declared the main settlement area of the Lubicon a hamlet, subdivided the area into 0.8 hectare lots, and proposed to lease or gift the lots to individual band members. The Lubicon were very concerned about how this "land tenure program" would affect their land claim and petitioned the federal government to look into the matter.

The minister of Indian Affairs discovered that the land in question could no longer be subject to a land claim because as a hamlet it was no longer classed as provincial Crown land.

In 1982, with the federal and provincial governments still unable to reach an agreement over the land allocation, the Lubicon filed a second legal action before the Alberta Court of Queen's Bench requesting the retention of Indigenous rights over their traditional area, which would void the leases provided by the province to oil companies. The band requested an immediate injunction to stop development until the land issues could be resolved. The concluding arguments in the case were heard on December 2, 1982, but the court postponed the delivery of its verdict until March 1983. At that time an injunction to stop development was received—too late. The companies had simply accelerated their exploration through the winter, and the area became irreversibly altered environmentally.

By 1983, 400 oil wells had been drilled within 15 kilometres of the Lubicon's main settlement. The typical trapper's income was reduced from $5,000 per year to $400, and the number of moose killed for food plummeted from 200 to 19. The Lubicon experienced a rash of suicides and rising alcoholism within the community. Welfare dependence in the community increased from 5 percent to 90 percent. The extreme poverty and a tuberculosis outbreak affecting one-third of the community demoralized the band even further.

Following the injunction, the companies returned to court to argue that the injunction was unnecessary since the drilling was already complete and the pumping process put in place would not cause any further environmental degradation. By 1987, it was estimated conservatively that oil and gas revenues from the area were in excess of $500 million per year.

In 1984, after the Supreme Court of Canada refused to hear their case, the Lubicon appealed to the United Nations Human Rights Commission. The United Nations conducted a study of the situation and concluded in 1987 that the Lubicon could not possibly achieve political redress in Canada. The United Nations appealed to Canada to do no further harm to Lubicon territory until a hearing could be held on human rights violations. However, in 1988, Alberta announced that it had granted timber rights in the Lubicon territory to a Japanese company, Daishowa, which planned to cut 11,000 trees daily to produce 1,000 tonnes of pulp per day.

In response to the news of the lease, the Lubicon toured Europe prior to the 1988 Olympics seeking support from other countries. Then, at the winter Olympics in Calgary, they boycotted the Indigenous art exhibition ("The Spirit Sings"), having discovered that its sponsors were the very oil companies that were undermining Indigenous land claims in Canada. Their boycott was supported by human rights organizations around the world. Also in 1988, the Lubicon, fed up with the system, withdrew all cases from Canadian courts, declared themselves a sovereign nation, and blockaded all roads leading into their territory. The RCMP arrested 27 people involved in the blockades, and the province refused to negotiate with the Lubicon until the blockades were removed.

Concerned that the situation could escalate into violence, Alberta returned to the negotiating table. Alberta negotiated the Grimshaw Accord, which called for the creation of a reserved land base for the Lubicon people that included subsurface rights to the land. The federal government disagreed, offering a reserved land base with no subsurface rights. The subsurface rights were critical for the Lubicon, since mining and drilling are the only ways they can now sustain their people—the degradation of the land made their traditional economy impossible. The subsurface rights are not forthcoming.

In 1989, the federal government exploited divisions within the band. Facing extreme poverty, with no resolution in sight, some members of the band wavered in their support of the band governance body. The federal government met with a dissident group and agreed to create a new band called the Woodland Cree, insisting that they have rights to the contested area. The federal government presented the rejected offer from the Lubicon band to the Woodland band, offering them an additional $1,000 each to sign the agreement that did not include subsurface rights. The federal government offered the same deal to the Loon Lake Cree, and subsequently pressured the Lubicon to sign the same agreement without subsurface rights. The chief of the Lubicon band, Bernard Omniyak, says the agreement is "deficient in the area of providing economic stability for the future. In essence, the Canadian government has offered to build houses for the Lubicon and support us forever on welfare like animals in the zoo who are cared for and fed at an appointed time" (Churchill, 1992).

In 1990, the United Nations charged Canada with human rights violations under article 27 of the *International Covenant on Civil and Political Rights*. Canada did not answer to the charges, which stand today.

In 1991, the Lubicon organized an international boycott of Daishowa. In response, Daishowa agreed to stay out of Lubicon territory until the land issue was resolved; however, in 1994, Daishowa sued the organizers of the boycott for $5 million in compensation for lost business. The suit was unsuccessful.

In 1994 the Lubicon protested oil and gas corporation Unocal's plans to build a sour gas processing plant within 4 kilometres of the proposed reserve. Alberta's energy board failed to convene a hearing on the matter until after the plant was built. The plant went into operation in 1995.

Following the opening of the sour gas plant, Alberta proposed that the size of the proposed reserve be reduced from the original 243 square kilometres specified in the Grimshaw Accord; their rationale was that the population of the Lubicon band had decreased due to the creation of the Woodland Cree band and the transference of members to that group (Gibson, Higgs, & Hrudey, 1998).

In 2002, an agreement was finally reached between the federal and provincial governments and the Lubicon Cree over the construction of a new reserve, although subsurface rights were still undetermined. On November 1, 2005, the United Nations Human Rights Committee reaffirmed its earlier conclusion that Canada is violating article 1 of the *International Covenant on Civil and Political Rights* insofar as it is denying the Lubicon basic subsistence by destroying their traditional economy and way of life. Furthermore, Canada is in violation of article 27 of the Covenant insofar as it is participating in the destruction of the Lubicon's culture, language rights, and way of life by refusing to negotiate a reasonable resolution to their land claim. The committee reiterated its 1987 recommendation (for which there is support in Canadian case law, established by the 1997 *Delgamuukw* decision) that Canada should consult with the band before granting licences for economic exploitation of the disputed land and ensure that in no case such exploitation jeopardizes the rights recognized under the Covenant. Canada has not responded to the committee's findings. However, Amnesty International provided the following statement:

> One of the most glaring failures to implement UN level human rights recommendations is the situation of the Lubicon Cree in Alberta. In 1990, the Human Rights Committee issued a detailed report documenting serious violations of the rights of the Lubicon, stemming from a decades-old failure to enter into an agreement with the Lubicon regarding their land rights. The Committee called on the government to ensure a prompt and just settlement of the dispute. Fifteen years later the dispute remains unresolved, the ability of the Lubicon to provide for themselves remains under threat, and there have been no negotiations between the government and the Lubicon for over two years. (Amnesty International, 2005; also see Friends of the Lubicon, 2006)

The issues regarding land rights have still not been resolved. The Lubicon band suffers economically and socially, and the resource that has brought economic wealth to the province of Alberta and Canada has led to economic collapse for the Lubicon. In 2009, the Alberta government approved the extension of an oil pipeline through the contested territory, and 2,400 kilometres of pipeline now snake through the Lubicon's traditional land. In May 2011, an oil spill leaked an estimated 28,000 barrels of oil onto the Lubicon's traditional territory, approximately 30 kilometres from the site of their community's main town, contaminating the surrounding areas.

While their land claim remains unresolved, the Lubicon are fighting not just for a resolution of their claim but for environmental protection for their community. In October 2014 Alberta Premier Jim Prentice met with the band to begin dialogue again on the 80-year outstanding claim. In December 2014 Aboriginal Affairs and Northern Development Canada signed a Negotiation Framework to move the claim forward after a long period of inaction on the claim. The framework sets out three priority issues identified by the band: the establishment of a reserve pursuant to the treaty; construction of the community on the future reserved land; and the resolution of claims to other treaty-related benefits. The next step will be to create an agreement-in-principle that can be signed and then negotiated into a binding legal decision in the form of a claim settlement that would then be protected under the Constitution. As we know from other claims examined in this chapter, settlement is years away, but progress continues.

9 Indian and Inuit Residential Schools

Cree child Thomas Moore, as he appeared in his traditional attire when admitted to the Regina Indian Industrial School in 1891, contrasted with his appearance afterward.

LEARNING OUTCOMES

After completing this chapter, you should be able to:

- Explain the Dominion of Canada's rationale for implementing residential schools.
- Understand the magnitude of the damage done to Indigenous societies by residential schools.
- Understand how the residential school experience led to the later seizure of children from Indigenous communities during the 1960s, 1970s, and 1980s.
- Understand why the Truth and Reconciliation Commission was created, what its goals were, and what it has recommended in its final report.
- Discuss the moral, legal, and ethical issues related to accountability and healing, as well as the current efforts being made by the government of Canada, in partnership with the Indigenous people, to promote healing.

Introduction

residential schools
church-run, government-funded boarding schools for Indigenous children, designed to prepare them for life in white society

Royal Commission on Aboriginal Peoples (RCAP)
a commission established by the federal government in 1991 to investigate the issues facing Indigenous people in Canada

From 1870 to 1940, Indigenous children were not allowed to attend any schools other than those designated specifically for their education. These schools were provided by the Canadian government in conjunction with the Roman Catholic, Anglican, United, and Presbyterian churches. The schools were chronically underfunded and poorly run, and the health of the children suffered. Due to poor nutrition and substandard living conditions, many children died of typhoid fever and tuberculosis. From the 1870s to the 1990s, when the last **residential school** was closed, a growing catalogue of crimes against humanity was compiled. The continued incidents of physical abuse, sexual abuse, emotional abuse, cultural extinguishment, and neglect resulted in psychological trauma for generations of Indigenous people in Canada. The forcible removal of First Nations children from their families to the schools was designed to "kill the Indian" but save the child and result in the assimilation of Indigenous children into white Canadian society.

Much of the information about residential schools and their impact on Indigenous communities was absent from the public consciousness until the final report of the **Royal Commission on Aboriginal Peoples (RCAP)** was released in November 1996. The commission's report gave society at large a clearer picture of the enormous damage done to Indigenous communities by the long-standing maltreatment and abuse of their children. The schools' presence in Canada and their effects on First Nations and Inuit children warrants careful study. Indigenous people working to heal their communities say that the education system's part in this damage cannot be overestimated.

The government of Canada made its first carefully worded apology in 1998, delivered by Indian Affairs Minister Jane Stewart. A second apology followed a decade later, in June 2008, delivered by Prime Minister Stephen Harper as he accepted responsibility on behalf of the Canadian government for the abuses that occurred in residential schools and concluded that the residential school system was wrong and had no place in Canada. Since the apologies, the government has partnered with Indigenous peoples to create both the Aboriginal Healing Foundation and the Truth and Reconciliation Commission (TRC) to improve the well-being of Indigenous communities and repair the relationship between Indigenous and non-Indigenous people in Canada. In 2015, after the release of the TRC's final report, Prime Minister Justin Trudeau committed to working with Indigenous communities to implement the TRC's recommendations (Prime Minister of Canada Justin Trudeau, 2015).

It is startling how many Canadians today are either unaware or only vaguely aware that Indigenous children, until relatively recently, were forced to attend residential schools. Many young non-Indigenous Canadians have not been taught—and many adults have chosen not to inquire—about the residential school legacy. This situation is very unfortunate. Just resolutions and reconciliation in the issues involving Indigenous people in Canada depend on all Canadians, Indigenous and non-Indigenous alike, having the same awareness of past and present.

This chapter examines and discusses the political environment that made this whole episode possible—and possible, moreover, in a country that is today renowned for its attention to civil rights. To help us understand the survivors' pain, we recount some of their stories. This chapter also examines some of the current efforts to help Indigenous people recover and to bring about reconciliation between them and the rest of Canada.

Education as a Tool for Subjugation, Socialization, and Assimilation

Indigenous and non-Indigenous people agreed from an early point in their relations that education was important. As a result, guarantees for education funding were set out in certain treaties. The Stone Fort Treaty (1871), for example, stated the following: "And further, Her Majesty agrees to maintain a school on each reserve hereby made, whenever the Indians of the reserve should desire it" (Morris, 1971, p. 315). Indigenous leaders recognized that their children would need new knowledge to cope with the rapidly changing environment. With the depletion of natural resources and with increasing white settlement, these leaders saw that their traditional hunting and trapping lifestyles were going to be severely disrupted. They envisioned state schools that would be run in partnership with Indigenous peoples to preserve traditional Indigenous culture while preparing children for new times and non-traditional labour markets.

John Tootoosis (1899–1989), a prominent Cree leader, wrote the following in his biography:

> The Indians who at treaty time had asked that their children be educated were asking that they be taught to read and write, to learn to work with figures, to be trained into useful skills to enable them to compete on an equal basis for a way of making a living with the children of the white men. … Poundmaker (chief at treaty time) had replied very clearly, "We want to be sure that life will be as good for them (our children) as it will be for your children." (Goodwill & Sluman, 1982, p. 113)

The federal government, however, had an altogether different vision for the schools. Canada viewed education as an efficient means of **subjugating** and **assimilating** the Indigenous people, a governmental ambition that we discussed in the previous chapter. While education in Canada has long been a provincial responsibility, the *British North America Act* gave the federal government jurisdiction over Indigenous people in this regard, a responsibility it bears to this day.

As early as 1830, four mission schools for Indigenous populations were established in Ontario, including the Shingwauk and the Mohawk institutes. A leader in this initiative was an Ojibwe man, Peter Jones, who was also a Methodist missionary. He had founded an agricultural settlement for the Mississaugas on the Credit River (near present-day Toronto), providing a reasonably successful education to young Indigenous people through the Credit River School. Jones wished to extend his education provisions to other Indigenous peoples by building residential schools that would provide manual training in addition to Christian teaching and English-language instruction.

The Mohawk Institute, which had been requested by the Indigenous leadership on the Six Nations of the Grand River, was established in 1833 by the New England Company and was dedicated to the Christianization, "civilization," and instruction of Indigenous people. The Mohawk

subjugation
forcing obedience to authority

assimilation
a process by which members of an ethnic minority group lose cultural characteristics that distinguish them from the dominant cultural group or take on the cultural characteristics of another group

Institute was a model for Jones. He asked four different bands in his area to help finance the schools by donating one-quarter of their treaty money. The Methodist church and the federal government also shared in the cost of establishing the schools. Jones envisioned that the schools would eventually be run by Christian Indigenous people. Neither the federal government nor the church shared his vision: both looked forward to using the school as an instrument of assimilation in keeping with the policies of the government of Canada.

Although Indigenous people supported the schools initially, they soon discovered that the goals of the church and the government were inconsistent with their own. Indigenous leaders recognized that schooling meant assimilation and a total rejection of all of their own values and traditions. They stopped financial support to the schools and withheld their children from them. The experiment was deemed a failure, but the precedent had been set—using partnerships with the church and missionaries in the education of Indigenous children (Grant, 1996).

When the question of education for Indigenous children arose again in 1870, the churches were recruited for the task for two main reasons. The first was that they could be expected to inculcate Indigenous children with the religious ideals of the day and have them reject all things associated with their own culture. The second reason was purely practical. The running of the schools and the instruction of the Indigenous children promised to be an expensive endeavour for the Indian department; the free labour of missionaries and priests would significantly reduce the cost. The federal government, in turn, would provide funding in the form of land grants drawn from reserved lands, per capita grants, and other material rewards to the four churches involved in Indian education. This partnership between church and state would last until 1969.

The decision to make education for Indigenous children "residential" rather than provide day schools on reserves was driven by similar motives. First, the cost of building a day school on each and every reserve, according to the Department of Indian Affairs, was too high (regardless of the wording within the treaty). Second, separating the children from the influence of their families and community was considered necessary if the children were to truly become "civilized" and internalize the religious teachings of the church. The "residential" component of Indian schools was considered critical to the achievement of their aims, as explained by Quebec politician Sir Hector-Louis Langevin, arguing before Parliament in 1883:

> Industrial schools have succeeded very well in the United States and it is quite likely they will succeed here as well. The fact is, that if you wish to educate the children you must separate them from their parents during the time they are being taught. If you leave them in the family, they may know how to read and write, but they will remain savages, whereas by separating them in the way proposed, they acquire the habits and tastes of civilized people. (Indian Tribes of Manitoba, 1971, p. 113)

Overview of the Residential School System

One of the first problems to surface in the residential school system was poor attendance. Parents opposed the curricula—the purpose of which, they saw, was assimilation—and rumours of abuse within the schools circulated quickly. In addition, health conditions were poor, and as many as 3,000 children died of diseases such as smallpox, tuberculosis, and polio. For these reasons, many Indigenous parents chose to withhold their children from residential schools.

Poor attendance resulted in a change to the *Indian Act* in 1894: school attendance became compulsory. Section 119 of the Act gave truant officers and Indian agents police authority to enforce attendance in day schools by removing children forcibly, if necessary, from their homes and families. In 1920, the Act was amended to give truant officers the same authority with respect to residential schools, and to make it an offence for parents to withhold their children from the schools.

In the following sections, we examine the general characteristics of residential schools and the many problems that existed within the system.

Age of Enrollment and Nature of Education

In addition to attendance, another problem that immediately surfaced concerned questions about what type of education should in fact be delivered, by whom, and to whom. The various agencies involved disagreed with one another about these matters.

Age of enrollment, for example, was a frequent source of dispute. Some Protestant ministers advocated enrolling students as young as three in residential schools, to "catch them early." Others argued that this would be a waste of money. Some argued the students should be kept until they were 14; some argued for 16, some 18, and some for 21. Enrollment ages did in fact change through the years. Bickering among the Catholic, Presbyterian, Anglican, and Methodist churches over who would get the students was common; each denomination viewed the contest for students as a battle for souls—or, in some instances, as a battle for per capita funding.

As far as curricula were concerned, some schools classed as "industrial schools" offered training in skilled trades such as carpentry, cabinet-making, and tailoring. Some of these schools produced a well-educated and literate group of graduates. However, these successes created two problems.

The first was that success in acquiring a skilled trade did not guarantee employment. In fact, there were no opportunities for employment for Indigenous people. One agent wrote to the department in December 1907, "Race prejudice is against them and I am afraid that it will take time, under the circumstances, before they can compete with their white brothers in the trades" (Malloy, 1999, p. 158). Critics of the system insisted that the more costly industrial school training was a waste of resources, since people in mainstream Canada were not prepared to accept working alongside Indigenous people. In response, the industrial schools were phased out.

The second problem with the early success of the schools was baldly expressed by the minister of the interior, Frank Oliver, in 1897: "We are educating these Indians to compete industrially with our own people, which seems to me a very undesirable use of public money" (Hall, 1983, p. 126). The attitudes expressed in these historical records may seem shocking to the average Canadian today, but they reflect the sentiments that were prevalent among many Canadians at the time. The status quo was being threatened by Indigenous people, who were showing that they could not only learn to read and write, but also become great craftsmen on par with non-Indigenous Canadians, and thus compete with the latter in the labour market for skilled jobs.

Staff and Quality of Instruction

As industrial schools were phased out and the number of residential schools increased, the quality of the education declined. By 1932, at the end of Duncan Campbell Scott's career as deputy superintendent general of Indian Affairs, there were 17,163 students enrolled in residential schools. Scott viewed this increase in attendance as proof of his success in the assimilation process. It was more likely due to the compulsory attendance legislation enforced by his government. The flipside of this statistic is that three-quarters of students enrolled were in grades 1 through 3. In 1932, only 100 students reached grade 6 (Malloy, 1999, p. 171).

In his autobiography, Indigenous scholar Basil Johnston (1989, p. 47) remembers having to repeat grades over and over in residential school and finally realizing, much to his dismay, that, as a matter of policy, Indigenous students' discharge from the school at the age of 16 had to coincide with their graduation from grade 8. In other words, no matter how they performed academically, Indigenous students were destined to repeat grades until they reached 16 and could be released from school.

Although there were some good and well-intentioned individuals among the staff at residential schools, it would be an understatement to say that the majority were unfit for the education of children. Bill Thomas (1991, p. 6), of the Peguis First Nation, described the staff in the school he attended as follows:

> The kooky clergy and even kookier staff make a shambles of any potential for effective development. … For the most part the "dedicated" staff I knew in the United Church school were old ladies trying to atone for earlier sins and mucking that up. Others were religious zealots or simply strange people who—under ordinary circumstances—could not get a job or fit in anywhere else.

Cree writer and lawyer Harold Cardinal (1969, p. 54) described his residential school experience as follows:

> In plain words, the system was lousy. The curriculum stank, and the teachers were misfits and second raters. Even my own elementary school days, in grade eight I found myself taking over the class because my teacher, a misfit, has-been or never-was sent out by his superiors from Quebec to teach savages in the wilderness school because he had failed utterly in civilization, couldn't speak English well enough to make himself understood. Naturally he knew no Cree. When we protested such inequities we were silenced as "ungrateful little savages who don't appreciate what is being done for you."

Complaints about the staff from residential school survivors are corroborated by studies conducted in the early 1960s. These studies indicate that, with few exceptions, staff fell into three categories:

1. relatively recent immigrants;
2. Canadians from lower socio-economic backgrounds; and
3. a small number of Indigenous people.

In 1967, researcher Richard King conducted a study of a Yukon Indian School at Mopass. King (1967) categorized staff as "generally deviant in the whiteman society." He found that many of the teachers lacked qualifications and many could not even speak English well. It seems that the reasonably generous pay in the residential schools—generous by comparison with other jobs such people would have been qualified for—attracted poorly educated and deficient personalities to work in them. As early as 1910, letters sent to school administrators by the Department of Indian Affairs addressed concerns over the quality of its teachers (Grant, 1996, p. 143).

Also damaging the academic standards of the residential schools was the requirement—based on the department's desire that the schools be self-sufficient—that students do long hours of manual labour. The students were supposed to spend half the day in class and half the day in manual labour, but the latter often took precedence. The records show that field workers and school inspectors were concerned from the first about this overemphasis on manual work. One letter, written in 1916, alerts the Department of Indian Affairs to the fact that the boys in one school had spent only 9 days out of 42 in class; the rest of their time was spent working on the farm to support the school (Malloy, 1999, p. 170). Poorly served by this regimen, many students left the school unable to read or even to converse well in English.

Health Conditions

The health of children in the schools was always a source of concern. Unsafe construction, overcrowding, inadequate food, and poor nutrition resulted in physical problems and a high death rate. In 2013, a report based on research of school documents estimated over 3,201 Indian children died in the schools. Nearly 500 of those children could not be identified.

At the time, the churches and the administrators at Indian Affairs were well aware of health problems associated with the schools, but funds were not readily available to provide more sanitary conditions in the schools through renovation. Dr. Peter Bryce was commissioned in 1903 to inspect residential schools and report on the health conditions. His report was scathing, indicating that some schools had a death rate of *50 percent*. He wrote as follows: "The sight of the ragged, ill-kempt and sickly looking children was enough to make me sick at heart" (Malloy, 1999).

Roger Cromarty said he had no memory of a doctor visiting the Sioux Lookout school during the seven years he spent there:

> Even though a lot of times once somebody caught something and it spread in the whole school like wildfire, and they would just more or less, we had to live out whatever it is that we caught, whether it's measles, mumps, sores, bedbugs, all that kind of stuff, we just had to live with it. We got some stuff from the matron. We used to have a matron that sort of acted as a nurse as well. So a medical doctor we never saw. (TRC, 2015b, p. 177)

In 1910, an Indian agent named MacArthur reported a 50 percent death rate at the Duck Lake residential school. S.H. Blake, a lawyer, conducted a review of the Anglican missions and reported as follows to Minister of Indian Affairs Frank Oliver: "The appalling number of deaths among the younger children appeals loudly to the guardians of our Indians. In doing nothing to obviate the preventable causes of death, brings the department within unpleasant nearness to the charge of manslaughter" (Malloy, 1999, p. 77).

Nutrition was lacking in many of the schools, and this left the children vulnerable to disease. In 1943, Dr. A.B. Simes conducted an inquiry into Elkhorn School in response to complaints from the Indians at The Pas, Manitoba. He reported (Malloy, 1999, p. 114) that the children were dirty, their clothes disgraceful, and that 28 percent of the girls and 69 percent of the boys were underweight. The menu he forwarded to the ministry had many omissions and few substitutions. Today, many residential school survivors remark about never having had enough to eat.

At File Hills Indian Residential School, Dr. Bryce found that 75 percent of the students on the discharge roll were dead. Of the 31 students on the roll, 15 had died in the school, and 7 had died at home within three years of discharge. At the time of first enrollment, all of these students had enjoyed good health. File Hills was certainly the worst case, but if its statistics are factored in with those of the other schools, the death rate in the 35 schools included in Dr. Bryce's study would be 42 percent. Those figures, projected throughout the 1907 school system, suggest that of the 3,755 children in the schools, 1,614—or 43 percent—would die prematurely (Malloy, 1999, p. 90).

This information was not restricted to government officials. Dr. Bryce's report made headlines in the newspapers; in other words, the Canadian public knew about the horrific conditions in the schools and about the unacceptable death rate. One reporter wrote that the death rate would be unacceptable even in war. Other efforts were made to attract public attention to the appalling conditions of the schools, but to no avail. It seems that the Canadian public was content to be complicit in the brutality of this process of forced assimilation. Up to 1922, Dr. Bryce continued to criticize the ministry for doing nothing to improve sanitation. Bryce was successful only in ensuring that he did not secure a position in Duncan Campbell Scott's administration as the department's minister of health.

Ultimately, modest measures were taken to improve conditions in the schools. But the communications between school administrators and Indian Affairs indicate that high death rates and poor sanitary conditions were constant problems throughout the decades the schools were in operation. Four decades after Dr. Bryce's first report, in 1948, Neil Walker, Indian Affairs superintendent, wrote as follows: "If I were appointed by the Dominion Government for the express purpose of spreading tuberculosis, there is nothing finer in existence than the average Indian residential school" (Malloy, 1999, p. 262).

Inhumane Conditions at Residential Schools

The following memo, dated October 21, 1953, was written by G.H. Marcoux, a regional inspector of Indian schools. It was addressed to the Indian Affairs Branch in Winnipeg, Manitoba.

I visited the school on October 19th and 20th and found the following situation:

From the front entrance to the corridor of the basement one was subjected to an unbearable odor. The floor of the boiler room was covered with liquid from the sewage system to a depth of 6 to 8 inches, some of the liquid was seeping into the boys' recreation room. At the other end of the building, in the girls' recreation room there are a number of trap openings on the floor. Upon opening these traps one could see the same kind of liquid containing raw sewage, direct from toilets, almost to the level of the floor.

It looks as if the entire sewage piping under the floor had collapsed and that the sewage piping leading to the outside has been blocked by some obstruction.

On Monday, October 19, the smell in the building was unbearable and no human being should be asked to live under such conditions. There is no doubt in my mind that such drastic action must be taken to remedy the situation and make sure it does not re-occur in the future. I, therefore, strongly recommend that the school be closed until such time as the necessary repairs are made. Should this condition continue or happen again at a later date, the health of the pupils and the members of the staff can be seriously affected. Furthermore, should there be an outbreak of disease in a school like this one, the Indian parents would blame the school and refuse to send their children there. This would be a ten year set back in the education plan.

This is respectfully submitted in the hope that the department be advised of the situation and that immediate appropriate action be taken.

Source: Indian and Northern Affairs Canada (1999).

EXERCISE 1

1. What value did mainstream society seem to place on Indigenous children? How did this change over time?
2. Consider the mandatory attendance legislation instituted by the government. How would you have felt about this legislation if you had been the parent of an Indigenous child in this era?

Abuse Within the Schools

Most people who write about abuse in residential schools divide the subject into four categories: sexual, physical, emotional, and spiritual and cultural. Here, we examine each category in turn, then look at the aftermath of the abuse and the efforts by the government and Indigenous communities to agree on liability and possible compensation.

Sexual Abuse

In 1964, 10-year-old Willie Blackwater was removed from his family home on Kispiox Reserve in British Columbia and taken to Alberni Indian Residential School on Vancouver Island, 1,600 kilometres away. Immediately, Blackwater was singled out by dorm supervisor Arthur Henry Plint, who sexually abused the boy during his years at the school. Blackwater revealed the abuse to several authorities, including a government official, none of whom believed him.

Furthermore, when news reached Plint that the boy had accused him of abuse, he beat the child so severely that Blackwater ended up in the infirmary.

After suffering greatly as an adult trying to cope with his childhood, Blackwater came forward again in the 1990s to initiate an investigation into his abuse at the school. Thirty other adult men also came forward in an attempt to make Plint accountable for his actions. After judgments against him in 1995 and 1997, Plint, at the age of 72, was convicted and sentenced to 12 years in prison; he showed no remorse. In his judgment, Supreme Court Justice Douglas Hogarth referred to Plint as a sexual predator and a sexual terrorist whose activities had been allowed to go on unchecked: "As far as the victims are concerned, the Indian residential school system was nothing more than institutionalized pedophilia" (Fournier & Crey, 1997, p. 72).

CLOSE-UP   George Clutesi

George Clutesi of the Tseshaht First Nation near Port Alberni, British Columbia was born in 1905 and died in 1988. He was widely acclaimed as an actor, artist, and writer. He exhibited his work in the 1940s with the support of Canadian artist Emily Carr. Expo 67 commissioned a mural of his work, and he received the British Columbia Centennial Award and the Canadian Centennial Medal. He appeared in nine feature films and the television series *The Beachcombers* and *Spirit Bay*. He attended the Alberni Indian Residential School.

The Alberni Indian Residential School operated as a day school when it opened in 1891 under Presbyterian management. The original school burned down in 1917 and was replaced by a new building funded by the government of

George Clutesi displaying Indigenous artwork, March 31, 1966.

Canada and operated by the United Church Women's Missionary Society in 1925. The school's survivors tell of suffering physical and sexual abuse and disease. The school closed in 1973.

This is only one of the thousands of incidents of sexual abuse in residential schools across Canada that came to light in the 1990s. In 1990, Phil Fontaine, who in 1991 was elected the Manitoba Grand Chief of the National Assembly of First Nations, talked publicly of his experience of sexual abuse while in residential schools in Manitoba. (See the Close-Up feature later in this chapter.) The Indigenous community was divided in its response to sudden public scrutiny. Some felt these experiences were so painful and shameful that they should not be brought forward, since they caused survivors to relive their pain. Others felt that the only way to begin the healing process was to openly face the harsh reality of what had been suffered.

The RCMP and other policing agencies became involved in uncovering information regarding past sexual assaults in the schools. They quickly uncovered thousands of victims. In 1994, the RCMP created a task force to deal with the many investigations required to address the complaints. Investigations were difficult because many of the perpetrators had died or could not be located. Many victims who made disclosures to police were unable to cope with dredging up the past; some committed suicide, and some turned to alcohol and drugs in order to deal with their pain.

No one can know for certain how widespread the sexual abuse was; we can count only those who have come forward voluntarily. In 1990, when residential school abuse became part of the political landscape, the *Globe and Mail* reported that Rix Rogers, who was then the special adviser to the minister of national health and welfare on child sexual abuse, indicated during a meeting of the Canadian Psychological Association that the abuse revealed to that date was believed to be just the tip of the iceberg. He believed that "a closer scrutiny of the past treatment of native children at Indian residential schools would show 100 percent of children at some schools were sexually abused" ("Reports of sexual abuse," 1990, p. A3).

Physical Abuse

Physical abuse, too, was rampant within the schools; the application of corporal punishment was difficult to monitor or contain. There are many stories of children being forced to eat their own vomit, having their faces rubbed in human feces, and being beaten for minor infractions of school rules. Many incidents of abuse are recorded in the Department of Indian Affairs files. Teachers who were sympathetic to the children and described or reported abuse by other teachers were dismissed for disloyalty.

One teacher described the physical abuse in a residential school as follows:

> Children's faces are slapped, [they are] hit on the head, struck across the nose causing nose bleeds. ... One teacher said a boy in her classroom had a swollen face for two days from being slapped. Another teacher reported that one of her pupils was slapped because he couldn't read the small print in the hymn books. One of my grade 8 boys was slapped on the head until he was pale, he staggered, complained of feeling dizzy and his nose bled profusely. This was witnessed by most of the school boys. He fainted five days later in prayers and again in my classroom. (Malloy, 1999, p. 282)

Eventually, in response to the various allegations and to the reports of the children's injuries that were observed when the schools were inspected, the Department of Indian Affairs issued a number of regulations to address the use of corporal punishment. These regulations seem to have had little effect; school administrators continued on the old course of physical punishments, set as policy when the schools were first established.

In 1965, in response to the widespread allegations of physical abuse, the department solicited an evaluation of the residential school system, to be presented at the first Residential Principals' Conference. The department handpicked as witnesses six residential school graduates who were of "impeccable authority and character," each successful in public service, education, or church service. One respondent was a graduate of the Mohawk Institute in Brantford, Ontario and he described (Malloy, 1999, p. 284) the conditions there as follows: 90 percent of the children suffered from dietary deficiency, evidenced by boils, warts, and general ill health. He reported seeing children eating from the garbage and from the bin intended to feed the pigs. Lice infestations were common and so children's heads were frequently shaved. Captured runaways were brought back to run a gauntlet where they were hit with anything found on hand. He reported that he had "seen boys crying in the most abject misery and pain with not a soul to care—the dignity of man!" (Malloy, 1999, p. 284).

The appraisal of the schools resulted in some positive comments; overall, though, the comments were unfavourable and difficult to ignore.

Emotional Abuse

Emotional abuse is among the most damaging kinds of abuse, and it was constantly meted out in the residential schools. Students were made to endure humiliation and ridicule by staff. At one school, as a punishment for bedwetting, children were made to wear the wet sheet draped over their heads. In another school, female students were stripped of their underwear and struck on the bare buttocks in front of the class. This disclosure came from the principal of a northern school who believed the punishment to be reasonable.

Children reported being locked in a room in only their underwear and restricted to a bread-and-milk diet as a punishment for running away. Two female runaways were forced to attend meals in the dining room in only their underwear. Children were ridiculed and taunted by staff and called derogatory names that specifically targeted their race.

Doris Young recalled that runaways from the Anglican schools she attended in Manitoba and Saskatchewan were punished in front of the assembled students:

> They both were brought back into the dining room, where we witnessed them getting their head shaved. And, and then they had to remove their clothes, they'd remove their clothes, and they strapped them in front of all of us. And we all had to go into the dining room, where, where the, where usually the, the boys' and the girls' dining rooms were separated, and but we, we were all taken into the dining room, and we were, we had to witness this beating, and I thought, oh, I hope it's not one of my brothers, but, but it wasn't, and still they, they were boys and girls that, the boys and girls, and everybody, the, the supervisors were all standing there witnessing this, these horrible beatings that these boys were getting because they ran away from school. (TRC, 2015b, p. 147)

The department was aware of the persistent problem of children running away. Many died while trying to escape, mainly due to exposure. The department also had to deal with the problem of children attempting suicide within the schools. These two problems were further symptoms of real problems within the school itself and the system at large. In 1920, nine boys attempted suicide by eating water hemlock; one died. In 1981, at Muscowequan school, five girls between the ages of eight and ten tied socks and towels together with a view to hanging themselves (Malloy, 1999).

Spiritual and Cultural Abuse

Spiritual and cultural abuse were implicit in the very purpose of the schools: assimilation. The schools were meant to eliminate the Indigenous way of life and spiritual beliefs for the next generation. Duncan Campbell Scott believed and hoped that within three generations the "Indian race" would no longer exist, as a result of the government's assimilation policies; residential schools were seen as an effective means to this end. Ultimately, Scott was mistaken. Though several generations of Indigenous children—as many as five, in some cases—did attend residential schools, Indigenous nations are alive and persevering in Canada today.

Residential schools vigorously tackled the ambitious goal of eliminating Indigenous culture. Many survivors report that the most severe punishments meted out by school staff were reserved for children who spoke their original language or attempted to carry on any Indigenous tradition. As children arrived at the schools, their birth name was replaced with an identification number and a new Christian name. Many of them spoke little or no English and so could not communicate with staff. A few schools would assign an interpreter from the older student population, but most schools expected the child simply to stop speaking in his or her original tongue until he or she could acquire sufficient English to communicate.

The idea to eliminate Indigenous languages came from the United States. In 1867, President Ulysses S. Grant called strongly for linguistic genocide:

> Through sameness of language is produced sameness of sentiment, and thought. ... In difference of language today lies two-thirds of our trouble. ... Schools should be established, which children should be required to attend; their barbarous dialect should be blotted out and the English language substituted. (Reyhner & Eder, 2004)

For the children, the psychological effects of this linguistic suppression were severe. As we will see in Chapter 10, the continuation or retention of language is a factor in the well-being of individuals and communities, whereas loss of language has been linked to higher rates of youth suicide. Erasing the child's language meant erasing his or her identity, concept of self, and world view, as well as the child's sense of his or her place in the world.

VOICES

That's where I had the most difficulty in school because I didn't understand English. My hand was hit because I wrote on my scribblers, the scribblers that were given on starting school, pencils, erasers, rulers and that, scribblers, and textbooks that were given. "Write your names," she said, "so they don't get lost." But I wrote on my scribblers in Cree syllabics. And so I got the nun really mad that I was writing in Cree. And then I only knew my name was Ministik from the first time I heard my name, my name was Ministik. So I was whipped again because I didn't know my name was Peter Nakogee.

Source: TRC (2015b, p. 48).

CALL TO ACTION

17. We call upon all levels of government to enable residential school Survivors and their families to reclaim names changed by the residential school system by waiving administrative costs for a period of five years for the name-change process and the revision of official identity documents, such as birth certificates, passports, driver's licences, health cards, status cards, and social insurance numbers.

A saying from this era expresses the non-Indigenous view of this erasure: "Kill the Indian and save the child/man." Once everything Indian in the child's life was destroyed, however, it was not replaced with any new values or world view. The original intention had been for Christianity to take the place of Indigenous culture and values, but the coercive way in which Christianity was taught belied its own values and detracted from its validity in the children's eyes, so that few of them internalized its ideals.

For many children, acquiring a new language under such stressful circumstances was difficult. Many children simply stopped speaking and ceased to express emotions such as frustration, fear, and anger; they learned to internalize emotion rather than express it. These self-protective barriers to communication remained in place after the child was discharged from the school. As the children returned to their home communities, the first generation of survivors could not communicate with any members of their community, even their own families. They had lost their language and now spoke only English, not widely spoken by members of their community. The emotional isolation thus continued.

We know that language is both the basis of culture and its conduit, and that if a language is forever lost, as is a risk for many Indigenous languages, the culture it conveys will be significantly diminished. Since the closure of the residential schools, various conditions have contributed to the decline of Indigenous languages. For example, there has been a significant influx of Indigenous people into large urban centres, where their original languages are inevitably eroded. The numbers are revealing (Statistics Canada, 2010):

- In 1941, less than 10 percent of Indigenous people claimed English as their first language.
- In 1971, by which point the schools had mostly been phased out after three generations of children had passed through them, 54 percent of Canadian Indigenous people reported English as their first language.
- By 1996, 75 percent of Canada's Indigenous population listed English as their mother tongue.
- According to the 2011 National Household Survey, there were 1,400,700 Indigenous people in Canada, but only 240,815 spoke an Indigenous language. (Indigenous and Northern Affairs Canada, 2011).

CLOSE-UP   Rita Joe

Rita Joe was born on a Mi'kmaq reserve on Cape Breton Island in 1932. When she was 12 years old, she went to Shubenacadie Indian Residential School in Nova Scotia, the only Indian residential school in Atlantic Canada. Rita recalled being told at school that she was "no good." She began writing as an adult to challenge this message, eventually publishing six volumes of poetry and song. She has been referred to as the "poet laureate" of the Mi'kmaq people. In the prologue to her memoir (1996), she states, "My greatest wish is that there will be more writing from my people, and that our children will read it. I have said again and again that our history would be different if it had been expressed by us."

She was made a member of the Order of Canada in 1989 and of the Queen's Privy Council for Canada in 1992. She died in 2007 after suffering from Parkinson's disease.

Source: *Canadian Encyclopedia* (2007).

I Lost My Talk

by Rita Joe, Mi'kmaq

I lost my talk
The talk you took away.
When I was a little girl
At Shubenacadie school.

You snatched it away;
I speak like you
I think like you
I create like you
The scrambled ballad, about my word.

Two ways I talk
Both ways I say,
Your way is more powerful.

So gently I offer my hand and ask,
Let me find my talk
So I can teach you about me.

Source: Joe (1998).

CALL TO ACTION

13. We call upon the federal government to acknowledge that Aboriginal rights include Aboriginal language rights.

Aftermath of Residential Schools

In 1948, the federal government undertook a review of Indian residential schools. It found that the schools were a dismal failure, and proposed phasing them out and integrating Indigenous students into mainstream schools. According to the review, a graduate from the residential school system was less prepared for life than an Indigenous person who had never attended any formal education institution. The federal government began funding provincial schools on a per capita basis to include Indigenous children. Nevertheless, many of the residential schools were kept open until the 1960s. The last one, the Gordon Residential School in Saskatchewan, did not close until 1996.

Effects on Individuals, Families, and Communities

The effect of the schools on Indigenous communities has been devastating. As many psychological and sociological studies have shown, those who are abused often become abusers, particularly in cases of sexual abuse. Indigenous leaders report that sexual abuse is like a disease ripping through their communities, where its incidence is currently reported to be very high.

Families have also been torn apart by violence—another legacy of the residential school experience. This system taught students that adults exert power and control over children by physical punishment, and the survivors of the system have carried this conditioning into Indigenous communities where, traditionally, few would ever have thought to raise a hand against a child for punishment or for discipline. The cycle is difficult to break. Residential school survivors never experienced nurturing, respectful parenting, and many, as a result, have faced difficulties raising their own children. Until recently, these struggles were being passed from one generation to the next without intervention.

In 1990, a First Nations leader wrote to Minister of Indian Affairs Tom Siddon regarding the far-reaching effects of residential school experiences on survivors:

> Social maladjustment, abuse of self and others and family breakdown are some of the symptoms prevalent among First Nations baby boomers. The graduates of Ste. Anne's Residential school are now trying and often failing to come to grips with life as adults after being raised as children in an atmosphere of fear, loneliness and self loathing. Fear of caretakers. Loneliness in knowing that elders and family were far away. Loathing from learning to hate oneself, because of repeated physical, verbal or sexual abuse suffered at the hands of various adult caretakers. This is only a small part of the story. (Indian and Northern Affairs Canada, 1990)

On a reserve in British Columbia, research was conducted to determine the health status and quality of life of Indigenous residential school survivors compared with Indigenous members of the community who had not attended residential schools. There was little difference between the two populations, but both groups suffered from worse health and a lower quality of life than non-Indigenous people. Researchers concluded that the effects of residential schools were disseminated through Indigenous communities. In other words, the trauma of the residential school experience was a contagion, spreading to collateral victims and from generation to generation (Barton et al., 2005).

VOICES

Genine Paul-Dimitracopoulos's mother was placed in the Shubenacadie residential school in Nova Scotia at a very early age. Paul-Dimitracopoulos told the [Truth and Reconciliation] Commission that knowing this, and what the school was like, helped her understand "how we grew up because my mom never really showed us love when we were kids coming up. She, when I was hurt or cried, she was never there to console you or to hug you. If I hurt myself she would never give me a hug and tell me it would be okay. I didn't understand why."

Source: TRC (2015a, p. 136).

Indigenous leaders called for a public inquiry into the residential school system to determine the breadth and depth of the damage it had caused and to suggest resolutions for their communities regarding how to begin the healing process. Initially, the federal government did not agree to such an inquiry. In 1992, however, the Royal Commission on Aboriginal Peoples (RCAP) was established by the federal government in response to a land claims issue that erupted into violence.

The RCAP devoted considerable effort to the residential school issue. The final report, released in 1996, recommended (among other things) a full investigation into the residential school system in the form of a public inquiry in order to "bring light and begin to heal the grievous harms suffered by countless children, families, and communities" (RCAP, 1996, p. 338). Specifically, the RCAP recommended that:

- the inquiry hold hearings across the country;
- funding be sufficient to allow all of those who were affected to testify;
- the inquiry be allowed to commission research and analysis to help better understand the nature and effect of residential school policies; and
- the inquiry be authorized to recommend remedial actions that governments and churches can take to mitigate the damage done by the schools. These might include apologies from those responsible; compensation to help heal and rebuild communities; and funding to treat those affected by the schools and their families.

Although not all of its recommendations were followed, the RCAP's findings put several processes in motion. We examine these later in the chapter under the heading "Attempts at Resolution."

The Sixties Scoop

The government's past involvement with Indigenous children did not end with the residential school system. A discussion of the government's mistreatment of Indigenous people and the terrible legacy of the residential schools would not be complete without addressing a related phenomenon—something that occurred as the schools were being phased out between the 1960s and 1980s. It has been dubbed the "**Sixties Scoop**" by sociologists, and refers to the removal, by well-intentioned social workers, of thousands of Indigenous children from their communities. The children were placed in foster care or put up for adoption in non-Indigenous homes in the belief that they were being rescued from a life of poverty and despair—from conditions that were, in fact, a legacy of the residential school system. Despite its name, the "Scoop" continued until the late 1990s.

The "Scoop" began as the schools closed, and a question arose about what to do with the children of school age and younger. This emerged as a significant problem. After three or four generations of Indigenous people had been raised in schools rather than in family homes, the ability of residential school survivors to raise their own children was severely handicapped. The prevalence of poverty, alcoholism, and other social problems on reserves left many children in need of protection or, at the very least, of intervention. After generations of the schools' efforts to break and destroy family ties, the communities had difficulty rebuilding harmonious family lives.

In 1947, the Canadian Welfare Council and the Canadian Association of Social Workers presented a brief to a federal special committee asserting that, under provincial social legislation, Indigenous children suffering from neglect were not afforded the same protections as white children. This was true: Indigenous children fell under the authority of the federal government, which was in the process of dismantling the school system. Child welfare services were provided to the mainstream population through provincial funds and under provincial jurisdiction and legislation; these services were not available to Indigenous children.

Changes to the *Indian Act* in 1951 addressed the concerns expressed by social workers. These changes provided that all provincial laws respecting child welfare were now to apply to Indigenous children as well, effectively bringing Indigenous child welfare services under the authority of provincial child welfare workers. The following question then arose: Who would fund the provision of these services to the Indigenous reserves and Indigenous children? There was considerable debate over this issue, which resulted in the postponement of intervention for Indigenous children. When the federal and provincial governments finally agreed to a cost-sharing process to finance these services, well-intentioned social workers quickly sprang into action. Although only 1 percent of all children in care in 1959 were Indigenous, this number

Sixties Scoop
the practice of removing Indigenous children from their communities and placing them in foster care or putting them up for adoption in non-Indigenous homes

rose by the end of the 1960s to 30 to 40 percent, even though Indigenous people made up only 4 percent of the population.

Reasons cited for removing Indigenous children from their communities included inadequate housing, unsafe drinking water, no running water, no available school, and poor health conditions. Instead of addressing these conditions, the federal government chose to remove the children from their communities. Services such as counselling and child care were not made available to intact Indigenous families; these services could be funded only if the child became a ward of the state.

> The caseloads in social service agencies were so high that workers did not have time to properly screen homes, nor was monitoring of either foster or adoptive homes usually feasible. But most social workers, none of whom were aboriginal, felt little harm could befall an aboriginal child rescued from poverty and placed with a nice, middle-class, white family. Yet behind the closed doors of their foster and adoptive homes, aboriginal children were even more isolated and vulnerable than they had been in residential school. … In many cases, children were taken from parents whose only crime was poverty and being aboriginal. (Fournier & Crey, 1997, p. 85)

In a holdover from the residential school days, siblings were separated. This was due not only to the large sizes of Indigenous families but also to the belief that the individual children would adjust more quickly to their new homes and new environments without the influence of siblings.

Bridget Moran, a social worker in British Columbia at the height of the Sixties Scoop, writes in *A Little Rebellion* (2002) that social service workers had no resources available that might have helped keep Indigenous families together. They had no family support workers, treatment centres, or transitional housing. Moran reports that when they found a child at risk, they had no alternative but to place the child in foster care. Ernie Klassen, former district superintendent for Indian Affairs, recalls that on one weekend a social worker chartered a bus to apprehend 38 children on the Spallumcheen reserve in British Columbia and was asking for 38 different foster homes to accommodate them (Fournier & Crey, 1997).

One result of the apprehension of children was the intensification of social problems on reserves that were experiencing the loss of their young. Indigenous leaders spoke out against the practice with vehemence, but their voices were rarely heard.

By the end of the 1970s, one in every four status Indian children could expect to be separated from his or her parents for all or part of childhood. In British Columbia in 1997, one in three legal wards was of Indigenous heritage. Many Indigenous children were shipped out of province and many went to families in the United States. Some private adoption agencies, mostly of a religious nature, sprang up to secure Canadian Indigenous children for adoption to US families. In all, Manitoba lost the greatest number of Indigenous children, an estimated 20,000, of which 55 percent were sent out of province, in comparison with 7 percent of non-Indigenous adoptions going out of province.

Because of this history, there is a movement toward Indigenous-run child welfare services available on reserves. Those services recognize the importance of placing children in need with Indigenous families within the community and supporting family reunification if possible. However, on-reserve child welfare services are underfunded compared with those for the rest of Canada. In 2007, the Assembly of First Nations supported the First Nations Child and Family Caring Society in bringing a complaint to the Canadian Human Rights Tribunal to assert that First Nations children are subject to discrimination because of their race in terms of the funds available to assist them and their families. In January 2016, the tribunal ruled that this is in fact discrimination and that the Ministry of Indigenous and Northern Affairs must take immediate action to correct the inequities of service. The federal government announced that it would not appeal the tribunal's ruling but would work toward making the necessary changes.

VOICES

The [Truth and Reconciliation] Commission heard many stories of mistreatment in foster homes. One woman told us that her foster parents physically and sexually abused her. Her Aboriginal identity was constantly disparaged. She said, "[My foster parents were] adamant about Aboriginal culture being less than human, living as dirty bush people, eating rats. It made me not want to be one of those people. And for years, I didn't know how to be proud of who I was because I didn't know who I was."

Source: TRC (2015a, p. 140).

In 1982, Manitoba judge Edwin Kimelman, at the insistence of Indigenous leaders, was appointed to investigate the apprehension of Manitoba's Indigenous children. He concluded that the child welfare services were well-intentioned but misguided and were guilty of **cultural genocide**. In response to his findings, a moratorium was placed on out-of-province adoptions, and the wholesale removal of children was stopped in the mid-1980s.

Tragically, a large number of these adoptions failed: many of the children suffered from identity crises in their teens; many had to endure racism in school and from society at large without the support of the Indigenous community; and many had been subjected to abuse while in the foster system prior to adoption and were unable to overcome that legacy. Others suffered from health complications, such as fetal alcohol syndrome (FAS) and fetal alcohol effects (FAE), that had not been diagnosed prior to adoption, and many adoptive parents were unable to cope with the challenges of raising such a child. Today, our court system and our jails are filled with Indigenous people who are casualties of the mistakes of this era.

Today, Indigenous children are still apprehended at disproportionate rates. Statistics Canada reported that of the 30,000 children across Canada in 2011 in care of child welfare services 14 years and younger, 48 percent were Indigenous: 3.6 percent of Indigenous children opposed to 0.3 percent for the general population (Statistics Canada, 2013).

Adoptees from this era have launched two class action lawsuits recently, in Ontario and Saskatchewan. In the Saskatchewan lawsuit, over 1,000 adoptees are represented by Merchant Law, who also represented many residential school survivors (Huck, 2015). Approximately 16,000 adoptees are represented in *Brown v. Attorney General of Canada* (Sixties Scoop Class Action Lawsuit, 2015). The plaintiffs were heard on August 23, 2016, but as of this printing, the federal government had yet to present its evidence. Indigenous Affairs Minister Carolyn Bennett expressed her hopes that the case could end in a negotiated settlement between the plaintiffs and the federal government.

cultural genocide
the destruction of those structures and practices that allow a group to continue as a group, such as language, spiritual practices, and cultural values

CALL TO ACTION

1. We call upon the federal, provincial, territorial, and Aboriginal governments to commit to reducing the number of Aboriginal children in care by:

i. Monitoring and assessing neglect investigations.

ii. Providing adequate resources to enable Aboriginal communities and child-welfare organizations to keep Aboriginal families together where it is safe to do so, and to keep children in culturally appropriate environments, regardless of where they reside.

iii. Ensuring that social workers and others who conduct child-welfare investigations are properly educated and trained about the history and impacts of residential schools.

iv. Ensuring that social workers and others who conduct child-welfare investigations are properly educated and trained about the potential for Aboriginal communities and families to provide more appropriate solutions to family healing.

v. Requiring that all child-welfare decision makers consider the impact of the residential school experience on children and their caregivers.

Cultural Genocide

The term *cultural genocide* has been used widely by academics studying the history of the relationship between Canada and Indigenous peoples. *Cultural genocide* can be defined as the deliberate and systematic destruction of the culture, traditions, language, and ways of being of a specific cultural group. More recently, academics have applied this term to the experiences of Indigenous people in Canada and around the world.

In response to the discovery of the atrocities committed against Jews during the Second World War, the international community rallied together through the United Nations to create the *Convention on the Prevention and Punishment of the Crime of Genocide*. Canada participated in this Convention in 1948, more than 50 years after the establishment of residential schools and prior to the proposed closure of the schools. The Convention reads as follows:

> **Article 1:** The Contracting Parties confirm that genocide, whether committed in time of peace or in time of war, is a crime under international law which they undertake to prevent and to punish.
>
> **Article 2:** In the present Convention, genocide means any of the following acts committed with intent to destroy, in whole or in part, a national, ethnical, racial or religious group, as such:
>
>> (a) Killing members of the group;
>> (b) Causing serious bodily or mental harm to members of the group;
>> (c) Deliberately inflicting on the group conditions of life calculated to bring about its physical destruction in whole or in part;
>> (d) Imposing measures intended to prevent births within the group;
>> (e) Forcibly transferring children of the group to another group.
>
> **Article 3:** The following acts shall be punishable:
>
>> (a) Genocide;
>> (b) Conspiracy to commit genocide;
>> (c) Direct and public incitement to commit genocide;
>> (d) Attempt to commit genocide;
>> (e) Complicity in genocide.
>
> **Article 4:** Persons committing genocide or any of the other acts enumerated in Article 3 shall be punished, whether they are constitutionally responsible rulers, public officials or private individuals. (United Nations, 1948)

EXERCISE 2

Based on the articles of the Convention on Genocide quoted above and on what you have learned about the experiences of Indigenous people in Canada, do you think the UN Convention's definition of genocide applies?
  If so, to what degree? Who should be held accountable, and how?
  If not, why not?

Attempts at Resolution

Before discussing the attempts at resolution, it is important to note that Indigenous communities and leaders agree that no amount of money can ever compensate Indigenous people for the suffering they endured. The question, then, is how Canadians can reconcile themselves to their past and partner with Indigenous people to promote recovery. What is the fair and just thing to do, considering all that has taken place? Financial compensation should not be construed as a punishment to Canada and viewed in terms of a fine. Compensation could be perceived in appropriate terms—as a dedication of resources to help residential school survivors overcome their pain and move toward health and wellness.

Legal Proceedings and the Indian Residential Schools Settlement Agreement

As discussed earlier in the chapter, Arthur Henry Plint was convicted of sexually assaulting Willie Blackwater and many other boys at Alberni Indian Residential School during the 1960s. In 1995 and 1997, he was sentenced to 12 years in prison. In 1998, Blackwater and 30 other residential school survivors embarked on a civil suit against Plint. The suit also named the federal government, which organized the residential school system, and the United Church of Canada, which ran the Port Alberni school.

The trial was difficult for survivors to endure, since they faced hard questioning by government and church lawyers. In 2001, the complainants chose to take an out-of-court settlement for a reported $180,000 to $290,000 each in order to end the trial. But the questions remain: Who was responsible for these atrocities? Was it Plint alone or was it the entire Indian Affairs Department, which appears to have turned a blind eye to the abuse of children? Should the government be held fully responsible for setting up an education system with very few formal accountability processes, thereby creating a situation that was destined to foster abuse? The Indian Affairs Department records made available to date have now been extensively examined, and it is clear that the department attempted to document complaints of abuse. But its attempts to stop the abuse were modest, and they failed. Should churches share in the responsibility because they supplied the unqualified staff who were the abusers?

Survivors have tried a variety of methods of redressing the wrongs done them. The first method is the criminal prosecution of offenders. One problem with this method is that police are frequently unable to locate the offenders, many of whom are now deceased. The survivors' second method of seeking redress—and the one that has proved most popular—has been civil litigation.

As the Plint case showed, legal proceedings can be difficult for survivors, who are forced to relive their traumatic experiences during the investigation and trial. There are a number of reasons for choosing to pursue criminal charges or civil litigation, however, aside from the prospect of financial reparation inherent in the latter:

- *Public recognition*
  Victory in the public forum of the court system signifies acknowledgment on the part of Canada's mainstream judicial system that a legitimate wrong has occurred and that a victim deserves compensation. This type of public recognition satisfies those who seek vindication on a matter of principle.

- *Level playing field*
  The court system is perceived as levelling the playing field between the plaintiff or complainant and the accused. Of course, the playing field cannot be perfectly level, since one side—in this case, the defendants (government and churches)—often has more financial resources for the litigation process than the other side. Still, in the case of criminal proceedings, the complainant can be assured that there will be no back-door, high-pressure negotiation, with the powerful strong-arming the powerless, as sometimes occurs—or is perceived to occur—in the alternative dispute resolution (ADR) process. The justice system, although imperfect, aspires to be unaffected by unequal distributions of power.

- *Establishment of precedent*
  Another reason for survivors to choose to litigate is that a court decision may establish precedents that other courts are bound to follow, thereby helping to ensure that survivors will be treated equally.

- *Awareness and understanding*
  The final reason for survivors of the residential school system to seek redress through the civil litigation process is that they want their stories heard. This desire was clear in the findings of the RCAP, which recommended a cross-country inquiry into the damage done by the residential schools—a recommendation that the federal government originally refused to follow, but much later did implement in the form of the Truth and Reconciliation Commission (discussed further below). The survivors desired to be heard and understood, and they wanted their experience to register in the consciousness of mainstream Canadian society. At that time, this could happen only if a resolution was sought in a public forum such as the court system, where the transcripts and outcome are part of the public record.

For the Indigenous plaintiffs, there were drawbacks to the civil litigation process. The most obvious was the cost. Some survivors resolved this through the use of contingency fees, although they were sometimes charged up to half of their financial settlement in legal fees (Tibbetts, 2000). Another drawback to the civil litigation route was that the acknowledgment of harm was offered only to the individual survivor; there was no recognition of the harm done to the survivor's family, to subsequent generations, and to the community. This second kind of recognition is particularly important to Indigenous people and to their communities.

Despite the difficulties they faced in seeking restitution for past wrongs, a growing number of survivors came forward through the 1990s. As of July 2003, there had been 12,000 claims filed, very few of which had been resolved. Many prospective claimants waited to see what resolutions would be reached before filing their own claims. It was predicted at the time that the number of claims could reach 30,000. At its height, the residential school system included 88 schools across Canada, and the 1991 census reported that there were 105,000 residential school survivors alive at that time. It was estimated in 2003 that, if the number of cases continued to grow at the current pace, the pursuit of civil litigation could stretch the time frame for settlement to over 50 years, by which time almost all the plaintiffs would be dead.

In order to address these timing problems, the government embarked upon an alternative dispute resolution process. This process was slow because many matters had to be settled, not the least of which was the division of responsibility between church and state. The federal government announced, after negotiations stalled, that it would accept responsibility for 70 percent of the claim amount, leaving the churches responsible for the remaining 30 percent. The churches insisted that being made responsible for this amount could in fact leave them bankrupt. When the Indian Residential Schools Settlement Agreement was approved, the churches were responsible for contributing up to $100 million in cash and services toward healing initiatives.

Another issue that arose in this process was the government's refusal to address the loss of culture and language suffered by Indigenous people as a consequence of the residential school experience. The government insisted it would address those losses through government-funded initiatives for Indigenous language and cultural renewal, and would provide compensation to survivors only for sexual and physical abuse suffered in the schools.

A major shortcoming of the ADR process, at least where residential school survivors were concerned, is that it moved the negotiation of these matters from the public to the private forum, so that only those directly involved were aware of the negotiations. In this way, the process became less accountable to the public, which could not be sure whether justice had in fact been served. The ADR process began in June 2001. In 2003, a lawyer representing some residential school survivors pointed out that of the $1.2 billion dedicated to the ADR process, $540 million was earmarked for legal costs rather than compensation (Frank, 2003). The survivors of residential schools grow older each year, and many have passed away without closure to this most life-altering experience.

On May 10, 2006, through the ADR process, the **Indian Residential Schools Settlement Agreement (IRSSA)** was reached. In the following sections we examine two of its components, financial compensation for survivors and the Truth and Reconciliation Commission.

Indian Residential Schools Settlement Agreement (IRSSA) an agreement by which Indigenous people who could prove their attendance in the residential schools became eligible to receive a "common experience payment" (CEP)

The Common Experience Payment

Under the IRSSA, Indigenous people who could prove their attendance in the schools became eligible to receive a "common experience payment" (CEP) of $10,000 for the first year of attendance and $3,000 for each subsequent year (known as the "10-plus-3" formula). As of June 2016, 79,309 applicants had been processed and paid, with an average payment of $20,457 per applicant (Indigenous and Northern Affairs Canada, 2016).

The IRSSA, which resulted from the largest lawsuit settled out of court in the history of Canada, began accepting applications in September 2007. The application process had a number of components. First, survivors applied to Indian Residential Schools Resolution Canada, whose role was to verify the applicant's years of attendance in one or more of the recognized schools. Following the verification, letters were mailed out and payment was made.

For those who were denied payment or were not happy with the results of their application, there was an appeal process. This process was put in place because the registration records of many students had been lost by the government, and the onus was on the survivor to prove his or her attendance. It is necessary to verify attendance and years of attendance in order to calculate entitlement. Attendance claims that could not be easily verified through archived records required additional research on the part of Indian Residential Schools Resolution Canada.

Another point of contention was that certain schools were not included on the list of residential schools. If we include the early mission schools and the final federally run schools, Indian education spanned 160 years and took many forms and had many partners. This meant that the survivors of these excluded schools did not qualify for the settlement process. Among the schools excluded were the Stirland Lake and Cristal Lake residential high schools in northern Ontario, which operated between 1971 and 1991. According to the Canadian government, these schools were private Mennonite schools and were not run with the direct involvement of the government of Canada (Residential Schools Settlement, 2012). A 2011 decision by the Ontario Superior Court confirmed that Stirland Lake must be added to the list and that all of the attendees must be considered for the CEP since the school met the definition of an Indian residential school (Nishnawbe Aski Nation, 2011).

The IRSSA included an independent assessment process (IAP) for certain kinds of survivors—those who identified themselves as survivors of sexual and physical abuse that had led to serious psychological trauma. In these cases, there was a hearing and an adjudicated judgment. This was done on a case-by-case basis; all records were to be fully disclosed by the government of Canada so that evidence could be collected to substantiate the alleged abuses in order to assess compensation. These records were intended to be kept as part of the TRC body of records for future archives. However, in 2014, the court had to clarify that the disclosure records for the IAP could be kept for the TRC records with permission of the survivor. In 2015, the court had to clarify for the federal government what "full disclosure" included, since police records were being withheld from those seeking settlement (Rennie, 2014).

Throughout this process, support services were put in place for the applicants, many of whom found that the application process triggered traumatic memories that led to depression, loneliness, fear, panic, and, in some cases, addictive behaviour and suicidal thoughts.

A further component of the IRSSA was the Aboriginal Healing Fund, administered by the Aboriginal Healing Foundation (AHF). The AHF had been created in 1998 following the apology issued by Cabinet minister Jane Stewart and was provided with a $350 million grant from the federal government for use over ten years for counselling programs and culture recovery initiatives. As part of the IRSSA, in 2007 the Aboriginal Healing Fund was assigned an additional $125 million over five years to operate healing initiatives and supports for survivors. The AHF closed in September 2014.

One of the AHF's initiatives was an evaluation of the common experience payment process. Its report was published in 2010, following interviews of 280 CEP recipients. The aim of these interviews was to determine whether the CEP had helped the survivors to heal and whether there were sufficient services in place to support them, practically and emotionally, in the application process.

The interviews conducted for this study produced many stories and reflections from survivors, some excerpts from which are included below. With regard to the application process, many found it straightforward enough, but some had difficulties on account of the poor education they had received in the residential schools. One survivor (AHF, 2010, p. 22) spoke as follows of his educational shortcomings:

> I didn't even get an education. I didn't go to a class or anything. … They made you work down there all the time. I didn't do any learning. I was on the farm, that's all I was doing. … There used to be rocks all over the fields, big boulders and they used horses and picked them all up. That's how they got that meadow there to make hay. We'd go out in the morning and first we'd clean the barn, pigs, chicken, we'd do that in the morning and then in the afternoon we'd go to the field. No time for the classroom. I can't even read or write, some of these heavy words [in the CEP application] I couldn't even understand.

A survivor in Nunavut (AHF, 2010, p. 29) spoke of the difficulty of finding school records to prove attendance at the schools, and of the skepticism with which their claims were often met:

> It was a waiting game, and you know, they don't believe you sometimes. They don't believe you went to the school. … Like us from before in the early 70's, we never keep all our records and our parents just threw them away. And that's what they want and that was hard. And then our school burnt down and all our records were in there and so for us around here it was kind of hard. I know there's still some people that are still waiting and trying.

Other survivors spoke about the long waiting times for the CEPs. Many of them—both for emotional reasons and for reasons of principle—were slow to apply, and then they had to wait a long time for the payment, sometimes for over a year. One survivor (AHF, 2010, p. 27) described this process as follows:

> I heard about [CEP] and it took me a long time. A lot of people applied for it right away but I didn't for a long time because I was angry, and I still am at the government because of what they have done to our Aboriginal people. I said, "they aren't going to buy me for what they have done to me." You know, it never replaces what we have lost … It took me quite a while and I thought about it for a long time. I wasn't going to apply for it in the beginning. No, I wasn't going to because I just felt that, "is that trying to replace what we lost?"

Another survivor described the emotional challenge of the application process, and the trauma of having to recall the details of his life in the school (AHF, 2010, p. 29):

> I waited a year and a half. It was a time consuming thing. They said to call back, asking the same questions over and over, and it was hard recalling names of people who died in school, who hung themselves, who died, who I grew up protecting. To bring it up again is kind of a hard thing to do.

The study asked participants whether the lump-sum CEP had had, overall, a positive or a negative impact on their lives. Of the 281 participants, 77 reported an overall positive experience,

38 a negative one, and 130 a mixed experience (AHF, 2010, p. 43). The remaining participants either did not respond or reported that their experience had been neither positive nor negative. Figure 9.1 lists the positive and negative effects of the CEP as described by the applicants.

A British Columbia survivor offered the following negative account of his CEP experience (AHF, 2010, p. 45):

> I want to mention about the negative experiences. I have lost about half a dozen cousins since we have gotten [CEP]. In my home community we are having funerals all the time. I have one cousin now who has wet brain and is in the hospital and he doesn't remember us. He drank and drank and drank and drank when the money came in. His younger brother died shortly after that money came in. He was young—he was 34 or 35 and he just drank and drank and drank. You know there is a lot more than just the half a dozen in my family and a lot of the people dying are younger than me. I'm 52 and many of them are my cohorts and were my cohorts in residential school and some of them are younger. There are Elders as well who passed away as a result. It is a common refrain in our territory. In our area there are three bands that speak the same language but culturally we are different. In the three bands, we were just having funerals and funerals and funerals. It is like the support people at the funerals just can't keep up. It has really done a lot of damage and destruction to our villages ... Everyone keeps dying.

Those who saw the CEPs in symbolic terms—that is, as an official acknowledgment by the government of the wrong done the Indigenous people—had a more positive experience of the process. The following quotation (AHF, 2010, p. 50) reflects a perspective of this sort:

> My kids understand a little of what we went through. ... The impact of being in that place [residential school], they didn't realize it. They put you in a strange place, they didn't see that. ... My kids were helped in a lot of ways. In a lot of ways they understood where the money was coming from. Everyone thinks it's just money, all the pain you went through, that the CEP is just about money. It's not.

FIGURE 9.1   Positive and Negative Impact of CEP Experience on the Aboriginal Participants

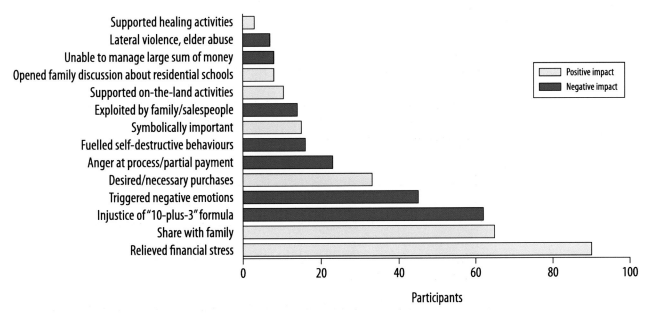

SOURCE: Aboriginal Healing Foundation (2010, p. 44).

Those who reported positive experiences tended to emphasize the benefits of sharing pain openly and of family healing, and they said the process gave them hope for future reconciliation with non-Indigenous Canada.

Survivors' efforts to heal themselves have taken various forms. Some have used Indigenous healing methods such as sweat lodges, traditional medicines, and other techniques for cultural reconnection. Some have adopted Western traditions of healing, such as therapy and counselling. Figure 9.2 shows the extent to which the recipients of the CEPs have been engaged in the healing process and—in cases where they have been engaged—how successful the process has been. Figure 9.3 shows the effects the CEPs have had on this process, according to the survivors themselves.

FIGURE 9.2   Residential School Survivors—Engagement in Healing

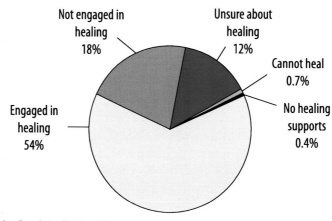

SOURCE: Aboriginal Healing Foundation (2010, p. 78).

FIGURE 9.3   Effects of CEPs on Healing and Well-Being

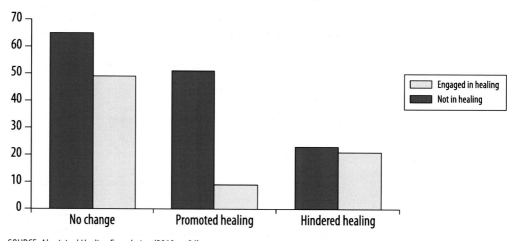

SOURCE: Aboriginal Healing Foundation (2010, p. 86).

The Truth and Reconciliation Commission

In addition to the CEP, part of the IRSSA's mandate was to create the Truth and Reconciliation Commission (TRC). The TRC had a five-year mandate (2008–2013) to accomplish the following, and to do so without holding any formal hearings, or acting as a public inquiry, or conducting any formal legal process:

1. Acknowledge residential school experiences, impacts, and consequences;
2. Provide a holistic, culturally appropriate, and safe setting for former students, their families and communities as they come forward to the commission;
3. Witness, support, promote, and facilitate truth and reconciliation events at both the national and community level;
4. Promote awareness and public education of Canadians about the Indian residential school system and its impacts;
5. Identify sources and create as complete an historical record as possible of the Indian residential school [IRS] system and its legacy. The record shall be preserved and made accessible to the public for future study and use;
6. Produce and submit to the parties of the agreement a report including recommendations to the Government of Canada concerning the IRS system and experience including: the history, purpose, operation and supervision of the IRS system, the effect and consequences of IRS (including systemic harms, intergenerational consequences and the impact on human dignity) and the ongoing legacy of the residential schools;
7. Support commemoration of former Indian residential school students and their families in accordance with the Commemoration Policy Directive. (TRC, 2011)

One of the TRC's tasks was to address concerns about the relative seclusion of the ADR negotiations—the fact that the records of abuse were not fully disclosed during this process. Canadians were not privy to the information that led to the various settlements. As mentioned, survivors want the rest of Canada to be aware of what they experienced in the residential schools. Only through a shared perspective—a common recognition of past and present—can Indigenous and non-Indigenous Canada be reconciled.

As part of its mission, the TRC travelled across Canada collecting statements from survivors of the residential schools. The commission received over 6,750 statements from survivors of residential schools, their families, and others who wished to share their stories. Seven major national events were held in Winnipeg, Inuvik, Halifax, Saskatoon, Montreal, Vancouver, and Edmonton between June 2010 and March 2014. As many as 155,000 people attended those events, in addition to 9,000 residential school survivors registered to attend them. These national events were also livestreamed to be accessible to Canadians everywhere. The TRC also held 238 days of local hearings in 77 communities across the country. Throughout its mandate the commission encouraged public participation in nearly 900 separate events.

The commission invited respected guests, both Indigenous and non-Indigenous, to the national events to represent all Canadians as "honorary witnesses" and partners in reconciliation. These witnesses included Michaëlle Jean, who was governor general of Canada at the start of the commission's mandate, and two former prime ministers, Paul Martin and Joe Clark.

Findings of the Truth and Reconciliation Commission

The TRC concluded its mandate in 2013 as scheduled and its final report, *Honouring the Truth, Reconciling for the Future*, was published in 2015. The report included 94 recommendations, or "calls to action," addressing, among other issues, the overrepresentation of Indigenous children in child welfare care; the overrepresentation of Indigenous people in the criminal justice system; jurisdictional disputes between provincial and federal governments over delivering health care for Indigenous people; discrepancies in the funding and delivery of education for Indigenous people; and strategies to maintain Indigenous languages and culture, and to recover what had been lost through the residential school era.

Concerning **reconciliation**, many recommendations aimed at healing the fractured relationship between Indigenous and non-Indigenous people in Canada. Many of these revolve around educating Canadians about the residential school era and commemorating the events so that we never forget this part of our history. One specific recommendation is the creation of mandatory, age-appropriate curricula on residential schools, treaties, and the contribution of Indigenous people, to be taught across Canada from kindergarten to grade 12, to ensure that all Canadians have a solid understanding of Indigenous history in Canada that includes Indigenous perspectives. Another recommendation calls for highly visible monuments to commemorate the residential school experience and the survivors of that era.

The University of Manitoba will become the permanent home of all of the research done by the commission as it establishes the National Centre for Truth and Reconciliation (NCTR). This centre will be available to survivors and researchers as well as the general public. Its purpose is to ensure that survivors and their families have access to their own history, much of which has been hidden from them, as well as to ensure that educators can share the true history of the residential school era with new generations of Canadians. The NCTR will house all TRC records, including survivors' oral history statements, artworks, and expressions of reconciliation, and other materials gathered by the TRC such as government and church records. It will be a site of collective public memory and consciousness, bearing permanent witness to survivors' testimonies to shape how the residential school era is understood and remembered within Canada (TRC, 2015a, p. 314).

The Missing Children Project

Many Indigenous children died at their residential schools. As Figure 9.4 shows, the death rate in the residential school system was far greater than that for children in the general Canadian population. The TRC supported the Missing Children Project, which was launched in 2008 with the aim of determining the number and causes of deaths, illnesses, and disappearances of Indigenous children at residential schools, and the location of burial sites of children across the country who were not interred in their school graveyard. Once their bodies are found, they can be repatriated to their communities.

The TRC concluded that it is unlikely that the exact number of students who died in residential schools will ever be determined, due to incomplete historical records. School enrollment records could be destroyed after five years and records of accidents in schools were kept for only ten years. Health records, including dental records and records of medical treatment and admission to hospital, were kept for only two years. Some principals reported annually how many children had died at their schools but often did not report the names of the deceased. To the best of its ability, given the system's ill-kept records, the TRC established a National Residential School Student Death Register.

The register contains three sub-registers:

1. the Register of Confirmed Deaths of Named Residential School Students;
2. the Register of Confirmed Deaths of Unnamed Residential School Students; and
3. the Register of Deaths That Require Further Investigation (for example, to discover names) (TRC, 2015a, pp. 90–92).

Recognition of Wrong

Beginning in the 1990s, those responsible for the implementation and running of residential schools began to express their regret in various ways. Churches and the Canadian government

FIGURE 9.4   Comparative Death Rates per 1,000 Population, Combined Residential Schools and the General Canadian Population of School-Aged Children, Using Five-Year Averages, 1921 to 1965

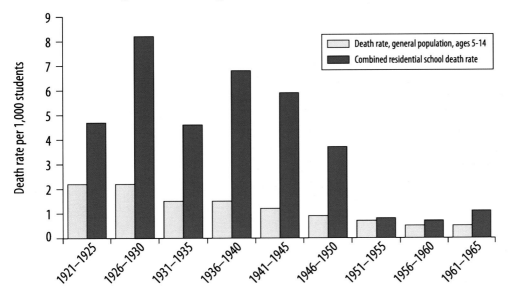

SOURCE: Truth and Reconciliation Commission of Canada (2015a, p. 91).

have both offered apologies. These differed in terms of the nature of the apology (that is, what was being apologized *for*) and in terms of the scope of the apology (that is, who was being apologized *to*). As with the CEP, individual reactions to the apologies have varied considerably.

Recognition by Churches

In 1994, the Roman Catholic Church recognized that terrible acts had been committed in the schools. The Catholic apology of 1994 was followed by an expression of "regret" for the Church and the "weaknesses of so many of her sons and daughters who sullied [the Church's] face." The acknowledgment of corrupted individuals acting on their own weaknesses implied no liability on the part of the Church. In reality, the Church apologized only to God for its agents' weaknesses— it neither apologized to former students, nor did it take responsibility for its larger role in the abuse in the schools. Individuals who were prosecuted would face secular civil proceedings, but the Church as an entity would not be held responsible. Survivors would be protected by the state.

Six years later, the Vatican issued a second apology, following a similar approach to that seen in the first. The "Day of Pardon" prayers of 2000 by Pope John Paul II included three prayers in his Mass that asked for the forgiveness of God for the weakness of the Church's clergy. Significantly, the Church did not ask for forgiveness from its victims. The Pontiff admitted that "Christians have often denied the Gospel; yielding to a mentality of power, they have violated the rights of ethnic groups and peoples, and shown contempt for their cultures and religious traditions." The Pope also acknowledged that "Christians have been guilty of attitudes of rejection and exclusion, consenting to acts of discrimination on the basis of racial and ethnic differences." Although not acknowledging sexual abuse committed by the Church's clergy, the Pope lamented "acts of injustice by trusting in wealth and power and showing contempt for the 'little ones'" (Pope John Paul II, 2000).

CALL TO ACTION

58. We call upon the Pope to issue an apology to Survivors, their families, and communities for the Roman Catholic Church's role in the spiritual, cultural, emotional, physical, and sexual abuse of First Nations, Inuit, and Métis children in Catholic-run residential schools. We call for that apology to be similar to the 2010 apology issued to Irish victims of abuse and to occur within one year of the issuing of this Report and to be delivered by the Pope in Canada.

In the years leading to the apology from the United Church of Canada in 1998, movement on the national political front included lobbying by national Indigenous lobby groups for the recognition of what had occurred in the schools. In 1998, the United Church's moderator, Bill Phipps, apologized to former students of United Church residential schools, their families, and communities:

> As Moderator of The United Church of Canada, I wish to speak the words that many people have wanted to hear for a very long time. On behalf of The United Church of Canada, I apologize for the pain and suffering that our church's involvement in the Indian Residential School system has caused. We are aware of some of the damage that this cruel and ill-conceived system of assimilation has perpetrated on Canada's First Nations peoples. For this we are truly and most humbly sorry. (Phipps, 1998)

Recognition by the Government of Canada

In 1998, the Canadian government issued a "statement of reconciliation," which included a carefully worded apology directed at those who had suffered physical and sexual abuse at the residential schools. The statement was delivered by Indian and Northern Affairs Minister Jane Stewart, working in cooperation with Assembly of First Nations (AFN) Grand Chief Phil Fontaine. Ms. Stewart signalled that the white population recognized the wrong that was committed in Canada, and expressed the profound regret of the government for its role:

> The government of Canada acknowledges the role it played in the development and administration of these schools. Particularly to those individuals who experienced the

CLOSE-UP   Robert Houle

Robert Houle, artist, art curator, intellectual, and arts educator, was born in 1947 and belongs to the Saulteaux First Nations in Manitoba. Houle earned a BA in art history from the University of Manitoba in 1972 and a degree in art education from McGill University in Montreal in 1975, and attended the Salzburg International Summer Academy. His work has been exhibited at the National Gallery of Canada in Ottawa, the Art Gallery of Ontario in Toronto, the Museum of Contemporary Art in Australia, the Canadian Cultural Centre in Paris, and the Stedelijk Museum in Amsterdam. He was featured in the 2011 film *Robert's Paintings*.

Houle attended the Sandy Bay Indian Residential School in Manitoba. The Sandy Bay Council had provided the Roman Catholic Church with 100 acres to build the school in 1905. In 1991, Reverend Doug Crosby of the Oblate Commission of Canada apologized for the way "children were usurped from their natural communities" and admitted that the school left a legacy of emotional and psychological chaos that has invaded entire communities. The school closed in 1970.

Source: Speaking My Truth (2012).

Robert Houle stands with his installation piece *Paris/ Ojibwa*, which reimagines a performance by a troupe of Ojibwe dancers in Paris, France in 1845.

CLOSE-UP   Phil Fontaine

Born in 1944, Phil Fontaine was a victim of abuse in the residential school he was forced to attend. A member of the Sagkeeng First Nation of Manitoba and the longest-serving grand chief of the AFN, Fontaine worked closely with the Indian and Northern Affairs Canada officials for the first resolution and settlement agreement for Indian and Inuit residential schools.

Phil Fontaine speaks in the House of Commons on the event of Prime Minister Stephen Harper's 2008 apology for the residential school system.

tragedy of physical and sexual abuse at residential schools, and who have carried this burden believing that in some way they must be responsible, we wish to emphasize that what you experienced was not your fault and should never have happened. ... For those of you who suffered this tragedy, we are deeply sorry. (Stewart & Goodale, 1998)

The statement was accompanied by an announcement that a new initiative would support community-based healing for people affected by residential schools, including those suffering the intergenerational impacts. The Aboriginal Healing Foundation, mentioned above, was established and the Aboriginal Healing Fund was granted $350 million to this end.

Indigenous people were divided in their sentiment regarding both the apology and the Aboriginal Healing Fund initiative. Many felt that the apology was a step forward; others felt that the healing fund was incapable of even scratching the surface of the social problems inflicted on Indigenous peoples by the schools. Others believed that neither the healing fund nor the apology was sufficient.

Despite the mixed response from the Indigenous community, this was a historic occasion in Canada; it was the government's first public acknowledgment that its former policies had harmed Indigenous people.

The 1998 apology was a prelude to Canada's official apology ten years later. In 2008, Prime Minister Stephen Harper delivered a full apology in Parliament for Canada's role in the residential school system. He called on the government to partner with Indigenous people in the healing of the latter's communities. Many survivors made their way to Parliament Hill to hear the apology in person, and they reflected that this was the most significant movement toward healing to date.

In contrast to the church apologies described above, the government's apology contained a plea for forgiveness from victims. The governing Conservative party's apology was followed by statements from the Liberals, the Bloc Québécois, and the New Democratic Party. Prime Minister Harper thanked NDP leader Jack Layton for continuously leading the call for the apology. Harper's statement addressed 150,000 residential school **direct victims** (Harper, 2008, 6849-6851). **Collateral victims** also received recognition. The extension of the suffering from direct victims to collateral victims marks a significant turning point in the residential school narrative.

direct victim
a targeted victim of an act

Prime Minister Harper asked forgiveness of Indigenous peoples on behalf of all Canadians. He said Canadians "recognize" the effect of attempts at assimilation and the residential schools on Indigenous peoples:

collateral victim
an unintentional but expected victim of an act

Today, we recognize that this policy of assimilation was wrong, has caused great harm, and has no place in our country. One hundred and thirty-two federally supported schools were located in every province and territory, except Newfoundland, New Brunswick, and Prince Edward Island. ... The Government of Canada built an educational system in which very young children were often *forcibly removed* from their homes and often taken far from their communities. … All were deprived of the care and nurturing of their parents, grandparents, and communities. (Harper, 2008, 6850; emphasis added)

Harper admitted the government failed to protect children from this abuse. Indigenous parents were powerless, in turn, "to protect your own children from suffering the same experience."

Harper pledged Canada's help on the new road to healing and reconciliation. The apology created a new vision for Canada–Indigenous relations:

- Canada recognized that direct and collateral victims of residential schools faced physical, social, and mental harm through the transmission of intergenerational trauma. Canada recognized "their resilience as individuals" and pledged to work with Indigenous people to repair the harm.
- The admission that it was wrong to *forcibly remove children* from their homes has international law implications. The 1948 UN Convention on Genocide prohibits the forcible transfer of Indigenous children.
- Canada admitted its "final solution" Indigenous assimilation policy. "Our object is to continue," wrote Duncan Campbell Scott, chief architect of the policy, in the early 1900s, "until there is not a single Indian that has not been absorbed into the body politic of Canada and there is no more Indian question. That is the whole purpose of our legislation" (Dickason, 1992, p. 327). Harper said early in Canada's apology that "this policy of assimilation was wrong, has caused great harm, and has no place in our country."

The apology created a path where Canada would work with Indigenous people to heal the pain caused by Canada's Indian and Inuit residential school system.

EXERCISE 3

Read or listen to a survivor story from the website Where Are the Children? (http://wherearethe children.ca/en/stories/). Assess the apologies in this section and identify what each apology means to your selected survivor. Is an apology and the CEP enough? Why or why not?

CHAPTER SUMMARY

All aspects of the assimilation process have been devastating to Indigenous communities: the seizure of resources and territory, which forced economic dependence; the influence of missionaries in undermining traditional Indigenous values and forcing an agricultural way of life; the suppression of culture through provisions of the *Indian Act*. But nothing has been so devastating to Indigenous people as the residential school system, which targeted their youngest, most vulnerable members. Among its destructive consequences are broken families, violence, substance dependency, and ill health.

The Aboriginal Healing Foundation and the Truth and Reconciliation Commission have concluded their mandates and have submitted recommendations to chart the path forward to reconcile all Canadians with this dark history and move toward a brighter future. And there is finally a real hope that Indigenous and non-Indigenous Canadians may reconcile their shared history and move forward into a brighter future. This can only happen if this history, rather than being suppressed or ignored, becomes part of the national consciousness.

REFERENCES

Aboriginal Healing Foundation (AHF). (2010). *The Indian Residential Schools Settlement Agreement's common experience payment and healing: A qualitative study exploring impacts on recipients*. Aboriginal Healing Foundation research series. Ottawa: Author. http://www.ahf.ca/downloads/cep-2010-healing.pdf.

Barton, S., et al. (2005, August). Health and quality of life of Aboriginal residential school survivors, Bella Coola Valley, 2001. *Social Indicators Research, 73*(2), 295–312.

Brown v. Attorney General of Canada. (2014). 2014 ONSC 6967.

Canadian Encyclopedia. (2007). Rita Joe. http://www.thecanadianencyclopedia.com/articles/rita-joe.

Cardinal, H. (1969). *The unjust society: The tragedy of Canada's Indians*. Edmonton: Hurtig.

Dickason, O.P. (1992). *Canada's First Nations: A history of founding peoples from earliest times*. Toronto: McClelland & Stewart.

Fournier, S., & Crey, E. (1997). *Stolen from our embrace: The abduction of First Nations children and the restoration of Aboriginal communities*. Vancouver: Douglas & McIntyre.

Frank, S. (2003, July). *Time Canada, 162*(4), 30.

Goodwill, J., & Sluman, N. (1982). *John Tootoosis: A biography of a Cree leader*. Winnipeg: Pemmican.

Grant, A. (1996). *No end of grief: Indian residential schools in Canada*. Winnipeg: Pemmican.

Hall, D.J. (1983). Clifford Sifton and the Canadian Indian Administration 1896–1905. In I.A.L. Getty & A.S. Lussier (Eds.), *As long as the sun shines and the water flows: A reader in Canadian native studies*. Vancouver: University of British Columbia Press.

Harper, Rt. Hon. S. (2008, June 11). Apology to former students of Indian residential schools. Canada, Parliament, House of Commons. *Hansard, 142*(10). 39th Parliament, 2nd session.

Huck, N. (2015, February 9). Merchant law firm launches class-action lawsuit for "60s scoop" adoptees. *CBC News*. http://www.cbc.ca.

Indian Act. (1985). RSC 1985, c. I-5.

Indian and Northern Affairs Canada (INAC). (1990, November 15). Letter to Tom Siddon. File E6575-18-2, vol. 4.

Indian and Northern Affairs Canada (INAC). (1999). G.H. Marcoux memorandum to Mr. R.S. Davis, October 21, 1953. File 501/25-1-019, vol. 1. Reprinted in J. Malloy, *A national crime: The Canadian government and the residential school system 1879 to 1986* (pp. 259–260). Winnipeg: University of Manitoba Press.

Indian Tribes of Manitoba. (1971). *Wahbung: Our tomorrows*. Manitoba: Manitoba Indian Brotherhood.

Indigenous and Northern Affairs Canada. (2011). 2011 National Household Survey: Aboriginal language knowledge. https://www.aadnc-aandc.gc.ca/eng/1377004468898/1377004550980.

Indigenous and Northern Affairs Canada. (2016). Statistics on the implementation of the Indian Residential Schools Settlement Agreement. https://www.aadnc-aandc.gc.ca/eng/1315320539682/1315320692192.

Joe, Rita. (1996). *Song of Rita Joe: Autobiography of a Mi'kmaq poet*. Lincoln, NE: University of Nebraska Press.

Joe, Rita. (1998). I lost my talk. In D.D. Moses & T. Goldie (Eds.), *An anthology of Canadian Native literature in English*. Toronto: Oxford University Press.

Johnston, B.H. (1989). *Indian school days*. Norman, OK: University of Oklahoma Press.

King, A.R. (1967). Case study of a Yukon Indian school: How education fails. *The school at Mopass: A problem of identity*. New York: Holt, Rinehart, & Winston.

Malloy, J.S. (1999). *A national crime: The Canadian government and the residential school system 1879–1969*. Winnipeg: University of Manitoba Press.

Moran, B. (2002). *A little rebellion*. Vancouver: Arsenal Pulp Press.

Morris, A. (1971). *The treaties of Canada with the Indians of Manitoba and the North West Territories*. Toronto: Coles.

Nishnawbe Aski Nation. (2011). Windigo and Nan applaud landmark decision for Stirland and Cristal Lake Schools. http://www.nan.on.ca.

Phipps, B. (1998). Apology to former students of United Church Indian residential schools, and to their families and communities. *United Church Social Policy Positions*. United Church of Canada, Toronto, Canada.

Prime Minister of Canada Justin Trudeau. (2015). Statement by prime minister on release of the final report of the Truth and Reconciliation Commission. http://pm.gc.ca/eng/news/2015/12/15/statement-prime-minister-release-final-report-truth-and-reconciliation-commission.

Pope John Paul II. (2000). Confession of sins and asking forgiveness. *L'Osservatore Romano*. Vatican, Rome.

Rennie, S. (2014, January 15). Ottawa agrees to give residential-school survivors Ontario police records. *The Globe and Mail*. http://www.theglobeandmail.com.

Reports of sexual abuse may be low, expert says. (1990, June 1). *The Globe and Mail*, p. A3.

Residential Schools Settlement. (2012). Stirland Lake & Cristal Lake notice. http://www.residentialschoolsettlement.ca/English_Main%20Page.pdf.

Reyhner, J., & Eder, J. (2004). *American Indian education: A history*. Norman, OK: University of Oklahoma Press.

Royal Commission on Aboriginal Peoples (RCAP). (1996). *The report of the Royal Commission on Aboriginal Peoples* (Parliamentary Research Branch of the Library of Parliament No. 99-24E). http://www.parl.gc.ca/Content/LOP/ResearchPublications/prb9924-e.htm.

Sixties Scoop Class Action Lawsuit. (2015). Update—July 2015. http://sixtiesscoopclaim.com/2015/07/08/update-july-2015/.

Speaking My Truth. (2012). Learning from the past: Documents of reconciliation and apology from Canadian government and churches. http://speakingmytruth.ca/?page_id=955.

Statistics Canada. (2010). Family, community, and Aboriginal language among young First Nations children living off-reserve in Canada. http://www.statcan.gc.ca/pub/11-008-x/2010002/article/11336-eng.htm#a14.

Statistics Canada. (2013). *Aboriginal peoples in Canada: First Nations people, Métis and Inuit*. http://www12.statcan.gc.ca/nhs-enm/2011/as-sa/99-011-x/99-011-x2011001-eng.pdf.

Stewart, J., & Goodale, R. (1998). Statement of reconciliation. Government of Canada. Ottawa.

Thomas, W.C. (1991, January 7). Letter, *Western Report*, p. 6.

Tibbetts, J. (2000, August). Lawyers agree to stop swooping in on victims. *Ottawa Citizen*, p. A4.

Truth and Reconciliation Commission of Canada (TRC). (2011). Our mandate. http://www.trc.ca/websites/trcinstitution/index.php?p=7.

Truth and Reconciliation Commission of Canada. (2015a). *Honouring the truth, reconciling for the future: Summary of the final report of the Truth and Reconciliation Commission of Canada*. http://www.trc.ca/websites/trcinstitution/File/2015/Honouring_the_Truth_Reconciling_for_the_Future_July_23_2015.pdf.

Truth and Reconciliation Commission of Canada. (2015b). *The survivors speak: A report of the Truth and Reconciliation Commission of Canada*. http://www.trc.ca/websites/trcinstitution/File/2015/Findings/Survivors_Speak_2015_05_30_web_o.pdf.

United Nations. (1948, December 9). *Convention on the prevention and punishment of the crime of genocide*, adopted by Resolution 260(III) A of the United Nations General Assembly.

REVIEW QUESTIONS

True or False?

____ **1.** Schools for Indigenous children in Canada were originally wanted both by Indigenous people and by the government of Canada.

____ **2.** Indigenous education in Canada today is funded by the provincial and territorial governments.

____ **3.** Access to education for Indigenous people is a treaty responsibility of the federal government.

____ **4.** From 1867 to 1945, Indian children were not permitted to attend any school other than those designated for Indian education.

____ **5.** In 1920 the *Indian Act* was amended to make attendance at residential school mandatory for all Indian children and provided for Indian parents to be charged criminally for withholding their children from the schools.

____ **6.** Training schools called industrial schools were set up to teach Indian children more advanced skills such as carpentry and cabinet-making. These schools were phased out because the children were unable to learn those skills.

____ **7.** Under the leadership of Duncan Campbell Scott, more students voluntarily enrolled at residential schools.

____ **8.** The decision to use clergy as instructors in residential schools stemmed from the genuine belief that they were the most skilled teachers and could provide the highest-quality education available.

_____ 9. Dr. Peter Bryce was commissioned in 1903 to inspect residential schools and report on health conditions. He found that the death rate of the student population exceeded 50 percent in some schools.

_____ 10. Under article 4 of the United Nations *Convention on the Prevention and Punishment of the Crime of Genocide*, constitutionally responsible rulers or public officials cannot be charged under any of the acts of genocide mentioned in article 3 of the Convention.

Multiple Choice

1. Those who write about abuse within Indian residential schools generally divide the abuse into four categories. Which of the following is not one of those categories?
   a. physical
   b. sexual
   c. mental
   d. financial

2. In the struggle to redress the abuses suffered at the residential schools, the federal government has agreed to discuss compensation for which of the following forms of abuse?
   a. spiritual
   b. sexual/physical
   c. cultural
   d. emotional

3. The most popular method of seeking redress for individual victims of abuse prior to the IRSSA was
   a. police investigation
   b. criminal prosecution
   c. protesting
   d. civil litigation

4. The Truth and Reconciliation Commission's Missing Children Project believes that it is unlikely that all of the children will ever be accounted for. The primary reason is:
   a. The bodies were purposely hidden.
   b. The federal government refuses to disclose records.
   c. Too many children escaped.
   d. The record-keeping protocol at the schools was incomplete and allowed for destruction of records.

5. Which of the following was not involved in the set-up and administration of Indian schools?
   a. the provincial governments
   b. the federal government
   c. the Catholic Church
   d. the United Church

6. The ultimate purpose of residential schools was to
   a. provide quality education to Indigenous children
   b. forcibly assimilate Indigenous populations
   c. develop employment skills in Indigenous communities
   d. fulfill treaty obligations

7. There was a significant delay between the time that the need for child welfare services on reserves was recognized and the time that services became available. This delay was due to
   a. Indigenous people's refusal to allow service staff to help their children
   b. the remote location of the reserves
   c. the inability of the federal and provincial governments to agree on a cost-sharing process to provide services
   d. problems identifying children at risk on reserves

8. Which of these statements is most accurate regarding Indigenous languages in Canada?
   a. Most Indigenous people today speak their original Indigenous language.
   b. Many Indigenous people today speak their original Indigenous language.
   c. Few Indigenous people today speak their original Indigenous language.
   d. No Indigenous people today speak their original Indigenous language.

9. The alternative dispute resolution process set up to deal with compensation finally produced a resolution in 2006 called the Indian Residential Schools Settlement Agreement. If you were a survivor who experienced serious psychological trauma as a result of physical abuse, what avenues would be available to you?
   a. the individual assessment process
   b. the common experience payment alone
   c. the IRSSA legal prosecution department
   d. the common experience payment dispute resolution mediator

10. Article 2 of the 1948 United Nations Convention on Genocide identifies acts that, if committed with intent to destroy a national, ethnic, racial, or religious group, constitute genocide. Which of the following acts is not contained within the definition of genocide?
    a. causing serious bodily or mental harm to members of a group
    b. deliberately inflicting on a group conditions of life calculated to bring about its destruction in whole or in part
    c. failing to provide education in the language of choice
    d. forcibly transferring children of a group to another group

Discussion Questions

1. Do you think the Truth and Reconciliation Commission has met its mandate of informing all Canadians about this experience? Why or why not? Explain your answer.

2. Do you think that the settlement of the residential schools lawsuits would have been achieved better through private and class action lawsuits than through the ADR process? Explain.

3. If you were Dr. Bryce or Dr. Simes inspecting residential schools between 1903 and 1943, what actions would you take to advocate for the children?

4. Of the various kinds of damage that resulted from the residential school experience, which do you think was most harmful to Indigenous people? Explain.

APPENDIX 9.1
Apology to Former Students of Indian Residential Schools

Prime Minister Stephen Harper, June 11, 2008

I stand before you today to offer an apology to former students of Indian residential schools.

The treatment of children in Indian Residential Schools is a sad chapter in our history.

For more than a century, Indian Residential Schools separated over 150,000 Aboriginal children from their families and communities. In the 1870's, the federal government, partly in order to meet its obligation to educate Aboriginal children, began to play a role in the development and administration of these schools. Two primary objectives of the Residential Schools system were to remove and isolate children from the influence of their homes, families, traditions and cultures, and to assimilate them into the dominant culture. These objectives were based on the assumption Aboriginal cultures and spiritual beliefs were inferior and unequal. Indeed, some sought, as it was infamously said, "to kill the Indian in the child." Today, we recognize that this policy of assimilation was wrong, has caused great harm, and has no place in our country.

One hundred and thirty-two federally-supported schools were located in every province and territory, except Newfoundland, New Brunswick and Prince Edward Island. Most schools were operated as "joint ventures" with Anglican, Catholic, Presbyterian or United Churches. The Government of Canada built an educational system in which very young children were often forcibly removed from their homes, often taken far from their communities. Many were inadequately fed, clothed and housed. All were deprived of the care and nurturing of their parents, grandparents and communities. First Nations, Inuit and Métis languages and cultural practices were prohibited in these schools. Tragically, some of these children died while attending residential schools and others never returned home.

The government now recognizes that the consequences of the Indian Residential Schools policy were profoundly negative and that this policy has had a lasting and damaging impact on Aboriginal culture, heritage and language. While some former students have spoken positively about their experiences at residential schools, these stories are far overshadowed by tragic accounts of the emotional, physical and sexual abuse and neglect of helpless children, and their separation from powerless families and communities.

The legacy of Indian Residential Schools has contributed to social problems that continue to exist in many communities today.

It has taken extraordinary courage for the thousands of survivors that have come forward to speak publicly about the abuse they suffered. It is a testament to their resilience as individuals and to the strength of their cultures. Regrettably, many former students are not with us today and died never having received a full apology from the Government of Canada.

The government recognizes that the absence of an apology has been an impediment to healing and reconciliation. Therefore, on behalf of the Government of Canada and all Canadians, I stand before you, in this Chamber so central to our life as a country, to apologize to Aboriginal peoples for Canada's role in the Indian Residential Schools system.

To the approximately 80,000 living former students, and all family members and communities, the Government of Canada now recognizes that it was wrong to forcibly remove children from their homes and we apologize for having done this. We now recognize that it was wrong to separate children from rich and vibrant cultures and traditions, that it created a void in many lives and communities, and we apologize for having done this. We now recognize that, in separating children from their families, we undermined the ability of many to adequately parent their own children and sowed the seeds for generations to follow, and we apologize for having done this. We now recognize that, far too often, these institutions gave rise to abuse or neglect and were inadequately controlled, and we apologize for failing to protect you. Not only did you suffer these abuses as children, but as you became parents, you were powerless to protect your own children from suffering the same experience, and for this we are sorry.

The burden of this experience has been on your shoulders for far too long. The burden is properly ours as a Government, and as a country. There is no place in Canada for the attitudes that inspired the Indian Residential Schools system to ever prevail again. You have been working on recovering from this experience for a long time and in a very real sense, we are now joining you on this journey. The Government of Canada sincerely apologizes and asks the forgiveness of the Aboriginal peoples of this country for failing them so profoundly.

Nous le regrettons

We are sorry

Nimitataynan

Niminchinowesamin

Mamiattugut

In moving towards healing, reconciliation and resolution of the sad legacy of Indian Residential Schools, implementation of the Indian Residential Schools Settlement Agreement began on September 19, 2007. Years of work by survivors, communities, and Aboriginal organizations culminated in an agreement that gives us a new beginning and an opportunity to move forward together in partnership.

A cornerstone of the Settlement Agreement is the Indian Residential Schools Truth and Reconciliation Commission. This Commission presents a unique opportunity to educate all Canadians on the Indian Residential Schools system. It will be a positive step in forging a new relationship between Aboriginal peoples and other Canadians, a relationship based on the knowledge of our shared history, a respect for each other and a desire to move forward together with a renewed understanding that strong families, strong communities and vibrant cultures and traditions will contribute to a stronger Canada for all of us.

Questions

1. What can you, personally, do today that will contribute to the reconciliation of Canada and Indigenous people?

2. What actions could be taken in conjunction with this apology that would improve the relationship between residential school survivors and other Canadians?

3. How much of the information in this chapter is new to you, a post-secondary student in Canada? Assuming that you were relying only on your previous level of knowledge of these matters, reflect on how effective you would be in helping to renew and redefine the relationship between Indigenous and non-Indigenous people in Canada into the future.

4. Do you think the entire system of attempting to assimilate Indigenous children, from the inception of residential schools to the end of the Sixties Scoop, fits the UN's definition of genocide? Defend your position.

10 Current Socio-Economic Issues

A forester on Texada Island, BC shows wild pine mushrooms to participants in the University of British Columbia's Aboriginal Forestry Initiative. According to the Intertribal Forestry Association of British Columbia, Aboriginal peoples view forestry "as one of the main ways out of economic depression and as a vehicle for job creation, community stability, and environmental and cultural enhancement … . For these reasons, forestry in the broadest sense of economic, social and environmental development is especially important to Aboriginal people."

LEARNING OUTCOMES

After completing this chapter, you should be able to:

- Identify the social and legal categories of Indigenous people in Canada and appreciate the challenges of researching Canada's diverse Indigenous groups and communities.

- Discuss trends in Indigenous educational achievement levels, population, income and labour market participation, health, language, living conditions, and social assistance, and the implications of these trends for Canada's future.

- Outline the contributing factors to the socio-economic trends analyzed in this chapter.

- Understand the connection between colonization and current challenges facing Indigenous people.

- Identify the relationship between Indigenous people and the federal and provincial governments with regard to funding, provision of services, and plans for economic renewal for Indigenous people in Canada.

- Understand the critical situation of many Indigenous languages and the link between language and Indigenous well-being.

Introduction

The socio-economic issues facing Indigenous people today are a legacy of colonization and forced assimilation. We have journeyed here together as mainstream Canada and Indigenous people in a dynamic relationship with power structures shifting over our 500 plus years of connection. As one Indigenous speaker put it, "We were not standing on the shores of Eastern Canada waiting for the white man to arrive in his sailing ship carrying a welfare check" (Geddes, Doxtater, & Krepakevich, 1997). Indigenous populations are growing rapidly, but economic growth in their communities is slow. In this chapter, we look at obstacles to that growth and to the ultimate goal of self-sufficiency for Indigenous people. We examine their overall social and economic capacity, as well as the health and resilience of their communities. Our aim is to understand how they can achieve greater mental and physical health, positive economic growth, and increased community cohesion and strength.

Case Study: Grassy Narrows

Prior to discussing demographics, let us look closely at a northern Ontario reserve—the Asubpeeschoseewagong First Nation, also known as Grassy Narrows—and at how this community came to its current socio-economic condition. There are many Indigenous communities in Canada, each with a distinct individual history shaped by particular events and crises, and all deserve our attention. But space constraints prevent us from discussing more than one of them.

Grassy Narrows is located 80 kilometres north of Kenora, Ontario, near the Manitoba border. The Ojibwe community living on the reserve today consists of 639 people. Almost half of them are children or youth 19 years of age or under.

The reserved area was set aside for the Grassy Narrows people in 1873, with the signing of Treaty No. 3. By this treaty, the people of this area relinquished 14 million hectares to the government while retaining their right to pursue their traditional occupations, such as hunting and fishing, on the surrendered tract of land, except on such areas as may "from time to time" be required for settlement, mining, or forestry. The government was to maintain schools for instruction and pay annuities to the band in the amount of $5 per person per year.

Missionaries began work in the Grassy Narrows area in the 1840s, accessing the area by canoe. On their arrival, most of the Indigenous people were out of their reach, following a traditional hunting and trapping way of life. The people would return from the traplines in May to their summer grounds, where they would plant gardens and live in their spaciously distributed summer cabins. Those who were taken to the residential schools at McIntosh or Kenora were the ones most influenced by the missions.

Land development came with the building of a railway to access forestry products, but few Indigenous people left the community. There was no welfare or social services; the Indian agent came to the reserve once a year to distribute treaty money. Until 1963, the relative isolation allowed the Indigenous people of this area to preserve their culture, way of life, self-sufficiency, and freedom. In the summer of 1963, Indian Affairs began the process of relocating the people of Grassy Narrows to a new community on the Jones logging road, which was linked to both the railway and the city of Kenora. Indian Affairs intended to provide the Indigenous people with the benefits of modern life and to end the isolation that had helped them resist assimilation.

The new community was built 8 kilometres from the old one, on the English-Wabigoon river system. The rivers were to supply their water needs (the government's promise of running water was not initially fulfilled). The housing provided on the new reserve was crowded and of poor quality. The hunting and trapping way of life became difficult to maintain; the government insisted that the children remain on the reserve and attend school, and this made the parents reluctant to leave for the traplines through the fall and winter.

Prior to the move, the government had been systematically dismantling the traditional economic system of the Ojibwe people. Harvesting wild rice for sustenance had been an activity of Ojibwe people from time immemorial. In the 1950s, however, the government began to issue licences for that harvest; the price of wild rice had increased, making it a possible source of income for the Ojibwe. Initially, only the Ojibwe people were issued licences to harvest wild rice, but in the 1970s non-Indigenous wild rice farmers took over many of those licences. Their mechanical methods of harvesting were more efficient than the traditional Ojibwe methods.

Access to the new reserve from Kenora made it easier for government officials to impose fishing regulations on the Grassy Narrows people. Amendments to the *Indian Act* made all laws of the province applicable not just to non-Indigenous people but to Indigenous people, too; this made the Ojibwe subject to fishing regulations even though this restriction was in direct violation of their treaty rights. Commercial fishing licences were issued to some Grassy Narrows people, but sport fishing licences were given priority because they brought more revenue to the area, predominantly in white communities.

With limited access to paid employment and new constraints on their traditional means of sustenance, the community began to sink into despair. During this time of social upheaval and vulnerability, the Jones logging road, intended to bring the benefits of modern life to the people of Grassy Narrows, brought an unregulated flow of alcohol. Alcoholism, violence, and suicide spiralled out of control in the community.

Studies conducted at Grassy Narrows in 1977–1978 concluded that 70 percent of adults in their child-bearing years and 80 percent in their child-rearing years were heavy drinkers. Alcohol has been, and continues to be, a disruptive influence on Indigenous communities such as the one at Grassy Narrows, where the parents' drinking is largely responsible for the children's substance abuse and resulting failure to achieve academically. Gasoline sniffing, in particular, is a major problem among young people who live in these communities.

The federal government brought extensive development to the North, in the form of forestry and mining, and by doing so brought more hardship to the people of Grassy Narrows. In the early 1920s, a pulp and paper mill was opened in Dryden, Ontario, 130 kilometres upstream from the traditional Grassy Narrows area. Between 1962 and 1970, this mill, operated by Dryden Chemicals Limited, with the sanction of the Ontario government dumped over 20,000 pounds of mercury into the river system, poisoning it. The commercial fisheries on the reserve had to be shut down, and the people were advised not to eat fish caught in the rivers. Those who held fishing licences were issued $300 in compensation for the loss of their livelihood. In the 1970s and subsequently, health officials conducted tests on the population and found that their mercury levels were 40 to 150 times higher than the average Canadian's, likely due to their consumption not only of fish but also of animals that had ingested the mercury in some form.

The government's expenditures on Grassy Narrows skyrocketed. Within 15 years of relocating the Grassy Narrows Ojibwe, the Department of Indian Affairs and Northern Development was spending almost $1 million annually on health, food, and housing for a community formerly visited once a year by an Indian agent and requiring little in the way of health care.

There were disputes between the provincial government and the mill as to who was responsible for the environmental disaster; neither wished to accept accountability. Because the mill had followed environmental practices that were acceptable according to provincial law, the band was ultimately unable to hold any agency accountable.

The band continued to appeal to the government for assistance in alleviating its severe social problems. In 1977, the federal government held a Royal Commission on the Northern Environment. The commission cited the following reasons for the severe physical, mental, and spiritual breakdown in the Grassy Narrows community (Shkilnyk, 1985):

1. the intentional undermining of its religion and way of life;
2. the loss of income from trapping due to flooding and hydroelectric development;
3. the Jones logging road disrupting the community's isolation upon relocation;
4. new access to alcohol;
5. the introduction of a foreign value system;
6. the loss of commercial fishing due to mercury poisoning;
7. the availability of welfare but no work; and
8. the inability to hold any agency accountable for the mercury disaster.

It was not until 1985 that the Grassy Narrows community received a negotiated settlement for the poisoning of their environment. By then, the community had already hit rock bottom and was beginning to recover. The situation at Grassy Narrows improved through the 1990s, and today the people are moving forward and taking control over many aspects of their community life.

Currently, the community is addressing logging issues in its traditional territories with some success. In April 2011, Grassy Narrows signed a memorandum of agreement with the province of Ontario over the management of the Whiskey Jack Forest resources. This forest, traditionally used by the Grassy Narrows First Nation, was licensed by the Crown to Abitibi Lumber until 2009, by which point 50 percent of the area had been clearcut. For the ten years prior to 2009, the band had been blockading roadways in an effort to force a negotiation to preserve the forest and gain some control over timber access on their traditional territory. In a 2005 lawsuit against the province of Ontario, the band asserted that the province does not have the right to harvest timber on Treaty No. 3 territories. The Ontario Court of Appeal in 2013 disagreed and ruled that the province has the rights to timber in the area (*Keewatin v. Ontario*, 2013). While the band awaited a Supreme Court ruling in 2014, one of the largest timber companies in Ontario, EACOM Timber Corporation, which owns six sawmills, announced its solidarity with the people of Grassy Narrows, stating it would not purchase timber logged in that area (Aulakh, 2014).

The Supreme Court of Canada affirmed the Ontario Court of Appeal's decision in July 2014. It confirmed that the province of Ontario can open the area for mining, timber, and other resource extraction without the involvement of the federal government. The Supreme Court did assert that the province must consult and, if appropriate, accommodate the First Nations living in the area in a manner consistent with the duty of the Crown toward them. Ontario must therefore justify any resource extraction that limits or eliminates First Nations treaty rights in the area. Grassy Narrows has the distinction of running the longest-lasting blockade in Canada, from 2002 until 2015. Its ongoing legal battles with the province appear to have been a galvanizing force in the community, adding a level of unity and purpose that has sped its recovery (Mandell Pinder LLP, 2014).

The situation at Grassy Narrows has improved since the 1970s; however, in August 2015 the band declared a state of emergency after two years without access to safe drinking water. The installation of the reserve's water and sewer lines began in 1990 but remains incomplete. The chemicals used to remove the mercury from the water have been shown to cause cancer, and therefore the water is still unsafe. In June 2015, news broke that mercury levels were still rising near the community, which galvanized protests outside Queen's Park in Toronto. As a result, the Ontario government committed to testing the groundwater and cleaning up the mercury (Porter, 2015; Vendeville, 2016).

Indigenous peoples, many from Grassy Narrows, protested in front of Queen's Park in Toronto on April 7, 2010, demanding action from the provincial government on mercury cleanup in the English-Wabigoon river system.

Economically, the community is still struggling. The unemployment rate in 2011 in Grassy Narrows was 37 percent, compared with the provincial average of 8 percent. Annual average income in the same year was $21,641, compared with the provincial average of $43,833 (Statistics Canada, 2015c).

Conclusion

This has been a very brief look at the recent history of the Grassy Narrows people. You are encouraged to look into this history more deeply. This community is an extreme case, but its dealings with non-Indigenous Canada are typical in some respects of the Indigenous experience in Canada. Almost every First Nations community in Canada has been relocated at some point from its traditional territory, usually because the government or some private interest, such as a logging company, wanted readier access to the region's resources. Some Indigenous groups have been moved hundreds of kilometres from their traditional land. In almost all cases, relocation has brought severe social problems and economic hardship to the Indigenous group involved. The Canadian government has known about the negative consequences of relocation since it first began to impose it on Indigenous people in the 19th century. Until recently, however, the government continued this destructive practice. Some Indigenous communities are still suffering deeply from economic instability and social problems, but many are in the recovery phase, rebuilding their economic bases, healing from historic trauma, and building resilience in their young people for a brighter future.

EXERCISE 1

As mentioned in Chapter 8, the federal government of Canada, through the treaty process, undertook the fiduciary responsibility for Indigenous people. Do you think the government met that responsibility in the case of Grassy Narrows?

Indigenous Ancestry: Social and Legal Categories

Trying to describe Canada's Indigenous people in statistical terms can be very confusing; there are various categories of people with Indigenous ancestry. Another complicating factor is that statistical data in this area comes from three sources—Statistics Canada, Indigenous and Northern Affairs Canada, and the Aboriginal Peoples Survey. Each of these organizations uses a different classification system. Statistics Canada information is derived from the census survey, for which identification is voluntary. The census uses the umbrella term *Aboriginal identity*, which includes Métis, Inuit, and First Nations (status and non-status) people. Indigenous and Northern Affairs Canada, in its statistical surveys of the Indigenous population, includes only those Indians who are registered under the *Indian Act*. The Aboriginal Peoples Survey is different again, including in its statistical count only Inuit, Métis, and *off-reserve* First Nations populations. Because of these divergent accounting systems, statistics regarding Indigenous populations vary from source to source. This can be confusing to researchers and readers alike.

It is not surprising, then, that the number of registered Indians recorded by the Indigenous and Northern Affairs Indian Register differs from Statistics Canada's census counts of registered Indians; the two sources of data do not count registered Indians in the same way or for the same reason. The Indian Register is an administrative database, while the census is a statistical survey. To complicate matters further, although many registered Indians are members of one of the more than 600 bands in Canada, many others are not. Some band members are registered as Indians, but others are not. Some bands are connected to treaties and therefore sometimes are referred to as Treaty Indians, but some bands have never signed any treaty (as discussed in Chapter 8). See Figure 10.1 for an overview of these categories.

There have always been significant statistical differences between Indigenous people who live on reserve and those who live off reserve; therefore, Statistics Canada and Indigenous and Northern Affairs Canada collect information for both of these categories. However, because the Indigenous population tends to be more mobile than the non-Indigenous population, these numbers change regularly as the people move back and forth between reserved territories and cities.

FIGURE 10.1 Social–Legal Categories of Indigenous Peoples Residing in Canada

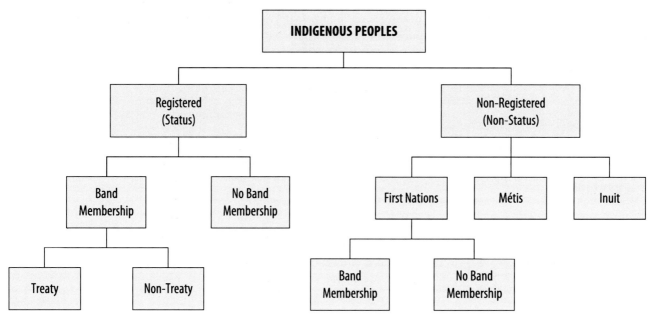

There is such diversity among Indigenous people that it is unwise to envision a homogeneous "Indigenous" population in Canada. A snapshot of census data covering all 600 bands, the Métis, and the Inuit cannot possibly capture the profound differences in all data areas among the various Indigenous groups. For example, there are profound differences between the Kanewake Mohawks of Quebec and the Lubicon Cree of Alberta, who differ from the Innu of Natuashish and the Cree Nation of Saskatchewan.

Size of the Indigenous Population

In the 2011 National Household Survey (NHS), 1,400,685 people identified themselves as having an Aboriginal identity, representing 4.3 percent of the total Canadian population. Of this number 851,560 or 60.8 percent report their identity as First Nations (North American Indian), 451,795 as Métis, and 59,445 as Inuit (see Tables 10.1 and 10.2).

The number of Canadians reporting Indigenous ancestry is growing rapidly; the growth rate between 2006 and 2011 was 20.1 percent, compared with only 5.2 percent for the non-Indigenous population. When the figures are broken down into categories of Indigenous identity types, First Nations' growth was 22.9 percent, Inuit growth was 18.1 percent, and Métis growth was 16.3 percent (see Table 10.1).

TABLE 10.1   Size and Growth Rate of Aboriginal Populations in Canada

Aboriginal identity population	2011 counts	Distribution (%) (2011)	Growth (%) (2001 to 2006)	Growth (%) (2006 to 2011)
Total population of Canada	**33,476,688**	**100.0**	**5.4**	**5.9**
Aboriginal identity population	1,400,685	4.3	20.1	20.1
Non-Aboriginal identity population	32,076,003	95.7	4.9	5.2
Total Aboriginal identity population	**1,400,685**	**100.0**	**20.1**	**20.1**
First Nations	851,560	60.8	14.6	22.9
Métis	451,795	32.3	33.3	16.3
Inuit	59,445	4.2	12.0	18.1

SOURCE: Statistics Canada (2013a).

TABLE 10.2   Size of the Indigenous Population, Canada, 2011

Aboriginal identity	Number	Percent
Total Aboriginal identity population	1,400,685	100.0
First Nations single identity	851,560	60.8
First Nations single identity (Registered or Treaty Indian)	637,660	45.5
First Nations single identity (not a Registered or Treaty Indian)	213,900	15.3
Métis single identity	451,795	32.3
Inuit single identity	59,445	4.2
Multiple Aboriginal identities	11,415	0.8
Aboriginal identities not included elsewhere	26,475	1.9

SOURCE: Statistics Canada (2013a, table 1).

It should be noted that the actual Indigenous population numbers may be higher than those reported in the NHS, because 36 Indian reserves and settlements did not participate in the 2011 census. In addition, some individuals may have chosen not to self-identify to government workers.

Factors Affecting Size

The growth rate of Canada's population is affected by three factors: the birth rate, the death rate, and the immigration rate. The growth rate of Indigenous populations is significantly affected by three factors: the birth rate, the death rate, and the rate at which individuals gain or lose status.

Status Loss and Gain

Canadian laws defining whom the government recognized as Indians pre-date the *Indian Act*. The earliest statutory definition of "Indian" did not discriminate on the basis of sex, but in 1869 provisions were introduced stating that women who "married out"—that is, who married non-Indians—would lose status, and their children would not be granted status. On the other hand, Indian men who married non-Indian women would not lose status. The 1876 *Indian Act* maintained these provisions; moreover, the 1876 Act also provided that an "Indian" included any woman who was married to "any male person of Indian blood reputed to belong to a particular band," whether or not the woman was Indian (Hurley & Simeone, 2010, p. 2).

The new *Indian Act*, enacted in 1951, established a national registry, with entitlement linked to band membership; it also maintained the provisions that discriminated, on the basis of sex, against women who married non-Indian men. Children born to an Indian mother and a non-Indian father were deemed non-Indian. However, the status of children born to an Indian father was determined by the "double-mother rule," which stated that if the child's mother and paternal grandmother had a right to Indian status only through having married an Indian man, the child had Indian status only up to the age of 21.

Prior to 1985, these provisions were strongly criticized by First Nations women's groups, human rights groups, and others, but these criticisms were ignored. However, when section 15 of the *Canadian Charter of Rights and Freedoms* came into force in 1985, the provisions were in clear violation of the new equality rights, which made it illegal to discriminate based on various categories, including sex. At this point, the government could not wait any longer to take action. In 1985, Bill C-31, *An Act to Amend the Indian Act*, was passed. Three principles guided the changes: (1) removing discriminatory clauses; (2) restoring status and membership rights; and (3) increasing control of Indian bands over their own membership (Aboriginal Affairs and Northern Development Canada, 2010).

With regard to entitlement to registration, sections 6(1) and 6(2) provided the following:

- Individuals entitled to registration prior to 1985 (including non-Indian women married to Indian men, and their children) retained full status (s. 6(1)(a)).
- Women who had lost status through marrying out or through an order of enfranchisement and persons who had lost status at 21 through the double-mother rule regained status (s. 6(1)(c)).
- Individuals with one parent entitled to registration under section 6(1) acquired status under section 6(2); persons with one parent registered under section 6(2) and one non-status parent were/are not entitled to registration.

Figure 10.2 shows the percentage change in Canada's registered Indian population from 1981 to 2015 and the effects of the 1985 amendments to the *Indian Act*.

The requirement that children registered under section 6(2) must partner with a registered Indian in order for their own children to be entitled to registration is often referred to as the

FIGURE 10.2   Percentage Change in Registered Indian Population, Canada, 1981 to 2015

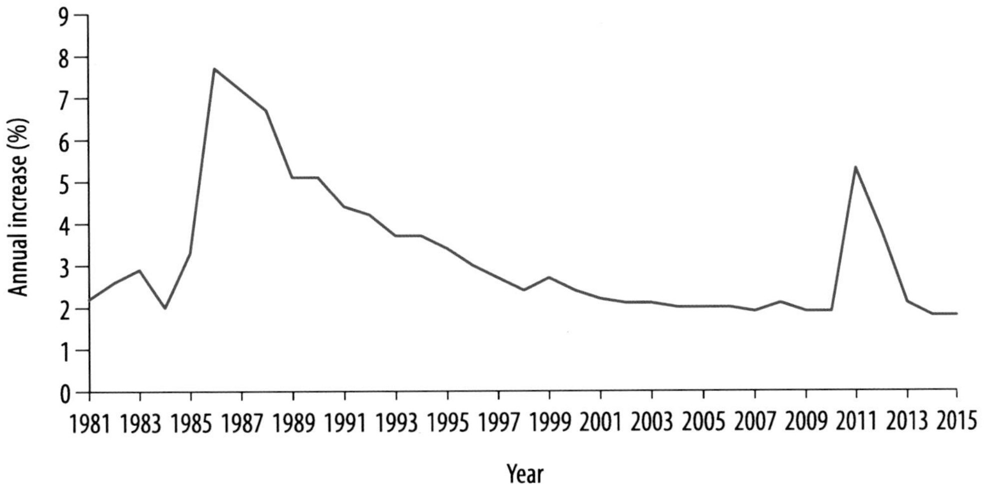

SOURCE: Indigenous and Northern Affairs Canada (2015a).

"second generation cut-off rule." This requirement was a primary target for charges that there was residual sex discrimination in the Act, and there were calls for the removal of this requirement (Hurley & Simeone, 2010, p. 4). In a 2005 statement, the Assembly of First Nations (AFN) commented that "[t]he Bill has not resolved any of the problems it was intended to fix … . Significant gender discrimination still remains, control over Indian status is still held by the Crown, and the population of Indians is declining as a direct result of Bill C-31" (Assembly of First Nations, 2005).

According to Indian and Northern Affairs Canada (2009, p. 3), between 1985, when Bill C-31 came into force, and 2007, over 117,000 persons who had lost status under discriminatory status provisions, as well as their descendants, had regained or acquired status. However, projections made several years ago warned of a "rapid decline" in the number of individuals entitled to registration. This decline would result from the section 6 rules and from marrying out, with one source predicting that sometime around the end of the fifth generation, the number of children born who would be entitled to Indian registration would fall to zero (Hurley & Simeone, 2010, p. 4).

Until recently, it was believed that applications for reinstatement had slowed to a trickle and that population growth in the future would no longer be affected by status reinstatement applications under Bill C-31. If this turns out to be the case, it will be largely owing to the 2009 BC Court of Appeal ruling in *McIvor v. Canada*, which has had a significant effect on the number of individuals who are eligible for registration.

To summarize the *McIvor* case, Sharon McIvor was not registered as an Indian prior to 1985. Had she been registered, she would have lost her registration because she married a non-Indian. McIvor became registered after 1985 under section 6(2), on the basis of having one parent registered under section 6(1) and one non-Indian parent. Her son, Jacob Grismer, has a child with a non-Indian woman. Because McIvor was registered under section 6(2) of the Act, her grandchild (Grismer's child) could not be registered as Indian.

The core of McIvor's argument on behalf of her grandson's registration was that if she had not been removed from status prior to 1985, she would have been registered as a section 6(1) Indian and thereby able to pass status on to her grandchild. If McIvor had been male (the court made use of a "hypothetical brother" of McIvor in considering this), she—or rather, "he"—

would have maintained status and been registered as a section 6(1) Indian once the changes to the Act took place in 1985. Any grandchildren of this hypothetical brother would be entitled to be registered. The BC Court of Appeal held that the "preferential treatment" enjoyed by Indian men who married prior to 1985—and whose grandchildren were afforded "enhanced status" as compared with those of a female who had married prior to 1985—was a violation of section 15 of the Charter. The court gave the government of Canada until April 2010 to amend the unconstitutional provisions in the Act.

In 2010, the government introduced amendments ensuring that eligible grandchildren of women who had lost status as a result of marrying non-Indian men would be entitled to registration under the Act. The current version of the Act, which came into force in January 2011, incorporates these amendments, in section 6(1)(c.1).

On January 8, 2013 the Federal Court of Appeal ruled in the case of *Daniels v. Canada*. The ruling in favour of Harry Daniels, a Métis, confirmed that non-status Indians and Métis are included as "Indians" within section 91(24) of the *Constitution Act*. This means they hold the rights accorded to Indigenous people within the context of the Constitution and extends the federal government's fiduciary duty to non-status Indians and Métis. Prior to this ruling, neither the federal government nor any provincial government claimed jurisdiction over these groups. The government of Canada appealed the Federal Court's decision. The Supreme Court of Canada heard the case and on April 14, 2016 it affirmed the lower court ruling. The decision will open access to services to about 200,000 Métis and 400,000 non-status Indians that were previously available only to status Indians. It will also allow the federal government to amend its policy of interpreting "Indian" under the Constitution, and obligate the federal government to negotiate equal treatment under the Charter in the same manner as for status Indians. It is unclear at this point how and when services will be extended to Métis and non-status Indians, as the process of clarifying these rights unfolds over the next several years.

Prior to the 2009, 2013, and 2016 rulings, the determination of status under the *Indian Act* was both a complex topic and a live issue. Many Canadians may find the matter merely confusing, but for Indigenous people it is critical. Through the federal government and provincial agencies, a wide range of programs and services are available to status Indians that are not available to non-registered individuals; status determines eligibility for living on reserves, eligibility for tax exemption, and access to health care and education.

In addition to these tangible benefits, being officially registered is for many individuals with Indigenous ancestry an important part of identification with their family and with the larger community.

Birth and Death Rates

Like the birth rate for Canada as a whole, the birth rate for Indigenous populations is declining over time. Despite this, the Indigenous birth rate is still higher than that of the non-Indigenous population. As a result, the Indigenous population is younger on average than the non-Indigenous population. In fact, the median age (the point where exactly half the population is older and the other half younger) is 28 years for Indigenous people, compared with 41 years for the non-Indigenous population. The Inuit population is younger still, with a median age of 23 years. The Métis population has a median age of 31 years (Statistics Canada, 2013a, table 4).

Life expectancy for Indigenous people still lags behind that of the general population. This results in fewer seniors in the Indigenous population. Seniors represent only 5.9 percent of Indigenous populations, compared with 14.2 percent of the non-Indigenous population. Issues that affect the mortality rate of Indigenous people are discussed later in this chapter.

Population Distribution

Geographical Distribution

According to the 2011 census (Statistics Canada, 2013a, table 2), 80 percent of Indigenous people live in Ontario, Manitoba, Saskatchewan, Alberta, and British Columbia. The next greatest number live in Quebec. The Western provinces and the territories have the greatest ratio of Indigenous people to the total population. For example, the 27,360 Indigenous people (mostly Inuit) in Nunavut make up 86.3 percent of Nunavut's population. Table 10.3 shows the percentage of the total population that Indigenous people represent, in Canada and in the respective provinces and territories.

TABLE 10.3   Number and Distribution of the Population Reporting an Aboriginal Identity and Percentage of Aboriginal People in the Population, Canada, Provinces and Territories, 2011

Provinces and territories	Aboriginal identity population	Percentage distribution	Aboriginal identity population as a percentage of the total population
Canada	1,400,685	100.0	4.3
Newfoundland and Labrador	35,800	2.6	7.1
Prince Edward Island	2,230	0.2	1.6
Nova Scotia	33,845	2.4	3.7
New Brunswick	22,615	1.6	3.1
Quebec	141,915	10.1	1.8
Ontario	301,425	21.5	2.4
Manitoba	195,900	14.0	16.7
Saskatchewan	157,740	11.3	15.6
Alberta	220,695	15.8	6.2
British Columbia	232,290	16.6	5.4
Yukon	7,705	0.6	23.1
Northwest Territories	21,160	1.5	51.9
Nunavut	27,360	2.0	86.3

SOURCE: Statistics Canada (2013a, table 2).

EXERCISE 2

Consider the name of the branch of the federal government charged with responsibility for Indigenous people during the 1970s: Department of Indian Affairs and Northern Development. Separate that title into two distinct interests: "Indian Affairs" and "Northern Development." Think about what these two had in common and the conflicting interests between the two. Then consider the current name of the branch: Indigenous and Northern Affairs Canada. What do these names tell you about the interests and priorities of the federal government?

Urban/Rural Distribution

Another trend shown by the 2011 census is that the Indigenous population overall is becoming increasingly urban. The 2011 census figures separate the urban population of First Nations people into status and non-status, since non-status First Nations people account for 25.1 percent of the First Nations population (Statistics Canada, 2013a). Forty-nine percent of First Nations with registered Indian status live on reserves, which means that 51 percent live in urban centres, including large cities and smaller towns. Even though a large percentage of First Nations registered Indians live in urban centres, they do not make up a very large percentage of the populations in these places. For example, in Winnipeg, where more First Nations registered Indians (25,970) reside than in any other Canadian city, they account for only 3.6 percent of the population. The cities with the next largest registered Indian population are Edmonton (18,210, or 1.6 percent of the city's population) and Vancouver (15,000, or 0.7 percent).

The census metropolitan areas with the largest populations of First Nations people without registered Indian status are Toronto (14,505, or 0.3 percent of the population), Vancouver (13,635, or 0.6 percent), and Montreal (10,540, or 0.3 percent).

The majority of people who identified themselves as Métis live in either the Western provinces or Ontario. The largest population of Métis is in Alberta, where 21.4 percent of all Métis live. The next largest population is in Ontario with 19 percent, followed by Manitoba with 17.4 percent, British Columbia with 15.4 percent, and Saskatchewan with 11.6 percent. Winnipeg has the highest number of urban-dwelling Métis, with 46,325, followed by Edmonton with 31,780, and Vancouver with 18,485. There are 11,520 Métis in Saskatoon and 9,980 in Toronto.

Inuit Nunangat
the four regions in which Inuit live, including land, water, and ice: Inuvialuit, Nunatsiavut, Nunavik, and Nunavut

According to the 2011 National Household Survey, 73.1 percent of Inuit in Canada live in the four regions of **Inuit Nunangat** (see Figure 10.3). There are 2,325 Inuit, or 3.9 percent of the total Inuit population, living in Nunatsiavut; they represent 89.1 percent of the total population of that region. Nunavik is home to 10,750 Inuit, or 18.1 percent of the Inuit population, and they too account for 89.1 percent of that region's population. The largest number of Inuit, 27,070, live in Nunavut and represent 45.5 percent of the Inuit population. Within Nunavut, the Inuit represent 85.4 percent of the total population. The Inuvialuit region is home to 3,310 Inuit or 5.6 percent of the total Inuit population, who account for 57.6 percent of the total population of this region. Inuit living outside these four regions predominantly dwell in Edmonton, Montreal, Ottawa, Yellowknife, and St. John's.

The trend toward urbanization among status Indians goes back over four decades. In 1966, only 19.5 percent of status Indians lived off reserve. By 1986, that figure had increased to 31.9 percent. By 2001, 42.5 percent of status Indians lived off reserve; by 2011, 51 percent lived off reserve. (Comparable data are not available for non-status Indians and Métis.)

A number of factors influence the decision to migrate to urban centres. Population increases on reserves can lead to overcrowding, lack of housing, and unemployment, which can cause individuals to look elsewhere for opportunity. Individuals may move to an urban centre to enter the labour market and/or to acquire education not readily available on a reserve. Individuals are more likely to migrate to an urban centre if there is one near their reserve.

Challenges for Urban Indigenous People

Among the challenges facing Indigenous migrants to urban centres are the ongoing jurisdictional disputes as to which level of government has legislative authority and responsibility for urban Indigenous people. The federal government acknowledges its responsibility for on-reserve registered First Nations people; however, the responsibility to provide services for other Indigenous people is often subject to disputes between provincial, municipal, and federal governments.

FIGURE 10.3   Inuit Nunangat (Inuit Regions of Canada)

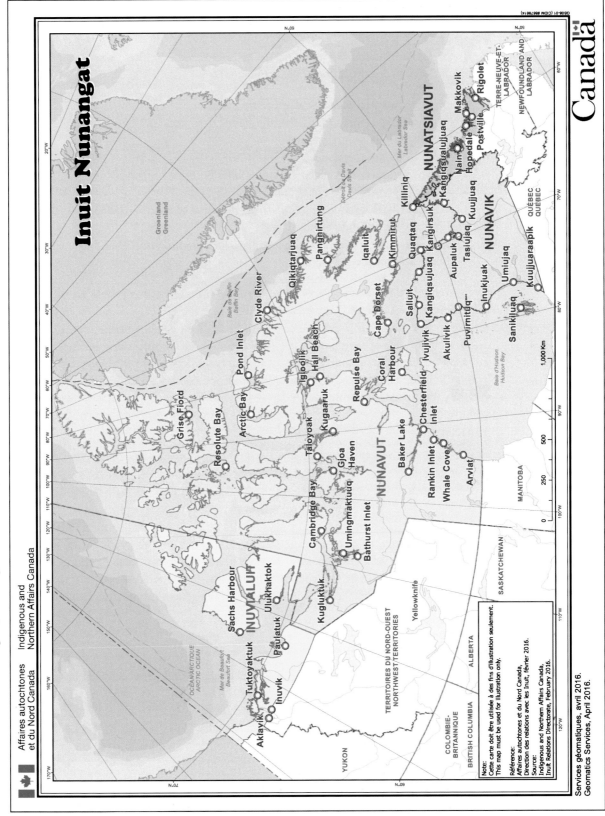

SOURCE: Indigenous and Northern Affairs Canada (2016a).

This situation often leads to a scarcity of services for Indigenous people living in urban areas. As a result of the *Daniels* case, however, improvements should begin to emerge over the next few years.

One analysis (Frideres & Gadacz, 2008, p. 170) has shown that urban Indigenous people, compared with their non-Indigenous counterparts,

- are more likely to have low levels of education;
- have low labour force participation rates;
- have high unemployment rates;
- have low income levels;
- have high rates of homelessness and greater housing needs;
- are overrepresented in the criminal justice system;
- have poor health status (particularly in the areas of mental health, suicide, HIV/AIDS, diabetes, and substance abuse); and
- are more than twice as likely to belong to lone-parent families and to experience domestic violence.

Currently in Canada, programs for urban-dwelling Indigenous people are offered through the National Association of Friendship Centres. There are 118 centres and seven provincial and territorial associations that provide services to urban Indigenous people, regardless of status. The Friendship Centres are funded federally through the Urban Aboriginal Strategy, which in 2014 implemented Community Capacity Support and Urban Partnerships programs. The programs offered at each centre depend on the specific needs of the communities they serve, but typically they focus on supporting education, economic development, cultural awareness, and youth initiatives. The goal is to encourage equal access to services and full participation in Canadian society for urban Indigenous people.

Education

The strong causal connection between education, participation in the labour market, and income has been well established by social science. Education is also connected to physical and mental health and to reduced criminal activity. There is also a generational spillover: the parents' educational level is connected to the educational attainment of their children. This is true for all Canadians, not just Indigenous populations. Indigenous people in Canada have had persistently low academic achievement relative to the general population, which has perpetuated their economic disadvantage.

Delivery and Funding

The history of Indigenous education in Canada is long and overshadowed by the residential school era. Since 2011 the federal government has been diligently working with First Nations people to overhaul the currently inadequate patchwork of First Nations education programming across the country. A panel was assembled in the fall of 2011, which, after extensive consultations with First Nations communities, submitted a report with recommendations for changes to the current system. The panel found that

> [i]n the early 1970s, following the dissolution of the residential school system, and the devolution of First Nation education to individual First Nations, virtually no thought was given to the necessary supporting structure for the delivery of First Nation education. There was no clear funding policy, no service provision and no legislation, standards or regulations to enshrine and protect the rights of a child to a quality education and to set

the education governance and accountability framework. (National Panel on First Nation Elementary and Secondary Education for Students on Reserve, 2013, p. 9)

The panel made five broad recommendations to improve First Nations education:

1. Co-create child-centred First Nations education legislation within 18 months of the panel's report, accompanied by an implementation plan and schedule that is consistent with the treaty and self-governing rights of First Nations people. The legislation was to include all necessary components of a high-quality education system, such as coordination of curriculum, standards, performance measures, and accountability.
2. Create a National Commission for First Nations Education to support education reform and improvement. The commission would take over the responsibility for First Nations education from Aboriginal Affairs and Northern Development Canada.
3. Facilitate and support the creation of a First Nation education system through the development of regional First Nation education organizations (FNEOs) to provide support services for First Nation schools and students. These FNEOs were seen as particularly necessary for northern or remote schools and those with needs unique to their area. Grouping schools under regional management would better provide for efficiencies and support.
4. Ensure adequate funding to support a First Nations education system that meets the needs of First Nations learners and communities, and of Canada as a whole. The panel found evidence of significant gaps in teacher compensation, a lack of equipment and supplies, inadequate supports for students with special needs, and school facilities in disrepair. Three recommendations address underfunding and were to be acted upon immediately:
   a. Increase education funding for 2012–13 to equal the funding increases in the provincial education system according to the location of each First Nations school.
   b. Increase teacher and administrator salaries to equal those in the provincial education system.
   c. Launch or expand early literacy programs with the goal of having all First Nations students reading by grade 3.
5. Establish an accountability and reporting framework to assess improvement in First Nations education by evaluating both the system and the students' progress. The panel found significant gaps in data tracking the progress of learners compared with that of provincial schools. These data are crucial to evaluating the progress and quality of education delivery. (National Panel on First Nation Elementary and Secondary Education for Students on Reserve, 2013, pp. 31–42)

By March 2012 the government of Canada had made a commitment to introduce a First Nations education act as part of its 2012 Economic Action Plan, and an intensive consultation process began in earnest in December 2012. In July 2013, the AFN passed a resolution to assert First Nations control over First Nations education. In October 2013 the government presented its proposal for a bill. The government and the AFN collaborated to produce Bill C-33, the *First Nations Control of First Nations Education Act*, which was introduced in April 2014. There was extensive debate in relation to Bill C-33 at both first and second reading; it was put on hold in May 2014. As we wait for a new national strategy to be agreed upon and implemented, we can review the current framework.

There are a number of paths to education for First Nations people in Canada. There are First Nations–managed (that is, band-operated) schools, funded by the federal government, which are predominantly on First Nations reserves across Canada and serve mostly First Nations students living on reserves. There are approximately 518 such schools, and approximately

61 percent of children who live on reserve attend band-operated schools. The band's degree of control over the education budget, curriculum, and staffing differs according to reserve and often depends on the numbers of students and staff involved. As well, the amount of funding per student allotted by the federal government is inconsistent region by region because it depends on the agreement between each First Nations group and the government, since a Canada-wide education strategy and legislation still do not exist. The goal for First Nations is and has always been to have the band exercise complete control over the education process, a goal that many bands have achieved (Laboucane, 2010, p. 18).

In 1988, the federal government created a Band Operated Funding Formula that sets out budgets for the operation of the schools. The formula, which was based on the number of students in the school multiplied by the cost of educational delivery, mirrored a similar funding formula in the provincial school systems throughout Canada. But there was tremendous growth in First Nations communities, and the federal government had not kept pace in funding either children who attended on-reserve schools or those who attended provincially run schools off reserve. In some cases provincial schools were paid more than double what on-reserve schools were paid for student tuition. In 2006–7, the support provided for First Nations students by the Elementary/Secondary Education Program was on average *$2,000 less per student* than the amount provided for provincial students (Laboucane, 2010, p. 18). Some estimates of the funding gap indicate the amount may in fact have been much greater (VanEvery-Albert, 2004, pp. 18–19). Teachers in band-operated schools were paid less than teachers in provincial schools. A Chiefs of Ontario report showed that the Ontario teacher's annual salary classed at year 5, level 5 on the grid was $54,079. First Nations teachers at the same level in band-operated schools had an average income of $46,179 (VanEvery-Albert, 2004, p. 7). This difference may have accounted for some of the funding shortfall, since salaries are a large part of education budgets. Robert Laboucane (2010, p. 21) paints a grim picture of reserve schools:

> There is no funding for on reserve school libraries or books. Schools are unable to provide competitive salaries for teachers on reserves. There is no funding for vocational training in secondary schools on reserves. There is no funding for extracurricular sports and recreation activities on reserves.

The failure of the federal government to adequately fund on-reserve K–12 schools, including a 2 percent cap on annual increases between 1990 and 2006, along with the increasing number of students attending First Nations on-reserve schools, has resulted in recent large increases in funding in order to catch up with provincial funding (see Figure 10.4).

These increases, however, have not managed to close the gap between First Nations schools and provincial schools, as is illustrated in Figure 10.5.

Of the 113,400 on-reserve students enrolled in K–12, 61 percent were in First Nations–managed schools, while 36 percent were in provincial schools and the remaining 3 percent in private schools (Bains, 2014). (These statistics exclude Nunavut, Northwest Territories, Atlantic Canada, and Quebec.) While many federally funded students attended band-operated schools from kindergarten through to grade 5, the number drops sharply by grade 12. This decrease is largely due to the fact that secondary schools are often unavailable in First Nations communities, so students transfer to the provincial system for secondary school, and the federal government transfers funds to the province to pay for the First Nations child's education.

In the past decades of neglect, many on-reserve school facilities had fallen into disrepair, many unsuitable for education. As part of Canada's Economic Action Plan in 2010, $200 million was committed over two years, with an additional $102 million over three years through the Building Canada Plan, toward renovating existing schools and to support new cost-efficient school projects. Funds have been allocated for construction of new schools and upgrades to current facilities. By March 2013, 110 school projects were in various states of completion (Indigenous and Northern Affairs Canada, 2016b).

FIGURE 10.4   AANDC Elementary/Secondary Education Expenditures, 2008–9 to 2013–14

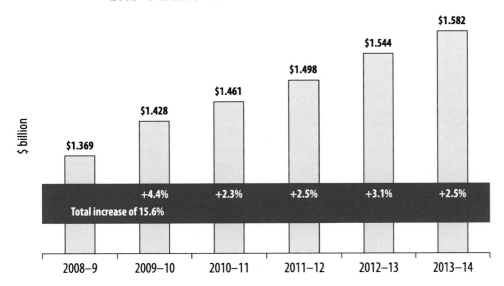

NOTE: INAC's investments in First Nations K–12 education on reserve, by fiscal year, from 2008–9 to 2013–14. It also outlines the year-over-year percentage increases to this funding over the same period.

SOURCE: Indigenous and Northern Affairs Canada (2016b).

FIGURE 10.5   Federal Funding for First Nations Schools

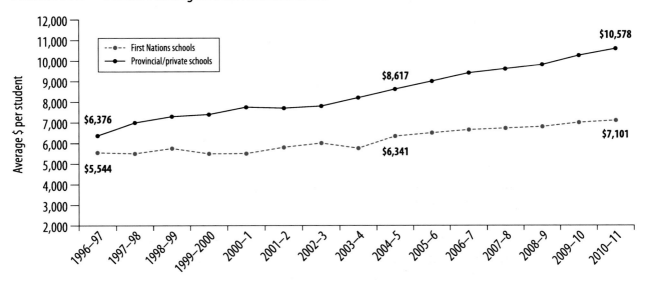

NOTE: Per-student funding is calculated using the following formula: Core funding allocated by the federal government for First Nations education (First Nations school or provincial/private school)/Nominal roll (First Nations school or provincial/private school).

SOURCE: Indian and Northern Affairs Canada, financial information (1996–2011); Indian and Northern Affairs Canada, nominal roll statistics (1996–2011).

Achievement Rates: A Comparison

Educational achievement rates for any population are strongly connected to the quality of education as well as to future labour participation and income rates. To examine the educational achievement rates of Indigenous people in Canada, we use the government data collected in both the 2011 National Household Survey (NHS) and the 2012 Aboriginal Peoples Survey (APS); however, the APS collects data from off-reserve Indigenous people only, so the statistics can be read differently. Off-reserve students attend provincial schools and thus are not surveyed within the First Nations school system. There are clear but less dramatic differences in educational achievement rates between First Nations students who are educated off reserve in provincial schools and non–First Nations children who attend the same schools. The differences in achievement rates are more dramatic when we compare First Nations students educated on reserve with non–First Nations students educated in provincial schools. Finally, there are differences among the achievement rates of First Nations, Métis, and Inuit students, both overall and when differences in location are factored in.

In 2012, 72 percent of First Nations people, 42 percent of Inuit, and 77 percent of Métis living off reserve aged 18 to 44 had a high school diploma. The figure for the non-Indigenous population in 2011 was 89 percent. Also in 2012, 43 percent of off-reserve First Nations people, 26 percent of Inuit, and 47 percent of Métis aged 18 to 44 had a post-secondary diploma or degree. The figure for the non-Indigenous population was 64 percent. Educational experiences correlate with employment experiences. According to the APS, in 2012, 72 percent of First Nations people who had completed high school were employed versus only 47 percent of those who had not. Of Inuit who had completed high school, 71 percent were employed versus 44 percent of those without a high school diploma; 80 percent of Métis who had finished high

FIGURE 10.6 Proportion of Aboriginal and Non-Aboriginal Identity Men and Women Aged 25 to 64 by Selected Levels of Educational Attainment, 2011

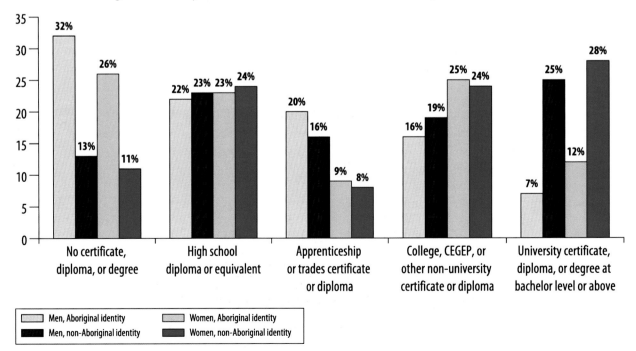

SOURCE: Employment and Social Development Canada (2013).

school were employed, versus 61 percent who had not. In addition, employed high school graduates were earning on average about $10,000 per year more than those who had not completed high school (Statistics Canada, 2013b).

The NHS collected statistics differently. The 2011 survey showed improved levels of educational achievement, with 68 percent of Indigenous people aged 35 to 44 having completed high school. In the same age category, 27 percent of Indigenous women and 18 percent of Indigenous men had a college diploma. Non-status Indigenous people generally have higher educational achievement rates than do status Indians (Bougie, Kelly-Scott, & Arriagada, 2015, Pt. A, s. 4).

FIGURE 10.7   Proportion of First Nations People Aged 25 to 64 Living On and Off Reserve by Selected Levels of Educational Attainment, 2011

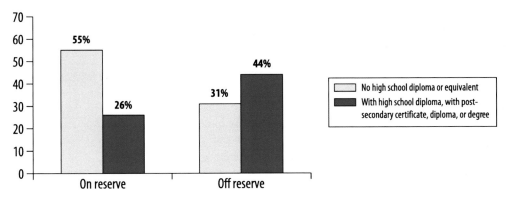

SOURCE: Employment and Social Development Canada (2013).

FIGURE 10.8   Proportion of Aboriginal People by Selected Levels of Educational Attainment and Age, 2011

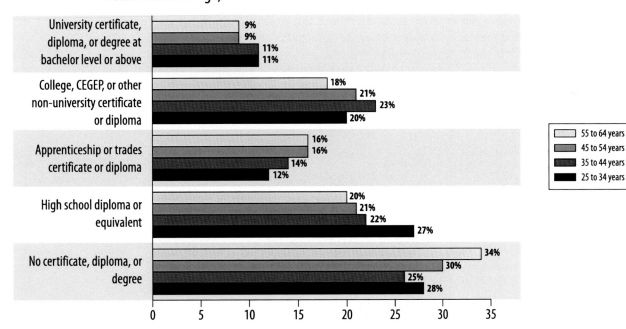

SOURCE: Employment and Social Development Canada (2013).

Factors Correlated with Success and Failure

A number of studies have been done to determine why Indigenous students perform as they do in the school system. These studies, along with more general research into the sources of academic achievement, confirm the role played by socio-economic status, parental education level, household living arrangements, and household income in determining student success.

The 2012 APS (Statistics Canada, 2012) identified a number of factors that are positively correlated with perceived academic achievement. (Recall that this survey considers only off-reserve status and non-status Indigenous people, Métis, and Inuit—in other words, those most likely to use provincial schools rather than band-operated schools.) These factors include:

- getting along with peers and having close friends with high educational aspirations;
- having parents with at least a high school education;
- having parents who spoke to and visited teachers and attended school events and activities;
- receiving support from school staff; and
- being involved in extracurricular activities.

The same survey identified a number of factors that correlated negatively with perceived academic achievement. These include:

- having close friends who missed school, smoked, or used drugs or alcohol;
- changing schools frequently;
- having parents who did not complete high school; and
- living away from home.

In Canada, British Columbia is the only province to publish standardized test results by various characteristics of schools and students, including Indigenous identity. In British Columbia, there are 60,000 self-identified Indigenous students in the provincial school system; they make up approximately 10 percent of the school population (Richards, Vining, & Weimer, 2010, p. 48). A study was conducted to examine Indigenous performance in the grades 4 and 7 standardized tests that assess the foundational skills of reading, writing, and numeracy. The study, focused on the period spanning the 2001–2 and 2005–6 school years, showed that a sizable gap exists by grade 4 between Indigenous and non-Indigenous student performance, and that this gap widens by grade 7 (Richards et al., 2010, p. 54).

In the BC study, the school catchment areas from which the results were drawn were measured in terms of socio-economic status. The improvement in test scores remained fairly constant for both Indigenous and non-Indigenous students when the catchment areas were in the highest income areas. Furthermore, the number of Indigenous students in each school was measured in relation to achievement levels, and it was found that a higher Indigenous student count in a school produced *lower* overall academic achievement for Indigenous students.

The BC study also looked for common denominators in the more successful districts, and it was found (Richards et al., 2010, p. 63) that these districts

- had school administrators and teachers who more consistently emphasized Indigenous educational success as a long-term priority;
- engaged Indigenous leaders from the broader community with greater success;
- made more consistent use of objective data on Indigenous student performance; and
- had a reputation for following through on policy implementation.

Clearly, this study has some implications for BC school system policy changes.

Generally speaking, the statistics indicate that the educational system is failing Indigenous students and failing Canada in the process. According to the Canadian Centre for the Study of Living Standards, Canada's economy would increase by $71.1 billion if Indigenous people achieved the same educational levels as other Canadians (Laboucane, 2010, p. 18). Among the various factors contributing to the underachievement of Indigenous students, an impoverished sense of identity is surely one. Certain factors contribute to such impoverishment: curricula that exclude Indigenous children's history, cultures, languages, and contributions to Canada, and educators' lack of knowledge about Indigenous culture and history.

Income and Labour Market Participation

According to the 2011 NHS, between 2006 and 2011, the number of Indigenous people of working age (that is, between the ages of 25 and 64) increased by 21 percent; for the general Canadian population, the increase was only 5 percent. The 2011 census enumerated 671,380 Indigenous people in this age group, of whom 481,325 participated in the labour force. Although the Indigenous employment rate (for individuals of working age) remained stable at 63 percent between 2006 and 2011, this rate is still much lower than the 76 percent employment rate for non-Indigenous people. The unemployment rate for Indigenous people of working age is more than twice the rate for other Canadians of the same age (13 percent versus 6 percent). The gap between the two groups narrowed by 8 percent between 2006 and 2011 (Bougie et al., 2015, Pt. A, s. 4).

There is also a difference in the employment rate between status and non-status Indigenous people. The employment rate for status Indians is only 55 percent, 20 percent lower than the rate for non-Indigenous Canadians. The overall unemployment rate for working-age status Indians is 17 percent; for those living on reserve the rate is 22 percent.

The Métis population has only a 9 percent unemployment rate; their lowest unemployment rates are in Manitoba and Alberta and the highest is in Newfoundland and Labrador.

For the Inuit population the employment rate is 59 percent, 17 percent lower than the rate for non-Indigenous Canadians. The overall unemployment rate for Inuit is 17 percent; for those living in Nunangat it is 20 percent.

Figure 10.9 shows the unemployment rate across several provinces for First Nations, Métis, all Aboriginal, and non-Aboriginal respondents for 2007. Figure 10.10 shows the employment rate of population aged 25 to 64, by Aboriginal identity and education, for 2011.

FIGURE 10.9 Unemployment Rate of Population Aged 25 to 54 by Province or Region and Aboriginal Identity, 2007

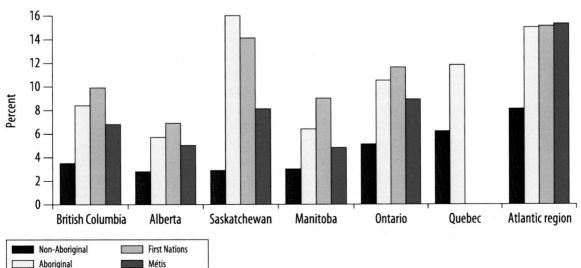

SOURCE: Statistics Canada (2008).

FIGURE 10.10   Employment Rate of Population Aged 25 to 64, by Aboriginal Identity and Education, Canada, 2011

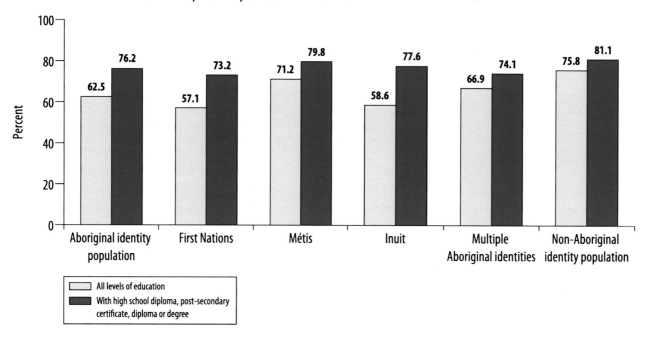

NOTE: Excludes data for one or more incompletely enumerated Indian reserves or Indian settlements. The three Aboriginal groups are based on the population reporting a single identity of "First Nations," "Métis," or "Inuit."

SOURCE: Statistics Canada (2015b, chart 15).

It appears that Indigenous people were hardest hit by the 2008 recession, with employment rates declining more steeply for the Indigenous population than for the non-Indigenous population (Statistics Canada, 2010). The unemployment rate in Canada for Indigenous people increased from 10.4 percent in 2008 to 13.9 percent in 2009, while the rate for non-Indigenous people rose from 6.0 percent to 8.1 percent. The manufacturing sector was hardest hit in this recession, with an 8 percent employment decline in 2009 from 2008; however, manufacturing employment fell for Indigenous people by 30 percent in the same year. In Alberta, the employment rate fell in 2008, at the start of the recession, from 75.1 percent to 65.1 percent, a steep decline for the province. The decline for Indigenous people was twice that.

As mentioned above, educational attainment is related to employability, and it is also related to income levels. This is true for all Canadians. The 2006 census (Statistics Canada, 2006) shows that Canadians who were employed full time and who had less than a high school education had an annual average income of $32,029. Canadians with a high school education made $37,403. Those with trades or apprenticeships made $39,996, and those with a college education earned $42,937. Canadians with some university education earned $47,253, while those with a bachelor's degree earned $56,048. The correlation between income and education levels is clear. Because Indigenous people's educational levels lag behind those of non-Indigenous people, so do their income levels—on average, by about $7,500 per year, according to the 2006 census (Statistics Canada, 2008). The gap between Indigenous and non-Indigenous education, employment, and income levels is closing, but slowly. Investment in Indigenous education will accelerate this process. Unfortunately, Statistics Canada's more frequent and detailed Labour Force Survey does not track on-reserve employment and unemployment; having these statistics gathered only in the census every five years makes the issue more difficult to address.

The labour force as a whole is important to Canada's economic future. Precisely because the Indigenous population is younger on average and its growth rate higher than the national average, it is an important resource for Canada's economic future. Key statistics in this regard include the following (Hull, 2008):

- Between 2001 and 2026, the number of Indigenous youth coming of age to enter the labour market will exceed 600,000.
- The 15–29 age group in the Indigenous population is projected to grow by 37 percent, compared with only 6 percent for this age group in the general Canadian population.
- By 2026, in Saskatchewan, 36 percent of the population between the ages of 15 and 29 is expected to be Indigenous; in Manitoba, the figure is expected to be 28 percent.

According to a medium growth rate projection, the Indigenous population will, by 2026, increase from its current 4 percent of Canada's population to 4.6 percent (Sharpe & Arsenault, 2010, p. 4). Because the Indigenous population is much younger than the rest of the population, it will be an increasing presence in the labour force as the aging population retires. If the current education (and, therefore, the employment) gap closes between the non-Indigenous and Indigenous populations, the latter will account for 19.9 percent of labour force growth between 2006 and 2026 (Sharpe & Arsenault, 2010, p. 4). Conversely, if the education gap remains as it is or becomes wider, given the projected increase in the Indigenous population, the result will be a higher social assistance dependency rate for that population and a negative economic effect for Canada as a whole.

The increased Indigenous population will have the greatest effect in the Western provinces. In Manitoba, Indigenous people are expected to account for 50 percent of the labour force growth and employment growth between 2006 and 2026 (Richards et al., 2010; Sharpe & Arsenault, 2010, p. 23). In Saskatchewan, the decrease in the non-Indigenous labour force (due to the aging population) between 2006 and 2026 means that Indigenous people are expected to account for more than 100 percent of all labour force and employment growth (Sharpe & Arsenault, 2010, p. 16). Clearly, investing in an educated and skilled Indigenous workforce is of paramount importance, in these two provinces and across the country.

Health

As with education and employment, Indigenous people suffer from a health gap; they are afflicted by certain illnesses more than the general population is, and overall life expectancy for Métis and status Indian populations is three years less than the general population's; the Inuit life expectancy is 10 years less for women and 14 years less for men. The causes of death differ by age category.

Delivery of Services

Before discussing Indigenous people's health issues, we need to discuss how health services are provided to Indigenous people. Health care is generally a provincial responsibility, but for status Indians living on reserve and for the Inuit in the North, it is a federal responsibility covered by Health Canada. For the rest of the Indigenous population—those living off reserve, whether status or non-status—health care is provided by the province. Federal funding for health services on reserves flows through the band. The federal funding formula for health care services and the itemized list of what is covered differ substantially from the provincial system.

Because hospitals and doctors bill the province for services, there has to be a way for the province to recoup from Health Canada the expenses it incurs for treating on-reserve status Indians. Different provinces have different policies concerning how this is done. Often, where the hospital or doctor prescribes or recommends a service that Health Canada does not ordinarily cover, Health Canada must pre-approve the expenditure. The levels of coverage differ between the provincial and federal systems; Health Canada does not fund all of the services the provinces do. As with education, there is a funding gap for the services provided to Indigenous people.

Because the provincial and federal systems are funded differently and have different operating budgets, disagreements sometimes arise over the financial obligations of service delivery. One such disagreement, central to events surrounding the death of five-year-old Jordan River Anderson in 2005, led to the passing of a private member's bill in the House of Commons known as Jordan's Principle. Jordan's story is about the inability of the federal and provincial governments to agree on who would cover the cost of his home care. While disagreements continued, Jordan remained in hospital, where he died while his family waited for a decision to be made. Jordan's story, and the tragic repercussions for his family, is the subject of Appendix 10.1.

The private member's bill, which passed in the House of Commons in 2007, proposed that, in the case of an on-reserve child who requires medical care, the level of government first contacted by the family, whether federal or provincial, should immediately pay to meet the child's medical needs, with the financial details to be worked out later.

Today formal agreements exist with each province on the administration of Jordan's Principle. These agreements and implementation protocols have not been without criticism. One complaint is that children's different identity categories influence whether Jordan's Principle is invoked. This may have the effect of creating disparities between different groups of Indigenous children in their access to health resources under Jordan's Principle. Furthermore, families have found navigating the formal case conferencing process lengthy and confusing (Blumenthal & Sinha, 2015). Figure 10.11 shows the process for New Brunswick's Jordan's Principle Agreement as summarized by the Assembly of First Nations.

In order to be covered for health benefits provided by Health Canada under the Non-Insured Health Benefits (NIHB) Program, an individual must be either a registered Indian according to the *Indian Act*, an Inuk recognized by an Inuit land agreement, or the infant of a qualified parent. As well, he or she must have no access to any other public or private health plan. In 2014, 808,686 people of Indigenous ancestry met these requirements (Health Canada, 2016). Although medical services are provided by all levels of government—municipal, provincial, and federal—the federal government, generally speaking, reimburses the other levels for services delivered to Indigenous people recognized under the NIHB program. All other people of Indigenous ancestry are covered under their respective provincial or private systems. The number of Indigenous clients served by Health Canada fluctuates depending on population and status, and will fluctuate into the future as the health services it provides go through the devolution process. For example, in 2014 responsibility for health services in British Columbia for Indigenous people was transferred to the First Nations Health Authority in that province (Health Canada, 2016; First Nations Health Authority, n.d.). Across the country, however, as a result of the creation of the Qalipu Mi'kmaq First Nation band and the *Gender Equity in Indian Registration Act*, an additional 51,267 registered Indians became eligible to receive benefits under the NIHB program. Of the clients served by Health Canada in 2014, 94.6 percent were First Nations people and 5.4 percent were Inuit (Health Canada, 2016).

On reserves, Health Canada also provides health promotion, nursing stations, transportation for health services, mental health and general health treatment, and many other services. Many First Nations and Inuit communities are taking more control over their own health services and programming; Health Canada is promoting the devolution—that is, the return—of administrative control over health care responsibilities to the respective communities.

FIGURE 10.11   Jordan's Principle: The 8 Steps to Get There

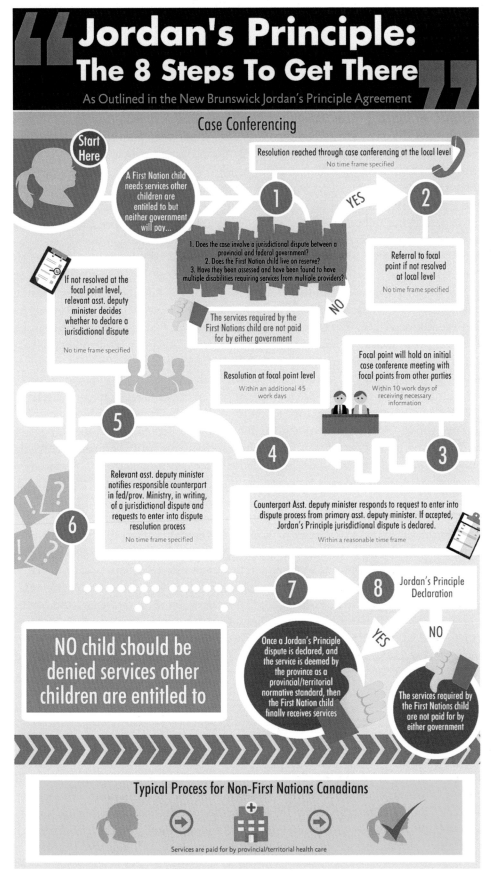

SOURCE: Assembly of First Nations (2015).

Physical Health

Currently, the major health concerns facing Indigenous people are diabetes, HIV/AIDS, heart disease, tuberculosis, mental health issues, and suicide. All of these problems are significantly more prevalent among the Indigenous population than among the general Canadian population.

Diabetes

The body of a person with diabetes, which is a chronic disease, either does not produce insulin (type 1 diabetes) or cannot properly use insulin (type 2 diabetes). Insulin is an essential hormone that regulates the amount of glucose in the blood. Those at greatest risk for developing type 2 diabetes are seniors, Indigenous people, baby boomers, and people who are prone to obesity, such as those who lead a sedentary lifestyle.

Indigenous people living on reserve have a prevalence rate of 17.2 percent of diabetes compared with 5 percent in the general public. The rate for the Indigenous population off reserve is lower at 10 percent but still double that of the general public. The prevalence rate for Métis is 7.3 percent. Indigenous people are generally diagnosed at a younger age, and the rate of gestational diabetes is also higher in Indigenous communities (Public Health Agency of Canada, 2011, "Report highlights").

In 2002, it was noted that rates of diabetes among the Inuit were lower than among the general population (Health Canada, 2002, p. 1). Since then, this statistic has changed dramatically. More recent research (Egeland, 2010, p. 17) has determined that Inuit are now diagnosed with diabetes at twice the rate of non-Indigenous Canadians. This same report indicates that 75 percent of Northern Labrador Inuit are overweight or obese—conditions linked to diabetes and other diseases. Forty percent of those surveyed who were over 40 had high blood pressure, compared with 20 percent of non-Indigenous Canadians in the same age category (Egeland, 2010, p. 17). It is interesting to note that food insecurity—that is, concern about the affordability or availability of food—was highest among the Inuit, with 13 percent of families reporting severe food insecurity and 34 percent reporting moderate food insecurity, compared with only 2.9 percent in the general population of Canada. Food insecurity among the Inuit is mostly a consequence of low incomes and the high cost of food in the regions where they live (Egeland, 2010, p. 20).

To address the diabetes epidemic, Health Canada implemented the Aboriginal Diabetes Initiative (ADI) in 1999. The ADI's primary purpose was to reduce the prevalence of type 2 diabetes by supporting health-promotion and disease-prevention activities and services, delivered by trained community diabetes workers and health service providers (Health Canada, 2011). The ADI comprised three phases. The first phase, from 1999 to 2004, focused on measuring the scope of the problem and developing strategies to increase awareness and health promotion to prevent diabetes; it received funding of $115 million. The second phase, from 2005 to 2010, included health promotion, primary prevention, screening and treatment, capacity building and training, and research surveillance evaluation and monitoring; it received funding of $190 million. The third and final phase, from 2011 to 2015, which received funding of $275 million, focused on initiatives for children and during pregnancy and pre-pregnancy, food security, and enhanced training for health practitioners. It included both on-reserve populations and off-reserve First Nations, Inuit, and Métis through partnerships with provinces. Now that all phases of the ADI are complete, Health Canada will assess its success over the next few years and provide statistics on its results.

It is now generally accepted that the increase in diabetes among Indigenous people is related to their rapid transition from traditional lifestyles of hunting and fishing to the more sedentary lifestyles and diet of the general population. The ADI partnered with tribal councils, First Nations organizations, Inuit community groups, and provincial and territorial governments to deliver a range of primary prevention, screening, and treatment programs for Indigenous people. The

ADI's aim was to implement strategies that were community-based and culturally appropriate. The programs that ADI promoted varied by community and included walking clubs, weight-loss groups, diabetes workshops, fitness classes, community kitchens, community gardens, and healthier food policies in schools. For example, vending machines that sell sugar-sweetened soft drinks and high-sugar, high-fat snacks were removed from many schools. The ADI also supported traditional activities such as drumming and dancing, canoeing, traditional food harvesting and preparation, and traditional games.

HIV/AIDS

As with many other health concerns, Indigenous people are overrepresented in the Canadian HIV/AIDS epidemic. They have

- a lower onset age for HIV/AIDS than other ethnicities do;
- a higher rate of new HIV infections than the general population has, and a high percentage of infections related to injection drug use; and
- much higher rates of infection among women than is the case in the general population.

It has been reported (Public Health Agency of Canada, 2010) that Indigenous people, who represented 3.8 percent of the Canadian population in the 2006 census, contracted 8.0 percent of all HIV infections in Canada—an estimated 4,300 to 6,100 cases. This represents a 24 percent increase over the 2005 numbers. With respect to new HIV infection rates, Indigenous people accounted for approximately 12.5 percent of new infections in 2008, an increase of 10.5 percent over the 2005 figure. In 2014, 10.8 percent of new HIV infections were in Indigenous people, bringing the number of Indigenous people living with HIV to 6,850—9.1 percent of all HIV cases in Canada in 2014. Due to the increase in Indigenous population, to 4.3 percent of the population total, Indigenous people's risk of contracting HIV in 2014 dropped; it is now only 2.7 times higher than that of the non-Indigenous Canadian population (Public Health Agency of Canada, 2015).

Figure 10.12 tracks the proportion of reported cases of HIV by race and ethnicity. Figure 10.13 shows the proportion of reported HIV cases among Indigenous subgroups (Public Health Agency of Canada, 2015).

Injection drug use (IDU) represents a significant exposure category for the HIV epidemic in Canada. "Exposure category" refers to the way in which individuals who test positive for HIV have acquired the virus—for example, through sexual activity or through injecting drugs. Statistics concerning exposure categories reveal that the HIV epidemic in Canada is complex in its sources, with different ethnicities acquiring the virus via different modes of transmission. For Indigenous people, IDU is a particularly important risk factor for HIV/AIDS. In 2014, the proportion of new HIV infections among those who inject drugs in the Indigenous population was 50.6 percent, while the rate among the non-Indigenous IDU population was 49.4 percent (Public Health Agency of Canada, 2014). IDU accounted for more HIV infections and cases of AIDS among Indigenous women than it did among Indigenous men—from 1979 to 2008, approximately double the number (Public Health Agency of Canada, 2010). This breakdown of statistics between men and women, however, was not repeated in the 2014 study.

The incidence of HIV/AIDS among young Indigenous people was a growing concern; positive HIV test reports and reported AIDS diagnoses were, in general, seen in the Indigenous population at younger ages than was the case with the general population. From 1998 to the end of 2008, nearly a third of the positive HIV test results among Indigenous people were for individuals aged 15–29 (32.6 percent of people diagnosed). Among other ethnicities, the rate was 20.5 percent (Public Health Agency of Canada, 2010). Age categories were not broken down by ethnicity in the 2014 study and therefore no comparison is possible.

FIGURE 10.12 Reported Cases of HIV, by Race and Ethnicity, by Year, Canada, 2009 to 2014

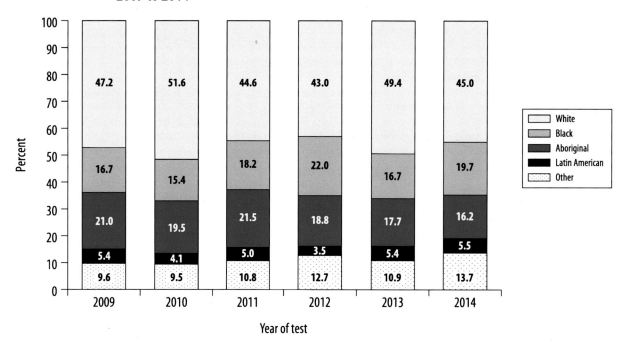

SOURCE: Public Health Agency of Canada (2015).

FIGURE 10.13 Proportion of Reported Cases of HIV/AIDS Among Aboriginal Subgroups, 2009 to 2014

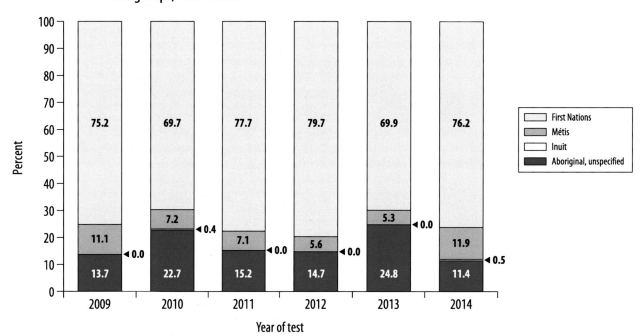

SOURCE: Public Health Agency of Canada (2015).

CLOSE-UP   Dr. Stanley Vollant

Dr. Stanley Vollant is a surgeon and First Nations coordinator in the Faculty of Medicine of the University of Montreal. Vollant is Innu, from Pessamit, Quebec. In 2010 he began a 6,000-kilometre series of treks on foot and by canoe through the Indigenous communities in Eastern Canada from Labrador to James Bay. The journey, called Innu Meshkenu (Innu Road), is meant to encourage young Indigenous people to excel and to stay in school, and to encourage healthy lifestyles and physical activity. Vollant experienced both poverty and racism as a child but had a passion for healing that he says comes from his grandparents, who raised him in the woods of Innu territory. He believes that obesity, diabetes, and school dropout rates are the most serious threats to Indigenous people in Canada. Vollant appeared in Ottawa in 2014 in support of an inquiry into missing and murdered Indigenous women in Canada.

Females are disproportionately represented in the HIV/AIDS epidemic among Indigenous people. Between 2009 and 2014, the percentage of females among the reported cases of Indigenous people with AIDS was 35.6 percent; in the non-Indigenous population for this same period, the percentage of women was 24.2 percent. In every year between 2001 and 2008, females have represented over 30 percent of reported AIDS cases among Indigenous people (Public Health Agency of Canada, 2015).

Tuberculosis

Tuberculosis (TB) is an infectious disease that affects the lungs. It is contagious, since it spreads through the air as a result of coughing and sneezing. TB is treatable through rounds of antibiotics and is most effectively treated when caught early. In Canada, TB has made a resurgence as a disease associated with poverty, easily spread in close living quarters and through neglect of treatment. The rates of TB infection for First Nations people were 8–10 times higher than for the non-Indigenous population (Health Canada, 2006). It was most prevalent among individuals aged 15 to 44. The rates of infection varied by community, but the highest rates were in British Columbia, Saskatchewan, Manitoba, Alberta, and northwestern Ontario. In 2013, Indigenous people made up 19 percent of all TB cases in Canada; they represented more than 65 percent of all cases in Manitoba and Saskatchewan, and 98 percent of all cases in the Northwest Territories, Nunavut, and Yukon. The rates broken down into Indigenous identity per 100,000 population are 3.3 for Métis, 21.8 for First Nations, and a shocking 154.2 for Inuit. The rate for the non-Indigenous Canadian-born population is 4.7 per 100,000. Risk factors associated with the contraction of TB include HIV and diabetes, as well as substance abuse, poor nutrition, and other factors that may weaken the immune system.

Overcrowded living conditions increase the rate of person-to-person transmission of TB. Living density among the general population of Canada is 0.4 persons per room (Health Canada, 2006). For First Nations people who live on reserve, the living density is, on average, 0.7 persons per room (Health Canada, 2006), but in many on-reserve communities the number is much higher. The First Nations communities that between 1996 and 2000 had the highest incidence of TB also had the highest living densities. TB is also more common in remote reserves, probably because these communities have restricted access to health professionals who can diagnose the disease early and restrict its spread.

Tuberculosis was an even more pressing issue for the Inuit, whose infection rate was 32 times the national average in 2008 (Zarate, 2010). This statistic is related to severe overcrowding in Inuit communities due to housing shortages.

Mental Health: Depression and Suicide

To be understood fully, Indigenous people's mental health issues must be considered in the light of the collective trauma through colonization that is part of their history, as well as the history of dispossession and oppression and the current state of struggle against poverty and the weakened social fabric of their communities. Indigenous populations in Canada face unique challenges in the area of mental health. Studies show that First Nations people experience depression at twice the rate of the average Canadian and that they more frequently report that the depression interferes with the activities of daily life (Kahn, 2008, pp. 6–7). The levels of reported depression among the Inuit are very low, but their suicide rate is very high. Indigenous people seek professional help in the form of treatment or counselling at twice the rate of the general Canadian population.

First Nations and Inuit communities experience higher rates of suicide, overall, than other communities in Canada do (see Figure 10.14). The rate varies from community to community, with some First Nations communities reporting no suicides or suicide attempts for years at a time, while others have annual suicide rates that are 11 times the national average. Suicide rates are highest for young Indigenous people aged 15–24; the rates for this age group are five to seven times what they are for people of this age group in the general population. Because of the relative youth of suicide victims in the Indigenous community, suicide accounts for the greatest number of potential years of life lost in Indigenous populations in Canada. As with the non-Indigenous population, rates of completed suicide are higher among Indigenous males than among Indigenous females (Kahn, 2008, p. 7).

Research (Statistics Canada, 2012) indicates that 24 percent of First Nations living off-reserve, 23.5 percent of Inuit, and 19.6 percent of Métis reported having suicidal thoughts. Thirty-nine percent of girls aged 12–17 and 17 percent of boys in the same age bracket have considered suicide. Young people with a close family member who had committed suicide in the last 12 months were more than twice as likely to report having had suicidal thoughts. A 2004 health survey (Anctil, 2008, p. 5) suggested that 20 percent of Inuit respondents had made a suicide attempt in their lifetime and that almost 7 percent had done so in the previous year. Having a parent who had attended a residential school increased the odds from 18 percent to 26 percent that a youth would have thoughts about suicide (Public Health Agency of Canada, 2006, p. 166).

FIGURE 10.14 Suicide Rates for First Nations, Inuit, and the General Population

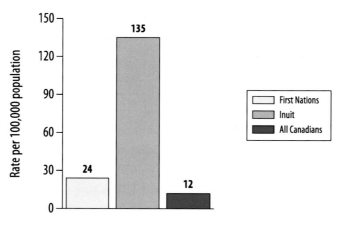

SOURCE: Public Health Agency of Canada (2006, p. 167).

Studies have identified suicide risk factors and protective factors at both the individual and the community levels (see Table 10.4). Anything that contributes to the risk of suicide is called a risk factor; any process that reduces the risk is referred to as a protective factor. Examining individual First Nations or Inuit communities with a view to these factors helps us to understand their suicide rates. Not all Indigenous communities experience high levels of suicide; some experience very few suicides or none at all. These healthy communities often have high protective factors, such as a strong sense of community and deep cultural connection. A study of bands in British Columbia found that those with a higher level of Indigenous language knowledge had fewer suicides. These features of a community are referred to as cultural continuity (Centre for Suicide Prevention, 2013, p. 5).

In January 2015, Health Canada introduced the First Nations Mental Wellness Continuum Framework (Figure 10.15). This was developed in partnership with Health Canada's First Nations and Inuit Health Branch, the Assembly of First Nations, and Indigenous mental health leaders. The centre of the model is the core of hope, belonging, meaning, and purpose, surrounded by a ring representing kinship, clan, elders, and community. The model is built and layered with elements foundational to supporting First Nations mental wellness. It recognizes cultural values such as sacred knowledge, language, and spiritual practices as foundations of strength and resilience. There are five key themes:

1. culture as foundation;
2. community development, ownership, and capacity building;
3. quality care systems and competent service delivery;
4. collaboration with partners; and
5. enhanced flexible funding.

TABLE 10.4   Suicide: Risk Factors and Protective Factors at the Community and Individual Levels

Community/social risk factors

- Historical trauma and loss
- Lack of meaningful activity or work available in the community
- Interpersonal conflict and crisis within the community
- Suicide common in community (clusters)
- Use/abuse of alcohol and other substances prevalent in the community
- Community social isolation
- Poverty
- Lack of community control over social services and finances

Individual risk factors

- Mood or other psychiatric disorder, including depression
- History of abuse (physical or sexual)
- Family history of suicide
- Hopelessness and pessimism
- Poor coping skills
- Impulsivity
- Influence of alcohol or other substances
- Access to lethal means

Protective factors

- Perception of family connectedness
- Intergenerational connectedness throughout the community
- Emotional well-being
- School/community involvement
- Academic success or meaningful work
- Spiritual connection and cultural continuity

SOURCE: Kirmayer, Fraser, Fauras, & Whitley (2010).

FIGURE 10.15   First Nations Mental Wellness Continuum Framework

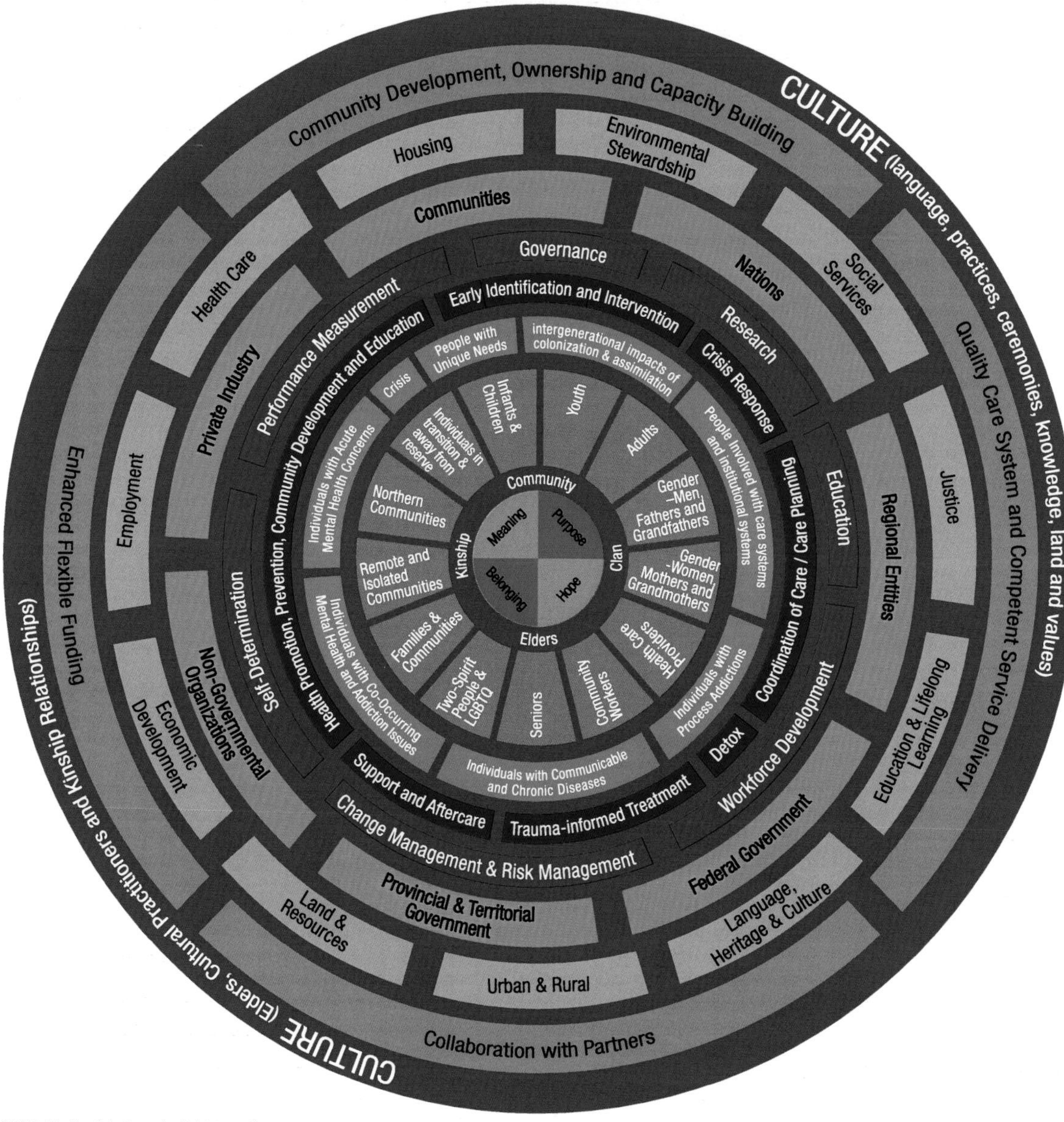

SOURCE: Health Canada (2014, p. 3).

The summary report recognizes the need for a full spectrum of culturally competent supports and services to support mental wellness, including health promotion, illness prevention, community development, and education as well as early identification and intervention, crisis response, and coordination of care and care planning. It recognizes the need for detox centres and for treatment that is informed by the trauma common in Indigenous communities and culturally appropriate, as well as the need for support and aftercare. It is hoped that the framework can help reduce suicides as well as substance abuse and addiction (Health Canada, 2014).

Substance Abuse and Addiction

The rate of alcohol-related deaths in the Indigenous population is twice that in the non-Indigenous population, and death due to illicit drugs is three times the rate in Indigenous populations. In a survey, one in five Indigenous youths reported having used solvents. Of those, one in three were under the age of 15. The rate of incarceration for Indigenous youth is eight times that of non-Indigenous youth in Canada. Of those incarcerated youth, eight in ten have a substance abuse problem (Chansonneuve, 2007, p. 25).

According to a survey conducted by Health Canada in 2003, 73 percent of First Nations and Inuit people consider alcohol a problem in their community, and 59 percent also report drug abuse as a problem (Kahn, 2008). Thirty-three percent indicate alcohol is a problem in their own family and 25 percent indicate that they have a personal problem with alcohol (Kahn, 2008). This is interesting, because fewer First Nations and Inuit people actually drink alcohol than do people in the general population: 66 percent of those living on reserve report consuming alcohol, compared with 76 percent of the general population. What is clear is that many of those First Nations and Inuit who do consume alcohol do so in quantities that present problems for themselves and their communities (Kahn, 2008).

Health Canada has funded the National Native Alcohol and Drug Abuse Program since the 1970s. In recent years, Indigenous people themselves have taken control of much of this program. There are 52 residential treatment centres across the country, equipped to treat Indigenous people in culturally appropriate programs. This program also focuses on prevention, intervention, and aftercare.

Once again, it is important to remember that all Indigenous communities are different. Some have few problems with alcohol and substance abuse, while others have severe problems. Communities that are in crisis need to be given culturally appropriate assistance and treatments. The First Nations Mental Wellness Continuum Framework will inform the delivery of assistance and treatment into the future.

Housing and Infrastructure Conditions

The 2006 census demonstrated that 25 percent of First Nations people on reserve were living in overcrowded conditions and 44 percent of the houses were in major need of repairs. The extent of the housing shortage differs, but all parties agree that it exists. The Assembly of First Nations reports the shortage as approximately 85,000 units across the country, while Aboriginal Affairs and Northern Development Canada estimates the shortage at only 35,000 to 40,000 units (Standing Senate Committee on Aboriginal Peoples, 2015, p. 6). The housing shortage leads to overcrowding and the use of inadequate shelter (such as people living in condemned units), which in turn leads to health problems. The type of housing can also interfere with cultural activities of the population, particularly if the population maintains traditional lifestyles such as hunting and preparing meat and hides. Housing that is considered appropriate for southern communities, city dwellers, or nuclear families may not provide the best opportunity for Indigenous peoples to maintain cultural continuity.

The housing shortage is difficult to address since the infrastructure must be in place to support the building of homes. Sewage systems, roads, and utilities must be available to develop serviceable lots on which to place new homes. There are major deficits in these areas on reserves, some of which have been under boil-water advisories for years because of inadequate water treatment or well systems.

As to the adequacy of the housing, the report of the Standing Senate Committee on Aboriginal Peoples (2015, p. 19) indicates that 37 percent of the 108,000 units on reserve need major repairs and 34 percent need minor repairs. Mould has been a significant problem in on-reserve housing. Many of the structures were poorly built out of materials inappropriate for the climate or environment.

In 2004 the government of Nunavut presented a 10-year action plan to address the housing crisis in its communities. The plan called for the immediate construction of 3,000 housing units and renovation of 1,000 existing units. It proposed an additional 2,730 new units by 2016 to address the projected population growth. It is unknown how many housing units have been built through this plan, since the program is completed but is yet to be reviewed. In 2010, however, the Nunavut Housing Needs Survey reported that 1,220 people in Nunavut were homeless (Nunavut Housing Corporation, 2010). The Conference Board of Canada in its 2011 map *Sleeping on the Couch* showed that Nunavut had the highest overcrowding rates in Canada. In March 2010, it was reported that 49 percent of people in Nunavik were living in overcrowded conditions (CBC News, 2010). The problem is made worse by the short lifespan of government housing, which is built to last only 15 years, in a region where weather conditions are extremely hard on the existing structures. Building costs are high due to the difficulty of transporting construction materials to areas accessible by road only at certain times in the year or not at all. In 2015, CBC News reported that 2,313 households in 25 communities in Nunavut were on social housing waiting lists, although the need is estimated as closer to 3,000 (Van Dusen, 2015).

Landownership in First Nations communities differs from the rest of Canada in important ways that complicate financial access to capital. Under the *Indian Act*, the lands of Indigenous people are held by the Crown. Section 89 of the Act restricts the use of Indian land as collateral against financing loans through traditional sources. As a result, many financial institutions are reluctant to grant traditional mortgages or loans to fund infrastructure on reserve territory. The Act also prohibits transfer of lands to any entity other than the band or another band member, which in effect limits any traditional for-profit housing on reserve.

The federal government's Ministerial Loan Guarantee (MLG) program backs loans up to a stated dollar limit for construction of on-reserve housing. Indigenous people taking advantage of these types of loans must demonstrate enough income to repay the loans. The diverse economic conditions on reserves means that home ownership is common in areas where unemployment rates are low and economic development provides sufficient income, but on remote reserves, where unemployment can be as high as 85 percent, home ownership and loan repayment are simply not feasible. The Canada Mortgage and Housing Corporation (CMHC) funds housing programs to provide social housing on reserve for those who require housing and cannot own their home; many of these people rent housing from the band through shelter allowances in their social assistance incomes. This funding also has limits set by the federal government.

In 2008, the federal government began the $300 million First Nations Market Housing Fund to promote private ownership of market housing on reserve. The fund secures mortgages for Indigenous people living on reserve to purchase or construct homes. CMHC is a financial partner in the fund with other lending institutions. One hundred First Nations communities have qualified for the program by demonstrating fiscal responsibility. The fund's goal was to help build 25,000 privately owned homes by 2018. As of May 2015, only 99 had been built. On-reserve housing has long been seen as a treaty responsibility of the federal government, and the new concept of market-based privately owned housing has not been immediately embraced by First Nations communities. The fund-backed mortgages still require a credit history from applicants and a demonstrated steady income, which many band members lack. Furthermore, in many remote communities there is no market history of housing prices and therefore no guarantee of a return on investment for a band member to personally finance the construction of a new home.

The Standing Senate Committee on Aboriginal Peoples began an investigation into the state of on-reserve First Nations housing in Canada in 2013. It released its report in February 2015. The introduction states:

> There was unanimous agreement among witnesses, including departmental officials, that there is a significant housing shortage in First Nation communities, and that the existing stock of housing in many communities is in deplorable condition. It is not an exaggeration to suggest that, in many First Nation communities, the housing situation is in a state of crisis. (Standing Senate Committee on Aboriginal Peoples, 2015, p. 3)

This report made a number of recommendations to address the housing and infrastructure problem on reserves. Here are just a few:

1. Indigenous and Northern Affairs should remove the 2 percent cap on annual increases in all department funding beginning in the 2016–17 budget.
2. CMHC should allocate sufficient funds to the On-Reserve Non-Profit Housing program to address the shortage of on-reserve housing and allow multi-year funding so that there is adequate time to organize construction and plan ahead.
3. The annual Band Support Program at Indigenous and Northern Affairs should fund the hiring of a qualified housing manager if a band finds it necessary.
4. Indigenous and Northern Affairs in consultation with First Nations should explore the implementation and enforcement of building codes.
5. Indigenous and Northern Affairs should assess whether the shelter allowance component of the Income Assistance Program is adequate to cover shelter costs, including rent and heating, and ensure consistency in funding across regions.
6. Indigenous and Northern Affairs and CMHC should collaborate to develop a housing strategy for remote and isolated communities that reflects the challenges and costs of building in remote areas.

The housing crisis in on-reserve housing has been decades in the making; it will not be resolved inexpensively or overnight. With community consultation, new plans are being developed that are consistent with the diversity in geography and social capacity across communities.

Social Assistance and Economic Renewal

Social Assistance

Income assistance is common for First Nations people, particularly those living on reserve, where there are few economic opportunities. It provides income for families to meet their basic needs such as housing and food and clothing if they cannot provide these for themselves through employment. According to Indigenous and Northern Affairs, in the 2012–13 fiscal year the government invested approximately $861 million in income assistance payments to 86,798 clients and their families living on reserve. In some communities the income assistance dependency rate is more than 80 percent. Across all communities the rate was 33.6 percent, compared with a little over 5 percent for the rest of the Canadian population (Indigenous and Northern Affairs Canada, 2012). Indigenous and Northern Affairs is currently working with 130 First Nations communities to fund projects aimed at reforming income assistance. As of January 2015, youth from 88 First Nations across the country were participating in skills training and job readiness programs to increase their employability (Indigenous and Northern Affairs Canada, 2015b).

Once again, it is important to realize that every Indigenous community is unique. Needs for income assistance vary tremendously between communities. For example, Indian and Northern Affairs Canada data for the Far North, including Yukon, Northwest Territories, and Nunavut, show that only about 50 percent of the Indigenous population had employment in 2001 compared with up to 90 percent of non-Indigenous people in the same regions (Indian and Northern Affairs Canada, 2005, p. 92, figure 7.5). In this case, the need for income assistance and government services is very high. In other areas of the country, such as southern Ontario, Indigenous people have had relative success in education and in the labour market, and this reduces the need for assistance.

Ultimately, economic development on reserves is one of the best methods of addressing the social ills that exist there. However, there are barriers to such development.

Land and Resource Management

Under legislation such as the *Indian Act*, the *Indian Oil and Gas Act*, and the *First Nations Land Management Act*, federal organizations still have considerable responsibility and control over First Nations' economic development, particularly when it comes to reserved land. There is no single land management regime that applies to all reserves in Canada. Each First Nations territory is governed by one of three types of land management: the *Indian Act* land management framework, the First Nations Land Management (FNLM) Regime, or a self-government arrangement as a stand-alone agreement or as part of a modern treaty. Of the 617 recognized First Nations bands, 550 adhere to the original *Indian Act* framework, which many find cumbersome, complicated, uncertain, and slow. This system does not inspire confidence in outside investors. The FNLM Regime gives bands greater control over their lands and resources. First Nations under this framework can pass laws for development and protection of lands, and issue licences and leases with community approval; ministerial involvement and approval are reduced. As of March 2014, 77 First Nations bands had joined the FNLM Regime and 48 were on a waiting list; of the 77, 36 had enacted land codes and 30 were preparing codes (Standing Committee on Aboriginal Affairs and Northern Development, 2014, p. 9). First Nations with stand-alone self-government agreements under modern, constitutionally protected treaties enjoy extensive land management and law-making authority, further reducing ministerial approval processes. There were 18 such agreements as of March 2014 (Standing Committee on Aboriginal Affairs and Northern Development, 2014, p. 8).

Under the *Indian Act*, by which most bands currently operate, there are different land tenure arrangements. Customary land holdings are the most common, in which individuals or families acquire tracts of land allotted by the band council. That individual or family can build a home or a farm or start a business on that land. The land cannot be sold in any formally documented manner since it belongs to the band. Land can also be held under a certificate of possession, which closely resembles **fee simple ownership**. These certificates are issued under the authority of the minister of Indigenous and Northern Affairs after the band council grants its permission. Such land can be leased to third parties, including non-band members, but land ownership is retained by the band. Finally, there are leasehold interests that can be leased to third parties for development purposes. These leases are completed by the minister as well, and income is managed by the minister on behalf of the band.

fee simple ownership
the right to exclusive use, possession, and disposal of a piece of land

First Nations are currently seeking to develop modern professionally managed land management systems that will allow their communities to tap into outside investments as well as develop the land's resources. Because of the complexity of the *Indian Act* land management framework, and to a lesser extent the FNLM Regime, simple on-reserve transactions can take up to five times longer than for off-reserve lands, which discourages outside investors. The procedure for leasing lands to outside third parties takes two to three years to pass through all the levels of approval. Investors are not usually prepared to wait so long, and First Nations are losing out on economic opportunities.

First Nations communities report difficulty in meeting the criteria of the federal government's business-development programs and thus obtaining program funding. These communities see access to natural resources as an important part of economic development, but they are having difficulty gaining that access. Many resources are on lands that are currently under claim and are therefore inaccessible until a resolution is reached.

First Nations people have difficulty accessing capital to invest in economic development. Many do not have large investment funds, and, owing to the nature of communal ownership and to the *Indian Act*, they cannot use reserved land to secure loans for capital ventures. In the past, banks and other capital lending institutions have been reluctant to learn about and accommodate their policies to First Nations organizations, which have unique legal status. First Nations people have found that their funding proposals are often rejected by federal officials, who view these proposals as high-risk. First Nations people have pointed out that approval for the funding of prospective Indigenous businesses moves more slowly than that for non-Indigenous businesses. At times, gaining funding approval can take years.

The *Indian Act* processes can be cumbersome, and the processes required by resource management are complex. For example, royalty payments from resource development on reserved lands are not paid to the band; they go to Indigenous and Northern Affairs, to be held in trust accounts. To access the money, the band must apply to the minister and detail how the money will be spent. This requirement, intended to ensure that the Crown meets its fiduciary duty to First Nations, is a complex system that can cause delays in accessing capital. To bypass the red tape involved in accessing government economic development programs, some First Nations seek partnerships with non-Indigenous business communities.

One of the greatest obstacles to the economic development of Indigenous society is the lack of land. Indigenous people are trying to boost their economies; however, in a country whose economy is based on natural resources, it is difficult for First Nations people to enter that economy when, until 2004, they had less than half of 1 percent of Canada's land mass. As a result of treaty entitlement and specific and comprehensive land claims, particularly in British Columbia and undeveloped northern regions, First Nations–held land mass has increased to 3.8 million hectares and is expected to increase by another 1.1 million hectares over the next decade. This will triple the 2004 level of First Nations landholdings. It is crucial that First Nations develop sustainable land management strategies consistent with their own values and traditions to make the most of the land and resources to boost their economies and provide hope for the future.

Access to Natural Resources

Resources that had supported First Nations people for thousands of years are now in the control and possession of private industry and governments that are not willing to allow First Nations to share in them; recall the Mi'kmaq lobster fishing dispute discussed in Chapter 8. Forestry and timber harvesting rights are another particular area of contention. First Nations have privileges for logging on only 3 percent of Crown land, with the remainder leased by the Crown to private industry. In 2005, a decision by the Supreme Court of Canada denied Indigenous people in Eastern Canada the right to access Crown land for logging to increase their presence in the logging industry (*R v. Marshall*; *R v. Bernard*, 2005). The Supreme Court ruled that logging for profit was not part of the pre-contact Indigenous economy and that therefore the Indigenous people concerned had no right to access the industry. In 2014, however, the Supreme Court of Canada unanimously ruled that the Tsilhqot'in Nation in BC had rights over ancestral lands outside of their reserve, including the right to use them for modern economic purposes, such as forestry, without destroying them for future generations (*Tsilhqot'in Nation v. British Columbia*, 2014). The right to access natural resources is conditional on establishing Indigenous title over the land, so as claims move forward, the landscape of Indigenous access to industry in natural resources may change.

Separating Indigenous people from their land and its resources has demoralized them and entrenched them in Canada's economy as wage labourers for the dominant culture and for Canada's private business interests. Major changes have recently occurred that will alter the trajectory of First Nations economies and their futures. Access to land and resources is the primary focus of Chapter 8.

EXERCISE 3

Casinos are one common opportunity for economic development on reserves. What do you think the potential benefits and possible pitfalls are of building casinos on reserves?

Language

In the 2011 census, over 60 different Indigenous languages grouped into 12 distinct language families were recorded as being spoken by First Nations people in Canada. Many of the 60 languages, those that are spoken by fewer than 500 people, are considered endangered for long-term survival. In 2011, according to the National Household Survey, only 17.2 percent of people who reported an Indigenous identity could conduct a conversation in an Indigenous language; this is a decrease from 21 percent in the 2006 census. The proportion of people who could speak an Indigenous language was highest among the Inuit, at 67 percent. The proportion among First Nations was 22.4 percent (5.6 percent lower than in the 2006 census) and 2.5 percent among the Métis. Many Indigenous people who speak an Indigenous language have learned it as a second language, since they did not report it as their mother tongue on the survey. However, of those who did report an Indigenous language as their mother tongue, 6.9 percent could no longer conduct a conversation in that language.

These figures represent a significant decrease overall since the 1940s. In 1941, English was the first language of less than 10 percent of Indigenous people; in 1971, it was the first language of approximately 54 percent; in 1991, of 60.4 percent.

According to the 2011 census, the ten most-reported languages account for almost 90 percent of the population who can speak an Indigenous language. Also, the number of people who speak an Indigenous language at home varies depending on where they live, with most Indigenous language speakers residing on reserve or in other areas with high proportions of Indigenous people.

A 2007 study shows that the continuation or retention of language is a factor in the well-being of individuals and communities (Hallett, Chandler, & Lalonde, 2007). This study tracked youth suicide rates in Indigenous communities in British Columbia, and found that bands in which a majority of members could converse in an Indigenous language experienced few youth

FIGURE 10.16   Proportion of the Population Whose Mother Tongue Is One of the Ten Most Reported Aboriginal Languages Who Speak Their Language Most Often or on a Regular Basis, Canada, 2011

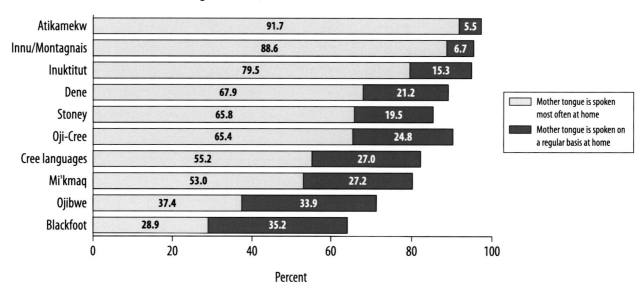

SOURCE: Statistics Canada (2015a, figure 3).

suicides. Youth suicide rates were *six times greater* for bands in which fewer than half of the members could converse in an Indigenous language. In sum, the study shows that "indigenous language use, as a marker of cultural persistence, is a strong predictor of health and wellbeing in Canada's Aboriginal communities" (Hallett et al., 2007, p. 398).

It is for these reasons that Heritage Canada has initiated the Aboriginal Languages Initiative to provide funds for programs that work for the preservation and revitalization of Indigenous languages for the benefit of Indigenous peoples and all Canadians.

Aboriginal Languages Initiative

One of the many programs financed by Heritage Canada's Aboriginal Languages Initiative is the Pre-School Language Nest Program in British Columbia. This program provides cultural immersion environments for pre-school children and their parents with the goal of creating new fluent speakers in their respective traditional languages. Indigenous communities across Canada can apply to the Aboriginal Languages Initiative for funding as they create their own language initiatives.

EXERCISE 4

In *Surviving as Indians*, Professor Menno Boldt (1993, p. i) defines *justice* in terms of "the survival and well-being of Indians as *Indians*, that is, defined by their traditional principles and philosophies." Boldt highlights the following five imperatives:

1. Moral justice for Indians.
2. Canadian policies that treat the needs, aspirations, interests, and rights of Indians as equal to those of Canadians.
3. Indian leadership committed to returning Indian government to the people.
4. The revitalization of Indian cultures, languages, and social systems within a framework of traditional philosophies and principles.
5. Economic self-sufficiency and independence through employment in the Canadian labour force.

Based on what you have read in this chapter, how does the reality of Indigenous people in Canada correspond to Boldt's imperatives? Do you see positive developments in certain areas? Where does Canada currently stand in relation to Boldt's definition of "justice"?

CHAPTER SUMMARY

In the case study that opened the chapter, we saw how the Grassy Narrows First Nations community lost control over its traditional territory. Its treaty with the federal government, the influence of nearby industry, and its relocation all contributed to serious and persistent socio-economic problems. But through activism and new agreements with government, the community has regained some control over its circumstances.

Counting the Indigenous populations in Canada and determining their needs are complicated by different categories of Indigenous ancestry and various survey methods used by government agencies. Legal changes in 1985 and 2009 allowed many Indigenous people who had lost or been denied registered Indian status to regain or acquire it. In 2016, the *Daniels* ruling extended the rights of status Indians to non-status Indians and Métis; it remains to be seen how this ruling will be put into practice.

While it is difficult to generalize about diverse Indigenous populations, it can be said that on the whole, they are younger than the non-Indigenous Canadian population and are becoming increasingly urban; both of these trends present socio-economic challenges.

Education is the chief means by which Indigenous people can improve their economic prospects. The fact that the federal government's funding of First Nations education has lagged behind that of the provincial education systems has led to a generally lower quality of education for First Nations children. Various federal programs and initiatives are attempting to improve the standards of First Nations schooling.

Statistics on the health of Indigenous people are cause for concern, since they show that several serious diseases disproportionately afflict Indigenous populations, as do mental health issues, addictions, and suicide. Again, the fact that the federal government funds and manages health care for many status Indians and Inuit leads to a different level of care from that available in the provincial health care systems, and sometimes to disputes about which level of government is responsible for care, as in the case of Jordan Anderson in 2005.

Housing on First Nations reserves and in Inuit communities is often substandard or in short supply, which contributes to health and social problems. Related infrastructure such as the water supply is often deficient as well. Land management on First Nations reserves, long under the control of the federal government, is being reformed so that the communities can benefit from the value of the land and its resources.

Language is key to culture and a sense of belonging. The Indigenous heritage of Canada includes over 60 languages, many of which are little spoken today and in danger of being lost forever. Various programs are encouraging Indigenous communities to learn, speak, and teach the languages of their people.

REFERENCES

Aboriginal Affairs and Northern Development Canada. (2010). How do the new legislative changes to the *Indian Act* affect me? http://www.aadnc-aandc.gc.ca/eng/1100100032501.

Anctil, M. (2008). Survey highlights. *Nunavik Inuit health survey 2004: Qanuippitaa? How are we?* Quebec: Institut national de santé publique du Québec (INSPQ) and Nunavik Regional Board of Health and Social Services (NRBHSS). http://www.inspq.qc.ca/pdf/publications/774_ESISurveyHighlights.pdf.

Assembly of First Nations. (2005, June 28). Bill C-31 twenty years later: AFN national chief calls for First Nations control of First Nations citizenship [Press release]. http://www.turtleisland.org/news/news-c31.htm.

Assembly of First Nations. (2012). Chiefs Assembly on Education: Information package—Federal funding for First Nations schools. http://www.treatysix.org/pdf/AFN Education Assembly Information Package_ENG.pdf.

Assembly of First Nations. (2015, February 10). Jordan's principle. http://www.afn.ca/en/jordans-principle-feb10.

Aulakh, R. (2014, March 25). Grassy Narrows First Nation greets Ontario lumber firm's decision. *The Toronto Star*. http://www.thestar.com.

Bains, R. (2014). *Myths and realities of First Nations education*. Centre for Aboriginal Policy Studies. Vancouver: Fraser Institute. https://www.fraserinstitute.org/sites/default/files/myths-and-realities-of-first-nations-education.pdf.

Blackstock, C. (2009). Jordan's story: How one boy inspired a world of change. *Canadian supplement to The state of the world's children 2009: Aboriginal children's health: Leaving no child behind*. Toronto: UNICEF Canada.

Blumenthal, A., & Sinha, V. (2015). No Jordan's Principle cases in Canada? A review of the administrative response to Jordan's Principle. *The International Indigenous Policy Journal, 6*(1), art. 6. http://ir.lib.uwo.ca/cgi/viewcontent.cgi?article=1206&context=iipj.

Boldt, M. (1993). *Surviving as Indians: The challenge of self-government*. Toronto: University of Toronto Press.

Bougie, E., Kelly-Scott, K., & Arriagada, P. (2015). *The education and employment experiences of First Nations people living off reserve, Inuit, and Métis: Selected findings from the 2012 Aboriginal Peoples Survey.* Statistics Canada catalogue no. 89-653-X. http://www.statcan.gc.ca/pub/89-653-x/89-653-x2013001-eng.htm.

Canadian Charter of Rights and Freedoms. (1982). Part I of the *Constitution Act, 1982*, being Schedule B to the *Canada Act 1982* (UK), 1982, c. 11.

CBC News. (2010, March 18). Nunavik housing shortage a "crisis": Inuit. *CBC News.* http://www.cbc.ca/news.

CBC News. (2013, November 1). Nunavut hamlet overcrowding nears breaking point. *CBC News.* http://www.cbc.ca.

Centre for Suicide Prevention. (2013). *Suicide prevention resource toolkit.* https://suicideinfo.ca/LinkClick.aspx?fileticket=MVIyGo2V4YY%3D&tabid=563.

Chansonneuve, D. (2007). *Addictive behaviours among Aboriginal people in Canada.* Ottawa: Aboriginal Healing Foundation. http://www.ahf.ca/downloads/addictive-behaviours.pdf.

Conference Board of Canada. (2011). *Sleeping on the couch* [Map]. Centre for the North Research Centre. Ottawa: Author.

Constitution Act, 1982. (1982). Being Schedule B to the *Canada Act 1982* (UK), 1982, c. 11.

Daniels v. Canada. (2013). 2013 FC 6, aff'd. 2016 SCC 12.

Egeland, G. (2010). *Inuit health survey 2007–2008: Inuvialuit settlement region.* Ste-Anne-de-Bellevue, QC: Centre for Indigenous Peoples' Nutrition and Environment, McGill University.

Employment and Social Development Canada. (2013, Fall). *Aboriginal Labour Market Bulletin.* http://www.esdc.gc.ca/eng/jobs/aboriginal/bulletins/fall2013.shtml#h2.4-h3.2.

First Nations Health Authority. (n.d.). About us. http://www.fnha.ca/about.

First Nations Land Management Act. (1999). SC 1999, c. 24.

Frideres, J.S., & Gadacz, R.R. (2008). *Aboriginal peoples in Canada: Contemporary conflicts* (8th ed.). Toronto: Pearson.

Geddes, C., Doxtater, M., & Krepakevich, M. (1997). *No turning back: The Royal Commission on Aboriginal Peoples.* Montreal: National Film Board of Canada.

Gender Equity in Indian Registration Act. (2010). SC 2010, c. 18.

Hallett, D., Chandler, M.J., & Lalonde, C.E. (2007). Aboriginal language knowledge and youth suicide. *Cognitive Development, 22*, 392–399. http://web.uvic.ca/psyc/lalonde/manuscripts/2007CogDevt.pdf.

Health Canada. (2002). First Nations, Inuit and Aboriginal health: Aboriginal diabetes initiative (ADI) evaluation framework. http://www.hc-sc.gc.ca.

Health Canada. (2006). First Nations, Inuit and Aboriginal health: Tuberculosis in First Nations communities. http://www.hc-sc.gc.ca.

Health Canada. (2011). First Nations, Inuit and Aboriginal health: Diabetes. http://www.hc-sc.gc.ca/fniah-spnia/diseases-maladies/diabete/index-eng.php.

Health Canada. (2013). First Nations and Inuit health. http://www.hc-sc.gc.ca/fniah-spnia/pubs/services/tripartite/framework-accord-cadre-eng.php.

Health Canada. (2014). First Nation mental wellness continuum framework—Summary report. http://www.hc-sc.gc.ca/fniah-spnia/pubs/promotion/_mental/2014-sum-rpt-continuum/index-eng.php.

Health Canada. (2016). *Non-insured health benefits program: First Nations and Inuit Health Branch—Annual report 2014–2015.* Ottawa: Author. http://healthycanadians.gc.ca/publications/health-system-systeme-sante/non-insured-health-benefits-annual-report-2014-2015-rapport-annuel-services-sante-non-assures/alt/nihb-ar-2014-2015-ra-ssna-eng.pdf.

Hull, J. (2008). Aboriginal youth in the Canadian labour market. *Horizons, 10*(1), 40–44.

Hurley, M.C., & Simeone, T. (2010, March 18; November 15). Bill C-3: Gender Equity in Indian Registration Act [Legislative summary]. Ottawa: Parliamentary Information and Research Service, Library of Parliament. http://www.lop.parl.gc.ca/Content/LOP/LegislativeSummaries/40/3/c3-e.pdf.

Indian Act. (1985). RSC 1985, c. I-5.

Indian and Northern Affairs Canada. (2005). *Basic departmental data 2004.* Ottawa: Minister of Public Works and Government Services Canada. http://dsp-psd.pwgsc.gc.ca/collection_2008/inac-ainc/R12-7-2004E.pdf.

Indian and Northern Affairs Canada. (2009). Discussion paper: Changes to the *Indian Act* affecting Indian registration and band membership—*McIvor v. Canada.* http://www.aadnc-aandc.gc.ca/DAM/DAM-INTER-HQ/STAGING/texte-text/mci_1100100032488_eng.pdf.

Indian Oil and Gas Act. (1985). RSC 1985, c. I-7.

Indigenous and Northern Affairs Canada. (2012). Income assistance program: Background. https://www.aadnc-aandc.gc.ca/eng/1334589796211/1334589859785.

Indigenous and Northern Affairs Canada. (2015a). Percentage change in registered Indian population, Canada, 1981 to 2015. http://www.aadnc-aandc.gc.ca.

Indigenous and Northern Affairs Canada. (2015b). Skills and job training: Income assistance program. https://www.aadnc-aandc.gc.ca/eng/1100100035256/1100100035257.

Indigenous and Northern Affairs Canada. (2016a). Inuit Nunangat map. http://www.aadnc-aandc.gc.ca/Map/irs/mp/index-en.html.

Indigenous and Northern Affairs Canada. (2016b). Kindergarten to grade 12 operating expenditures 2013–2014 overview. http://www.aadnc-aandc.gc.ca/eng/1349140116208/1349140158945.

Intertribal Forestry Association of British Columbia. (1990). *Lands, revenues and trusts forestry review.* Kelowna, BC: Author.

Kahn, S. (2008). Aboriginal mental health: The statistical reality. *Visions: BC's Mental Health and Addictions Journal, 5*(1), 6–7. http://heretohelp.bc.ca/publications/aboriginal-people/bck/3.

Keewatin v. Ontario (Natural Resources). (2013). 2013 ONCA 158, aff'd. (*sub nom. Grassy Narrows First Nation v. Ontario (Natural Resources)*), 2014 SCC 48, [2014] 2 SCR 447.

Kirmayer, L.J., Fraser, S.-L., Fauras, V., & Whitley, R. (2010). Current approaches to Aboriginal youth suicide prevention. Canadian Mental Health Research Unit working paper no. 14. Montreal: Jewish General Hospital. http://www.namhr.ca/pdfs/Suicide-Prevention.pdf.

Laboucane, R. (2010, October). Canada's Aboriginal education crisis. *Windspeaker, 28*(7), 18–19. http://www.ammsa.com/publications/windspeaker/canada%E2%80%99s-aboriginal-education-crisis-column.

Mandell Pinder LLP. (2014, July 21). *Grassy Narrows First Nation v. Ontario (Natural Resources)* 2014 SCC 48—Case summary. http://www.mandellpinder.com/grassy-narrows-first-nation-v-ontario-natural-resources-2014-scc-48-case-summary/.

Marshall, R. v; R v. Bernard. (2005). 2005 SCC 43, [2005] 2 SCR 220.

McIvor v. Canada (Registrar of Indian and Northern Affairs). (2009). 2009 BCCA 153.

National Panel on First Nation Elementary and Secondary Education for Students on Reserve. (2013). *Nurturing the learning spirit of First Nation students: The report of the National Panel on First Nation Elementary and Secondary Education for Students on Reserve.* Ottawa: Aboriginal Affairs and Northern Development Canada. https://www.aadnc-aandc.gc.ca/DAM/DAM-INTER-HQ-EDU/STAGING/texte-text/nat_panel_final_report_1373997803969_eng.pdf.

Nunavut Housing Corporation. (2010, October 29). *An analysis of the housing needs in Nunavut: Nunavut Housing Needs Survey 2009–2010* [Working paper prepared by Income Statistics Division, Statistics Canada]. http://www.stats.gov.nu.ca/Publications/Housing/NHNS Pubs/Analysis of the Housing Needs in Nunavut, 2009-2010.pdf.

Porter, J. (2015, June 15). Mercury levels still rising near Grassy Narrows First Nation, report says. *CBC News.* http://www.cbc.ca.

Public Health Agency of Canada. (2006). *The human face of mental health and mental illness in Canada 2006.* Ottawa: Minister of Public Works and Government Services Canada. http://www.phac-aspc.gc.ca/publicat/human-humain06/pdf/human_face_e.pdf.

Public Health Agency of Canada. (2010). HIV/AIDS among Aboriginal people in Canada. In *HIV/AIDS epi updates—July 2010.* http://www.phac-aspc.gc.ca/aids-sida/publication/epi/2010/pdf/EN_Chapter8_Web.pdf.

Public Health Agency of Canada. (2011). *Diabetes in Canada: Facts and figures from a public health perspective.* Ottawa: Author. http://www.phac-aspc.gc.ca/cd-mc/publications/diabetes-diabete/facts-figures-faits-chiffres-2011/index-eng.php.

Public Health Agency of Canada. (2014). Chapter 8: HIV/AIDS among Aboriginal people in Canada. In *HIV/AIDS epi updates.* Ottawa: Author. http://www.phac-aspc.gc.ca/aids-sida/publication/epi/2010/8-eng.php.

Public Health Agency of Canada. (2015). HIV and AIDS in Canada: Surveillance report to December 31, 2014. http://healthycanadians.gc.ca/publications/diseases-conditions-maladies-affections/hiv-aids-surveillance-2014-vih-sida/index-eng.php.

Richards, J.G., Vining, A.R., & Weimer, D.L. (2010, February). Aboriginal performance on standardized tests: Evidence and analysis from provincial schools in British Columbia. *Policy Studies Journal, 38*(1), 47–67.

Sharpe, A., & Arsenault, J.-F. (2010, December). Investing in Aboriginal education in Canada: An economic perspective. *CPRN research report.* Ottawa: Canadian Policy Research Networks. http://www.cprn.org/documents/51980_EN.pdf.

Shkilnyk, A. (1985). *A poison stronger than love: The destruction of an Ojibwa community.* New Haven, CT: Yale University Press.

Standing Committee on Aboriginal Affairs and Northern Development. (2014). *Study of land management and sustainable economic development on First Nations reserve lands.* http://www.parl.gc.ca/content/hoc/Committee/412/AANO/Reports/RP6482573/AANOrp04/aanorp04-e.pdf.

Standing Senate Committee on Aboriginal Peoples. (2015). *Housing on First Nations reserves: Challenges and successes.* http://www.parl.gc.ca/Content/SEN/Committee/412/appa/rms/08feb15/home-e.htm.

Statistics Canada. (2006). Earnings and incomes of Canadians over the past quarter century, 2006 census: earnings. Higher education: Gateway to higher earnings. http://www12.statcan.gc.ca/census-recensement/2006/as-sa/97-563/p8-eng.cfm.

Statistics Canada. (2008). Aboriginal people living off-reserve and the labour market: Estimates from the Labour Force Survey, 2007. http://www.statcan.gc.ca/pub/71-588-x/71-588-x2008001-eng.htm.

Statistics Canada. (2010, May 13). Study: Aboriginal labour market update. *The Daily.* http://www.statcan.gc.ca/daily-quotidien/100513/dq100513b-eng.htm.

Statistics Canada. (2012). Aboriginal peoples survey (APS). Catalogue no. 89-653-X. http://www5.statcan.gc.ca/olc-cel/olc.action?objId=89-653-X&objType=2&lang=en&limit=0.

Statistics Canada. (2013a). *Aboriginal peoples in Canada: First Nations people, Métis and Inuit.* http://www12.statcan.gc.ca/nhs-enm/2011/as-sa/99-011-x/99-011-x2011001-eng.pdf.

Statistics Canada. (2013b). The education and employment experiences of First Nations people living off reserve, Inuit, and Métis: Selected findings from the 2012 Aboriginal Peoples Survey. http://www.statcan.gc.ca/daily-quotidien/131125/dq131125b-eng.htm.

Statistics Canada. (2015a). Aboriginal languages in Canada. https://www12.statcan.gc.ca/census-recensement/2011/as-sa/98-314-x/2011003/fig/fig3_3-2-eng.cfm.

Statistics Canada. (2015b). Employment. In *Aboriginal statistics at a glance* (2nd ed.). Catalogue no. 89-645-X. http://www.statcan.gc.ca/pub/89-645-x/2015001/employment-emploi-eng.htm.

Statistics Canada. (2015c). NHS Aboriginal population profile, 2011. https://www12.statcan.gc.ca/nhs-enm/2011/dp-pd/aprof/index.cfm?Lang=E.

Tsilhqot'in Nation v. British Columbia. (2014). 2014 SCC 44, [2014] 2 SCR 257.

Van Dusen, J. (2015, September 30). Nunavut housing crisis: "Dire straits" in Igloolik. *CBC News.* http://www.cbc.ca.

VanEvery-Albert, C. (2004). A review of the band operated funding formula. http://chiefs-of-ontario.org.

Vendeville, G. (2016, July 7). Protesters march on Queen's Park over mercury poisoning in Grassy Narrows First Nation. *The Toronto Star.* https://www.thestar.com.

Zarate, G. (2010, March 10). Inuit TB infection rate 32 times above national average in 2008. *Nunatsiaq Online.* http://www.nunatsiaqonline.ca/stories/article/9879_inuit_org_wants_tuberculosis_strategy/.

REVIEW QUESTIONS
True or False?

_____ 1. The federal government relocated the Ojibwe of Grassy Narrows in 1963 because it wanted to end the isolation that had helped this community resist assimilation.

_____ 2. Most Indigenous communities have been relocated from their original territories.

_____ 3. With the 1951 changes to the *Indian Act*, Indian women who "married out" no longer lost their Indian status.

_____ 4. The *Canadian Charter of Rights and Freedoms* has had little effect on Canada's registered Indian population.

_____ 5. Government funding of on-reserve schools has kept pace with the rapid growth in Indigenous communities.

_____ 6. By 2026, over one-third of Saskatchewan's population between the ages of 15 and 29 is expected to be Indigenous.

_____ 7. The passing of Jordan's Principle in the House of Commons in 2007 put an end to jurisdictional disputes over the funding of government services to on-reserve Indigenous children.

_____ 8. The increase in diabetes among Indigenous people is related to their rapid transition from traditional lifestyles of hunting and fishing to a more sedentary lifestyle.

_____ 9. The proportion of people in the Indigenous population who drink alcohol is smaller than the proportion of people in the general population who do so.

_____ 10. All Indigenous languages are in sharp decline and will soon be lost.

Multiple Choice

1. Which of the following calamities came to the people of Grassy Narrows in the 1960s?
   a. HIV/AIDS
   b. competition in the wild rice market from non-Indigenous farmers
   c. the *Indian Act*
   d. mercury poisoning from a pulp and paper mill

2. Among the people in Canada reporting Indigenous ancestry, the fastest growing population is
   a. Cree
   b. Inuit
   c. Métis
   d. Indian

3. The growth rate of Canada's Indigenous population is significantly affected by which of the following factors?
   a. the birth rate
   b. the death rate
   c. the rate at which individuals lose or gain status
   d. all of the above

4. Which of the following Canadian cities has the largest population of Indigenous people?
   a. Kenora
   b. Montreal
   c. Winnipeg
   d. Vancouver

5. Which of the following factors is negatively correlated with academic achievement?

   a. playing sports every day

   b. living in a household with a high income

   c. strong social skills

   d. none of the above

6. For status Indigenous people living on reserve and for the Inuit, health care is

   a. a provincial responsibility

   b. a community responsibility

   c. a federal responsibility covered by Health Canada

   d. none of the above

7. Compared with people in the general population, how likely are Indigenous people to be diagnosed with type 2 diabetes?

   a. no more likely

   b. twice as likely

   c. less likely

   d. three times as likely

8. Which of the following Indigenous populations has an infection rate for tuberculosis that is 32 times the national average?

   a. the Métis

   b. those who live in cities

   c. the Inuit

   d. the Ojibwe of Grassy Narrows

9. One path to economic development for Indigenous communities is to access the natural resources in the land, but they are having trouble doing so because

   a. the equipment required is expensive

   b. the resources are on lands that are currently under claim

   c. the resources have been used up

   d. it goes against their conservationist beliefs

10. Which of the following is thought to contribute to Indigenous communities' sense of continuity and their ultimate well-being?

   a. facilities for preserving cultural artifacts and traditions

   b. a degree of self-governance

   c. secure access to traditional lands

   d. all of the above

APPENDIX 10.1
Jordan's Story: How One Boy Inspired a World of Change

Jurisdictional Disputes and the Denial of Government Services

Jordan was born in 1999 to a large family in Norway House Cree Nation, Manitoba. ... He was born with complex medical needs and remained in a Winnipeg hospital for the first two years of his life while his medical condition stabilized. While Jordan's mother, Virginia, stayed with him in Winnipeg, his father, Ernest, returned to Norway House First Nation in northern Manitoba to look after the couple's other children. ... Shortly after Jordan's second birthday, his doctors agreed that he was ready to go home. But Jordan never made it. ...

Provincial and federal governments do not always agree on which level of government is responsible for the payment of government services for First Nations children living on reserve, services that are routinely available to other children. When one of these jurisdictional disputes occurred, the typical practice of both levels of government was to deny or delay the provision of services to the child until the payment issue could be sorted out. ...

For Jordan, this amounted to provincial and federal bureaucrats arguing over every item related to his at-home care—while he stayed in hospital at about twice the cost. ...

Jordan died while waiting for a resolution. He was only five, and he had never spent a day in his family's home.

We can say that two lives were lost as a result of this jurisdictional dispute. Jordan's mother, Virginia, did not have a history of substance abuse prior to Jordan's hospitalization, but the heartbreak of seeing her young son remain needlessly in hospital, and enduring the long separation from her husband and other children, likely contributed to Virginia's subsequent slide into substance abuse. Just months after Jordan passed away, Virginia died in a Winnipeg bus shelter. ...

A Groundswell of Advocacy for Change

Buoyed by the strength of his son's spirit, Ernest Anderson vowed this type of discrimination would never happen to another First Nations child in Canada. Those touched by Jordan and the Anderson family were galvanized by the compelling need for change, but uncertain about how to address federal and provincial government policies to make Ernest's dream come true. There was no money and only a small group of Jordan's Principle supporters at the beginning, but all knew Ernest was right, and they were determined to succeed.

When Jordan passed away in 2005, the First Nations Child and Family Caring Society of Canada was conducting a research project on First Nations child welfare, which provided a platform to study the incidence of jurisdictional disputes affecting First Nations children. This study ... suggested that each year, thousands of First Nations children were being denied on the basis of their race and residency the government services that are routinely available to other children.

Just as these findings were coming to light in June 2005, UNICEF Canada hosted the North American consultation on violence against children, during which Jordan's Principle to resolve jurisdictional disputes was announced for the first time. Simply put, Jordan's Principle puts the child's interests first in any jurisdictional dispute within and between federal and provincial/territorial governments. When a dispute arises around the provision or payment of government services (such as health care, education, child welfare, recreation, and other services normally enjoyed by all Canadian children) to a status Indian or Inuit child, Jordan's Principle requires that the government of first contact pays the bill immediately—and then resolves the payment issue later. ...

In 2005, all of the provinces/territories and the federal government were notified of Jordan's Principle and asked to take immediate steps to implement it. ...

Although the federal government and provinces/territories were slow to act, hundreds of Canadians and Canadian organizations stepped forward to support an online declaration for Jordan's Principle, calling on governments to move quickly to adopt and implement the principle. ... By the time Jordan's Principle came for a vote in the House of Commons, more than 1,400 Canadians and organizations had officially registered their support.

Ernest Anderson and his daughter Jerlene, along with other families from Norway House Cree Nation who were also affected by jurisdictional disputes, flew to Ottawa to watch the vote take place. At 5:30 p.m. on December 12, 2007, members of Parliament stood in unanimous support of Private Members' Motion-296 supporting Jordan's Principle and followed with a standing ovation for the Anderson family and all those who supported Jordan's message. It was, by all accounts, a wonderful day, but, as Ernest Anderson warned, the good that was accomplished in Jordan's name that day would be little more than a victory in name only if Canada and the provinces/territories did not immediately move to implement Jordan's Principle. The result? The federal government decided to strike a working committee to discuss implementation.

Gathering Provincial/Territorial Government Support for Jordan's Principle

On January 24, 2008, British Columbia Premier Gordon Campbell announced that B.C. could become the first province to endorse Jordan's Principle. ... More recently, the government of Ontario announced its support for Jordan's Principle and although it plans to begin implementation for children with special needs, it has acknowledged the need to apply Jordan's Principle across health and social programmes in the province.

Meanwhile, jurisdictional disputes continue to negatively affect the lives and health of First Nations children. As of May 2008, as the governments of Manitoba and Canada engaged in a jurisdictional dispute concerning payment for children's special-needs care, 37 children in Norway House Cree Nation faced unnecessary placement in foster care. Norway House Cree Nation used their own revenue to provide the life-saving and wellness services these children needed, while the governments continued to argue that they lacked sufficient funds. ...

Jordan's Lasting Legacy

Jordan's Principle is now the most widely supported child policy movement in recent Canadian history. It is an example of what can be accomplished when a group of committed people stand up against injustice for the best interests of children, leveraging their networks and talents to bring about change, even without financial resources. However, the question remains: Why won't Canada vigorously and fully implement Jordan's Principle without delay? We must have an immediate answer: First Nations children are dying, and their best interests and safety are being jeopardized while waiting for governments to do the right thing.

Source: Blackstock, C. (2009). Jordan's story: How one boy inspired a world of change. *Canadian supplement to The state of the world's children 2009: Aboriginal children's health: Leaving no child behind.* Toronto: UNICEF Canada.

11 Indigenous People and the Criminal Justice System

The Okimaw Ohci Healing Lodge provides a safe and empowering environment where Aboriginal women can begin their individual healing journeys, while being supported and encouraged through daily interaction with Aboriginal spiritual leaders, community representatives, and Healing Lodge staff. Healing for Aboriginal women means the opportunity, through Aboriginal teachings, programs, spirituality, and culture, to recover from histories of abuse, regain a sense of self-worth, gain skills, and rebuild families. Through healing, Aboriginal women are able to change or release negative behaviours such as addictions and criminal behaviour. Delving deep into issues allows for an intensive healing experience, which improves their ability to re-establish themselves in their community.

Introduction

The incarceration rate for Indigenous people in Canada is high, as is their victimization rate. Both statistics have been linked to socio-economic issues and institutionalized discrimination. In this chapter, we will examine the relationship between the criminal justice system and Indigenous people in Canada, the advent of Indigenous policing and alternative justice, the role of Correctional Service Canada in delivering services to Indigenous people, and the unique challenges that Indigenous people face within the justice system. This chapter addresses a variety of issues and should prompt discussion on how to improve the relationship between Indigenous people and the criminal justice system.

Case Study: Hobbema (Maskwacis)

Like Chapter 10, this chapter begins with a case study—in this instance, a description of the Maskwacis reserve (formerly known as Hobbema reserve), taken from a CBC News article (2008, pp. 31–32). Just as Grassy Narrows is not representative of all Indigenous communities, Hobbema is not typical of all reserves; it is an extreme case.

A Community Fights Gangs and Guns

Two-year-old Asia Saddleback was eating a bowl of soup at her family's kitchen table when a bullet ripped through the side of her house, striking her in the stomach. Asia was taken by air ambulance to an Edmonton hospital. The bullet hit her kidney and her spine, but the resilient girl survived—despite the fact that doctors were unable to remove the bullet. Within days, two teenage boys, one 15 and one 18, were charged in the drive-by attack. While it was clear the boys didn't intend to shoot Asia, police struggled to find out why they fired on the house in the first place. The incident horrified people living in Hobbema, and soon all of Canada would learn of the serious gang problem in the small Alberta town.

Descent into Chaos

The descent of Hobbema into chaos can be traced to a number of factors: substance abuse, shattered families, poverty, unemployment, and the erosion of Aboriginal traditions to name a few. Couple these socio-economic factors with evidence of systemic racism (much of which was revealed in the now defunct residential school system that openly tried to destroy Aboriginal culture over its 100-year history) and it becomes clear why First Nations communities are in what seems to be a state of perpetual crisis. Hobbema appears to be the current epicentre of this crisis, as an array of troubles have hit the town.

Hobbema, Alberta

Hobbema is a town of about 12,000 people located within a one-hour drive south of Edmonton. It is the home of four First Nations communities, including the Samson Cree reserve where Asia lives with her family. What might come as a surprise to most Canadians is that the RCMP office in Hobbema is arguably the busiest police detachment in all of Canada. They are dealing with a high volume of violent crime brought on by Hobbema's 13 gangs, who are fighting for drug turf in the town. In fact, Hobbema has the highest ratio of gang members in Canada, with 18.75 members for every 1,000 people living in the town (compared with Toronto's 1.15 members for every 1,000 people). Of all calls received by the RCMP, two-thirds of them come from the Samson Cree reserve. How did a town of 12,000 become a gang hub, producing so much violence in such a concentrated area?

Squandered Cash

One would think that Hobbema would be sitting pretty. Located on prime Alberta oil land, local residents have historically been the beneficiaries of royalty money collected by the federal government and redistributed to each citizen of the town. Instead of saving the money, most residents squandered the cash, going on shopping sprees—with more than a few spending their money on drugs, drinking, and gambling. Despite the fact that oil revenues on the reserve have been steadily declining, Aboriginal youth still manage to receive a large, lump sum royalty payment when they turn 18. Candace Saddleback, Asia's mother, received a cheque for $234,000 when she turned 18 and she has nothing left to show for it. This is common in Hobbema.

Gang Formation

The royalty cheques are one way that gangs are putting Hobbema's youth under their control. Drug dealers give kids under 18 free drugs for years on condition that they pay for the drugs when they get their royalty cheque when they turn 18. By the time the dealers come to collect, many of the youth are fully fledged gang members who willingly turn over their mountain of cash. With over half of Hobbema's population under the age of 18, gangs have no shortage of targets on which to set their sights. The gang life inevitably draws the attention of the police, and many of Hobbema's youth find themselves in young offenders' institutions or, after they turn 18, provincial and federal prisons. It is in prison that gang members get their real education. Surrounded by other professional criminals, novices enter incarceration ignorant and leave with skills that will serve them in their later criminal endeavours.

Once released, gang members return to their surrogate families—the gang itself—and Hobbema has no shortage of places for gang members to find a safe haven. With 13 known gangs in the town, many of which are on the Samson Cree reserve, the RCMP have their hands full keeping a lid on the high level of violence brought on by the gangs. Whether it's Redd Alert, the Alberta Warriors, the Indian Posse, or one of the up-and-coming gangs, Hobbema is a community held on the ropes by the two-punch combination of violence and intimidation.

Community Activism

In the meantime, the citizens of Hobbema have rallied together in response to the shooting of little Asia Saddleback. Abandoned homes are being torn down to prevent the gangs from turning them into crack houses. Graffiti, one of the main ways that gangs use to mark their turf and communicate their messages, is being painted over almost as soon as it goes up. In the summer of 2008, the RCMP declared a four-month gun amnesty, allowing gang members to turn in their weapons and ammunition without being charged with weapons offences. Despite these measures, Hobbema is still mired in gang violence, with almost daily reports of shots being fired and three gang-related shooting deaths in the summer of 2008.

Conclusion

Hobbema has become the flashpoint for communities rallying to keep gangs from taking over their neighbourhoods. The gangs didn't just show up one day and declare Hobbema to be their own. They established themselves over time, feeding on the general state of decay on the reserves and capitalizing on the oil money that many people were happy to party away. While lessons can be learned from Hobbema, it will be interesting to see if anyone is taking note.

Since the shooting of Asia Saddleback, violence has continued to haunt Hobbema. A four-month gun amnesty was introduced in August 2008 in response to Asia Saddleback's shooting, but two homicides occurred that month. One of those homicides, the death of Delena Lefthand, was a result of a gang-related shooting. In 2011, five-year-old Ethan Yellowbird was killed as he slept by shots fired outside his house; two months later, his aunt, Chelsea Yellowbird, was shot in the back yard of the house next door.

In January 2014, Hobbema changed its name to Maskwacis to reflect the heritage of the community, since Hobbema is not a Cree name. However, the name change did not change the cycle of tragedy in the community; the same month, teenager Jacob Soosay was shot and killed by a 16-year-old shooter. RCMP reported that the shooting was gang-related. In 2014, the federal government announced that it would put $2 million toward an existing anti-gang violence program in the community. The program's strategy includes the promotion of community involvement, education, employment skills training, and counselling programs. Case workers assigned to the community each mentor 25 youth for school, family, and social issues. The funding meant that the program could continue for another five years. As of this writing, it is too early to assess its effect on the community.

EXERCISE 1

Consider the case of Maskwacis in light of what you have learned so far in this text about the Indigenous experience in Canada. Explain, in broad terms, how the community has reached its current condition. What possible strategies could be used to intervene? How would you design a new anti-gang violence program with $2 million in funding?

Indigenous Overrepresentation in the Criminal Justice System

Indigenous people are overrepresented in the criminal justice system, both as perpetrators and as victims of crime. In 2012 the Office of the Correctional Investigator released a report announcing that 21.5 percent of federally incarcerated individuals are Indigenous. The Indigenous proportion of federally incarcerated females dropped slightly to 31.9 percent from 33 percent in 2009. However, in the period from 2002 to 2012, the increase in Indigenous incarcerated women was 85.7 percent, while the increase for all incarcerated Indigenous people was 43 percent (Office of the Correctional Investigator, 2012).

In addition to higher rates of incarceration, Mann (2009) notes that, compared with non-Indigenous inmates, Indigenous inmates

- are released later in their sentences,
- are overrepresented in solitary confinement,
- are more likely to have previous sentences, and
- are classified as higher risk and are more likely to reoffend.

CALL TO ACTION

30. We call upon federal, provincial, and territorial governments to commit to eliminating the overrepresentation of Indigenous people in custody over the next decade, and to issue detailed annual reports that monitor and evaluate progress in doing so.

Just as Indigenous people are overrepresented among the accused in the justice system, they are also overrepresented among victims, especially victims of violent crime. The best measure of victimization comes from Statistics Canada's General Social Survey—Victimization (GSS), which collects information from a sample of Canadians in the provinces regarding their victimization in eight categories of crime in the last 12 months: sexual assault, robbery, assault, break and enter, theft of motor vehicle, theft of household property, vandalism, and theft of personal property (Statistics Canada, 2015b). The GSS also rates opinions and satisfaction with the criminal justice system in its various forms.

The GSS reports that, in 2015, 30 percent of Indigenous people living in the provinces had been a victim of one of the identified eight types of crime in the past 12 months. This is 11 percent higher than the figure for the non-Indigenous population.

Violent crime is divided into two areas: spousal violence and non-spousal violence. In 2009, 12 percent of Indigenous people reported being the victim of non-spousal violence in the past 12 months. This is more than double the rate of the non-Indigenous population. The most commonly reported violent crime was assault, where Indigenous people were twice as likely to be victimized; however, for sexual assault, Indigenous people were three times more likely to be victimized (see Figure 11.1).

FIGURE 11.1   Self-Reported Non-Spousal Violent Victimizations, Canada's Ten Provinces, 2009

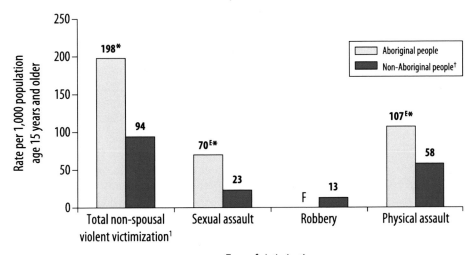

NOTES:

†   reference category

*   significantly different from reference category (p < 0.05)

E   use with caution

F   too unreliable to be published

1.   Includes robbery and excludes all incidents of spousal sexual and physical assault. Includes incidents that occurred during the 12 months preceding the survey.

SOURCE: Perreault (2011, p. 8).

CALL TO ACTION

39. We call upon the federal government to develop a national plan to collect and publish data on the criminal victimization of Aboriginal people, including data related to homicide and family violence victimization.

The Homicide Survey collects data on all reported homicides in Canada (Statistics Canada, 2015c). In 50 percent of cases, the cultural identity of the accused is unknown. Nonetheless, in 2014, police reported that Indigenous people made up 23 percent of homicide victims and 32 percent of persons accused of homicide. While no relevant data were available in the 2014 Homicide Survey, earlier reports indicated that most homicides involved the use of alcohol or drugs. In 73 percent of these cases, the victim was under the influence of drugs or alcohol, as was the accused in 91 percent of these cases (Perreault, 2011, p. 8). Eighty-six percent of the accused were young males, with an average age of 34.

The GSS also collects data regarding socio-demographic factors in connection with violent victimization, such as age, marital status, and the lifestyle characteristics of victims (for example, alcohol and recreational drug use). A number of factors associated with a high risk of victimization were reported more frequently by Indigenous people than by others. It was concluded that, with these risk factors taken into account, Indigenous people are three times more likely to be victimized than are non-Indigenous people (Statistics Canada, 2015b).

Missing and Murdered Indigenous Women

Helen Betty Osborne was born in Norway House Cree Nation, in northern Manitoba in 1952. Helen Betty left her reserve to attend school in the town of The Pas, Manitoba with dreams of becoming a teacher. On November 13, 1971 she was brutally murdered by four young men. It took 18 years to bring the perpetrators to trial, and only one was convicted of the abduction and brutal murder. The matter was reviewed in the Aboriginal Justice Inquiry in 1992. The inquiry revealed that her death and the barriers to justice that followed her death were the direct result of racism, sexism, and indifference, which took the form of sloppy police work and the disinterest of citizens toward resolution of the case. The government of Manitoba apologized to the Osborne family for the failure of the justice system, and in 2001 a foundation was created to honour her memory and her educational dreams.

Helen Betty Osborne came to symbolize hope for all families of missing and murdered Indigenous women in Canada—hope that the justice system would evolve to equally serve all Indigenous women in Canada through the elimination of racism and sexism within the system. Helen Betty's story has been told in the film *A Conspiracy of Silence* as well as in a graphic novel.

In late 2013 the commissioner of the RCMP led a study of reported incidents of missing and murdered Indigenous women across all police jurisdictions throughout Canada. This was a response to the Native Women's Association of Canada Sisters in Spirit initiative (2010), which asserted that 600 Indigenous women in Canada had been murdered or reported missing in the previous three decades. The RCMP study used a similar time frame as the Sisters in Spirit initiative, 1980 to 2012, in order to compare or corroborate its findings. The RCMP found that, in fact, 1,017 Indigenous women had been murdered over that period. Overall, Canadian women in general accounted for 32 percent of all homicide victims in that 33-year span; of that number,

16 percent were Indigenous. This is a serious overrepresentation, since Indigenous women made up only 4.3 percent of the total female population during this time. The RCMP also reported 120 unsolved cases of murdered Indigenous women and 105 unsolved cases of missing Indigenous women. The report did, however, conclude that the solve rates for Indigenous and non-Indigenous female homicides were equal at 90 percent (Royal Canadian Mounted Police, 2014).

The 2012 Missing Women Commission of Inquiry in British Columbia, led by Justice Wally Oppal, was established in light of the serial slayings of Downtown Eastside Vancouver sex-trade workers. Robert Pickton was convicted of the deaths of six of the missing women in 2007, but the DNA of 33 missing women were found on his pig farm outside the city. Pickton was recorded by police during an undercover sting asserting that he had killed up to 50 women over the years. Many of Pickton's victims were Indigenous women, as confirmed through DNA. The inquiry did not address exclusively Indigenous women, but many of the 63 recommendations produced by the commission addressed the overrepresentation of Indigenous women among the missing. At the conclusion of the inquiry, Justice Oppal made statements to the press asserting that Pickton got away with murder for years because of a systemic bias against poor Indigenous drug-addicted victims, who as a group were dismissed by police (Missing Women Commission of Inquiry, 2012).

Inequities in the justice system regarding the protection of vulnerable Indigenous women date back to the murders of Helen Betty Osborne in 1971 and Pamela George, a sex-trade worker, in 1995. In the George case, one of two young men convicted of her killing was reported to have said, "She deserved it. She was an Indian." The court's direction to the jury on the charge of first-degree murder, that they consider the issue of consent to sexual activity because of George's work in the sex trade, came under fire from both Indigenous and non-Indigenous rights organizations. Ultimately, George's killers—19 and 20 years of age—were convicted of only manslaughter and sentenced to 6.5 years' imprisonment for the murder (Commercial Sex Information Service, 2000).

Indigenous organizations, as well as Amnesty International, have called on the government of Canada to undertake a national inquiry into the missing and murdered Indigenous women. Following the 2015 federal election, the new government announced the first phase of a national inquiry, with the goal of beginning the inquiry itself in 2016.

The "Highway of Tears" awareness walk kicked off a 2005 symposium to address the issue of missing women who disappeared or were found murdered along the 724-kilometre stretch of British Columbia's Highway 16 between Prince Rupert and Prince George. The number of missing women combined with those confirmed murdered is believed to exceed 30; all but one of these victims were Indigenous (Highway of Tears Symposium, 2006). The communities in this area have struggled to bring the issue to the attention of law enforcement and government agencies since the pattern of disappearances began to emerge as far back as 1989. The long-term goals of the symposium echo many of the issues addressed throughout the chapters of this text:

1. Reduce Indigenous intergenerational poverty and post-secondary student temporary poverty, since poverty is the factor that makes both groups vulnerable to predators.
2. Increase outreach services to Indigenous communities along the highway specifically, and Indigenous communities in general, to reduce their need to hitchhike (due to poverty) to the nearest town or city.
3. Increase Indigenous youth recreation and social activities in the communities along the highway and generally, to prevent these youth from travelling (hitchhiking) to recreation and social activities in the nearest town or city.

Source: Highway of Tears Symposium (2006).

EXERCISE 2

Review the results of BC's Missing Women Commission of Inquiry and find three families' stories of their experience of a loved one going missing. Look for commonalities in the stories, then reflect on (1) how they could have been helped at the time of the disappearance, and (2) what measures could have prevented the disappearance.

Indigenous people are also twice as likely as non-Indigenous people to be the victims of spousal violence (Perreault, 2011, p. 10). Most of this violence is directed at women. For Indigenous victims of spousal assault, the frequency and severity of the assaults was found to be greater than for victims in the non-Indigenous population (Perreault, 2011, pp. 10–11). Twice as many Indigenous victims reported having been injured, and 48 percent (compared with 18 percent for non-Indigenous victims) reported that they feared for their lives (see Figure 11.2).

Causes of Overrepresentation

According to Aristotle, "poverty is the mother of crime." If he was correct, then the overrepresentation of Indigenous people in the criminal justice system is a natural consequence of the poverty and marginalization of Indigenous people in Canada today, as discussed in Chapter 10. The systemic failure to address this overrepresentation is also related to the vast difference between Indigenous and European concepts of justice, Canada's system being based on the latter.

There is good reason to associate Indigenous criminality with the effects of colonization, which has led to poverty and marginalization. Carole LaPrairie (2002) has sought to refine this general notion, asserting that if colonization and cultural conflict are the main source of Indigenous criminality, there should be no variation across the country in the levels of Indigenous overrepresentation, since all Indigenous people suffered colonization.

FIGURE 11.2   Self-Reported Spousal Victimizations, in the Preceding Five Years, Canada's Ten Provinces, 2009

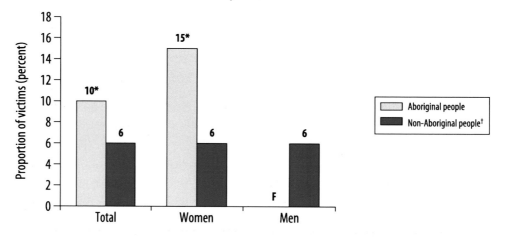

NOTES:

† reference category

* significantly different from reference category (p < 0.05)

F too unreliable to be published

SOURCE: Perreault (2011, p. 10).

LaPrairie looked at provincial differences in Indigenous admissions to custody. The greatest overrepresentation, she noted, is in Saskatchewan, where Indigenous people are incarcerated at 10 times the rate of non-Indigenous people; in Alberta, at 9 times the rate; and in Manitoba, at 7 times the rate. According to McGillivray and Comaskey (1999), the highest enrollment rates at residential schools were also in these provinces. This suggests that assimilation and colonialism are primary factors in the overrepresentation of Indigenous criminality in Canada. Figure 11.3 demonstrates the overrepresentation of Indigenous people across Canada admitted to provincial or territorial custody in 2011 and 2012.

The crime statistics for urban Indigenous people, a fast-growing population, are higher than for Indigenous people living on-reserve. According to the 2011 census, 49 percent of Indigenous people live on reserves. A 1992 study revealed that only 19 percent of federally sentenced Indigenous offenders were from a reserve. In 1992, the Edmonton Inner-City Violent Crime Task Force found that 50 to 60 percent of incarcerated Indigenous offenders in Alberta came from urban areas (LaPrairie, 2002). LaPrairie conducted studies in 1992 and 2000 on urban Indigenous crime in Winnipeg; the results led her to argue that high Indigenous crime rates were related to disadvantaged living conditions. This hypothesis was tested again in 2008 by researchers Fitzgerald and Carrington (2008). Their results confirmed LaPrairie's earlier findings: the high level of police-reported Indigenous crime is related to the characteristics of the neighbourhoods in which Indigenous people tend to live—namely, neighbourhoods that experience low incomes, unemployment, low academic achievement, and a high incidence of family breakdown.

Enforcement directives differ greatly between on-reserve policing and urban policing. Urban police are more likely than on-reserve police to resolve criminal behaviour by laying charges; they are less likely to seek other means of resolving a situation. As a result, a relatively high number of charges are laid against urban Indigenous people. Many urban Indigenous people suffer from low socio-economic status and marginalization, and are isolated in high-crime

FIGURE 11.3   Admissions to Sentenced Custody by Aboriginal Identity and Proportion of Aboriginal People in Total Population, by Jurisdiction, 2011–12

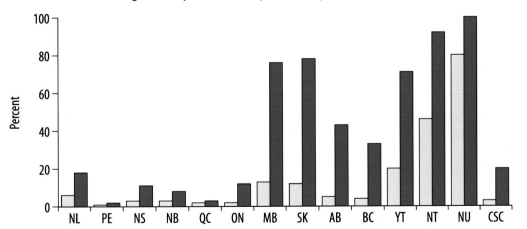

NOTE: The calculation of percentages excludes admissions for which Aboriginal identity was unknown. The term "Aboriginal identity" designates individuals who reported being an Aboriginal person, that is, First Nations (North American Indian), Métis, or Inuk (Inuit), and/or those who reported *Registered or Treaty Indian status*, that is, registered under the *Indian Act* of Canada, and/or those who reported membership in a First Nation or Indian band. The provincial/territorial figures represent admissions in provincial/territorial facilities. Correctional Services Canada (CSC) figures represent admissions to federal facilities.

SOURCE: Perreault (2014).

urban communities. This puts them doubly at risk—of being victimized and of engaging in criminal activity themselves.

Figure 11.4 shows the employment and education status of the prison population aged 20 to 34 in Alberta on census day, 2006. The figures suggest that lacking a high school diploma or a job contributes to the incarceration rate of Indigenous adults in this age bracket. But even when education and employment deficits for Aboriginal people are factored out, the risk of incarceration is still higher for Indigenous people than for non-Indigenous. This points to the likelihood that other factors are contributing to the high incarceration rate for Indigenous people, such as low income, inadequate housing, and the criminal justice process itself (Perreault, 2011).

Indigenous people see the family as central to the social health of their communities. Other marginalized groups view the family similarly. The assimilation process enforced by the federal government severely disrupted family relationships in First Nations communities. Residential schools caused the greatest damage; the abuse left the children with serious emotional scars. Those who escaped the worst abuse still suffered the loss of both language and family relationships. Some were unable to develop healthy relationships with their own children.

As the residential school system wound down in the 1960s, a new form of family dislocation occurred: the child welfare system. Cross-cultural adoptions and foster placements were so common that many communities lost almost an entire generation of children (see Chapter 9). Those adoptions rarely worked out; adoptive parents were often unprepared for the challenges of rearing an already troubled child whose problems were then compounded by discrimination (Wagamese, 1996). Communities reeling from the loss of their children continued to unravel (Fournier & Crey, 1997). In some penitentiaries, 95 percent of Indigenous prisoners are victims of the child welfare system, having been separated from family, culture, and community through adoption, foster care, and, eventually, custody (Royal Commission on Aboriginal Peoples [RCAP], 1996, p. 129). Figure 11.5 shows the statistics concerning involvement in the child welfare system for Indigenous and non-Indigenous inmates. In the Prairie provinces, an attempt was made to quantify the number of inmates who had been through the child welfare system

FIGURE 11.4   Incarceration Rate on Census Day, by Employment and Education Status, Population Aged 20 to 34, Alberta, May 16, 2006

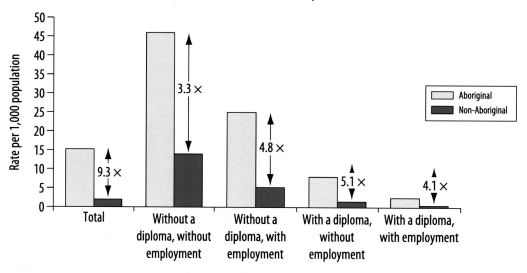

SOURCE: Perreault (2009).

FIGURE 11.5   Inmate Involvement in the Child Welfare System

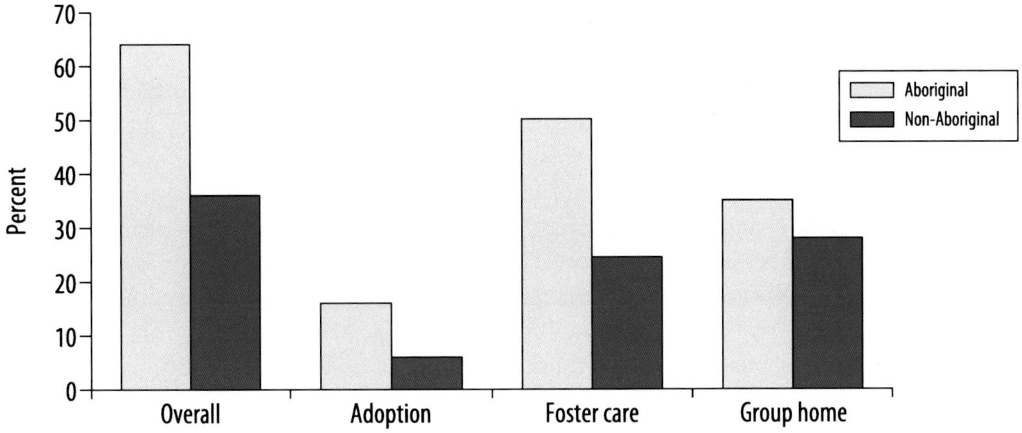

SOURCE: Trevethan, Auger, & Moore (2001).

compared with their non-Indigenous counterparts. It was found that 50 percent of Indigenous inmates had been through the system—twice the rate of non-Indigenous inmates (Trevethan, Auger, & Moore, 2001).

Loss of land through the colonization process and economic collapse in Indigenous communities led to extreme poverty and economic reliance on the Canadian government. At the conclusion of the era of colonization—an era that arguably continues to this day—Indigenous people endured "ill health, run-down and overcrowded housing, polluted water, inadequate schools, poverty and family breakdown/violence at rates found more often in developing countries than in Canada" (RCAP, 1996, p. 129). These problems reinforce one another, creating a circle of disadvantage for Indigenous people; swirling amid this circle is the prevalence of alcohol and substance abuse (discussed below).

Joan Sangster (1999) examined the historical overrepresentation of Indigenous women in custody at the Mercer Reformatory in Toronto between 1920 and 1960. Her study of admissions records at the Mercer Reformatory in the 1950s indicated that 70 percent of Indigenous women's admissions were for alcohol-related offences. Sangster (1999) writes, "When a middle aged woman, who lost all her eight siblings to disease and her father to alcoholism, told the Mercer doctor that her drinking is 'unfortunate but unchangeable' one can perhaps understand her tone of resignation." Sangster attributes the overrepresentation of Indigenous women in the criminal justice system to three factors. The first is material and social dislocation due to colonization. The second is gender and race **paternalism**, which translates into loss of autonomy and therefore agency over one's own actions. The third is the cultural gap between Indigenous ideas of justice rooted in healing and restoration and European ideas of justice rooted in crime and punishment. The three factors Sangster cites are rooted in the Indigenous experience of colonization.

paternalism
a system in which a dominant person or institution assumes authority for supplying the needs and regulating the conduct of those under its control

Alcohol, Substance Abuse, and Criminality in Indigenous Communities

In the past, alcohol problems in Indigenous communities were examined from a biological perspective; problem drinking was seen as a weakness of race, and Indigenous people were believed to have a genetic predisposition to alcoholism. Several studies in the 1970s disproved this theory, but it continues to surface today. The disease model of alcoholism gained popularity after the demise of genetic- or race-based theories. Indigenous addiction workers quickly embraced this model, since it not only offered a reprieve from the victim blaming and racial bias intrinsic in the genetic theory, but also held out hope for treatment and recovery. More recent examinations of the disease model question its validity; they indicate that many problem drinkers are not alcoholics but binge drinkers who engage in violent behaviour (Thatcher, 2004, p. 21).

This chapter addresses the issue of alcohol because its use has a strongly positive correlation with crime and violence, particularly family violence. As mentioned previously, alcohol is very often a factor in homicides in which Indigenous people are involved, whether as victims or as accused. There are two theories on the prevalence of alcoholism in Indigenous communities. The first is that alcohol and substance abuse is a symptom of social problems such as poverty, ill health, and family breakdown. The second theory inverts the first: alcoholism is the primary factor in the ill health, family breakdown, and violence in Indigenous communities (Whitehead & Hayes, 1998, pp. 6–7). All things considered, it seems most likely that alcoholism among Indigenous people stems from their experience of colonization and the consequent social upheaval they endured.

For some Indigenous communities, alcohol-related crime and family violence have been the norm and not deemed to be criminal. In 2009, Correctional Service Canada reported that substance abuse was a problem for 80 percent of all adult male inmates, but for 95 percent of Indigenous inmates. Domestic violence, similarly, was not seen as criminal or deviant; it was ordinary. It was a situation where denunciation and deterrence (section 718 of the *Criminal Code*) as one of the aims of criminal sentencing in criminal law had become irrelevant. With domestic violence, there is a strong intergenerational correlation; that is, children who witness or experience abuse are more likely to become abusers. The intergenerational correlation likewise exists with alcohol and substance abuse; its onset takes the form of gas sniffing, which is a particular problem in more isolated and economically desperate Indigenous communities. Gas sniffing has been reported in children as young as four years of age.

This cycle seems almost impossible to stop. Nonetheless, many Indigenous communities are currently making serious efforts to confront these issues. Inuit communities in Nunangat, for example, have attempted to regulate alcohol in their communities, and others have done the same (see Figure 11.6). Other communities have prohibited alcohol altogether. Statistics show that the prohibition of alcohol has significantly reduced the incidence of violent crime in these communities, including cutting the rates of serious assault and homicide by more than half (Wood, 2011).

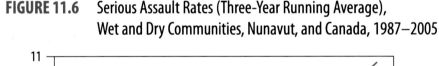

FIGURE 11.6 Serious Assault Rates (Three-Year Running Average), Wet and Dry Communities, Nunavut, and Canada, 1987–2005

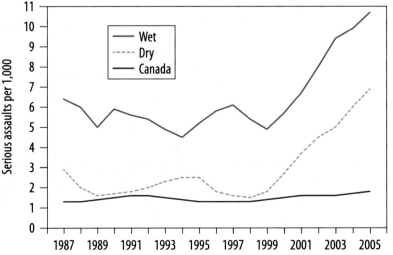

SOURCE: Wood (2011, p. 24).

Systemic Problems

Much attention has been paid in the last two decades to the overrepresentation of Indigenous people in the criminal justice system, including correctional facilities. Of grave concern are the matters of justice and economics. As we discussed in Chapter 10, the Indigenous population is increasing; according to the 2011 National Household Survey, between 2006 and 2011 the increase was 20.1 percent. The demographic statistics for Indigenous communities show an average age much younger than that of non-Indigenous Canadians. For example, in Maskwacis (Hobbema), more than half the population is 18 or younger (Offman, 2008). Since youth is recognized to be a contributing factor in criminal behaviour (most who engage in criminal activity are aged 18 to 35), there is cause for serious concern about the Indigenous population; the overrepresentation of Indigenous people in the criminal justice system will increase unless significant interventions occur. Inaction could have serious financial repercussions, too. The cost of incarceration in a federal penitentiary is approximately $111,000 per year for males and $214,000 per year for females (Office of the Correctional Investigator, 2013).

A number of studies have been undertaken with a view to establishing policy and action for intervention. One such study (Aboriginal Justice Implementation Commission [AJIC], 1991, p. 86) discovered the following:

- More than half of the inmates of Manitoba's jails are Indigenous.
- Indigenous people accused of a crime are more likely to be denied bail than are non-Indigenous people.
- Indigenous people spend more time in pre-trial detention than non-Indigenous people do.
- Indigenous people accused of crimes are more likely to be charged with multiple offences than are non-Indigenous people.
- Lawyers spend less time with their Indigenous clients than with their non-Indigenous clients.
- Indigenous offenders are more than twice as likely as non-Indigenous offenders to be incarcerated.

A report of the Office of the Correctional Investigator published in October 2012 repeated these same themes, indicating that little had changed since 1991. It showed that 21 percent of the federal inmate population was Indigenous and found the following facts:

- Indigenous offenders serve disproportionately more of their sentences behind bars before first release than non-Indigenous offenders do.
- Indigenous offenders are underrepresented in community supervision populations and overrepresented in maximum-security institutions.
- Indigenous offenders are more likely to return to prison on revocation of parole than non-Indigenous offenders are.
- Indigenous offenders are disproportionately involved in institutional security incidents, use-of-force interventions, segregation placements, and self-injurious behaviour. (Office of the Correctional Investigator, 2012)

CALL TO ACTION

31. We call upon the federal, provincial, and territorial governments to provide sufficient and stable funding to implement and evaluate community sanctions that will provide realistic alternatives to imprisonment for Aboriginal offenders and respond to the underlying causes of offending.

32. We call upon the federal government to amend the Criminal Code to allow trial judges, upon giving reasons, to depart from mandatory minimum sentences and restrictions on the use of conditional sentences.

33. We call upon the federal, provincial, and territorial governments to recognize as a high priority the need to address and prevent Fetal Alcohol Spectrum Disorder (FASD), and to develop, in
collaboration with Aboriginal people, FASD preventive programs that can be delivered in a culturally
appropriate manner.

**systemic
discrimination**
the enforcement
of laws and the
enforcement of
policies that are inher-
ently prejudicial to
a group or culture

These findings support the concept of systemic discrimination against Indigenous people.
Systemic discrimination is the enforcement of laws and the creation of policies that, while they
apply equally to all people, are inherently prejudicial to a group or culture. Sometimes treating
all people as equals does not amount to justice. The clearest example of this inequality is in the
sentencing process. Factors that judges must consider in providing custodial or non-custodial
sentences include socio-economic factors such as education level, family situation, having a
fixed address, and employment or prospects of employment. On the surface, these appear to be
neutral factors; however, as you will recall from Chapter 10, Indigenous people are most often
the unemployed, the transient, and the poorly educated, making them prime candidates for
custodial sentences. Manitoba's AJIC (1991, chap. 4) observed the following:

> Historically, the Justice system has discriminated against Aboriginal people by providing
> legal sanction for their oppression. This oppression of previous generations forced Ab-
> original people into their current state of social and economic distress. Now, a seemingly
> neutral justice system discriminates against current generations of Aboriginal people ...
> of lower socio-economic status. This is no less racial discrimination; it is merely "laun-
> dered" racial discrimination. It is untenable to say that discrimination which builds upon
> the effects of racial discrimination is not racial discrimination itself. Past injustices cannot
> be ignored or built upon. ... These statistics [of overincarceration] are dramatic. There is
> something inherently wrong with a system that takes such harsh measures against an
> identifiable minority. It is also improbable that systemic discrimination has not played a
> major role in bringing this state of affairs into being.

Racial profiling in policing is a problem faced by many minority groups in Canada, and
Indigenous people are no exception. This overpolicing of their populations generates more
charges against Indigenous people. Indigenous people are also overrepresented as victims of
crime; nevertheless, in the past, police have at times given less consideration to Indigenous
victims of crime than to non-Indigenous victims, such as in the cases of missing and murdered
Indigenous women.

Consider also the conclusions of the Royal Commission on the Donald Marshall, Jr., Prosecution (1989). Donald Marshall was falsely accused and convicted of murder and spent 11 years
in jail until witnesses heard the real murderer bragging about his deeds. The case was re-opened,
and Marshall was acquitted after witnesses in the original trial admitted to giving false evidence. The Royal Commission came to the following conclusion:

> Donald Marshall, Jr.'s status as a Native contributed to the miscarriage of justice that has
> plagued him since 1971. We believe that certain persons within the system would have
> been more rigorous in their duties, more careful, or more conscious of fairness if Marshall
> had been White.

Cultural Conflict and Alternative Justice

Besides systemic discrimination, the fact that Indigenous people's traditional notions of justice
differ from those of the dominant system is considered to be another cause of their overrepresentation in the criminal justice system. Recall that before European contact, Indigenous people
did not have jails, police officers, or courts. Each group had its own methods of social control
and its own manner of dealing with people who behaved outside what was accepted in the

community. Disputes were resolved through mediation, with elders playing a primary role. The focus was on restoring harmony within the community. Offenders were encouraged to accept responsibility for their offence and to make amends to the victim and the community. All community members played a role in restoring the offender to a harmonious relationship within the community.

Table 11.1 presents the broad principles of Indigenous justice, although each community had distinct ways of handling justice. Can and should pre-colonial systems be resurrected, and would they be successful in today's environment? Mary Ellen Turpel-Lafond addresses this question in the RCAP report on justice issues (RCAP, 1996, p. 65):

> Can the pre-colonial regime ever be reconstructed? In my own view no, not except as a relic of the past. It cannot be resurrected because we have all been touched by imperialism and colonialism, and there is no simplistic escape to some pre-colonial history except a rhetorical one. In my view, we [Aboriginal people] need to regain control over criminal justice, indeed all justice matter, but in a thoroughly post-colonial fashion. … One cannot erase the history of colonialism, but we must, as an imperative, undo it in a contemporary context. … We have to accept that there are profound social and economic problems in Aboriginal communities today that never existed pre-colonization and even in the first few hundred years of interaction. Problems of alcohol and solvent abuse, family violence and sexual abuse, and youth crime—these are indications of fundamental breakdown in the social order in Aboriginal communities of a magnitude never known before. A reform dialogue or proposals in the criminal justice field have to come to grips with this contemporary reality and not just retreat into a pre-colonial situation.

TABLE 11.1   Traditional Western Justice Versus Traditional Indigenous Justice

Traditional Western Justice	Traditional Indigenous Justice
Crimes as offences against the state	Crimes as offences against the family of the victim
Punishment for the protection of society	Restoration of peace and equilibrium within the community
Punishment as a means of making the deviant person conform	Reconciliation of the accused with his or her own conscience and with the person(s) who have been wronged
Laws enacted by elected or appointed members of government	Laws enacted by government, with governance structure differing between nations
Formal administration of justice, including policing	No specialized apparatus of law enforcement; justice informally administered by chiefs, appointed persons, or kin groups
Existence of "victimless crime," such as deviant sexual or religious conduct	Crimes defined by harm caused to the victim
Sanctions may include fines, imprisonment, or death	Sanctions may include compensation to the victim, corporal punishment, banishment, or death
Atonement or reparations made by the individual offender to the individual victim	Atonement or reparations made by the offender's family or clan to the victim's family or clan

SOURCE: Aboriginal Justice Implementation Commission (1999).

Indigenous people are infusing different approaches into criminal justice programs directed at their communities. In the traditional Indigenous justice system, authority is dispersed among many people, with consensus as a goal. This approach contrasts with the mainstream one, whereby sole authority for sentencing rests with one individual, such as a justice or a judge, and decision-making power is confined to the Crown, the defence attorney, and the justice. Another difference in the Indigenous justice system is that Indigenous women play a primary role in all stages of the process. Finally, when it comes to mediation or sentencing, the Indigenous process considers a large web of relationships, far beyond victims and offenders. This reflects the Indigenous world view that all things are connected and nothing can be addressed in isolation (RCAP, 1996).

The major changes we have seen in the last two decades within the court system in Canada have been largely borrowed from original themes in pre-contact Indigenous justice. We give them new names, such as "alternative justice" or "restorative justice," but they are ways of justice that have existed since time immemorial. Alternative justice and restorative justice programs include victim–offender mediation, sentencing circles, and traditional Indigenous justice.

Justice in Nunavut

Due to its majority Inuit population, Nunavut has had the unique opportunity to make major structural changes to its justice system. Upon the creation of the territory of Nunavut in 1999, the *Nunavut Judicial System Implementation Act* took effect. Whereas all other provinces and territories in Canada have a three-tier justice system composed of provincial, appeals, and superior or supreme courts, Nunavut has a one-tier court system. Due to the size of the territory and the sparseness of the population, through extensive community consultation and consultation with justice professionals, it was decided that Nunavut would have a one-tier system so that all judges would have the power to hear any case.

The per capita crime rate in Nunavut exceeds that of any other area in Canada. The police-reported crime rate is 9 times greater than in the rest of Canada, and the violent crime rate is 7.1 times higher. Between 1999 and 2004, while the rest of Canada saw a decrease in youth court cases due to the creation of the *Youth Criminal Justice Act*, Nunavut saw a 93 percent increase in youth court cases (Clark, 2011). This increased crime rate is influenced by social factors, including the age of the population, which is younger than the rest of Canada. Additionally, police service (the RCMP) has expanded in remote areas since 1999, which accounts for some of the increase in reported crime. Finally, the high crime rate is connected to colonization and the community relocations brought about in the last 50 years.

The Nunavut Court of Justice must cover the entire territory of Nunavut, which is 20 percent of Canada's landmass. There are 25 communities across the territory that must be served by the court. The court travels to communities based on need—it can hold court in each community anywhere from once every six weeks to once every two years, depending on the number of cases. The circuit court consists of a judge, clerk of the court, court reporter, Crown prosecutor, and defence attorney. Interpreters are often present, since for many Inuit, English is not their first language—in fact, they may not speak English at all. Court is held in schools, community centres, and other locations as they are available, and the circuit court almost always flies into each community.

In addition to this circuit court, there are justices of the peace (JPs) who reside in the communities. Ideally, these are Inuit from the communities they represent who also speak the language. The JPs can deal with summary conviction matters and show cause hearings, and issue search warrants when necessary.

CLOSE-UP   Community Justice in Iqaluit

The Government of Nunavut has breathed new life into restorative justice efforts in Iqaluit by resurrecting its community justice committee. "Crimes concern a whole community and that's why I'm part of the committee—because I feel that personal responsibility," said Romani Makkik, who will chair Iqaluit's committee.

"I grew up in Igloolik, where I'd like to think I'm a prime example of that saying, 'it takes a community to raise a child.' Everybody in town had a part in the person I've become," Makkik added during a July 14 interview.

"And that's grounded in Inuit societal values, which this committee is very much grounded in."

Iqaluit-Niaqunnguu MLA Pat Angnakak has been a vocal supporter of restorative justice measures to divert offenders from what she called Nunavut's "inadequate" corrections system June 1 in the territorial legislature.

The outspoken MLA said the revival of Iqaluit's justice committee is welcome news.

"I think it's very good news, and a long time coming. ... Justice committees provide a really important contribution to justice in Nunavut. If we can send some of those people who've broken the law to the justice committees instead of through court, all the better," Angnakak said July 14.

The Iqaluit Alluriarvik justice committee—which means in English "a place to step forward to"—will work alongside elders to incorporate three main Inuit social values, Makkik said: respect for others; serving family and community; and working together for a common cause.

Both the RCMP and Nunavut's Crown prosecution office can refer those accused of a summary crime to the committee, explained Lisa Tootoo, a community justice specialist with the GN.

Summary crimes are generally less serious crimes than indictable offences such as homicide, sexual assault and crimes against children.

If the accused admits to the crime, and is willing, his or her case will be dealt with by two facilitators and one or two elders on the local justice committee, Makkik said.

Unlike the court system, the community justice model is a collaborative process, Tootoo said, because it brings victims, if they so choose, and others impacted by a crime, together with community members to talk about how it affected their lives.

That collaborative process includes the offender, Tootoo added.

"Offenders have a direct say in what they can do to make things right, and are involved with coming up with an agreement. It's a safe place for them to discharge some of that shame that comes with offending and allows them to be a part of the solution."

The agreement will be unique to each case, Tootoo said, and could include things like community volunteer work, financial restitution or hunting on the land for those impacted by the offence.

In the court system, by contrast, lawyers speak on behalf of accused offenders and the judge hands out a sentence if the accused is found guilty, Tootoo said.

"In court, it's justice that's done to people, and here in community justice, it's justice that's done with people."

Source: Rohner (2015).

This system is far from perfect. Some of the inherent flaws are as follows:

- In isolated communities, the circuit court visits are infrequent, which places strain on victims, witnesses, and the accused while they await closure from the court. This strain is increased if the matter is a domestic abuse situation.
- Funding for legal aid and Inuit court workers comes from the Nunavut Legal Services Board. The salaries are significantly lower than those of professionals who work for other legal organizations, so retaining quality staff is difficult.
- The Nunavut court faces a higher cost of delivery per case due to isolation travel expenses and the volume of legal aid cases.
- Circuit courts may lack credibility in the community because members of the court are not from the communities that they serve and are thus viewed as having a limited stake in those communities. Therefore, the sanctions imposed by the court may also lack legitimacy in the community's view.

As previously mentioned, due to the majority Inuit population, there is an opportunity to infuse traditional justice into the system. In 2015 the four regions of Nunavut had 25 justice committees providing both adult and youth diversion and victim support services. In 2012–13,

137 cases were diverted using community justice committees. By the end of that year, 92 cases had been completed, 29 were pending completion, and only 12 were referred back to court (Nunavut Tunngavik, 2014).

Proposed Solutions

recidivism
the process of re-lapsing into crime

According to a 2009 report released by the Office of the Correctional Investigator (Mann, 2009), Correctional Service Canada has not done enough to ensure that Indigenous offenders have sufficient access to culturally sensitive programming and services—factors that may reduce incarceration and **recidivism**. Ongoing problems include delays in the implementation of Indigenous programming, a shortage of links to the Indigenous community at the time of release, a shortage of Indigenous elders within the prison system, and insufficient staff to deliver programming.

There are a number of proposed solutions to address the failure of Canada's mainstream criminal justice system. Patricia Monture-Angus (2000, p. 167) suggests creating one autonomous Indigenous system. This has been recommended in many comprehensive studies and inquiries. Another option involves creating autonomous but government-funded Indigenous agencies to work within the dominant system or, preferably, to integrate Indigenous ideas and people into the dominant system (Monture-Angus, 2000, p. 167).

Creating an autonomous Indigenous system has been recommended by academics, policy advisers, and both the Royal Commission on Aboriginal Peoples and the AJIC of Manitoba. Community justice initiatives, such as the one used in the Hollow Water community (see Close-Up: Hollow Water later in this chapter), hold great promise, but they must have points of contact with the mainstream criminal justice system. For this reason, a two-track approach is recommended: reform of the non-Indigenous system and creation of an Indigenous system. These two efforts must occur simultaneously, with close attention to how they will work in partnership.

CALL TO ACTION

42. We call upon the federal, provincial, and territorial governments to commit to the recognition and implementation of Aboriginal justice systems in a manner consistent with the Treaty and Aboriginal rights of Aboriginal peoples, the *Constitution Act, 1982*, and the *United Nations Declaration on the Rights of Indigenous Peoples*, endorsed by Canada in November 2012.

Autonomous government-funded agencies have been created to work within the dominant system. Examples of this include Indigenous court liaison officers and corrections inmate liaison officers. These agencies will be discussed in the following sections.

The integration of Indigenous ideas and people into the dominant system is happening currently as Indigenous people gain entry into all levels of the system, as police officers, justices, lawyers, and correctional officers. Currently, however, Indigenous people are underrepresented in all these areas.

The solutions generated in the past 15 years have been developed in consultation with Indigenous political organizations. Some suggested solutions are as follows:

- "Indigenizing" existing criminal justice structures by increasing Indigenous representation within the system. This includes creating a policing policy for Indigenous-run law enforcement agencies on reserves, and other initiatives.

- Implementing sentencing reforms, such as new sentencing directives, including section 718.2(e) of the *Criminal Code* and the subsequent creation of alternative measures, sentencing circles, and diversion programs.
- Amending the *Corrections and Conditional Release Act* (including ss. 79 to 84) to recognize the needs of Indigenous offenders.
- Implementing the Correctional Service Canada (CSC) Strategic Plan for Aboriginal Corrections, which provides for culturally appropriate rehabilitation programs in custody facilities (CSC, 2011).
- Developing programs through the Department of Justice Canada's Aboriginal Justice Strategy to build community capacity to prevent crime and provide community justice solutions to ongoing crime problems (see Department of Justice Canada, n.d.).

Indigenization

Indigenization—that is, the incorporation of Indigenous people as employees into the justice system—currently presents a number of challenges. First, as some academics have argued, the incorporation of a people does not guarantee the incorporation of their values and thought. The incorporation of Indigenous police officers, court workers, lawyers, and judges does not change the adversarial nature of the judicial system, which is intrinsically opposed to Indigenous values.

indigenization
the incorporation of Indigenous people into a social system, such as the justice system

Policing

The evolution of First Nations policing began in 1969 when the Department of Indian Affairs and Northern Development (DIAND) encouraged bands to hire "band constables" to enforce band bylaws. In 1971, DIAND extended this authority, encouraging bands to hire "special constables." The authority of these officers was limited; they did not carry firearms and received very low pay. In 1973, a study by DIAND led to the prospect of employing Indigenous people in a comprehensive policing role. One option was to establish autonomous police forces on reserves; another was to develop the role of special Indigenous constables attached to existing police forces. The latter was the most common choice, with larger forces including Indigenous contingents.

In 1991, the federal government announced a new on-reserve policing policy, making Indigenous policing increasingly autonomous. First Nations reserve policing would now come under the authority of the solicitor general. With the assistance of the solicitor general's office, provincial, federal, and First Nations governments now partner in agreements over police services that will meet the needs of each community. Agreements must be reached regarding cost-sharing for the creation and maintenance of police services.

Under the federal government's First Nations policing policy, created in 1991, a number of forms of policing can exist. One is the First Nations–administered police service—for example, the Nishnawbe Aski Police Service, which serves 35 Ojibwe and Cree communities in northern Ontario. A First Nations–administered police service is run by a board of directors consisting of representatives from First Nations communities, and its officers either are Indigenous or are trained in policing in an Indigenous context. It is modelled on the structure of an independent municipal police service: it has its own police services board, is accountable to the community it polices, and is not governed by a provincial or federal service. Another option is to have Indigenous officers employed within the RCMP, the provincial police, or the many municipal police services across Canada with dedicated responsibilities to Indigenous communities, including urban Indigenous communities—since, as we saw in Chapter 10, more than 50 percent of Indigenous people now live in urban centres. The governance of these specialized units or branches comes through the chain of command of the larger services to which they belong, with consultation for special community needs.

Today, 118 of the 134 Indigenous communities in Ontario have their own police services, with additional support units provided by the OPP. Of the 55 First Nations in Quebec, 51 are served by police services under community policing agreements with additional support units available through Quebec's provincial police (Sécurité publique Québec, 2013). In Alberta, the RCMP provides 36 members located in 12 Indigenous communities. However, three Indigenous communities have tripartite agreements with the province for the creation and maintenance of an on-reserve police service, with 52 percent of the cost coming from federal funds and 48 percent from provincial funds designated for policing services.

Currently, northern Manitoba is served by the RCMP, but communities are demanding expanded police services that could include fully trained Indigenous police services rather than the current band constable model. This is possible under contract provisions allowed under the provincial *Police Services Act*.

In British Columbia, there are 55 community tripartite agreements that provide policing services to 130 Indigenous communities and one Indigenous-administered policing service, the Stl'atl'imx Tribal Police.

Clearly, as Indigenous communities chart their path toward self-governance, self-administered police services will be a goal for many Indigenous communities. In March 2013, there were concerns that as part of budget cutbacks, the federal Ministry of Public Safety was intending to discontinue funding the First Nations Policing Program, which would force the disbanding of tripartite and First Nations–administered policing, but at the end of March, the ministry committed to funding the program for another five years.

EXERCISE 3

Choose a First Nations police service to research online. Consider the positive and negative consequences of its funding being discontinued and a non-Indigenous police service taking over its role in the community. Would it be more cost-effective? Would it be better or worse for the community? Would it be better or worse for the police officers themselves?

The Royal Commission on Aboriginal Peoples identified as a matter for concern the fact that Indigenous police agencies are often modelled on mainstream police agencies. Indigenous communities must have more input into the structure, the function, and the mission statements of their police services. This can be accomplished only when control over policing and justice is connected to self-government. As discussed in Chapter 10, self-government requires an economic base.

Indigenous Court Workers and Gladue Courts

Recently there has been an emphasis on recruiting Indigenous people into all levels of the court system, including Indigenous justices of the peace, judges, and jury members, particularly in areas of the country where there is a large Indigenous population.

Most provinces also have an Aboriginal Courtworker Program funded jointly by the provincial and federal governments. The need for the program was identified in a number of studies of Indigenous people in the justice system. One such inquiry in Toronto, in 1989, quoted a judge as saying, "Unfortunately, Indians are the ideal accused in the courts. They are quick to accept blame for their offences and they accept their punishment very passively. In many ways they appear to be the victims of the system" (RCAP, 1996, p. 97). Whether Indigenous defendants' easy admissions of guilt are based on culture or an unfamiliarity with the criminal justice system is unclear; however, the Aboriginal Courtworker Program was initiated to address these specific issues. The program's purpose is to have the system feel less alienating for Indigenous accused and to ensure they have a clear understanding of their rights as well as a person to advocate on their behalf as they make their way through the system. Low socio-economic status among Indigenous people has, in the past, forced offenders to rely almost solely on the legal aid process, which may partly explain why Indigenous accused spend less time with a lawyer and more time in pre-trial detention than do non-Indigenous accused. Furthermore, if they spend less time with legal counsel, they are less likely to be informed of available alternative justice programs.

Indigenous court workers are intimately familiar with the issues that are likely to bring Indigenous offenders into court; they have a unique perspective on both Indigenous and non-Indigenous culture and can advocate for their clients to try to make the justice system work to their benefit in terms of healing and recovery.

Another initiative is the use of *Gladue* reports and the subsequent creation of *Gladue* courts. The implementation of the requirements under the *Gladue* case law differs from province to province; only a limited examination can be provided in this section. The *Gladue* reports, named for the 1999 Supreme Court of Canada decision in *R v. Gladue*, were initiated in Ontario by Aboriginal Legal Services of Toronto. In *Gladue*, an Indigenous woman who was charged with manslaughter as a result of a domestic dispute was not given access to sentencing reforms under section 718.2(e) of the *Criminal Code* because she was urban-dwelling, and the offence happened in a large urban centre. The court found fault with this; the sentencing reforms had been aimed at all Indigenous people. The *Gladue* decision marked the first time the court interpreted the amended section 718.2(e), which reads:

> A court that imposes a sentence shall ... take into consideration the following principles: ...
>   (e) all available sanctions, other than imprisonment, that are reasonable in the circumstances and consistent with the harm done to victims or to the community should be considered for all offenders, with particular attention to the circumstances of Aboriginal offenders.

According to the court, these amendments required a change in the way that judges should approach the sentencing process.

A more recent Supreme Court decision, *R v. Ipeelee* (2012), dictates that *Gladue* principles must be included in all sentencing. Manasie Ipeelee was of Inuit descent and had an extensive criminal record as both a young offender and an adult. His alcoholism began when he was only 12 years old. Ipeelee had spent most of his life in a correctional facility and was out on a long-term supervision order when he breached the conditions to abstain from alcohol. He was sentenced to an additional three years in custody as a result of the breach; he appealed the sentence because *Gladue* principles had not been considered by the judge. The appeal court confirmed that *Gladue* principles must be considered in all sentences, even in relation to breach of long-term supervision orders.

The onus for obtaining sufficient information on the Indigenous offender to satisfy section 718.2(e) of the *Criminal Code* lies with counsel and the judge. Case law demands that if counsel does not supply sufficient information to meet the *Gladue* requirement, the onus is on the sentencing judge to obtain the information. If the information is not procured by the sentencing judge, it will be grounds for appeal according to case law (*R v. Kakekagamick*, 2006, paras. 44–45).

Furthermore, the *Gladue* principles are not limited to minor crimes but must be met in all cases. The principles must be considered in all aspects of the justice system that involve incarceration, including bail, release, and parole hearings.

Prior to *Gladue*, various studies had pointed out the ways in which the Canadian justice system had failed the Indigenous peoples of Canada, due primarily to "the fundamentally different world views of Aboriginal and non-Aboriginal people with respect to such elemental issues as the substantive content of justice and the process of achieving justice" (RCAP, 1996, p. 309).

Gladue Reports

A *Gladue* report exceeds the depth of a pre-sentence report since it considers the specific experiences of the Indigenous offender, detailing family history, historical family participation in residential schools, community dysfunction, intergenerational trauma, and community supports available to the offender. In Ontario, these labour-intensive reports are researched and written by Aboriginal Legal Services of Toronto (ALST) rather than by probation officers. *Gladue* report writers are available in a number of Ontario cities, including Toronto, Guelph, Sarnia, Manitoulin Island, Thunder Bay, and London. These reports are less widely used than might be expected, since Aboriginal Legal Services of Toronto reports the creation of only 169 *Gladue* reports in 2012 (Ibbotson, 2013).

In British Columbia, trained Indigenous court workers create a detailed report, at the request of defence counsel or the court, to cover all "*Gladue* impact factors." These reports are funded by the Legal Services Society of BC. All provinces have processes in place to meet the criteria set out in legislation and the ability to produce reports that detail the *Gladue* factors. It is important to recognize that the purpose of the reports is not to reduce jail time but to look at the options available to provide the accused's best chance of rehabilitation in order to prevent recidivism.

Gladue Courts

The first *Gladue* court began functioning in October 2001, in Toronto. At the time of writing, for Ontario there are four *Gladue* courts operating in Toronto, Sarnia, Brantford, and London. A *Gladue* court is one in which all Crown attorneys, defence counsel, and judges have received supplemental training with respect to the decision in *R v. Gladue* and to the history, culture, and experiences of discrimination of the Indigenous peoples of Canada, as well as the alternative programs available to Indigenous offenders. The court is available to all Indigenous persons—status and non-status Indians, Métis, and Inuit—who wish to identify as such and have their matter heard in a *Gladue* court. The accused is assigned a *Gladue* caseworker, who does extensive background investigation to determine what strategy would best ensure rehabilitation. In some cities, such as Hamilton, Milton, and Kitchener-Waterloo, Indigenous offenders can apply for a *Gladue* caseworker and a *Gladue* report will be prepared, but their cases will not be heard in a dedicated *Gladue* court, since none is available there at the time of writing.

In British Columbia, dedicated Indigenous courts (*Gladue* courts) are in Vancouver, Duncan, and New Westminster, and a part-time Indigenous court has opened in Kamloops. In Manitoba, where much sentencing of Indigenous offenders takes place but where there are neither *Gladue* reports nor *Gladue* courts, probation officers still try to cover the *Gladue* principles by adding Indigenous-specific considerations into their pre-sentence reports (University of Manitoba Faculty of Law, 2012).

Gladue courts accept guilty pleas, conduct remands and trials, sentence offenders, and carry out bail hearings. Judges consider the unique factors that may have contributed to the offender's being charged and the sentencing procedures that may be appropriate, given the offender's Indigenous heritage. This includes examining alternative justice processes such as restorative justice.

Jury Selection

An area of the justice system that is noticeably lacking Indigenous participation is the jury selection process. This concern was raised in relation to fielding a jury in Ontario for an inquest into the 2007 death of 15-year-old Reggie Bushie. Bushie, from the Nishnawbe Aski Nation, like other teens in his community had to live in Thunder Bay in order to get a high school education. Bushie was the seventh teen from Nishnawbe Aski to die while attending school in

Thunder Bay; six teens drowned and one was asphyxiated. Bushie's family asked that the inquest proceedings be stopped so that Indigenous people could be part of the jury pool.

This incident led to an independent review of the jury selection process in Ontario by former Supreme Court justice Frank Iacobucci, who completed his report in February 2013. Iacobucci identified five key reasons why Indigenous people are reluctant to become involved in the jury selection system:

1. the perception that the legal system is not consistent with Indigenous traditional values, laws, or ideas;
2. the perception that the justice system discriminates against Indigenous people;
3. a lack of knowledge among Indigenous people about the functioning of the criminal justice system in general and the jury system in particular;
4. Indigenous people's desire for more control over the justice system as it pertains to them in their communities and to not have a jury selection system imposed on them from outside; and
5. concern in many Indigenous communities over the underresourcing of their police services, which contributes to an overall negative view of the justice system. (Iacobucci, 2013)

Iacobucci made 17 recommendations as a result of his consultation with Indigenous service groups and his meetings with the leadership of 32 different First Nations communities in Ontario. Some of these include:

- recommendations for economic support to overcome hardship for time spent on juries, including transportation and accommodation;
- instituting a process for Indigenous people to volunteer as jurors for inquests;
- instituting a process whereby Indigenous people with minor criminal records could still serve as jurors;
- embarking on an educational initiative with Indigenous communities to provide information on the jury selection process and the requirements and benefits of sitting on a jury;
- the creation of an advisory committee to the attorney general on matters affecting Indigenous people in the criminal justice system; and
- the creation and implementation of cultural training for justice system workers on Indigenous culture. (Iacobucci, 2013)

Cultural Awareness Training

Within the last ten years, there has been a focus on Indigenous awareness training for non-Indigenous employees of the criminal justice system. Studies in Indigenous issues have been included in college courses for prospective police officers and correctional workers. Police services and correctional staff now in the field have received training in Indigenous issues and in the Indigenous world view, so as to promote understanding and collaboration. This training continues in most provinces and territories, although much work remains to be done.

Recommendations for this training were put forward in the 1996 RCAP report and endorsed by the First Nations Chiefs of Police Association's 2000 study. In 2007, as a result of Justice Linden's report on the Ipperwash crisis, all OPP officers receive education in Indigenous issues. OPP crisis negotiators and tactical response unit officers also receive additional training on Indigenous matters, including history and legal and socio-economic issues. This training includes a one-week "Native Awareness Training" program, which includes Indigenous elders and Indigenous community partners in setting curricula. *Spirit Matters* (Office of the Correctional Investigator, 2012) recommends ongoing training for corrections workers in applying legislation that affects Indigenous inmates as well as in cultural issues.

Outside Ontario, First Nations–administered police services are less common. The RCMP serves 634 Indigenous communities across Canada. The RCMP reports that currently 67 percent of its detachments serve Indigenous communities and more than 1,500 of its members are Indigenous (Royal Canadian Mounted Police, 2011). The RCMP also provides its staff with training in Indigenous perspectives to help them understand and serve Indigenous communities.

Sentencing Reforms

As mentioned above, section 718.2(e) of the *Criminal Code* states that "all available sanctions, other than imprisonment, that are reasonable in the circumstances and consistent with the harm done to victims or to the community should be considered for all offenders, with particular attention to the circumstances of Aboriginal offenders." This provision, added in 1996, was intended to address the excessively high incarceration rate for Indigenous people.

Section 718.2(e) states that sanctions other than incarceration must be available; these include sentencing circles, alternative measures, and diversion programs. Since many offenders are in large urban centres, programs are required both on- and off-reserve. This is supported by the Supreme Court's decision in *R v. Gladue* in 1999, which states that urban Indigenous people must be considered in accordance with section 718.2(e) even if they are not connected to a particular Indigenous community. The alternatives created for sentencing by section 718.2(e) have been used widely by both Indigenous and non-Indigenous offenders, allowing for a more individualized and restorative approach to justice. There is concern, however, that these sentencing options, particularly conditional sentences, are being used more often as an extension of punitive power than as an alternative to incarceration. In the two years following the addition of section 718.2(e), 28,000 conditional sentences were ordered, but prison populations were not proportionately reduced (Roach & Rudin, 2000).

Alternative Measures

The alternative sentencing options under section 718.2(e) include approaches other than conditional sentences. Diversion programs are common for both Indigenous and non-Indigenous offenders, either pre-charge or post-charge. Diversion programs are used for a variety of criminal offences, particularly minor thefts. In a non-Indigenous context, a diversion approach might involve the offender's being required, for example, to attend an education session or write letters of apology. In an Indigenous context, cases more serious than minor theft may be subject to diversion, at the discretion of the Crown. The Crown may suspend the disposition of the case until the Indigenous panel or deliberative body has settled on an appropriate resolution for the case. In the case of minor and non-violent offences, charges against the accused are then generally withdrawn, having been adequately dealt with by the community.

Sentencing circles and elders' panels are common alternative sentencing options. They are based on traditional Indigenous justice structures and allow communities to have control over rehabilitation efforts for offenders. (Sentencing circles have also become commonplace for non-Indigenous youth offenders under the *Youth Criminal Justice Act*, although they are known as "youth justice committees.") This initiative addresses the problem of having an outside person pass sentence over an Indigenous person in an Indigenous community; people who, as well as sharing their culture, know the accused and the victim and have relationships with their families have insight that an outsider may not possess and that may be difficult to translate into a pre-sentence report.

An elders' panel consists of elders or clan leaders who sit with the judge and provide advice regarding an appropriate sentence. In a sentencing circle, community members are invited to sit in a circle with the accused and a judge to decide the sentence. There are prerequisites for a

CLOSE-UP Hollow Water

The area of Manitoba in which Hollow Water is located is one hundred fifty miles northeast of Winnipeg and has a combined population of approximately one thousand people. The people live in four neighbouring communities (Manigotogan, Aghaming, and Seymourville, which are Métis settlements, and Hollow Water, which is a status Indian Reserve).

In 1984, a Resource Team was formed to work on healing and development in these four communities. The first disclosure of sexual abuse came in 1986. Before that time, no one talked about it. When Hollow Water people looked at their community before 1986, alcohol and drug abuse loomed large as a problem, as did unemployment and a need to reroute the education of their children in the cultural ways of their people. It became very clear that there had been a great deal of sexual abuse going on for many years, but that talking about it was taboo. They gradually discovered that as the blanket of alcohol abuse was removed, many of the people were holding on to acute anger, hurt and dysfunctional behaviour patterns that were related to sexual abuse or to some other violation that had been done to them in their past.

What followed was a very active period of learning and healing. The Resource Team soon realized that there was a fundamental conflict between what the justice system does with offenders and what the community needed to do. What was actually needed, they realized, was a new negotiated relationship with all the agencies who have a stake in dealing with sexual abuse cases. The new negotiated relationship would have to spell out a strict set of procedures about what to do at the time of disclosure and how a disclosure would be dealt with by the courts to allow for the healing process to take place. This model was named Community Holistic Circle Healing (CHCH), and works basically as follows:

1. An intervention team consisting of representatives of CHCH, Child and Family Services, and Band Constable conducts an initial investigation to find out what really happened.

2. Once it has been determined (beyond reasonable doubt) that abuse has taken place, the abuser is confronted and charged. At this stage, the combined power of the law and the community are used to force the abuser to break through his or her own denial to admit to the abuse, and to agree to participate in a healing process.

3. If the abuser agrees to the healing road, he or she then begins a three to five year journey, which ends in restitution and reconciliation between the abuser and the victim, the victim's family and the whole community. Abusers are asked to undergo a process of looking deeply into themselves to admit to themselves and others what they have done and how their actions have hurt others.

In all, the CHCH process for dealing with abusers has thirteen steps as follows:

1. Disclosures
2. Establish safety for the victim
3. Confront the victimizer
4. Support the spouse or parent of the victimizer
5. Support the families that are affected
6. A meeting between the Assessment Team and the RCMP
7. Circles with victimizers
8. Circles with the victim and the victimizer
9. Prepare the victim's family for the Sentencing Circle
10. Prepare the victimizer's family for the Sentencing Circle
11. A special gathering for the Sentencing Circle
12. A sentencing review
13. A cleansing ceremony

Today Hollow Water enjoys a fairly high level of sobriety (around eighty percent) and they are actively dealing with the sexual abuse issue.

Source: Bushie (1999).

---

sentencing circle. First, the accused must recognize his guilt and have a clear intention to rehabilitate and become a good citizen of his community. Second, the community must have a desire to intercede on behalf of one of its members. Third, the victim must also support the initiative.

Youth

All of these options are also available for youth sentencing. Although the absolute numbers of Indigenous youth in custody decreased from 1,128 to 720 between 2000 and 2003, Indigenous youth are still overrepresented in the criminal justice system. Statistics Canada reported that in 2014, 3,468 Indigenous youth were in custody, compared with all youth at 8,945 (Statistics Canada, 2015a). In the nine jurisdictions covered by this report, 41 percent of youth admitted to custody were Indigenous, even though they make up only 7 percent of the total youth population in the jurisdictions under study. A greater number of Indigenous youth are incarcerated for serious offences than are their non-Indigenous counterparts. Indigenous youth are also more likely than their non-Indigenous counterparts to receive custodial sentences and to re-ceive longer periods of probation. In a 2009 study, it was found that 22 percent of youth gang members in Canada are Indigenous (Totten, 2009). Figure 11.7 shows Aboriginal youth admis-sions to correctional services for eight jurisdictions in 2010–11.

Without intervention, these youth will make their way into the adult system. To combat this, family group conferencing is available to all youth, particularly Indigenous youth. It is a pro-cess by which the youth and members of his or her family, a youth advocate, a police officer, a social worker, and other community members meet to decide what types of intervention are available to the youth and what strategies can assist him or her to become a productive mem-ber of the community. Family group conferencing can take place pre-charge or post-charge. Unfortunately, family support is often unavailable for Indigenous youth due to estrangement or family dysfunction, and often there is no youth advocate, particularly for those who are homeless.

In the one-day snapshot of youth in custody in 2001 reported by the Department of Justice Canada, it was found that only 23 percent of youth in custody were living on a reserve directly prior to admission; however, 65 percent of youth in custody spent the majority of their time on the reserve in the two years prior to their incarceration (Bittle, Quann, Hattem, & Muise, 2002).

Corrections and Conditional Release Act

Amendments to the *Corrections and Conditional Release Act* (CCRA), including sections 81 and 84, which recognize the needs of Indigenous offenders, provide for early release consider-ations by parole boards. This would reduce the cost of incarceration, but the processes must be in place within the community to assist the offender in successful readjustment. Considering the high rate of recidivism for Indigenous offenders, this has not been an area of strength for our corrections system. Efforts to partner with Indigenous communities and to allow their input into the release process are currently under way.

FIGURE 11.7   Aboriginal Youth Admissions to Correctional Services, by Province/Territory, 2010–11

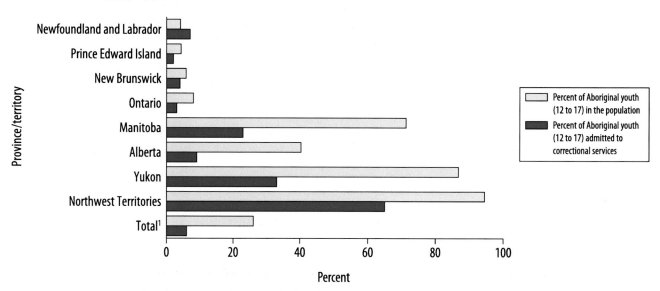

NOTE:

1. Excludes data from Nova Scotia, Quebec, Saskatchewan, British Columbia, and Nunavut.

SOURCE: Munch (2012).

Sections 81 and 84 were reviewed and evaluated by the Office of the Correctional Investigator in its 2012 report, *Spirit Matters*. These sections of the Act specifically deal with policy and structural adjustments that address the needs of Indigenous inmates. The report was critical of the action taken thus far to reduce the incarceration rate of Indigenous people in Canada. It asserted that the incarceration rate for Indigenous people had increased by 50 percent in the last decade, despite the *Gladue* reporting requirements and sections 81 and 84 of the CCRA. Although corrections is only one piece of the criminal justice system, it has serious influence over incarceration and recidivism rates for all clients, including Indigenous clients.

Section 81 Transfers

Section 81 of the CCRA provides for the transfer of an Indigenous offender from a correctional facility to an Indigenous community in a non-institutional setting where supervision, treatment, and programming are provided under the 24-hour supervision of community members for the term of sentence. Other types of arrangements can also be made under this section; an offender may be transferred to a spiritual or healing lodge, or a treatment facility in an urban centre or on reserve territory.

Section 81 reads as follows:

> 81(1) The Minister, or a person authorized by the Minister, may enter into an agreement with an aboriginal community for the provision of correctional services to aboriginal offenders and for payment by the Minister, or by a person authorized by the Minister, in respect to the provisions of those services. ...
>
> (3) In accordance to any agreement entered into under subsection (1), the Commissioner may transfer an offender to the care and custody of an aboriginal community, with the consent of the offender and of the aboriginal community.

To support these provisions included in the CCRA, eight healing lodges have been constructed. Four are run by Correctional Service Canada and funded under its model, and four are contracted and operated by the Indigenous communities themselves under section 81 of the Act. It is important to recognize the difference between the two types of lodges. For section 81 lodges, jurisdictional responsibility for corrections is not transferred to Indigenous communities; rather, the Act allows for certain services and programming funded by the Crown, including care and custody, to be delivered by Indigenous communities. Below are listed the four section 81 funding agreements between CSC and Indigenous communities. A total of 68 beds are available, and plans are under way to increase bed capacity (Office of the Correctional Investigator, 2012).

Facility	Opening date	Region	Bed capacity
Prince Albert Grand Council (PAGC)		Prairie—	
Spiritual Healing Lodge	1995	Saskatchewan	5
Stan Daniels Healing Centre	1999	Prairie—Alberta	30
O-Chi-Chak-Ko-Sipi Healing Lodge . . .	1999	Prairie—Manitoba	18
Waseskun Healing Centre	2001	Quebec	15

The CSC has established four healing lodges that it operates as minimum-security institutions. They have significantly greater bed capacity: a total of 194 beds, with plans under way to soon increase spaces for both men and women. These are funded under a different model.

The plan for these lodges was not to compete with section 81 facilities but to ultimately transfer these facilities to community control under section 81 agreements. The negotiations for transfer were discontinued for three reasons according to the Office of the Correctional Investigator:

- The Indigenous communities enjoy the benefit of having the healing lodges without assuming full responsibility for them.
- The CSC healing lodges provide long-term stability rather than the five-year contracts negotiated under section 81.
- The funding for section 81 healing lodges is considerably lower than that for the CSC-run facilities.

Permanency and funding are two major factors affecting the operation of healing lodges. The discrepancy in funding between section 81 and CSC-operated lodges is significant despite the fact that CSC lodges provide more beds and also contribute to the operational funding of the department. In 2009–10, CSC's four facilities had a budget of $21.6 million, whereas the four section 81 lodges had a budget of $4.8 million. The cost per offender in CSC-run lodges is $113,450, compared with $70,845 in section 81 lodges. Since section 81 lodges pay lower wages, sometimes up to $30,000 less than in CSC lodges, their staff turnover rate is high. The five-year contracted budget means that staff are often laid off or transferred depending on budgetary needs and negotiations.

The CSC healing lodges are listed below.

Facility	Opening date	Region	Capacity
Okimaw Ohci Healing Lodge	1995	Prairie—Saskatchewan	30
Pê Sâkâstêw Centre	1997	Prairie—Alberta	60
Kwìkwèxwelhp Healing Village	2001	Pacific—British Columbia	50
Willow Cree Healing Lodge	2003	Prairie—Saskatchewan	80

According to the Office of the Correctional Investigator, Correctional Service Canada has received funding to enter into new section 81 agreements to increase the number of facilities and beds. The department changed direction in 2001–2 and decided to reallocate funds to create new Pathways healing units in medium-security penitentiaries. "In other words, the investigation found that Effective Corrections funding originally earmarked to enhance Aboriginal community reintegration was used largely to create new penitentiary-based interventions for Aboriginal inmates" (Office of the Correctional Investigator, 2012, p. 15).

CALL TO ACTION

35. We call upon the federal government to eliminate barriers to the creation of additional Aboriginal healing lodges within the federal correctional system.

This shift in direction may be occurring for two reasons. The existing healing lodge beds do not run at maximum capacity. CSC allows only minimum-security offenders to be transferred to a lodge. This restriction is not set out in the CCRA; however, it is meant to minimize risk. This poses some problems since in 2010–11, for example, only 22 percent of Indigenous offenders were classed as minimum risk under the custody rating scale. Furthermore, only 11 percent were housed in minimum-security institutions. The policy for transfer to healing lodges effectively excludes 90 percent of federal prisoners. The lodges could operate at maximum capacity based on the number of eligible inmates; it is unclear why this is not happening.

Facility	Capacity	2009–10		2010–11	
		Count	%	Count	%
PAGC Spiritual Healing Lodge	5	4	80%	4	80%
O-Chi-Chak-Ko-Sipi Healing Lodge	18	13	72%	13	72%
Stan Daniels Healing Centre	30	13	43%	22	73%
Waseskun Healing Centre	15	13	86%	10	66%
Total/Average Percentage	68	43	63%	49	72%

(Office of the Correctional Investigator, 2012, p. 19.)

The second reason for the shift in direction is the recognition that there are too few successful culturally appropriate in-custody healing programs that would speed Indigenous inmates' progress toward minimum-security assessment and possible release. These in-custody initiatives will be discussed later in this section.

Section 84 Release Plans

Section 84 of the CCRA mandates that Indigenous communities be provided with the opportunity to participate in an offender's release plan once he or she is out of custody and on parole. The release plan balances the needs of the community with the needs of the offender. Successful reintegration is the primary goal for all parties: the victim, the offender, and the community.

Section 84 reads as follows:

> 84. If an inmate expresses an interest in being released into an aboriginal community, the Service shall, with the inmate's consent, give the aboriginal community
>
> (a) adequate notice of the inmate's parole review or their statutory release date, as the case may be; and
>
> (b) an opportunity to propose a plan for the inmate's release and integration into that community.
>
> 84.1 Where an offender who is required to be supervised by a long term supervision order has expressed an interest in being supervised in an aboriginal community, the Service shall, if the offender consents, give the aboriginal community
>
> (a) adequate notice of the order; and
>
> (b) an opportunity to propose a plan for the offender's release on supervision, and integration, into the aboriginal community.

To assist in the implementation of section 84, 12 Indigenous community development officers are responsible for bridging the best interest of the community and the offender prior to release. A section 84 release planning kit is available for those seeking this release option. The process is lengthy and time-consuming: there are 25 tasks to complete in a section 84 release application. A major obstacle in this process is that the community that receives the offender is not given resources to monitor the offender's compliance with release. Program and transportation costs must be listed in the release plan, but there is no guarantee that CSC will cover these costs, and the expense could fall to the community. As we know, over 50 percent of Indigenous people live in urban centres; this is true for Indigenous offenders as well. Many, other than Inuit who are mostly released into Inuit communities, would seek release to the urban centre they call home. There are organizations to help released offenders access services in urban centres, such as the Circle of Eagles Lodge in Vancouver and Friendship Centers in Saskatchewan, but many urban centres do not have the capacity to embark on a section 84 release with CSC. For these reasons, the number of section 84 release plans fluctuates. In 2010–11, for example, there were 593 offenders who expressed interest in section 84 release plans but only 99 were successful (Office of the Correctional Investigator, 2012, para. 67).

CALL TO ACTION

37. We call upon the federal government to provide more supports for Aboriginal programming in halfway houses and parole services.

Indigenous community involvement in justice issues marks the beginning of mainstream Canada's devolution of control over these matters where Indigenous people are concerned. However, it is only a beginning. The communities require funds to compensate members for the work of taking on these new responsibilities.

Culturally Appropriate Programs in Custody

CSC's *Strategic Plan for Aboriginal Corrections* (CSC, 2011) involves providing culturally appropriate rehabilitation programs to Indigenous people in custody. Under section 80 of the CCRA, CSC is required to provide programs designed to address the particular needs of Indigenous offenders. This section authorizes the solicitor general to enter into agreements with Indigenous communities to provide services to offenders, such as traditional healers and elders. Furthermore, it mandates the establishment of a national Indigenous advisory committee to advise CSC on how best to provide services to Indigenous inmates.

This is an important initiative for Indigenous inmates, since the chaplaincy program funded by CSC and other counselling programs are ill-equipped to deal with Indigenous experiences. Furthermore, some evidence supports the fact that exposure to Indigenous spirituality and connection to culture has been effective in the healing and rehabilitation of Indigenous offenders. In the Cawsey report, which was studied by RCAP, Justice Cawsey noted that "[e]verything that has worked for Aboriginal people has come from Aboriginal people" (RCAP, 1996).

CALL TO ACTION

36. We call upon the federal, provincial, and territorial governments to work with Aboriginal communities to provide culturally relevant services to inmates on issues such as substance abuse, family and domestic violence, and overcoming the experience of having been sexually abused.

In its quest for appropriate initiatives for Indigenous offenders, CSC (2011) has acknowledged the particularities of the Indigenous population in the criminal justice system and recognized that, compared with the average non-Indigenous offender, the Indigenous offender

- is younger;
- is more likely to have served a previous youth or adult sentence;
- is incarcerated more often for a violent offence;
- is at a higher risk of being placed in increased security institutions, which limits access to rehabilitative programs;
- is more likely to have gang affiliations;
- more often has increased health problems, including fetal alcohol disorders and mental health issues; and
- has a higher need rating when first admitted to custody.

With regard to needs, CSC assesses the needs of people who are admitted to custody in the following categories: employment, marital/family relationships, social interaction, substance abuse, community functioning, personal/emotional situation, and attitude. Because an assessment of these needs as medium or high is correlated with a greater risk of reoffending, these are areas in an offender's life that must be improved to increase the chances that the offender will be successfully reintegrated into his or her community. Currently, Saskatchewan and CSC collect data regarding offenders' needs (see Figure 11.8). In data collected for 2007–8, Indigenous adults admitted into custody had a higher number of needs on average than non-Indigenous people, in all areas of assessment (Perreault, 2009).

Table 11.2 compares the proportion of Indigenous and non-Indigenous offenders in Saskatchewan and federal institutions that demonstrate a particular need. The figures may go some way in explaining the overrepresentation of Indigenous offenders in custody; they suggest that the risk of recidivism—that is, the risk of returning to a correctional facility—may be higher for Indigenous offenders.

In addition to the fact that, compared with non-Indigenous offenders, a higher proportion of Indigenous offenders demonstrate needs, Indigenous offenders more often score as high risk (41 percent, compared with 22 percent among non-Indigenous inmates) on the Reintegration Potential Reassessment Scales (RPRS). According to measures of "low potential for integration," the non-Indigenous population has a 36 percent rating, whereas the Indigenous population has a 69 percent rating. It has been a priority of CSC to assess the risk-scoring process for bias against Indigenous people in custody. Because of the risk ratings, Indigenous inmates are paroled later than non-Indigenous inmates and less often complete sentences under community supervision. Indigenous inmates are more likely to be denied applications for full parole (24 percent, compared with 5 percent for their non-Indigenous counterparts). Finally, Indigenous inmates are more likely to waive parole application because of incomplete programs in custody (Mann, 2009).

Initiatives from CSC to address these matters include its Aboriginal Corrections Continuum of Care model, developed in consultation with Indigenous communities in 2003. The model was built around the traditional medicine wheel because research has indicated that connection to culture teachings and ceremonies is key in rehabilitation of Indigenous offenders. The model includes the following goals:

- Begin at intake to identify Indigenous offenders and encourage a reconnection with cultures and communities.
- Enable paths to healing in institutions to better prepare for transfer to lower security for eventual release.

FIGURE 11.8   Average Number of Needs by Aboriginal Identity, 2007–8

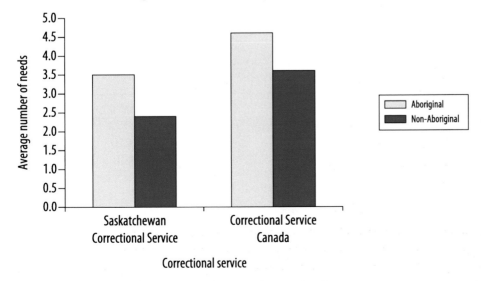

SOURCE: Perreault (2009).

TABLE 11.2   Proportion of Aboriginal and Non-Aboriginal Adults Admitted to Custody and Assessed as Having Needs, by the Type of Need, Saskatchewan and Correctional Service Canada, 2007–8

Type of need	Saskatchewan Correctional Service		Correctional Service Canada	
	Aboriginal	Non-Aboriginal	Aboriginal	Non-Aboriginal
	percent			
Employment	63	33	73	49
Marital/family relationships.	48	33	51	32
Social interaction	76	51	72	61
Substance abuse	81	58	82	67
Community functioning	..	..	39	27
Personal or emotional.	10	8	82	72
Attitude	71	52	58	55
Average number of needs.	3.5	2.4	4.6	3.6

NOTE: Represents individuals who were assessed as having either medium or high needs. For those who were admitted more than one time during the fiscal year 2007–8, information is based on the most recent admission.

SOURCE: Perreault (2009, July).

FIGURE 11.9   Corrections Continuum of Care

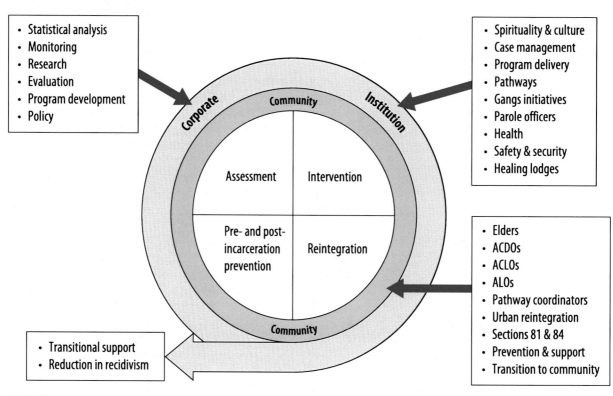

SOURCE: Correctional Service Canada (2012).

- Engage Indigenous communities to receive offenders back into the community and support integration.
- Create community supports for offenders to reduce risk of reoffending (Correctional Service Canada, 2012).

Under the institutional part of the model, during the initial intake the offender may indicate that he or she would like to work with an elder who would visit the inmate, review his or her circumstances, and submit a report based on these observations. The elder may continue to work with the offender and the case management team and incorporate into the offender's correctional plan any Indigenous-specific intervention programs that are available in the institution. If the offender demonstrates a commitment to traditional healing and ceremonies, he or she may request transfer to a Pathways unit in a medium-security institution.

The inmate must meet the criteria to gain access to a Pathways unit. These units provide a culturally appropriate environment for healing in intensive programs such as traditional talking circles, traditional parenting, and the "In Search of Your Warrior" program. Elders and spiritual advisers play key roles, and participants must verifiably abstain from substance abuse during their stay. Approximately 18 percent of the total Indigenous inmate population spent time in a Pathways unit with promising results. In a 2004 audit to justify the funding redirected from healing lodges to the Pathways units, it was found that Pathways participants' recidivism rate was 17 percent compared with 35 percent for non-participants one year after release from custody. The same audit revealed that Pathways participants were more likely to receive discretionary releases from custody: 37 percent of participants versus 22 percent of non-participants. In 2012, CSC reported that the service was planning for expansion to 17 Pathways units over the following five years (Office of the Correctional Investigator, 2012, paras. 75–78).

CLOSE-UP   Pathways

After two hours heading north on winding roads, the buildings of La Macaza Institution appear in the distance. The institution sprawls over a large area, which in the 1960s was the site of a U.S. army base, and later, an Aboriginal school. From there, you can see a longhouse and the tip of a great white tepee that pierces the blue sky. This medium-security institution houses about 257 offenders, of which nearly half are sex offenders undergoing intensive treatment.

According to the small team working on Pathways, the unit fosters a way of living that takes into account the actual experiences of Aboriginal, Métis and Inuit offenders—experiences marked by residential schools, life on reserves, forced assimilation, broken family ties and a pervading feeling of helplessness in the face of change.

Pierre Gervais explains: "Pathways is an initiative that tries to offer solutions to alleviate certain social problems by recreating a way of life that enables offenders to reconnect to Aboriginal culture and philosophy and take their needs—such as self-esteem—into account." Darryn Roy, Acting Manager, Aboriginal Initiatives Branch, National Headquarters, adds: "Pathways tries to create a special healing environment that encourages only positive behaviour. It is a considerable challenge, when considered in the context of a medium-security institution."

The Pathways team consists of three Elders, a liaison officer, two program officers and Coordinator Pierre Gervais. Together, they work with nearly 60 offenders, providing them with individual counselling, organizing sweat lodges and other ceremonies and crafts workshops, and preparing traditional meals. In addition, the team works with parole officers, building a relationship of increased trust that is essential to achieving positive outcomes.

"Pathways is a healing tool," says one offender, "a way to reconnect with my cultural heritage and with who I am. I used to be in a maximum-security institution in Kingston. I am here now, and I hope that the progress I've made will help me get into a minimum-security institution. I would rather talk to the Elders than to correctional officers. Their teachings are fantastic: respecting the land and the people. I prefer that to meetings with psychologists. Now, I make objects that are part of my culture and that I'm really proud of."

Gervais explains that offenders wishing to participate in Pathways must show genuine motivation and commit to making positive emotional, mental, physical and spiritual changes. They must also demonstrate responsibility and show respect for others and themselves. "An inmate interested in Pathways has to fill out the participation request form, explaining why he is interested in joining Pathways," he says. "After consultations with the Elders, the coordinator, the liaison officer, the correctional officer and the parole officer, the case is discussed by the Pavilion Board, and if the decision is favourable, we hold a welcome ceremony for the new member."

Elders Pierre Papatie, Colette Sabourin and Elizabeth Alikashuak work side by side with Pierre Gervais. When asked how they fit into Pathways, Elder Papatie says: "I think God chose me to play a role here. Pathways harmonizes body and soul through various activities. We must listen to them because their past is holding them back."

Métis Colette Sabourin, another Elder and former midwife, says that being there for offenders in their troubled times is crucial to the healing process. "I have been here with the team for two years. I was sent by the Creator. I have lived the cultural duality and today I'm proud of it, but it hasn't always been easy.

Self-acceptance is important. In Pathways, we focus on the offenders' best inner qualities rather than on their negative side."

Elizabeth Alikashuak has been in the institution for 13 years and works closely with Inuit offenders: "I try to work within a spiritual base. I talk to them about the old ways of life; I used to live in a tent in the middle of nowhere and I'm proud of who I am. I also encourage them to speak their mother tongue."

Offenders find that the arrival of Elders at the institution in 1997 changed their life for the better.

Source: Ammelal (2006).

EXERCISE 4

Read the box "A Community Fights Gangs and Guns," below, which discusses the Pê Sâkâstêw Healing Lodge, established by CSC in Maskwacis (Hobbema). How does the information further your understanding of the crisis in Maskwacis and some of the steps that can be taken to address it?

A Community Fights Gangs and Guns: The Pê Sâkâstêw Healing Lodge

In an effort to address the need for a more culturally specific approach to helping Aboriginal Canadians rehabilitate after becoming involved in criminal behaviour, the Correctional Service of Canada (www.csc-scc.gc.ca) constructed eight healing lodges across the country, including the Pê Sâkâstêw Healing Lodge in Hobbema, Alberta. All of the healing lodges strive to embrace Aboriginal traditions in an effort to allow the inmates to reconnect with their roots and find a way out of the criminal justice system and back into society. The Pê Sâkâstêw Healing Lodge is a 40-bed, minimum-security facility that has been serving Aboriginal inmates since 1997.

Counselors at the Pê Sâkâstêw Healing Lodge find they are teaching many Aboriginal inmates their traditions for the first time. Most inmates arrive without a real knowledge of their social, historical, and spiritual roots. The teaching of traditions takes the form of practical participation in Aboriginal rituals in what has been called the "In Search of Your Warrior" (ISYW) program. Pê Sâkâstêw Program Director Sharon Bell explains the rationale behind the program: "ISYW was created to treat traumatic experiences, to heal the scars of abuse, to get rid of the blinding rage and anger that inmates carry deep inside. Some of them, for example, are suffering from the effect that residential schools have had on their lives or on their parents'—residential schools established by the Canadian government that in the past aimed to assimilate Aboriginal people into white society. The scars from abuse and the loss of identity can have a terrible impact on a human being. That is why some of them strongly feel the need to refocus on themselves, to get back in touch with their real selves, to be able to face the future with hope."

So Bell and her staff help inmates to participate in Aboriginal rituals like the cleansing ceremonies known as smudging. In a smudging ceremony, those gathered form a circle. Sweetgrass is burned and carried around the circle. All participants wash themselves in the smoke of the burning grass, drawing the smoke toward them with their hands. After the smudging, inmates take turns holding an eagle's feather and giving voice to their thoughts and feelings while everyone gathered listens intently. This is just one of 75 healing activities that inmates can take part in at the healing lodge.

There are six units in the Pê Sâkâstêw Healing Lodge. The units are designed to capture some of the main teachings of Aboriginal spirituality. Circular patterns represent influence, unity, and social interaction. If you were to fly over the lodge, each unit is shaped like an eagle, which symbolizes the embracing of life and the effort to ward off evil. The colours used on the outside of each unit represent the all-pervasive presence of the Creator, with red representing the east, yellow representing the south, blue representing the west and white representing the north.

Overall, the Pê Sâkâstêw Healing Lodge provides a unique approach to rehabilitation. It strives to embrace the ideals of Aboriginal spirituality and give the inmates a sense of their own traditions. While people working at the lodge recognize that the program is not a cure for the Aboriginal community's ills, it does bring hope to a few of the community members who need help the most.

Source: CBC News (2008).

In regular institutions, there are a number of programs specifically intended for Indigenous inmates, including the "In Search of Your Warrior" program mention above, which is aimed at reducing serious violence. A review of this program (CSC, 2005) showed that offenders who completed the program were 19 percent less likely to be readmitted to custody. CSC seems to be making some progress in its rehabilitation focus for Indigenous offenders, but there is still much work to be done, and key resources are still lacking in many areas. For example, some institutions report that they do not have the services of an elder for extended periods of time, and the burnout of elders and spiritual advisers—due to lack of recruitment, retention, and operational requirements—means that the way in which services are delivered in practice is not in line with what was originally envisioned (Mann, 2009, p. 25). The incarceration rate of Indigenous people in Canada has increased in the past few years, and considering the social conditions and the demographics of the Indigenous population in Canada, the rate of incarceration can only increase if the criminal justice system and CSC do not make considerable efforts.

The Aboriginal Justice Strategy

Indigenous people are seeking to be responsible for their own populations and for addressing crime in their communities, and they should be empowered to find solutions in partnership with all levels of government. The Department of Justice Canada has developed the Aboriginal Justice Strategy to work in partnership with Indigenous communities. The goals are:

- To contribute to a decrease in the rate of victimization, crime and incarceration among Aboriginal people in communities operating AJS programs
- To assist Aboriginal people in assuming greater responsibility for the administration of justice in their communities
- To provide better and more timely information about community-based justice programs funded by the AJS
- To reflect and include Aboriginal values within the justice system. (Department of Justice Canada, n.d.)

The Aboriginal Justice Strategy has a very strict and onerous grant application system and does not cover any capital expenses for programs such as land, buildings, or vehicles. It limits administration costs to 20 percent of the funding grant. In 2014 its budget was $11 million for all of Canada to both support ongoing justice initiatives and create new ones.

The Department of Justice offers two funding streams for which Indigenous communities can apply. Both include only partial funding since the community must contribute either on its own or in partnership with provincial and territorial governments. One funding stream is the Capacity Building Fund for one-time funds to engage in studies, create capacity-building events, and provide training for existing programs. The other is the Community-Based Justice Fund, which supports Indigenous community-based programs including diversion programs, developing pre-sentencing and sentencing options, victim support programs, offender reintegration services, and Indigenous court worker programs. As of 2011–12 the Aboriginal Justice Strategy was funding 214 programs, up from 100 programs in 2006–7. One such program is the Community Council in Toronto operated through the Aboriginal Legal Services of Toronto. This is a criminal diversion program for youth and adult Indigenous offenders who live in Toronto. The project takes Indigenous offenders out of the criminal court system and brings them before members of the Toronto Indigenous community. The council develops a plan by consensus that will allow the offender to take responsibility for his or her actions and address the root of the problem, be it family dysfunction, drug or alcohol abuse, or any other personal matter that may have led to the offence. The concept of a community council reflects the way justice was delivered in Indigenous communities before the Canadian criminal justice system reached these communities.

This program reflects the truth of Justice Cawsey's statement, quoted earlier and repeated here: "Everything that has worked for Aboriginal people has come from Aboriginal people" (RCAP, 1996).

CHAPTER SUMMARY

The mainstream criminal justice system has been very slow to include traditional Indigenous forms of justice. In the last ten years it has begun to evolve much more quickly, to the benefit not only of Indigenous people but of all Canadians, as restorative justice processes become available to non-Indigenous as well as Indigenous people. Current measures for rehabilitation of Indigenous offenders appear to be lagging behind, though, as the number of Indigenous offenders incarcerated increases daily. Changes are not coming fast enough for those from Indigenous communities who are languishing in prison.

Indigenous efforts to create new programs for treatment of offenders and their communities are often hindered by lack of funding. Ultimately, if Indigenous communities were more affluent and economically independent they could finance those efforts themselves and have more autonomy and creative independence in community problem-solving.

Economic development and recovery are therefore vitally important in Indigenous communities. It is all interconnected: economic renewal and prosperity are tied to self-government and self-determination, which are tied to Indigenous control over justice service delivery. Economic renewal itself would address one of the root causes of crime, which is poverty.

The current legislative reforms in justice have shown some positive results but are not the only answer to the problem of Indigenous overrepresentation in the criminal justice system. First Nations territories and Indigenous communities Canada are diverse, complex, and various in their needs. Indigenous people need to lead the way in areas that are fundamental to their well-being. Indigenous people in Canada are working on all fronts to improve their situation; they need a strong partnership with the Canadian government, but one in which the government is willing to follow their lead.

REFERENCES

Aboriginal Justice Implementation Commission (AJIC). (1999). *Report of the Aboriginal Justice Inquiry of Manitoba* (Vol. 1). Winnipeg: Statutory Publications. http://www.ajic.mb.ca/volume1/toc.html.

Ammelal, D. (2006). The Pathways unit at La Macaza Institution: The path to personal growth and healing. *Let's Talk, 31*(1), 8-9. http://www.csc-scc.gc.ca/publications/lt-en/2006/31-1/pdf/letstalk_31-1_e.pdf.

Bittle, S., Quann, N., Hattem, T., & Muise, D. (2002, March). *A one-day snapshot of Aboriginal youth in custody across Canada.* Ottawa: Department of Justice Canada, Youth Justice Research.

Bushie, B. (1999, August 7). *Community holistic circle healing.* International Institute for Restorative Practices. http://www.iirp.edu/article_detail.php?article_id=NDc0.

CBC News. (2008, November). A community fights gangs and guns. *CBC News in Review.* https://media.curio.ca/filer_public/33/f7/33f77dcb-80f2-41de-a095-8e60a7e01422/nov-08-gangs.pdf.

Clark, S. (2011). The Nunavut Court of Justice: An example of challenges and alternatives for communities and for the administration of justice. *Canadian Journal of Criminology and Criminal Justice, 53*(3), 343-370.

Commercial Sex Information Service. (2000). Pamela George murder trial. http://www.walnet.org/csis/news/regina_96/pam_george.html.

Correctional Service Canada (CSC). (2005). The "In Search of Your Warrior" program for Aboriginal offenders: A preliminary evaluation. http://www.csc-scc.gc.ca/research/r172-eng.shtml.

Correctional Service Canada (CSC). (2011). *Strategic plan for Aboriginal corrections: Innovation, learning, and adjustment 2006–07 to 2010–11.* Ottawa: Correctional Service Canada. http://www.csc-scc.gc.ca/aboriginal/092/002003-1000-eng.pdf.

Correctional Service Canada. (CSC). (2012). Commissioner's directive 702—Aboriginal offenders. http://www.csc-scc.gc.ca/text/plcy/cdshtm/702-cde-eng.shtml#aB.

Corrections and Conditional Release Act. (1992). SC 1992, c. 20.

Criminal Code. (1985). RSC 1985, c. C-46.

Department of Justice Canada. (n.d.) Aboriginal Justice Strategy. http://justice.gc.ca/eng/fund-fina/acf-fca/ajs-sja/.

Fitzgerald, R., & Carrington, P.J. (2008). The neighbourhood context of urban Aboriginal crime. *Canadian Journal of Criminology and Criminal Justice, 50*(5), 523–557.

Fournier, S., & Crey, E. (1997). *Stolen from our embrace: The abduction of First Nations children and the restoration of Aboriginal communities.* Vancouver: Douglas & McIntyre.

Gladue, R v. (1999). [1999] 1 SCR 688.

Highway of Tears Symposium. (2006). *Highway of Tears Symposium recommendations report.* Prince George, BC: Author. http://www.turtleisland.org/healing/highwayoftears.pdf.

Iacobucci, F. (2013, February). *First Nations representation on Ontario juries: Report of the independent review conducted by the Honourable Frank Iacobucci.* Toronto: Ministry of the Attorney General.

Ibbotson, H. (2013, April 8). Gladue reports: Boon or bane? *Brantford Expositor*. http://www.simcoereformer.ca/2013/04/08/gladue-reports-boon-or-bane.

Ipeelee, R v. (2012). 2012 SCC 13, [2012] 1 SCR 433.

Kakekagamick, R v. (2006). 81 OR (3d) 664 (CA).

LaPrairie, C. (2002). Aboriginal overrepresentation in the criminal justice system: A tale of nine cities. *Canadian Journal of Criminology, 44*(2), 181–208.

Mann, M.M. (2009). *Good intentions, disappointing results: A progress report on federal Aboriginal corrections*. Ottawa: Office of the Correctional Investigator.

McGillivray, A., & Comaskey, B. (1999). *Black eyes all of the time: Intimate violence, Aboriginal women, and the justice system*. Toronto: University of Toronto Press.

Missing Women Commission of Inquiry. (2012, November 22). Media statement from Commissioner Wally Oppal, Q.C. http://www.missingwomeninquiry.ca/media-releases/.

Monture-Angus, P. (2000). Lessons in decolonization: Aboriginal overrepresentation in the Canadian criminal justice system. In D. Long & O.P. Dickason (Eds.), *Visions of the heart: Canadian Aboriginal issues*. Toronto: Harcourt Canada.

Munch, C. (2012). Youth correctional statistics in Canada, 2010/2011. *Juristat*. http://www.statcan.gc.ca/pub/85-002-x/2012001/article/11716-eng.htm#a4.

Native Women's Association of Canada (NWAC). (2010). *What their stories tell us: Research findings from the Sisters in Spirit Initiative*. Ohsweken, ON: Author.

Nunavut Tunngavik. (2014). *Annual report on the state of Inuit culture and society 13-14: Examining the justice system in Nunavut*. Iqaluit, NU: Author. https://www.tunngavik.com/files/2014/10/2013-14-SICS-Annual-Report-ENG.pdf.

Office of the Correctional Investigator. (2012, October). *Spirit matters: Aboriginal people and the Corrections and Conditional Release Act*. Ottawa: Author. http://www.oci-bec.gc.ca/cnt/rpt/oth-aut/oth-aut20121022-eng.aspx.

Office of the Correctional Investigator. (2013). *Segregation in Canadian federal corrections: A prison ombudsman's perspective*. Ottawa: Author. http://www.oci-bec.gc.ca/cnt/comm/presentations/presentations20130322-23-eng.aspx.

Offman, C. (2008, April 15). Hobbema, Alberta: A town in a "state of crisis." *The National Post*. http://www.nationalpost.com.

Perreault, S. (2009, July). The incarceration of Aboriginal people in adult correctional services. *Juristat*. http://www.statcan.gc.ca/pub/85-002-x/2009003/article/10903-eng.htm.

Perreault, S. (2011). Violent victimization of Aboriginal people in the Canadian provinces, 2009. *Juristat*. http://www.statcan.gc.ca/pub/85-002-x/2011001/article/11415-eng.pdf.

Perreault, S. (2014). Admissions to adult correctional services in Canada, 2011/2012. *Juristat*. http://www.statcan.gc.ca/pub/85-002-x/2014001/article/11918-eng.htm.

Roach, K., & Rudin, J. (2000). Gladue: The judicial and political reception of a promising decision. *Canadian Journal of Criminology, 42*(3), 355–388.

Rohner, T. (2015). Nunavut's capital resurrects restorative justice committee. *Nunatsiaq Online*. http://www.nunatsiaqonline.ca.

Royal Canadian Mounted Police. (2011). Serving Canada's Aboriginal people. http://www.rcmp-grc.gc.ca/aboriginal-autochtone/index-eng.htm.

Royal Canadian Mounted Police (RCMP). (2014). *Missing and murdered Aboriginal women: A national operational overview*. Ottawa: Author. http://www.rcmp-grc.gc.ca/en/missing-and-murdered-aboriginal-women-national-operational-overview.

Royal Commission on Aboriginal Peoples (RCAP). (1996). *Bridging the cultural divide: A report on Aboriginal people and criminal justice in Canada*. Ottawa: Supply and Services Canada.

Royal Commission on the Donald Marshall, Jr., Prosecution. (1989). *Commissioners' report, findings and recommendations* (Vol. 1). Halifax: Province of Nova Scotia.

Sangster, J. (1999). Criminalizing the colonized: Ontario Native women confront the criminal justice system, 1920–1960. *Canadian Historical Review, 80*(1), 32–60.

Sécurité publique Québec. (2013). Aboriginal nations police forces. http://www.securitepublique.gouv.qc.ca/en/police-prevention/aboriginal-police.html.

Statistics Canada. (2015a). Youth correctional statistics in Canada, 2013/2014, Table 5. *Juristat*. http://www.statcan.gc.ca/pub/85-002-x/2015001/article/14164/tbl/tbl05-eng.htm.

Statistics Canada. (2015b, November 23). Criminal victimization in Canada, 2014. http://www.statcan.gc.ca/pub/85-002-x/2015001/article/14241-eng.htm.

Statistics Canada. (2015c, November 25). Homicide in Canada, 2014. *The Daily*. http://www.statcan.gc.ca/daily-quotidien/151125/dq151125a-eng.htm.

Thatcher, R. (2004). *Fighting firewater fictions: Moving beyond the disease model of alcohol in First Nations*. Toronto: University of Toronto Press.

Totten, M. (2009, March). *Preventing Aboriginal youth gang involvement in Canada: A gendered approach*. Paper prepared for Aboriginal policy research conference, Ottawa.

Trevethan, S., Auger, S., & Moore, J.-P. (2001). *The effect of family disruption on Aboriginal and non-Aboriginal inmates*. Ottawa: Correctional Service Canada. http://www.csc-scc.gc.ca/research/r113-eng.shtml.

University of Manitoba Faculty of Law. (2012). *Gladue handbook: A resource for justice system participants in Manitoba*. Winnipeg: Author.

Wagamese, R. (1996). *The terrible summer: The national newspaper award-winning writing of Richard Wagamese*. Toronto: Warwick.

Whitehead, P.C., & Hayes, J.J. (1998). *The insanity of alcohol: Social problems in Canadian First Nations communities*. Toronto: Canadian Scholars' Press.

Wood, D.S. (2011). Alcohol and violence in Nunavut: A comparison of wet and dry communities. *International Journal of Circumpolar Health, 70*(1), 19–28. http://www.justice.gov.yk.ca/pdf/4_Alcohol_controls__violence_in _Nunavut_comparison_of_wet__dry_communities.pdf.

REVIEW QUESTIONS
True or False?

1. Statistics show that most incarcerated Indigenous offenders come from reserves.
2. The incarceration level of Indigenous people in relation to non-Indigenous people is declining.
3. Indigenous people are more frequently victims of crime than are other Canadians.
4. The report of the Royal Commission on Aboriginal Peoples stated that an exclusive pre-colonial Indigenous justice system can successfully be resurrected in today's society.
5. The Royal Commission on the Donald Marshall, Jr., Prosecution concluded that Donald Marshall Jr.'s status as an Indigenous person contributed to his false conviction for murder.
6. The Manitoba Aboriginal Justice Inquiry found that more than half the inmates of Manitoba's jails were Indigenous.
7. Alternative sentencing measures reflect Indigenous values and therefore are only available to Indigenous offenders.
8. Section 718.2(e) of the *Criminal Code* states that "all available sanctions other than imprisonment that are reasonable in the circumstances should be considered for only Aboriginal offenders."
9. To qualify for a sentencing circle, the accused must recognize his or her guilt and have a clear intention to rehabilitate.
10. The *Corrections and Conditional Release Act* has changed to allow Indigenous communities to participate in an offender's release plan.

Multiple Choice

1. Which of the following has not been a factor in Hobbema's descent into chaos?
   a. unemployment
   b. substance abuse
   c. the erosion of Indigenous traditions
   d. lack of access to natural resources
2. Joan Sangster attributed the overrepresentation of Indigenous women in the criminal justice system to three things. Which of the following is not one of those three?
   a. material and social dislocation due to colonization
   b. gender and race paternalism
   c. the isolation of Indigenous communities from the main cities
   d. the cultural gap between Indigenous ideas of justice and mainstream ideas of justice
3. The biological perspective of examining alcohol problems in Indigenous communities was popular prior to 1970. This perspective relies on the belief that
   a. problem drinking is a weakness of race and Indigenous people have a genetic predisposition to alcoholism
   b. all people have a predisposition to alcoholism; some people simply have more self-control
   c. problem drinking is not race-based but gender-based
   d. predispositions to alcoholism depend on the age of the drinker
4. The 1991 *Report of the Aboriginal Justice Inquiry of Manitoba* made several findings. Which of the following is not one of their conclusions?
   a. Indigenous offenders are more than twice as likely to be incarcerated as non-Indigenous offenders are.
   b. Lawyers spend less time with their Indigenous clients than with their non-Indigenous clients.
   c. Indigenous people spend more time in pre-trial detention than non-Indigenous people.
   d. Indigenous offenders are more likely to have their sentences reduced.
5. Which of the following is the definition of *systemic discrimination* as it pertains to the justice system?
   a. discrimination against a particular race in the delivery of any governmental service
   b. the enforcement of laws and policies that are inherently prejudicial to a group or culture
   c. lack of attention to the needs of a specific group in drafting legislation
   d. a purposeful exclusion of a group from certain sentencing options

6. Most comprehensive studies of the criminal justice system in relation to Indigenous people recommend

   a. an autonomous Indigenous system

   b. a dependent Indigenous system

   c. healing circles

   d. a system in which the Indigenous system and the dominant system are interrelated

7. Which of the following is not a feature of Indigenous traditional justice?

   a. Laws are formulated by the community through tradition and consensus.

   b. Traditional spirituality is the foundation of codes of behaviour.

   c. Personal offences are seen as transgressions against the state.

   d. Personal offences are seen as transgressions against the victim and the victim's family, and against the community when the peace is threatened.

8. Which of the following is the definition of *race paternalism*?

   a. a system under which the dominant group takes authority to supply the needs and regulate the conduct of a minority group

   b. an insistence that a group adopt the religion of the dominant culture

   c. an institutionally approved form of racism

   d. there is no such term

9. *Gladue* courts are

   a. mostly in Toronto

   b. courts where all Crown attorneys, defence counsel, and judges have received specialized training in Indigenous issues

   c. courts where only summary offences involving Indigenous accused can be heard

   d. courts where all Crown attorneys, defence counsel, and judges are Indigenous

10. One of the aims of Indigenous healing lodges is to

   a. increase the recidivism rate of Indigenous offenders

   b. help Indigenous offenders stay connected to their communities

   c. formally address the issue of substance abuse

   d. train Indigenous people to become elders

Glossary

acculturation: process of change in the cultural patterns of an ethnic group as a result of contact with other ethnic groups

agnostic: a person who believes it impossible to know God or to determine how the universe began

assimilation: a process by which members of an ethnic minority group lose cultural characteristics that distinguish them from the dominant cultural group or take on the cultural characteristics of another group

assimilation ideology: ideology that expects people of diversity to relinquish their culture and linguistic identity and adopt the culture of the host state

assimilationist: intolerant of immigrants' heritage culture, demanding that they relinquish the culture and adopt the host culture

atheist: a person who does not believe in a higher power

authoritarianism: policy of demanding obedience to authority

bipolar disorder: a mood disorder, previously known as manic depression, that involves emotional swings between depression and mania

***British North America Act*:** a statute enacted on March 29, 1867, by the British Parliament providing for the Confederation of Canada

***Canadian Charter of Rights and Freedoms*:** the part of the Canadian Constitution that protects the rights and freedoms that are deemed essential to maintaining a free and democratic society and a united country

***Canadian Human Rights Act*:** the federal statute that prohibits discrimination based on race, national or ethnic origin, colour, religion, age, sex, sexual orientation, marital status, family status, disability, or conviction for an offence for which a pardon has been granted

Canadian Human Rights Commission: the federal body responsible for investigating and adjudicating complaints concerning violations of the *Canadian Human Rights Act*

Canadian Human Rights Tribunal: a quasi-judicial body that hears complaints of alleged discrimination referred by the Canadian Human Rights Commission

child abuse: physical and psychological abuse of children

child sexual abuse: the sexual exploitation of a child under the age of 18

civic ideology: ideology that subscribes to multiculturalism ideology principles but does not support state funding to maintain and promote ethnocultural diversity

claims arising from Indigenous title: claims based on the allegation that lands traditionally used and occupied by Indigenous people were never surrendered to the Crown by Indigenous people

claims arising from the surrender for sale of reserve land: claims occurring when First Nations seek compensation for, or the return of, land that had been surrendered to the Crown for sale for the benefit of the band

claims relating to the fulfillment of terms of treaties: claims that are usually a result of disagreement between the Crown and First Nations about the size and location of reserves set aside by treaties

collateral victim: an unintentional but expected -victim of an act

community policing: policing that is associated with the police services approach and with the mandate of policing for and with communities

comprehensive land claims: claims to territory that are not covered by treaty or land -cession agreements

consensus government: a form of government that requires all parties to agree with a decision

constructive discrimination: a kind of discrimination that may not be obviously discriminatory and may seem to be based on reasonable criteria, but that effectively excludes, restricts, or favours some people contrary to human rights laws

covenant chain: first agreement entered into between the Five Nations of the Iroquois and the British; a clear recognition by both sides that their political systems would remain separate even as their systems of trade and alliance bound them

cultural genocide: the destruction of those structures and practices that allow a group to continue as a group, such as language, spiritual practices, and cultural values

culture: the patterns of behaviour and behavioural consequences that are shared and transmitted among members of a particular society

cycle of abuse: a social cycle theory that describes four stages of behaviour in an abusive relationship

dating violence: violence committed by a current or former dating partner or by a person with whom the victim had a sexual relationship or a sexual attraction

delusions: ideas that have no basis in reality; a common symptom of schizophrenia

democratic rights: rights to vote and to run in an election and the assurance that no government has the right to continue to hold power indefinitely without seeking a new mandate from the electorate

depression: a mood disorder characterized by extended periods of despair and hopelessness and a lack of interest in life

direct victim: a targeted victim of an act

discrimination: a process by which a person is deprived of equal access to privileges and opportunities available to others because of prejudice

diversity: the variety of human qualities among different people and groups

diversity competency: possessing the cultural knowledge and understanding to serve diverse communities effectively

diversity equity: a value according to which there are no superior or inferior cultural groups

diversity policing: the use of effective policing practices in response to the issues of diverse populations

elder abuse: the physical, sexual, emotional, or psychological abuse or neglect, or the financial exploitation, of an older person by a caregiver, a staff member in an institution, or a criminal

equality rights: the rights of all Canadians, regardless of race, national or ethnic origin, colour, religion, sex, sexual orientation, age, or mental or physical disability, to be equal before the law and to enjoy equal protection and benefit of the law

ethnic group: group of individuals with a shared sense of peoplehood based on presumed shared socio-cultural experiences and/or similar characteristics

ethnicity: the culture of origin with which an individual or group identifies within a multicultural context

ethnist ideology: ideology that expects people of diversity to assimilate, but the state defines which groups should assimilate and thus which ones are not rightful members of the state

exclusionary: intolerant of immigrants' heritage culture and of immigration in general

family violence: the different forms of abuse, mistreatment, or neglect that adults or children may experience in their intimate, kinship, extended, or dependent relationships

fee simple ownership: the right to exclusive use, possession, and disposal of a piece of land

fiduciary responsibility: the legal or ethical responsibility to manage something, usually money or property, in trust for another person (or people) and act in their best interests

formication: a hallucinatory experience, sometimes undergone by stimulant users, that involves feeling that insects or snakes are crawling over or under one's skin

freedom from discrimination: the standard set out in part I of the Ontario *Human Rights Code*, granting freedom from discrimination with respect to services, goods, facilities, accommodation, contracts, employment, and vocational associations, and freedom from sexual solicitation in the workplace and by those in a position of power

fundamental freedoms: freedom of conscience and religion; freedom of thought, belief, opinion, and expression, including freedom of the press and other media of communication; freedom of peaceful assembly; and freedom of association

gender: the culturally constructed roles, attitudes, feelings, and behaviours that are associated with a person's biological sex

gender identity: a person's self-perception of their gender, which may or may not be the same as their birth-assigned sex; involves self-image, physical appearance, behaviour, and gender-related conduct

gender roles: culturally informed norms of how males and females are expected to feel, think, and behave

gendered apartheid: a policy of segregation, followed in certain religions, based on a belief that women are inferior to men and constitute a subordinate class of human being

hallucinations: delusional sensory experiences that may be disturbing to the person having them; a common symptom of schizophrenia

harassment: unwelcome comments or conduct toward another person

homelessness: the condition of having no fixed, regular, and adequate address

host community: comprises groups of people who have the power and influence to shape attitudes toward the remaining groups in society

Indian Act: a statute created in 1876 to consolidate all policies aimed at the administration of Indian populations in Canada and giving the federal government exclusive jurisdiction over Indians and reserves

Indian agent: a federal employee of Indian Affairs in charge of administration on reserves

Indian Residential Schools Settlement Agreement (IRSSA): an agreement by which Indigenous people who could prove their attendance in the residential schools became eligible to receive a "common experience payment" (CEP)

indigenization: the incorporation of Indigenous people into a social system, such as the justice system

Indigenous rights: the rights of Canada's Indigenous peoples to preserve their culture, identity, customs, traditions, and languages, and to maintain any special rights that they have currently or may acquire in the future

integration: embrace of the host culture and maintenance of the culture of origin

integrationist: supportive of immigrants' adopting features of the host culture while maintaining aspects of their heritage culture

intellectual disability: a condition characterized by significantly subaverage intelligence, significant limitation in adaptive functioning, and onset before the age of 18 years

intimate partner violence: violence committed within an intimate relationship

Inuit Nunangat: the four regions in which Inuit live, including land, water, and ice: Inuvialuit, Nunatsiavut, Nunavik, and Nunavut

Islamophobia: irrational fear of or hostility toward Muslims that results in fear or dislike of all or most Muslims or those who are perceived to be Muslims

legal rights: the basic legal protections granted to all Canadian citizens in their dealings with the state and justice system

mandatory arrest policy: a policy dictating that arrest must take place in family violence cases

mania: a mood disorder characterized by an emotional high, agitation, and impulsivity

marginalization: simultaneous rejection of the culture of origin and the host culture

mediative policy: a non-arrest police approach to family violence calls

mental illness: a group of disorders marked by disturbances in thinking, feeling, and relating

mobility rights: the freedom to enter, remain in, or leave the country, and to live and seek employment anywhere in Canada

mood disorders: mental disorders, including depression and bipolar disorder, that affect a person's mood

multicultural heritage: the unique and constitutionally enshrined character of Canadian society

multiculturalism: a policy relating to or designed for a combination of several distinct cultures

multiculturalism ideology: ideology that recognizes and supports people of diversity in maintaining or promoting their diversity, provided that their practices do not clash with the laws of the nation

not criminally responsible: a criminal defence that may apply when a person, at the time of committing a crime, was unable by reason of a mental disorder to appreciate the nature or quality of the crime or to know that it was wrong

official languages: English and French, as confirmed by the Charter, which guarantees that the federal government will serve members of the public in the official language of their choice

Ontario *Human Rights Code*: the Ontario statute that protects the dignity and worth of every person and provides for equal rights and opportunities without discrimination that is contrary to law

Ontario Human Rights Commission: the provincial body that promotes, protects, and advances human rights by engaging in research, education, legal actions, and policy development to prevent discrimination

Ontario *Police Services Act*: a statute requiring that the police services provided throughout Ontario reflect the safeguards enshrined in the *Canadian Charter of Rights and Freedoms* and the Ontario *Human Rights Code*

paternalism: a system in which a dominant person or institution assumes authority for supplying the needs and regulating the conduct of those under its control

patriation: the process by which Canada gained control over the Constitution; previously, amendments to the Canadian Constitution required an act of British Parliament

police force approach: the approach to policing that emphasizes the crime-control, enforcement aspect of the job, on the assumption that police need to be hard on crime

police services: the name given to policing that emphasizes the helpful, supportive aspect of the role, with a focus on problem-solving, crime prevention, and partnership between police and communities

prejudice: an adverse judgment or opinion formed with little or no knowledge or experience or examination of the facts; a predetermined preference, idea, or bias

pro-arrest policy: a policy that favours arrest in family violence cases but leaves the decision to the discretion of the officers

psychosis: a form of mental disturbance that involves a person's losing touch with reality

race: a classification based on ancestry or origin as indicated by physical characteristics

radicalization: process by which individuals or groups become socialized to radical or extreme views or beliefs

recidivism: the process of relapsing into crime

reconciliation: an ongoing process of establishing and maintaining respectful relations

refugee policy: humanitarian policy, based on the United Nations definition of a refugee, that assesses eligibility for entry to a country based on refugee status

religion: a spiritual belief system that addresses matters of ultimate reality, such as life and death, and instructs people in how to live

religious beliefs: tenets of particular faiths

religious practices: concrete expressions of religious beliefs

religious profiling: the targeting of an individual, for safety or security reasons, on the basis of stereotypes about the person's religion, including ethnic and racial stereotypes, rather than on the basis of reasonable suspicion

residential schools: church-run, government-funded boarding schools for Indigenous children, designed to prepare them for life in white society

Royal Commission on Aboriginal Peoples (RCAP): a commission established by the federal government in 1991 to investigate the issues facing Indigenous people in Canada

Royal Proclamation of 1763: the cornerstone of Indigenous land claims today; has been called the "*Magna Carta* of Indian Rights" and has been deemed by the courts to have the "force of a statute which has never been repealed"

schizophrenia: a serious mental illness marked by a breakdown in the connection between thoughts, feelings, and actions, and often accompanied by strong psychotic disturbances and delusions

scrip: a one-time payment issued to Métis to discharge treaty rights

segregationist: opposed to immigrants and other cultures, preferring that immigrants return to their countries of origin

seigneurial farms: a system in which a man, usually a soldier, was granted land in the name of France

separation: individual rejection of the host culture and maintenance of the culture of origin

settlement patterns: the variety of ways people physically establish themselves in a country, whether born there or as immigrants

sex: a person's biological status as assigned at birth, typically categorized as male, female, or intersex, and associated with physical attributes such as chromosomes, hormonal prevalence, and external and internal anatomy

sexual diversity: variations in sexual behaviours, orientations, and identities

sexual orientation: a person's sexual preference, whether heterosexual, gay or lesbian, or bisexual

Sixties Scoop: the practice of removing Indigenous children from their communities and placing them in foster care or putting them up for adoption in non-Indigenous homes

specific land claims: claims that relate to specific misdealings of the Crown with relation to land or resources

spousal violence: violence or mistreatment suffered at the hands of a marital or common law partner

stereotype: conventional, formulaic, and usually oversimplified conceptions that falsify reality through overgeneralization and strip their subjects of individuality

subjugation: forcing obedience to authority

substance-related disorders: mental disorders caused by substance dependence and abuse, and by substance withdrawal

suicide: a consequence of mood disorder, with suicidal mood disorder taking the possible forms of ideation, threat, gesture, attempt, and completed suicide

systemic discrimination: the enforcement of laws and the enforcement of policies that are inherently prejudicial to a group or culture

terrorism: an act committed in whole or in part for a political, religious, or ideological purpose, objective, or cause

thought disorders: a pattern of vague or disorganized thinking that may appear illogical to others

transgender: a person whose gender identity, gender expression, or behaviour differs from that typically associated with the biological sex that was assigned at birth

transsexual: a person whose gender identity differs from the biological sex that was assigned at birth

treaty: an agreement between two states that has been formally concluded and ratified

unfit to stand trial: a determination that a person is unable on account of a mental disorder to understand the nature, object, and possible consequences of a criminal proceeding, and that the person is unable to communicate with counsel

values: standards or principles; ideas about the worth or importance of certain qualities, especially those accepted by a particular group

visible minority: individuals, other than Indigenous peoples, who are non-Caucasian in race or non-white in colour

white machismo culture: a culture that values white skin colour, masculinity, and hierarchy while devaluing non-whites, women, and non-traditional sexual orientation

Index

Credits

Figure 8.1: Implementation Monitoring Committee.

Figure 8.2: Indigenous and Northern Affairs Canada.

Figure 8.3: Indigenous and Northern Affairs Canada.

Indigenous Protestors (photo): JULIE OLIVER/Postmedia News.

The Nishiyuu Walkers (photo): Fred Chartrand/The Canadian Press.

CHAPTER 9

Chapter-opening photos: Provincial Archives of Saskatchewan R-A8223(1)-(2).

Inhumane Conditions at Residential Schools (box): Indigenous and Northern Affairs Canada.

George Cultesi (photo): University of Victoria, "George Clutesi presenting display of First Nations art," 1966, Item 038.0407.

I Lost My Talk (poem): Joe, R. (1998). I lost my talk. In D.D. Moses & T. Goldie (Eds.), *An anthology of Canadian Native literature in English*. Toronto: Oxford University Press.

Robert Houle (photo): TYLER BROWBRIDGE/Postmedia News.

Phil Fontaine (photo): Tom Hanson/The Canadian Press.

Appendix 9.1: Indigenous and Northern Affairs Canada.

CHAPTER 10

Chapter-opening photo: Mychaylo Prystupa.

Grassy Narrows (photo): Peter Power/The Canadian Press.

Figures 10.2–10.5: Indigenous and Northern Affairs Canada.

Figures 10.6–10.8: Employment and Social Development Canada.

Figure 10.11: Assembly of First Nations.

Figures 10.12–10.13: Public Health Agency of Canada © All rights reserved. *HIV and AIDS in Canada. Surveillance Report to December 31, 2014*. Public Health Agency of Canada, 2015. Adapted and reproduced with permission from the Minister of Health, 2016.

Dr. Stanley Volant (photo): Projet Innu Meshkenu. Reprinted with permission.

Table 10.4: Kirmayer, L.J., Fraser, S-L, Fauras, V., & Whitley, R. (2009). Current approaches to Aboriginal youth suicide prevention. Working Paper 14. Culture and Mental Health Research Unit, Institute of Community and Family Psychiatry, Jewish General Hospital, Montreal, Quebec.

Figure 10.15: © All rights reserved. *First Nations Mental Wellnessw Continuum Framework—Summary Report*. Health Canada and the Assembly of First Nations, 2015. Adapted and reproduced with permission from the Minister of Health, 2016.

Appendix 10.1: Blackstock, C. (2009). Jordan's story: How one boy inspired a world of change. *Canadian supplement to The State of the world's children 2009: Aboriginal children's health: Leaving no child behind*. Toronto: Unicef Canada. Reprinted with permission from Unicef Canada.

CHAPTER 11

Chapter-opening photo: Dave McCord/The Canadian Press.

A Community Fights Gangs and Guns (excerpt in case study): CBC News in Review November 2008. Reprinted with permission.

Figure 11.5: © Source: Correctional Service Canada, Inmate Involvement in the Child Welfare Systems. S. Trevethan, S. Auger & J-P Moore. http://www.csc-scc.gc.ca/research/r113 -eng.shtml. Reproduced with the permission of the Minister of Public Services and Procurement Canada, 2016.

Community Justice in Iqaluit (close-up box): Rohner, T. (2015). Nunavut's capital resurrects restorative justice committee. Nunatsiaq Online. http://www.nunatsiaqonline.ca.

Hollow Water (close-up box): Bushie, Berma. (1999, August 7). *Community holistic circle healing*. International Institute for Restorative Practices.

Figure 11.9: © Source: Correctional Service Canada, Strategic Plan for Aboriginal Corrections - Aboriginal Continuum of Care Model. http://www.csc-scc.gc.ca/text/pa/ev-ahl-394-2-49/ healing-lodges-eng.shtml. Reproduced with the permission of the Minister of Public Services and Procurement Canada, 2016.

Pathways (close-up box): © Source: Correctional Service of Canada, 2006. Let's Talk: Vol. 31, No. 1. http://www.csc-scc .gc.ca/publications/lt-en/2006/31-1/6-eng.shtml. Reproduced with the permission of the Minister of Public Services and Procurement Canada, 2016.

A Community Fights Gangs and Guns (box): The Pê Sâkâstêw Healing Lodge: CBC News in Review November 2008. Reprinted with permission.

Royal Commission on Aboriginal Peoples (excerpt): RCAP. (1996). *Bridging the cultural divide: A report on Aboriginal people and criminal justice in Canada*. Ottawa: Supply and Services Canada. Permission granted by the Privy Council Office © Her Majesty the Queen in Right of Canada (2016).